D1360836

TIMELINES ‧ OF ‧ WAR

Also by David Brownstone and Irene Franck

Timelines of the Twentieth Century

Women's World

Timelines of the Arts and Literature

Dictionary of 20th Century History

20th Century Culture:
A Dictionary of the Arts and Literature of Our Time

Parents' Desk Reference

Women's Desk Reference

People in the News

The Green Encyclopedia

Island of Hope, Island of Tears:
The Great Migration Through Ellis Island to America
Told by Those Who Made the Passage

The Silk Road: A History

To the Ends of the Earth:
The Great Travel and Trade Routes of Human History

America's Ethnic Heritage series

Work Throughout History series

Historic Places of Early America

Natural Wonders of America

Great Historic Places of America

On the Tip of Your Tongue:
The Word/Name/Place Finder

Where to Find Business Information

TIMELINES · OF · WAR

A Chronology of Warfare
from 100,000 BC to the Present

David Brownstone and Irene Franck

LITTLE, BROWN AND COMPANY

Boston • New York • Toronto • London

Copyright © 1994, 1996 by David M. Brownstone and Irene Franck

All rights reserved. No part of this book may be reproduced in any form or by any electronic or mechanical means, including information storage and retrieval systems, without permission in writing from the publisher, except by a reviewer who may quote brief passages in a review.

First Paperback Edition

Library of Congress Cataloging-in-Publication Data

Brownstone, David M.
    Timelines of war : a chronology of warfare from 100,000 B.C.
to the present / David Brownstone and Irene Franck. — 1st ed.
        p.   cm.
    Includes index.
    ISBN 0-316-11403-0 (HC)   0-316-11447-2 (PB)
    1. History, Military — Chronology.   I. Franck, Irene M.
II. Title.
D25.A2B76   1994
902′.02 — dc20   94-203

                    10 9 8 7 6 5 4 3 2 1

                                SEM

Published simultaneously in Canada by Little, Brown & Company
(Canada) Limited

Printed in the United States of America

PREFACE

War continues to be one of humankind's chief occupations and preoccupations; we celebrate the end of the Cold War and the emergence of a score of newly freed nations in a huge territory that stretches from the Danube to the Pacific, and see civil wars break out in Bosnia and Georgia, resurgent wars in Angola and Rwanda, growing insurrection in northern India, and continuing low-level wars and new threats of war in scores of other countries. War continues to be endemic, a long, continuing worldwide plague that in our time of nuclear, chemical, and biological weaponry can very well end in destroying the human race. Yet it is also one of humankind's most enduring activities; to be chronicled, studied, dissected, and reduced to its elements so that it may be better understood and better controlled, even though the creation of a world fully at peace may be very difficult for some time to come.

Timelines of War is a chronology of the wars, revolutions, battles, leaders, and weapons that have played such an enormous role in human history, from Megiddo, the rise of Assyria, the siege of Troy, and the century-long Chinese-Hun war 2,000 years ago to the massive world wars, revolutions, and superpower conflicts that have dominated the life of our century; and from Alexander, Caesar, Genghis Khan, Napoleon, Shaka, Eisenhower, and Schwarzkopf to Salamis, Cannae, Waterloo, Gettysburg, Ypres, Normandy, and Iraq. Also included are landmarks in the development and introduction of weapons, and war-related developments in science, technology, and medicine. Peace is to some extent covered, as well, in the form of a considerable number of treaties, such international organizations as the League of Nations and the United Nations, and key peace movements.

Timelines of War is organized chronologically, from the earliest to the most recent times. In early sections, entries are grouped into time periods, such as centuries and later decades. Then, from 1700 on, the information is carried year-by-year. The work is also organized geographically, in four parallel columns lined up across each two-page spread, so that the reader can link or compare events and people across the whole world in any given period.

With this organization, all the theaters of war can be linked chronologically and geographically, as for example during the Napoleonic Wars or the two 20th-century world wars, or earlier during the Greco-Persian Wars, the Roman-Carthaginian Wars, or the Mongol conquests. Similarly, this organization provides a fascinating look at the four-centuries-long European invasion and conquest of the Americas, the centuries-long European conquests of Africa and much of Asia, and the long struggle for dominance in Europe.

Using the headings on each page as a guide, you can easily find the time period or geographical area you are seeking. If, for example, you want to know what military events were occurring in Europe at the time of the Columbus voyages, you can look on the lefthand page for the period 1490–1499. Alternatively, you can go into the book directly through the index.

For ease of use, we have kept abbreviations to a minimum, using only these: *b.* for born; *d.* for died, and *ca.* for circa, in addition to BC and AD. One other editorial note: For Japanese names, we have retained the traditional Japanese name order — family name first, surname second — up to 1700, but from then on have adopted Western-style name order — surname first, family name second — since that is the pattern used in many military works on modern wars.

Our thanks to editors Tracy Brown, Mary South, and Catherine Crawford; editorial assistant Jennifer Stein; copyeditors Barbara Jatkola, Peggy Freudenthal, and David Coen; book designer Janis Owens; and jacket designer Debra Morton, who have all worked so capably to see the book through to publication. Our thanks also to Mary Racette, who was so very helpful in preparing and organizing the material; and as always to the librarians of the northeastern library network, in particular to the staff of the Chappaqua Library — Director Mark Hasskarl; the expert reference staff, including Martha Alcott, Teresa Cullen, Carolyn Jones, Paula Peyraud, Mary Platt, and Carolyn Reznick; and the circulation staff, including Marilyn Coleman, Lois Siwicki, and Jane McKean — who are ever helpful in fulfilling our research needs.

David Brownstone
Irene Franck

TIMELINES · OF · WAR

100,000 ~ 501 BC

Europe and Anatolia

Africa

Southwest Asia (except Anatolia)

East, Central, and South Asia,
the Pacific, and the Americas

Europe and Anatolia	Africa

100,000-5001 BC

Spears were used in Europe; oldest known surviving spear was found in Germany (ca. 120,000 BC), but some fragments may date much earlier, such as an English spear tip (ca. 300,000 BC).

Bow and arrow may have been used on the Iberian Peninsula and in northern Africa (ca. 25,000 BC), though possibly much later.

Mechanical spear-throwers, essentially rigid slings, were used in southern Europe, as depicted at the Lascaux cave (by 15,000 BC); earliest surviving spear-throwers found in southern Europe (from ca. 12,000 BC).

Bow and arrow were used in northern Europe (by 9000 BC); earliest surviving arrow shafts (ca. 8500 BC), in Germany, and bows, in Scandinavia.

Earliest known use of copper as a melted, cast metal (ca. 6400 BC), in Anatolia.

Bow and arrow may have been developed in northern Africa and southern Europe (ca. 25,000 BC; possibly much later), as suggested by possible stone arrow tips and drawings of what seem to be archers found in the Sahara. Other common weapons, developed earlier, included clubs; rocks thrown or hurled (as from a sling), the first missiles; throwing sticks, including javelins, darts, and boomerangs; pikes, or thrusting spears; clubs with sharpened edges, the predecessor of the sword; and axes (tomahawks). Shields of wood or wicker, sometimes covered with leather, were commonly used on the left arm, the right being used to hold the weapon itself. Head, body, and legs might be protected by leather, wicker, cloth (often padded or quilted), or wood.

5000-2501 BC

Wooden palisades and earthen walls were used as fortifications in northern Europe, as at Köln-Lindenthal, in Denmark (ca. 4500 BC).

Polished stone axes and adzes were used in Europe (ca. 4000 BC).

Horse was domesticated by Indo-European-speaking peoples living in eastern Europe, north of the Black Sea, and on the Russian steppe (possibly as early as ca. 4000 BC). Horsedrawn two-wheeled vehicles (chariots) may even have been in use here this early.

Copper tools and weapons began to replace stone ones in Europe, especially in Iberia (from ca. 3000 BC).

Earliest surviving examples of copper weapons (ca. 5000 BC), from Egyptian graves.

Egyptians mined and smelted copper for weapons, tools, and ornaments (ca. 4500 BC).

Egyptians smelted gold and silver (ca. 4000 BC); they also used iron, but of poor quality and apparently only in decorative jewelry, not weapons.

Earliest surviving African bowstave, from what is now Zambia (ca. 3500 BC).

Numerous small regions were combined into the single kingdom of Upper Egypt (ca. 3500 BC).

Egypt's Upper and Lower Kingdoms were unified (ca. 3100 BC) by the warrior-king Menes (Narmer), the first historical figure known by name.

Egyptians used simple boats, essentially modified rafts, propelled by paddles or sails (ca. 3000 BC).

Egypt, which had long traded in the upper Nile Valley, began sending expeditions down the Red Sea to the land of Punt, probably in East Africa or southwest Arabia (by 2800 BC).

Egypt's Old Kingdom, especially under the Third to Seventh Dynasties, had numerous civil wars, while extending its military power into Palestine and Nubia (southern Egypt and the Sudan) (ca. 2630-ca. 2000 BC).

Egyptian pharaoh Snefru (r. ca. 2613-ca. 2589 BC) undertook a military expedition into Nubia, reportedly bringing back 7,000 captives and 200,000 cattle (after 2613 BC), and also conquered the Sinai. Under him the first true pyramids were built. He was succeeded by his son Khufu.

100,000–5001 BC

Jericho, on what is now the West Bank, on the Jordan River, became the first known permanent settlement surrounded by walled fortifications (by ca. 8000 BC).

Copper may have seen limited use (by 8000 BC), though worked like stone, not cast like later metals.

Mesopotamian peoples made axes with stone heads wedged and tied into notches on heavy sticks (before ca. 5000 BC).

Fine chipped tools, including spear points, were being made by the Folsom culture in America (ca. 100,000 BC); they are named for the site in New Mexico where they were first discovered.

Polished stone axes, instead of flaked stone heads, began to be used eastward from Persia through India (before 5000 BC).

Peoples of the Americas used a type of spear-thrower called an atlatl (before 5000 BC).

5000–2501 BC

Sumerians, people of unknown ancestry, settled in southern Mesopotamia, in modern Iraq (by ca. 3500 BC), establishing Ur and other city-states, which were often at war with each other. They smelted gold and silver.

Bronze Age developed, as civilizations in Mesopotamia and the eastern Mediterranean began to use bronze for weapons, tools, and ornaments (3500–3000 BC); a poor quality iron, known as metalworking by-product, was used largely for ornaments.

Carts with solid wheels were in use in Mesopotamia, possibly developed first there but perhaps borrowed from earlier developments on the Russian steppe. Heavy and awkward, they were pulled by beasts of burden such as oxen (ca. 3500 BC).

Assyrians emerged as a power in northern Mesopotamia (ca. 3000 BC); for centuries they would engage in battles with their neighbors — the Hittites to the north, the Sumerians and Babylonians to the south.

Two-wheeled vehicles called chariots — still awkward and cumbersome — came into use in Mesopotamia, perhaps first in Sumer (ca. 3000 BC); wheels were sometimes strengthened with a wooden rim.

Peoples of Mesopotamia made axes with heads of copper or bronze, not stone, containing a hole into which the shaft was fitted (ca. 3000 BC).

Semilegendary warrior-king Gilgamesh, whose history is told in the epic poem *Gilgamesh,* ruled the Sumerian city-state of Uruk (Erech) (ca. 2675 BC).

Nomadic peoples of Central Asia gradually domesticated horses, breeding larger, stronger animals (3000–2000 BC).

Mohenjo-daro and Harappa developed as city-states in the Indus River valley (ca. 3000–1500 BC).

Regular trading route ran between Melukkha, probably in the lower Indus Valley; colonies along the Persian Gulf, notably Dilmun, in Bahrain, and Magan (near Muscat?), on the Omani coast; and the peoples of southern Mesopotamia (by 3000 BC).

According to Chinese annals, the semilegendary Huang Ti (Yellow Emperor) founded the Chinese nation (r. ca. 2697–ca. 2597 BC), introducing innovations such as writing, mathematical calculations, money, the compass, oxcarts, and much more; Chinese tradition suggests that he came "from the West," out of Central Asia.

Bronzeworking techniques were being used in the Indus Valley civilizations of Mohenjo-daro and Harappa (by ca. 2500 BC) and in China's Yellow River basin (before ca. 2500 BC).

2500-2001 BC

Tin was smelted in Anatolia, probably first near the oldest known tin source, at Goltepe (ca. 2500 BC), beginning the Bronze Age in southwestern Asia.

Copper knives, daggers, and ornaments were being made by peoples in central, northern, and eastern Europe (late 3d millennium BC).

Peoples from mainland Europe invaded Britain, settling on Salisbury Plain (ca. 2500 BC).

Peoples from the eastern Mediterranean settled colonies on the coast of southern spain (ca. 2500 BC).

Earliest known iron weapon, probably ceremonial, a dagger from Alaca Hüyük, in Anatolia (ca. 2200 BC).

Egyptians used an early form of phalanx, a close-knit formation of soldiers — in this period archers and spearmen (ca. 2500 BC); they also used ladders with wheels to help them climb over walls.

Egyptians developed seagoing wooden vessels propelled by rowers, with which they sailed on the Mediterranean (ca. 2500 BC).

In Egypt, the Middle Kingdom, with its capital at Thebes, began to maintain professional standing armies, often with Nubian auxiliary units (ca. 2100-ca. 1600 BC).

2000-1501 BC

Chariots with lighter wheels, using 8 to 12 spokes, rather than solid disks, were used on the Russian steppe (ca. 2000 BC).

Indo-European-speaking peoples, probably from the Russian steppe north of the Black Sea, began to spread in all directions, fighting from horses and using chariots (ca. 2000 BC). Developing distinct languages and cultures — as Iranians, Hittites, Greeks, Celts, Cimmerians, Slavs, Balts, and many other peoples — they would send waves of migrations, sparking many wars and cultural changes in Eurasia, resulting in their languages being spoken from Britain to India.

Celts, an Indo-European-speaking people, became known as a distinct people in the upper Danube region (2d millennium BC).

Seagoing wooden ships with high sterns were made by the Minoan people of Crete (ca. 2000 BC), then the dominant trading center of the eastern Mediterranean, with maritime supremacy.

Latins, an Indo-European-speaking people closely related to the Greeks, invaded Italy by way of the Alps, bringing with them bronzeworking techniques (ca. 2000 BC).

Hittites, an Indo-European-speaking people, established their rule in northern and central Anatolia (Asia Minor) (ca. 2000 BC), also pressing neighbors to the east and south.

Peoples later called "Beaker folk" invaded Britain (by ca. 2000 BC).

Battering rams, covered with hides or reeds, were used in Egypt (ca. 2000 BC); at least one fortress, at Buhen, in Nubia, had a drawbridge equipped with rollers.

Hyksos (shepherd-kings) made the first known foreign invasion of Egypt (ca. 1800 BC), bringing with them from southwest Asia the horse, the horse-drawn chariot, and bronze weapons superior to the Egyptians' copper ones.

Hyksos completed their conquest of Egypt by taking the southern regions (ca. 1700 BC), ruling for another century.

Wheels with spokes were used in Egypt (by ca. 1600 BC).

Egyptian pharaoh Amosis (r. 1580-1557 BC) reestablished native rule in Egypt, driving the Hyksos into Palestine, and reconquered northern Nubia; he had adopted the Hyksos war chariot and developed a well-trained permanent army of archers.

Under Amenhotep I (r. ca. 1546-ca. 1526 BC) and his son-in-law and successor, Thutmosis I (r. ca. 1526-ca. 1512 BC), Egyptian power was extended into Libya, southern Nubia, Palestine, and Syria, to the Euphrates River.

Southwest Asia (except Anatolia)	East, Central, and South Asia, the Pacific, and the Americas

First Dynasty of Ur, in Mesopotamia, was founded by Mesanni-Padda (whose royal tombs were excavated in 1922 AD) (ca. 2500 BC).

First Dynasty of Lagash was founded by Ur-Nanshe (ca. 2500 BC); his dynasty produced some of the earliest known historical documents.

Chariots came into common use for warfare in Mesopotamia, generally carrying a driver — the charioteer — and a warrior armed with a spear, ax, or javelin (ca. 2500 BC).

An early form of the phalanx, a close-knit formation of soldiers — in this period archers and spearmen — was used in Mesopotamia (ca. 2500 BC).

Lugalzaggisi of Erech (Umma) (r. ca. 2375-ca. 2350 BC) created the temporarily unified Sumerian Empire in Mesopotamia, including parts of Syria and Anatolia.

Sargon of Akkad (r. ca. 2334-ca. 2249 BC) conquered Sumer and built an empire extending into Anatolia and the Mediterranean coast, which lasted for two centuries. In addition to bows and arrows, Akkadians use spears as projectiles; their desert-fighting style made them more mobile than the Sumerians, who mostly used unwieldy lances and heavy shields.

Akkadian Empire collapsed, and the independent empire of Sumer was reestablished in southern Mesopotamia (ca. 2200 BC).

Sumerian Empire was destroyed by Elamite invaders from the east (ca. 2006 BC).

Copper was used in China, although whether it was only worked or also smelted is unclear (ca. 2500 BC).

Traditional date for the settlement of Korea by people of Mongol stock (ca. 2300 BC).

Chariots were used in China (ca. 2100-1600 BC), at first only by military leaders as mobile command posts, generally accompanied by a driver, several archers, and a drummer for signaling.

Peoples of Mongol stock migrated from northern Asia to Japan (before 2000 BC), pushing the Ainu people off the main southern islands.

Amorites established the First (Old) Babylonian Empire, centered on Babylon (ca. 2000 BC), in southern Mesopotamia.

Wheels with spokes were used in Mesopotamia (ca. 2000 BC); some also now had rims of copper, not wood.

Indo-European-speaking peoples from the north began their invasions of Iran (ca. 2000 BC).

Metalworkers began to use hammering and alloys to harden metals for tools during the Copper Age (ca. 1850-1650 BC).

One-humped camel was domesticated in Arabia (ca. 1800 BC); when and where the two-humped Bactrian camel was domesticated is unclear.

Babylonian warrior-king Hammurabi (r. 1792-1750 BC) extended his empire's rule to all Mesopotamia, also establishing a famous code of law.

Under Murshilish I (r. ca. 1620-ca. 1590 BC), the Hittites persistently raided the Old Babylonian Empire, bringing it to near collapse; the Hittites took Aleppo and extended their empire deep into Syria (by ca. 1590 BC).

As the Old Babylonian Empire fell to invaders (ca. 1530 BC), Kassites from Iran took southern Mesopotamia, establishing a kingdom that retained the Babylonian code of civil justice.

Peoples in what is now Thailand were making bronze objects (by ca. 2000 BC), possibly centuries earlier.

Aryans, an Indo-European-speaking people closely related to the Persians, began to press into India; they brought chariots and military weapons and techniques superior to those of the Dravidians who lived there (from ca. 2000 BC).

Central Asian horses were used to pull two-wheeled carts, or chariots, originally with solid wheels soon made lighter by the use of spokes (after ca. 2000 BC). Central Asian peoples also developed a compound bow designed to be shot powerfully and accurately from a moving vehicle. These gave them a distinct military advantage until their more settled neighbors developed similar vehicles, weapons, and horses.

Aryans invaded the Indus Valley (by 1800 BC), completing the fall of the already-weakened Mohenjo-daro and Harappa cultures; from the merged peoples would develop the Hindu civilization in the Ganges Valley (after ca. 1400 BC). For some centuries, their primary weapon was a long (four- to five-foot) bow with a metal-tipped arrow; generally unshielded, bowmen were fronted by a row of shield-carrying javelin throwers.

2000-1501 BC (cont.)

Greece experienced waves of invasions by Indo-European-speaking peoples called Achaeans — later simply called Greeks (from ca. 1900 BC).

Tin was used and bronze made in western Europe (ca. 1900 BC).

Celts, an Indo-European-speaking people, invaded the British Isles from mainland Europe, apparently bringing with them knowledge of copperworking (ca. 1800 BC).

1500-1251 BC

Iron of sufficiently high quality for use in weapons was first developed on the Anatolian plateau, probably by the Mitanni people in iron-rich Armenia (ca. 1500 BC); the secret technology would gradually spread through captured ironworkers.

Minoan trading civilization on the island of Crete was invaded and conquered by Mycenaean Greeks (ca. 1450 BC).

Peoples from the European mainland invaded the Wessex area of England (ca. 1450 BC).

Seagoing ships with actual hulls were introduced on the Mediterranean (by ca. 1400 BC).

Hittites conquered the Mitanni kingdom in Armenia (ca. 1370 BC), learning their ironworking secrets.

Greeks probably besieged Troy (ca. 1300-ca. 1180 BC), the trading center in northwestern Anatolia, main gateway into Asia; tales of this siege, encrusted with myth and legend, survived primarily through Homer's *Iliad* and *Odyssey* (written ca. 800 BC).

By the reign of Hattushilish III (r. ca. 1281-1260 BC), though possibly as early as 1100 BC, the Hittites were using iron weapons, armor, and chariots; their initial advantage over their rivals would soon be lost because of internal weakness in the kingdom.

Egyptians made more sophisticated types of wooden ships, some with double rudders (ca. 1500 BC).

d. Thutmosis III (?-ca. 1449 BC), Egyptian pharaoh (r. ca. 1504-ca. 1449 BC) who was victorious at the Battle of Megiddo (ca. 1469 BC); he expanded the empire to its greatest extent, to the frontiers of the Hittite Empire in Anatolia.

Under Pharaoh Akhenaton (Ikhnaton) (r. ca. 1380-ca. 1365 BC), Egypt was convulsed by religious conflict, weakening its hold on outlying territories, especially Syria, taken by the Hittites, and much of Palestine, retaken by local leaders.

Bronze weapons and tools, as well as horse-drawn carts, were used in the Sahara (ca. 1300 BC).

Egyptian chariots were built with six, not just four, spokes (ca. 1300 BC).

d. Seti I (?-1299 BC), Egyptian pharaoh (r. ca. 1318-ca. 1299 BC) who succeeded his father, Ramses I; he fought in Palestine, Libya, and Syria. He was succeeded by Ramses II (r. ca. 1299-ca. 1232 BC), who reexpanded the boundaries of the Egyptian empire.

1250-1001 BC

Dorians, an Indo-European-speaking people, began to move into Greece (ca. 1250 BC), their iron weapons giving them an advantage over the bronze-using Mycenaeans, whom they overwhelmed.

Egypt's Ramses III (r. ca. 1198-ca. 1167 BC) reconquered Palestine and held off invaders, including Libyans and "Peoples of the Sea," raiders from Medi-

Southwest Asia (except Anatolia)	East, Central, and South Asia, the Pacific, and the Americas
	In China, Yu founded the Hsia dynasty (ca. 1800-1500 BC).
	At the Battle of Ming Chiao (in Honan, near modern Shang Chu), the Shang defeated the semilegendary Shao dynasty (ca. 1523 BC), establishing the Shang dynasty, with its capital at Anyang. Horses and chariots were used; bronze weapons, tools, and helmets were made by then or soon after; the bow remained the main weapon, with arrows (probably bamboo) tipped with metal.
Cire-perdu (lost wax) method of metalworking was developed (ca. 1500 BC), allowing production of more refined weapons, tools, and ornaments in the Near East.	Bronzeworking techniques were used in western Siberia (ca. 1500 BC) and then in central Siberia (ca. 1200 BC).
King of Kadesh, a Hyksos kingdom in northern Palestine, spearheaded a revolt in Palestine and Syria against Egyptian rule (1472 BC).	Chinese axes and lances were made in imitation of Siberian styles (ca. 1400 BC).
Egyptians invaded southwest Asia with a great army, and at the Battle of Megiddo, the first battle described in historical records, Thutmosis III led his troops to victory against rebels in central Palestine, the two forces clashing near Megiddo fortress, north of Mount Carmel (ca. 1469 BC).	Chinese chariots were made with wheels having more than four spokes (ca. 1300 BC).
Egypt's Thutmosis III reconquered much of Syria from the Hittites, forcing them to pay tribute (ca. 1460 BC).	
Mitanni people of northwest Mesopotamia established sway over the weakened Old Assyrian Empire (ca. 1450 BC).	
Under Eriba-adad (r. ca. 1390-ca. 1364 BC), the Assyrians became independent from the Mitanni, establishing the Middle Assyrian Empire; as the Assyrians expanded, they forced mass deportations from their erstwhile Hittite allies, including blacksmiths who possessed ironworking techniques; they would give the Assyrians a significant edge in weapons technology.	
Egypt's Seti I defeated a coalition of small Palestinian states at Beisan in Galilee (ca. 1315 BC), then dominated Palestine but failed to reconquer Syria from the Hittites.	
Mesopotamians began to ride animals, notably horses and donkeys, rather than simply using them to haul loads or pull chariots and carts (ca. 1300 BC).	
Pharaoh Ramses II and his Egyptian forces defeated the Hittite army near Kadesh (1294 BC), on the Orontes River in northern Palestine; unable to take Kadesh itself, Ramses left the Hittites controlling part of Syria.	
Egypt's Ramses II and the Hittite king Hattushilish III concluded a peace treaty and alliance, recognizing Egyptian control in Palestine and Hittite control in Syria (1271 BC).	
Jewish people who had been held in Egypt were led by Moses on a migration from Egypt into Palestine, the Promised Land, in what was called the Exodus (ca. 1250 BC).	Cast bronze bells and other objects were made in China (by ca. 1200 BC).

Europe and Anatolia

Africa

1250-1001 BC (cont.)

"Peoples of the Sea," raiders from eastern Mediterranean islands and southern Europe, sent waves of invaders to eastern Mediterranean coastal regions; most were driven off, but some established themselves, notably the Philistines in Palestine (by ca. 1200 BC).

Distinct culture of the Scythians, an Indo-European-speaking people, developed on the Russian steppe (ca. 1200 BC).

Cimmerians, an Indo-European-speaking people, settled on the Crimean peninsula, north of the Black Sea (ca. 1200 BC).

Phoenician colonists founded Gadir (Agadir; Cadiz) on the southern Atlantic coast of Spain, past Gibraltar, according to traditional dating (ca. 1200 BC); this is now thought to have occurred a century or two later, with the Phoenicians possibly preceded by Greek settlers.

Phoenicians founded colonies on Cyprus and Rhodes (11th c. BC).

terranean islands and southern Europe, some of whom gained footholds on the Egyptian coast.

Phoenicians (Canaanites) settled Utica (Utique) on the coast of North Africa, guarding The Narrows of the Mediterranean (ca. 1100 BC); they also founded Hadrumetum and Leptis (Lepcis) Magna, near modern Tripoli, in Libya, in the same period.

1000-801 BC

Greeks founded the city-state of Sparta (ca. 1000 BC), originally a group of villages in the Eurotas Valley on Greece's Peloponnesian peninsula; it would later be noted as a military society.

Phoenicians established more colonies along the North African coast, from the Gulf of Syrtis to the Atlantic Ocean (1st millennium BC).

| Southwest Asia (except Anatolia) | East, Central, and South Asia, the Pacific, and the Americas |

Ironworking techniques became widely known and used in southwestern Asia, as at Jaffa, in Israel (ca. 1250 BC).

Various city-states in coastal Palestine, including Ashdod, Ashkelon, Ekron, Gaza, and Gath, formed an alliance against attacks by the "Peoples of the Sea," the most successful of these being the Philistines (ca. 1200 BC).

With Egypt and the Hittites in decline and Assyria on the rise, the peoples of Palestine and Syria formed many small, independent states in the "Warring States" period (ca. 1200-ca. 800 BC); most notable of these would be the Philistines, the Phoenicians, the Aramaeans, and the Jews, who met at Schechem (ca. 1200 BC) to celebrate conquering the Promised Land, Palestine.

League of the Twelve Tribes (Amphictyony) was formed by the Jews in Palestine to provide protection for themselves and a central shrine (ca. 1200 BC).

Elamites defeated the Kassites in southern Mesopotamia and sacked Babylon (1160 BC).

Under Tiglath-Pileser I (r. ca. 1116-ca. 1093 BC), Assyria again became a major military power, dominating southwest Asia from the headwaters of the Tigris River in Anatolia through northern Syria to the Mediterranean, largely maintaining the empire for most of five centuries; with its highly trained standing armies (charioteers, infantry, and troops specially armed with helmets, mail, and shields) instead of earlier militias, Assyria had the first-known thoroughly military society.

Warrior-leader Gideon briefly united most of the independent Jewish states to defeat the invading Midianites (ca. 1100 BC).

Chariots in Mesopotamia began to have six, instead of just four, spokes, and the axle was moved farther to the rear, for increased mobility (ca. 1100 BC).

d. Tiglath-Pileser I (?-ca. 1093 BC), Assyrian ruler (r. ca. 1116-ca. 1093 BC) who rebuilt the Assyrian Empire.

Philistines, one of many "Peoples of the Sea," invaded and came to dominate lands inhabited by Jewish peoples (ca. 1080-1025 BC).

Aramaean invaders shook the Assyrian Empire (ca. 1050 BC) but were eventually halted, some being absorbed into the existing empire.

Under Saul (r. 1028-1013 BC), the Jews fought against the Ammonites of eastern Jordan and revolted against the Philistines, with some success; Saul was killed in the Battle of Mount Gilboa, on the Plain of Jezreel (1013 BC).

Under David (r. ca. 1010-ca. 973 BC), the Jews resisted Philistine attempts to reestablish domination, bringing many Philistines into the Jewish army as mercenaries, taking the Philistine coastal cities, and defeating the Ammonites, Moabites, and Edomites to rule all Palestine.

In the Battle of Mu Yu (in southern Honan, China), the Chou people from the Wei and Yellow River region, led by the "Martial King" Wu Wang, defeated the Shang (ca. 1027 BC; possibly ca. 1057 BC), establishing the Chou (Zhou) dynasty, which would last for eight centuries.

During Solomon's relatively peaceful reign (r. ca. 973-ca. 933 BC) in Israel, the Aramaeans and Edomites became independent; according to the Bible, the queen of Sheba (Saba), in southwest Arabia, visited Solomon, possibly seeking a trading alliance.

Chou dynasty extended its control east to the sea and north to near today's Manchurian border, then south into the lower Yangtze Valley and the central coastal regions (ca. 1000-900 BC). Chinese explorers or mer-

1000-801 BC (cont.)

Use of iron began in Italy, believed to have been brought in by migrations of various peoples, including the Latins, Sabines, and Illurians (ca. 1000 BC).

Etruscans, possibly originally from Anatolia, invaded and colonized northwestern Italy, establishing a distinct culture (by ca. 900 BC).

Mediterranean sailors, Greeks or Phoenicians first, added rams to their warships; instead of boarding for hand-to-hand combat, as previously, they tried to sink the opposing ship (ca. 850 BC).

Kingdom of Urartu (Ararat in the Bible) was established by Sadur I in the Armenian highlands near Lakes Van and Urmia, in eastern Anatolia (ca. 835-825 BC), becoming a major power.

Phoenicians founded Carthage on the North African coast (814 BC), east of Utica; this would be the basis of the Carthaginian Empire, lasting long after the "mother city" of Tyre, in Phoenicia, was eclipsed; in Virgil's *Aeneid*, Carthage was founded by dissenting Tyrians, including Dido, who met Aeneas when he was shipwrecked at Carthage on his way from fallen Troy to Italy.

800-701 BC

Kingdom of Phrygia was established in Anatolia, with its capital at Gordium (ca. 800 BC); its best-known king would be Midas (in Assyrian, Mita), famed for his gold.

Rome was founded in west-central Italy, according to tradition (ca. 753 BC), though perhaps somewhat later.

Greeks from Corinth took the island of Corcyra (Corfu) (753 BC).

Greeks founded Cumae in southwestern Italy, north of Naples; it is the oldest known Greek colony on the peninsula (750 BC).

Scythians, an Indo-European-speaking people out of Turkestan, pushed their relatives, the Cimmerians from the Crimean peninsula, ahead of them through the Caucasus Mountains into Anatolia, where both clashed with the Assyrians and were then driven back by the Medes (ca. 750 BC); many Scythians settled in the region north of the Black Sea, while others pressed on into the Danube Basin, the Balkans, and eastern Germany. Scythians were mounted archers, using light composite bows and arrows tipped with stone, bone, bronze, or iron; their fighting techniques were so effective

Ethiopian invaders led by Piankhi, king of Kush (r. ca. 751-ca. 716 BC), conquered Egypt (ca. 730 BC), making their capital at Napata, on the Nile.

Southwest Asia (except Anatolia)

East, Central, and South Asia, the Pacific, and the Americas

After Solomon's death (ca. 933 BC), the Jewish kingdom split into two rival parts: Israel in the north and Judah in the south, with its capital at Jerusalem; the two would be involved in a series of wars over the next 200 years.

Under Ashurnasirpal II (r. 883-859 BC), the Assyrians used cavalry, plus mass executions, impalements, deportations, and other brutalities, in major offensives in Mesopotamia, Syria, and the Kurdish mountains, where they sacked the city of Nishtun (Nusaybin) (883 BC).

Omri, head of the army, became king of Israel (r. ca. 876-ca. 869 BC) after conflict with Egypt, the Aramaeans, Damascus, and the Philistines; he made the strategic site of Samaria the capital. He was succeeded by his son Ahab (r. ca. 869-ca. 853 BC).

Ashurnarsirpal II and his Assyrian forces campaigned against Babylonia and took Suhu (878 BC).

d. Ashurnasirpal II (Assur-nasirpal) (?-ca. 859 BC), Assyrian ruler (r. 883-859 BC). His son and successor, Shalmaneser III (r. ca. 859-ca. 824 BC), solidified Assyrian control over Syria and Palestine but was unable to take the Aramaean capital of Damascus.

At Qarqar (Karkar), the allied forces of Ahab of Israel and Ben Hadad II of Damascus defeated the Assyrians under Shalmaneser III (854 BC).

chants may have traveled far to the west in Central Asia, to the domains of the largely or wholly mythical Hsi Wang Mu (Royal Mother of the West), linked by some to the queen of Sheba; these journeys were ascribed to the semilegendary Emperor Mu in the *Bamboo Annals*.

According to legend, the Iranian king Jamshid married a daughter of the king of Machin (Great China) (ca. 1000 BC) and was pursued through China and India by his enemies; other legends from the same period tell of Iranian kings willing parts of China or Central Asia to their sons, suggesting contact between western and eastern Asia.

In a series of small wars with various city-states (ca. 1000-ca. 600 BC), Aryan Hindus became dominant in northern and central India, with their influence extending into southern India and Ceylon.

Two-humped Bactrian camels came into use in China (early 1st millennium BC).

Central Asian nomads, who had for a millennium been experimenting with riding horses, learned how to control horses with the bottom half of the body (without saddle or stirrups), leaving the arms free for shooting; so the cavalry was born (ca. 900 BC), which would gradually make the chariot obsolete.

Central Asian invaders of Mongol stock — the first of many — raided extensively into the north Indian plain (ca. 900 BC).

King Hsuan of the Western Ch'u, one of many Chinese warlords, temporarily defeated the Chou in the field (823 BC); he reportedly had 3,000 chariots and a highly organized military structure, which was adopted by many other warlords.

Assyrians conquered Palestine and Syria (ca. 750 BC), which would not become independent again until the 20th century.

Under Tiglath-Pileser III (r. 745-727 BC), the Assyrians — after a period of weakness — once again extended their rule, taking Syria, Palestine, and territories east of the Jordan River and even invading Babylonia. Assyria's professional armies included masses of spearmen, archers using powerful bows and iron-tipped arrows, cavalry (many of them Scythian mercenaries), and horse-drawn chariots, as well as siege craft equipment, such as battering rams and wooden towers to bring archers into range and give their projectiles greater velocity; their main advantage was not technological, but the highly organized use of these forces.

d. Tiglath-Pileser III (?-727 BC), Assyrian ruler (r. 745-727 BC) who rebuilt Assyria as a major power.

Israel revolted against the Assyrians, who under Shalmaneser V besieged Samaria; after Shalmaneser's death, Sargon II besieged the city, then captured and destroyed it, ending the revolt (724-722 BC).

Chou central power declined in China, leading to persistent wars among numerous warlords (from ca. 800 BC).

Chou rulers were driven out of the Wei Valley (771 BC), according to tradition because the emperor had too often "cried wolf," lighting the army's alert fires to amuse his mistress; when real danger threatened, the army failed to respond to the signal fires. The succeeding Eastern Chou dynasty (ca. 770-256 BC), with a new capital at Loyang, saw the rise of the religious philosophers Confucius (ca. 551-479 BC) and Lao-tzu (6th c. BC), founder of Taoism. The Chou built numerous roads, along which sped chariots, generally drawn by four horses and carrying a driver, a lancer, and an archer.

800-701 BC (cont.)

that the Scythians became prized mercenaries, changing battle techniques, especially in the Middle East.

Greeks founded the colony of Naxos on Sicily (735 BC).

Greeks from Corinth founded the colony of Syracuse on Sicily, key to the western Mediterranean (733 BC).

Tiglath-Pileser III and his Assyrian army conquered the kingdom of Urartu (Ararat), in the Armenian highlands of Anatolia (714 BC).

After a long conflict, the Anatolian kingdom of Phrygia bowed to Assyrian control (709 BC).

Greeks founded the coastal colony of Tarentum (Tarento), on the bay west of the "heel" of southern Italy's "boot" (708 BC).

Mediterranean sailors, probably Phoenicians or Greeks first, developed biremes, war galleys containing two banks of oars (before 700 BC).

700-651 BC

Lycurgus, a semilegendary figure, became leader of Sparta (ca. 700 BC), transforming it into a thoroughly military society in which citizenship and army service were virtually indistinguishable.

First Messenian War (ca. 700-680 BC): Greek city-state of Sparta became dominant over the southern Peloponnesian peninsula, notably the Messenian plain.

People of Rome waged persistent wars with their Etruscan neighbors (ca. 700-ca. 500 BC), developing a strong military system.

Major iron-manufacturing center developed at Hallstatt, Austria (ca. 700 BC).

Under Gyges and his son Ardys (ca. 680-652 BC), the western Anatolian kingdom of Lydia attempted to take control of Ionian Greek cities on the coast, with little success; the Lydians developed coined money.

Greeks founded Byzantium (later Constantinople; Istanbul) as a colony and trading center on the Bosporus, the strait that forms the vital gateway to the Black Sea and Asia (ca. 660 BC).

Under a succession of leaders (called tyrants) (657-580 BC), Corinth became Greece's leading sea power.

Major iron-manufacturing center developed at Meroë, in Nubia (the Sudan) (ca. 700 BC).

Under Essarhaddon (r. 681-668 BC), the Assyrians conquered Egypt from the Ethiopians (671 BC); he was killed three years later during an Egyptian rebellion led in the field by Taharqa (668 BC). Assyrian leader Ashurbanipal finally put down the revolt, taking the Egyptian capital of Memphis (668-667 BC).

Assyrian leader Ashurbanipal put down a second Egyptian revolt led by Tantamun, nephew of earlier rebel leader Taharqa; the Assyrians sacked Thebes (El Karnak) (663 BC).

Under Psamtik I (r. ca. 663-ca. 609 BC), the Egyptians freed themselves from foreign rule by defeating Ashurbanipal's Assyrians (ca. 658-ca. 651 BC).

Greeks, who had come to Egypt as mercenaries and remained as colonists, temporarily took Thebes (654 BC).

650-601 BC

Greek traders settled the colony of Tartessos (mid-7th c. BC), on the Atlantic coast of Spain, in a region rich with copper, gold, silver, and precious tin, needed to make bronze; this put them in direct conflict with the Phoenicians, who had settlements all around them.

Trireme, triple-banked war galley, first developed, probably by the Greeks (ca. 650 BC); possibly earlier, by Ameinokles of Corinth (704 BC).

Second Messenian War (ca. 640-620 BC): Sparta renewed its dominance over Messenia, enslaving its surviving opponents. Sparta developed its characteristic military state, based on hoplites, armored foot soldiers operating in closely formed units called phalanxes.

Phoenician sailors sailed around Africa, from the Red Sea south along the continent's east coast and up along the Atlantic coast through the Strait of Gibraltar and back to Egypt, going ashore seasonally during the three-year voyage to grow grain for food, according to Herodotus (ca. mid-7th c. BC).

Southwest Asia (except Anatolia)	East, Central, and South Asia, the Pacific, and the Americas

Under Sargon II (r. 722-705 BC), Assyria defeated an alliance of its northern neighbors, extending its power into northern Anatolia and suppressing an uprising in Babylonia.

Palestine, Syria, and Babylonia rebelled, dealing the Assyrians a notable defeat at Jerusalem (701 BC).

Phoenicians introduced the first vessels designed primarily for fighting — longer, narrower, faster biremes, oar-propelled galleys named for their two banks of oars (ca. 700 BC).

Assyrians reconquered the rebel provinces of Palestine, Syria, and Babylonia, in the process destroying Babylon (689 BC).

Under Ashurbanipal (r. 668-627 BC), son of Essarhaddon, the Assyrians conducted various campaigns on their northern frontier and fought off persistent attacks from other neighbors; from then on, the Assyrians largely relied on Scythian mercenaries.

Ashurbanipal and his Assyrian forces took Tyre (Sur) (ca. 658 BC), the great Phoenician port and (with Sidon) center of its "royal purple" dye factories.

Ashurbanipal's half-brother Shamash-shu-mukin led a revolt in Babylon (652-648 BC).

An informal trading network stretched across the Eurasian steppe, with Greek metalworkers from the Black Sea colonies trading their weapons and ornaments for gold, grain, and furs from the Scythians; the Scythians also traded eastward, providing the Chinese with camels, horses, furs, and jade in exchange for Chinese silk (by ca. 700 BC).

According to tradition, Jimmu Tenno (Kamu-yamato-ihare-biko), a semilegendary warrior from Kyushu, conquered neighboring peoples to establish the first unified Japanese empire, based in Yamoto province, near modern Nara (ca. 660 BC); he is regarded as the ancestor of all succeeding Japanese emperors.

Assyrian forces under Ashurbanipal besieged and took Babylon (650-648 BC).

d. Ashurbanipal (Ashur-bani-apli) (?-627 BC), king of Assyria (r. 668-627 BC) who lost Egypt to Psamtik I (ca. 658-ca. 651 BC).

Allied with Cyaxares of Media, Satrap (governor) Nabopolassar led Babylonia in a successful revolt against Assyrian rule (626 BC).

Under Cyaxares (r. 625-585 BC), the Medes built an empire that stretched from Lydia, on the Aegean Sea in northest Anatolia, to the Indus River, the largest known empire up to that time.

Assyria's domination ended with a successful invasion by the Medes and Babylonians, using many Scythian mercenaries (616 BC); the

Greek adventurer Aristeas claimed to have traveled with Scythian caravans eastward across the Eurasian steppe to their gold source in the Altai (Golden) Mountains (7th or 6th c. BC).

650-601 BC (cont.)

Under Alyattes (r. 605-560 BC), the Anatolian kingdom of Lydia expanded, bringing it into conflict with its neighbors.

600-551 BC

Phocaean Greeks, originally from the Anatolian coast, founded Massalia (Marseilles), the prime port near the Rhône delta in southern France (ca. 600 BC).

Various peoples in Italy founded the League of Twelve Cities (ca. 600 BC).

Tarquin royal line of Etruscans ruled Rome, which came to dominate the whole region of Latium (ca. 600-509 BC), and began to develop a strong military bent.

Sparta, with its military civilization, was the strongest of the Greek states, although others — notably Argos, Athens, Corinth, and Thebes — formed shifting alliances to challenge its dominance (ca. 600 BC).

Avars moved into the Hungarian plain from Central Asia (ca. 600 BC).

Anchor was developed, possibly by Anarcharis the Scythian (by ca. 600 BC).

After a long border war (600-585 BC), the Medes and Lydians finally settled on the Halys River as the boundary between them.

Croesus (active ca. 560-546 BC), ruler of Lydia, son of Alyattes, and famed for his wealth, reportedly attacked the Persians (547 BC) after being told that if he did so, he would "destroy a great kingdom" — not realizing it would be his own.

Domesticated Arabian camels began to be used in Egypt (by 6th c. BC).

Egyptian pharaoh Psamtik II (r. ca. 595-ca. 589 BC) campaigned inconclusively in lower Nubia (Kush) (ca. 590 BC).

Egyptian pharaoh Apries (r. ca. 589-570 BC) failed to defeat the Greek colony of Cyrene, west of Egypt (ca. 570 BC); he was then deposed in a revolt led by Ahmose II, dying shortly afterward (ca. 568 BC).

Ahmose II led Egyptian forces in an invasion of Palestine but was defeated by the Chaldeans under Nebuchadnezzar II (567 BC).

550-501 BC

Greek city-states formed a mutual-protection alliance called the Peloponnesian League, dominated by the strongest member, Sparta (from ca. 550 BC).

Lydia's ruler Croesus took control of all Ionian Greek cities on the coast of Anatolia except Miletus (ca. 550 BC).

b. Miltiades (ca. 550-489 BC), Athenian general.

Croesus of Lydia, allied with the Egyptians, Chaldeans, and Spartans, crossed the Halys River to invade Persia (547 BC), meeting the Persians under Cyrus the Great in the inconclusive Battle of Pteria (547 or 546 BC); he then retired to the Lydian capital, Sardis.

On the plain of Thymbra, Croesus and his Lydian army were routed by Cyrus the Great, who pursued the retreating forces into Lydia, taking Sardis (546 BC). Heavy infantry from Lydia's ally

d. Ahmose II (Amasis) (?-ca. 525 BC), Egyptian pharaoh (r. ca. 570-526 BC); he had served as a general under both Psamtik II and Apries, whom he then deposed (ca. 570 BC); his forces also defeated Nebuchadnezzar II of Babylon (567 BC) and fought with Croesus of Lydia against Cyrus the Great of Persia (547-546 BC). He was briefly succeeded by his son Psamtik III (r. 526-525 BC).

Persians, under Cyrus's son Cambyses, defeated Psamtik III at Pelusium and conquered Egypt (525 BC), which was destined to remain under foreign rule for the next 2,400 years. Cambyses also captured the Greek colony of Cyrene but failed in his Nile expeditions against Nubia and Ethiopia.

Southwest Asia (except Anatolia)	East, Central, and South Asia, the Pacific, and the Americas

Assyrian capital, Nineveh, was taken and razed (612 BC). The Chaldeans then took the former Assyrian lands west of the Tigris River, founding the New Babylonian (Chaldean) Empire. Territories east of the Tigris went to the Medes.

At the second Battle of Megiddo — called Armageddon — Necho and his Egyptian army decisively defeated a Jewish army under Josiah, then advanced to the Euphrates (609 BC).

At Carchemish, Babylonian forces under Nebuchadnezzar II crushed Necho's Egyptian army, driving them out of Syria and Palestine (605 BC).

600-551 BC

As predicted by the prophet Jeremiah, Jerusalem was besieged, captured, and destroyed by Nebuchadnezzar II (587 BC), ending the kingdom of Judah; many Jews were deported to the newly rebuilt Babylon, beginning the "Babylonian captivity" (586-538 BC) and the Diaspora (dispersal) of Jewish people from their homeland.

Babylonians under Nebuchadnezzar conducted a long, unsuccessful seige of Tyre (585-573 BC), although Nebuchadnezzar succeeded in putting down revolts in Syria, Palestine, and Phoenicia.

b. Cyrus II (the Great) (ca. 585-ca. 530 BC), king of Persia.

Egyptian pharaoh Apries was defeated at Jerusalem by Chaldean leader Nebuchadnezzar, who then took Palestine (ca. 580 BC).

Persians, an Indo-European-speaking people related to the Medes, deposed Astyages of Media (559 BC), establishing their independence under Cyrus the Great, who quickly consolidated his control over Media (559-550 BC).

In India's Ganges River plain, 16 kingdoms and republics emerged, known collectively as the Mahajanapandas (ca. 600 BC). This was the century of the religious leaders Siddhartha Gautama (ca. 560-ca. 483 BC), called the Buddha (Enlightened One), and Vardhamana (ca. 540-ca. 468 BC), called Mahavira (Great Hero) or Jina (Victor), whose followers were called Jains.

Zoroaster (Zarathrustra; Camel-Driver) founded the Zoroastrian religion, adopting some ideas from Jewish colonists along the old Silk Road (6th c. BC); it would spread throughout Central Asia, later becoming the official religion of the Persian Empire.

550-501 BC

b. Darius I (the Great) (550-486 BC), king of Persia (r. 522-486 BC).

Cyrus the Great of Persia took Chaldea, besieging Babylon for two years (539-538 BC) and taking that great walled city only after diverting the waters of the Euphrates and mounting a surprise offensive across the remaining river. As Babylon was annexed to the Persian Empire, the Jews hailed Cyrus as the liberator who ended their "Babylonian captivity" (586-538 BC); some Jews returned to Palestine.

d. Cyrus II (the Great) (ca. 585-ca. 530 BC), king of Persia who created the largest empire yet known, bequeathing it to other Persians and eventually to Alexander the Great; he was killed battling the Massagetae people near the Caspian Sea.

Darius campaigned for and took the Persian throne (522-521 BC), beginning his own long reign as Darius the Great.

Cyrus the Great of Persia took Media's former eastern provinces, which had sought independence, including Parthia, Sogdiana, Bactria, and Arachosia (modern Afghanistan and Turkestan) (545-539 BC).

Cyrus the Great and his Persian forces campaigned in Central Asia as far as the Jaxartes River and took most of the territory up to the Indus River, reaching at least to near modern Peshawar (537-530 BC).

China's states of Wu and Ch'u were at war (519-506 BC); the conflict started when Wu attacked the Ch'u city of Zholai (modern Fenglai in Anhwei); this was part of a wider battle for dominance — also including the state of Ch'in — in an effort to replace the weakened Chou dynasty.

Egypt held firm at Thymbra and made a separate peace with Persia. Thymbra marked the first known use of the square formation, introduced by Cyrus.

After Persia's defeat of Croesus, Ionian Greek coastal cities attempted to reestablish their independence but were subdued by the Persian general Harpagus (546 BC).

Etruscans and their Carthaginian allies defeated Greek forces at Alalia, on Corsica (ca. 540 BC), securing Etruscan naval power in the northwestern Mediterranean.

b. Cleomenes I (ca. 540-490 BC), king of Sparta (r. ca. 521-490 BC).

b. Hiero (Hieron) I (ca. 535-ca. 467 BC), ruler of Syracuse (r. 478-ca. 467 BC).

Phoenicians razed the Greek trading city of Tartessos (ca. 530 BC), on Spain's Atlantic coast, and set up a blockade of the Strait of Gibraltar (to the Greeks, the Pillars of Hercules); this would virtually close that vital passageway to all but their own ships until the early 3d century BC.

Now-prominent Athens was at war with Thebes (519-507 BC), which had attempted to form the Boeotian League with Plataea against Athens.

b. Themistocles (ca. 514-ca. 449 BC), Athenian Greek admiral.

Persian forces crossed the Hellespont (Dardanelles) on a temporary bridge formed by boats, capturing territory between Macedonia and the Black Sea (513 BC).

Persian forces under Darius the Great invaded southeastern Europe (511 BC), taking Thrace and Macedonia. The army of 70,000 to 100,000 soldiers, personally led by Darius, crossed the Bosporus on a floating bridge, while the Persian fleet patrolled the western Black Sea. Another floating bridge was constructed over the Danube, allowing the Persian army to push northward, aided by the Ionian Greek fleet, but the Persians later returned to the south, stymied by mounted Scythians who rejected pitched battles, preferring harassment.

Ionian Greek cities unsuccessfully revolted against Persian dominance, mistakenly believing that Darius had been defeated by the Scythians (510 BC).

Sparta's King Cleomenes I intervened in Athens, helping to overthrow the Athenian leader Hippias, who found refuge with Darius of Persia (510 BC).

In their earliest known treaty, Rome agreed to limit its trade to Italy, while Carthage agreed not to expand into Italy (509 BC).

After popular revolutions overthrew the Tarquin monarchs, the Roman Republic was established (509 BC).

Tarquins attempted to regain the throne, resulting in persistent conflicts; during one battle Horatius Cocles reportedly held the bridge over the Tiber River against the Etruscans led by Lars Porsena (508 BC), a feat enshrined in legend as "Horatio at the bridge."

Spartans under Cleomenes I took Athens (507 BC), but the often-quarreling Athenians united under Cleisthenes to oust the invaders.

Persians developed composite bows, no longer of wood but of horn and animal sinew, which better retained their strength and elasticity over time and climatic variations (before 500 BC).

Darius the Great and his troops conquered Gandhara and Sind in northwestern India and annexed them to the Persian Empire, including the west bank of the Indus River and some areas east of it (517 BC). The Greek admiral Skylax was sent to explore the Indus down to the Arabian Sea (517-509 BC).

Sun Tzu (Sun Wu; Honorable Sun), Chinese general and military theorist (active ca. 511-500 BC) who wrote *The Art of War* (ca. 511 BC), the earliest known book on strategy and military theory; this was the first great military work.

In China, general Sun Tzu was brought in by King He Lu to lead the Wu forces; in the decisive Battle of Bai Ju (modern Ma-Zhang, in Hubei), Wu forces ambushed two converging Ch'u armies, defeating them and pursuing them to their capital of Ying (modern Jiang-ling, Hubei), which they sacked and destroyed (506 BC).

500 BC - 999 AD

Western Europe

Eastern Europe

Africa and Southwest Asia

East, Central, and South Asia, the Pacific, and
the Americas

500-476 BC

After the Latin war (498-493 BC), Rome recognized the autonomy of Latin cities but was established as dominant.

Greco-Persian Wars: Phoenician city-state Tyre, subject to Persia, directed its North African daughter colony, Carthage, to attack Syracuse and other Greek city-states in Sicily. The result was the Battle of Himera, pitting an alliance of Greek-Sicilian states under Gelon, ruler of Syracuse, against a large Carthaginian army under Hamilcar, killed in battle (480 BC). The Carthaginians withdrew, paying an indemnity.

Metalworkers in Noricum (Austria) first learned how to make steel (ca. 500 BC).

b. Pericles (ca. 495-429 BC), Athenian general.

Cleomenes I of Sparta won the Battle of Sepeia, gaining control of Argos (494 BC).

Greco-Persian Wars: A Persian fleet headed for Greece was destroyed on a rocky shore by a sudden storm (491 BC), temporarily saving European Greece from attack for aiding the Ionian Greek revolution.

Greco-Persian Wars: The Persians assembled what they claimed was the largest fleet the world had ever seen, including specially designed landing craft carrying horses for the Persian cavalry; the force landed on the coastal plain of the Bay of Marathon and there met Athenians, led by Callimachus, and other Greeks, although Sparta arrived too late. Despite being outnumbered four or five to one, the Greeks, under general Miltiades, who correctly guessed the enemy's plans, defeated the Persians; the news was reported to Athens by the original marathon runner, probably Pheidippides (490 BC).

d. Cleomenes I (ca. 540-490 BC), king of Sparta (ca. 521-490 BC).

d. Miltiades (ca. 550-489 BC), Athenian general who led the Greeks to victory at Marathon (490 BC); he died of wounds suffered in battle.

Greco-Persian Wars: Preparing for the next invasion of Greece, the Persians built bridges over small rivers in areas they controlled on the European side of the Hellespont (Dardanelles), to ease passage by their armies; they also built a double floating bridge across the Hellespont itself, reportedly using almost 700 boats (484 BC).

Greco-Persian Wars: Under Themistocles, the Athenian Greeks expanded their fleet, building new forms of triremes, ships propelled by three banks of oars (ca. 483-481 BC).

Greco-Persian Wars: Greek city-states, led by Sparta, established a defensive alliance called the Hellenic Symmachy (481 BC).

Greco-Persian Wars: In its long-awaited invasion, the Persian army — perhaps 200,000 soldiers under Xerxes and his general Mardonius — crossed the Hellespont in parallel columns and marched across Thrace, Macedonia, and Thessaly, accompanied offshore by a fleet of several thousand warships and transport ships (spring 480 BC). The Greeks abandoned northern Greece as indefensible with their resources and took up defensive positions at the pass of Thermopylae, with an estimated 6,000 to 7,000 soldiers supplemented by archers, under Sparta's King Leonidas.

Greco-Persian Wars: At Thermopylae, the far-outnumbered Greeks succeeded in holding off the Persians for three days, until the Persians learned of a mountain path around the narrow pass; Xerxes's bodyguard, called the Immortals, used the path to surprise and envelop Greek forces; some of the Greeks surrendered, but others, notably Leonidas and his

Greco-Persian Wars (499-448 BC): A long series of conflicts began when Ionian Greek cities, led by Aristagoras of Miletus and aided by Athens and Eretrie (on the island of Euboea), revolted against Persian rule (499-493 BC).

Greco-Persian Wars: Ionian Greek rebels and their allies temporarily took Sardis, capital of the Persian province of Lydia, but were quickly driven out and defeated at Ephesus (498 BC).

Greco-Persian Wars: In a sea battle off the island of Lade, near Miletus, the Persians decisively defeated the Ionian Greeks, cutting them off from their European allies and effectively ending the revolt; Miletus surrendered and was destroyed; many of its inhabitants were deported to Mesopotamia. In this period some captive Greeks were settled as far east as Bactria (Bukhara) (494 BC).

d. Darius I (the Great) (550-486 BC), king of Persia (r. 522-486 BC) who organized the Persian Empire; he built the Persian Royal Road, basis for an empire-wide communications system, and fought long wars with the Greeks; he was succeeded by his son Xerxes I (r. 486-465 BC).

Egyptians revolted against Persian rule, temporarily diverting Persian attention away from Greece (486-484 BC).

d. Hamilcar (?-480 BC), Carthaginian general who was killed in battle on Sicily; he was the grandfather of an early Hannibal.

Greco-Persian Wars: Greek forces under Pausanias took the island of Cyprus and then the city of Byzantium (479 BC). European Greek city-states (except for Athens) then ceased fighting Persia, urging that Ionian Greeks emigrate and settle in mainland Greece.

Metalworkers in Hyderabad, in south-central India, discovered how to make a high-quality steel, producing superior weapons; the metal was transported to Damascus and there made into weapons of so-called Damascus steel (by ca. 500 BC).

In India's Ganges Valley, the dominant states were the kingdoms of Magadha, Kosala, and Kasi and the republic of Vrjji (ca. 500 BC).

Under Ajatusatra, Magadha became the leading state in northern India, winning a series of wars against nearby Kosala (ca. 490-350 BC). By the end of this period, the elephant had become common in Indian warfare, and special heavy iron arrows and fire arrows were developed for use against them. Presumably inspired by Persian success, Indians also developed cavalry rather than relying primarily on chariots.

Exiled Hindu prince Vijaya landed on the island of Ceylon (Sri Lanka) (ca. 483 BC), founding the Vijayan kingdom in the northeast; its history would be marked by struggles with the resident Tamils, a Dravidian people.

Western Europe	Eastern Europe

500-476 BC (cont.)

	bodyguard, fought to the death (Aug. 480 BC). Other Greeks retreated to the fortifications across the narrow Isthmus of Corinth, defending the Peloponnesian peninsula. Stationed off Artemisium, the Greek fleet, under Sparta's Eurybiades, had prevented the Persian fleet from joining in or bypassing the conflict at Thermopylae, but the Greeks sailed for Athens when they received news of their army's defeat.
	d. Leonidas (?-480 BC), ruler of Sparta (r. ca. 490-480 BC) who held the pass at Thermopylae, where he and all his troops were killed.
	Greco-Persian Wars: Persians under Xerxes took and sacked Athens, many of whose inhabitants had been evacuated to the nearby island of Salamis (Sept. 480 BC).
	Greco-Persian Wars: At Salamis (Sept. 23?, 480 BC) the Greek fleet, led by Sparta's general Eurybiades but following plans laid out by Themistocles, met the Persian fleet, which was drawn into a narrow portion of the channel and crowded together; the crowding allowed for hand-to-hand combat, giving the Greeks an advantage because their fewer ships carried virtually all their soldiers. Greeks took or sank half the Persian fleet; the rest retreated, and Persian land troops left Athens. Some Persian troops remained in northern Greece under Mardonius; Xerxes returned to Asia.
	Greco-Persian Wars: Persian troops under Mardonius again took Athens (spring 479 BC), destroying it but retreating when faced with the main Greek army under Sparta's King Pausanias. The two forces met at Plataea where, after the death of Mardonius, the Persian troops were defeated, retreating with enormous losses (July? 479 BC).
	Greco-Persian Wars: Warriors from a Greek fleet under Sparta's Leotychidas attacked Persian troops on the island of Mycale, near Samos, and might well have been defeated, except that Ionian Greeks who had been among the Persian troops switched sides; the Greeks then burned the Persian fleet dry-docked nearby, allowing the Ionians to revolt successfully (Aug.? 479 BC).
	Greco-Persian Wars: Athens built city walls, over the objections of Sparta (479 BC); some two decades of peace followed in Greece.
	Greco-Persian Wars: Athens and the Ionian Greek city-states allied themselves against the Persian threat, forming the first Attican Maritime Alliance, also called the Delian League, dominated by Athens (477 BC).

475-451 BC

| Off Cumae (Cyme), in southern Italy, a Greek fleet from Syracuse, led by Hiero, brother of Gelon, destroyed the Etruscan fleet, ending the Etruscans' expansion into the Campania and their control of the Tyrrhenian Sea — and creating a vacuum that Rome would fill (474 BC).

d. Hiero (Hieron) I (ca. 535-ca. 467 BC), ruler of Syracuse (r. 478-ca. 467 BC) who won at Cumae (474 BC). | b. Cleon (ca. 470-422 BC), Athenian general.

d. Pausanias (?-ca. 470 BC), Spartan general who led allied Greek forces at Plataea (479 BC), then took Cyprus and Byzantium (479 BC); fleeing treason charges for communication with the Persian king, he sought sanctuary in the Temple of Athena, where he was reportedly walled in to die. |

Africa and Southwest Asia

East, Central, and South Asia, the Pacific, and the Americas

475-451 BC

Greco-Persian Wars: Cimon of Athens defeated the Persian army and fleet off the Eurymedon River in Anatolia, ending the Greco-Persian conflict in the Aegean (466 BC).

Athenians aided Egyptian rebels in throwing off Persian rule (460 BC); they took the capital, Memphis, but the citadel held out for almost four years until relieved by Persian reinforcements (456 BC); the Athenians and rebels were themselves besieged for two years on a Nile island, finally surrendering when the river was diverted (454 BC).

Several kingdoms vied for dominance in China during the Chan-kuo period (Era of the Warring States) (ca. 475-221 BC); at the start the strongest was Wei and the weakest and most backward Ch'in; other contenders included Ch'i, Ch'u, Yen, Ch'ao, and Han. The battlefield was dominated by infantry — spearmen, swordsmen, crossbowmen, and halberdiers (their

Western Europe	Eastern Europe

475-451 BC (cont.)

Farmer-warrior L. Quinctius Cincinnatus was tapped to be dictator of Rome, leading the Romans in their defeat of the neighboring Aequians (458 BC).	Athens ended its alliance with Sparta, allying itself instead with Sparta's rival Argos (461 BC); on the Spartan side were Corinth, Thebes, and Aegina.
	Athens made itself a fortress by beginning to build its famous "long walls" connecting the city with its port, Piraeus (460-457 BC); during this period Athens and Sparta concluded various shifting alliances against each other.
	First Peloponnesian War (460-445 BC): Athens went to war with Corinth and other Peloponnesian states.
	First Peloponnesian War: Athens defeated the fleet of the Greek city-state Aegina (458 BC), besieging and taking the city itself (457 BC).
	First Peloponnesian War: Sparta joined the alliance against Athens, leading an allied army to victory over the Athenians at Tanagra, near Thebes; the Thebans then lost to the Athenians at Oenophyta (457 BC).
	b. Thucydides (ca. 456-ca. 400 BC), Athenian Greek general, admiral, and historian.

450-426 BC

L. Quinctius Cincinnatus was again called from his farm to be dictator, this time leading Rome to victory against the neighboring Volsci (439 BC).	b. Alcibiades (ca. 450-404 BC), Athenian admiral and politician.
After a long siege, the Romans defeated the Veii, an Etruscan people from across the Tiber (438-425 BC).	d. Themistocles (ca. 514-ca. 449 BC), Athenian Greek admiral who orchestrated the victory at Salamis (480 BC) and rebuilt Athens's city walls (480 BC), then began construction of the city's famed long walls (from 460 BC); later charged with bribery, he took refuge in the Persian Empire, where he died.
Aequians were again defeated by the Romans, under dictator A. Postumius Tubertus (431 BC).	Greco-Persian War: The war finally ended with the Peace of Callias, recognizing Greek hegemony over the Aegean Sea and allowing the Ionian Greek city-states some autonomy (448 BC); the Delian League effectively became the Athenian Empire.
b. Dionysius (ca. 430-367 BC), ruler of Syracuse (r. 405-367 BC).	First Peloponnesian War: Weakened by fighting both Persia and Sparta, Athens experienced numerous revolts within its empire (Delian League), losing some of its northern Greek territories to Sparta and its allies, which even invaded Attica from their conquered territory in mainland Greece (446 BC).
	First Peloponnesian War: Under the leadership of Pericles, Athens concluded the Thirty Years' Peace with Sparta (445 BC).
	b. Agesilaus II (444-360 BC), Spartan ruler (r. 399-360 BC).
	Corinth, a Spartan ally, had a naval war with Corcyra, an Athenian ally (435 BC); Athens intervened on the side of Corcyra (433 BC).
	Second Peloponnesian War (432-404 BC): Sparta, joined by the Peloponnesian and Boeotian leagues, declared war, charging that Athens had broken the Thirty Years' Peace by supporting Corcyra against Corinth (433 BC).
	b. Xenophon (ca. 430-ca. 355 BC), Athenian soldier and historian.

| | weapon a combination spear and battle-ax), with chariots generally used as mobile command posts; cavalry was used only toward the end of the era. Prisoners who might once have been held for ransom were now routinely executed; Ch'in soldiers were paid on delivery of the losers' heads. This was the age of the great Chinese philosopher K'ung Fu-tzu (Kung the Master), in the West known as Confucius. | |

| Carthaginian navigator Hanno explored down the west coast of Africa, possibly reaching as far as the Cameroons and establishing some colonies (by mid-5th c. BC).

Carthaginian navigator Himilco explored the Atlantic coast of Europe, north from the Carthaginian colony of Gades (Cadiz) and perhaps as far as Cornwall, possibly seeking sources of tin for making bronze (450 BC). | b. Wu Ch'i (ca. 430-381 BC), Chinese general. | |

Western Europe	Eastern Europe

450-426 BC (cont.)

	Second Peloponnesian War: Athenian admiral Phormio twice defeated superior Peloponnesian fleets, at Chalcis and Naupactus (Lepanto), and was able to establish a blockade of the Gulf of Corinth, but he died shortly after (429 BC).
	Second Peloponnesian War: Spartan and Theban allied forces besieged Athens's ally Plataea; on capturing it, they destroyed the city and killed its inhabitants (429-427 BC). This was the first known instance of besieging forces having lines facing both inward toward the city being besieged (contravallation) and outward against possible attackers (circumvallation).
	d. Pericles (ca. 495-429 BC), Athenian leader during the Peloponnesian Wars, under whom Athens completed building its long walls (457 BC); he was succeeded by Cleon.
	Second Peloponnesian War: Athenian general Demosthenes failed in his attempt to take Thebes and Boeotia but ambushed and defeated the Spartans at Olpae (426 BC).

425-401 BC

Western Europe	Eastern Europe
Second Peloponnesian War: Athenians launched an expedition against Syracuse, on Sicily, led by Nicias, Lamachus, and Alcibiades, who had suggested the move; recalled to face blasphemy charges that might mean execution, Alcibiades defected to Sparta, which then warned Syracuse. Nicias failed to attack before Syracuse had been alerted, then won one battle (in which Lamachus was killed), finally settling into a siege of Syracuse (415 BC).	Second Peloponnesian War: Demosthenes established a fortified Athenian base at Pylos (Navarino), holding off Spartan attacks and capturing a Spartan fleet; reinforced by Cleon, the Athenians decisively defeated the Spartans but refused Spartan offers of peace (425 BC).
Second Peloponnesian War: In narrow waters near Syracuse, the Athenian fleet was defeated by the Corinthian-Syracusan fleet, which then blockaded and annihilated the remaining Athenian fleet. Athenian land forces, including reinforcements under Demosthenes, were captured while attempting to retreat. Both Nicias and Demosthenes were killed; the surviving Athenians were enslaved in stone quarries (413 BC).	Second Peloponnesian War: Spartan general Brasidas invaded Thrace, taking Amphipolis, the most important colony protecting the Athenian supply route from the Black Sea (424 BC); Athenian admiral Thucydides, later known as a war historian, prevented the loss of nearby Eion.
Avenging his grandfather's defeat at Himera (480 BC), Hannibal captured and destroyed Himera, Selinus, and other northern and western Sicilian cities (409 BC), then took Agrigentum (406 BC), threatening Syracuse and the remaining Greek-Sicilian city-states (400 BC). This began the long series of Greek-Carthaginian wars in Sicily.	Second Peloponnesian War: Athens agreed to a truce (423 BC), but it was ignored by Sparta's Brasidas, who took other Athenian colonies.
Romans besieged the city of Veii for nine years (405-396 BC); on the point of defeat, they appointed as their general Marcus Furius Camillus, who tunneled under the city walls, attacking with select troops, while an external diversionary attack was launched (396 BC); the city was destroyed, and its people and territory were absorbed into Rome.	Second Peloponnesian War: Cleon and Nicias met Brasidas in Thrace, pushing him back into Amphipolis; Brasidas counterattacked, decisively defeating the much larger Athenian forces; both Cleon and Brasidas were killed (422 BC).
Greek cities on Sicily united under Dionysius of Syracuse to halt a Carthaginian offensive (405 BC); Syracuse then became dominant on Sicily.	d. Cleon (ca. 470-422 BC), Athenian leader killed by Spartan general Brasidas near Amphipolis.
	d. Brasidas (?-422 BC), Spartan general who killed Athenian general Cleon at Amphipolis and was then himself killed.
	Second Peloponnesian War: Athens and Sparta concluded the Peace of Nicias, intended as a Fifty Years' Peace (421 BC).
	Second Peloponnesian War: Technically at peace, Athens and Sparta fought again at Mantinea, after Sparta's King Agis invaded Argos and Mantinea and Athens came to their defense; the Spartans won decisively (418 BC).
	Second Peloponnesian War: Advised by Alcibiades, Sparta declared war on Athens and besieged the city (414 BC).
	Gylippus (active 414-404 BC), Spartan general known for his defense of Syracuse, especially his virtual annihilation of the Athenian fleet (413 BC).

Funded by Persia, Sparta built a new fleet at Ephesus, in Anatolia, directed by Spartan general Lysander (408 BC).

Alcibiades captured Byzantium, giving Athens clear control of the Bosporus, gateway to the Black Sea (408 BC).

After the Athenian fleet was defeated off Notium, the port of Colophon, Alcibiades was relieved of command (407 BC).

Callicratidas, who temporarily replaced Lysander in the Spartan rotation for leader, blockaded the Athenian fleet at Mitylene. Raising yet another fleet, the Athenians decisively defeated the Spartans at Arginusae (Aug. 406 BC) but refused Spartan peace offers. Athenian fleet leaders were executed (against Socrates's advice) for failing to rescue shipwrecked c

d. Hannibal (?-406 BC), Carthaginian general who d   ıring Carthage's campaign in Sicily; he was the grandson of Hamilcar.

Artaxerxes II became king of Persia (r. 404-358 BC).

Cyrus the Younger, satrap (governor) of Persia's province of Lydia, revolted against his brother, Persian emperor Artaxerxes II (401 BC). At Cunaxa, near Babylon, Cyrus was killed and most of his rebel supporters were routed. The large Greek portion of his army then defeated Artaxerxes's troops, but at a feast afterward, the Greek leaders were seized and executed by Artaxerxes.

Their senior officers gone, the Greek remnants of Cyrus's army — now led by young Spartan and Athenian officers — fought their way over 1,000 miles of often-mountainous terrain to reach a safe haven at the Greek colony of Trapezus (Trebizond), on the Black Sea (401-400 BC); this March of the 10,000 was celebrated in *Anabasis (Upcountry March)*, the classic military book written by Xenophon, one of those young Athenian officers.

Some individual Chinese states built defensive walls (before 400 BC) against the Hsiung-nu (Terrible Slaves), raiders from Central Asia, who lacked the siege craft to breach them. The Chinese also attempted to buy peace with lavish gifts and marital alliances with the Hsiung-nu, later known to Europe as the Huns.

425-401 BC (cont.)

d. Nicias (?-413 BC), Athenian general who, after failing to take Syracuse (415-414 BC), died during an attempted retreat overland.

d. Demosthenes (I) (?-413 BC), Athenian general who was executed after being captured in battle against Epipolar, part of Syracuse, on Sicily.

Second Peloponnesian War: With Alcibiades acting for them, the Spartans attempted to spark an Ionian revolt against Athenian rule, gaining Persian support (412 BC); Athens produced another fleet, however, and continued to assert its claim to the Aegean.

Second Peloponnesian War: Alcibiades, who had secretly been angling for a return to Athens, was recalled to the city to command the Athenian fleet after the Athenians had overthrown their ruling oligarchy for a broader democracy (411 BC).

Second Peloponnesian War: At Cyzicus, Alcibiades won a double victory over the Peloponnesian fleet in the Sea of Marmara and the Persian army (410 BC). Sparta's peace offer was rejected by the new Athenian leader, Cleophon.

b. Epaminondas (ca. 410-362 BC), Theban general.

Second Peloponnesian War: Returning to Spartan command after serving in Persia, Lysander orchestrated a total victory over the Athenians at Aegospotami, striking the Athenian fleet at night, with crews mostly ashore, in the decisive action of the war. The vessels were destroyed; the crews were mostly captured and killed. While Sparta's King Pausanias besieged Athens by land, Lysander blockaded its port, Piraeus (405 BC).

Second Peloponnesian War: After a six-month siege, Athens, cut off from supplies, surrendered to Sparta, and the Second Peloponnesian War ended; Athens was occupied, its long walls were razed, and the Delian League was dissolved, with the Athenian Empire coming under Spartan control (Apr. 404 BC).

d. Alcibiades (ca. 450-404 BC), Athenian admiral and politician, a controversial figure who served Athens and Sparta alternately during the Peloponnesian Wars.

400-376 BC

From its North African base, Carthage expanded into the central and western Mediterranean, sending expeditions and founding colonies in Iberia, both on the Mediterranean and, through the Strait of Gibraltar (Pillars of Hercules), on the Atlantic (from ca. 400 BC).

As new waves of Celts moved across Europe from the east, some groups made their way through the Alps and into Italy (ca. 400 BC).

Carthaginian troops led by Himilco besieged Syracuse under Dionysius, but their losses were so heavy that they had to withdraw not only from the siege but also from most of their Sicilian colonies (398-397 BC). This conflict may have seen the

Sparta and Persia were at war (400-387 BC) over Sparta's support of the Ionian Greek cities that had lent support to Cyrus the Younger's rebellion against Artaxerxes II. It was in this period, in a troubled Athens, that the philosopher Socrates was condemned to death for corrupting youths and presenting new gods (399 BC).

b. Parmenion (Parmenio) (ca. 400-330 BC), Macedonian general.

d. Thucydides (ca. 456-ca 400 BC), Athenian Greek general and admiral during the Peloponnesian Wars whose *History* gave an extraordinary account of that conflict.

400-376 BC

Carthage expanded westward, establishing colonies along the North African coast (from ca. 400 BC).

Agesilaus II led Spartan troops successfully against Persian forces in Anatolia (Asia Minor) (396-394 BC) until being recalled to deal with threats at home.

Corinthian War: Off Cnidus, near the island of Rhodes, the Athenian-Persian fleet, led by the Athenian admiral Conon, destroyed the Spartan fleet, largely ending Sparta as a maritime power (394 BC).

Corinthian War: In the face of a renewed threat from Athens, Persia secretly switched its support to Sparta; a joint Persian-Spartan fleet blockaded the Bosporus, cutting off Athens's grain supply from southern Russia (390 BC).

d. Wu Ch'i (ca. 430-381 BC), Chinese general serving several kingdoms during the Era of the Warring States; his military meditations were later widely read.

400-376 BC (cont.)

first use of the catapult, introduced around this time by Dionysius. The catapult was the first of many crew-operated siege machines. A bow under tension from twisted animal sinew was used to deliver arrows, rocks, or spears with force. Lighter versions would later be used in the field.

In their second war against Dionysius, the Carthaginians again lost to Syracuse, which maintained control of most of Sicily (392 BC).

Celts (Gauls), who had been pressing into the Po Valley and down the Adriatic coast (from ca. 400 BC), ravaged much of Etruria (391 BC).

Celts (Gauls) led by Brennus defeated a Roman army at the Allia River (390 BC), sacking the city of Rome except the citadel, on Capitoline Hill. They left after payment of a large tribute but continued to raid central Italy for decades.

Romans under Marcus Furius Camillus decisively defeated the Aequians and Volsci, expanding and consolidating their leadership of a Latin confederacy (389 BC).

Dionysius of Syracuse established his domination over the Greek states of the central and western Mediterranean, called Magna Graecia (Greater Greece) (ca. 390-379 BC), leading them to victory over the Italiote League at the Elleporus (389 BC).

In their third war against Dionysius, Carthaginians were able to capture and hold some territories in western and central Sicily, though not Syracuse (385-376 BC).

Romans built defensive fortifications — the Servian Wall — around the Seven Hills (from 380 BC).

Corinthian War (395-387 BC): While Sparta was occupied against the Persians in Anatolia, Athens, Corinth, Thebes, Argos, and other city-states formed an alliance against Sparta, effectively allying themselves with Persia; at Haliartus the allies defeated the Spartans, whose leader, Lysander, was killed (395 BC).

d. Lysander (?-395 BC), Spartan admiral and general during the Peloponnesian Wars (431-404 BC); killed at Haliartus.

Corinthian War: Spartans under Agesilaus II defeated the forces of Thebes, Athens, and the other Greek allies at Coronea (394 BC).

Corinthian War: Agesilaus II and the Spartans besieged Corinth (394 BC).

Corinthian War: Athens, which had taken advantage of Spartan reverses to reestablish some of its power and rebuild its long walls, relieved the Spartan siege of Corinth (390 BC).

Corinthian War: The largely stalemated conflict ended with the Peace of Antalcidas (King's Peace) (387 BC).

b. Philip II (ca. 383-336 BC), Macedonian ruler (r. 359-336 BC).

Spartans took the Theban citadel, Cadmeia (382 BC).

b. Antigonus I (Cyclops; Monophthalmus; One-Eyed) (382-301 BC), Macedonian general and ruler (r. 306-301 BC).

In a revolt against Sparta (379-371 BC), Thebes was joined by Athens; Sparta was pushed out of central Greece.

Second Athenian Naval League was formed by some 60 member states allied against Sparta (377 BC).

Under Chabrias, Athens decisively defeated the Spartan fleet off Naxos (376 BC).

375-351 BC

Fourth Carthaginian war against Dionysius of Syracuse was inconclusive, ending with his death (368-367 BC).

d. Dionysius (ca. 430-367 BC), ruler of Syracuse (r. 405-367 BC) who made his Sicilian city-state dominant, introducing new military technology.

Romans under Marcus Furius Camillus repelled a second invasion of the Celts (Gauls) (367 BC).

b. Agathocles (361-289 BC), ruler of Syracuse (r. 317-289 BC).

Romans and Samnites formed a defensive alliance against the Celts (Gauls) and other neighboring peoples (354 BC).

At Leuctra (371 BC), Theban troops under Epaminondas defeated Sparta so decisively as to permanently end its reputation as a military power. Though heavily outnumbered, Epaminondas outsmarted the Spartans by using an unconventional, oblique battle order, with some forces concentrated to attack in one area but others refusing to engage the Spartans early on and coming in unexpectedly later; the Thebans suffered minimal casualties. This was the first known use of the column of attack and the refused flank.

b. Craterus (ca. 370-321 BC), Macedonian general.

Temporarily a hostage in Thebes, Philip of Macedonia (later Philip II) studied military techniques under Epaminondas (367-365 BC).

At Mantinea (362 BC) Theban forces led by Epaminondas met allied forces, including both Spartan and Athenian troops; Epaminondas appeared likely to win again with his unconventional military tactics, but after he was killed in the field, Theban forces were defeated.

400-376 BC (cont.)

d. Himilco (?-ca. 389 BC), Carthaginian general during the wars with Sicily; he committed suicide on returning home after his disastrous defeat by Dionysius of Syracuse (396 BC).

As central power in the Persian Empire declined, the satrapies (provinces) of Anatolia became largely autonomous (ca. 386-358 BC).

375-351 BC

b. Ptolemy I Soter (ca. 367-283 BC), Greek general serving Macedonia, later ruler of Egypt (r. 323-285 BC).

Under Artaxerxes III (r. ca. 358-338 BC), Persian authority was somewhat restored, mainly through the efforts of Greek general Mentor.

In China the Wei army under general P'ang Chuan invaded the state of Han (ca. 354-353 BC), which called in the Ch'i army. Advised by the celebrated military strategist Sun Ping, general T'ien Chi led the combined Han-Ch'i armies, feigning a retreat to draw Wei forces into an ambush; in this Battle of Ma Ling, Ch'i crossbowmen virtually destroyed the Wei army.

375-351 BC (cont.)

d. Epaminondas (ca. 410-362 BC), Theban general and noted military tactician who orchestrated the victory at Leuctra (371 BC); killed at Mantinea.

d. Agesilaus II (444-360 BC), Spartan ruler (r. 399-360 BC) who fought most notably at Coronea and the siege of Corinth (both 394 BC).

Initially as regent for his nephew (359-356 BC), then as king himself (r. 356-336 BC), Philip II led a series of wars to secure and expand the Macedonian kingdom. His army was noted for its highly organized phalanxes (closely formed infantry units) with overlapping round shields and long spears, division of the cavalry into regiments, use of catapults as both siege and field machines, and use of the oblique battle order introduced by Epaminondas of Thebes.

b. Cassander (ca. 358-297 BC), Macedonian general and ruler (r. 305-297 BC).

Second Athenian Naval League was disbanded during the War of the Allies (357-355 BC) after the withdrawal of Chios, Rhodes, Cos, and Byzantium from the alliance.

Macedonians under Philip II took the Athenian colony of Amphipolis on the Chalcidian peninsula (357 BC).

b. Alexander III (the Great) (356-323 BC), Macedonian king (r. 336-323 BC) and conqueror.

b. Lysimachus (ca. 355-281 BC), Macedonian general.

d. Xenophon (ca. 430-ca. 355 BC), Athenian soldier; one of the young officers leading the famous retreat (401-400 BC) described in his *Anabasis (Upcountry March);* he also wrote *Hellenica (A History of My Times), Hipparchicus* (on cavalry duties), and other works.

Intervening in a Greek war over an offense to the Temple at Delphi, Philip II of Macedonia defeated the Phocian Greeks under general Onomarchus at Volo, effectively conquering Thessaly (352 BC); Philip was then blocked at Thermopylae.

Philip II and the Macedonians turned northeast to take Athens's ally Thrace (351 BC).

350-326 BC

Rome and Carthage reaffirmed their earlier treaty (ca. 509 BC) restricting Roman trade to Italy and accepting Carthaginian hegemony in the western Mediterranean, except in Italy or cities allied with Rome (ca. 347 BC).

War Against Timoleon (344-339 BC): Sicily's Greek cities were in disorder after Timoleon of Corinth overthrew key leaders (tyrants), including Syracuse's Dionysius II. Carthaginian forces besieged Syracuse, taking it all except the citadel, but were afflicted by a plague and internal dissension; Syracusan Greeks under Timoleon revived to drive them out (341 BC), crushing them at the Crimissus River (340 BC).

In the First Samnite War (343-341 BC), Romans led by Marcus Valerius Corvus defeated the Samnites at Mount Gaurus (342 BC), acting as defenders of other cities in the Campania.

Macedonians under Philip II took Athens's ally Chalcidice (348 BC).

War between Athens and Philip II of Macedonia ended with the Peace of Philocrates (346 BC); Athens remained powerful at sea, while the Macedonians continued to expand to the north and west.

Athens was divided about strategy: Isocrates advised the Greeks to unite with Philip II and the Macedonians against the Persians; Demosthenes, notably in his *Philippics,* promoted Greek unity against the "barbarian" Macedonians (343 BC).

Greeks formed the Hellenic League against Philip II after the Macedonians threatened the Black Sea supply lines and mainland Greece (340 BC).

350-326 BC

Artaxerxes III's Persian forces retook Egypt (342 BC).

Alexander the Great: Alexander invaded Persia, crossing the Hellespont with an army of 30,000 infantry and 5,000 cavalry; after paying homage to Achilles at the site of Troy, he won a quick victory over the Persian army of some 40,000 soldiers, perhaps half of them Greek, at the Granicus River (334 BC). The Ionian Greek cities were freed equally quickly, except a brief siege was required at Miletus, as part of a plan to cripple the Persian fleet by taking its bases.

Alexander the Great: Causing small, temporary setbacks to Alexander, the Persians took the islands of Chios and Mitylene (333 BC).

Alexander the Great: Following the Persian Royal Road inland, Alexander exacted submission from local princes at Gordium, in Phrygia, by cutting (rather then untying) the Gordian knot, signifying that he would rule all Asia. After completing his conquest of the Anatolian interior, he left Macedonian officers in charge. Forcing his way through the Cilician Gates in a daring night

In China, Shang Yang, a refugee from the kingdom of Wei, introduced military and political reforms that strengthened the state of Ch'in (ca. 350 BC).

Persian territories in India became largely independent (ca. mid-4th c. BC).

In China the Wei army invaded the state of Ch'ao (ca. 342-341 BC), which (as the Han had earlier done) called in the Ch'i army, still advised by strategist Sun Ping; as before, the Wei were ambushed and defeated, this time at Guai Ling (ca. 341 BC).

350-326 BC (cont.)

In the Latin War (340-338 BC), Romans under Publius Decius Mus met an alliance of Latin and Campanian cities, fighting them to a draw at Vesuvius (339 BC) but defeating them decisively at Trifanum (338 BC); these cities thereafter formed the core of Roman support.

Greek colonists in southern Italy obtained help from Archimadus of Sparta in their long fight against the Italians (338 BC).

Alexander of Epirus, uncle of Alexander the Great, campaigned in Italy for the Greek colony of Tarentum (Tarento), allied with the Romans against the Samnites; he was killed at Pandosia (331 BC).

In the Second Samnite War (327-304 BC), the Romans again battled the Samnites, with some initial success.

Philip II of Macedonia failed in his attempts to take the fortified seaports of Perinthus and Byzantium (339 BC), although he succeeded in taking the Propontis (Sea of Marmara).

At Chaeronea, on mainland Greece, Macedonians under Philip II defeated a much larger Athenian-Theban army, completing their conquest of Greece; Philip's son Alexander (later the Great) made a decisive contribution heading the left cavalry (338 BC).

In a meeting at Corinth, Philip established himself as head of the Hellenic League of all Greek cities (except Sparta) and laid out plans for war against Persia, ostensibly to free Ionian Greek cities from Persian domination (337 BC).

d. Philip II (ca. 383-336 BC), Macedonian ruler (r. 359-336 BC) who created the Macedonian Empire, bequeathed to his son Alexander the Great; he was murdered, possibly at the behest of his estranged wife, Olympias.

Alexander the Great: Alexander quickly put down a revolt of Greek cities, emboldened by his youth to try for freedom; instead he replaced his father at the head of the Hellenic League (336 BC).

b. Demetrius I Poliorcetes (336-283 BC), Macedonian general and ruler (r. 294-288 BC).

Alexander the Great: Alexander carried out campaigns to reaffirm Macedonian control of the northern and eastern territories; when the central Greek cities revolted, he captured and destroyed Thebes, enslaving its inhabitants; Athens then surrendered (335 BC).

Alexander the Great: Moving against Persia, Alexander left an army of approximately 10,000 soldiers under Antipater to hold his European conquests (335 BC).

Alexander the Great: Sparked and financed by the Persians, several Greek states, under Sparta's King Agis II, revolted against Macedonian rule (332 BC); Alexander's general Antipater defeated the rebels at Megalopolis (331 BC), then sent reinforcements to Alexander's main army.

Alexander the Great: Alexander's adoption of Persian royal titles and dress sparked opposition in Macedonia (331 BC).

d. Parmenion (Parmenio) (ca. 400-330 BC), Macedonian general under Philip II and Alexander the Great; served most notably at Granicus (334 BC), leading the left cavalry wing, and Issus (333 BC), as second in command; appointed satrap of Media (330 BC), he was executed after his son Philotas had been executed for plotting against Alexander.

d. Coenus (?-326 BC), Macedonian general serving Alexander; the army's main spokesman, he urged consolidation, not more expansion, after Hydaspes (326 BC); he died in India.

attack, he also took the southern coast of Anatolia, conducting a siege of Halicarnassus (333 BC).

Alexander the Great: Using oblique battle tactics introduced at Leuctra by Epaminondas (371 BC), Alexander overcame great odds — some 30,000 Greeks against 100,000 Persians — to defeat Darius III on the coastal plain of Issus (333 BC). Perhaps half the Persians fell; the rest fled with Darius, whose family was captured by Alexander.

Alexander the Great: Alexander took the Syrian and Palestinian coasts, establishing military garrisons in key cities. To take the old Phoenician stronghold of Tyre (Sur), the Persian navy's main base, he had to conduct a siege (Jan.-Aug. 332 BC), in the end building a mole from the mainland to the island fort and fighting Tyrian ships with a fleet formed from the ships of other captured ports; the city was destroyed, and its people were enslaved. The other key resister, Gaza, also was taken after a siege (Sept.-Nov. 332 BC), ended when Alexander used catapults and ballistae to bombard the city from a specially built 250-foot-high earthen mound. Darius III offered Alexander all of his empire west of the Euphrates, 10,000 gold talents, and his already-captive daughter in marriage; Alexander refused.

Alexander the Great: Alexander moved on to take Egypt (Dec. 332-Mar. 331 BC), where he founded Alexandria, the first of many cities to be named for him; at the end of his 200-mile campaign into the Libyan Desert, to Siwa Oasis, priests at the Temple of Zeus Ammon welcomed him as the son of Zeus.

Alexander the Great: The main Persian and Macedonian armies — estimated at 47,000 and 200,000 soldiers, respectively — met on the plain of Gaugamela, west of Arbela (Erbil), near the ancient Assyrian capital of Nineveh. Darius III renewed his peace offer, upping the cash amount to 30,000 gold talents; it was again refused. Instead, Alexander attacked, using an oblique battle line and, perhaps for the first time in history, holding troops in tactical reserve; using concentrated force, he drove a wedge in the line directly toward Darius, who fled eastward through the Caspian Gates, followed by many of his troops (Oct. 1, 331 BC).

Alexander the Great: The ancient capital of Babylon surrendered to Alexander without resistance, yielding a treasure of 50,000 gold talents (331 BC); the city of Susa also surrendered.

Alexander the Great: Heading southwest, Alexander destroyed the Persian capital of Persepolis (330 BC) in supposed retribution for the Persians' burning of the Acropolis in Athens (480 BC); this ended the Hellenic portion of Alexander's campaign. In pursuit of the remnants of the Persian army, he also took Ecbatana (Hamadan) (330 BC).

Alexander the Great: In flight after his army was routed at Arbela (Gaugemela), Darius III of Persia was murdered by one of his own people — Bessus, satrap of Bactria — who took the royal title. Alexander also proclaimed himself Persian emperor, thereafter adopting Persian all-purple royal dress (331 BC); he also took the provinces of Aria, Drangiana, and Arachosia.

The state of Ch'u expanded in the lower Yangtze Valley, and the Ch'in became powerful in north and west China (ca. 330 BC).

Alexander the Great: Marching east through Parthia into Bactria, Alexander caught and executed Darius III's murderer, Bessus. Fighting to establish his rule over the Scythians of Central Asia, Alexander crossed the Oxus River into Sogdiana and traveled past Maracanda (Samarkand) to Bukhara, winning a notable victory after crossing the Jaxartes River on improvised rafts made of sewn tents (329 BC); he founded his easternmost city, Alexandria the Farthest, near modern Khojent, then moved on into India.

Alexander the Great: In Sogdiana, to which he returned to put down a revolt, Alexander married Roxana, daughter of Sogdian leader Oxyartes, who was named Alexander's viceroy; some Greeks and Macedonians opposed Alexander's policy of reconciliation with his Asian subjects (328 BC).

Alexander the Great: Against strong resistance, Alexander and his army forced their way through the mountain passes guarding northwest India, including the Khyber Pass, reaching the Indus River (327 BC); he formed an alliance with the king of Taxala, near modern Rawalpindi, against Porus, dominant ruler in the Punjab.

Alexander the Great: Alexander contrived to make Porus think he would not cross the flood-swollen Hydaspes (Jhelum) River, but he crossed upstream to make a surprise attack, using harassment to disrupt the war elephants and break the Indian lines (326 BC).

Alexander the Great: Continuing his campaign to rule the known world, Alexander was pressing into north-central India toward the Ganges when, at the Hyphasis (Beas) River, his key Macedonian troops refused to proceed (July 326 BC). Leaving Greek governors behind him, Alexander acceded to their wishes and turned south-

350-326 BC (cont.)

325-301 BC

Second Samnite War: At the Caudine Forks (321 BC), Roman forces under consuls Spurius Postumius and T. Veterius Calvinus were decisively defeated by Samnites under Gavius Pontius; after this the Roman army was reorganized.

Second Samnite War: Samnites defeated the Romans at Lautulae (316 BC) but were defeated at Ciuna (315 BC).

Second Samnite War: Using the newly constructed Via Appia (Appian Way) to supply their forces, the Romans largely won the Campania from the Samnites (312 BC).

Carthaginians under Hamilcar defeated Syracusan Greeks under Agathocles at Himera, on Sicily (311 BC), then besieged Syracuse (311-310 BC).

Second Samnite War: Led by Q. Fabius Rullianus, the Romans defeated the Etruscans, Samnite allies since 311 BC, at Lake Vadimo (310 BC).

Second Samnite War: Romans under L. Papirius Cursor defeated the Samnites in their mountain homeland (309 BC).

Second Samnite War: In their first known use of sea power (308 BC), the Romans fought by both land and sea against the Umbrians and other southern mountain peoples allied with the Samnites.

War between Syracuse and Carthage ended with Carthaginian victories in North Africa and on Sicily (306 BC).

Romans and Carthaginians signed their third treaty (306 BC).

Second Samnite War: Roman forces decisively defeated the Samnites at Bovianum (305 BC).

Second Samnite War: Under the peace treaty ending the war, Romans kept the Campania, and further expansion of the Samnite League was barred (304 BC).

Syracusan Greek leader Agathocles proclaimed himself king of Sicily (304 BC); he also attacked the Italians of southern Italy, at the request of the Greek colony of Tarentum, with indecisive results (305?-302 BC).

d. Alexander III (the Great) (356-323 BC), Macedonian king and son of Philip II, who took and expanded beyond the Persian Empire; when only 33 years old, he died in Babylon of a fever, probably resulting from malaria (June 13).

Wars of the Diadochi (Successors) (323-281 BC): A long series of conflicts began as Alexander's key generals fought over pieces of his empire. In Macedonia his chief of staff, Perdiccas, was named regent for his infant son Alexander IV (r. 323-321 BC), replacing the former regent, Antipater. Lysimachus took control of Thrace.

Wars of the Diadochi: In the Lamian War, Alexandrian generals Antipater and his son-in-law Craterus suppressed a revolt by Athens and many other Greek cities at Crannon and permanently destroyed Athenian sea power at Amorgos. As the Macedonians occupied Athens, the revolt's leader, Demosthenes, committed suicide (322 BC).

Wars of the Diadochi: Macedonian regent Perdiccas was murdered, his assassins paid by Ptolemy I (Soter); Antipater again became regent, controlling Macedonia and Greece (321-319 BC); Antigonus I and Cassander were named imperial generals.

d. Craterus (ca. 370-321 BC), Macedonian general in Alexander's army who was killed near the Hellespont by his rival Eumenes.

b. Pyrrhus (319-272 BC), king of Epirus.

Wars of the Diadochi: Olympias, mother of Alexander the Great and still a power in Macedonia, was murdered by Cassander, who then ruled Macedonia (316 BC).

d. Nearchus (?-312 BC), admiral from Crete serving Philip II and Alexander the Great; he was killed in the Wars of the Diadochi at Gaza.

Wars of the Diadochi: The contenders agreed to a truce, under which Cassander would control Macedonia until Alexander IV came of age, Lysimachus would rule Thrace and the Chersonese peninsula, and Antigonus would rule Greece and Anatolia.

Wars of the Diadochi: Cassander murdered Alexander the Great's wife, Roxana, and heir, Alexander IV, ending the Alexandrian line (310 BC).

Wars of the Diadochi: Demetrius, son of Antigonus I, invaded Greece, taking Athens and most of the other cities; thereafter he was called Poliorcetes (Conqueror of Cities) (307 BC).

350-326 BC (cont.)

east, fighting his way down the Indus River. At the river's mouth, he built a fleet and sent it, under Nearchus, to explore the sea route back to the head of the Persian Gulf. Alexander himself returned, with most of his army, by land, apparently making contact with the coast-hugging fleet at least twice (326-324 BC).

325-301 BC

Alexander the Great: Alexander reorganized his empire from Babylon, his new capital, making plans for the fusion of peoples through intermarriage and resettlement, symbolized by a five-day marriage festival in which he married perhaps 10,000 of his soldiers to Asiatic wives and himself took a second wife, Darius's daughter Statira. Persians were accepted into the army, and at his death he was planning new campaigns against Carthage and the western Mediterranean (324 BC).

After Alexander's death, Antigonus I took control of Phrygia and Lycia, in central and southwest Turkey (323 BC); Seleucus I (Nicator) was governor of Babylon.

Wars of the Diadochi (Successors): Macedonian general Craterus was killed by another Alexandrian general, Eumenes, during an invasion of Cappadocia, in northwest Anatolia (321 BC).

Wars of the Diadochi: Alexandrian generals Antigonus I and Eumenes fought to a draw at Paraetakena, in Iran (317 BC).

Wars of the Diadochi: Macedonian general Antigonus I, seeking undivided power, was blocked by an alliance, including Cassander, Ptolemy I (Soter), Lysimachus, Seleucus I, and Eumenes; he was murdered by some of his own men, who had been bribed by Antigonus (316 BC).

Wars of the Diadochi: Under the successors' truce, Ptolemy I would retain Egypt, Palestine, and Cyprus; Antigonus I would rule Anatolia and Greece; and Seleucus I would control the lands from the Euphrates River to India (311 BC).

While Carthaginians were besieging Syracuse, on Sicily, Syracusan Greeks sent an expedition under Agathocles to besiege Carthage (310-307 BC); defeated, Agathocles was forced to return to Sicily.

Wars of the Diadochi: After taking most of Greece, Demetrius I took Palestine (307-306 BC).

Wars of the Diadochi: Demetrius I decisively defeated Ptolemy I's brother Menelaeus at Salamis, gaining control of Cyprus (306 BC).

Wars of the Diadochi: Ptolemy I fought off Demetrius I's invasion of Egypt (305 BC).

Wars of the Diadochi: Demetrius I besieged Ptolemy I's garrison on the island of Rhodes, but after two years he was forced to withdraw (305-304 BC).

Wars of the Diadochi: At the crucial Battle of Ipsus, in western Anatolia, Seleucus I and Lysimachus, supported by Cassander, defeated Demetrius I and his father, Antigonus I, by then over 80; Antigonus was killed in the fighting (301 BC). The victors were helped by their use of war elephants. The result was four kingdoms: Cassander ruled Macedonia, soon succeeded by his son (300 BC); Ptolemy ruled Egypt; Seleucus I ruled Persia; and Lysimachus ruled Thrace and Anatolia, soon losing western Anatolia to Demetrius I (300 BC).

Alexander the Great: Alexander's Asian dominions were thrown into turmoil after his death, at which his key generals — the successors (diadochi) — divided his empire (323 BC).

Chandragupta, a general of Magadha, deposed the Nanda rulers and took the throne (323 BC), founding the Mauryan dynasty; influenced by Alexander the Great, whom he had reportedly met, he expanded his kingdom, taking northwestern India back from the Macedonians. The classic work on government and war, *Arthasastra (Manual of Politics),* is believed to have been written in this period by Kautilya, Chandragupta's key aide.

Seleucus I (Nicator), one of Alexander's generals and successors, embarked on a program (321-302 BC) to reconquer the empire's eastern provinces, which had struggled free during the Wars of the Diadochi.

The Ch'ao, under King Wu Ling, became the first Chinese army to have separate cavalry forces, their soldiers abandoning the traditional long robes for nomad-style short jerkins and trousers (ca. 320 BC).

Seleucus I campaigned in the Indus Valley, attempting to reestablish Macedonian rule (305 BC); instead, he and Chandragupta formed an alliance, with northwest India going to Chandragupta in exchange for 500 war elephants.

325-301 BC (cont.)

d. Antigonus I (Cyclops; Monophthalmus; One-Eyed) (382-301 BC), Macedonian general and ruler (r. 306-301 BC) who fought with Alexander and was a key figure in the Wars of the Diadochi; he was killed while fighting at Ipsus; his son was Demetrius I Poliorcetes.

300-276 BC

Pytheas, a Phocaean Greek, managed to slip through the Phoenician blockade of the Strait of Gibraltar and sailed north to Britain and beyond, the first Mediterranean sailor known to have done so (ca. 300 BC).

Third Samnite War (298-290 BC): Romans again fought the Samnites, allied with Etruscans, Gauls, and Umbrians.

Third Samnite War: Romans under Q. Fabius Rullianus and Publius Decius Mus (son of the Latin War consul) defeated the Samnite alliance at Sentinum (295 BC), after which the Gauls, Umbrians, and Etruscans made a separate peace.

Third Samnite War: At Aquilonia (293 BC), Romans under Manius Curius Dentatus decisively defeated the Samnites, who joined the Roman confederation at war's end (290 BC).

d. Agathocles (361-289 BC), ruler of Syracuse (317-289 BC) and self-proclaimed king of Sicily (304 BC).

b. Archimedes (ca. 287-212 BC), Greek scientist and inventor.

Etruscans and Gauls rebelled against Roman domination; the Gauls destroyed a Roman army under Lucius Caecilius at Arretium (285 BC).

Romans under P. Cornelius Dolabella defeated a combined rebel force of Etruscans and Gauls at Lake Vadimo, north of Rome (283 BC).

Etruscan rebellion was ended by the Romans at Populonia (282 BC).

Called in by the Greek city-state of Tarentum, concerned over Roman expansion, Pyrrhus of Epirus came to southern Italy with a Macedonian-style infantry and cavalry, as well as war elephants (281 BC).

Pyrrhus of Epirus first met the Romans in southern Italy at Heraclea, driving them across the Siris River, but at so great a cost that he reportedly said, "One more such victory and I am lost," referred to in the phrase *Pyrrhic victory* (280 BC).

Facing the Romans under consuls Caius Fabricius and Quintus Aemilius at Asculum, Pyrrhus — joined by some Samnites, other Italians, and Greek colonists — had another extremely costly victory and was badly wounded (279 BC).

Pyrrhus of Epirus assisted the Syracusan Greeks in ending the Carthaginian encirclement of Syracuse (278 BC), but the Carthaginians remained in western and central Sicily.

Carthage and Rome made an alliance against Pyrrhus of Epirus (277 BC).

Greeks developed the torsion catapult using twisted animal sinew or human hair (by 300 BC).

d. Cassander (ca. 358-297 BC), Macedonian general and son of Antipater; he killed Roxana and Alexander IV (310 BC), becoming ruler of Macedonia (r. 305-297 BC).

Wars of the Diadochi: Demetrius I took control of Macedonia, murdering Cassander's son (294 BC).

Wars of the Diadochi: Demetrius I, who also had taken Athens, was defeated and driven from Macedonia by Lysimachus, Seleucus (Nicator), Ptolemy I (Soter), and Pyrrhus of Epirus (288-286 BC), dying in prison three years later.

d. Demetrius I Poliorcetes (336-283 BC), Macedonian general who captured the throne (ca. 294-ca. 288 BC); son of Alexander's general Antigonus I, he was involved in the Wars of the Diadochi; captured by Seleucus I (285 BC), he died in captivity.

Wars of the Diadochi: At the wars' end, Macedonia was ruled by the Antigonids, descendants of the Alexandrian general Antigonus (281 BC).

d. Lysimachus (ca. 355-281 BC), Macedonian general, a key commander, fighting with Alexander from Persia through Central Asia to India; governor of Thrace, he was killed at Corus (281 BC).

Celtic peoples invaded Macedonia, Greece, and Thrace (279-277 BC); Ptolemy Keraunos, Ptolemy I's disinherited son, was killed fighting against them.

Antigonus II Gonatus, son of Demetrius I, regained control of Macedonia from the invading Celts, some of whom were driven into Anatolia (276 BC).

d. Ptolemy I (Soter) (ca. 367-283 BC), Greek general serving Alexander the Great who later founded the Ptolemaic line in Egypt (r. 323-285 BC); a key figure in the Wars of the Diadochi, defeating Antigonus I's son Demetrius I at Gaza (312 BC), he was called Soter (Savior) for his relief of Demetrius's siege of Rhodes (304 BC).

Wars of the Diadochi: At Corus (Corupedion), Seleucus I, aided by Ptolemy's disinherited son Ptolemy Keraunos, defeated the 75-year-old Lysimachus, who died in hand-to-hand combat, ending the wars (281 BC). Seleucus, the last surviving successor, ruled the remaining Asian lands until his murder by Ptolemy Keraunos (280 BC).

Wars of the Diadochi: At the wars' end, Egypt was ruled by the Ptolemys, descendants of the Alexandrian general Ptolemy I (281 BC).

Damascene War (280-279 BC): Ptolemy II, Ptolemy I's second son, defeated Antiochus I, as the descendants of Ptolemy and Seleucus began a long series of wars for control of Syria and Palestine.

Mithridates established the kingdom of Pontus on the Black Sea (ca. 280 BC).

Celtic peoples invaded Anatolia by way of Macedonia, Greece, and Thrace, founding the kingdom of Galatia (279 BC); they aided Nicomedes in establishing the kingdom of Bithynia.

First Syrian War (276-272 BC): Ptolemy II defeated Antiochus I.

d. Chandragupta Maurya (?-286 BC), Indian ruler (r. 323-286 BC) who blocked the invasion led by Seleucus I (305 BC).

In China, the state of Ch'in conquered the formerly dominant Wei (ca. 280 BC).

On returning from Sicily, Pyrrhus of Epirus again led his allied forces against the Romans at Beneventum (275 BC) and seemed poised to win, but the Romans under M. Curius Dentatus counterattacked, driving him from the field; Pyrrhus soon returned to Epirus.

Italian mercenaries called Mamertines (Sons of Mars) revolted against the Greek colony at Syracuse, led by Hiero II (ca. 275 BC); they later settled the colony of Messana (Messina), raiding by sea and land from their vital position near the Strait of Messina.

Romans took Rhegium, completing their hold on southern Italy (270 BC).

b. Marcus Claudius Marcellus (ca. 268-208 BC), Roman consul.

b. Quintus Fabius Maximus Verrucosus (ca. 266-203 BC), Roman consul.

In their running battle against Syracuse, the Mamertines of Messana sought aid from two different sources: Rome and Carthage (a Phoenician colony); by the time the Romans arrived, the Carthaginians had garrisoned Messana (265 BC); this triggered the First Punic War, *Punic* being the Roman version of the Greek *poeni*, "royal purple," which gave the Phoenicians their name.

First Punic War (264-241 BC): Romans drove the Carthaginians out of Messana, occupying the city themselves, but were quickly besieged by Carthaginians and their Syracusan Greek allies under Hiero II; Romans, under consul Appius Claudius Caudex, broke the siege of Messana, then besieged Syracuse, without success (264 BC).

First Punic War: Hiero II of Syracuse made a separate peace and alliance with the Romans, who under consul Marcus Valerius Maximus had won victories in eastern Sicily (263 BC).

First Punic War: Carthaginians led by Hannibal Gisco were besieged by Romans in Agrigentum, in western Sicily; Carthaginian relief forces led by Hanno were decisively defeated, leaving Rome in control of most of Sicily; Hannibal and his army escaped (262 BC). (Many other Hannibals and Hannos would follow in Carthaginian history.)

First Punic War: No seamen, the Romans had built a navy modeled on Carthaginian ships, called *quinquiremes*, adding a special invention of their own: the *corvus*, a boarding bridge with a grappling hook at the end, which attached to an enemy ship and allowed for hand-to-hand combat, at which Roman legionaries excelled. Overcoming the Carthaginians' historical naval advantage, the Romans under C. Duillius won at Mylae, becoming a dominant sea power, and quickly invaded Corsica and Sardinia (260 BC).

First Punic War: A Roman invasion fleet headed for Carthage, under consuls M. Atilius Regulus and L. Manlius Volso, was met off Sicily by Carthaginians, led by Hamilcar and Hanno; Roman innovations again carried the day at the Battle of Cape Ecnomus.

d. Pyrrhus (319-272 BC), king of Epirus, originally allied with Demetrius I Poliorcetes of Macedonia and later with Ptolemy I, during wars against Rome and Carthage in Sicily; notable for his costly Pyrrhic victories at Heraclea (280 BC) and Asculum (279 BC); he was killed fighting in Argos.

In the Chremonidean War (265 BC), Ptolemy II sponsored invasions of Macedonia by Athens, Sparta, and Epirus; Antigonus II defeated the allies, led by Chremonides of Athens.

Sparta was decisively defeated by Antigonus II near Corinth and withdrew from the alliance against him (265 BC).

Alexander of Epirus, son of Pyrrhus, took much of Macedonia (263 BC).

Antigonus II and his Macedonian forces besieged Athens, which surrendered after two years (262 BC).

Antigonus II and his troops recaptured Macedonia, forcing Alexander of Epirus to withdraw (255 BC).

b. Philopoemen (ca. 252-182 BC), Greek general.

Antiochus I, son of Seleucus, established his domination of the Celtic kingdom of Galatia (275 BC).

Eumenes I established the independent kingdom of Pergamum in Anatolia (ca. 263 BC); the great library there would be built under his successors, Eumenes II and Attalos II.

Second Syrian War (260-255 BC): Antiochus II, who had succeeded his father, Antiochus I (261 BC), invaded Syria (260 BC).

Second Syrian War: Ptolemy II defeated Antiochus II's ally Antigonus II in a sea battle off the island of Cos (258 BC).

First Punic War: Roman invasion fleet landed an army under M. Atilius Regulus near Carthage, where they won a decisive land victory at Adys (256 BC). The Carthaginians made a peace offer but found Regulus's terms too severe to accept.

First Punic War: Carthaginians, reinforced by Greek mercenaries under Spartan soldier of fortune Xanthippus, decisively defeated the Romans at Tunes (Tunis), capturing Regulus and half his army. The rest of the army was evacuated by a Roman relief fleet but was largely destroyed in a storm between Africa and Sicily, with the reported loss of almost 100,000 Roman warriors and 284 of 364 ships (256 BC).

Second Syrian War: Unable to win Syria and Palestine, Ptolemy II sued for peace (255 BC).

Asoka, grandson of Chandragupta, won the throne of the Mauryan Empire (ca. 274 BC), with its capital at Pataliputra; he mounted a campaign to the Ganges River and the Deccan, but, appalled by warfare — especially the carnage at the taking of Kalinga, in which 100,000 people were reportedly killed — he gave up expansionist aims and became a Buddhist.

The Ch'in army decisively defeated the state of Ch'ao at Ch'an-P'ing (Gao Ping), in China's Shansi province (260 BC).

b. Shih Huang Ti (Cheng) (259-210 BC), Chinese emperor (r. 221-210 BC).

Diodotus, satrap of Bactria, successfully rebelled against Seleucid rule, then took Sogdiana and expanded both west toward India and east into Parthia (255 BC).

Driven from Bactria by Diodotus, Scythian leader Arsaces moved into western Parthia, founding an independent kingdom (250-249 BC).

|

275-251 BC (cont.)

First Punic War: Romans under consul L. Caecilius Metellus defeated Carthaginians under Hasdrubal at Panormus, in northwest Sicily (251 BC).

250-226 BC

First Punic War: The rebuilt Roman fleet blockading the Carthaginian colony of Lilybaeum on Sicily was attacked by Carthaginians under Adherbal at Drepanum (Trapani); the Romans, under P. Claudius Pulcher, suffered a disaster, losing nearly half their ships, while the Carthaginians lost none. The Romans lost again to Hamilcar Barca off Eryx later that year, then lost the rest of their fleet in a storm (249 BC).

First Punic War: Under Hamilcar Barca, Carthaginians regained their strongholds in western Sicily, holding them against all Roman attacks (247-242 BC).

First Punic War: Romans under L. Lutatius Catulus captured the Carthaginian colonies of Lilybaeum and Drepanum, in western Sicily (242 BC).

First Punic War: With yet another rebuilt fleet, the Romans under Catulus met a Carthaginian fleet under Hanno off Sicily, taking 70 and sinking 50 of their 200 ships in the decisive Battle of the Aegates Islands (241 BC). Carthage gave up western Sicily, which became Rome's first overseas province.

Romans, aided by rebellious Carthaginian mercenaries, took Sardinia from the Carthaginians (238 BC); it later became a Roman province (227 BC).

From Carthaginian colonies on the coast of Spain, Hamilcar Barca conquered most of the Iberian Peninsula up to the Tagus and Ebro rivers (237-228 BC).

b. Scipio Africanus (Publius Cornelius Scipio Major) (ca. 236-184 BC), Roman consul and general.

b. Marcus Porcius Censorinus Cato (Cato the Elder; the Censor) (234-149 BC), Roman political and military leader.

Hasdrubal continued the conquests in Spain begun by his father-in-law, Hamilcar Barca (228-221 BC), founding Carthago Nova (Cartagena) (227 BC); under the Ebro Treaty (226 BC), Romans recognized Carthaginian rule south of the Ebro River.

War of Demetrius (238-229 BC): Macedonia's Demetrius II fought against the revived Achaean and Aetolian leagues; this was part of a long series of battles for control of Greece.

b. Philip V (238-179 BC), king of Macedonia (r. 221-179 BC).

First Illyrian War (229-228 BC): Roman forces, called in by the Greek city-states, defeated the Illyrians, pirates on the Adriatic and Ionian seas; Illyrian queen Teuta paid tribute to Rome.

Achaean League was defeated by the Spartans under Cleomenes III (228-227 BC).

225-201 BC

Gauls invaded central Italy, defeating the Romans at Faesulae (225 BC).

Roman forces under Aemilius Papus and Caius Atilius Regulus defeated the Gauls at Telamon; Regulus was killed (224 BC).

Pursuing the Gauls north to the Po River, Romans under M. Claudius Marcellus won at Clastidium and took the Gauls' capital, Mediolanum (222 BC); Rome established colonies in the north, building the Via Flaminia.

Macedonia's Antigonus III defeated Sparta's Cleomenes III at Sellasia (222 BC).

Social War (219-217 BC): Philip V of Macedonia decisively defeated the Aetolian League.

Second Illyrian War (219 BC): The Romans again delivered a sharp defeat to the Illyrians, under King Scerdilaidas, effectively taking control of the Illyrian coast.

First Macedonian War (215-205 BC): Philip V of Macedonia and Hannibal of Carthage, later joined by the Achaean League, allied themselves against Rome (215 BC).

Africa and Southwest Asia | East, Central, and South Asia, the Pacific, and the Americas

250-226 BC

b. Hannibal Barca (247-183 BC), Carthaginian general.

Third Syrian War (246-241 BC): Ptolemy III, who had succeeded his father, Ptolemy II (246 BC), lost a naval battle at Andros (245 BC) to Antigonus III, but he eventually took most of Syria and much of southern Anatolia from Seleucus II.

b. Antiochus III (the Great) (242-187 BC), king of the Seleucid Empire (r. 223-187 BC).

An estimated 25,000 unpaid mercenaries revolted against the rule of Hanno, besieging Carthage; inducing the rebels to meet him on the field, Hamilcar Barca defeated one group at Utica and another near Tunes (Tunis) (238 BC).

In a civil war in Anatolia, Seleucus II was defeated at Ancyra (Ankara) by his brother Antiochus Hierax, supported by the Galatians (236 BC).

Under Arsaces I Parthia expanded, taking eastern portions of the Seleucid Empire, then in a period of decline (235 BC).

Attalus I of Pergamum, who had succeeded his uncle, Eumenes II (241 BC), defeated Antiochus Hierax and the Galatians (groups of Gauls), securing the positions of Pergamum and Seleucus (by 230 BC).

In the state of Ch'in, King Cheng (later Shih Huang Ti) came to power (r. 247-210 BC), proceeding to conquer his rival states.

The Parni people, a branch of the Scythians, founded the kingdom of Parthia, east of the Persian highlands, under Arsaces I (ca. 247 BC).

Diodotus and Arsaces I became allies against Seleucus II's attempts to retake the eastern Alexandrian provinces (239-238 BC).

d. Asoka (?-ca. 232 BC), last ruler of the Mauryan Empire (r. ca. 273-ca. 232 BC), which swiftly collapsed after his death.

Diodotus was deposed by the Greek-Macedonian Euthydemus, who became king of Bactria (230 BC).

225-201 BC

Attalus I of Pergamum had initial success in a war against the Seleucid Empire (224-221 BC) but lost most of recently acquired central Anatolia to the new Seleucid emperor, Antiochus III (the Great) (r. 223-187 BC).

d. Hasdrubal (?-221 BC), Carthaginian general during the First Punic War and the conquest of Spain; son-in-law of Hamilcar Barca, he was assassinated; his brother-in-law Hannibal Barca succeeded him.

Fourth Syrian War (221-217 BC): Antiochus III suppressed a revolt in Mesopotamia and became embroiled in a conflict with Egypt's Ptolemys.

Fourth Syrian War: Ptolemy IV defeated Antiochus III at Raphia (Rafa), retaining Egyptian control of Palestine (217 BC).

Having unified the region from the Yangtze River north, Cheng declared himself emperor of China, calling himself Shih Huang Ti; in his brief Ch'in dynasty, he laid the groundwork for the centralized government that would thereafter dominate China (222 BC). He also introduced iron to supplement bronze weapons, generally metal-tipped spears or swords, and placed special emphasis on the use of the crossbow by mounted horsemen. The army of life-

Intending to complete the conquest of the Iberian Peninsula — and to avenge the defeat of his father, Hamilcar Barca, in the First Punic War — Hannibal Barca led Carthaginian forces in a successful eight-month siege of Saguntum (Sagunto) (219 BC), a Greek colony allied with Rome, triggering the Second Punic War.

Second Punic War (218-202 BC): Leaving his brother Hasdrubal Barca protecting Carthaginian territories in Spain, Hannibal took an army overland through southern Gaul toward northern Italy, hoping to make a surprise invasion and also avoid sea engagements, in which Rome was now superior (218 BC).

Second Punic War: Unaware of Hannibal's invasion plans, the Romans readied three armies: one, under consul Titus Sempronius, to attack Carthage; a second, under consuls Publius Cornelius Scipio and his brother Gnaeus Cornelius Scipio, to invade Spain; and the third to protect northern Italy from attacks by the Celts (Gauls) in the Alps (218 BC).

Second Punic War: Learning of Hannibal's plans, the Scipio brothers landed their Roman army at Massilia (Marseilles), hoping to cut them off; Hannibal had turned inland to make a northerly detour through the Alps, taking his war elephants across the Rhône River on a temporary bridge made of rafts. The Scipios divided their forces, sending the larger part to Spain and the smaller along the coast to northern Italy (218 BC).

Second Punic War: Gnaeus Scipio's Roman army landed in northern Iberia, defeating Carthaginian forces under Hanno Barca (possibly another brother of Hannibal's) and gaining control of the territory between the Ebro River and the Pyrenees (218 BC).

Second Punic War: The Carthaginians made a difficult late-year crossing through the Alps, facing not only harsh wintry conditions but unanticipated attacks from the Alpine Celts (Gauls), who also defeated Manlius's Roman forces when they arrived in northern Italy. The Carthaginians met the Romans, now under Publius Scipio, at the Ticinus River, where the Romans were defeated and Scipio was wounded (Nov. 218 BC).

Second Punic War: Roman forces, reinforced by Sicilian forces under Sempronius, fought Hannibal's Carthaginians, reinforced by Gauls at the Trebia River; the Romans lost three-quarters of their troops, some 30,000 soldiers (Dec. 218 BC).

Second Punic War: After resting over the winter and recruiting more Gauls, the Carthaginians made a surprise spring march over the Alps and through the Arnus (Arno) marshes to cut off the Roman army of Gaius Flaminius, positioned to block the main road to Rome. En route to intercept Hannibal, Roman forces were ambushed in a defile near Lake Trasimene; in the resulting disaster, three-quarters of the Roman troops were killed or captured, some 30,000 soldiers, including Flaminius (217 BC). Hannibal headed for southern Italy, where he expected to establish a base and find allies among Rome's subject peoples. Under a new dictator, Quintus Fabius, the Romans harassed the Carthaginians but mostly avoided direct combat.

First Macedonian War: In their conflict with Philip V of Macedonia, the Romans allied themselves with Greece's Aetolian League (212 BC); Sparta, Mantinea, and Elis also joined the alliance (211 BC), as did Attalus I of Pergamum (209 BC).

First Macedonian War: At Mantinea, the Achaeans, under Philopoemen, considered the last great general of the early Greeks, decisively defeated Sparta (207 BC). The war petered out inconclusively.

Antiochus III suppressed a revolt in Anatolia (216-213 BC), then began to rebuild Seleucid strength.

Second Punic War: Encouraged by the Romans, Numidia (roughly modern Algeria) revolted against Carthaginian rule; Hasdrubal Barca (son of Hamilcar, brother of Hannibal) returned from Spain to put down the revolt, aided by Numidian prince Massinissa (213 BC); later he returned to Spain with Numidian reinforcements.

Antiochus III defeated Armenia (212-211 BC), forcing it to acknowledge Seleucid domination.

Antiochus III regained control of Media (210 BC).

d. Hasdrubal Barca (?-207 BC), Carthaginian general during the Second Punic War (219-202 BC), son of Hamilcar Barca and brother of Hannibal; he commanded in Spain while Hannibal traversed the Alps and was killed at the Metaurus River en route to join Hannibal (summer 207 BC).

Antiochus III sent an amphibious expedition from Mesopotamia down the Arabian coast of the Persian Gulf and took Gerha (Bahrain) (205-204 BC).

Second Punic War: Roman proconsul Scipio (Africanus), son of Publius Scipio, invaded Africa with a veteran army, besieging Utica until stalled by the Carthaginians under Hasdrubal Gisco and Numidian king Syphax (204 BC); the two armies wintered under a truce. Numidian prince Massinissa, Syphax's rival, was allied with the Romans.

Second Punic War: Unilaterally breaking the winter truce, Scipio's Roman forces attacked unsuspecting Carthaginian and Numidian camps, destroying them and renewing the siege of Utica; a new Carthaginian army, under Hasdrubal Gisco and Syphax, confronted the Romans at Bagbrades, near Utica, but was utterly defeated, and Syphax was captured; the Carthaginians sued for peace and recalled Hannibal from Italy (203 BC).

Fifth Syrian War (203-195 BC): Antiochus III and Philip V of Macedonia agreed to split Egypt's overseas possessions after the infant Ptolemy V inherited the Egyptian throne (r. 203-180 BC).

Second Punic War: Having raised a new army and broken off peace negotiations, Hannibal's Carthaginians met Scipio's Roman forces at Zama, inland from Carthage, but were decisively defeated (202 BC), ending the Second Punic War. Peace terms called for the Carthaginians to pay extensive reparations, to cede warships to Rome, to give up any claim to Spain, and not to make war without Roman permission; Massinissa became king of Numidia, and Syracuse was absorbed into the Roman province of Sicilia (Sicily).

d. Hasdrubal Gisco (?-202 BC), Carthaginian general in the Second Punic War; accused of treason, he committed suicide before the Battle of Zama.

Fifth Syrian War: Philip V of Macedonia lost to Ptolemaic forces at Chios, in the Aegean Sea (201 BC), also losing to Pergamum and Rhodes, both allies of Egypt.

size terra-cotta statues found buried near Xian (1974 AD) were guarding his tomb.

Shih Huang Ti's forces, generally led by generals Ming T'ien and Chao T'o, expanded China's borders into northern Korea and south of the Yangtze River, taking the regions of modern Fukien, Kwantung, Kwangsi, and Tonkin (221-214 BC).

Shih Huang Ti unified the various defensive walls on the Ch'in Empire's northern borders into one Great Wall (later much expanded) against the Hsiung-nu, Central Asian nomads whom he temporarily defeated (by 210 BC).

d. Shih Huang Ti (Cheng) (259-210 BC), Chinese emperor (r. 221-210 BC) who unified China (222 BC), founding the short-lived but influential Ch'in dynasty, with a centralized government; he introduced many beneficial reforms but ordered massive destruction of all unapproved books and records, an irreplaceable loss (213 BC).

Chinese general Chao T'o established an independent kingdom, Nam-viet, including Tonkin, northern Annam, and briefly the Canton region (ca. 210 BC).

Seleucid emperor Antiochus III invaded Parthia, defeating Arsaces III at Arius (209 BC) and forcing him to accept Seleucid rule. Antiochus also campaigned in Bactria, defeating Euthydemus, descended from Alexander the Great's army (208-206 BC), gaining his nominal submission. Following Alexander's path, Antiochus campaigned to the Indus River, possibly into the Punjab (208-206 BC).

Ch'in dynasty ended, after the murder of Shih Huang Ti's son Hu Hai (207 BC) by Hsiang Yü and Liu Pang; the two then fought a civil war (207-202 BC), during which northern Korea became independent.

Antiochus III invaded the Kabul Valley, accepted as nominal sovereign by Indian ruler Sophagasenous (206 BC).

d. Ch'en Yü (?-205 BC), Chinese general; he unsuccessfully led Ch'ao royal forces against Liu Pang (Kao Tsu), who beheaded Ch'en after the battle.

Revolutionary leader Liu Pang finally defeated general Hsiang Yü in the contest for power in China; Liu then took the name Kao Tsu, founding the Han dynasty (202 BC).

225-201 BC (cont.)

Second Punic War: A new Roman army, under consuls Aemilius Paulus and Terentius Varro, met Hannibal's smaller Carthaginian army at Cannae, in southeastern Italy; during the battle Hannibal's central forces made a planned withdrawal into a curve of the Autidus River, using his wings to encircle the Romans; in their worst defeat in history, the Romans lost 50,000 to 60,000 of their 87,000 soldiers, including Paulus (Varro had fled) (Aug. 2, 216 BC).

Second Punic War: Another new Roman army, under proconsul M. Claudius Marcellus, defeated Hannibal's Carthaginians at Nola (216 BC), slowing the defection of Italian allies to Hannibal.

Second Punic War: Hannibal raided in Italy's Campania but was hampered by a lack of support from Carthage; the Romans generally avoided engagement (215 BC).

After the death of Hiero II, the Greek city-state of Syracuse allied itself with Carthage (215 BC); southern Italy came back under Roman control.

Second Punic War: In Iberia, the Romans took Saguntum from the Carthaginians while Hasdrubal was away in Africa (213-212 BC).

Second Punic War: Romans under Marcellus besieged and took Syracuse (213-212 BC), a Carthaginian ally; the city's defense was aided by machines invented by Archimedes, including tonglike grapplers to use against battering rams.

d. Archimedes (ca. 287-212 BC), Greek scientist and inventor who developed new military technology for the defense of Syracuse; he was killed (against orders) by Roman troops after the city fell.

Second Punic War: Hannibal took Tarentum after great effort, while the Romans besieged Capua, a Carthaginian ally; other Greek colonies in southern Italy declared their independence (212 BC).

Second Punic War: In Iberia, Hasdrubal's reinforced Carthaginian forces defeated Romans under the Scipio brothers in the upper Baetis Valley (211 BC), again taking control of Spain south of the Ebro River.

Second Punic War: Hannibal marched toward Rome, apparently hoping that the Romans would end their siege of Capua; that did not happen, and Capua surrendered, a blow to the Carthaginians (211 BC).

d. Publius Cornelius Scipio (?-211 BC), Roman consul who fought Hannibal and Hasdrubal Barca; he took Saguntum but was killed in battle soon after.

Second Punic War: Romans conquered and sacked Syracuse, then annexed all of Sicily, abandoned by the Carthaginians (210 BC).

Second Punic War: Romans under Fabius Cunctator retook Tarentum (209 BC), which Hannibal had made his main base; Roman troops retained the citadel, being supplied by sea.

d. Hsiang Yü (Hsiung Chi) (?-202 BC),
Chinese rebel leader who originally served
the Ch'in emperor Shih Huang Ti; after
the emperor's death, he led the anti-Ch'in
rebellion and later committed suicide.

Hsiung-nu forces, recently unified under
Mo Du, invaded China (201 BC) and
defeated Kao Tsu (200 BC), who ceded to
them the border regions and gave his
daughter in marriage to Mo Du.

Bactrian leader Euthydemus mounted an
expedition to the East, attempting to make
direct contact with the source of silk, the
Chinese, known to him as the Seres (late
3rd c. BC); the Hsiung-nu stopped him.

225-201 BC (cont.)

Second Punic War: The Carthaginian capital of Carthago Nova was surprised and captured by Roman forces in Spain, led by Publius Scipio (later called Africanus), named after his father (209 BC).

Second Punic War: After fighting Scipio in the inconclusive Battle of Baecula (near modern Cordova), Hasdrubal took his forces overland to Italy, to reinforce Hannibal (208 BC).

d. Marcus Claudius Marcellus (ca. 268-208 BC), Roman consul, who was a field commander against Hannibal at Nola (216 BC); after the siege of Syracuse (213-212 BC), his troops killed Archimedes, against his orders.

Second Punic War: Scipio (Africanus) extended Roman control to much of Spain, defeating Carthaginian forces under Mago Barca (another of Hannibal's brothers) and Hasdrubal Gisco, most decisively at Ilipa (or Silpia) (207-206 BC), and ending Carthaginian rule of Spain; Mago retreated to the Balearic Islands and then to Italy, near modern Genoa.

Second Punic War: Learning from intercepted communications that Hasdrubal Gisco was arriving in northern Italy, a Roman army under Caius Claudius Nero and M. Livius Salinator surprised the Carthaginians at the Metaurus River, employing the flanking techniques that Hannibal had used so successfully at Cannae; Hasdrubal was killed and his army effectively destroyed (207 BC).

Recalled to Carthage, Hannibal and Mago withdrew from Italy; Mago died en route; their army numbered approximately 18,000 soldiers, mostly Italians (203 BC).

d. Quintus Fabius Maximus Verrucosus (ca. 266-203 BC), Roman consul noted for his tactics of delay and attrition.

Manius Acilius Glabrio (active 201-189 BC), Roman general and statesman who would be a key commander at Thermopylae (191 BC).

200-176 BC

Romans won the Battle of Cremona (200 BC), part of the reconquest of the Po Valley after Hannibal's defeat, building the Via Aemilia to take their main west coast highway to Placentia (187 BC).

A more powerful siege machine, called the onager because it delivered a powerful "kick" when fired, came into use (ca. 200 BC).

d. Scipio Africanus (Publius Cornelius Scipio Major) (ca. 236-184 BC), Roman consul and general who defeated Hannibal's Carthaginians in the decisive battle at Zama (202 BC); he was the son of Publius Cornelius Scipio, nephew of Gnaeus Cornelius Scipio, and grandfather of Scipio the Younger (Africanus Minor).

b. Scipio the Younger (Publius Cornelius Scipio Aemilianus Africanus Minor Numantinus) (ca. 184-129 BC), Roman consul and general.

Second Macedonian War (200-196 BC): Philip V of Macedonia sought to expand in the eastern Mediterranean, while his ally Antiochus III of Syria focused on Egypt; the Romans were called in by Pergamum, Rhodes, and Athens, while Sparta joined Philip.

Second Macedonian War: At Cynoscephalae (197 BC), in Thessaly, Roman forces under Titus Quinctius Flamininus defeated Philip V so badly that he was forced to give up any claim to Greece and also lost his territories in Thrace, Anatolia, and the Aegean at the end of the war (196 BC). Cynoscephalae is notable because it was the first open-field confrontation between the Roman legion and the Macedonian phalanx.

Antiochus III of Syria and the Romans were at war (192-188 BC) after Antiochus invaded Greece; though not actively involved, Ptolemy V was allied with Rome because of Antiochus's designs on Egypt.

Antiochus III's forces lost to the Romans on land, at Thermopylae, and at sea, between Ionia and Chios (both 191 BC).

200-176 BC

Greek geographer Eudoxus is reported to have sailed around Africa from the Red Sea to Gades (Cadiz), Spain (ca. 2nd c. BC); in this period, and possibly earlier, Phoenicians from Carthage were trading along the coast of West Africa.

Fifth Syrian War: Antiochus III defeated Ptolemaic forces at Panium (198 BC), then occupied Palestine and other Ptolemaic territories in Syria and southern Anatolia, except for Cyprus.

Too successfully leading the Carthaginian recovery, Hannibal was accused by Rome of breaking the peace (196 BC) and took refuge with Antiochus III in Syria.

Roman forces under Scipio Africanus and his brother Lucius Cornelius Scipio invaded Anatolia, joining with troops from Pergamum under Eumenes II; at Magnesia, south of Pergamum, they met and routed Antiochus III's Syrian army, partly by stampeding the Syrians' war elephants (190 BC).

Under the Peace of Apameax, Antiochus III lost his territories in Greece and in Anatolia west of the Taurus Mountains, which were mostly divided between Rhodes and Pergamum (188 BC). Armenia proclaimed its independence (188 BC).

Euthydemus, Bactrian king of Greek-Macedonian ancestry, expanded his control into Gandhara and the Punjab (200-195 BC), beginning a second major wave of Greek influence on the Indian subcontinent.

Succeeding his father Euthydemus, Bactrian king Demetrius expanded his control into the Indus Valley and perhaps beyond (ca. 195-ca. 175 BC).

Hsiung-nu (later the Huns) of Mongolia expanded into the Kansu (Gansu) Corridor and western Mongolia, defeating and driving before them the Indo-European-speaking people called the Yüeh Chih (Meat-Eaters), a red-haired, blue-eyed people later called the Kushans (from ca. 176 BC).

Western Europe	Eastern Europe

200-176 BC (cont.)

	Admiral Lucius Aemilius Regillus led a combined fleet of Roman and Rhodian ships against a Syrian fleet under Hannibal (in his only sea battle) at Eurymedon; the Syrians lost there and at Myonnessus (both 190 BC).

d. Philopoemen (ca. 252-182 BC), Greek general who became general (*strategus*) of the Achaean League (208 BC); he reorganized the Achaean troops using Macedonian weapons and techniques and was killed fighting rebels from Messena.

Romans founded a fort at Aquileia (181 BC), at the head of the Adriatic Sea.

d. Philip V (238-179 BC), king of Macedonia (r. 221-179 BC) and son of Demetrius II, who led his country in various wars until his decisive defeat (197 BC); he then became allied with Rome.

175-151 BC

Western Europe	Eastern Europe
In their attack on Heracleum (169 BC), the Romans used (perhaps for the first time) the *testudo* (tortoise) formation, in which groups of infantry approached in close formation, with their shields held high and overlapping, forming a protective roof (akin to tortoiseshell) over them.	Third Macedonian War (172-167 BC): After Perseus of Macedonia, son of Philip V, tried to murder Eumenes II of Pergamum, the Romans took Pergamum's side, though suspicious of its recent expansion.
b. Gaius Marius (156-86 BC), Roman general.	Third Macedonian War: Macedonian forces under Perseus defeated invading Roman forces under P. Licinius Crassus at Callicinus, near Larissa (171 BC), foiling two more invasion attempts in the next two years.
Roman troops under Marcus Claudius Marcellinus put down a rebellion by the Lusitanians and Iberians (154-151 BC).	Third Macedonian War: Under a new general, Lucius Aemilius Paulus, the Romans decisively defeated the Macedonians in an impromptu battle near the Pydna River (June 22, 168 BC); more than half of the Macedonian forces — some 20,000 soldiers — died, and many more were captured; Perseus escaped but later surrendered and died in captivity. Many Greeks were then brought to Rome, including the historian Polybius. Macedonia was divided into four republics, and Rome became dominant in the eastern Mediterranean.
	Andriscus, possibly a son of Perseus's, led a rebellion against Roman power, temporarily uniting Macedonia and proclaiming himself king (152 BC).

200-176 BC (cont.)

d. Antiochus III (the Great) (242-187 BC), king of the Seleucid Empire (r. 223-187 BC) who at times controlled much of southwest Asia. He was succeeded by his sons Seleucus IV (r. 187-175 BC) and then Antiochus IV (r. 175-164 BC).

d. Hannibal Barca (247-183 BC), Carthaginian general during the conquest of Spain (237-220 BC) and the Second Punic War (218-202 BC); son of Hamilcar Barca and brother of Hasdrubal Barca, he took his army, including elephants, over the Alps to Italy. He committed suicide in Bithynia, in flight from the Romans.

175-151 BC

Antiochus IV of Syria invaded Egypt twice (171-170; 168 BC), conquering most of the country and besieging Alexandria; however, warned by Rome to restore Ptolemaic rule, he withdrew.

Mithridates I of Parthia and Eucratides of Bactria carried on a long war, slightly favoring Parthia (ca. 170-ca. 160 BC).

In his retreat from Egypt, Antiochus IV of Syria occupied Jerusalem, destroying the city walls and suppressing the Jewish religion; the result was the revolt of the Maccabees, led by the priest Mattathias and his five sons, one of them Judas Maccabeus (168 BC).

Judas Maccabeus led Jewish forces against the Seleucid Syrians, winning notably at Beth Horon and Emmaus (both 166 BC) and at Beth Zur, near Hebron (165 BC), then also taking Jerusalem, including the temple but not the citadel.

Antiochus IV reestablished Seleucid rule over Armenia and other eastern territories (166-163 BC) lost by his father's defeat two decades earlier.

While Jewish forces maintained a siege of Seleucid Syrians in the Jerusalem citadel, the main Syrian forces, under the regent Lysias, invaded Judea, defeating the Jews at Beth Zachariah (164 BC).

Judas Maccabeus and his Jewish forces were defeated and driven from Jerusalem by Syrian troops (162 BC).

Judas Maccabeus and the Jews defeated Syrians under general Nicanor at Adasa but lost to Bacchides at Elases; Judas was killed in battle (161 BC). His brother Jonathan Maccabeus continued leading guerrilla activity based in Jerusalem (from 152 BC).

During a time of dynastic strife, Timarchus, governor of Babylonia, declared his independence from the Seleucid Empire, conquering the province of Media and calling himself the "Great King"; he was defeated by Demetrius I, who restored Seleucid rule in Babylonia and Media (ca. 161-159 BC).

While Bactrian king Demetrius was campaigning in India, general Eucratides led a revolt; during the resulting civil war, he conquered most of Bactria's Indian territories, except those in the Punjab east of the Jhelum River (ca. 175-ca. 162 BC).

Phraates I of Parthia took the region south of the Caspian Sea, formerly Seleucid territory (ca. 175 BC).

Now directly on China's borders, the Hsiung-nu raided deeply into northwest China, at one point approaching the Han capital, Loyang (ca. 166 BC).

In Bactria, Eucratides was assassinated, setting off a power struggle (ca. 162-ca. 150 BC) eventually won by Menander, a descendant of Bactrian king Demetrius, although his domains were limited to southern Bactria, Gandhara, and parts of Arachosia and the Punjab; the line of Eucratides continued in parts of northern India.

Tamil peoples of Ceylon (Sri Lanka) were briefly united by Elara (Elala), leader of the Cholas from the southeast, soon defeated and replaced by Prince Duttha-Gamani (Dutegemunu) (161 BC).

Pushed westward by the Indo-European-speaking Yüeh Chih, who were themselves being pushed by the Hsiung-nu, Scythians invaded and took parts of Bactria (from ca. 160 BC).

b. Wu Ti (Liu Ch'e) (156-87 BC), emperor of China (r. 140-87 BC).

150-126 BC

Lusitanians and Iberian Celts, led by Viriathus, revolted against the Romans, at first occupied in fighting Carthage (149-139 BC).

d. Marcus Porcius Censorinus Cato (Cato the Elder; the Censor) (234-149 BC), Roman political and military leader who pronounced, *"Delenda est Carthago"* ("Carthage must be destroyed") (149 BC); with Manius Acilius Glabrio, he won at Thermopylae (191 BC).

Romans under Q. Caecilius Metellus suppressed the decade-long revolt of the Iberian Celts and Lusitanians after the assassination of their leader, Viriathus, probably engineered by the Romans (139 BC).

b. Lucius Cornelius Sulla (138-78 BC), Roman general.

Numantian War (137-132 BC): Iberian Celts again revolted against the Romans, with initial success; the conflict ended when Publius Scipio Aemilianus captured Numantia, their key city on the Durius (Douro) River.

First Servile War (135-132 BC): Led by the Syrian Eunus, slaves — some estimate as many as 200,000 — revolted in Sicily, eventually being suppressed by Publius Rupilius, with perhaps 20,000 slaves being crucified.

Popular tribune Tiberius Sempronius Gracchus was assassinated in Rome, which then saw widespread riots (133 BC).

d. Scipio the Younger (Publius Cornelius Scipio Aemilianus Africanus Minor Numantinus) (ca. 184-129 BC), Roman consul and general who led the final siege and destruction of Carthage (146 BC) and won the Numantian War (137-132 BC); adopted grandson of Scipio Africanus, he received the honorary titles "Africanus Minor" and "Numantia."

Andriscus's Macedonian revolt was suppressed by Romans under Q. Caecilius Metellus (148-146 BC); Macedonia became a Roman province.

While Rome was occupied with Carthage, the Achaean League attacked Sparta, a Roman ally, but the league was decisively defeated by Romans under consul Lucius Mummius; Corinth was taken and destroyed, the Achaean League was dissolved, and all of Greece came under direct Roman control (146 BC).

125-101 BC

Romans under consul Marcus Fulvius Flaccus began to press into Transalpine Gaul, between the Alps and the Rhône River (125 BC).

b. Quintus Sertorius (ca. 125-72 BC), Roman general.

In Latium, Italy's second-largest city, the Fregellae people revolted, seeking the vote; the Romans took the city and destroyed it (124 BC).

The Cimbri, Teutones, Ambrones, and other Germanic peoples, who had recently migrated from the region of Jutland, defeated a Roman army at Noreia, in Carinthia (now southern Austria). The Cimbri invaded the Carnic Alps, reaching the Drava Valley, where they were stopped by a Roman army under G. Papirius Carbo (113 BC).

Carthage and Massinissa of Numidia moved from their long disputes into open war (150 BC).

As dynastic strife continued among the Seleucids, the Parthians, under Mithridates I, took Media (150 BC).

Third Punic War (149-146 BC): Rome ordered Carthage to cease war with Numidia, give up its hostages, and dismantle the city's fortifications; when asked to abandon their city, the Carthaginians refused; the Romans declared war, at which time Cato said, "Carthage must be destroyed" (149 BC).

Third Punic War: Carthaginians put up a strong defense against initial Roman attacks by land and sea (148 BC).

Third Punic War: Carthage was besieged and blockaded by land and sea by Roman troops under Publius Scipio Aemilianus, son of L. Aemilius Paulus and adopted grandson of Scipio Africanus (147 BC).

Third Punic War: Its people starved by the Roman blockade, Carthage fell; survivors either died or were enslaved, and the city itself was utterly destroyed, ending the war (146 BC). Carthage became the Roman province of Africa.

Jonathan Maccabeus, Jewish guerrilla leader and brother of Judas Maccabeus, was killed in an ambush at Ptolemais (Acre) (143 BC).

Simon Maccabeus, brother of guerrilla leaders Jonathan and Judas Maccabeus, was accepted as king of independent Judea by the Seleucids (143 BC).

Mithridates I and the Parthians took Babylonia (141 BC).

Scythians, Yüeh Chih, and Parthians struggled for the former Hellenic Greek kingdom of Bactria (ca. 140-ca. 100 BC).

b. Tigranes (Dikran) (ca. 140-55 BC), king of Armenia (ca. 95-55 BC).

After winning a dynastic struggle for the Seleucid throne, Demetrius II retook Mesopotamia from the Parthians (139 BC), although he was later betrayed and captured (138 BC).

Attalus III willed his kingdom of Pergamum to the Romans at his death; the Romans had to suppress the pretender, Aristonicus, before making it the province of Asia (133-129 BC).

Antiochus VIII and his Seleucid forces retook Babylonia (130 BC), forcing Parthian leader Phraates II to release Antiochus's brother Demetrius II; Antiochus then pushed eastward, until he was defeated and killed by the Parthians at Ecbatana (129 BC); with this the Seleucid Empire lost all its territory east of the Euphrates River.

While the Parthians under Phraates II were pushing against the Seleucids in southwestern Asia, they were themselves attacked from Central Asia by the Tochari, a Scythian people (ca. 130 BC), who killed Phraates II and wasted much of Parthia.

Bactria's Greek-descended leader Menander (in India called Milinda) invaded India's Ganges Valley and expanded his control as far as the old Mauryan capital of Pataliputra, although he lost most of Bactria to Scythian and Parthian invaders (ca. 150-ca. 140 BC).

Emperor Wu Ti, called the "Martial Emperor," came to power in China (ca. 140 BC).

Chinese emperor Wu Ti sent Chang Ch'ien with a caravan of more than 100 people across Central Asia (138 BC) to seek an alliance with the Yüeh Chih against the Hsiung-nu; Chang was captured and held for more than ten years by the Hsiung-nu.

b. Chao Ch'ung-kuo (137-52 BC), Chinese general.

Han An-kuo (active 135-129 BC), Chinese general during the wars with the Hsiung-nu.

Chinese forces under general Wei Ch'ing attacked the Hsiung-nu, eventually retaking the northern border regions (133-119 BC).

d. Menander (Milinda) (?-ca. 130 BC), ruler of Bactria and son of Demetrius, of Greek ancestry; he invaded India's Ganges Valley and ruled an Indo-Greek kingdom (ca. 150 BC).

Escaping from the Hsiung-nu, Chinese ambassador Chang Ch'ien continued across Central Asia to Bactria, new home of the Yüeh Chih; they declined an alliance with the Chinese; again captured and imprisoned for a year, Chang returned home with a stock of highly prized "Heavenly Horses of Ferghana," accompanied only by his Hsiung-nu wife and one of his original party; Chang had opened what would be known as the Silk Road (138-126 BC).

Tochari Scythians again defeated the Parthians, killing their new leader, Artabanus I (124 BC).

Under Mithridates II the Parthians gradually drove the Tochari Scythians from their lands (ca. 123-100 BC).

To settle a dynastic struggle in Numidia, after the death of Massinissa, the Romans divided the kingdom between the two contestants, Jugurtha and Adherbal (119 BC).

Wei Ch'ing's nephew Ho Ch'un Pang extended Chinese control into the Kansu region, leading Chinese forces in a major victory over the Hsiung-nu at He Si, capturing their king and some 40,000 soldiers (121 BC).

Q. Fabius Maximus led Roman forces, allied with the Aedui, to victory against the Arverni and Allobroges near the Rhône and Isere rivers (121 BC), establishing the province of Transalpine Gaul, called Provincia (the Province; modern Provence).

b. Lucius Licinius Lucullus (ca. 117-56 BC), Roman general.

b. Marcus Licinius Crassus (ca. 115-53 BC), Roman political leader.

Cimbri and Teutones arrived in southern Gaul, badly defeating a Roman army under M. Junius Silanus near the Rhône River (109 BC).

b. Pompey (the Great) (Gnaeus Pompeius Magnus) (106-48 BC), Roman general.

Pressing farther south into Gaul, the Cimbri and Teutones gave the Romans one of their worst defeats ever, at Aruasio (Orange) (105 BC); the army of some 80,000 Romans, led by consul Mallius Macimus, was destroyed, with an estimated 40,000 noncombatants also killed; the invaders then moved southwest, but the disaster rocked Rome, leading to military reform under Gaius Marius and P. Rutilius Rufus, replacing militias with a professional army.

Second Servile War (104-99 BC): Another slave revolt in Sicily was put down by Romans under consul Manius Aquillius.

As the Cimbri and Teutones turned east by different routes, Marius led the reorganized army against the Teutones, killing tens of thousands at Aquae Sextae (Aix-en-Provence) (102 BC). The Cimbri, who came through the Brenner Pass into northern Italy, defeated Roman troops under consul Q. Lutatius Catulus (102 BC).

b. Quintus Tullius Cicero (102-43 BC), Roman general.

At Vercellae, Marius's Roman troops effectively destroyed the Cimbri people, killing an estimated 140,000, including noncombatants, and capturing 60,000 (101 BC).

Jugurthine War (112-106 BC): Jugurtha declared war on Adherbal and the Romans, intending to take all of Numidia.

Jugurthine War: Caecilius Metellus, nephew of Q. Caecilius Metellus (Macedonicus), reorganized Roman troops, which then invaded Numidia at the Muthul (108 BC), defeating Jugurtha, who began a desert guerrilla campaign.

Jugurthine War: Roman troops led by Lucius Cornelius Sulla captured Jugurtha, ending the war (106 BC), with part of Numidia becoming a Roman province; Sulla and his superior Marius (successor to Caecilius Metellus) clashed personally during the campaign and would later lead rival factions in Rome.

Wei Ch'ing and Ho Ch'un Pang led Chinese forces in attacks on the Hsiung-nu, driving them beyond the Gobi Desert to near modern Ulaan Bataar (Ulan Bator); their victory at Mo Bei was so decisive that it ended for decades the Hsiung-nu threat to China proper (119 BC).

The way now open to the West, Chang Ch'ien was again sent to establish contacts with the western countries and alliances against the Hsiung-nu; he left in place various Chinese ambassadors and returned with reciprocal ambassadors and various gifts (ca. 115-105 BC) including many new fruits, flowers, and spices, as well as military and commercial intelligence.

d. Chang Ch'ien (?-114 BC), Chinese diplomat and general who opened the Silk Road across Central Asia (138-126 BC) in his search for allies against the Hsiung-nu.

China's Emperor Wu Ti took control of the kingdom of Yüeh, in southern China, extending into Tonkin and Annam, and also of Yunnan, in the mountains of southwest China (111-109 BC); having learned of the existence of India from Chang Ch'ien's western journey (138-128 BC), he vainly attempted to reach it through the Southeast Asian mountains and jungles.

Wu Ti's forces defeated the kingdom of Ch'ao Hsien in southern Manchuria and northern Korea, incorporating it into the Chinese Empire (108 BC).

A Chinese ambassador arrived at An-hsi (Parthia), on the Iranian plateau, opening direct relations with the Iranians and beginning what would be eight centuries of alliances between the peoples (106-105 BC); from this time, the Chinese would try unsuccessfully to reach the Roman Empire, of which they seem to have just learned.

d. Wei Ch'ing (?-106 BC), Chinese general who was a key commander in the wars against the Hsiung-nu.

Seeking more "heavenly horses," the Chinese emperor sent an army westward under Li Kuang-li across the Tarim Basin and the Pamir Mountains, obtaining submission (and supplies) from oasis-cities en route. Kokand, in Ferghana, refused to supply any more horses, and the weakened army was unable to force the issue. A second massive army of 60,000 soldiers, not counting support personnel, was sent to besiege Kokand, which fell after 40 days, when its water supply was diverted. The

125-101 BC (cont.)

100-76 BC

b. Julius Caesar (Gaius Julius Caesar) (100-44 BC), Roman general.

Social War (War of the Allies) (91-89 BC): Many Italian states allied with Rome revolted because they had not been given citizenship; they established a new Italian state, with its capital at Corfinium (91 BC); in response, Rome granted citizenship to allies who had not rebelled, notably the Latins, Etruscans, and Umbrians.

Social War: Roman forces were defeated at Fucine Lake, and their leader, consul Lucius Porcius Cato, was killed; troops under C. Pompeius Strabo won decisively at Asculum (both 89 BC); the rebellious allies were offered and accepted citizenship, ending the revolt.

Roman Civil War (88-82 BC): War grew out of rivalry between the political factions of Marius and Sulla; en route to Greece to deal with Mithridates VI of Pontus, Sulla came to Rome to quell a democratic revolt, led by P. Sulpicius Rufus and supported by Marius, who fled to Africa (88 BC).

Roman Civil War: Roman democrats again seized power (87 BC), under Lucius Cornelius Cinna and Marius, murdering their political opponents until Marius's death (86 BC).

d. Gaius Marius (156-86 BC), Roman general who as consul reformed the Roman army from a citizen to a professional force (104 BC), leading them at Aquae Sextiae (102 BC) and later leading a democratic revolt (88 BC).

b. Decimus Junius Brutus Albinus (ca. 84-43 BC), Roman general and politician.

Roman Civil War: Sulla returned to Italy with his veteran army, defeating troops under consul Caius Norbanus at Mount Tifata, near Capua (83 BC).

Roman Civil War: Sulla defeated the Marius faction and their allies, notably the Samnites and the Lucans, at the Colline Gate (82 BC), then made himself dictator of Rome, ending the war.

b. Mark Antony (Marcus Antonius) (ca. 82-30 BC), Roman soldier.

Sertorian War (80-72 BC): Quintus Sertorius, a supporter of the Marius faction, founded an independent country in Lusitania; though defeated by Romans under Lucius Fufidias at the Baetis (Guadalquivir) River (80 BC), Sertorius remained at large and active, holding off two Roman armies, one led by Quintus Metellus Pius, the other by Pompey.

d. Lucius Cornelius Sulla (138-78 BC), Roman general whose rivalry with Gaius Marius led to civil war (88-82 BC), which ended with Sulla's victory and dictatorship.

First Mithridatic War: Sulla, briefly recalled to Rome, returned to defeat the Pontic and Greek armies in Greece under Archelaus and Ariston, retaking Athens; at sea the Romans, under Lucius Licinius Lucullus, defeated the fleet of Mithridates VI of Pontus off Tenedros. Archelaus escaped to the island of Boeotia, north of the Gulf of Corinth, where he was defeated by Sulla at Chaeronea (86 BC).

First Mithridatic War: Archelaus, with reinforcements from other Greeks and from Mithridates VI of Pontus, again lost to Sulla, this time decisively at Orchomenus (85 BC); the Peace of Dardanos (84 BC) provided for the return of Rome's province of Asia and various payments.

Second Mithridatic War (83-81 BC): This was essentially a regional affair, primarily to enforce the terms of the Peace of Dardanos.

hinese got their desired horses and al
on the whole of Sinkiang (New Domi
n), fully opening the Silk Road to t
est (105-102 BC).

100-76 BC

Parthians under Mithridates II defeated Artavasdes, forcing Armenia to acknowledge Parthian control (ca. 100 BC).

Under Tigranes, the Armenians expanded to take Media and northern Mesopotamia (from ca. 95 BC), establishing their influence over other neighboring regions as well.

Tigranes of Armenia invaded Cappadocia, a Roman protectorate in Anatolia; as Rome's praetor in Asia, Sulla made an alliance with Mithridates II of Parthia against Tigranes, but in the end he defeated the Armenians without outside help (92 BC).

First Mithridatic War (89-84 BC): In Anatolia regional disputes previously mediated by Rome flared into war when Mithridates VI of Pontus, on the Black Sea, invaded Bithynia and Cappadocia, taking the Roman province of Asia, and then invaded Greece, calling for an uprising against Rome (89 BC).

First Mithridatic War: In the Ephesian Vespers, an estimated 80,000 Romans were killed in Rome's province of Asia, then under Mithridates VI of Pontus (88 BC).

Tigranes of Armenia invaded Syria, heartland of the once-powerful Seleucid Empire (83 BC).

Sulla sent Pompey (Gnaeus Pompeius Magnus) to suppress supporters of the Marius faction in Sicily and Africa (83 BC).

Tigranes invaded Cappadocia and annexed it to Armenia (78 BC).

Having lost their western regions to Tigranes of Armenia, the Parthians were so weakened that the Scythians installed a puppet ruler (77 BC).

During China's Han dynasty, the old bow-trap used in hunting was developed into a crossbow, using a lock that, when a trigger was pulled, shot an arrow (by ca. 100 BC); either through military contact or trade, this device gradually reached the West.

Yüeh Chih, an Indo-European-speaking people from Central Asia, gradually won the struggle for Bactria, repelling the Parthians and diverting the Scythians toward India (100-1 BC).

The last of the many small Hellenic Greek kingdoms in India proper disappeared (ca. 100 BC).

d. Li Kuang-li (?-90 BC), Chinese general who helped consolidate Han influence in the Tarim Basin, especially along the Silk Road.

d. Wu Ti (Liu Ch'e) (156-87 BC), emperor of China (r. 140-87 BC) who was called the "Martial Emperor" and led a series of major expeditions, breaking Hsiung-nu power and vastly expanding the Chinese Empire.

Pushed by the Yüeh Chih, Scythians invaded India (there called the Sakas), reaching the Indus Valley (by ca. 80 BC); later waves were joined by Parthians (called Pahlavas).

Third Servile War (73-71 BC): The Roman gladiator Spartacus led a slave revolt based near Mount Vesuvius (73 BC).

Third Servile War: Spartacus's slave army defeated the Romans on several occasions, his people raiding at will throughout Italy, especially southern Italy and the Campania (72 BC).

d. Quintus Sertorius (ca. 125-72 BC), Roman general and supporter of Marius in the Roman Civil War (88-82 BC), who formed a Marian government in exile in Spain (80 BC); his assassination was engineered by sometime ally and rival M. Peperna Vento, who then quickly lost to Pompey.

Third Servile War: Spartacus's revolutionaries, who had swelled to perhaps 90,000, were defeated by M. Licinius Crassus and finally quashed by Pompey (71 BC).

d. Spartacus (?-71 BC), Thrace-born Roman rebel and fugitive from a gladiator school; he led a slave revolt (73-71 BC).

After a half century of ineffectual Roman attacks on piracy, Pompey took over the campaign, conquering the main pirate bases throughout the Mediterranean and being given command in the East as a result (67 BC).

b. Sextus Pompey (Sextus Pompeius Magnus Pius) (ca. 67-35 BC), Roman general.

b. Marcus Vipsanius Agrippa (64-12 BC), Roman general.

Attempted coup by Lucius Sergius Catiline was discovered and publicly exposed (63 BC) by consul Cicero (Marcus Tullius Cicero); fleeing to Etruria, Catiline and his supporters were defeated near Pistoria (62 BC).

b. Augustus (Octavian; Gaius Julius Caesar Octavianus Augustus) (63 BC-14 AD), Roman general and emperor (r. 27 BC-14 AD).

Julius Caesar, governor of Spain, put down a revolt, bringing Lusitania into the empire (61-60 BC).

In troubled Rome, Pompey, Caesar, and Crassus (who had defeated Spartacus) privately agreed to share power in the First Triumvirate (60-50 BC); they also divided colonial responsibilities, with Caesar taking Gaul, Pompey Spain, and Crassus Syria.

Gallic Wars (58-51 BC) began after Caesar became Roman governor of Gaul (58 BC).

Gallic Wars: Caesar's Roman forces destroyed a Helvetian army crossing the Arar (Saône) River (June 58 BC), then defeated the Helvetians at Bibracte (Mount Beuvray), killing more than 100,000 Helvetians, including noncombatants (July 58 BC).

Gallic Wars: Caesar's forces campaigned against Germanic tribes under Ariovistus (Aug.-Sept. 58 BC), routing them near modern Belfort, Mulhaus, or Cernay and pursuing survivors back across the Rhine, completing the Roman conquest of central Gaul.

Gallic Wars: Caesar invaded Belgica, scattering a much larger coalition of Belgae (Gallic-Germanic) forces with his 40,000

Third Mithridatic War (75-65 BC): Mithridates VI of Pontus invaded the Anatolian regions of Cappadocia, Paphlagonia, and Bithynia (just willed to Rome on the death of the king, Nicomedes III), also encouraging revolt in Rome's province of Asia; a Roman army under consul Lucius Licinius Lucullus suppressed provincial revolts, but another under M. Aurelius Cotta was trapped in Chalcedon on the Bosporus, its fleet destroyed by Mithridates (75 BC).

Third Mithridatic War: At Cyzicus the two Roman armies under Lucullus and Cotta trapped Mithridate VI's Pontic forces near Brusa, on the Cyzicus peninsula, inflicting a severe defeat (74 BC). Mithridates escaped by sea, while his army cut its way overland, with huge losses. Lucullus immediately pursued into Pontus (74 BC).

Third Mithridatic War: Pursuing Mithridates VI into Pontus, Lucullus completely conquered the country; Mithridates took refuge with his son-in-law Tigranes of Armenia, who refused Roman demands to return him (72 BC).

Third Mithridatic War: Lucullus invaded Armenia (70 BC), defeating Tigranes's army, tenfold larger than the Roman force, at Tigranocerta (69 BC).

Seeking to regain Parthian power, Phraates III allied the Parthians with Rome (69 BC).

b. Cleopatra (69-30 BC), Egyptian queen of Greek ancestry.

Third Mithridatic War: Lucullus's Roman army won again at Artaxata, in northeastern Armenia (68 BC), then retreated when his troops refused to proceed.

Third Mithridatic War: Taking command of the Roman army in the East, Pompey won a total victory at the Lycus (66 BC); Mithridates VI of Pontus fled to the Crimea and committed suicide (64 BC), while Tigranes of Armenia was captured and had to give up his conquered territories.

Tigranes the Younger attempted to overthrow his father (65 BC); he was supported by Phraates III of Parthia but defeated and captured by Pompey (65 BC), who annexed some of Armenia's former territories to Rome.

Pompey and his Roman troops added Syria and Palestine to the empire, capturing a resistant Jerusalem and annexing Palestine (64 BC); afterward he reorganized Rome's eastern territories, provinces, and protectorates.

In Parthia, Phraates III was overthrown and killed by his sons, Mithridates III and Orodes I (57 BC); after a power struggle, Mithridates fled, taking refuge in Roman Syria.

Leading forces supplied by the Romans, Mithridates III of Parthia invaded Mesopotamia, attempting to take the Parthian throne from his brother Orodes I; he was defeated at Seleucia by Parthian forces under general Surenas (55 BC), then captured and killed after a siege of Babylon (54 BC).

d. Tigranes (Dikran) (ca. 140-55 BC), king of Armenia (ca. 95-55 BC) who defeated the Seleucids in Syria (83 BC) and expanded his kingdom (78-70 BC) to include much of Media (Persia) and northern Mesopotamia, even invading Egypt; he lost at Tigranocerta (69 BC) and at Artaxata (68 BC) but retained his throne.

Rome's support of Mithridates III of Parthia was the trigger for Marcus Licinius Crassus's campaign against the Parthians (54-53 BC); at Carrhae (Haran) (53 BC) the Roman infantry was largely destroyed by the Parthian cavalry during the battle itself and a two-day fighting retreat; only 5,000 of the 39,000 Roman soldiers returned; some 10,000 were captured and taken east, possibly to Antiocheia Margiana (Merv), some perhaps even to the frontiers of China; the rest died, including Crassus, killed during negotiations with the Parthians.

Hsiung-nu invaded Turkestan but were defeated by allied forces of the Chinese and the Wu Sun, an Indo-European-speaking people related to the Yüeh Chih (73 BC).

Chinese and Wu Sun forces again combined to defeat Hsiung-nu forces invading Turkestan (54 BC).

d. Chao Ch'ung-kuo (137-52 BC), Chinese general who was active during the wars against the Hsiung-nu.

Eastern Hsiung-nu were defeated so thoroughly that their leader came to China's capital, Ch'ang-an, to kowtow — literally, to knock his head on the ground — before the Chinese emperor (51 BC); the leader of the western Hsiung-nu was captured and decapitated; with these losses, the Hsiung-nu would not revive for four centuries, until Attila.

Roman legionaries and 20,000 Gallic auxiliaries (57 BC). The Romans fought the Belgae at the Axona (Aisne) River, accepting surrender from some and pursuing others farther north into Belgica (Apr.-May). A Belgae coalition led by the Nervii ambushed the Romans encamped on the Sabis (Sambre) River; both sides had heavy losses (July).

Gallic Wars: Caesar's Roman forces besieged and took Aduatuca (Tongres), capital of the Aduatuci (Sept. 57 BC).

Gallic Wars: Caesar's Roman army campaigned in Armorica (Brittany) against the Veneti on land and water (56 BC). Caesar's autumn campaign in northwestern Belgica virtually completed the Roman conquest of Gaul, except for some peoples sheltered in the coastal marshes (especially the Morini and Menapii) and the Ardennes forest (56 BC).

d. Lucius Licinius Lucullus (ca. 117-56 BC), Roman general who fought against Mithridates VI of Pontus.

Gallic Wars: Caesar's Roman forces reportedly killed more than 400,000 Germans, three-quarters of them noncombatants, who had settled on the west bank of the Rhine, near Maastricht (55 BC). They then crossed the Rhine to campaign against other Germans, building a bridge at Bonn, which they destroyed on their return to Gaul (June).

Gallic Wars: Caesar led two legions in the first Roman invasion of Britain, meeting strong opposition at their landing site near Dubra (Dover); the Romans returned to Gaul after three weeks (Aug. 55 BC). War chariots were still being used by the Celts in Kent, although they had become obsolete among the Romans.

Gallic Wars: Caesar led five legions and perhaps 22,000 cavalry in the second invasion of Britain, then returned to Gaul (July 54 BC).

Gallic Wars: After suppressing Belgae uprisings, notably by the Nervii under Ambiorix, Caesar rescued besieged Roman forces in northern Gaul, near Binche (54-53 BC).

Gallic Wars: Caesar's army crushed Belgae rebellions, pursuing some Belgae across a temporary Rhine bridge into Germany (spring-summer 53 BC).

Gallic Wars: Arverni ruler Vercingetorix led revolts in central Gaul (53-52 BC). Caesar's Roman forces retook Cenabum (Orléans), center of Gallic rebellion; Vercingetorix retreated (53 BC).

d. Marcus Licinius Crassus (ca. 115-53 BC), Roman general killed by the Parthians while retreating at Carrhae (53 BC).

Gallic Wars: Caesar besieged and took Avaricum (Bourges), despite Vercingetorix's attempts to relieve it (Mar. 52 BC), then unsuccessfully besieged Vercingetorix at Gergovia (Apr.-Mar.) before temporarily retreating to the Province (Provence).

Gallic Wars: Caesar besieged Vercingetorix at Alesia (Alise-Ste.-Reine), fighting off Gallic relief attempts behind his own newly built walls; the Gallic surrender effectively ended the rebellion (52 BC); Vercingetorix was paraded in Rome and later executed (ca. 46 BC).

Roman eagles, standards of the defeated legions, were taken to decorate Parthian palaces. The Parthians, who used bows so powerful that they sometimes skewered two soldiers with one arrow, had perfected the Central Asian fighting technique of turning on horseback and shooting over one shoulder while in retreat; this technique was called the Parthian shot.

Emboldened after Carrhae, the Parthians campaigned unsuccessfully against the Romans in Syria (53-38 BC).

Pompey had himself declared sole consul of Rome by the Senate, which recalled Caesar, ordering him to disband his army; this triggered the Great Roman Civil War.

Great Roman Civil War (50-44 BC): Understanding that he was directly disobeying the Roman Senate, Caesar crossed the Rubicon River with his veteran army at night, proclaiming *"Ilea jacta est!"* ("The die is cast!") (Jan. 11, 49 BC). Pompey retreated ahead of him to Brundisium (Brindisi) and across the Adriatic to Epirus, leaving Italy to Caesar but maintaining control of the Roman navy.

Great Roman Civil War: The Senate — those who had not left with Pompey — declared Caesar dictator of Rome, ending the Roman Republic (49 BC).

Great Roman Civil War: Leaving Marcus Aemilius Lepidus in Rome and Mark Antony (Marcus Antonius) covering the rest of Italy, Caesar headed overland toward Spain to confront Pompey's legions there. En route he found that Massilia (Marseilles) was occupied by troops supporting Pompey; leaving some troops to besiege the city (Mar.-Sept. 49 BC), he continued on to Spain. Decimus Junius Brutus won a naval battle off Massilia, then took the city for Caesar (Sept. 6).

Great Roman Civil War: Having sent advance troops to secure passes through the Pyrenees, Caesar met Pompeian forces under L. Afranius and M. Petreius at Ilerda (Lerida), in Spain, eventually obtaining a surrender after he cut off their water (Aug. 2, 49 BC). The defeated legions were disbanded, some joining Caesar.

d. Pompey (the Great) (Gnaeus Pompeius Magnus) (106-48 BC), Roman general who fought against Mithridates VI of Pontus and Tigranes of Armenia; part of the First Triumvirate (60 BC), he then opposed Caesar, winning at Dyrrhacium (48 BC) but losing disastrously at Pharsalus; fleeing to Egypt, he was killed by a supposed follower.

Great Roman Civil War: Back in Italy, many of Caesar's veterans mutinied, but most were persuaded to go with him to Africa (47 BC).

d. Vercingetorix (?-ca. 46 BC), Arverni leader from central Gaul who unsuccessfully revolted against Caesar's Roman legions (53-52 BC); having been paraded, then held, in Rome, he was executed.

Great Roman Civil War: Caesar took a veteran army to Spain to confront the remaining Pompeian forces, now led by Pompey's son Gnaeus Pompey and general Labienus; after some skirmishing, the Pompeians lost disastrously at Munda (possibly near modern Montilla) (Mar. 17, 45 BC); Labienus was killed; Gnaeus Pompey was captured and executed.

Caesar completed the reconquest of Spain (Mar.-July 45 BC), then returned to Rome, of which he was now sole leader; he began planning a war against the Parthians to retrieve the Roman eagles, legion standards lost at Carrhae (53 BC).

d. Julius Caesar (Gaius Julius Caesar) (100-44 BC), Roman general famed for his Gallic Wars (58-51 BC); part of the First Triumvirate and then the Great Roman Civil War, defeating his rival Pompey; Caesar was assassinated by conspirators,

Great Roman Civil War: Caesar and his forces, later supplemented by Mark Antony's, sailed from Brundisium to attack Pompey at his base in Dyrrhachium (Durazzo), besieging the city (Apr.-July 48 BC); Pompey took the offensive, defeating Caesar, but allowed Caesar's forces to withdraw into Thessaly (July 10). There the two sides met in the decisive Battle of Pharsalus (Aug. 9), where Caesar, with half as many soldiers as Pompey, surprised and broke Pompey's legions, of whom some 15,000 were killed, compared to about 230 of Caesar's soldiers. Pompey fled to Egypt in disguise, where he was murdered. Roman territories in Greece and Asia quickly announced their support for Caesar.

Wars of the Second Triumvirate: Roman forces under Octavian and Antony crossed the Adriatic from Brundisium to Epirus and headed east, meeting Marcus Junius Brutus and Gaius Cassius Longinus near Philippi. In the first battle (Oct. 3, 42 BC), the two sides fought largely to a draw, although Cassius committed suicide thinking he was defeated. In the second battle (Oct. 23), Brutus's forces were routed, after which he committed suicide.

As the Romans extended their rule into Germany, they established the city of Colonia Agrippinensis (Cologne; Köln) as the base for their push across the Rhine (38 BC).

After Mark Antony's marriage to Cleopatra, the Roman Senate stripped him of his official powers and declared war on her (32 BC); Antony and Cleopatra sent a fleet and army to Greece, quartered near Actium (Punta).

Octavian's forces won the sea battle off Actium, aided by the new *harpax* and the unreliability of Antony's forces (Sept. 2, 31 BC); Antony and Cleopatra both fled to Egypt; on land, the couple's army, led by P. Crassus Canidus, mutinied and defected to Octavian.

Great Roman Civil War: Gaius Curio, Julius Caesar's deputy in Africa, faced a Pompeian force under Attius Varus, allied with Juba, king of Numidia; Gaius Curio won near Utica but lost at the Bagradas River (Aug. 24, 49 BC), giving Pompey control of Africa.

Great Roman Civil War: Pursuing his rival to Egypt, Julius Caesar learned that Pompey had been assassinated (Sept. 48 BC) but faced a revolt from Egypt's corulers, brother and sister, Ptolemy XIII and Cleopatra VII; he was besieged in a section of Alexandria (Aug. 48-Jan 47 BC) and finally relieved by his ally Mithridates of Pergamum. The allied forces then decisively defeated the Egyptians in the Battle of the Nile, in which Ptolemy was killed (Feb. 47 BC); Cleopatra and her younger brother Ptolemy XIV remained on the throne, under Caesar's and Rome's control.

Pharnaces, king of Bosporus Cimmerius (the Crimea), seeking to reestablish the kingdom of his father, Mithridates VI of Pontus, expanded along the northern Anatolian coast and into Cappadocia, where he defeated Caesar's deputy Domitius Calvinus at Nicopolis (Nikopol) (Oct. 48 BC).

Caesar's forces, reinforced from Syria, defeated Pharnaces at Zela; Caesar reported to Rome, *Veni, vidi, vici* ("I came, I saw, I conquered") (May 47 BC); Pharnaces's kingdom was given to Rome's ally Mithridates of Pergamum.

Great Roman Civil War: At Thapsus, Caesar decisively defeated the remaining Pompeian forces and their Numidian allies (Feb. 46 BC); some of the defeated forces fled to Spain.

Wars of the Second Triumvirate: From their respective provinces of Macedonia and Syria, Marcus Junius Brutus and Gaius Cassius Longinus raised armies, meeting at Sardis (July 42 BC), then crossing the Hellespont into Thrace.

Roman leader Mark Antony met Egypt's Queen Cleopatra VII and followed her back to Egypt (42 BC).

At Gandarus, in northern Syria, Romans repelled the last of a series of invasion attempts by the Parthians (38 BC), killing Parthian general Pacorus.

Wars of the Second Triumvirate: Mark Antony invaded Parthia, losing half his army — some 30,000 soldiers — and control of Armenia in an unsuccessful attack on Phraates IV (June-Oct. 36 BC). Repudiating his wife, Octavia, he married Cleopatra of Egypt (36 BC).

Wars of the Second Triumvirate: Mark Antony again invaded Parthia, which had been making incursions into Syria; the Romans resumed control of Armenia (34 BC).

Under Phraates IV the Parthians retook the region of Atropatene (32-31 BC).

Octavian's forces invaded Egypt; Antony and Cleopatra committed suicide (July 30 BC).

d. Cleopatra VII (69-30 BC), Egyptian queen of Greek ancestry, who, kept on the throne by Julius Caesar (47 BC), later married Mark Antony (36 BC), committing suicide after losing their bid for power.

The small Hindu kingdom of Andhra, under semilegendary leader Vikramaditya, stopped the Saka invasion, reestablishing Indian control over northern and central India and founding the Satavahana dynasty (ca. 50 BC).

The last of the Hellenic Greek kingdoms in Asia — Gandhara, ruled by descendants of Eucratides at Kabul — fell to Scythian invaders (ca. 40 BC).

Chinese forces fighting the Hsiung-nu in Sogdiana (36 BC), near the Talas River, besieged and defeated what was apparently a camp of Roman legionaries, judging by their distinctive camp guarded by a defensive ditch and double wooden palisade and by what the Chinese called their "fish-scale" formation, probably describing the *testudo* formation in which soldiers marched as a group, their shields interlocked overhead for protection. Probably legionaries originally taken at Carrhae (53 BC), some 145 were taken by the Chinese to the Kansu Corridor, there founding a city called Li-Kan (an old Chinese name for lands beyond Parthia, meaning Rome).

Chinese ambassadors were sent to the state of Chi-Pin (30 BC), possibly newly taken by the Sakas; nearly a century earlier (ca. 120 BC), the state had killed Chinese envoys; more recently they had sent ambassadors to apologize, but the Chinese had refused to admit them (ca. 48-33 BC).

including both Pompeians and his own former supporters, such as Marcus Junius Brutus and Decimus Junius Brutus, to one of whom he is supposed to have said, *"Et tu, Brute"* (Mar. 15, 44 BC).

A power struggle followed Caesar's assassination; the rivals were Mark Antony, Caesar's key surviving subordinate; Octavian (Gaius Julius Caesar Octavianus; later Augustus), Caesar's nephew and personal heir; and the assassins, who went unpunished, some even being given key governorships, including Decimus Brutus in Cisalpine Gaul, Marcus Brutus in Macedonia, and Gaius Cassius Longinus in Syria. Octavian allied himself with Decimus Brutus against Mark Antony, who besieged the allies at Mutina (Modena) (Dec. 44-Apr. 43 BC).

Coming to the aid of Octavian and Decimus Brutus, two Roman armies marched north; while his brother Lucius Antonius maintained the siege at Mutina, Mark Antony marched south to meet them at Forum Gallorum; he defeated one army, under consul C. Vibius Pansa, who was killed, but was routed by the other, under consul Aulus Hirtius (Apr. 14, 43 BC).

Hirtius's army pursued Mark Antony's forces back to Mutina, defeating them there, where Hirtius was killed (Apr. 21, 43 BC); Antony retreated farther, into Transalpine Gaul, where he joined forces with an old Caesarean lieutenant, Aemilius Lepidus.

d. Decimus Junius Brutus Albinus (ca. 84-43 BC), Roman general who fought with Julius Caesar in Gaul but later joined in his assassination, then fighting with Octavian against Mark Antony; en route to join Cassius and Marcus Brutus, he was captured and executed.

Back in Rome, after the defeat of Antony and the death of Decimus Brutus, Octavian convinced the Senate to name him sole consul (Aug. 43 BC). He then reached an agreement with Mark Antony and Aemilius Lepidus to share rule, establishing the Second Triumvirate, and to pursue Caesar's assassins, now declared outlaws, beginning the Wars of the Second Triumvirate (43-34 BC).

d. Quintus Tullius Cicero (102-43 BC), Roman general who supported Pompey in the Great Roman Civil War (50-44 BC); his assassination was reportedly ordered by Mark Antony and Octavian.

Wars of the Second Triumvirate (43-34 BC): Disagreement between Octavian and Lucius Antonius broke into civil war; Octavian defeated Lucius and Mark Antony's wife, Fulvia, in Perusia (Perugia) (41 BC); she died shortly after.

d. Cassius (Gaius Cassius Longinus) (?-42 BC), Roman general who was a key figure in the conspiracy to murder Julius Caesar (44 BC); he committed suicide at Philippi, mistakenly thinking that his cause was lost.

b. Tiberius (Tiberius Claudius Nero Caesar Augustus) (42 BC-37 AD), Roman emperor.

Wars of the Second Triumvirate: Sextus Pompey, son of Pompey the Great, took Sardinia, Corsica, Sicily, and the Pel-

50-26 BC (cont.)

oponnesian peninsula; Mark Antony declared for Pompey, landing in Brundisium. However, Octavian negotiated the Treaty of Brundisium, under which Antony would fight against Pompey, Octavian would assist Antony against the Parthians, and Lepidus's responsibility was diminished to Africa. Antony's wedding to Octavian's sister Octavia confirmed the agreement (40 BC).

Roman forces under M. Vipsanius Agrippa suppressed uprisings in Gaul and Germany (38 BC).

Wars of the Second Triumvirate: Lepidus landed an army on Sicily, but it mutinied, taking the side of Octavian (36 BC); he surrendered and was kept under house arrest in Rome for 23 years, until his death.

Wars of the Second Triumvirate: At Naulochus (Mylae), near Messana, Octavian's forces, under Agrippa, defeated Sextus Pompey (Sept. 3, 36 BC). The sea battle saw the introduction of the *harpax* or *harpago,* a long pole with a hook at one end and a rope at the other; the predecessor of the harpoon, the harpax was shot from a catapult into a ship's side and the rope winched, to bring the ships close together for boarding.

d. Sextus Pompey (Sextus Pompeius Magnus Pius) (ca. 67-35 BC), Roman general who, after the defeat of his father, Pompey the Great, joined anti-Caesar forces; after Caesar's assassination, he allied himself with the Senate and Mark Antony; after being decisively defeated at Naulochus (36 BC), he was caught and executed at Miletus.

d. Mark Antony (Marcus Antonius) (ca. 82-30 BC), Roman soldier who served Julius Caesar and later aroused the Romans to avenge Caesar's assassination (43 BC); long a rival of Octavian, he joined with Cleopatra against Octavian; both he and Cleopatra committed suicide after their loss to Octavian's forces.

Returning to Rome, Octavian was named imperator, as Caesar had been before him (29 BC); this is the traditional beginning of the Pax Romana (Roman Peace) (29 BC-ca. 162 AD), perhaps less peaceful than all-powerful.

Octavian was given the title Augustus (27 BC), Rome's first emperor, although he retained republican forms. He reorganized the army, placing the regular troops in outlying provinces and creating a private army, the Praetorian Guard, to serve as the imperial bodyguard in Rome and Italy; the Praetorian Guard would later have the power to make or break emperors.

An embassy from India, presumably from the Hindu kingdom of Andhra, arrived in Rome at the court of Augustus after a reportedly six-year journey (ca. 26 BC).

25-1 BC

d. Marcus Vipsanius Agrippa (64-12 BC), Roman general who served Octavian in Rome's power struggles, defeating Sextus Pompey's forces at Naulochus (Mylae) (36 BC) and Mark Antony's at Actium (31 BC).

Roman forces under Marcus Lollius were defeated by Germanic invaders (16 BC), after which punitive expeditions were launched in Gaul by Augustus (Octavian) and in the central European regions of Raetia and Pannonia by his stepsons Drusus and Tiberius.

50-26 BC (cont.)

25-1 BC

After the Romans captured a son of Parthia's Phraates IV, Augustus exchanged him for the Roman eagles, standards taken in the disastrous battles between the Parthians and Crassus (53 BC) and Mark Antony (36 BC); he also negotiated a peace treaty with Phraates (20 BC), accepting Roman control of Armenia and upper Mesopotamia, with four Parthian princes living in Rome as hostages under the treaty.

Gondopharnes was king of an empire in northwest India; according to Christian legend, he was one of the "three wise men of the East" who visited the infant Jesus in Bethlehem (ca. 6 BC).

25-1 BC (cont.)

Western Europe	Eastern Europe
	Romans under Tiberius and Drusus put down another revolt in Pannonia (12-9 BC).
	Romans under Drusus defeated Germanic forces at the Lupia (Lippe) River (11 BC); Roman control was extended by Drusus, until he died (9 BC), and then by Tiberius, to the Elbe River (7 BC).
	Germanic peoples revolted against Roman rule (from 1 BC); Augustus sent Tiberius to suppress the revolts, with expeditions reaching the Elbe River (4-5 AD).

1-24

Western Europe	Eastern Europe
Roman emperor Augustus established the *aerarium militare,* a permanent fund to pay soldiers' retirement benefits (6), also fostering settlement of retirees in frontier provinces.	Tiberius and his Roman forces put down revolts in Pannonia and Illyricum (6-9).
b. Vespasian (Titus Flavius Vespasianus) (9-79), Roman emperor (r. 69-79).	Battle of the Teutoberg Forest: En route to their winter base in Germany, five Roman legions under P. Quintilius Varus were attacked and annihilated by their erstwhile German auxiliaries under Arminius, supported by other German guerrillas (Sept. or Oct. 9); almost all the Roman soldiers, as well as the noncombatants traveling with them, were killed; the Romans lost central Germany, establishing their frontier on the Rhine and Danube rivers; Arminius (Herman) became a German hero.
d. Augustus (Octavian; Gaius Julius Caesar Octavianus Augustus) (63 BC-14 AD), general and first Roman emperor (r. 27 BC-14 AD), named for his uncle Julius Caesar; he won the Wars of the Second Triumvirate (43-34 BC). He was succeeded by Tiberius.	
	Romans under Germanicus defeated Arminius and his German forces east of the Weser River near Minden, recovering the Roman eagles, standards of Varus's legions, taken at Teutoberg (16).
	In a contest for leadership of the Germanic peoples, Marboduus, leader of the Marcomanni, was defeated by Arminius and others (19) and fled to the Roman Empire for refuge.
	German leader Arminius was assassinated amid warfare among various Germanic peoples (21).

25-49

Western Europe	Eastern Europe
Lucius Aelius Sejanus, Praetorian Guard commander, was executed after a failed conspiracy against the Roman emperor Tiberius (31).	b. Decebalus (ca. 40-106), ruler of Dacia (ca. 85-106).
b. Nero (Nero Claudius Caesar Drusus Germanicus) (37-68), Roman emperor (r. 54-68).	
d. Tiberius (Tiberius Claudius Nero Caesar Augustus) (42 BC-37 AD), second Roman emperor (r. 14-37), who campaigned extensively in Germany. He was succeeded by Nero.	
b. Gnaeus Julius Agricola (40-93), Roman general.	
Cassus Chaerea, prefect of Rome's Praetorian Guard, assassinated insane emperor Caligula, installing instead his uncle Claudius (41).	
Suetonius Paulinus (active 41-69), Roman consul who, campaigning in Mauritania, became the first Roman to cross the Atlas Mountains (41); later governor of Britain (58-61), putting down Boadicea's revolt (61).	

25-1 BC (cont.)

1-24

Chinese forces, continuing to expand in Central Asia, opened their shorter New Route to the North (2).

Wang Mang, regent under the Han dynasty, proclaimed himself emperor of the Hsin (New) dynasty (9-23); invasions of Mongolia and Turkestan failed, and China lost much of Central Asia, as Wang Mang faced the "Red Eyebrow" peasant revolt, during which he was killed.

Han dynasty was reestablished in China after Kuang Wu Ti retook Chang'an (Xian) from Wang Mang (24).

25-49

After the crucifixion of Jesus Christ, riots and revolts were widespread in Judea, where Pontius Pilate was Roman governor (ca. 30).

Hippalus was the first known Greek seaman to sail from the Red Sea across the Indian Ocean to India (ca. 45), rather than following the shore.

Kushans, descendants of the Yüeh Chih, expanded from Central Asia into Afghanistan (by ca. 25).

b. Pan Ch'ao (32-102), Chinese general.

Han forces led by Ma Yuan suppressed a revolt in Tonkin and went on to take Annam and Hainan (40-43).

Western Europe	Eastern Europe

25-49 (cont.)

Roman forces invaded and conquered southern Britain (43); four legions plus auxiliaries under Aulus Plautius landed in Kent, with Emperor Claudius himself leading reinforcements, including elephants (44).

Romans under Plautius defeated Caractacus, leader of the Catuvellauni, driving him into Wales (47).

50-74

After persistent raids from his refuge in Wales, Caractacus was defeated at Caer Caradock (modern Shropshire) and sent to Rome a captive (50).

b. Domitian (Titus Flavius Domitianus) (51-96), Roman emperor (r. 81-96).

b. Trajan (Marcus Ulpius Traianus) (53-117), Roman emperor (r. 98-117).

Revolt by the Iceni people (of modern Norfolk and Suffolk, in Britain), led by Queen Boadicea (Boudicca), was defeated by the Romans under Suetonius Paulinus near modern Towcester; Boadicea committed suicide (61).

Paul, Peter, and many others were killed during the persecution of Christians under Nero (ca. 64).

d. Nero (Nero Claudius Caesar Drusus Germanicus) (37-68), Roman emperor (r. 54-68); he committed suicide after the Senate declared him a public enemy for misgovernment.

In the "Year of the Four Emperors" (68-69) the Praetorian Guard and Senate first recognized Spanish legate Servius Sulpicius Galba as emperor, then switched to Marcus Salvus Otho, who had Galba murdered. German legate Aulus Vitellius declared himself emperor and marched toward Rome; at Bedriacum (near Cremona) he defeated Otho, who committed suicide (Apr. 69). Other legates nominated Vespasian emperor; their forces defeated Vitellius at the second Battle of Bedriacum (Oct. 69).

Roman auxiliaries and some legions revolted in Roman-held German areas and northeastern Gaul; rebels under Claudius Civilis were defeated near Augusta Treverorum (Trèves; Trier) by troops under Petillius Cerialis (69-71).

75-99

b. Hadrian (Publius Aelius Hadrianus) (76-138), Roman emperor (r. 117-138).

Under Gnaeus Julius Agricola, the Romans extended their control into southern Scotland and Wales (77-84), winning a notable victory over the Caledonians at Mons Graupius (possibly Mount Kathecrankie) (84).

d. Vespasian (Titus Flavius Vespasianus) (9-79), Roman emperor (r. 69-79) who as general put down a revolt in Judea (66-70). He was succeeded by his son Titus, killed at Pompeii (81), himself succeeded by Domitian.

d. Gnaeus Julius Agricola (40-93), Roman general who won at Mons Graupius (84); father-in-law of Tacitus.

Under emperor Domitian (r. 81-96), the Romans began to build the Limes, their fortified line along the Rhine and Danube rivers.

Dacian forces led by Decebalus invaded Moesia, south of the Danube, but were defeated by Romans under Domitian (85).

Domitian's Roman forces, campaigning north of the Danube, were defeated by combined Dacian, Marcomanni, and Quadi forces led by Decebalus (89).

Africa and Southwest Asia	East, Central, and South Asia, the Pacific, and the Americas	

50-74

Vologases of Parthia invaded Armenia, a Roman protectorate, installing his brother Tiridates as ruler (56).

Roman forces under Gnaeus Domitius Corbulo invaded Parthian-occupied Armenia, taking Artaxata (58), then defeated the Parthians in Mesopotamia (59).

Combined Parthian and Armenian forces under Vologases and Tiridates defeated Roman forces under L. Caesennius Paetus at Rhandeia (62), then lost after Corbulo returned to command the Romans; Armenia was reestablished as a Roman protectorate (63).

Successful revolt in Judea drove the Roman garrison out of Jerusalem (66).

Vespasian arrived to lead Roman forces in reconquering Judea (67), notably in the taking of Jotapata from the Jewish defenders, led by Josephus, the historian (68).

Romans under Vespasian (and later his son Titus) besieged and finally took Jerusalem (69).

Romans besieged Masada, the last stronghold of rebellion in Judea (72-73); at its fall the defenders — some 900 men, women, and children, led by Eleazar ben Yair — committed suicide rather than be taken.

Kushans conquered the Kabul Valley (by ca. 50).

Hsiung-nu forces, who had returned to the Kansu Corridor, were once again driven north by the Chinese (ca. 50-60).

d. Kuang Wu Ti (Liu Hsiu) (?-57), Chinese ruler who reestablished the Han dynasty and directed the reconquest of China (40-43).

Lambakanna dynasty came to power on Ceylon (Sri Lanka) (65).

In a series of campaigns, Chinese general Pan Ch'ao retook Sinkiang, then expanded into western Turkestan as far as the Caspian Sea, defeating numerous nomadic tribes (ca. 73-90) and requiring even the powerful Kushans to pay tribute.

75-99

Klings, Hindu traders from India, founded colonies on Java, according to tradition (ca. 75).

Chinese forces under Tou Shien finally drove the Hsiung-nu from China's borders (89-91); as the Hsien Pi replaced them, the Hsiung-nu moved onto the Kirghiz steppe, from which they would later move west as the Huns.

Chinese forces under Pan Ch'ao defeated the Kushan army in Central Asia (90), part of a series of Kushan-Chinese conflicts

Western Europe	Eastern Europe

75-99 (cont.)

d. Domitian (Titus Flavius Domitianus) (51-96), Roman emperor (r. 81-96) who was assassinated by a court conspiracy. Thereafter, the Romans chose the emperor by "adoption" of the one fittest to rule.

100-124

Crossbows came into use in southern France (ca. 100), probably inspired by earlier Chinese models.

d. Trajan (Marcus Ulpius Traianus) (53-117), Roman emperor (r. 98-117) who brought Dacia, Arabia Petraea, and Mesopotamia into the empire.

b. Marcus Aurelius (Marcus Aurelius Antoninus; Marcus Annius Verus) (121-180), Roman emperor (r. 161-180).

Romans built a defensive line in northern Britain called Hadrian's Wall, after the emperor who ordered and inspected it (122).

Romans conquered the Dacians under Decebalus (101-102) and then again after another rebellion (103-107); this took the Roman frontier to the Carpathian Mountains and the Dniester River.

d. Decebalus (ca. 40-106), ruler of Dacia (ca. 85-106) who unified Dacia (Romania) but was ultimately defeated by the Romans, reportedly committing suicide after a failed revolt.

125-149

d. Hadrian (Publius Aelius Hadrianus) (76-138), Roman emperor (r. 117-138) during the Dacian Wars, for whom Britain's wall was named (122). He was succeeded by Antoninus Pius (r. 138-161).

Under Antoninus Pius, the Romans extended their northern fortifications, the Antonine Wall, to Scotland's Firth of Forth (142).

Romans under Q. Lollius Urbicus suppressed a revolt of the Brigantes (in modern Yorkshire) (142-143).

b. Septimius Severus (Lucius Septimius Severus Pius Pertinax) (146-211), Roman emperor (r. 193-211).

150-174

After the death of Antonius Pius (161 BC), Marcus Aurelius became Roman co-emperor with his brother Commodus (L. Aurelius Verus), then sole emperor (168-180 BC) after his brother's death.

Marcomanni, Langobardi, and Quadi peoples invaded south of the Danube into Pannonia and Noricum (Austria), with some invaders reaching as far as Verona, Italy; Romans under Marcus Aurelius and Lucius Verus forced the invaders to a temporary halt (166-168).

there. Under Kanishka (r. ca. 78-ca. 103) the Kushan Empire reached from Bactria and Turkestan into India as far as Pataliputra on the Ganges and south through Rajputana.

Chinese forces under Pan Ch'ao took control of the Tarim Basin, allowing for open trade on the Silk Road (91); Pan Ch'ao was named protector general of the Western Regions (91-102).

Chinese sent an ambassador, Kan Ying, seeking direct contact with the Roman Empire (which they called Ta-Ch'in); he apparently traveled all the way through Parthia to the Persian Gulf but was dissuaded from continuing (ca. 94-97).

Roman forces annexed Petra, the kingdom of the Nabataeans, and Arabia, as the province Arabia Petrea (107).

Reviving old conflicts, Osroes of Parthia took control of Armenia (113).

Romans under Trajan defeated the Parthians in Armenia, Assyria, and Mesopotamia (114), taking their capital, Ctesiphon, and surviving a strong counterattack by Osroes of Parthia (115) to stretch the Roman Empire to its greatest extent.

Jews in the North African colony of Cyrene revolted against the Romans (115); defeated, they retreated to oasis settlements in the Sahara, some possibly reaching West Africa.

Trajan's successor, Hadrian, made peace with the Parthians, giving up conquests east of the Euphrates; he also put down a revolt in Judea (both 117).

d. Pan Ch'ao (32-102), general under the Han dynasty who established Chinese domination of the Tarim Basin (91), becoming protector general.

Romans faced yet another revolt in Judea, this one led by Bar Kochba (132-135); forces personally led by Roman emperor Hadrian crushed the rebellion and began the Diaspora — the dispersal of the Jewish people around the world.

In the Eastern War (162-165), Parthians under Vologases III invaded Roman Syria and declared Armenia their puppet; Romans under Lucius Verus and Avidius Cassius decisively defeated the Parthians, taking Artaxata, Seleucia, and Ctesiphon. Returning Roman troops brought a deadly plague back to Europe.

Chinese courts recorded the arrival of an ambassador from Roman emperor Marcus Aurelius (ca. 166), though more likely a freebooting trader.

Western Europe	Eastern Europe
150-174 (cont.)	
	Marcomanni forces again invaded across the Danube; after being defeated by the Romans, they were settled inside imperial borders (169-171). It was during this campaign that Marcus Aurelius is believed to have composed his *Meditations*.
	Romans under Marcus Aurelius decisively defeated the Quadi and other invaders from across the Danube (174).
175-199	
d. Marcus Aurelius (Marcus Aurelius Antoninus; Marcus Annius Verus) (121-180), Roman emperor (r. 161-180) who reestablished the Danubian frontier; also a noted philosopher. He was succeeded by Commodus (r. 180-192).	Septimus Severus besieged and took Byzantium, which had resisted his assumption of Roman imperial authority (196).
b. Caracalla (Marcus Aurelius Antoninus; Septimius Bassianus) (186-217), Roman emperor (r. 211-217).	
Roman emperor Commodus was assassinated in a court conspiracy (192); there followed another "Year of the Four Emperors," during which the Praetorian Guard murdered one emperor and sold the throne to the highest bidder (193); after Septimus Severus won the succession struggle (193-194), he disbanded the Praetorians, founding a new guard drawn from frontier soldiers.	
200-224	
Faced with revolts in northern Britain, Septimus Severus took personal control of the Roman troops, largely abandoning the region north of Hadrian's Wall (208-211).	
b. Severus Alexander (Marcus Aurelius Severus Alexander) (208-235), Roman emperor (r. 222-235).	
d. Septimus Severus (Lucius Septimius Severus Pius Pertinax) (146-211), Roman emperor (r. 193-211) during the Parthian War (195-202); died in northern Britain, at York (Feb. 4); he was succeeded by his son Caracalla, who quickly killed his coruler and other rivals (212).	
b. Claudius II Gothicus (Marcus Aurelius Claudius Gothicus) (214-270), Roman emperor (r. 268-270).	
d. Caracalla (Marcus Aurelius Antoninus; Septimius Bassianus) (166-217), Roman emperor (r. 211-217), son of Septimus Severus, nicknamed Caracalla for the goatskin coat he wore during the German wars (213-214); while preparing for a Parthian invasion, he was killed by Roman officers, including his immediate successor, Marcus Opelius Macrinus (r. 217-218). His successor was Elagabalus (r. 218-222), Caracalla's nephew, who was murdered by the palace guard and succeeded by his cousin Severus Alexander (r. 222-235).	
225-249	
b. Probus (Marcus Aurelius Probus) (ca. 232-282), Roman emperor (r. 276-282).	Goths raided virtually at will in Moesia and Thrace (238).
d. Severus Alexander (Marcus Aurelius Severus Alexander) (208-235), Roman emperor (r. 222-235); he was killed during	Romans under Gaius Trajanus Decius defeated the Goths along the Danube (245-249).

Africa and Southwest Asia	East, Central, and South Asia, the Pacific, and the Americas	

175-199

| At the end of a struggle for the Roman imperial throne, Septimus Severus defeated his rival Niger in three battles — Cyzicus, Nicaea, and Issus (193-194) — finally killing him outside Antioch.

Parthians under Vologases IV invaded Roman-ruled Mesopotamia but were pushed out by the Romans under Septimus Severus (195-197); punitive expeditions against Parthia continued. | In China general Tung Cho, de facto military dictator under the Han emperor, was assassinated (192), leading to a period of civil war. | |

200-224

| Roman emperor Caracalla defeated the Parthians to regain lost territories, including Armenia, Osrhoene, and Mesopotamia (216).

Parthian emperor Artabanus V defeated Romans under their new emperor, Macrinus, at Nisibis (217).

Varius Avitus led a revolt against Macrinus, defeating and killing him at Antioch (218).

Trading state of Aksum (modern Tigre province, Ethiopia) arose on the Red Sea (ca. 220), gradually expanding to cover most of Ethiopia, eastern Sudan, northern Somalia, and, across the Red Sea, the Minaean and Sabaean kingdoms of Yemen.

In Parthia's civil war, Artabanus V defeated (and likely killed) his brother Vologases V in southern Babylonia (222). | Fan Shih-man led the kingdom of Funan, centered on the lower Mekong Valley, in an expansion that came to include Cochin-China (southern Vietnam), Cambodia, and possibly Thailand (ca. 200).

The Cham, an Indonesian people, founded the independent kingdom of Champa in southern Annam (ca. 200).

Ts'ao Ts'ao, a general of the much-weakened Han dynasty, was defeated on the Yangtze River in the Battle of the Red Cliff by southern warlords who refused to accept his personal authority (208).

Ts'ao P'ei, son of Ts'ao Ts'ao, deposed the last Han emperor, founding the Wei dynasty (220), but he could establish his authority only north of the Yangtze River; the rest of China split into two other kingdoms, the Shu under Liu Pei in the southwest, centered on Ch'engtu, and the Wu under Sun Ch'uan in the southeast, centered on Nanking. | |

225-249

| Sassanid Persian ruler Ardashir (Artaxerxes) rose to power near Persepolis; he took advantage of Parthia's weakness, defeating and killing Artabanus V at Ormuz, on the Persian Gulf (226); Ardashir founded the Sassanid Empire, successor to those of Cyrus and Darius, incorporating Parthia and expanding | Pallava family took the throne in the Indian state of Andhra (ca. 230), then expanded into the eastern Deccan, toward the Ganges, and south against the Tamil Cholas. | |

Western Europe	Eastern Europe

225-249 (cont.)

a soldiers' riot. He was followed by a line of "soldier-emperors," most ruling only briefly.

b. Maximian (Marcus Aurelius Valerius Maximianus) (245-310), Roman coemperor (r. 286-305).

Widespread persecution of Christians was carried out in Rome under Decius (249-251).

250-274

b. Diocletian (Gaius Aurelius Valerius Diocletianus) (ca. 250-ca. 313), Roman general and emperor (r. 284-305).

Alemanni and other frontier peoples raided widely in Gaul and Italy (from 254), where they defeated Romans under Valerian and reached Ravenna (257). In the inner Roman Empire long-unnecessary city walls were repaired or rebuilt.

After widespread raiding in Gaul, Spain, and North Africa, the Franks defeated a Roman army led by Valerian in Gaul (256).

Under the Roman emperor Valerian (r. 253-260), Christians were strongly persecuted (257-258).

Various military and senatorial claimants fought each other for the Roman throne in the "Age of the Thirty Tyrants" (259-268). During this succession struggle, M. Cassianus Postumus established an independent empire including Gaul, Britain, and Spain (259-274).

Rome's succession fight was won by Gallienus (r. 260-268), who ended persecution of Christians under his Edict of Toleration (260) and reformed the army to reestablish the empire's frontiers.

d. Claudius II Gothicus (Marcus Aurelius Claudius Gothicus) (214-270), Roman emperor (r. 268-270), nicknamed "Gothicus" for his victories over the Goths.

The Alemanni, defeated by Aurelian's Roman forces south of the Danube, escaped and headed for Rome, badly defeating the pursuing Romans at Placentia before losing twice more, decisively, at Fano and Pavia (271). After this threat, Rome's city walls were rebuilt.

The independent empire of Gaul, Britain, and Spain, now under Tetricus, was brought back into the empire by Aurelian (r. 270-275), who won at Châlons (late 273).

First Gothic War (250-252): Goths, led by King Cuiva, bested a Roman army at Philippopolis (250); the Roman emperor Decius then pushed them southeast to the lower Danube.

At Forum Terebronii, Roman forces were beaten badly by the Goths; Decius was killed, succeeded by C. V. Tribonianus Gallus, whose failure was largely responsible for the defeat (251); peace terms called for Rome to pay tribute to the Goths for staying east of the Danube.

Breaking the just-concluded peace, the Goths crossed the Danube but were defeated by Romans under Aemilianus (252).

Gothic land and sea rovers raided widely in Greece, taking and sacking key cities such as Athens, Sparta, Corinth, and Argos (265-267).

Romans under Publius Herennius Dexippus pushed the Goths out of central Greece toward the north (267) but left the Goths and the Heruli virtually controlling the Aegean Sea.

New Roman emperor Claudius II diverted a threatened Gothic invasion of Italy from the Alps, driving them to the east and defeating them in the Morava Valley near Naissus (Nish), then destroying the Gothic fleet at Thessalonika (269).

Romans under Aurelian halted a new Gothic invasion across the Danube, established once again as the border, and abandoned efforts to hold Dacia (270).

its borders eastward to the Oxus River and beyond, even taking some land from the Kushans and pushing into Afghanistan and Baluchistan.

Challenging Rome, Ardashir invaded Syria and Armenia, a Roman client (230), raiding into Anatolia (230-231).

Severus Alexander's Roman forces retook Mesopotamia from the Sassanid Persians (233), also helping Armenian ruler Chosroes fight off the Persians.

Shapur I, son and successor of Ardashir, invaded Roman-held Mesopotamia (241), took Nisibis (Nusaybin) and Carrhae (Haran), and was sharply defeated at Resaena, on the upper Araxes (Araks) River, by Romans under Gordianus III and G. F. Sabinus Aquila Timesitheus (243); Gordianus was murdered, and his successor, Philippus Arabus, called for peace.

b. Wu Ti (Ssu-ma Yen) (236-290), founder of the Chin (Ch'in) dynasty.

Shapur I's second war with Rome was triggered by his murder of Armenian ruler Chosroes, conquest of Armenia, and sacking of Antioch (all 258).

Valerian and his Roman forces defeated Shapur I, driving the Persians back across the Euphrates (259).

Shapur I decisively defeated and surrounded the Romans at Edessa (Urfa) (260); during negotiations the Roman emperor Valerian was captured, dying in captivity in Persia. After the Roman army surrendered, Shapur's troops raided freely in Syria, Cilicia, and Cappadocia, finally taking Caesarea, whose notable defense was orchestrated by Demosthenes (261).

West of the Euphrates River, Septimus Odaenathus, prince of Roman-dominated Palmyra, routed Shapur I's Persian army, heavy with loot from Roman cities (261).

Odaenathus of Palmyra defeated and killed Roman soldier Quietus, who was trying to take Syria as a step to the Roman throne; Odaenathus was then named Dux Orientalis — ruler of the East — by Emperor Gallienus (262).

Commanding Roman and Palmyran forces, Odaenathus invaded Persia, relieving a siege of Edessa, retaking Nisibis and Carrhae (262), and campaigning in Armenia and Mesopotamia, twice taking Ctesiphon (262-264).

After raiding the coast of the Black Sea and in the Caucasus Mountains and Georgia, Goths penetrated into Anatolia, reaching the Aegean Sea, where, at Ephesus, they destroyed the Temple of Diana, famed as one of the Seven Wonders of the World (262).

Odaenathus was murdered (267) and nominally succeeded by his son Vaballathus, but the real ruler of Palmyra became his widow, Zenobia, who had accompanied him on campaigns against Persia.

Forces under Palmyra's Queen Zenobia and her general Zobdas conquered Egypt and then defeated an army sent to bring them under Roman control (267).

Roman forces led by Aurelian defeated Palmyra's Queen Zenobia and general Zobdas in two battles, at Immae, near Antioch, and Emesa; Romans then besieged Palmyra until the queen surrendered (271-272), bringing the eastern provinces back into the empire.

After Zenobia once more revolted (272), Aurelian besieged, took, and sacked Palmyra, later parading the queen as a captive in Rome (274).

Sassanid Persian leader Shapur I appointed the Han Chinese refugee prince Mamgo as his governor in Armenia (ca. 272-288) rather than return him to China as his enemy, Emperor Wu Ti (Ssu-Ma Yen), demanded.

Shapur I defeated the Kushans under Vasuveda (ca. 250), possibly in Bactria, ending the great days of the Kushan Empire.

Wu kingdom of southeast China sent an exploratory merchant fleet into the Indian Ocean (ca. 250).

China's weakened Shu kingdom was defeated by Wei general Ssu-Ma Yen (264); some survivors fled to Persia, joining Shapur I's army; one, a Han prince named Mamgo, became his governor of Armenia.

Wei general Ssu-Ma Yen placed himself on the throne as Wu Ti, first emperor of the Western Chin dynasty (265).

250-274 (cont.)

275-299

Roman emperor Probus (r. 276-282) campaigned in Gaul against the Franks, Burgundians, and Lygians (276) and in Germany as far as the Elbe River (277); he also rebuilt the Limes fortifications along the Rhine and Danube rivers.

b. Constantine I (Flavius Valerius Aurelius Constantinus) (ca. 282-337), Roman emperor (r. 306-337).

d. Probus (Marcus Aurelius Probus) (ca. 232-282), Roman emperor (r. 276-282); assassinated by his own troops, who were reportedly unhappy at his harsh discipline. He was succeeded by Carus (r. 283-284), who fought in the East, where he died, possibly assassinated.

After yet another power struggle for the throne (284-285), Diocletian became emperor, winning a civil war against Carinus at the Margus (Morava) River. He reorganized the empire with two equal emperors — himself in the East, ruling from Nicomedia, in Anatolia, and Maximian in the West (286).

Marcus Aurelius Carausius, commander of the Roman fleet at Gessariacum (Boulogne), put down a peasant revolt in Gaul (286).

Becoming marauder instead of protector, Carausius and his Roman fleet raided the German coasts (287); he then proclaimed himself emperor of northern Gaul and Britain; the revolt was eventually suppressed, but only after Carausius was killed (294).

To the coequal emperors, Diocletian added two assistant rulers (caesars), creating effectively four divisions of the Roman Empire, none ruling from Rome itself (292), which would further exacerbate problems of succession. Maximian ruled Italy and Africa from Mediolanum (Milan). One of the new caesars, Flavius Valerius Constantius, ruled Gaul, Spain, and Britain from Augusta Treverorum (Trier) (292).

A major Alemanni invasion was twice defeated by Constantius, at Lingones (Langres) and Vindonissa (Windisch, Switzerland) (298).

One of the new Roman caesars (assistant rulers), Gaius Galerius Valerius, ruled Illyria and the Danube frontier from Sirmium (Mitrovica), in Yugoslavia (292).

300-324

Christians were again strongly persecuted under Diocletian (303-311).

Diocletian and Maximian abdicated as emperors, initiating a succession struggle (305); contenders included Constantius's son Constantine (Flavius Valerius Aurelius Constantinus) and Maximian's son Marcus Aurelius Valerius Maxentius.

Informed that his Roman coemperor, Licinius, was plotting against him, Constantine I marched first; the two armies met indecisively at Cibalae (possibly Vinkovci), in southeastern Pannonia, and again at Mardia, in Thrace, where Licinius gave up Illyricum and Greece to Constantine, though retaining control of Asia, Egypt, and Thrace (314).

Once again openly at war, Licinius and Constantine I met with massive armies at Adrianople (July 3, 323); Licinius lost

d. Shapur I (?-272), Persian king (r. 241-272) who captured the Roman emperor Valerian (260); he made Persia a center of learning.

While the Romans were besieging Palmyra, the Egyptians also revolted against Roman rule; the revolt was quickly suppressed by Aurelian (273).

Under their new emperor, Tacitus, Roman forces defeated Goths and Alans, a Scythian-Germanic people, in Anatolia (276).

Saturninus, commander of Roman forces in the East, proclaimed himself emperor but was quickly defeated and killed by the reigning emperor, Probus (279).

New Roman emperor Marcus Aurelius Carus twice defeated Bahram I's Persian forces in Mesopotamia, the second time near their capital, Ctesiphon, but died while campaigning east of the Tigris (282-283).

Tiridates III, son of Chosroes, returned to Armenia to claim his throne, supported by the Romans, the Armenian nobility, and eventually Persia's governor, Chinese refugee prince Mamgo; he then invaded Assyria (293).

New Persian emperor Narses, son of Shapur I, retook Assyria and Armenia from the Romans, sending Tiridates III back to the Romans for refuge (294-295).

Proclaiming himself emperor of northern Egypt, Achilleus established himself in Alexandria (294), later besieged and taken by Diocletian; Achilleus was executed (296).

Coastal Mauretania (Morocco) was invaded by desert and mountain peoples; they were defeated by Romans under Maximian, who took their strongholds and deported the inhabitants to other parts of the empire (295-297).

Rome declared war on Persia (295-297), under Galerius winning some small fights but losing decisively at Callinicum, near Carrhae (296).

Reinforced, Galerius pursued the Persians into Armenia, winning so thoroughly that he captured Narses and his family (297); under the peace terms, the Persians accepted Roman authority in Mesopotamia and the Caucasus. Tiridates III returned to the Armenian throne; he would soon convert to Christianity.

Wei emperor Wu Ti temporarily reunited China (280-290).

d. Wu Ti (Ssu-ma Yen) (236-290), founder of the Chin (Ch'in) dynasty; at his death, the empire was divided among his 25 sons.

b. Shapur II (the Great) (309-379), Persian ruler (r. 309-379), born enthroned, with a long regency (309-325).

Valerius Licinianus Licinius, appointed emperor of the East by Constantine I, defeated rival Roman forces under Galerius Valerius Maximinus Daia at Tzirallum, near Heraclea Pontica, in western Anatolia, checking a planned invasion of Europe (313).

Thair, king of Arabia (Yemen), campaigned successfully against Persia (ca. 320).

Hsiung-nu and Hsien Pi peoples raided widely in China for more than two centuries (from ca. 300), controlling parts of the area north of the Yangtze. After two Western Chin emperors were killed (311; 316), the Chin emperors moved south of the Yangtze, founding the Eastern Chin dynasty at Nanking (317).

Western Europe	Eastern Europe

300-324 (cont.)

d. Constantius I (Aurelius Valerius Constantius; Constantius Chlorus) (?-306), Roman general and caesar; he was the father of Constantine I.

d. Maximian (Marcus Aurelius Valerius Maximianus) (245-310), Roman coemperor (r. 286-305); he died after conspiring against Constantine.

Persecution of Christians was ended under the Edicts of Toleration, issued by Galerius Valerius Maximinus Daia and Valerius Licinianus Licinius, briefly corulers (311).

Roman succession struggle degenerated into civil war; to forestall Maxentius's planned invasion of Gaul, Constantine I marched through the Alps to win key battles at Susa, Turin, Milan, Brescia, and Verona (312). Finally meeting Maxentius directly near Rome, Constantine won a decisive victory at the Milvian Bridge, converting to Christianity reportedly because he had seen a sign before the battle.

d. Marcus Aurelius Valerius Maxentius (?-312), Roman emperor who was defeated at the Milvian Bridge and drowned in the Tiber River.

Edict of Toleration in Milan confirmed the end of persecution of Christians (313).

d. Diocletian (Gaius Aurelius Valerius Diocletianus) (ca. 250-ca. 313), Roman emperor (r. 284-305) who instituted divided rule (286).

b. Constantius II (Flavius Julius Constantius) (317-361), Roman emperor (r. 337-361).

badly, taking refuge in Byzantium, then besieged by Constantine.

In the Battle of the Hellespont, Constantine I's elder son, Crispus, decisively defeated Licinius's fleet (July? 323); unable to retreat across the Bosporus, Licinius took refuge in Chalcedon, where, at Chrysopolis (Scutari), he surrendered (Sept. 18, 323); he was later executed (324).

Constantine I became sole emperor of the Roman Empire, making his capital in the old Greek city of Byzantium (324), massively rebuilt and named for him: Constantinople (330).

325-349

d. Valerius Licinianus Licinius (?-325), Roman emperor (r. 308-324) who fought against his rival Constantine (314; 323-324); he eventually surrendered and was executed.

b. Julian (Flavius Claudius Julianus) (332-363), Roman emperor (r. 361-363).

d. Constantine I (Flavius Valerius Aurelius Constantinus) (ca. 282-337), Roman emperor (r. 306-337) who adopted Christianity (313) and transferred the imperial capital to Constantinople (324). Another succession struggle followed, this time involving his three surviving sons, among whom he had divided the empire; Constantine II in Britain, Gaul, and Spain; Constans I in Illyricum, Italy, and Africa; and Constantius II in Thrace, Greece, and the East, who would survive.

Fighting over the imperial succession, Constantine II invaded Italy but was killed at Aquileia, at the head of the Adriatic; his brother Constans I added Constantine's territory to his own (340).

Picts and Scots raided in northern Britain, while the Saxons raided along the coasts of Britain and Gaul (343).

b. Theodosius I (the Great) (ca. 346-395), Roman emperor (r. 379-395).

In alliance with the beleaguered Sarmatians, a Scythian-Germanic people, Constantine I led his Roman forces against the Goths who, under Araric, had been raiding across the Danube into Moesia (332).

After the breakup of the Roman-Sarmatian alliance, the Goths under Geberic decisively defeated the Sarmatians under Wisumar (334); many of the defeated Sarmatians settled within the Roman Empire.

	300-324 (cont.)
	Szechuan, in southwest China, became independent (304).
	In Magadha the Gupta dynasty was founded by Chandragupta (r. ca. 320-ca. 330), who claimed descent from the early Mauryan dynasty, and revived his kingdom's strength in India's central Ganges Valley.

	325-349
Under Ezana, the Red Sea kingdom of Aksum defeated the old Cushite kingdom of Meroë, on the Nile, and took firm control of Yemen (ca. 325); Christianity spread widely in the land.	Under Samudragupta (r. ca. 330-ca. 375), son of Chandragupta, Magadha expanded to include Rajputana, the northern Deccan, and the coast south of the Ganges; its influence also extended into Nepal, Assam, the Punjab, and Gandhara.
Sassanid emperor Shapur II defeated King Thair of Arabia (Yemen) (328).	
Sassanid emperor Shapur II invaded Roman Mesopotamia (337), beginning a series of ill-recorded conflicts (337-350) between the two. Romans under general Lucilianus successfully fought off three Persian sieges of the fortress at Nisibis (337; 344?; 349).	
Several Scythian peoples, most notably the Massagetae and the Chionites, raided widely in northeastern Persia (349-358); gradually Shapur II subdued them, bringing some into the Persian army.	

350-374

In Gaul, Roman general Magnentius revolted against Constans I, who was killed in flight to Spain; Magnentius proclaimed himself emperor (350).

After losing at Mursa (351), Magnentius and his forces returned to Italy, pursued by Constantius II, whom he defeated at Pavia; Magnentius faced popular revolts in both Italy and Gaul, to which he fled; he committed suicide, leaving Constantius as undisputed Roman emperor (351).

b. Flavius Stilicho (ca. 355-408), Roman general of Roman-Vandal ancestry.

Julian (Flavius Claudius Julianus), named caesar by his cousin Constantius II, campaigned against invaders along the west bank of the Rhine. Constantius sometimes operated on the east bank; he lost to the Alemanni at Reims but later defeated them at Sens (356).

At Argentorate (Strasbourg), Julian and his Roman forces were far outnumbered by the Alemanni but won a surprising victory (357), capturing the Alemanni king, Chnodomar, then subduing the rest of the Rhine's west bank.

Conflict between Julian and Constantius II broke into civil war (360-361); asked to send some veteran troops to Constantius in the East, Julian instead proclaimed himself emperor, swiftly marching east to take his rival's stronghold at Sirmium, then heading toward Constantinople; Constantius died en route to meet him, leaving Julian as sole emperor.

d. Constantius II (Flavius Julius Constantius) (317-361), Roman emperor (r. 337-361), third son of Constantine I, who won the succession wars following his death.

d. Julian (Flavius Claudius Julianus) (332-363), Roman emperor (r. 361-363) who challenged and briefly succeeded Constantius II; he was killed fighting the Persians and was succeeded by Valentinian I (r. 364-375).

Valentinian I led campaigns against the Alemanni, with notable victories at Châlons and Solicinium (Sulz) on the Neckar River (365-367).

Valentinian's general Theodosius campaigned in Britain, in turmoil because of raids by Saxon sea rovers and revolts by the Scots and Picts (368-369).

b. Alaric (ca. 370-410), Visigothic leader.

Under Ermanaric, the Ostrogoths built a major kingdom stretching from the Black Sea to the Baltic and east to the Dnieper Valley (ca. 350-376).

Seeking to avenge the death of his brother Constans, killed fleeing Magnentius, Constantius II returned from the East and, in Illyria, persuaded general Vetranio to change sides and join him against Magnentius (350). The opposing forces met at Mursa (Osijek, Yugoslavia), with extremely heavy losses on both sides (351).

Constantius II campaigned successfully along the Danube, notably against Quadi and Sarmatian invaders (355).

Aided by Gothic mercenaries, Procopius took control of Constantinople and the surrounding areas, declaring himself emperor, but was then defeated by the Eastern Roman emperor Valens, brother of Valentinian I (366).

Visigoths, led by Athanaric, invaded across the Danube; the Romans pushed them back and reestablished the Danube as the frontier (367-369).

Huns, descendants of Asia's Hsiung-nu, began pressing into Europe (ca. 372), invading the lands between the Volga and Don (Tanais) rivers occupied by the Alans, whom they decisively defeated at the Tanais (373?); the Alans were dispersed, some staying with the Huns, some joining the Goths, and others becoming Roman mercenaries.

Gabinus, king of the Quadi, was killed by Roman general Marcellinus during negotiations over disputed land, leading to a widespread revolt by the Quadi and Sarmatians (374-375).

375-399

Magnus Clemens Maximus, Roman general in Britain, proclaimed himself emperor and invaded Gaul (383); Roman coemperor Gratian (r. 375-383) was murdered at Lugudunum (Lyon) en route to confront him. Maximus then controlled Britain, Gaul, and Spain; Italy was held under a regency for Valentinian II.

After Maximus invaded Italy (387), Valentinian II took refuge with Theodosius I in the East, who bested Maximus at the Save River, in Illyricum (388), and then pursued and besieged Maximus at Aquileia, where he was killed.

Huns crossed the Dnieper River to invade the Gothic Empire, which lost both its venerable leader, Ermanaric, and his successor, Withimer; hundreds of thousands of refugees fled across the Danube, where many Visigoths, led by Fritigern and Alavius, settled; Ostrogoths, led by Alatheus and Saphrax, followed suit. Other Visigoths under Athanaric fled into the forests of Carpathia and Transylvania (376).

During peace negotiations, Romans attacked the Visigothic leaders, killing Alavius; Fritigern then led his people in battle

350-374

War between Sassanid Persia and the Romans ended with the inconclusive Battle of Singara (Sinjar) in Iraq, as both Constantius II and Shapur II faced other external threats (350).

Aksumite forces destroyed the old Cushite kingdom of Meroë (ca. 350).

Shapur II again challenged Rome by invading southern Armenia (358), launching a successful but very costly 73-day siege of the Roman fortress of Amida (Diyarbekir), in Turkey.

Shapur II's Persians took the Roman fortresses of Singara and Bezabde (359).

Constantius II tried unsuccessfully to retake Bezabde and was awaiting reinforcements from his cousin Julian when he died (361).

Julian led Roman forces against Persia, bringing a reported 1,000-ship supply fleet onto the Euphrates River to take two forts guarding the Persian capital of Ctesiphon and defeating Shapur II's army outside its walls (363). Pursuing the Persians overland, the Romans were weakened by their enemy's "scorched earth" policy; Julian was killed in battle, and, lacking food and supplies, his successor, Jovian, was forced to give up key Roman fortified towns in Mesopotamia and all territory and influence east of the Tigris River (364).

Shapur II captured Armenian king Arsaces III, who committed suicide (364); the Persians established uncertain control over Armenia, while the Romans supported Arsaces's son Para (Pap) as an exiled ruler.

In Mauretania (Morocco), Firmus revolted against the Romans but was swiftly defeated by Valentinian I's general Theodosius (himself later emperor) and committed suicide (371-372).

Roman forces defeated the Persians in southern Armenia, but the Roman general Trajan killed exiled Armenian leader Para instead of placing him on the throne (374).

India's kingdom of Andhra, under the Pallava dynasty, was defeated by Samudragupta of Magadha (ca. 350).

Ch'iang people from Tibet became the most prominent among the Central Asians in China north of the Yangtze River (ca. 350).

b. Liu Yü (356-422), Chinese general and ruler.

After numerous expeditions to Korea, Japan established colonies on its southern coast, between the states of Paekche and Silla (ca. 360).

Eastern Chin dynasty began to revive after general Huan Wen retook Szechuan (370).

375-399

Jewish Sabaeans in northeastern Yemen successfully revolted against Aksumite rule (ca. 375).

As Persia and Rome each failed to win decisively, their conflict ceased, with Persia still having uneasy control of Armenia (377).

d. Shapur II (the Great) (309-379), Persian ruler (r. 309-379) from birth who fought long wars with the Romans.

Romans under Theodosius I and Sassanid Persians under Bahram IV ended a long series of conflicts by dividing the country of Armenia between them (390).

Under Chandragupta II (r. ca. 375-ca. 413), son of Samudragupta, Magadha expanded into the Punjab, also annexing Malwa, Saurashtra, and Gujarat.

Avars (Juan Juan; Gougen), a Mongol people, defeated the Hsiung-nu, pushing them south and west in Central Asia (ca. 380); Avar leader Toulun proclaimed himself khan (cagan).

Western Europe | **Eastern Europe**

375-399 (cont.)

d. Alatheus (?-387), Ostrogothic chieftain and general; killed in battle by Roman general Promotus.

Gaul was reestablished within the Roman Empire by the Frankish general Arbogast (388-389).

Christianity became the official state religion of Rome, with other religions suppressed (391).

Arbogast arranged for the murder of the young coemperor Valentinian II (392), in his place installing his own man, Eugenius; accepting neither, the Roman coemperor Theodosius I sent troops under his Roman-Vandal general Stilicho, who decisively defeated the rebels at Aquileia (Sept. 5-6, 394); Eugenius died in the fighting; Arbogast killed himself. Theodosius briefly became sole Roman emperor.

b. Flavius Aëtius (ca. 395-454), Roman general.

d. Theodosius I (the Great) (ca. 346-395), Roman emperor (r. 379-395).

---

at Marianopolis (Shumla), in eastern Bulgaria, defeating Roman troops under Lupicinus (377).

Forming a united front with the Ostrogoths, the Visigoths met a hastily assembled Roman force under Valens at the Salices (Willows), in the southern Danube Delta; at first blockaded behind their wooden wagons, the Visigoths, led by Fritigern, then broke out, forcing Valens to retreat to Thrace and leaving the way open for raids by Sarmatians, Alans, and Huns (377).

As conflicts erupted along the Rhine, as well as the Danube, Valens's nephew and coemperor, Gratian, defeated a large Alemanni army, killing their leader, Prianus, at Argentaria (Colmar) (378); Romans then campaigned on the river's east bank before reinforcing Valens in Thrace.

Roman troops led by Sebastian defeated the Gothic allies at the Maritza River, driving them into a group of wagon-camp forts, where they were joined by Gothic mercenaries defecting from the Romans. At this second Battle of Adrianople (Aug. 9, 378), the Romans suffered one of their worst defeats in history; an estimated 40,000 soldiers died, including Valens. The Goths failed to take Adrianople or Constantinople but otherwise were the only remaining power in Thrace. Gratian, who succeeded Valens as emperor of the West, had not yet arrived; Theodosius I became emperor of the East.

Roman forces, rebuilt in Greece and Thrace under Theodosius I, defeated the Goths in two campaigns, during one of which Fritigern died (382-383); Roman general Promotus successfully campaigned south of the Danube against the Ostrogoths, under Alatheus and Saphrax; many Goths were forced back across the Danube, some settling within the Roman Empire — Ostrogoths in Pannonia, Visigoths in Macedonia.

Goths again invaded across the Danube but were defeated by Promotus; their leader, Alatheus, was killed (387).

Visigoths crossed the Danube to raid Thrace; their leader, Alaric, made his first appearance in history; Theodosius I defeated them and brought Alaric and many of his troops into the Roman army (390).

Alaric and his Visigoths raided widely through Thrace and Greece; they were stopped briefly by Stilicho, who had arrived from Italy but was asked by Eastern emperor Arcadius to leave (396).

400-424

Raiding widely with his Gothic-Roman army, Alaric invaded northern Italy, in his first season taking Aquileia, Istria, and Venetia (401).

Alaric besieged Honorius's capital, Milan, then raised the siege to follow the fleeing emperor Honorius; with troops (including Alan cavalry) brought from Gaul through the Alps in winter, the Roman-Vandal general Stilicho pursued Alaric to Asta (Asti), where they fought inconclusively (Mar. ? 402).

Proclaiming his allegiance to Honorius, Alaric was appointed master-general of Illyricum (as he had previously been for the Eastern Roman emperor Arcadius), charged with acting as a bulwark against invaders (404).

b. Attila (406?-453), king of the Huns (r. 434-453).

Huns under King Uldin invaded Thrace but were pushed back across the Danube by Romans under Anthemius (409).

Africa and Southwest Asia	East, Central, and South Asia, the Pacific, and the Americas

Ostrogoths under Tribigild and Visigoths under Gainas, previously a Roman general, raided widely in Anatolia and around Constantinople (399).	Led by Fu Chien, the Ch'iang invaded Chin territory but were decisively defeated at the Fei River (383); their northern power then collapsed. T'upa (To Pa; Toba), a people related to the Hsien Pi, replaced the Ch'iang as the power north of the Yangtze River (ca. 386); over the next century, their Northern Wei dynasty would include much of Mongolia and Turkestan.

Visigoth forces under Gainas were defeated in Anatolia by Roman forces under another Gothic general, Fravitta; Gainas then fled north and was killed by King Uldin of the Huns (400). Kingdom of Ghana, with its capital at Kumbi, was founded in West Africa (by 400). After a brief war (421-422), Romans agreed to grant freedom of worship to Zoroastrians, and Persians agreed to do the same for Christians.	In the time of the Three Kingdoms (ca. 400), Korea was divided among Kokuryo in the north, Paekche in the southwest, and Silla in the southeast, with some small Japanese colonies on the southern coast. Cham forces under King Bhadravarman campaigned in Chinese-controlled Namviet (Tonkin and northern Annam) (ca. 400).

400-424 (cont.)

Alaric, losing at Pollentia to Stilicho after a surprise attack (Apr. 6, 402), retreated to Tuscany, agreed to leave Italy, and moved on to winter at Istria.

Learning that Alaric planned to invade Gaul, with its depleted garrisons, Stilicho launched a devastating surprise attack, winning the Battle of Verona in the Athesis (Adige) Valley, although Alaric was able to retreat with his forces (June 403); Honorius moved his capital from Milan to the more defensible Ravenna.

A great migration, including predominantly Vandals, Suevi, and Burgundians, but also Goths, Alans, and many other peoples (all probably being pushed westward by the Huns), invaded from the Baltic through the Alps and into the Po Valley, led by Radagaisus (405).

Invading forces under Radagaisus surrounded Florence but were trapped by a series of blockhouses and trenches built by the Romans under Stilicho; most of the losers were enslaved; Radagaisus was executed (406).

The rest of the invading immigrants retreated into southern Germany, except the Vandals, who, under King Godigisclus, were defeated by the Franks under Marcomir, then moving on into Gaul (406-410).

Roman forces abandoned Britain when soldiers there elected one of their number, Constantine, as emperor (406?), then followed him across the English Channel to take Gaul and Spain (407-408); in Britain, communities prepared their own defenses against Saxon invaders.

d. Flavius Stilicho (ca. 355-408), Roman general of Roman-Vandal ancestry who led the fight against Alaric and his Gothic forces (396-408); he was convicted of treason and executed (Aug.), apparently on trumped-up charges by Honorius; his auxiliaries then went over to Alaric.

Alaric again invaded Italy (409), advancing without hindrance to Rome, while Honorius remained in fortified Ravenna. Paid heavy tribute to lift the siege of Rome, Alaric attacked Ravenna, without success.

Alaric and his Gothic troops besieged and took Rome, the first invaders ever to do so, then sacked the city (Aug. 24, 410). Marching southward in Italy, Alaric was planning an invasion of Sicily and Africa when he died.

d. Alaric (ca. 370-410), Visigothic leader who captured Rome (410); he was succeeded by his brother-in-law Athaulf (Adolphus).

Army-proclaimed emperor Constantine, attempting to hold Gaul, was besieged at Arelate (Arles) by Honorius's general Constantius but eventually surrendered and was executed (411).

Athaulf won a four-way battle for control of Gaul (412-414), with his Visigothic forces taking all of Gaul except Massilia (Marseilles); he was defeated by Roman general Constantius but proclaimed Gaul part of the Roman Empire, marrying the emperor's half-sister Galla Placidia (412-414).

Avars conducted border wars with the Northern Wei dynasty in China (from ca. 400).

Ephthalites (White Huns; in India, called Hunas), relatives of the Kushans, established themselves in Bactria (ca. 420), controlling the lands southeast of the Aral Sea (modern Russian Turkestan) and raiding into Gandhara and the Punjab.

Chin general Liu Yü defeated rebel forces, taking Nanking and declaring himself the first emperor of the Liu (Former) Sung dynasty (420).

d. Liu Yü (356-422), Chinese general and ruler who founded the Liu (Former) Sung dynasty.

400-424 (cont.)

Athaulf led his Visigoths in a reconquest of Spain (415), where he was murdered (416).

Athaulf's successor, Wallia, defeated the Alans, Suevi, and Vandals, pushing them into northwestern Spain (Galicia) (419); king of Toulouse (Aquitaine), he became the first of the invading peoples to rule a kingdom within the Roman Empire. His successor was Alaric's son Theodoric I (r. 419-451); his widow, Placidia, married general Constantius.

Under King Gunderic, the Vandals defeated Suevi and Roman forces in Spain under Castinus (421).

425-449

Flavius Aëtius, leading Roman auxiliary forces composed mostly of Huns, blocked the attempt by King Theodoric I of Toulouse, to take Provence, defeating him at Arles (425).

Placidia became de facto ruler of the Western Roman Empire when her son Valentinian III was placed on the throne by Eastern emperor Theodosius II, who had put down other claimants (425).

In Spain the Vandal king Gaiseric (Genseric), Gunderic's half-brother and successor, defeated a Suevi revolt at Mérida on the Anas (Guadiana) River (428).

Aëtius completed the reconquest of Gaul for the Roman Empire (430); Toulouse remained under the Visigoths.

Aëtius and his forces invaded Italy from Gaul, defeating imperial forces at Ravenna (432) and becoming effective ruler of the Western Roman Empire.

Aëtius and his army of Huns and Alans blocked the invasion of Provence by Theodoric I's Visigoths, defeating them at Arles and again at Narbonne (436).

In Spain the Suevi under King Rechila revolted against Roman rule, taking Mérida (439) and Seville (441).

Vandals under King Gaiseric raided Sicily (440), beginning a century-long reign of piracy in the Mediterranean.

Eastern Roman emperor Theodosius II sent a fleet against the Vandals in Sicily (441) but withdrew them to meet Attila's Hun invasion.

Rechila and his Suevi forces came to control all of Spain except Tarraconensis (Catalonia) (447).

Recognizing effective Hun control of Pannonia, the Eastern Roman emperor Theodosius I paid tribute to the Huns, making their leader, Ruas, a general in the Roman army (432).

Huns under Attila invaded the Eastern Roman Empire, reaching all the way to Constantinople and largely destroying the main defending army (441-443); Emperor Theodosius I bought temporary peace with a larger tribute.

Having murdered his brother Bleda, Attila became sole leader of the Huns (445).

Attila again invaded the Eastern Roman Empire, this time turning toward Greece and reaching Thermopylae (447); Theodosius I granted the Huns the Danube's right bank, from Singidunum (Belgrade) to Novae (Svistov), in Bulgaria (447), and tripled his monetary tribute, paid until his death (450).

450-474

Angles, Saxons, and Jutes from the Continent's coastal lowlands settled on the coasts of southeastern Britain (ca. 450-500).

Attila and his army besieged Orléans (May-June 451) but on the verge of success withdrew at the arrival of the combined Roman and Visigothic armies. At Châlons, in one of the key battles in history, Roman and Visigothic armies under Aëtius and Theodoric I defeated Attila's invading troops, who retreated back across the Rhine (mid-June 451); among the

After tribute payment stopped, Attila and his Huns (and other light cavalry forces, including the Ostrogoths, Thuringi, and Bavarians) crossed the Rhine to invade the Western Roman Empire (451), sacking most of the towns of northern Gaul, except Paris.

d. Attila (406?-453), king of the Huns (r. 434-453) who raided widely in Europe; he died preparing to invade Italy. In the power struggle following his death, Hun power collapsed.

Africa and Southwest Asia	East, Central, and South Asia, the Pacific, and the Americas	
		400-424 (cont.)
		425-449
Vandals and Alans under King Gaiseric invaded Africa, defeating Roman forces twice near Hippo (Bône), Algeria (430), then besieging and taking the city (431); St. Augustine, bishop of Hippo, was killed.	The Cham fought off a Chinese naval attack on Champa (431).	
Attila and Bleda, joint rulers of the Huns after the death of their uncle Ruas (433), expanded Hun control into Scythia (southern Russia), Media, and Persia (433-441).	India's kingdom of Pandya invaded and conquered Ceylon (Sri Lanka), replacing the Lambakanna dynasty (432).	
Vandals completed their conquest of northwest Africa, except for eastern Numidia (Tunisia) (435).	Chinese expeditionary forces under Tonkin's governor T'an Ho-ch'u invaded Champa and sacked the capital (446).	
Gaiseric and his Vandal forces took Carthage and eastern Numidia (Oct. 439).		
After another brief war (441), the Romans and Persians reaffirmed religious toleration.		
		450-474
Eastern Roman emperor Leo I sent two forces against the Vandals in North Africa. One, under Heraclius, captured Tripoli from the Vandals (468), then marched overland toward Carthage. The other, under Basiliscus, landed near Cape Bon but, having granted Visigothic leader Gaiseric a truce, were forced to withdraw after he mobilized the whole Visigothic fleet against them.	China's Northern Wei (T'upa) dynasty annexed part of Sinkiang (ca. 450).	
	Invading the Punjab, the Hunas (Ephthalites) were soundly defeated by the Gupta Empire under Skandagupta (457).	
	Persians under Yazdegird II were defeated near the Oxus River (457) by the Ephthalites.	

Western Europe	Eastern Europe

450-474 (cont.)

defenders was Meroveus, who founded the Merovingian dynasty of the Salian Franks.

Attila and his army invaded Italy, wasting cities like Padua and driving Venetians (according to tradition) to flee to coastal islands, founding Venice; visited by a mission from Pope Leo I, Attila withdrew, probably because of his weakening position and possibly after a tribute was paid (452).

d. Flavius Aëtius (ca. 395-454), Roman general who stopped Attila at Châlons (451); he was murdered by Emperor Valentinian III, who was apparently jealous of his success.

Vandal sea raiders entered the Tiber River, taking and sacking Rome, then returning to Carthage (June 2-16, 455).

Roman forces under the Swabian-Visigothic general Ricimer drove the Vandals from Sicily (456).

Visigoths under Theodoric II invaded Spain, decisively defeating the Suevi under Rechiari at the Urbicas, in Galicia (456).

Roman forces under general Majorian defeated Alemanni invaders at the Campi Cannini, in southern Switzerland (456); Majorian became Western Roman emperor. The Romans then invaded Toulouse, defeating King Theodoric II and bringing Visigothic Gaul back into the Western Roman Empire (458), and completed the reconquest of Gaul and Spain (460).

Majorian's Roman fleet, preparing for an invasion of Africa, was destroyed by the Vandals at Cartagena, Spain (461).

Theodoric II led the Visigoths in retaking Toulouse (461), expanding to the Mediterranean at Narbonne; he and (after his 466 assassination) his brother Euric campaigned widely in Gaul and Spain.

d. Majorian (Julius Valerius Majorianus) (?-461), Western Roman emperor (r. 457-461). He abdicated and was murdered after general Ricimer revolted against him.

b. Clovis (Chlodwig; Chlodowech) (ca. 466-511), king of the Salian Franks (r. 481-511).

In Spain Visigoths under Euric defeated the Suevi under King Remismund (468), then came to control all of Spain and much of Gaul, to the Loire and Rhône rivers.

Vandals led by Gaiseric continued to raid widely in the Mediterranean (468-477).

Under Gundobad (r. 473-516), Burgundy became an independent kingdom in the Rhône and Saône valleys.

Ostrogoths led by the brothers Walamir, Theodemir, and Widemir joined the Eastern Roman army (454); they had fought with Attila at Châlons (451).

b. Theodoric (Dietrich) I (the Great) (454?-526), Ostrogoth chieftain and ruler of Italy (r. 474-526).

Huns invaded Dacia from across the Danube but were defeated by the Romans under general Anthemius (466).

475-499

Part-Hun general Odoacer led a revolt by mercenaries in the Roman army, defeating Roman forces at Pavia (Aug. 23, 476) and killing their leader, Orestes; Odoacer assumed control of Italy (Sept. 4, 476), taking the title emperor; this is generally regarded as the end of the Western Roman Empire.

Odoacer annexed Dalmatia to his Italian territories (481).

---

b. Besas (Bessas) (ca. 480-ca. 560), Ostrogoth general serving the Byzantine Empire.

Winning a succession struggle, Theodoric the Great came to power (484), then raided widely in Thrace (486).

	450-474 (cont.)	
	Peroz (Firuz) allied himself with the Ephthalites to overthrow his brother Hormizd III for the Persian imperial throne (459).	
	Sinhalese under Dhatusena drove the Pandya out of Ceylon (Sri Lanka), founding the Moriya dynasty (459).	
	Persians under Peroz were involved in a long series of wars (464-484) with his erstwhile allies, the Ephthalites, who took Bactria and most of the eastern Persian territories.	
	475-499	
Vandal leader Hunneric (r. 477-484), son and successor of Gaiseric, persecuted his Catholic subjects, practices continued under his successors, also Arian Christians. b. Justinian I (the Great; Flavius Justinianus) (483-565), Byzantine emperor (r. 527-565).	Apparently developed in Central Asia, the stirrup was introduced into China, probably by the Northern Wei (T'upa) dynasty (ca. 477). Under King Jayavarman (ca. 480-514), the kingdom of Funan expanded from the	

475-499 (cont.)

Clovis, grandson of Meroveus, who fought at Châlons (451), became king of the Salian Franks (481), between the Somme and the lower Rhine rivers.

Clovis led the Salian Franks against Syagrius, a Roman general in northern Gaul, defeating him at Nogent (Soissons) (486); expanding in the region, Clovis married a Burgundian princess, Clotilda, and through her his people adopted Christianity.

In their first direct confrontation, Theodoric the Great, King of the Ostrogoths, defeated Odoacer at the Sontius (Isonzo) River (Aug. 28, 489) and at Verona (Sept. 30); Odoacer withdrew to Ravenna.

Forced to divide his forces after the Visigoths and Burgundians invaded northwestern Italy, Odoacer was defeated at the Adda River (Aug. 11, 490); he took refuge at Ravenna, besieged by Theodoric the Great. With reinforcements, Odoacer left still-besieged Ravenna to defeat Theodoric at Faenza (490).

After a three-and-a-half-year siege, Odoacer was forced to surrender Ravenna (Feb. 27, 493); he agreed to share power, but Theodoric the Great murdered him (Mar. 15), becoming sole ruler of Italy and soon taking Raetia, Noricum, and Dalmatia.

Clovis aided the Ripuarian Franks in decisively defeating the Alemanni at Tolbiac (Zulpich), near Cologne (496), effectively becoming leader of all the Franks, including those of the upper Rhine.

Italian leader Odoacer crossed the Alps to defeat Fava (Feletheus), king of the Rugi, and annex the region of Noricum (Austria), south of the Danube (487).

Spurred on by Eastern Roman emperor Zeno, Theodoric the Great and his Ostrogoths headed toward Italy, defeating the Gepidae at Sirmium (Sirmione) (488).

500-524

Angles, Saxons, and Jutes — first raiders, then invaders — came to control southeastern and central Britain (500-534); some historians place the semilegendary King Arthur in this period (r. ca. 516?-ca. 537?) as leader of the Roman-Briton defenders.

Intervening in Burgundy, Clovis supported Godegesil against Gundobar, whom he eventually besieged and defeated at Avignon (500); Burgundy became a dependency of the Franks.

Clovis and the Franks went to war with the Visigoths, defeating them and killing their leader, Alaric II of Toulouse, at Vouillé, and extending the Frankish kingdom to the Pyrenees (507).

Theodoric took Provence and defeated the Burgundians in Gaul (507), temporarily halting the Franks short of the Mediterranean.

d. Clovis (Chlodwig; Chlodowech) (ca. 466-511), king of the Salian Franks (r. 481-511) who united the Franks and adopted Christianity; his empire was divided among his four sons.

At Mount Badon (Badbury, Dorset, England), King Arthur's Roman-Briton forces may have defeated the Saxons under Cerdic (ca. 517?).

Lombards (Langobardi), under Tato, defeated the Heruli, led by Rodulf, in the central Danube Valley (508).

475-499 (cont.)

Succeeding his brother Peroz as Persian emperor, Balash agreed to stop the persecution of Christians in Armenia, ending a three-year revolt (481-484).

In the Isaurian War (492-496), Eastern Roman emperor Anastasius suppressed the rebellion of mountain peoples of Isauria, in south-central Anatolia, winning at Cotyaeum (Kutahya) (493).

Mekong Valley, possibly to the Irrawaddy River.

In a campaign to reconquer his lost eastern territories, Peroz and his Persian army were annihilated by the Ephthalites (484).

500-524

Two Arab kingdoms — Ghassan in Arabia's northwest and Hira in the northeast — were long at war, often supported by the Eastern Roman Empire and the Persian Empire, respectively (ca. 500-583).

Seeking access to the Black Sea, Kavadh of Persia allied himself with Ephthalites from Central Asia against the Eastern Roman Empire, fighting along the Armenian and Mesopotamian frontiers (502-505).

Huns invading south through the Caucasus Mountains caused the Eastern Romans and Persians to end their war and become allies against a common threat, sharing the defense of passes through the Caucasus (505).

b. Belisarius (ca. 505-565), Byzantine general.

Eastern Roman emperor Anastasius built the Anastasian Wall, a line of fortifications from the Black Sea to the Sea of Marmara (Propontis), aimed against the Persians (512).

In Justinian I's First Persian War (524-532), Persian emperor Kavadh I and his Arabian general al Mondhir fought well against the Romans but were stopped by their fortresses.

In India the military classic *Siva-Dhanurveda* was written, drawing heavily on Kautilya's earlier *Arthasastra;* the book emphasized archery, as the bow and arrow were still the main Hindu weapons (ca. 500).

Under Toramana the Hunas conquered Malwa (500-510), carving out a new kingdom as the Gupta Empire weakened.

Northern Wei (T'upa) dynasty invaded southern China but was decisively defeated (507).

Hunas under Mihiragula (r. 510-530) expanded south and east in the Punjab and Rajputana.

500-524 (cont.)

Franks, under Clovis's four sons, conquered Burgundy and Provence (523-532), also at times invading Germany, Italy, and Spain.

525-549

In the Italian (Gothic) War (534-553), the Eastern Roman Empire battled against the Ostrogoths in what had been the Western Roman Empire. Belisarius led Justinian's forces against the Ostrogoths, first taking Sicily, including the Gothic stronghold at Palermo (535).

Cynric, son of Cerdic, led Saxon expansion into Wiltshire (from ca. 534), in south-central Britain; his son, Ceawlin, apparently won a key battle at Dearham, near the Severn River (577?).

Italian (Gothic) War: Belisarius and his imperial forces invaded Italy from Sicily across the Strait of Messina, besieging and taking Naples (536).

Italian (Gothic) War: The Goths ceded Provence to the Franks, to forestall them from joining their Eastern Roman allies (536).

Italian (Gothic) War: Belisarius took Rome (Dec. 10, 536), abandoned by the Goths before his arrival, and began to rebuild the city's defenses.

Italian (Gothic) War: Goths under Vitiges besieged Belisarius's much smaller imperial forces in Rome (Mar. 2, 537-Mar. 12, 538), finally retreating when an Eastern Roman fleet arrived with reinforcements.

Italian (Gothic) War: On raising the siege of Rome, Vitiges and his Goths pursued a smaller Eastern Roman force under John the Sanguinary, besieging them in Rimini (538). As other Eastern Roman reinforcements arrived, Vitiges raised the siege of Rimini and took refuge in Ravenna, where the Goths themselves were besieged, finally surrendering (late 539); Vitiges surrendered and was sent to Constantinople.

Italian (Gothic) War: Belisarius had largely completed the Eastern Roman conquest of Italy, except for Pavia and Verona, when he was recalled to Constantinople, apparently because Emperor Justinian feared his success (541).

Italian (Gothic) War: Under their new king, Ildibad, Gothic forces broke the siege of Verona and defeated imperial forces at Treviso, regaining the Po Valley (541).

Italian (Gothic) War: Goths under Totila (Baduila), nephew of Vitiges, defeated Eastern Roman forces at Faenza and again at Mugello (both 542), then retaking much of central and southern Italy, including Naples (by 543).

Italian (Gothic) War: Rome was besieged and taken by the Goths under Totila (545), but it was quickly retaken by imperial forces after the return of Belisarius, who fought off several attempts to retake the city (546).

Italian (Gothic) War: After Belisarius was recalled to Constantinople again (549), Totila and his Gothic forces reconquered most of Italy, as well as Sicily, Sardinia, and Corsica.

d. Theodoric (Dietrich) I (the Great) (454?-526), Ostrogoth chieftain (r. 474-526) who conquered Italy (488-493) and stayed to become its ruler, extending his rule into Provence.

Pushed from the east by the Avars, a Central Asian people, many Bulgars and Slavs began to invade across the Danube and move into the Balkans (from ca. 530).

Roman imperial forces, under Belisarius, Narses, and Mundas, suppressed the Nika uprising against Justinian in the Eastern Roman capital of Constantinople (532).

Italian (Gothic) War: Imperial forces under Mundas were defeated by Goths at Salona (near Split), Dalmatia (536).

In Arabia the forces of Ghassan under Harith Ibn Jabala won a major victory over Hira (528).

Romans under their new Eastern commander Belisarius defeated a much larger combined Persian-Arab army at Dara, in Persian-held Armenia (530), but later lost at Calinicum (531), then fighting to a draw.

Belisarius invaded North Africa with an Eastern Roman imperial army, defeating the Vandals under King Gelimer at Ad Decimum (Sept. 13, 533); Carthage then surrendered without a fight.

Vandal forces under Tzazon (Zano), brother of King Gelimer, put down a revolt in Sardinia encouraged by Justinian I (533).

Though reinforced by Tzazon's forces, the Vandals were routed when Belisarius mounted a surprise attack at Tricameron (Dec. 533); Tzazon was killed; King Gelimer surrendered (534) and was taken back to Constantinople; the Vandal kingdom ended; and North Africa was once again Roman.

b. Maurice (Flavius Tiberius Mauricius) (539-602), Eastern Roman emperor (r. 582-602).

Justinian I's Second Persian War (539-562): Chosroes I of Persia declared war on the Eastern Roman Empire.

Justinian I's Second Persian War: Persians under Chosroes I invaded and conquered Syria, including Antioch, taking many captives (540).

Justinian I's Second Persian War: Persians took Petra (near Phasis) (541), in coastal Armenia.

Justinian I's Second Persian War: Eastern Roman forces under Belisarius, just returned from Italy, joined by Ghassanid troops under Harith Ibn Jabala, retook Mesopotamia and raided Persia, forcing Chosroes I to leave Armenia (542).

Abraha became viceroy of Himyar (southwestern Yemen) (ca. 545), appointed by Aksum's King Ella-Abeha (Caleb).

Justinian I's Second Persian War: Fighting to a stalemate, Chosroes I and Justinian agreed to an armistice (545).

Justinian I's Second Persian War: Responding to Persian persecution of Christians in coastal Armenia, Eastern Roman forces under general Dagisteus besieged Petra (549-551).

In China, civil war wracked the Northern Wei (T'upa) dynasty (529-534), resulting in the Eastern and Western Wei empires.

Hunas under Mihiragula were defeated by a Hindu coalition, including forces under princes Balditya of Magadha and Yasodharman of Ijjain (530); the Huna kingdom never recovered and gradually disappeared (by ca. 550).

Vietnamese led by Li-bon briefly threw off Chinese rule (541-547).

King Rudravarman led the Cham in an unsuccessful attack against Li-bon's Vietnamese forces (543).

Parts of China's Great Wall were rebuilt by the Eastern Wei against threats from the Avars of Central Asia (543).

The Turks, a people of Mongol and Indo-European ancestry, revolted against the Avars under their chief Tuman (Tumere) (ca. 546-553), establishing themselves as a Central Asian power; some Avars went east into China, but most migrated toward Europe.

Chinese put down Li-bon's Vietnamese revolt (547).

Western Europe   **Eastern Europe**

550-574

Italian (Gothic) War: Goths under Totila attacked Ravenna by land and sea but were badly defeated in the Adriatic (551), also losing Sicily to Eastern Roman forces under Artaban.

Italian (Gothic) War: Imperial forces, now under Narses, won a major victory at Taginae (near modern Gubbio), where the Gothic leader Totila was killed; the Eastern Romans then besieged and took Rome (552).

Frankish-Alemanni forces under the brothers Lothaire and Buccelin, along with some Gothic troops, invaded Italy, defeating imperial forces at Parma to take the Po Valley (553); the army then divided, with Buccelin's forces going to southern Italy.

Italian (Gothic) War: The Goths were decisively defeated by Narses's imperial forces at Monte Lacteria (Samus), near Cumae, where their new king, Teias, was killed (553).

Italian (Gothic) War: Imperial forces under Narses destroyed Buccelin's army at Casilinum, on the Volturno River, near Capua (554); Lothaire's army, decimated by disease, ceased to be a threat; Italy — though much wasted — was again part of the Roman Empire.

Justinian called Belisarius out of retirement to consolidate Eastern Roman conquests in southern Spain (554).

Clotaire I, son of Clovis, briefly reunited his father's Frankish Empire (558-561).

Justinian imprisoned his key general, Belisarius, accusing him of treason (562), presumably fearing and envying his success; Belisarius was later released and restored to honor (563).

Lombards, joined by some Saxons, invaded Italy; led by Alboin, they defeated the imperial general Longinus, from Ravenna (568), then took the Po Valley and Milan.

Lombards took Pavia after a three-year siege (572), making it the capital of Lombardy; in northern Italy the Eastern Roman emperor retained control of some coastal cities.

Germanius, nephew of Eastern Roman emperor Justinian, temporarily stopped an invasion of the Slavs at Sardica (Sofia) (550).

Driven westward when their homelands were taken by the Turks, Avars began to invade Europe (ca. 555).

Bulgars led by Zabergan raided widely in southeastern Europe, arriving at the walls of Constantinople, where they were stopped (near Melanthius) by Roman general Belisarius, brought out of retirement a second time for his final victory (559).

d. Besas (Bessas) (ca. 480-ca. 560), Ostrogoth general serving the Byzantine Empire.

Under their leader Baian, the Avars invaded Germany from the Danube Valley but were defeated by the Franks (562).

Allied Avar and Lombard forces destroyed the Gepidae people and took Transylvania (567).

575-599

Roman-Briton forces blocked Saxon expansion into Wales, defeating Ceawlin at Faddiley (near Nantwich) (583).

A long series of conflicts between the Visigoths, believers in Arian Christianity, and their Catholic Iberian subjects was ended when the Visigoths converted to Catholicism (589).

Under King Aethelbert (r. 597-616), the Jute kingdom became dominant in Kent.

Avars under Baian took Sirmium (Sirmione) (580) and campaigned as far as the Aegean Sea (591; 597).

Shortly before he became Eastern Roman emperor, Maurice wrote the military treatise *Strategikon* (580).

Romans under emperor Maurice and general Priscus stopped an Avar invasion in a series of campaigns in southeastern Europe (595-601).

Africa and Southwest Asia	East, Central, and South Asia, the Pacific, and the Americas

Persians under Chosroes I allied themselves with a new Central Asian power, the Turks, together defeating the Ephthalites (ca. 554-ca. 560).

Justinian I's Second Persian War: After Eastern Roman forces decisively defeated the Persians under Nacoragan at the Phasis River, the two sides agreed on a peace (562).

d. Belisarius (ca. 505-565), Byzantine general who served notably under Emperor Justinian, though sometimes out of imperial favor.

d. Justinian I (the Great; Flavius Justinianus) (483-565), Byzantine emperor (r. 527-565) who rebuilt the empire; he was involved in numerous wars, many directly commanded by his generals Belisarius and Narses. He was succeeded by his nephew, Justin II (r. 565-574).

Abraha, Aksumite viceroy who had come to control most of Yemen, invaded the Hejaz with initial success, but he failed to take Mecca (570).

Eastern Roman emperor Justin II allied himself with the Turks of Central Asia against Persian leader Chosroes I, whose grandson Chosroes II successfully campaigned in Syria (572-573).

Persians under Chosroes II sent a naval expedition against Aksum's colony of Himyar (southwestern Yemen), landing at Aden (572), then gradually winning most of Arabia from Aksum and its Eastern Roman allies (572-585).

Eastern Roman emperor Justin II abdicated in favor of general Tiberius (r. 574-582).

In India's western Deccan, Pulakesin I founded the Chalukya dynasty, based near Bijapur (550); it would gradually overwhelm the Pallava dynasty and control the central Deccan (ca. 550-608).

Funan king Rudravarman was overthrown by two brothers from Chenla, Chitrasena and Bhavavarman, who took most of Cambodia (ca. 550); Rudravarman retained only a small southern region.

After another Chinese civil war, the Eastern Wei dynasty ended, replaced by the Northern Ch'i dynasty (550).

After further victories over the Chinese, the Avars, and the Ephthalites, the Turks briefly established a Central Asian empire (553-582).

In its long expansion, primarily against Paekche, the kingdom of Silla reached Korea's west coast (554).

b. Kao Chiung (Gao Jiong) (555-607), Chinese general.

China's Great Wall was further rebuilt by the Northern Ch'i dynasty (successor to the Eastern Wei), facing new threats from Central Asia, notably the Turks (556).

China's Northern Chou dynasty defeated and replaced the Western Wei dynasty (556), which then also conquered the Northern Ch'i (557).

Kingdom of Silla conquered the last Japanese colonies on Korea's south coast (562).

Eastern Roman forces under Maurice drove the Persians from Cappadocia (575).

b. Heraclius (ca. 575-641), Byzantine emperor (r. 610-641).

Eastern Roman general Justinian defeated the Persians under Chosroes II at Melitene (576).

Eastern Romans invaded Persian Armenia (577), conquering much of Armenia and the Caucasus Mountains.

d. Chosroes I (Khosrow; Anushirvan) (?-579), Persian king (r. 531-579) who contended with the Romans for power in southwest Asia.

After the death of Tiberius (582), Maurice became Eastern Roman emperor, (r. 582-602).

b. 'Amr Ibn Al-'As (al-Aasi) (ca. 585-664), Arab general.

b. Omar I ('Umar ibn al-Khattab) (ca. 586-644), Muslim caliph (r. 634-644).

In India's eastern Deccan, King Simhavishnu of the resurgent Pallava dynasty defeated the Chola kingdom, driving the Chola south (575).

Kingdom of Pandya became dominant in southernmost India (575-600).

Turks, allied with the Eastern Romans, attacked Persia's eastern territories, taking most of Khorasan and reaching Hyrcania, on the Caspian Sea (ca. 579-587).

All of northern China was unified by Yang Chien, founder of the Sui dynasty (581), who further rebuilt the Great Wall.

Persians under Bahram Chobin decisively defeated the Turks in an ambush at Hyr-

Western Europe	Eastern Europe

575-599 (cont.)

600-624

At Daegsastan, invading Dalriad Scots were defeated by King Aethelfrith of Northumbria, an Angle kingdom in northwest England (603).

Merovingian ruler Lothair II temporarily united the Frankish kingdoms of Austrasia, Neustria, and Burgundy (613).

King Aethelfrith of Northumbria defeated the Britons at Chester (615), expanding westward to the Irish Sea.

Raedwald, king of East Anglia, defeated and killed Aethelfrith at the Idle River (616). Aethelfrith's successor, Edwin, Northumbria's first Christian king, defeated the Britons in northern Wales and Anglesea (616).

Eastern Roman Empire lost its last remaining Spanish territories to the Visigoths (616).

In the Frankish kingdom of Austrasia, Pepin I became mayor of the palace (prime minister) (623-629) under King Dagobert, the last Merovingian.

Romans halted Avar invaders at Viminacium (601), on the Danube, but the Avars still had an empire stretching east and north from the Danube to the Volga River and the Baltic Sea.

Phocas, a centurion serving on the Danube, led a mutiny against Eastern Roman emperor Maurice, forcing him to abdicate, then killing him and his two sons (602).

Slavs revolted successfully against Avar rule in Moravia (603).

d. Bajan (Baian) (?-609), Avar ruler who led his people's expansion into modern Romania and Hungary (558-563).

Avars raided in the Balkans, reaching the walls of Constantinople (617-619) but leaving after payment of a heavy tribute.

Kurt (Kubrat), the first Bulgarian ruler known by name, traveled to Constantinople seeking an alliance against the Avars (619).

575-599 (cont.)

Bahram Chobin led Persian forces to victory against the Eastern Romans at Martyropolis (Mus), Turkey, but was then defeated by Maurice at Nisibis and at the Araxes River, in Armenia (all 589).

Bahram Chobin refused to accept dismissal by Persian emperor Hormizd, instead overthrowing him and taking the throne himself (590); Hormizd's son and heir, Chosroes II, took refuge with the Romans.

Eastern Roman forces under general Narses invaded Persia on behalf of Chosroes II; Bahram Chobin was decisively defeated near the Zab River, as many of his troops defected to Chosroes, the rest being destroyed in Media (591). Chosroes II took the Persian throne and made peace.

b. Sa'd (Saad) Ibn Abi Waqqas (ca. 596-ca. 660), Arab general.

canian Rock (588), then regained territories south of the Oxus River.

Under Yang Chien, Sui forces invaded southern China (589), defeating the Ch'en dynasty and reuniting China for the first time since the Han dynasty (220). Yang Chien also took Korea's northern kingdom, Kokuryo.

b. Harsha (Harshavardhana) (ca. 590-ca. 648), Indian king (r. 606-ca. 648).

Under the regency of Prince Shotoku (r. 593-621), ruling for Empress Suiko, the Soga clan fell from power in Japan, which began to develop a more centralized government; the ruler also continued the wars with the Ainu people in northern Honsu.

b. Li Shih-min (T'ai Tsung) (ca. 598-649), Chinese emperor (r. 626-649).

600-624

b. 'Ali ('Ali ibn Abi Talib) (ca. 600-661), fourth Muslim caliph (r. 656-661).

d. Maurice (Flavius Tiberius Mauricius) (539-602), Eastern Roman emperor (r. 582-602) who fought the Persians and the Avars, winning at Viminacium (601); he was killed by Phocas during an army revolt.

Chosroes II of Persia declared war on Phocas, murderer of Byzantine emperor Maurice, to whom he owed his throne; he campaigned in Mesopotamia and Syria, stopped only at Antioch and Damascus, and then in Anatolia, reaching the Bosporus (603-608).

Heraclius the Elder sent Byzantine forces under his son Heraclius from Carthage to Constantinople, where they deposed and killed Phocas (610); the younger Heraclius became the new emperor, under whom Greek became the official language of the empire, now generally called the Byzantine Empire.

Arab forces raided Persian lands south of the Euphrates, winning at Dhu-Qar, then being pushed back into the Arabian Desert (610).

Continuing its war with the Byzantine Empire, Persia took Antioch and Armenia (611), Damascus (613), Jerusalem (614), and Chalcedon (616), directly across the Bosporus from Constantinople.

Persian forces under Chosroes II conquered Egypt (616-619), cutting off Constantinople's grain supply.

Visigoths took the Byzantine territory of Ceuta, in Morocco opposite Gibraltar (618).

Persian forces took Ancyra (Ankara), in Anatolia; Byzantine fortresses in Armenia; and the island of Rhodes (620).

Surprising the Persians, who thought he was considering their peace terms, Heraclius landed an invasion army from Constantinople near Alexandretta, in Syria; at Issus he defeated the much larger Persian army, under general Shahr Baraz (622), then routed the Persians at the Halys River (Jan. 623).

Mohammed, founder of Islam, led his followers on the Hegira, from Mecca to Medina (622), marking the start of the Islamic calendar.

Briefly reunified under Tardu (ca. 600-603), Central Asia's Western Turkish Empire threatened the Chinese capital of Ch'ang-an.

General Lui Fang renewed Chinese control of Tonkin and Annam and sent a punitive expedition against the Cham (602-605).

d. Yang Chien (?-604), Chinese emperor who founded the Sui dynasty (581), reunited China (589), and took northern Korea (589); he may have been murdered by his son and successor, Yang Ti.

Chinese naval forces fought off an invasion of Tonkin by the Cham (605).

Under King Harsha (r. 606-648), the Punjab state of Thaneswar expanded to include most of northern India down to the Narbada River.

Chinese naval forces ravaged Formosa island (Taiwan) (606).

Chinese forces defeated the T'ai people of Yunnan (607-610).

d. Kao Chiung (Gao Jiong) (555-607), Chinese general who supported Yang Chien in the reunification of China (589), becoming chief minister; he was executed by Emperor Yang Ti.

Chinese general P'ei Chu drove the Western Turks from the border regions of Kansu and Koko Nor, occupying Hami (Khamil) (608) and campaigning into Sinkiang (609).

600-624 (cont.)

625-649

At Hatfield Chase (632), Edwin of Northumbria was defeated and killed by the allied forces of Cadwallon, a Briton king from northern Wales, and Penda, an Angle king from Mercia.

Oswald of Northumbria, Edwin's successor, defeated and killed Cadwallon at Hefenfelth (Rowley Water), conquering northwest England (633).

At Maserfeld (Oswestry), in Shropshire, Oswald was defeated and killed by Penda of Mercia, which became the dominant Anglo-Saxon kingdom (641).

Bulgars became independent of Avar rule in the Volga Basin (ca. 634).

Slavonian Croats successfully rebelled against Avar control (640).

Moving into the Mediterranean, Arab Muslims captured Cyprus (649).

600-624 (cont.)

Moving his Byzantine army by water to Trapezus (Trebizond), on the Black Sea, Heraclius invaded Armenia and Media; Chosroes II abandoned the capital, Tauris (Tabriz), to Heraclius (623).

Byzantine forces under Heraclius invaded deep into central Persia to Ispahan, farther than any other Roman forces had gone; at this, Chosroes II withdrew the Persian forces camped opposite Constantinople, in Chalcedon; in a surprise attack, Heraclius defeated Shahr Baraz's army, wintering in captured cities in northwest Persia (624).

Mohammed and his followers from Medina defeated the forces of Mecca at Badr (624) but lost at Ohod (625).

Pulakesin II of Chalukya expanded his rule to the Bay of Bengal (609).

Chinese emperor Yang Ti campaigned with little success in Manchuria and northern Korea (611-614).

Attempting to suppress rebellions, Yang Ti was defeated and trapped in Yenmen (615); he was rescued by the young general Li Shih-min, whose father, Li Yuan, later founded the T'ang dynasty.

d. Yang Ti (Yang Kuang) (?-618), Chinese emperor (r. 604-618) who may have murdered his father, Yang Chien; forced out of his capital, Loyang, by rebellions, he was murdered. His successor was Li Yuan, who as Kao Tsu (r. 618-626) founded the T'ang dynasty.

Pulakesin II of Chalukya turned back the Indian king Harsha's invasion of the Deccan (620).

Under Song-tsan Gampo (r. ca. 620-650), Tibet became a major power, with its capital at Lhasa.

After Prince Shotoku's death, the Soga clan temporarily returned to power in Japan (621-645).

Western Turks, allied with Heraclius and the Byzantines, took Khorasan and the Oxus Basin from Persia (ca. 622).

Chinese general Li Shih-min defeated the Eastern Turks, who had reached the gates of China's capital, Ch'ang-an (Sian) (624-627).

Under Chitrasena's son Isanavarman I (r. ca. 611-635), Funan was reconquered and reunited (ca. 627), expanding to include most of Cambodia.

625-649

After campaigning in Corduene (Kurdistan) and Mesopotamia, Heraclius and his Byzantine forces defeated Shah Baraz's army at the Sarus River (625), then retook Cappadocia and Pontus.

A huge Avar army, including Slavs, Germans, and Bulgars, besieged Constantinople (June 29-Aug. 10, 626) while their new allies, the Persians, attacked by sea. Heraclius's son Constantine led an extraordinarily successful defense, repelling both land and sea assaults and inflicting heavy losses, especially on the Avars, who withdrew (626).

Heraclius, reinforced by troops under his brother Theodore, completed the reconquest of Anatolia and retook Syria, Mesopotamia, and southern Armenia (627), cutting off Shahr Baraz's Persian army in Chalcedon, which surrendered; Heraclius then invaded Assyria and, at Nineveh, destroyed the Persian army, personally killing the army's general, Rhazates (Dec. 627). He pursued

Pulakesin II of Chalukya defeated the rival Pallava dynasty to become dominant in southern India (625-630).

After Kao Tsu abdicated, his son Li Shih-min took the Chinese throne as T'ai Tsung (r. 626-649).

T'ai Tsung and his Chinese forces fought a series of campaigns that eventually broke the Eastern Turks (626-641).

Aided by the Uigher Turks, T'ai Tsung defeated the Western Turks (641-648), reestablishing Chinese power in Sinkiang

625-649 (cont.)

Chosroes II to his capital, Ctesiphon, but did not attempt to take it, instead offering peace.

Mohammed and his followers fought off an attempt by rival Arabs to take Medina (627).

When Chosroes II rejected Byzantine peace terms, the Persians deposed him in favor of his son Kavadh II (Siroes); the Persians were obliged to give up their conquests, including religious items (such as the relic of the True Cross) taken in the sacking of Jerusalem (628).

Byzantine forces defeated the first Muslims to attack them, at Muta, in Palestine (629).

Mohammed and his followers took Mecca (630), while also conquering other nearby Arab peoples.

At the death of Mohammed (632), Abu Bakr became the first caliph (successor); Khalid ibn al-Walid led forces suppressing rival claimants Tulayha and Musaylima, who were finally defeated at Akraba (633).

Arab Muslims under 'Amr ibn al-'As invaded Palestine and Syria (633). Others under Khalid ibn al-Walid invaded Persian territories, taking Hira and Oballa (633).

Arab Muslim forces left in Mesopotamia by Khalid were checked by the Persians under general Mihran in the Battle of the Bridge, at the Euphrates River (634), then repelled Persian pursuit at Buwayb, south of Kufa (635).

Khalid's Arab Muslims defeated Byzantine forces at Ajnadain, between Jerusalem and Gaza (July 634), at Fihl (Pella or Gilead), near Baisan (Jan. 635), and at Marjal-Saffar (near Damascus) (635). Khalid then took Damascus and Emesa (Homs), temporarily abandoning them, won decisively at the Yarmuk River (Aug. 636), then retook the cities.

Arab Muslims under Sa'd ibn abi-Waqqas defeated a far larger Persian force under Rustam, at the Qadisiyah (June 637), then took the capital of Ctesiphon and won at Jalula, north of Madain (Dec. 637).

In Syria, Arab Muslims besieged and took Jerusalem and Antioch (638), then Aleppo (639).

Arab Muslims under 'Amr ibn al-'As invaded Egypt (639), defeating Byzantine defenders at Babylon, near Heliopolis (July 640), then besieging and taking Babylon (Apr. 641) and Alexandria (Sept. 642).

Arab Muslims decisively defeated the Persians at Ram Hormuz (640), near Shushtar, and Nahavend (641), both in the Persian highlands, gradually extending control to the Oxus River. They also besieged and took the Syrian cities of Caesarea and Gaza (640), Ascalon (644), and Tripoli (645), by this time controlling all of Syria and Mesopotamia.

d. Heraclius (ca. 575-641), Byzantine emperor (r. 610-641) whose most notable victory was at Issus (622).

Moving westward, Arab Muslims led by Abdulla ibn Zubayr took Cyrene and Tripoli, even raiding near Carthage (642-643).

d. Omar I ('Umar ibn al-Khattab) (ca. 586-644), second Muslim caliph (r. 634-644), who fought in the conquest of Syria, Palestine, Mesopotamia, and Egypt (634-645); the first to call himself *Amir-al-Mu'minin* (Commander of the Faithful), he set the model for the Islamic state.

'Amr ibn al-'As suppressed a revolt in Alexandria, retaking the city and repelling a Byzantine fleet (645).

and receiving tribute from beyond the Pamir Mountains.

Chinese forces under T'ai Tsung decisively defeated a Tibetan invasion force led by Song-tsan Gampo (641); both Tibet and Nepal began paying tribute.

d. Pulakesin II (?-642), who founded the Chalukya dynasty (608); he was defeated and killed outside his capital, Vatapi, fighting Narasimharvarman I of the Pallava dynasty (642).

Chinese naval forces campaigned against Korea (643).

In Japan the Soga clan was once again driven from power by Prince Kotoku (645); he and Nakatomi-no-Kamatari, founder of the Fujiwara clan, continued the centralizing reforms of Prince Shotoku.

Chinese forces invaded Korea but were repelled by the northern state of Kokuryo (645; 647).

d. Harsha (Harshavardhana) (ca. 590-ca. 648), Indian king (r. 606-ca. 648) who founded the Pushyabhuti dynasty, consolidating several smaller kingdoms.

After Harsha's death, a key aide, Arjuna, took control of Bihar and Bengal (648); he then attacked Chinese ambassador Wang Hsuan-Tsu, who raised an army from the Chinese protectorates of Nepal and Tibet and defeated Arjuna on the Ganges, taking him back to China as a prisoner (649).

d. Li Shih-min (T'ai Tsung) (ca. 598-649), second T'ang emperor (r. 626-649), who led the expansion of Chinese power in Central Asia. He was succeeded by his son Li Chih (Kao Tsung) (r. 649-683), who was increasingly dominated by Empress Wu Chao.

625-649 (cont.)

650-674

Swedes invaded the land now named for them; from their center at Uppsala, they gradually came to dominate the Goths and other peoples they found there (ca. 650-ca. 800).

Oswy, Oswald's younger brother, defeated and killed Penda of Mercia at Winwaed (655), making Northumbria dominant again.

Emperor Constans II led Byzantine forces against the Lombards in Italy and was killed in a revolt there (662-668), suppressed by his son and successor, Constantine IV.

Under their new leader Isperich, Bulgars invaded the Danube Basin (ca. 650-ca. 670).

Arab Muslims invaded north through the Caucasus Mountains into the land of the Khazars, a Turkish people, taking Derbent on the Caspian Sea (661).

675-699

In Austrasia Pepin II led a revolt that became a civil war; he then became mayor of the palace (ca. 675-678).

Byzantine forces fought off Slav attacks on Thessalonika (675-681).

Africa and Southwest Asia	East, Central, and South Asia, the Pacific, and the Americas
	625-649 (cont.)
b. Abd al-Malik (Abd-al-Malik ibn Marwan) (646-705), Omayyad caliph (r. 685-705). Arab Muslims invaded the Byzantine province of Africa (647).	
	650-674
After six years of fighting, Arab Muslims took Cyprus (653) and attacked Rhodes (654). Arab Muslims conquered part of Byzantine Armenia (653). Arab Muslim naval forces under Dhat al-Sawari defeated a Byzantine fleet commanded by Emperor Constans off Phoenix, in Lycia (655). After the third Muslim caliph, Othman ('Uthman), was murdered (656) by his opponents, Mohammed's adopted son 'Ali became caliph; at the Battle of the Camel (Dec.), near Basra, in Mesopotamia, he defeated opposing forces, including Talha, Zubayr, and Mohammed's widow, Ayesah. d. Zubayr ibn Al-Awwam (?-656), Arab general, a key figure in the dissension among Mohammed's successors; part of the group that killed Othman, he later rebelled against 'Ali and was killed at the Battle of the Camel (Dec. 656); his son Abdulla later became caliph (683). Othman's cousin Mu'awiya, governor of Syria, led another rebellion against 'Ali, the two sides fighting to a draw at Siffin, in Syria (657); this civil war echoes into modern times, for supporters of Mu'awiya's line were called Sunni Muslims, while those supporting 'Ali were Shi'ites. Byzantine Empire and Muslim Caliphate negotiated a temporary peace (659). d. Sa'd (Saad) Ibn Abi Waqqas (ca. 596-ca. 660), Arab general who led Islamic forces in Arabia (631-633) and Mesopotamia (634-638). d. 'Ali ('Ali ibn Abi Talib) (ca. 600-661), fourth Muslim caliph (r. 656-661), whom Shi'ites revere as Mohammed's true successor, murdered by his opponents; his son and successor, Hassan, abdicated. Mu'awiya was named Muslim caliph at Jerusalem (661), founding the Omayyad dynasty. d. 'Amr Ibn Al-'As (al-Aasi) (ca. 585-664), Arab general who conquered Egypt (659), becoming its governor. Arab Muslims invaded Anatolia and reached Chalcedon (668) but failed in their attack on Constantinople (669); their army was annihilated at Armorium. Byzantine forces fought off an Arab Muslim naval assault on Constantinople, then destroyed the Arab fleet at Cyzicus, in the Sea of Marmara (672); this was the first known use of Greek fire, a secret chemical preparation (including niter, petroleum, pitch, and sulfur) that the Byzantine Greeks used to set fire to their enemies' ships; an early use of chemical weapons, it would save them for centuries. Arab Muslims mounted a sea and land blockade, and sometime siege, of Constantinople (673-677), which was saved several times by Greek fire.	Arab Muslims conquered Baluchistan (ca. 650-707). Gurjaras, a nomadic people from Central Asia, conquered Rajputana (ca. 650). Under Jayavarman I (r. ca. 655-695), Funan (Chenla) expanded to include southern and central Laos. Vikramaditya, son of Pulakesin II, defeated the southern India kingdoms of Chola and Pandy (655). Chinese forces suppressed a rebellion of the Western Turks in the Oxus Basin, capturing their khan (657-659). Chinese naval forces attacked Korea (658). Chinese land and sea forces, with the Korean state of Silla, defeated the Korean state of Paekche and its Japanese allies; Silla became a Chinese dependent (660-663). Arab Muslims under Ziyad ibn Abihi raided as far as the Indus Valley (661-663). After Tibet rebelled against China, taking the Tarim Basin, China's western territories — now cut off — declared their independence, as did Korea, the Western Turks, the Eastern Turks, and Nanchao, the T'ai state in Yunnan (663-683). Arab Muslims campaigned to Kabul, which they temporarily took (664). China and Silla defeated Kokuryo, unifying Korea under Silla's rule and China's control (668); Silla later declared its independence (ca. 670). Arab Muslims invaded Transoxiana, briefly taking Bukhara (674) and Samarkand (676). Avenging his father's loss (642), Vikramaditya of Chalukya defeated the Pallava dynasty, destroying its capital, Kanchi (674).
	675-699
After long-term Muslim raiding, especially focused on Dongola (Dunqalah), the Christian kingdom of Nabotia, on the Nile, signed a peace treaty with Arab Muslims under 'Abd Allah ibn S'ad (ca. 675).	At the death of Emperor Li Chih (Kao Tsung), Empress Wu Chao effectively took control of China (683), then formally took

Western Europe	Eastern Europe

675-699 (cont.)

After invading Scotland, Egfrith (Oswy's successor) was defeated and killed by the Scots at Dunnichen Moss, north of the Tay River in Forfar (685).

Pepin II defeated the kingdom of Neustria at Tertry, near St. Quentin (687), then defeated the Frisians, Alemanni, and Burgundians to create a kingdom equal to Clovis's, except for Aquitaine.

b. Charles Martel (the Hammer) (ca. 688-741), Frankish leader.

Bulgars under Isperich invaded across the Danube, defeating Byzantine forces to win Moesia (679-680).

Byzantine emperor Constantine IV recognized Bulgarian independence (680).

Byzantine emperor Justinian II, son and successor of Constantine IV, was overthrown by Leontius (695), himself overthrown by Tiberius Absimarus (698).

700-724

Muslims under Tarik ibn Ziyad invaded Spain at Gibraltar (711), giving the rock its name: Gebal el Tarik. Visigothic forces were defeated at the Guadalete River (near Medina Sidonia) (July 19), where their leader, Roderick, drowned in flight, and at Ecija. Toledo, the Visigothic capital, fell without a fight.

After Tarik ibn Ziyad's death, Musa ibn Nusair took command of Muslim forces, completing the conquest of Spain, except for some isolated mountain pockets (712).

Muslims made their first recorded raid north of the Pyrenees (712).

Charles Martel won the succession struggle that followed the death of Pepin II (714) with victories over his rivals at Amblève, near Liège (716), and Vincy, near Cambrai (717).

b. Pepin III le Bref (the Short) (714?-768), king of the Franks (r. 751-768).

Justinian II, with the support of Bulgar king Terbelis (Tervel), returned to take Constantinople in a surprise attack (705), executing the rebels who had taken his throne.

Bulgar forces led by Terbelis defeated the Byzantines at Anchialus (708).

Troops dispatched to the Crimea (where Justinian II had been exiled) mutinied under Bardanes Philippicus (711); aided by the Khazars, from north of the Caucasus Mountains, Philippicus defeated and killed Justinian in Anatolia, taking the Byzantine throne himself (711).

Under Terbelis, Bulgar forces raided widely in Thrace, reaching the walls of Constantinople (712).

Byzantine troops deposed Philippicus, replacing him with Anastasius II (713). Other Byzantine forces rebelled against Anastasius (715), instead supporting Theodosius III, who besieged and took Constantinople, sending Anastasius to a monastery.

Byzantine forces destroyed the Arab Muslim fleet off Syllaeum, in southern Anatolia (679), after which Caliph Mu'awiya made peace, agreeing to leave Cyprus and pay an annual tribute.

Hussein I, 'Ali's second son, rebelled against Omayyad rule and was defeated and killed at Kerbela, on the Euphrates (680).

b. Leo III the Isaurian (ca. 680-741), Byzantine emperor (r. 717-741).

Egyptian Arab Muslims under Okba ibn Nafi invaded Morocco, reaching the Atlantic before the Berbers and their Byzantine allies from Carthage pushed them back to Cyrene (681-683).

Abdulla ibn Zubayr revolted against Omayyad rule, successfully defending against a siege of Mecca (682-683); he was proclaimed caliph of Arabia, Iraq, and Egypt.

Omayyad leader Marwan ibn Hakam defeated supporters of Abdulla ibn Zubayr at Marj Rahit, near Damascus, confirming himself as caliph (684). He took Egypt from Zubayr's faction (685); his son Abd al-Malik succeeded him at his death (685).

Counterattacking Arab Muslims, Khazars invaded through the Caucasus Mountains into Armenia, Georgia, and Azerbaijan (685-722).

Abd al-Malik defeated Mus'ab ibn Zubayr, Abdulla's brother, on the Tigris River, near Basra (690), to retake Iraq for the Omayyads.

In the Arab War (690-692), Muslims took Byzantine territories beyond the Taurus Mountains after winning at Sebastopolis (Phasis) (692); Byzantines and Muslims then shared control of Cyprus.

General Al-Hajjaj ibn Yusuf led Omayyad armies in retaking Arabia from supporters of Abdulla ibn Zubayr, killed in the siege of Mecca (692).

d. Abdullah ibn Zubayr (?-692), Omayyad general and ruler; he died during the final assault on Mecca.

Arab Muslims took Carthage (698), the last Byzantine stronghold in North Africa (698).

the throne (r. 690-705), becoming China's only woman empress; under her, China again defeated the Tibetans, recovering its rebellious territories.

Pallava forces, including Tamil mercenaries, invaded Ceylon (Sri Lanka), ending the Moriya dynasty and beginning the second Lambakanna dynasty, with Manavamma on the throne (684).

Al-Hajjaj ibn Yusuf, governor of the Muslim eastern provinces, suppressed a revolt by Arabs under Ibn al-Ash'ath in Afghanistan (699-701).

Aksum raided the Arabian port of Jiddah (702).

Berbers in Algeria defeated Arab Muslims led by Hassan ibn No'man (703), then made an alliance with them.

d. Abd al-Malik (Abd-al-Malik ibn Marwan) (646-705), Omayyad caliph (r. 685-705) who reconquered Iraq and Arabia.

Musa ibn Nusair led Arab Muslims in conquering northwest Africa (708-711).

Muslim forces under Musa ibn Nusair reached the Strait of Gibraltar, initially failing to take Ceuta, on the Moroccan side (710).

Arab Muslims invaded Byzantine territories in Anatolia, taking Cilicia (711) and part of Galatia (714).

Arab Muslim invaders took Pergamum (716).

Leo III and his Byzantine forces crossed the Bosporus and defeated the Arab Muslim army at Chalcedon (June? 718). Muslims gave up the siege of Constantinople (Aug. 718), some retreating through Anatolia, pursued by Leo; the rest, evacuated by sea, were almost all lost in a great storm; only an estimated 30,000 of 200,000 Muslims returned.

b. Abu Muslim (720-755), Abbasid general.

Kingdom of Srivijaya became dominant on the island of Sumatra, with its capital in the south, at Palembang (by 700), later taking western Java and becoming a power in the region for several centuries.

Iceland was settled by Irish monks (ca. 700) exploring westward from the Faroe Islands.

Japanese produced the first known translation of Sun Tzu's *The Art of War* (8th c.; originally written ca. 511 BC).

Qutayba ibn Muslim led the Omayyad dynasty's eastern expansion, taking Bukhara, Samarkand, Khwarizm, Ferghana, and Tashkent and campaigning as far as Kashgar (705-713).

Kingdom of Funan (Chenla) split and collapsed (ca. 706).

Western Europe	Eastern Europe

700-724 (cont.)

Muslims under Hurr raided Aquitaine and southern France (717-719), capturing the Mediterranean port of Narbonne (719).

After defeating the Muslims at Covadonga (718), the Visigoths, under Prince Pelayo, established the Christian kingdom of Asturias.

Samah, governor of Spain, led Muslim forces invading Aquitaine; they surrounded Toulouse but were defeated, and Samah was killed by Eudo of Aquitaine (721). Samah's successor, Abd er-Rahman (Abdul Rahman), repeatedly raided Aquitaine and southern France (721-725).

Facing an Arab Muslim threat, Leo III (the Isaurian) deposed and replaced Theodosius III as Byzantine emperor (717).

Arab Muslim forces under general Maslama crossed the Hellespont to besiege Constantinople (July 717), sending part of their army to Bulgaria to block Byzantine reinforcements from the west; a major assault in August was repelled, with heavy Muslim losses.

A huge Muslim armada under Suleiman, seeking to blockade Constantinople, was decisively defeated and driven back into the Sea of Marmara by Leo III's Byzantine forces and their use of Greek fire (Sept. 717), keeping supply lines open to the Black Sea.

Suleiman was able to establish a partial blockade of Constantinople, until Leo III destroyed the Muslim fleet in a surprise attack (June? 718).

Bulgarians under King Terbelis attacked and defeated Arab Muslim forces under Maslama at Adrianople (July? 718).

725-749

Under Anbaca (Anabasa), Muslims invaded southern France (725-726), taking Carcassonne, Nîmes, and Septimania (the coast between the Rhône River and the Pyrenees).

Charles Martel led a series of campaigns into Germany (726-732), conquering Bavaria and parts of Thuringia and Frisia.

Ravenna revolted against Leo III (726), encouraged by Pope Gregory, after Leo's ban against image worship; Leo tried unsuccessfully to retake Ravenna (731), losing part of his invasion fleet in a storm; Lombards also attacked the city, taking but then losing part of it (728).

Charles Martel invaded Aquitaine (731), taking Berry, in the region of Bourges.

b. Abd er-Rahman I (Abd-al-Rahman ibn Mu'awiyah) (731-788), Arab leader.

Abd er-Rahman (Abdul Rahman) and his Muslim forces invaded Aquitaine; at Bordeaux (732) they defeated Eudo, who quickly allied himself with Charles Martel's Christian forces. Muslim and Christian armies met near Tours (Poitiers), on the Vienne River (732), where Abd er-Rahman was decisively defeated and killed. Their expansion halted, the Muslims were pushed back to Spain, retaining only Septimania. Here Charles won the name Martel, meaning "hammer."

King Aethelbald of Mercia conquered the Saxon kingdom of Wessex (733).

Eudo's sons and successors revolted unsuccessfully against Charles Martel's rule of Aquitaine (735).

Muslim invasions of Frankish lands were stopped by Charles Martel at Valence (737) and Lyon (739).

Berbers in Morocco and Spain revolted against Muslim rule (740).

After Leo III instituted reforms directed against religious images (726), earning him the nickname "Iconoclast," Pope Gregory encouraged revolt in Byzantine territories; those in Italy, including Ravenna, increasingly came under papal control. Leo defeated a rebel fleet bound for Constantinople, then suppressed a revolt in Greece (726-727).

Arab Muslims again invaded through the Caucasus Mountains, taking Georgia and defeating the Khazars (727-731); at some point in this period, the Khazar leaders, pressed by both Christians and Muslims, converted to Judaism; Khazaria became the only independent Jewish state in existence between the time of the Romans and the 20th century.

700-724 (cont.)

b. Abu al-Abbas (Abu'l Abbas) (ca. 721-754), Abbasid ruler (r. 750-754).

Muslim forces under Maslama suppressed a revolt against Omayyad rule led by Yazid ibn Mohallib, who was defeated at Akra, on the Euphrates (721).

Muslim forces under Mohammed ibn al-Kassim took Kabul and Sind, defeating India's King Dahar after a successful siege of Multan; they then campaigned in the Punjab, failing to defeat the Gurjaras in Rajputana and Gujarat (708-712).

Under Hsuan Tsung (r. 712-756), the Chinese confirmed their dominance over Central Asia's Oxus and Jaxartes valleys.

d. Qutayba ibn Muslim (?-715), Omayyad general who led the expansion into Central Asia (705-715); he was killed in a troop mutiny.

Muslim armies under Yemenite general Yazid ibn Mohallib conquered the region between the Oxus River and the Caspian Sea (716).

725-749

Arab Muslims unsuccessfully invaded eastern Anatolia (726).

Again counterattacking against the Arab Muslims, Khazars invaded through the Caucasus as far as Mesopotamia before being pushed back to their homeland (731-733).

Byzantine forces led by Leo III defeated invading Arab Muslims at Akroinon (Afyon Karahisar), in Anatolia (739).

Berbers and Kharijites successfully revolted against Omayyad Muslim rule in Morocco (741-742).

d. Leo III the Isaurian (ca. 680-741), Byzantine emperor (r. 717-741) who staved off an Arab attack on Constantinople (718). He was succeeded by his son Constantine V.

Under Constantine V, Byzantine forces invaded Syria (741), were repelled, and invaded again (745), taking some borderlands.

After widespread revolts and dynastic battles, Omayyad caliph Marwan II regained control of Syria, Iraq, Arabia, and most of Persia (744-748).

Constantine V's Byzantine fleet defeated the Arab Muslims near Cyprus, driving them from the island (746).

Abbasid revolt against the Omayyads spread to Persia and Mesopotamia, where Abu al-Abbas proclaimed himself caliph at Kufa (749).

Muslim forces were defeated by Turkish troops with Chinese leaders near Samarkand (730) and Kashgar (736), but under Nasr ibn Sayyar, they won near Balkh (737).

Under Yasovarman, the Kanauj Empire conquered Bengal (730) and the Ganges Valley. Its drive north was blocked by Kashmir, the dominant power in the Punjab, under Lalitaditya.

Chalukya's Vikramaditya II, grandson of Vikramaditya I, overwhelmed the Pallava dynasty (ca. 730-740).

China reconquered the T'ai state of Nanchao in Yunnan (730).

Gurjaras, under King Nagabhata, founded the Pratihara dynasty (740), foiling numerous Arab Muslim attacks on Rajputana and Gujarat.

Uighur Turks of northern Mongolia defeated the Eastern Turks, ruling the lands between lakes Balkash and Baikal (ca. 745), allied with China.

Last written record of Li-Kan (ca. 746), the city settled in Chinese borderlands (36 BC) apparently by Roman legionaries, taken first by the Parthians and then by the Chinese.

Descendants of Mohammed's first cousin and companion Al-Abbas led an Abbasid revolt in Khorasan against Omayyad rule (747); under Abu Muslim they took Merv

725-749 (cont.)

d. Charles Martel (the Hammer) (ca. 688-741), Frankish leader who halted the Muslim advance at Tours (732). His two sons — Carloman and Pepin III (Pepin the Short) — became co-mayors of the palace.

b. Charlemagne (Karl der Grosse; Carolus Magnus) (742-814), Frankish king (r. 768-814) and Holy Roman Emperor, effectively emperor of the old Western Roman Empire (r. 800-814).

Pepin III conquered Septimania for the Franks, driving Muslim forces back across the Pyrenees (743-759).

Mercians led by King Aethelbald conquered Northumbria (744).

750-774

In Spain the Christian kingdom of Asturias expanded to include Galicia (750).

Sole mayor of the palace after his brother's resignation (747), Pepin III deposed the last Merovingian, Childeric III, and was himself crowned king of the Franks (751).

Lombards under Aistulf took Ravenna, the former Byzantine capital in Italy (752); they had held it briefly in 728.

Pepin III and his Frankish forces invaded Italy at the request of Pope Stephen II, retaking Ravenna (754) and winning Aistulf's promise to cease raiding Rome.

Abd er-Rahman, an Omayyad who had fled the Abbasids, founded the Emirate of Cordova (755), largely blocking Christian expansion in Spain.

After Aistulf again attacked Rome, Pepin III invaded Italy, defeating the Lombards near Ravenna (756); captured lands were donated to Pope Stephen II, establishing the Catholic Church as a temporal power.

Pepin III suppressed a Bavarian revolt led by Duke Tassilo III (757).

Under Offa (r. 757-769), Aethelbald's successor, Mercia established its dominance over the lands south of Scotland — a first, brief unification of England.

d. Aistulf (?-757), Lombard ruler who took Ravenna (752) but was blocked from further conquests by the Franks under Pepin III.

After a long campaign, Pepin III suppressed a revolt in Aquitaine led by Duke Waifer (760-768).

Tassilo III, duke of Bavaria, led a successful revolt against the Franks (763).

d. Pepin III le Bref (the Short) (714?-768), king of the Franks (r. 751-768) and son of Charles Martel. His two sons, Carloman and Charles, succeeded him as corulers, with Charles (Charlemagne) then becoming sole ruler (r. 771-814).

Charlemagne began a long series of campaigns against the Saxons (772-799).

Byzantine emperor Constantine V defeated Slav forces in Thrace (758).

Constantine V's Byzantine troops defeated Bulgar forces at Marcellae (759) and Anchialus (763), in eastern Thrace.

Constantine V again defeated Bulgar forces in Thrace (772).

725-749 (cont.)

from the Omayyad governor, Nasr ibn Sayyar (748), who was also defeated at Nishapur, Jurjan, Nehawand, and Kerbela.

750-774

Omayyad caliph Marwan II, who had fled to Egypt during the Abbasid revolt, was defeated and killed at the Greater Zab by Abu al-Abbas, who founded the Abbasid dynasty (750) and killed most of his surviving Omayyad opponents.

During the Muslim civil wars, Byzantine forces campaigned in Mesopotamia (750-754) and retook Armenia (751-752).

d. Abu al-Abbas (Abu'l Abbas) (ca. 721-754), Muslim caliph (r. 750-754) and founder of the Abbasid dynasty; called al-Saffah (the Bloodshedder) for his execution of many rivals. He was succeeded by Al-Mansur, who, with Abu Muslim's help, suppressed revolts against him (754).

d. Abu Muslim (720-755), Abbasid general who commanded the Arab army at the Talas River (751).

Abbasid forces suppressed a rebellion by Shi'ite Muslims at Bakhamra (762); Al-Mansur established his capital at Baghdad.

b. Harun ar-Rashid (Harun ar-Rashid ibn Muhammad al-Mahdi ibn al-Mansur al-Abbasi) (ca. 763-809), Abbasid caliph (r. 786-809).

Gopala established the Pala dynasty (750), ruling all of Bengal.

Allied Arab and Tibetan forces defeated Chinese forces under Chinese-Korean general Kao Hsien-chih at the Talas River, in Kirghizia (751); one of the key battles of history, it ended Chinese westward expansion; Chinese forces were saved from disaster by their Uighur Turk allies.

Khitan Mongols, descendants of the Hsien Pi, invaded northern China (751-755); while Chinese forces under general An Lu-shan held them off, Tibet, Korea, and Nan-chao all declared their independence.

Dantidurga defeated Chalukya ruler Kirtivarman II, founding the new Rashtrakuta dynasty (753) and quickly expanding.

Northern Chinese warlord An Lu-shan and his rebel army took Loyang, making it his capital; An Lu-shan proclaimed himself emperor (755), then took the T'ang capital, Chang'an (Xian); the rebellion was defeated by Chinese and Uighur Turk forces at Sui Yang (757) and, after An Lu-shan's death (757), at Loyang (763). During the war Tibetan troops under Khrisong Detsen sacked Ch'ang-an (763).

d. Kao Hsien-chih (?-755), Korean-born Chinese general who led T'ang forces at the Talas River (751).

Arab and Persian traders sacked Canton (758), ending foreign trade until 792.

750-774 (cont.)

After Desiderius, king of the Lombards, threatened papal lands, the pope called in Charlemagne, who besieged Pavia, captured Desiderius, and annexed Lombardy (773-774).

775-799

Frankish forces invaded northern Spain, initially with some success against the emir of Cordova (777).

Frankish army was forced to retreat from Spain, attacked by both the Muslims and the Christian Basques; Charlemagne's nephew Roland and his rear guard, who covered the retreat, were annihilated in the pass of Roncesvalles (778), an event commemorated in the epic poem *Chanson de Roland (Song of Roland)*, told in various versions throughout Christian Europe for centuries.

Charlemagne suppressed a Saxon rebellion led by Widukind (779-780).

In the massacre of Verden, at the Aller River, Charlemagne and the Franks reportedly killed thousands of Saxon rebels surrendered to them by the Saxon nobles (782).

Charlemagne made peace with the Saxon noble Widukind, who was baptized (785); mass baptisms followed; many Saxons were deported to the Frankish lands, while some Franks settled in Saxony.

In Bavaria, Charlemagne suppressed another revolt by Tassilo III (787-788), who was sent to a monastery.

d. Abd er-Rahman I (Abd-al-Rahman ibn Mu'awiyah) (731-788), Arab ruler and commander who stopped Charlemagne's forces in Spain, pursuing them through the pass of Roncesvalles (778).

Vikings made their first recorded raid on Britain, near Dorchester (789).

Danish Vikings raided Lindisfarne Island, off Northumbria (793).

Vikings made their first recorded raids against Scotland (794) and Ireland (795), followed by many more.

Slav forces were defeated in Macedonia and Greece by Byzantine general Staurakios (783).

Over objections from the Byzantine Empire, Charlemagne conquered Istria, around modern Trieste, on the northeastern Adriatic (789).

Deposed by an army mutiny (790), Byzantine queen Irene returned to share power with her son (792), becoming sole ruler (797) after blinding him.

Campaigning in the central Danube Valley, Charlemagne and his son Pepin defeated Avar forces and, farther south, Slavs, conquering parts of Croatia and Slovenia (791-796).

800-824

Charlemagne was crowned Holy Roman Emperor (*Romanorum gubernans imperius*) in Rome by Pope Leo III (800).

Having defeated the Basques and driven the Muslims south of the Ebro River, Charlemagne besieged and took Barcelona (800-801).

Danish Vikings raided up the Elbe River (809-812) but were largely held in check by the Frankish fleet at Boulogne.

Charlemagne drove back Danes under Godfred, who were invading Frisia (the Netherlands) (810).

After widespread raids on islands and coastal regions (from ca. 810), the Vikings took and sacked Dorstadt and Utrecht (834).

Byzantine queen Irene was deposed for the second time and exiled to Lesbos (802).

Charlemagne campaigned against the Byzantine Empire in Dalmatia and on the Adriatic (803-810), finally giving up his eastern conquests, except Istria, when the Byzantine emperor Nicephorus I recognized him as emperor of the Western Roman Empire (810).

Nicephorus I led Byzantine forces in an invasion of Bulgaria (809), taking the capital of Pliska, but he was defeated and killed by Bulgarian leader Krum (811).

b. Basil I (the Macedonian) (812-886), Byzantine emperor (r. 867-886).

		750-774 (cont.)

		775-799

Byzantine forces defeated Arab Muslims at Germanicopolis (Gangra) (778), turning back another invasion of Anatolia.

During the regency of Queen Irene (r. 780-790), the Byzantine Greeks paid tribute to Arab Muslims, who had reached the Bosporus.

Khazar forces raided Georgia, held by Arab Muslims (790).

Caliph Harun ar-Rashid led Arab Muslim forces on another invasion of Anatolia (797-798), defeating Byzantines under Nicephorus I at Heraclea, again receiving tribute.

Sakanoue Tamuramaro (active 780-806), Japanese general who led expansion campaigns against the Ainu people of northern Honshu island (780-800), pushing Japanese borders to the Tsugaru Strait.

After a period of succession wars and defeats by the Ainu, central power was restored in Japan under Emperor Kammu (781).

		800-824

Idris ibn Abdulla founded an independent Arab-Berber emirate in Morocco and western Algeria (ca. 800).

Abbasid governor Ibrahim ibn Aghlab established the independent Aghlabid dynasty, centered at Kairouan, in Tunisia (801).

Muslims under Harun ar-Rashid invaded Byzantine dominions in Anatolia (803, 804, 805-807), winning at Crasus (805) against Nicephorus I.

Arab Muslim fleets devastated Rhodes and took Cyprus (805-807).

Nicephorus I and his Byzantine forces retook much of Anatolia, driving Harun ar-Rashid eastward into Khorasan (808).

d. Harun ar-Rashid (Harun ar-Rashid ibn Muhammad al-Mahdi ibn al-Mansur al-Abbasi) (ca. 763-809), Abbasid caliph (r. 786-809) who expanded his empire

Dharmapala, son of Gopala, expanded from Bengal to the Punjab, taking the remains of the Kanauj Empire (ca. 800).

In Southeast Asia, Lower Chenla (Funan) was revived under Jayavarman II (r. 802-805) as the Khmer kingdom, famed for its later temples and palaces at Angkor.

Harun ar-Rashid retreated into Khorasan after a Byzantine offensive (808) and was killed trying to suppress a rebellion (809).

General Tahir ibn Husain was made viceroy of Khorasan and the eastern Muslim provinces, founding the Tahirid dynasty (821).

Western Europe	Eastern Europe

800-824 (cont.)

d. Charlemagne (Karl der Grosse; Carolus Magnus) (742-814), Frankish king (r. 768-814) who was crowned Holy Roman Emperor in Rome by Pope Leo III (800), becoming emperor of the old Western Roman Empire.	Led by Krum, Bulgarians defeated Byzantine forces in several battles, notably at Versinikia (813), then took Adrianople and threatened Constantinople; after Byzantine general Leo the Armenian deposed and replaced the new emperor, Michael, the Byzantines decisively defeated Bulgarians under Krum's son Omortag at Mesembria (817).
Under Abd ar-Rahman II (r. 822-852), Spanish Muslims fought off Christian invasions by Alfonso II from Asturias and by the Franks.	
b. Charles II le Chauvre (the Bald) (823-877), Frankish king (r. 840-877) and Holy Roman Emperor (r. 875-877).	

825-849

At Ellandun, Beornwulf of Mercia was defeated by Egbert of Wessex (825), then the dominant kingdom in England.	Arab Muslims took Crete (825-826) and invaded Sicily (827).
Aghlabid forces from Tunisia invaded and took most of Sicily, leaving the Byzantines only Syracuse and Taormina (827-831).	Bulgars raided widely in Croatia and Pannonia (827-829).
Vikings under Thorgest first raided beyond the coast of Ireland (832).	b. Michael III (838-867), Byzantine emperor (r. 842-867).
Norwegian Vikings began to make permanent settlements on the Scottish mainland (ca. 835).	Byzantine forces campaigned against Slavs and Arabs, retaking Crete (843).
Aghlabids from Tunisia raided widely in southern and central Italy (836-909), even sacking part of Rome (846).	
Christian and Jewish revolt against Muslim rule in Toledo was put down by Abd-er-Rahman II (837).	
Egbert, Saxon king of Wessex, defeated Welsh and Viking invaders at Hingston Down (838).	
Vikings conquered Frisia (ca. 840-ca. 890).	
At Fontenay (Fontenat) near Sens, two of Charlemagne's grandsons, Louis the German and Charles the Bald, defeated their older brother and king, Lothair I (841); the Treaty of Verdun divided the empire among the three (843), with Lothair taking Italy, Burgundy, and Lotharingia; Louis Germany; and Charles France.	
Thorgest and his Norwegian Vikings captured fortified Dublin and Annagassan (841), coming to rule half of Ireland.	
Vikings first settled around the Loire River (843).	
In Ireland, Norse leader Thorgest was killed in battle by Mael Sechnaill, king of Mide (845).	
Vikings first raided Paris (845).	

850-874

Vikings sacked London and Canterbury before being defeated at Ockley by the Saxon king of Wessex, Aethelwulf (850).	Young Byzantine emperor Michael III threw off his regency to take full power, influenced by his uncle Bardas (858).
Vikings made their first permanent settlement in England, near Margate (851).	Swedish Vikings (Rus; Varangians) conquered the region of Novgorod (ca. 862), under their semilegendary leader Rurik.
Vikings sailed up the Elbe and sacked Hamburg (851).	Magyars, a Eurasian people related to the Finns and Turks, made their first foray west of the Danube (862), pushed out

800-824 (cont.)

to include northern Africa and all southwest Asia, making Baghdad a major cultural center. Civil war followed his death.

Khurramite Muslims from Azerbaijan, led by Babek, raided widely in Persia and Mesopotamia (from 816).

Muslim pirates from Spain captured Alexandria (ca. 817).

d. Leo V (the Armenian) (?-820), Byzantine emperor (r. 813-820) who fought the Bulgarians.

825-849

Arab Muslims from Spain took Crete, making it a pirate base (825-826).

Abbasid general Abdullah ibn Tahir retook Alexandria from Muslim pirates based there (827).

Arabs and Christian Copts rebelled in Egypt (828-832) but were suppressed at Basharud in the Nile Delta.

Abbasid caliph Abu Ishak al-Mu'tasim formed a new, primarily Turkish imperial bodyguard (ca. 833).

Abbasid forces under general Afshin finally turned back Khurramite Muslim invaders (835-837).

Byzantine troops under Emperor Theophilus invaded deep into Syria (837), taking and sacking Samosata and Aibatra (837).

Caliph al-Mu'tasim led an Abbasid army into Anatolia, defeating Theophilus's Byzantine army at the Halys River, at Dasymon (Anzan), then taking and sacking Amorium and Ancyra (838).

Muslim fleet bound for Constantinople was destroyed in a storm (839).

Abbasid imperial bodyguard, under Turkish general Bogha, put down a rebellion in Arabia (844-845).

T'ang forces fought off an invasion by the Nanchao, from Burma, defeating them at Ch'engtu (829).

Under Nagabhata II, the Indian state of Pratibara defeated the Pala to take Kanauj (ca. 830).

Under King Vijayala (r. 836-870), Chola was the dominant state in southern India.

Kirghiz and Karluk Turks defeated the Uighur Turks, driving them into the southern Tarim Basin (ca. 846).

Tibetans, who had gradually resumed control of Kansu, were expelled by T'ang forces (848).

850-874

Zinj (Black African) slaves revolted and sacked Basra, the main port of southern Mesopotamia, ruling the region for more than a dozen years (mid-9th c.).

Byzantine forces attacked Egypt, sacking Damietta (853).

Emperor Michael III's Byzantine army lost to the Muslims in northern Syria (860).

Caliph Ja-far Al-Mutawakkil was killed by his Turkish bodyguard (861).

Norse explorers reached Iceland (ca. 850), soon beginning substantial settlement.

b. Chu Wen (Chu Ch'üan-chung) (852-912), Chinese rebel general and warlord.

Kingdom of Sanjaya won a battle for dominance in central Java, defeating the state of Sailendra on the Ratubaka plain (856).

850-874 (cont.)

Frankish king Charles the Bald was defeated by the Vikings at Givald's Foss (852) and failed to take the Viking base at Oiselle, an island in the Seine (858).

Charles the Bald blocked a Viking attack up the Marne, aimed at Paris (862).

Irish king Aed Findliath temporarily drove the Vikings out of northern Ireland (862-879).

Vikings sailed up the Rhine, raiding widely (863).

Under Alfonso III (r. 866-910), Asturias expanded Christian Spain to the Duero (Douro) River, later called León after its capital.

Danish Vikings under Halfdan defeated Northumbria at York (867), also conquering and settling in Mercia and East Anglia.

Aethelred and Alfred (the Great) of Wessex unsuccessfully tried to retake Mercia from the Vikings (868).

Edmund (later Saint) of East Anglia was killed fighting the Vikings at Hoxne (870).

Aethelred and Alfred of Wessex defeated the Danish Vikings at Englefield (Dec. 870); they lost badly at Reading, won again at Ashdown, then lost again at Marton and, after Aethelred's death, Wilton (all 871).

of the Don Basin by a Turkish people called the Pechenegs (Patzinaks).

Swedish Vikings first raided as far south as the Bosporus, threatening Constantinople (865).

Michael III proclaimed as coemperor Basil, who had killed Michael's uncle Bardas (865).

Byzantine emperor Michael III invaded Bulgaria, successfully pressing King Boris I and his Bulgarian subjects to convert to Christianity (866).

d. Michael III (838-867), Byzantine emperor (r. 842-867); he was assassinated by his coemperor, who became Basil I.

Orthodox Church of Byzantium, under Bishop Photius, who had been excommunicated by the pope in Rome, separated itself from Rome (867); the East-West religious split was formalized at the Council of Constantinople (869).

875-899

Under Basil I, Byzantine forces retook Bari (875), Tarentum (880), and Calabria (885) from the Arab Muslims; at Bari they were aided by the Holy Roman Empire under Louis II; they failed to recapture Sicily.

Danish Vikings under Guthrum invaded Wessex, taking Wareham (876) and Exeter (877) and defeating Alfred at Chippenham (Jan. 878) before losing badly to Alfred at Edington (May 878), then abandoning Wessex.

After the death of Louis the German (876), Charles the Bald tried to take Germany but was stopped at Andernach.

d. Charles II le Chauvre (the Bald) (823-877), Frankish king (r. 840-877) and Holy Roman Emperor (r. 875-877).

Aghlabids took Syracuse from the Byzantines (878).

Vikings again sacked Hamburg (880).

Vikings defeated the Franks under Charles the Fat at Ashloh (882).

Charles the Fat briefly resurrected Charlemagne's empire (884-887), except for Burgundy, before being deposed for his handling of the Viking attack on Paris (886); he was replaced by Count Odo.

Vikings under Siegfried and Sinric besieged Paris, successfully defended within its fortifications by Count Odo (Eudes)

d. Rurik (Ryurik; Rörik) (?-ca. 879), Swedish Varangian (Rus) ruler; a semilegendary figure who took Novgorod and established the state that would become Russia.

Byzantine naval forces took control of the eastern Mediterranean from the Arab Muslims (880-881).

Under Prince Oleg (r. ca. 880-912), the Swedish Viking (Rus) states of Kiev and Novgorod were combined, forming the state of Russia.

d. Basil I (the Macedonian) (812-886), Byzantine emperor (r. 867-886) who took the throne after murdering his predecessor, Michael III; he retook southern Italy (875-885).

Arnulf and his German forces, assisted by Magyars, stopped an invasion of Slavs, led by Sviatopluk of Moravia (892-893).

Symeon of Bulgaria was at war with the Byzantine Empire (894-897).

Defeated by Pechenegs and Bulgars, Magyar forces under Arpad drove into the central Danube Basin (ca. 895).

Africa and Southwest Asia	East, Central, and South Asia, the Pacific, and the Americas
Abbasid general Omar's Muslim army campaigned widely in Anatolia before being destroyed by the Byzantines under Petronas (863). Turkish governor Ahmed ibn Tulun proclaimed his independence, founding the brief Tulunid dynasty in Egypt (r. 868-876). After Turkish guards presided over a period of anarchy, Ahmad Al-Mu'tamid and his brother Abu Ahmad al-Muwaffak restored central authority in Mesopotamia and Iraq (870-883). Byzantine emperor Basil I invaded Abbasid territory, winning a key victory at Samosata (873).	Kingdom of Nanchao, centered in Burma, attacked Chinese dominions in south China and Tonkin (858-863) but were defeated by T'ang forces at Hanoi (863). Under Fujiwara Yoshifusa, the Fujiwara clan became the first to control the emperor, and therefore the whole of Japan (858). Huang Ch'ao led an initially successful rebellion against China's T'ang dynasty (868-884). Norwegian Vikings made their first permanent settlement on Iceland (ca. 870). Saffarids led by Yakub ibn Laith threw off Tahirid rule in the East (872), later threatening Baghdad (876). b. A-Pao-Chi (Ye-lu A-pao-chi) (ca. 872-926), Khitan ruler. Chinese general Kao P'ien drove Nanchao invaders from Tonkin and then from Szechuan, to which they fled (874).
Tulunids from Egypt conquered most of Syria (878-884). Carmathian Muslims, a Shi'ite sect led by Abu Sa'id al-Jannabi, rebelled against Abbasid rule (899-903); though defeated in Syria by general Mohammed ibn Sulaiman, they founded an independent kingdom in northeastern Arabia.	Huang Ch'ao's Rebellion: Chinese rebels in Canton (Guangzhon) reportedly killed an estimated 120,000 Christian, Muslim, Jewish, and Persian traders (878), ending foreign trade for nearly a century. Huang Ch'ao's Rebellion: Rebel forces took Loyang (Nov. 880) and the imperial capital, Ch'ang-an (Dec. 880), but the rebels were finally defeated by T'ang forces under Li K'o-yung, a general of Turkish ancestry (882-884), after which Huang Ch'ao committed suicide. Under King Yasovarman (r. 889-900), the Khmer (Angkor) Empire reached its widest extent, including Cambodia, southwestern Vietnam, southern Burma, and most of Laos and Thailand. Under Mahendrapala (r. 890-910), Pratihara became the dominant state of northern India.

Western Europe	Eastern Europe

875-899 (cont.)

and Bishop Gozelin (885-886); the attackers eventually left after payment of a large ransom.

At Hafrs Fjord, near Stavanger, Harald I Harfager (Fairhair) won a power struggle to become Norwegian king (ca. 886).

Vikings under Sinric conducted an unsuccessful siege of Sens (886-887).

Muslim raiders took parts of Provence, some of which they would hold for more than a century, as they also took more (890-975).

Arnulf, king of the East Franks (Germans), successfully assaulted the Vikings' fortified base at Louvain (891), largely ending raids into Germany.

b. Abd er-Rahman III (Abd-al-Rahman al-Nasir) (891-961), Moroccan-Spanish ruler.

Alfred of Wessex and his son Edward repelled Danish land and sea invasions of Kent and Wessex; the defeated invaders then settled in Danish-held regions of England (893-896).

After an expedition to Italy, Arnulf was crowned Holy Roman Emperor (896).

Magyars made their first raids into northern Italy (899).

900-924

Aghlabids took Taormina, the last Byzantine territory in Sicily (902).

Muslims under Isam-al-Khamlami took the Balearic Islands from the Franks (903).

A new invasion of Danish Vikings was stopped by Edward of Wessex (905), who then campaigned in Danish England, winning notably at Tetlenhall (910).

After extensive raiding in northern France, Vikings under Rollo were granted the Duchy of Normandy by the Frankish king Charles the Simple in the Treaty of St. Clair-sur-Epte (911).

Norwegian Vikings captured and fortified Waterford (914) and Limerick in Ireland (920).

Vikings from Brittany invaded up England's Severn River but were driven off by Edward of Wessex (914).

After a long conflict, the Byzantines effectively ended Muslim control in southern Italy, winning at the Garigliano River (915).

At Tempsford, Edward of Wessex defeated and killed Guthrum II, Danish king of East Anglia (918), largely ending the Viking threat to southern England.

Irish king Niall Glundub was defeated and killed in an assault on Viking-held Dublin (919).

Count Robert of Paris, Odo's brother, revolted against France's Charles III (921); Robert defeated Charles but later was killed at Soissons (923).

Leo the Wise wrote the military treatise *Tactica* (900).

Magyars first raided Bavaria (900).

Magyars defeated the kingdom of Moravia (906), pushing the Slavs out of the Danube and Theiss valleys to found Hungary (906).

At Augsburg Magyars defeated German forces (910).

b. Otto I (the Great) (912-973), German emperor (r. 936-973).

Again at war with the Byzantines (913-924), Symeon of Bulgaria took Macedonia, Thessaly, and Albania (ca. 914) and then Serbia (918), temporarily taking Adrianople (914) but only threatening Constantinople; meanwhile, he lost territory to others, notably Transylvania and Pannonia to the Magyars and Wallachia to the Pechenegs.

Magyars raided widely in the Rhine and Danube valleys (924).

900-924

Empire of Ghana conquered the Sanhajah Berber peoples, gaining control of the trans-Sahara salt trade (10th c.).

Shi'ites led by Abu Abdullah al-Husain (al-Shi'i) successfully revolted against the Aghlabids of Tunisia, founding the Fatimid dynasty (so-named because its rulers were descended from Mohammed's daughter, Fatimah), with 'Obaidallah al-Mahdi as caliph (r. 902-909).

Abbasid forces under general Mohammed ibn Sulaiman retook Egypt from the Tulinids (904-905).

b. Nicephorus II Phocas (912-969), Byzantine soldier-emperor (r. 963-969).

Fatimid forces under Abu'l Kasim al-Kaim twice invaded Egypt and took Alexandria before being driven back by the Abbasid general Mu'nis (914-915; 919-921).

Fatimids under 'Obaidallah al-Mahdi defeated the Idrisids, taking their Moroccan emirate (922).

Carmathian Muslims, in continuing rebellion, sacked Basra (923), Kufa (925), and Mecca (929).

Muslim pirates led by Leo of Tripoli were decisively defeated by the Byzantine navy at Lemnos (924).

b. John I Zimisces (Tzimisces) (924-976), Byzantine emperor (r. 969-976).

Chinese general Chu Wen ended the T'ang dynasty by killing the last emperor (907), triggering the Wars of the Five Dynasties (907-959).

Under Ye-lu A-pao-chi (r. 907-926), the Khitans, a Mongol people, conquered Inner Mongolia, southern Manchuria, and much of northern China.

Gunpowder was developed in China; it was not initially used for weapons (ca. 908).

d. Chu Wen (Chu Ch'üan-chung) (852-912), Chinese rebel general and warlord who ended the T'ang dynasty, founding the Later Liang dynasty (907).

In central Korea general Wanggun founded the Wang dynasty in the kingdom of Koryo, with its capital at Kaesong (918); Koryo absorbed Silla, as its last king abdicated.

Western Europe	Eastern Europe

900-924 (cont.)

Aethelstan of Wessex, son of Edward, reconquered Danish-held lands in northern England (924-939).	

925-949

Western Europe	Eastern Europe
Magyars raiding in northern Italy were defeated by Rudolph of Burgundy and Hugh of Vienne, then went on to raid Provence and Septimania (926).	Under Prince Chaslav, part of Serbia again became independent (931).
Abd er-Rahman III reunited Muslim Spain, naming himself caliph of Córdoba (Jan. 16, 929), asserting his independence from the Omayyads in Baghdad.	German king Henry the Fowler defeated Magyar forces at Riade (Merseberg), near Erfurt (933).
Ramiro II of León defeated Abd er-Rahman III at Simancas (934) and Zamora (939).	Otto I (the Great), son of Henry the Fowler, came to power in Germany (936), winning two civil wars to secure his throne.
Aethelstan of Wessex invaded Scotland (934), defeating Constantine III of Scotland and his Welsh and Irish-Norse allies at Brunanburgh (937) in Dumfrieshire and unifying Britain (937).	Byzantine navy defeated Russian raiders at the Bosporus (941).
Fatimid Muslim fleet captured and sacked Genoa (934).	Magyar raiders reached Constantinople (942) but left after being paid a tribute.
b. Brian Boru (941-1014), high king of Ireland (r. 1002-1014).	Otto I suppressed a revolt (944-947) led by Bertold, duke of Bavaria, whom he defeated at Wels (947).

950-974

Western Europe	Eastern Europe
Deposed Norwegian king Eric Bloodax, son of Harald I Harfager, invaded northern England, ruling briefly in Northumbria (950; 952-954) before being defeated and killed at Stanmore (954).	Germany's Otto I established his control over Bohemia by defeating Duke Boleslav (950).
German king Otto I led an expedition to Italy, called in by Adelaide, widow of King Lothair, whom he married, also taking the title king of the Lombards (951-952).	Though defeated and captured, Otto I later escaped to put down a revolt led by his son Ludolf; Conrad, duke of Lorraine; and Frederick, bishop of Mainz (953-955).
Again called into Italy, this time by the pope, Otto defeated King Berengar II (961) and was crowned Holy Roman Emperor by Pope John XII (962), whom he then deposed and replaced with Pope Leo VIII (963).	In the Great Magyar Raid, tens of thousands of invading Magyars brought devastation to Bavaria, France, Italy, and the Drava and Danube valleys (954).
Haakon I Den Gode (the Good), who had tried unsuccessfully to bring Christianity to Norway, was killed at Fitjar, an island off Norway, by several of his nephews, aided by the Danish king Harald I Blatand (Bluetooth) (961).	Magyars besieging Augsburg were attacked by a much smaller German army under Otto I; they were defeated, with heavy losses, at Lechfeld (955), effectively ending Magyar raids into Germany.
d. Abd ar-Rahman III (Abd-al-Rahman al-Nasir) (891-961), Moroccan-Spanish ruler, self-proclaimed caliph of Córdoba (r. 929-961).	Slavic Wends were defeated by Otto I at the Recknitz River (955).
	b. Vladimir I (Saint Vladimir) (ca. 956-1015), grand prince of Kiev (r. 980-1015).

925-949

From their center at Dailam, Shi'ites under Merdawj ibn Ziyar expanded southward in Persia (ca. 925).

As the Abbasid dynasty crumbled, the Hamdanid dynasty established itself in northeastern Syria and Kurdistan (ca. 929).

Ziyarids were overthrown and pushed into the Caucasus by other Shi'ites led by three brothers, who founded the Buyid dynasty (932).

After a series of campaigns, Byzantine forces under John Kurkuas pushed the imperial frontier eastward, taking Theodosiopolis (Erzerum) (928) and Melitene (Malatya) (934).

After years of anarchy, Abbasid general Mohammed ibn Tughj took control in Egypt, founding the Ikhshid (Ruler) dynasty (935).

Ikhshid dynasty of Egypt won a scramble for Syria (941).

Hamdanid prince Saif al-Dawla took Aleppo and most of northern Syria from the Ikhshidites (944).

Buyids of Persia, led by Mu'izz al-Dawlam, took the Abbasid capital of Baghdad (946).

d. A-Pao-Chi (Ye-lu A-pao-chi) (ca. 872-926), Khitan ruler who created an empire in north China, Manchuria, and Mongolia.

Under Te-kuang (r. 927-947), the Khitans, now as the Liao dynasty, expanded farther, exercising power even in anarchic China.

b. T'ai-Tsung (Chao K'uang-yin) (927-976), Chinese emperor (r. 960-976).

Clan rivalries in Japan broke into open civil war (935-941), with the most notable figures being Taira Masakado, finally defeated in eastern Japan (940), and Fujiwara Sumitomo, who temporarily controlled the Inland Sea until his defeat by the Taira League (941).

Koryo suppressed a rebellion by the state of Paekche (935), unifying Korea (936).

Nanchao armies conquered the Pyu kingdom in central Burma and Mon regions in the south before being driven back by the Mons (935).

Annam finally won its independence from a weakened China (939).

Ravendravarman II overthrew the Khmer ruler Harshavarman II and then ruled from Angkor (944), mounting an unsuccessful attack on Champa (945-946).

950-974

Byzantine troops under general Nicephorus Phocas retook eastern Anatolia and Crete (960-961), then invaded Cilicia and Syria, briefly taking Aleppo (962-963).

Hamdanid prince Saif al-Dawla, contending with the Byzantines and Ikhshidites for Syria, was defeated at Maghar-Alcohl by Leo Phocas, Nicephorus's brother (963).

Nicephorus II Phocas, now Byzantium's coemperor, took Cilicia and its key cities of Adana (964) and Tarsus (965) from the Muslims.

General Nicetas recaptured Cyprus for Byzantium (965).

Fatimid Muslims under Ja'far defeated the Ikhshidites at Ramleh, between Jerusalem and Jaffa, driving them from Syria and Palestine (969).

Under general Jauhur, the Fatimids finally conquered Egypt, defeating the Ikhshidites at Gizeh (969).

Invading Mesopotamia and Syria, Nicephorus II Phocas took Antioch and Aleppo (969); the Muslims sued for peace.

Mons, apparently allied with the Pyus, expanded into central Burma, establishing their capital at Pagan (ca. 950).

Under Krishna III (r. 939-968), Rashtrakuta crushed Chola power in India, killing their king, Parantaka (953).

Rejecting Srivijayan claims to Java, according to tradition, East Java's King Dharmauamsa (ca. 958-ca. 1000) unsuccessfully attacked the Srivijayans on Sumatra.

Chinese general Chao K'uang-yin was proclaimed the new emperor by the army; as T'ai Tsung, he founded the Sung dynasty (960), reunifying much of China, except the northern Liao dynasty, and ending the Wars of the Five Dynasties (907-959).

950-974 (cont.)

b. Olaf I Tryggvasson (ca. 964-1000), king of Norway (r. 995-1000).

Byzantine forces retook Taormina (965).

Otto I made a third expedition to Italy (966-972), campaigning successfully against the princes of southern Italy and the Byzantines, to whom he returned some territories in exchange for their recognition of him as emperor.

Byzantines, now under Nicetas, failed again to retake Sicily (966-967).

Ireland's king of Muster, Mathgamain, took the fortified city of Limerick from the Vikings (968).

Norwegian king Haakon Siggurdsson den Store (the Great) allied himself with Denmark's Harald I Blatand against the German emperor Otto II (ca. 974).

b. Basil II Bulgaroctonos (Bulgar-butcher) (ca. 958-1025), Byzantine emperor (r. 976-1025).

Under its first recorded ruler, Mieszko I (ca. 960-992), Poland expanded west to the Oder River.

Russians under Prince Sviatoslav defeated the Khazars on the lower Volga River (965); in doing so, they laid themselves open to raids from the Pechenegs, whom the Khazars had held back.

Bulgaria was overwhelmed by a Byzantine land attack under Nicephorus II Phocas and a Russian naval attack led by Prince Sviatoslav (967-969), who captured Bulgarian king Boris II; Byzantium annexed eastern Bulgaria.

Russians under Prince Sviatoslav repelled an invasion by Pechenegs (967-968).

Byzantines under coemperor John I Zimisces defeated Prince Sviatoslav and his Russian forces at the battles of Arcadiopolis (970), near Adrianople, and Dorostalon (971), forcing them out of Bulgaria.

d. Sviatoslav I (?-972), grand prince of Kiev (r. 945-972), probably Rurik's grandson; he was defeated and killed fighting Pecheneg forces; a succession struggle ensued among his three sons, Oleg, Yaropolk, and Vladimir (972-980).

d. Otto I (the Great) (912-973), German emperor (r. 936-973), who developed a strong central monarchy and conducted three expeditions into Italy (951-972). He was succeeded by his son Otto II, who faced widespread revolts (973-978), notably by his cousin Henry II (the Wrangler) of Bavaria and Duke Boleslav of Bohemia.

975-999

Mathgamain, king of Muster, in Ireland, was killed by a rival prince, Mael Muaid (975), who was himself killed and succeeded by Mathgamain's brother Brian Boru (976).

Lothair of France invaded Germany, temporarily occupying Aachen before being driven back and besieged by Otto II in Paris (978-980), thus failing to gain his aim: Lorraine.

Campaigning in Italy, Otto II lost badly to allied Muslim and Byzantine forces on land at Crotona and at sea off Stilo (982).

Sweyn I Tveskaeg (Forkbeard) killed his father, Harald I Blatand, succeeding him as Danish king (ca. 985).

After the Carolingian (Charlemagne's) line ended, the French elected Hugh Capet, count of Paris, as king, a title assumed after he won a civil war against Charles of Lorraine (987).

Ibin Abi Amir al-Mansour, military dictator of Muslim Spain, defeated the Spanish Christians, taking and sacking León.

Danish king Sweyn I Tveskaeg and his son Canute mounted a major invasion of England, winning numerous victories, most notably at Maldon in Essex (991).

b. Olaf II Haraldsson (ca. 995-1030), king of Norway (r. 1016-1028).

Prince Vladimir won an eight-year fight with his brothers to take the Russian throne (980).

In a series of wars, Vladimir and his Russian forces conquered Chervensk (modern Galicia) (981), the region of modern Belarus (983), and most of Bulgaria (985), later adopting Christianity (988) and then forcibly converting his people.

Bulgarians under Samuel defeated Basil II's invading Byzantine forces near Sofia (981).

Generals Bardas Phocas and Bardas Skleros led a rebellion (987-989); although they threatened Constantinople (988), they were defeated at Abodys by the Byzantine emperor Basil II (989).

Bulgarians under Samuel began to win back eastern Bulgaria from the Byzantines (989-996).

Poland's Boleslav the Brave, son of Mieszko, took eastern Pomerania (994) and then Silesia, Moravia, and Cracow (999).

Byzantines led by Basil II retook Greece and Macedonia from the Bulgarians, defeating Samuel at the Spercheios River (996).

950-974 (cont.)

d. Nicephorus II Phocas (912-969), Byzantine soldier-emperor (r. 963-969) who served other emperors before becoming coruler (961); he was assassinated.

Carmathian Muslims invaded Palestine, defeating and killing Fatimid general ja'far (970).

Carmathian Muslims invaded Egypt and were defeated by Fatimid general Jauhur at Cairo (Victory) (971), there building the new capital of the Fatimid dynasty.

Byzantine forces under John I Zimisces reconquered lands west of the central Euphrates and took Damascus, but they were blocked by Muslims from taking Jerusalem (973-976).

Under al-Hakam II, son of Abd-er-Rahman III, Omayyad Muslims from Spain conquered Morocco (973), which for decades would be contested by the Omayyads, Fatimids, Idrisids, and Berbers.

Fatimid caliph Mu'izz repelled a new invasion of Egypt by Carmathian Muslims (974), driving them from Palestine and Syria (974-975); his empire now stretched from the western Mediterranean across North Africa to Syria and western Arabia.

Alptagin, a Turkish slave refugee from Bukhara, founded the Ghaznevid dynasty in Afghanistan (ca. 962).

Chalukya dynasty revived under Taila II (r. 973-997), supplanting Rashtrakuta.

975-999

Forces from Damot, in southern Ethiopia (possibly a Jewish kingdom called Demdem), personally led by Queen Esato (Judith), raided widely in Aksum (976).

d. John I Zimisces (Tzimisces) (924-976), Byzantine emperor (r. 969-976) who fought against the Russians, Bulgarians, and Muslims.

Persians and Arabs from the Persian Gulf, especially from Muscat, Shiraz, and Bushire, settled the East African coast, founding many cities, including Mogadishu, Melinde, Mombasa, Kilwa (Quiloa), and Sofala (ca. 980).

Though threatened by the Fatimid Muslims, the Byzantines under Basil II reconquered all of Syria (995-996).

d. T'ai-Tsung (Chao K'uang-yin) (927-976), Chinese emperor (r. 960-976) who founded the Sung dynasty (960).

Under Sabuktagin (r. 977-997), Alptagin's son-in-law and successor, Ghazni conquered much of Khorasan.

Annam fought off an invasion by the Cham king Paramesvaravarman (979).

Norse explorers, including Eric the Red and his father, Thorvald, reached Greenland (ca. 980), soon founding settlements there.

b. Suryavarman I (ca. 980-ca. 1050), Cambodian ruler (r. ca. 1010-ca. 1050).

Annamese under King Le Hoan invaded Champa, sacking the capital and killing the Cham king Paramesvaravarman (982).

Under Tamil king Rajaraja I (r. 985-1014), the southern Indian state of Chola expanded in the Deccan and on the coast

975-999 (cont.)

Muster's King Brian Boru defeated the king of Leinster and his Norse allies from Dublin at Glen Mama, in Ireland (999).

of the Bay of Bengal, conquering Pandya, Kerala (Chera), Vengi, and Kalinga.

Khitans pressing from Central Asia into northern China failed to take Peking (986).

In Annam, rebels overthrew King Le Hoan, who was eventually replaced by King Hrivarman II (989).

Sabuktagin of Ghazni pushed into India, taking Peshawar (ca. 990).

Persia's Saminid dynasty was driven out of Transoxiana by the Ilak Turks (ca. 990-999).

Tanguts, a Tibetan people, settled in Kansu, founding the Western Hsia kingdom (ca. 990).

b. Fan Chung-yen (990-1053), Chinese general.

Under Rajaraja I, India's Chola dynasty took Ceylon (Sri Lanka) (993) and the Maldive Islands.

1000 - 1699

Atlantic and Northern Europe

Central, Southern, and Eastern Europe

Africa and Southwest Asia

East, Central, and South Asia,
the Pacific, and the Americas

1000-1009

At Svolder (Svalde), Norway's Olaf I Tryggvasson was defeated and killed by the combined forces of Eric, Jarl of Lade; Olaf Skötkonung of Sweden; and Sweyn I of Denmark (1000), with Sweyn then effectively controlling Norway. The sea battle was the subject of numerous Scandinavian sagas.

d. Olaf I Tryggvasson (ca. 964-1000), king of Norway (r. 995-1000) who brought Christianity to his land; he led his troops against the Anglo-Saxons at the Battle of Maldon (991) and a siege of London (994), returning home to become king.

Brian Boru defeated Mael Sechnaill II to become Ireland's high king (1002).

Under King Sweyn I and his son Canute, the Danes conquered England (1003-1013); Saxon king Aethelred fled to Normandy.

Scotland was united under King Malcolm II (r. 1005-1034). Malcolm later lost at Nairn to invading Danish forces under Sweyn Forkbeard (1009) but repelled a second invasion at Mortlack (1010).

Holy Roman Emperor Henry II had persistent conflicts with Ardoin, king of Lombardy (1002-1014), finally deposing him.

Venetians captured Bari from the Muslims (1002).

The city-state of Pisa defeated Lucca (1003).

Boleslav of Poland defeated Germans under Henry II to take Lusatia and Silesia (1003-1017).

Basil II and his Byzantine forces retook Thrace and Macedonia from the Bulgarians (1007).

1010-1019

Saxon king Aethelred died in London while attempting to retake England from Canute (1014).

Danes from the Orkney Islands invaded Ireland and, though joined by Dublin's Danes, were defeated at Clontarf by Brian Boru, who was killed during the fight (1014).

d. Brian Boru (941-1014), high king of Ireland (r. 1002-1014); he died successfully fighting off invading Danes.

Edmund, Aethelred's son, continued the Saxon attempt to retake England from the Danes under Canute. Edmund won the Battle of Pen, in Somersetshire; fought to a draw in the Battle of Sherston, in Wiltshire; forced Canute to raise his siege of London; and lost badly at Assandun (Ashington). Edmund then died, leaving Canute sole ruler (1016).

Scotland's Malcolm II invaded Northumbria, winning the Battle of Carham on the Tweed River, which became Scotland's southern border (1018).

Muslims raided Pisa, their last successful attack on Italy (1011).

Byzantine emperor Basil II invaded Bulgaria, winning the decisive Battle of Balathista (Belasica) (1014); afterward he reportedly had 15,000 Bulgarian prisoners blinded, for which he was named "Bulgaroctonos" (Bulgar-butcher); he then completed taking the country (1018).

In Kiev the death of Vladimir (1015) sparked a dynastic war (1015-1019) among his sons, won by Prince Yaroslav; as Yaroslav the Wise (r. 1019-1054), he led Kiev in fighting off Polish and Pecheneg invaders. His rival Prince Mstislav maintained some independence east of the Dnieper River.

d. Vladimir I (Saint) (ca. 956-1015), grand prince of Kiev (r. 980-1015) who expanded his domain from the Ukraine to the Baltic, forcibly bringing Christianity to the area.

A combined Pisan-Genoese fleet drove Mogahid and his Muslim pirates from Sardinia, from which they had dominated the northwestern Mediterranean (1015-1016).

b. Robert Guiscard (Robert de Hauteville) (ca. 1015-1085), Norman general.

1000-1009

Mesopotamia and Syria were a battleground, the main contenders for control being the Byzantine Empire, most powerful in the north and northwest, especially around Antioch; the Fatimids, centered on Damascus; and the Buyids, based in Baghdad (from ca. 1000).

Chinese developed a projectile-throwing device called the *huo-pa'o*, in Europe later called a trebuchet (ca. 1000).

Norse reached North America and settled on the coast in at least one known site, L'Anse Aux Meadows, in northern Newfoundland (by ca. 1000).

Mahmud (Muizz ad-Din Mohammed) of Ghazni, in Afghanistan, completed his conquest of Khorasan (1000), settling his Turkish subjects, led by Seljuk, north of the Oxus River. He then campaigned widely in northern India (1000-1030), winning notable victories over Jaipal, raja of Lahore (1001), and Jaipal's son Anang-pal at Peshawar (1009); he also expanded into eastern Persia and Transoxiana.

Intermittent wars were fought by China, the Khitan Mongols' Liao dynasty in Manchuria, and the Tanguts of the Western Hsia kingdom in Kansu (1000-1004); the Khitans reached the Sung capital of Pien Liang (Kaifeng) before being bought off.

In Vietnam the kingdom of Champa was at war with Annam (1000-1044).

1010-1019

Under Suryavarman I (r. ca. 1010-ca. 1050), Cambodia expanded in the Mekong Valley north to Luang Prabang (ca. 1015-1025).

Ranging through northern India, Mahmud of Ghazni sacked Thaneswar (1014) and Kanauj (1018).

Under Rajendra I (r. 1014-1042), son of Rajaraja, Chola invaded the lower Ganges Valley, defeating the Pala king of Bengal (1014).

Srivijaya attacked and destroyed the kingdom of East Java (1016-1017).

1020-1029

b. Magnus I Olafsson (1024-1047), king of Norway (r. 1035-1047) and Denmark (r. 1042-1047).

Canute, who already held England and Denmark, attacked Norway, initially losing the sea battle of Stangebjerg (1026) but winning decisively at Helgeaa (Helga Å; Holy River) (1028), after which Norway's Olaf II Haraldsson took refuge in Russia.

Sancho III (the Great) of Navarre and Aragon completed the conquest of Christian Spain, including Castile, León, and Barcelona (1027), although his domains were divided at his death.

b. William I (the Conqueror) (1027-1087), Anglo-Norman ruler.

Poland's Boleslav defeated Russia's Prince Yaroslav at the Bug River (1020), briefly occupying Kiev.

d. Basil II Bulgaroctonos (Bulgar-butcher) (ca. 958-1025), Byzantine emperor (r. 976-1025) whose nickname stemmed from his reported blinding of Bulgarian prisoners (1014).

Byzantine forces under Constantine Diogenes repelled a Pecheneg invasion, pushing them back across the Danube (1027).

Normans made their first permanent settlement in Italy, under Rainulf at Aversa (1027).

1030-1039

Allied with Sweden's Anund Jakub, Olaf II Haraldsson attempted to regain the Norwegian throne, but at the Battle of Stiklestad (Aug. 31, 1030), he was defeated and killed by Canute, who then took full control of Norway and the Baltic's southern coast.

d. Olaf II Haraldsson (ca. 995-1030), king of Norway (r. 1016-1028) who fought with Danish troops against England (from 1009) before taking the throne.

France's Henry I put down a rebellion by his brother Robert (1032), also campaigning against nobles in northern France (1033-1043).

d. Canute (the Great) (?-1035), king of England (r. 1016-1035) and of Denmark (r. 1018-1035), son of Sweyn I. A complicated struggle began over his empire; Sweyn took Norway, Harthacanute Denmark, and Harold Harefoot England; England also was claimed by Harthacanute and two of Aethelred's sons — Alfred, who was killed by Harold, and Edward (later called "the Confessor") — both of whom had been raised in Normandy.

On becoming duke of Normandy, William (later called "the Conqueror") suppressed a revolt (1035-1047), finally succeeding at the Battle of Val-des-Dunes, near Caen, with help from France's Henry I.

Stephen I of Hungary (later Saint Stephen) fought off an invasion by German forces under Conrad II (1030).

Byzantine fleets largely cleared Muslim pirates from the Adriatic (1032) and the western Mediterranean, employing Norse mercenaries (1032-1035).

Byzantine-Norman forces under George Maniakes invaded Muslim-held Sicily, taking Messina (1038) and winning the battles of Rametta (1038) and Dragina (1040).

Bratislav I of Bohemia took Silesia from the Poles (1038), briefly occupying Cracow (1039).

1040-1049

Macbeth killed King Duncan and took the Scottish throne (1040).

Harthacanute took the English throne (r. 1040-1042); when he died, he was succeeded by Edward (the Confessor) (r. 1042-1066).

Norway's Magnus I Olafsson defeated Wendish (Slav) invaders of Jutland at the Battle of Lysborg (1043).

b. Rodrigo Díaz de Vivar (El Cid Campeador) (ca. 1043-1099), Spanish general.

Sweyn Estridsen, nephew of Canute, revolted against Magnus I Olafsson of Denmark and Norway (ca. 1045-1047), taking the throne to found the Valdemar dynasty.

d. Magnus I Olafsson (1024-1047), king of Norway (r. 1035-1047) and Denmark (r. 1042-1047).

William of Normandy fought off an invasion by his erstwhile ally Henry I of France (1049).

Muslims recaptured Sicily from Byzantium (1040).

Peter Deljan led an unsuccessful Bulgarian revolt against Byzantine rule (1040-1041).

Henry III and his German forces defeated Bratislav I of Bohemia (1041).

Byzantine forces under George Maniakes repelled a Norman invasion of Byzantine southern Italy, winning at Monopoli (1042). Maniakes then led a revolt, but he died advancing on Constantinople (1043).

Hungarians under Andrew I fought off several German invasion attempts (1049-1052).

Africa and Southwest Asia	East, Central, and South Asia, the Pacific, and the Americas	

1020-1029

Armenia, threatened by the Seljuk Turks, was annexed by the Byzantine Empire (1020).

Fatimids under Anush-takin al Dizbiri defeated Salih ibn Mirdas, one of many contenders for Syria, at Ukhuwanah (1029).

Mahmud of Ghazni campaigned overland to the coast of Gujarat, killing an estimated 50,000 Hindus (1025).

Rajendra I's kingdom of Chola attacked Srivijaya (1025), soon taking the capital, Palembang, and other key ports, then reopening Indian trade routes to China.

Mahmud of Ghazni invaded Persia, conquering the eastern territories of the Buyids (1029).

1030-1039

Byzantine losses in Syria under Romanus (1030) were regained by general George Maniakes (1031).

b. Alp Arslan (Mohammed ibn Da'ud Alp Arslan) (ca. 1030-1072), Seljuk Turk sultan (r. 1063-1072), son of Chaghrai Beg.

Tughril Beg and Chaghrai Beg, grandsons of Seljuk, successfully revolted against Ghazni (1034), decisively defeating Mahmud's son Mas'ud at Nishapur (1038) and near Merv (1040).

Under Yuan Ho, the Tanguts' Western Hsia kingdom of Kansu successfully revolted against Chinese domination, despite aid given to the Chinese by Uighur Turks; China then paid the Tanguts tribute (1038-1043).

1040-1049

Seljuk Turks under Tughril Beg invaded eastern Persia and northern Mesopotamia (1043).

Seljuk Turks invaded Armenia, winning the Battle of Kars, but fought to a draw against Armenia's Byzantine protectors at Kapitron before being defeated at Stragna and, most decisively, at Manzikert (Malazgirt) (1048-1049).

b. Alexius I Comnenus (1048-1118), Byzantine general and emperor (r. 1081-1118).

Zirids, former Muslim pirates from Sardinia, rejected Fatimid rule, founding an independent state in central North Africa (1049) centered on Mahadia.

b. Minamoto Yoshiie (1041-1108), Japanese general.

Chinese forces under general Fan Chungyen repressed a rebellion by Tangut nomads in western China (1044).

Burmese ruler Anawrahta annexed Arakan and Lower Burma (1044-1056), building the unified state of Burma.

Khitan Mongols fought off an invasion of Manchuria by the Tanguts of Kansu's Western Hsia kingdom (1044).

Wang dynasty of Koryo built a defensive wall in northern Korea against Khitan Mongols (1044).

1040-1049 (cont.)

1050-1059

Godwine, earl of Wessex, and his son Harold unsuccessfully rebelled against the Norman-influenced rule of Edward the Confessor (1051).

In Scotland, Malcolm III Canmore, son of Duncan, defeated Macbeth at the Battle of Dunsinane (1054), eventually deposing and replacing him (1057).

Pope Leo IX's troops, seeking to halt raids by the Normans, were defeated at Civitella (Civitate), in Apulia, by Norman forces under the brothers Humphrey and Robert Guiscard (1053); the pope was captured.

Poles under Casimir I (the Restorer) retook Silesia (1054).

Cumans, a Turkish people, invaded Kiev after Yaroslav's death (1054).

1060-1069

Norway's Harald III Hardraade (the Ruthless) defeated Sweyn II of Denmark in the sea battle of the Nissa (Niz) (Aug. 9, 1062).

At the death of Edward the Confessor (1066), Harold (Godwine's son) succeeded as king, but Edward's cousin William, duke of Normandy, proclaimed himself the rightful king.

English king Harold's brother Tostig rebelled, allying himself with Norwegian invaders under Harald III Hardraade, who landed near the Humber River; at Fulford they defeated Edwin, earl of Mercia, and Morkere, earl of Northumbria (Sept. 20, 1066), then took York.

At Stamford Bridge (Sept. 25, 1066), England's King Harold defeated the Norwegian invaders, who returned with only 24 of their original 300 ships; Harold also suffered heavy losses; both Harald III Hardraade and Tostig were killed.

Normans under William invaded England, landing at Pevensey, in Sussex (Sept. 28, 1066); King Harold marched to meet them at the decisive Battle of Hastings (Senlac) (Oct. 14, 1066), which hung in the balance until Harold was killed, leaving William the victor; he was crowned at Westminster Abbey (Dec. 25, 1066).

England's King William I suppressed a rebellion in the north (1069-1071), led by Hereward the Wake and aided by the Danes, who took York but were then driven out.

Normans under Robert Guiscard and his brother Roger took Sicily (from 1060); Roger would later become Roger I of Sicily (1072).

Pisans took and sacked the Muslim stronghold of Palermo (1062).

Cumans invading from across the Danube reached Thessalonika (1064-1065).

1040-1049 (cont.)

Four-decade Annam-Champa war ended when the Annamese took the Cham capital of Vijaya (Binh Dinh) and killed the king (1044).

1050-1059

Empire of Karanga ruled in southern Africa, now Zimbabwe (11th c.).

Western Sahara oases (1053-1056) were taken by Tuaregs, led by Yana ibn Omar, who founded the Almoravid dynasty.

Almoravids under Abdallah ben Yassin crossed the Sahara to take some parts of West Africa, bringing Islam to the region (1054-1076).

Seljuk Turks took Baghdad, ending the Buyid dynasty (1055). Turkish general Al-Basasiri, formerly in Buyid service, led a Fatimid-supported revolt against the Seljuk Turks (1055-1060), temporarily taking Baghdad (1058) before being suppressed.

Under abu-Bakr ibn-'Umar and his cousin Yusuf ibn Tashfin, the Almoravids took Morocco and most of Algeria (1056-1080).

d. Suryavarman I (ca. 980-ca. 1050), Cambodian ruler (r. ca. 1010-ca. 1050) who took the Mekong Valley (ca. 1015-1025).

In northern Japan the Minamoto clan put down a revolt by the Abe clan (1051-1062).

Chola's King Rajadahira I, son of Rajendra I, was defeated and killed at Koppan (1052) by a Hindu alliance under Chalukya's King Somesvara I and his sister Akkadevi, one of history's few female generals.

d. Fan Chung-yen (990-1053), Chinese general who commanded Chinese forces against the Tanguts.

Burmese ruler Anawrahta conquered the Mon kingdom of Thaton, in the Irrawaddy and Salween valleys (1057).

1060-1069

Seljuk Turks took much of Syria and Palestine from the Fatimids (1060-1071).

Turks sparked numerous revolts within the Fatimid army in Egypt (1060-1074) until they were suppressed by the Armenian general Badr al-Jamali.

Seljuk Turks led by Alp Arslan took Armenia from Byzantium (1064) and campaigned in Anatolia (1065-1067).

Alp Arslan led a Seljuk Turk invasion of Armenia, taking the capital, Ani (1064), and also attacking Byzantine lands, notably in northern Syria (1068-1071).

b. al-Afdal Shahinshah (al-Afdal ibn Badr al-Jamali; al-Malik al-Afdal; Abu-al-Qasim Shahinshah) (ca. 1066-1121), Fatimid Egyptian general.

Romanus and his Byzantine forces drove the Seljuk Turks out of most of their Byzantine conquests; their most notable victories came over Alp Arslan at Sebastia (Sivas) and Heraclea (Eregli) (1068-1069).

Defeating the Chalukya dynasty, Virarajendra made his kingdom of Chola once again dominant in southern India (1062-1070).

1070-1079

During dynastic wars in Castile and León, Alfonso VI of Castile came to power (1072) and turned against the Muslims, his key general being Rodrigo Díaz de Vivar (later El Cid Campeador).

English forces under William I invaded Scotland, establishing dominance over King Malcolm (1072).

Scots and Anglo-Normans were at war (1077-1080).

Civil war erupted at Constantinople; released on a promise to pay the Turks a ransom, Emperor Romanus was taken by his rivals, notably Andronicus Ducas, and blinded (Aug.-Sept. 1071); he then died (1072). Chaos continued for a decade.

Robert Guiscard and his Norman forces took Bari, the last Byzantine foothold in Italy (1071).

Pisa came to effectively control Corsica (1077).

Under Henry IV, Germany was wracked by civil war (1077-1106), during which Henry defeated rivals for the throne.

At Calavryta (1079), in Thessaly, general Alexius Comnenus (later himself emperor) helped suppress rivals of the Byzantine emperor Nicephorus III.

1080-1089

Rodrigo Díaz, exiled by a jealous Alfonso VI of Castile, served against Christian Spain with the Muslims (1081), who called him *sidi* (lord), which became El Cid.

Castile took Toledo from the Spanish Muslims (1085).

Weakened Spanish Muslims called in the Almoravids of Morocco, whose Moorish army under Yusuf ibn Tashfin soon took most of Muslim Spain (1086-1091) and defeated Alfonso VI at Zallaka, near Badajoz (1088).

d. William I (the Conqueror) (1027-1087), Anglo-Norman ruler who landed at Hastings (1066) to take the English throne, introducing Continent-style feudalism and a central government, which prepared the Domesday (Doomsday) Book (1086) as a record of his holdings; he died in an accident while at war with Philip I of France (Sept. 9).

William's second son, William II, became the English king (1087), involved in running battles with his older brother, Robert, who became duke of Normandy.

El Cid returned to fight for Castile (1088-1089) before being exiled again.

With a private army including both Christians and Muslims, El Cid took Valencia (1089-1094), ruling independently.

Alexius Comnenus, who had helped bring the Byzantine emperor Nicephorus III to power, took the throne (1081), as Alexius I Comnenus, temporarily making peace with the Seljuk Turks while dealing with other threats.

Normans under Robert Guiscard attacked the Byzantine Empire, taking Corfu and besieging Durazzo (Dyrrachium); they were then defeated by a Byzantine-Venetian fleet (1081). Despite the arrival of Byzantine reinforcements, led by Emperor Alexius Comnenus, the Normans fought and won a second battle, on land, at Durazzo (1082). Robert Guiscard then returned to Italy at the pope's request, while Normans under his son Bohemund campaigned through Thessaly, besieging Larissa.

Henry IV and his German forces invaded Italy (1081-1085; 1090-1095), briefly taking Rome (1083). Pope Gregory VII, besieged in Rome, called in Robert Guiscard and his mostly Norman troops; after Henry retreated without a fight, the Normans took and sacked Rome (1083-1084).

d. Robert Guiscard (Robert de Hauteville) (ca. 1015-1085), Norman general, brother of Roger I of Sicily. After his death, his son Bohemund withdrew Norman forces from Byzantine territory, returning to Italy.

Africa and Southwest Asia

Byzantine forces under Manuel Comnenus were defeated by two Turkish armies led by Alp Arslan and his brother-in-law Arisiaghi (1070).

Possibly weakened by treachery within their own ranks, Byzantine forces under Emperor Romanus were surprised by Alp Arslan's Seljuk Turk army, then overwhelmed at the fortress of Manzikert, all being either killed or captured (Aug. 19, 1071); Romanus was taken but later released. The Seljuk Turks then took nearly all of Anatolia, except for a few coastal cities (1071-1081).

Seljuk Turks took Jerusalem from the Fatimids (1071).

At Berzem (1072), Alp Arslan's Seljuk Turks fought off an invasion by forces from Khwarezm (Khiva) led by Yakub, who was captured but managed to assassinate Alp after the battle.

d. Alp Arslan (Mohammed ibn Da'ud Alp Arslan) (ca. 1030-1072), Seljuk Turk sultan (r. 1063-1072), who conquered Armenia (1064) and defeated the Byzantines at Manzikert (1071); he was killed by his captive, Yakub of Khwarezm. Alp was succeeded by his son Malik-shah.

d. Romanus IV Diogenes (?-1072), Byzantine emperor who was defeated at Manzikert (1071); captured by the Seljuk Turks, then released, he surrendered to Michael VII, his rival for the throne, was blinded (1071), and died.

Somali forces, many under Arabic leaders, took the Horn of Africa from the Bantu kingdom of Zanj (ca. 1075-1200), there fighting with Ethiopian Christians.

Almoravids took Kumbi, massacring its citizens and imposing Islam on the region of Ghana (1076).

b. Tancred (1078?-1112), Norman Crusader.

After Virarajendra's death led to a succession struggle in Chola, his daughter married a Chalukya prince; the Chalukya-Chola dynasty then ruled most of India's Deccan (1070).

Under Harivarman IV, Champa fought off Annamese and Khmer invasions (1070-1076).

Vijhaya Bahu led the successful campaign to end Chola (Tamil) domination of Ceylon (Sri Lanka) (1070).

Under Malik-shah (r. 1071-1092), the Seljuk Turks expanded into Central Asia.

d. Anawrahta (?-1077), Burmese ruler (r. 1044-1077) under whom Pagan conquered the whole central Irrawaddy Basin, Arakan, Lower Burma, and the Mon kingdom, building a string of fortresses to guard their eastern frontier.

Antioch, the last Byzantine stronghold in Syria, fell to the Seljuk Turks under Sulaiman ibn Kutalmish (1084).

Seljuk Turk forces, led by Atsiz the Khwarezmian, campaigned in Syria, taking Damascus (1086).

Combined Pisan-Genoese fleet took the Zirid stronghold of Mahadia (1087), ending Muslim control of the western Mediterranean.

b. John II Comnenus (1088-1143), Byzantine emperor (r. 1118-1143).

In northern Japan the Minamoto clan eliminated the rival Kiyowara clan (1083-1087).

b. Suryavarman II (ca. 1085-1150), Cambodian ruler (ca. 1113-1150).

1080-1089 (cont.)

In Bulgaria, the Bogomils (a Christian sect), Pechenegs, and Cumans revolted against Byzantine rule; they defeated Alexius I Comnenus at Dorostorum (Silistra) (1086) but were eventually suppressed.

1090-1099

Scotland's King Malcolm invaded England and was killed at the first Battle of Alnwick (1093).

Under Magnus III Barfot (Bareleg) (r. 1093-1103), so called because he wore Scottish kilts, the Norse attempted to reconquer the Orkneys and the Hebrides.

El Cid fought off Almoravid invasions at the battles of Cuarte (1094) and Bairen (1097).

Pedro I expanded Aragon, taking Huesca (1096), later his capital.

d. Rodrigo Díaz de Vivar (El Cid Campeador) (ca. 1043-1099), Spanish general who fought for both Christians and Muslims and was the subject of numerous epics. After his death the Almoravids retook Valencia (1099-1102).

Pechenegs lost to Byzantine forces at Leburnion and were pushed back across the Danube (1091).

Using a Cuman army, Constantine Diogenes tried to capture the Byzantine throne, besieging Adrianople but finally losing to Alexius I Comnenus at Taurocomon (1094).

Pope Urban II called for Christians to make a Crusade to free the Holy Land, especially Jerusalem, from Muslim control (1095), partly responding to Byzantine appeals for aid.

b. Roger II (1095-1154), Norman king of Sicily and Naples (r. 1130-1154).

First Crusade (1096-1099): In the People's Crusade, thousands of unarmed and untrained pilgrims marched through central and eastern Europe, some loosely led by Peter the Hermit or Walter the Penniless; pillaging en route, they attacked and massacred Jews in many cities, such as Cologne, Mainz, and most notably Prague. Largely unprovisioned, many pilgrims died on the march (Apr.-Oct. 1096).

King Calomar I of Hungary defeated Venice, taking most of the Dalmatian coast (1097-1102).

1080-1089 (cont.)

1090-1099

Muslim followers of Hasan ibn al-Sabbah took the fortress of Alamut (ca. 1090), in the Persian mountains, south of the Caspian Sea, founding their secret Islamic sect the Assassins; he took the title Sheikh al-Jabal, widely known to westerners as the "Old Man of the Mountains."

At the death of Malik-shah (1092), the Seljuk Turk Empire was weakened by civil wars (1092-1098) and split: Kilij Arslan, son of Sulaiman ibn Kutalmish, headed the Sultanate of Rum (Roum), centered at Iconium (Konya), in Anatolia; Mohammed ibn Danishmend ruled the area around Sivas; and Ridwan led the Emirate of Aleppo, in Syria and northern Mesopotamia.

b. 'Abd-al-Mu'min ibn-'Ali (al-Kumi) (ca. 1094-1163), Berber (Moorish) general and ruler.

First Crusade: Many of the People's Crusaders attacked in Asia indiscriminately, Christians as well as Muslims; in the end most who survived the march through Europe were killed or enslaved by the Turks (1096).

First Crusade: The trained, armed forces of the First Crusade — some 50,000 of them — gathered in Byzantium (1096-1097); their leaders included the French bishop Adhemar du Pay; Norman duke Bohemund; his nephew Tancred; Count Raymond of Toulouse; Duke Godfrey de Bouillon of Lorraine; his brother Baldwin; Robert, duke of Normandy; Hugh, duke of Vermandois, brother of the French king; Count Robert of Flanders; and Count Stephen of Blois. Byzantines under Alexius I Comnenus guided and aided them; they agreed to give him any former Byzantine lands.

First Crusade: The Crusaders besieged and took Nicaea (Iznik) (May 14-June 19, 1097), turning it over to the Byzantines but unhappy at not being allowed to sack it.

First Crusade: At Dorylaeum (Eskisehir), the Crusaders, notably led by Bohemund, Raymond, and Godfrey, routed the Seljuk Turks under Kilij Arslan of Rum, with heavy losses on both sides (July 1, 1097); they then took the capital of Iconium (Konya), while the Byzantines retook western Anatolia.

First Crusade: Traveling through Syria, the Crusaders under Baldwin took Edessa, which became a Crusader state under Baldwin (late 1097).

First Crusade: Christian forces besieged Antioch, defended by Muslims under Yagi Siyan (Oct. 21, 1097-June 3, 1098); they defeated two Muslim relief armies, both at Harenc (Dec. 31, 1097; Feb. 9, 1098), but were close to defeat — indeed, Stephen and his forces had already left. The Crusaders were saved when small English and Pisan fleets took the ports of Laodicea (Latakia) and St. Simeon (Samandag), providing desperately needed provisions.

First Crusade: The Crusaders were besieged in Antioch only two days after taking it, by Turkish forces under Emir Kerboga of Mosul; they rallied under Bohemund to attack the Muslims across the Orontes River, finally routing them (June 5-28, 1098). Bohemund there established an independent state, refusing to cede the city to Byzantium, so he and Tancred became involved in a long conflict with Count Raymond and Alexius I Comnenus in Syria (1098-1108).

First Crusade: Fatimid forces under general al-Afdal Shahinshah retook Palestine and southern Syria, including Jerusalem (1098), from the Seljuk Turks before finally losing Jerusalem to the Crusaders (1099).

During civil war in the Seljuk Turk Empire (1092-1098), and ensuing unrest, the eastern provinces struggled free.

1090-1099 (cont.)

1100-1109

First known depiction of the projectile-throwing device called a tre-buchet, modeled on the Chinese *huo-pa'o* (early 12th c.).

d. Roger I (?-1101), Norman leader who, over thirty years — from Messina (1061) to Noto (1091) — conquered the island of Sicily, installing himself formally as grand count of Sicily and Calabria (southern Italy).

Norse leader Magnus III Barfot campaigned in Ireland, during which he was killed (1103).

England's Henry I (r. 1100-1135), William the Conqueror's fourth son, continued the conflict with his eldest brother, Robert of Normandy, eventually defeating him at Tinchebrai (1106) and adding "duke of Normandy" to his own titles.

Holy Roman Emperor Henry IV was overthrown by his sons and other rebels; he died attempting to regain his throne (1105-1106).

Leaving his nephew Tancred in Antioch, Bohemund raised an army in Italy and attacked the Byzantines at Durazzo (1106); defeated by Alexius I Comnenus several times, Bohemund finally ceded Antioch to Byzantium (1108), but Tancred refused to accept it.

Under Henry V (r. 1106-1125), Germans made inroads into Bohemia (1107-1110), but their invasions of Hungary (1108) and Poland (1109) were repelled.

Poles under Boleslav III fought off a German invasion of Silesia led by Emperor Henry V, winning the Battle of Glogau (Hundsfeld), near Breslau, and retaking Pomerania at the Battle of Naklo (both 1109).

1110-1119

Pisan fleets raided Muslim bases on the Balearic Islands (1113; 1115).

Louis VI and his French forces, who had aided the Norman rebels against England, were defeated by England's Henry I at Bermule (1119) as part of their running wars (1109-1112; 1116-1130).

Under Vladimir II Monomakh (r. 1113-1125), Kiev fought the Cumans.

1090-1099 (cont.)

First Crusade: Now supported by the Pisan fleet, the Crusaders — except for Bohemund and Bishop Adhemar, who had died at Antioch — besieged Jerusalem (June 9-July 18, 1099); they were led primarily by Godfrey, who became guardian of Jerusalem; captured defenders and noncombatants — both Muslims and Jews — were massacred.

First Crusade: At Ascalon, Godfrey led the Crusaders in a notable victory against Muslim forces five times larger, led by Fatimid general al-Afdal Shahinshah (Aug. 12, 1099). After this, many Crusaders returned to Europe, but some remained in the Crusader states, joined by new waves of Crusaders.

Knights of St. John (Sovereign and Military Order of the Knights Hospitaller of Saint John of Jerusalem) established themselves in Jerusalem (1099); the religious and military order had been founded earlier in the century, originally to care for sick and wounded pilgrims.

1100-1109

Bohemund was captured and held by the Seljuk Turks near Aleppo (1100-1104).

Baldwin, who after Godfrey's death became king of Jerusalem (1100), defeated a far larger Egyptian force under Saad el-Dawleh at the first Battle of Ramleh (1101); at the second Battle of Ramleh (1102), against even greater odds, his army was virtually destroyed, although he revived for another win at Jaffa.

Three separate Crusader expeditions into Anatolia were crushed by the Seljuk Turks (1101-1102); the first, seeking to rescue Bohemund, was destroyed by Mohammed ibn Danishmend at Mersevan (1101); the second and third were turned back at Heraclea (1101; 1102).

Kilij Arslan of Rum took Mosul from Ridwan (1102) but later lost and was killed at the Khabur River (1107).

While various groups fought for Syria (1102-1127), the Assassins moved into the area from Persia and came to control the mountains northeast of Tripoli, Lebanon.

Sigurd I of Norway became the first European king to arrive in the Holy Land, where he and the Venetians helped Baldwin take Sidon (1109).

d. Minamoto Yoshiie (1041-1108), Japanese general whose clan eliminated their Kiyowara rivals.

1110-1119

In their renewed war (1110-1117), the Byzantines defeated the Seljuk Turks at Philomelion (Akshehr) (1116), regaining the Anatolian coast.

d. Tancred (1078?-1112), Norman who fought in the First Crusade, helping to take Jerusalem (1099); he became prince of Galilee and regent of Antioch, for his uncle Bohemund.

Baldwin died in the Sinai Desert during an aborted invasion of Egypt (1118).

d. Alexius I Comnenus (1048-1118), Byzantine general and emperor (r. 1081-1118) who fought the Normans and Seljuk Turks, in an uneasy relationship with the Crusaders, some of whom had been his enemies. He was succeeded by his son John II Comnenus; his biography, *Alexiad,* was written by his daughter Anna Comnena.

Count Roger of Salerno was surprised and his force annihilated at Aleppo by Muslims under Ilghazi (1119).

Templars (Poor Knights of Christ and of the Temple of Solomon), a military religious order, was founded in Jerusalem (1119-1120) under the leadership of Hugues de Payens to protect Christian pilgrims there.

China's Sung dynasty, allied with the Juchen Mongols, conquered the Khitan Mongol kingdom (1115-1122).

Aided by the Chinese, the Juchen Mongols conquered Manchuria; the Liao leader, Ye-lu Ta-shih, withdrew to the Tarim Basin, there (with Uighur Turks) forming the Kara Khitai kingdom (1115-1123).

b. Taira Kiyomori (1118-1181), Japanese general.

1120-1129

France's Louis VI fought off a German invasion (1124).

Under David I (r. 1124-1153) Scotland largely conquered Northumberland and Cumberland.

b. William I (the Bad) (ca. 1120-1166), Norman king of Sicily and Naples (r. 1154-1166).

b. Enrico Dandolo (ca. 1120-1205), Venetian doge.

Byzantine forces led by John II Comnenus smashed a final Pecheneg invasion of Bulgaria (1121-1122).

Byzantium and Venice engaged in an inconclusive naval war (1122-1126).

b. Frederick I Barbarossa (Red Beard) (ca. 1123-1190), German emperor (r. 1152-1190).

The election of Lothair II as Holy Roman Emperor over Frederick Hohenstaufen, duke of Swabia, led to civil war (1125-1135), the basis for a long struggle between two factions: the Guelphs (Welf) and Ghibellines (Waiblingen).

1130-1139

b. Henry II (1133-1189), English king (r. 1154-1189).

England's Henry I was succeeded by his nephew Stephen, sparking a series of dynastic conflicts (1135-1154), notably involving Henry's daughter Matilda (his named successor), her half-brother Robert, and her son Henry.

Scotland's David I was defeated by English forces at the Battle of the Standard (Northallerton) (1138).

Count Affonso (Alfonso) Henriques won the Battle of Ourique (1139), capping a sequence of victories against the Spanish Muslims, then declared himself king of Portugal (1140), independent of Castile and León.

After a period of complicated warfare in Italy involving all the major European powers, Roger II firmly established Norman control over southern Italy and Sicily (1137-1139).

1140-1149

Almohad forces from Morocco, under 'Abd al-Mu'min ibn-'Ali (al-Kumi), invaded and took Muslim Spain (1145-1150).

Portugal's Affonso took Lisbon from the Muslims and set his southern boundary at the Tagus River (1147); the first known use of a trebuchet, a projectile-throwing device, was in this battle.

Roger II's Normans, their seaborne forces led by admiral George of Antioch, attacked Byzantine territory, taking Corfu and sacking Athens, Corinth, and Thebes (1147-1149). A Byzantine-Venetian fleet then defeated the Normans (1148), retaking Corfu (1149).

1120-1129

Muslim Berbers under Mohammed ibn-Tumart founded the Almohad dynasty in the Atlas Mountains (ca. 1120-1130).

Under John II Comnenus the Byzantines recaptured most of Anatolia from the Seljuk Turks (1120-1121).

d. al-Afdal Shahinshah (al-Afdal ibn Badr al-Jamali; al-Malik al-Afdal; Abu-al-Qasim Shahinshah) (ca. 1066-1121), Fatimid Egyptian general who, after taking Jerusalem (1099), was surprised by the Crusaders and defeated at Ascalon (1099).

Declaring themselves the Chin dynasty, the Juchen Mongols under T'ien Fu (Tsu) invaded China, reaching Pien Liang (Kaifeng), the Sung capital, before being defeated (1126); the next year they took the capital and the emperor (1127); one of the emperor's sons, Kao Tsung, escaped to found the Southern Sung dynasty, centered at Nanking, but the Juchens attacked across the Yangtze, taking Nanking and driving the Southern Sung into Hangchow (1127).

Now incorporating the Western Liao, the Kara Khitai expanded westward through the Pamir Mountains all the way to Transoxiana (1126-1141).

Sung forces under general Yueh Fei, coordinating with the Yangtze River fleet, pushed the Chin (Juchen) army north beyond the river nearly to the Chin capital of Pien Liang (1128-1140).

1130-1139

b. Saladin (Salah-al din Yusuf ibn Ayyub) (ca. 1138-1193), Kurdish general and sultan of Egypt (r. 1174-1193).

After initial success against Champa, Khmer forces under Suryavarman II failed to conquer the kingdoms of Champa and Annam (1130-1132).

Chinese general Ch'en Gui invented the first known weapon using gunpowder, a long bamboo musket (ca. 1132).

Central Asian Mongols under khan Kabul raided China (1135).

1140-1149

d. John II Comnenus (1088-1143), Byzantine emperor (r. 1118-1143), son of Alexius I Comnenus; he reconquered much of the Anatolian territory previously taken by the Seljuk Turks, as well as Antioch (1137-1138), much of which was soon lost again. He was succeeded by Manuel Comnenus (r. 1143-1180).

Forces led by Imad-al-Din Zangi, ruler of Mosul, took Edessa from Crusaders under Count Joscelin II (1144), sparking the Second Crusade.

In the continuing conflict over Antioch, Manuel Comnenus defeated Raymond of Antioch (1144).

Operating from Sicily, George of Antioch established a Norman presence in North Africa, taking Muslim strongholds such as Tripoli and Mahadia, as well as Malta (1146-1152).

In Morocco and western Algeria, the Almoravids were overthrown by the Almohads under 'Abd Al-Mu'min ibn-'Ali (al-Kumi), who proclaimed himself caliph (1147-1160); the Almohads expanded into Algeria, Tunisia, and western Tripolitania, gradually taking Norman territories (1147-1160).

Sanjar and his Seljuk Turks were defeated near Samarkand and swept out of Transoxiana (1141) by local rebels allied with the Kara Khitai.

Khmer forces under Suryavarman II conquered Champa (1145) but were later ousted (1149).

b. Minamoto Yoritomo (1147-1199), Japanese shogun.

1140-1149 (cont.)

1150-1159

Atlantic and Northern Europe	Central, Southern, and Eastern Europe
Under the truce of the Battle of Wallingford (1154), Henry, duke of Normandy (Matilda's son and Henry I's grandson), succeeded Stephen on the English throne as Henry II (r. 1154-1189), founding the Plantaganet dynasty.	Manuel Comnenus (r. 1143-1180), son of John II, suppressed a Serbian rebellion against Byzantine rule (1150-1152).
b. Alfonso VIII (1155-1214), ruler and general of Castile and León.	Byzantine forces under Manuel Comnenus invaded Hungary (1151-1153; 1155-1168).
Under Malcolm IV (r. 1153-1165), grandson of David I, Scotland was obliged to cede Northumberland and Cumberland to England's Henry II.	Byzantium took Ancona, in southern Italy (1151).
England's Henry II, who on his own and through his marriage to Eleanor of Aquitaine held most of western France, was at war with France's Louis VII (1157-1180).	Under Frederick I Barbarossa, Germans campaigned widely in Europe — in Poland, Bohemia, Hungary, and six times in Italy (1156-1173).
Alfonso VII of Castile and León invaded Muslim Spain but was defeated and killed during the Battle of Muradel (1157).	b. William II (1153-1189), Norman king of Sicily and Naples (r. 1166-1189).
Civil war among dynastic contenders ended in Denmark when Valdemar I (the Great) came to the throne (1157), expanding his nation's influence in the Baltic.	d. Roger II (1095-1154), Norman king of Sicily and Naples (r. 1130-1154), son of Roger I; he fought the Byzantine Empire (1147-1149) but was stopped short of Constantinople. He was succeeded by his eldest son, William I (r. 1154-1166).
In Sweden's first expansion, King (later Saint) Erik III Eriksson led a crusade to Finland (1157).	William I of Sicily was defeated by Byzantine forces in a sea battle off Apulia, the "heel" of southern Italy (1155), but won decisively at the Battle of Brindisi (1156), again expelling the Byzantines.
b. Richard I (1157-1199), English king (r. 1189-1199).	
England's Henry II gradually conquered Wales (1158-1165).	

1160-1169

Atlantic and Northern Europe	Central, Southern, and Eastern Europe
b. Philip II (Augustus) (1165-1223), French king (r. 1179-1223).	On Frederick I Barbarossa's fourth expedition to Italy, the Germans took Rome (1166-1168); they were later forced to leave the city when sickness decimated the army.
Henry II's Norman knights, led by Richard of Clare, took Ireland (1167-1171).	d. William I (the Bad) (ca. 1120-1166), Norman king of Sicily and Naples (r. 1154-1156), eldest son of Roger II, who defeated the Byzantine fleet at Brindisi (1156) but lost Norman territories in Tunisia and Algeria (1158-1160). He was succeeded by his son William II.
	After long campaigning in Hungary, Manuel Comnenus and his Byzantine forces won the Battle of Semlin (Zemun) and annexed Dalmatia and other territories (1168).

1140-1149 (cont.)

Second Crusade (1147-1149): Crusaders under German emperor Conrad III, short of food, were crushed by the Turks in Anatolia, near Dorylaeum; the survivors returned to the coast, going to Palestine by ship. The other main force, under French king Louis VII, traveled along coastal Anatolia but lost to the Turks at Laodicea; the cavalry was then sent to Palestine by sea, but the infantry was wiped out by the Turks.

Second Crusade: Surviving Crusaders and those of Jerusalem's Baldwin III ineffectively besieged Damascus (1148).

Nur-ed-din, son of Zangi, took Muslim Syria, also defeating Raymond of Antioch (1149-1150).

1150-1159

Shirazi people from Oman, on the Persian Gulf, invaded the East African coast, gradually taking Kilwa, Pemba, Zanzibar, and the Comoro Islands (ca. 1150-1200).

Crusaders under Baldwin III took Ascalan, the last Muslim stronghold on the Palestinian coast (1153).

Abbasid caliphs revived to regain control of south and central Mesopotamia from the Seljuk Turks (1155-1194).

Almohads completed their conquest of Norman territories in Tunisia and Algeria (1158-1160).

Between Persia and the Punjab, Saif ud-din Suir and Ala-ud-din of Ghor defeated Bahram, shah of Ghazni; when the Seljuk Turks under Sanjar defeated and temporarily captured Ala-ud-din, Bahram revived to defeat and kill Saif (1150); Ala-ud-din then destroyed Ghazni (1152).

Khmer forces attacking Annam were crushed near Tonkin (1150).

d. Suryavarman II (ca. 1085-1150), Cambodian ruler (r. 1113-1150) who led several campaigns of expansion.

In Japan's Hogen War (1156), the main clans were divided by a struggle for the imperial throne between two brothers — Goshirakawa II, the victor, and Sokotu, who was exiled.

Japan's Minamoto clan initiated the Heiji War by taking power, but they were overthrown by the Taira clan (1159-1160).

b. Minamoto Yoshitsune (Ushiwaka) (1159-1189), Japanese general.

1160-1169

Nur-ed-din's Turkish forces under general Asad ud-Din Shirkuh went to Egypt, ostensibly to aid the Fatimids in suppressing a revolt (1163); fearing they wanted to take Egypt themselves, the Fatimids formed an alliance with Crusader King Amalric I of Jerusalem, then defeated Shirkuh and his nephew Saladin near Cairo (Apr. 11, 1167).

d. 'Abd-al-Mu'min ibn-'Ali (al-Kumi) (ca. 1094-1163), Berber (Moorish) general and founder of the Almohad dynasty in North Africa.

First known use of explosives in battle, by Sung general Yu Yun-wen at Ts'ai-shih (near Nanking), where the Sung army and Yangtze River fleet blocked an invasion of southern China, this one led by Chin emperor Liang, who was hanged by mutinous troops after ordering a fresh attack (1161).

b. Genghis Khan (Temujin; Chingghis; Jenghis) (1162-1227), Mongol ruler.

Sinhalese king Parakram Bahu fought off a Tamil invasion of Ceylon (Sri Lanka) (1168); he later invaded the Indian mainland at Madura (ca. 1170).

1170-1179

Norman knights of England's Henry II murdered Thomas à Becket (1170), archbishop of Canterbury, part of a continuing struggle between church and state; Henry later did penance at a shrine for Thomas (1174).

Portugal's Affonso took Santarem from the Muslims (1171).

England's Henry II was involved in a series of wars with France under Louis VII (from 1173).

Henry II put down England's last major Anglo-Saxon rebellion against Norman rule (1173-1174), possibly triggered by Becket's murder. William the Lion, brother of Scotland's Malcolm IV, joined in the rebellion; he was defeated, captured, and ransomed at the second Battle of Alnwick (1174).

At war with Byzantium (1170-1177), Venice was temporarily swept from the Aegean (1170); with Norman help, it came back to take Chios and Ragusa (1171), but the Byzantines held Ancona, Italy (1173).

Hungarians under King Bela III fought off Venice's attempts to retake the Dalmatian coast (1172-1196).

On Frederick I Barbarossa's fifth expedition to Italy, the Germans were badly defeated by the Lombard League at Legnano (May 29, 1176).

1180-1189

England's Henry II was involved in a series of conflicts with France's Philip II (Augustus) (1180s), sometimes joined in rebellion by one or more of Henry's sons.

Philip II established his dominance over the northern French nobles (1180-1186).

Canute IV of Denmark fought off a German invasion (1182), confirming Danish supremacy in the Baltic by winning the sea battle of Strela (Stralsund) (1184).

Jews were expelled from France (1182).

d. Henry II (1133-1189), English king (r. 1154-1189) and founder of the Plantaganet dynasty; among the children of Henry and Eleanor of Aquitaine were the English kings Richard I (the Lion-Hearted), his immediate successor, and John I.

Stephen Nemanya led a successful Serbian revolt against Byzantine rule (1180-1196).

William II of Sicily and his Norman forces invaded Byzantine-held Greece (1184), taking Durazzo and Thessalonika before being decisively defeated on land by forces under Emperor Isaac II Angelus at the Strymon River (Sept. 7, 1185) and at sea by Alexius Branas at Demetritsa (1185). The Normans were finally cleared from Greece (1191).

Ivan and Peter Asen led a successful Bulgarian revolt (1186-1187), founding the Bulgarian Empire, under Ivan Asen I; the brothers also raided in Thrace and defeated the Byzantines at Berrhoe (1189).

d. William II (1153-1189), Norman king of Sicily and Naples (r. 1166-1189), son of William I; he was stopped short of Constantinople at the Strymon River (1185).

1170-1179

Saladin took Tripolitania from the Almohads (1172).

After an international struggle for Egypt, Saladin became regent and then ruler of Egypt (r. 1174-1193), founding the Ayyubid dynasty and making Egypt a Sunni Muslim nation.

At the death of Nur-ed-din, Saladin, ruler of Egypt, proclaimed himself heir to Zangid Turk lands in southwest Asia, enforcing his claim with effective military campaigns (1174-1183); his regular army was largely composed of Turkish slaves called Mamelukes.

Crusaders defeated Saladin's forces at Ramleh (1177).

b. Subotai (Subodei) (ca. 1172-1245), Mongol general.

Penetrating into the Punjab, Muhammad of Ghor defeated the Ghaznevids (1175) but was forced to end his campaign in Gujarat after being defeated by the Hindu raja (1178).

In the Champa-Angkor war, the Cham invaded Angkor, taking and sacking the capital (1177). Khmer led by Jayavarman VII scored a notable naval victory over the Cham (1178?), possibly on the Mekong River.

Muhammad of Ghor took Peshawar (1179) and brought Islam to the Punjab.

1180-1189

As part of a jihad (holy war) (1187-1192), Saladin invaded Palestine, at Hattin (July 4, 1187) smashing a Crusader army, then taking most of the region, including Tiberias, Acre, and Ascalon (July-Sept. 1187). Blocked at Tyre by newly arrived Crusaders, Saladin turned to take Jerusalem (Sept. 20-Oct. 2, 1187) before turning back toward Tyre.

Third Crusade (1189-1192): Frederick I Barbarossa led his German forces across Europe to Constantinople, then across Anatolia.

Third Crusade: Supplied from the sea by Genoese and Pisan fleets, Crusaders under Guy of Lusignan besieged Acre, fighting numerous battles nearby against Saladin's forces (1189-1191).

In Japan the Minamoto clan under Minamoto Yoritomo led a revolt against the Taira clan (1180-1184), defeating them at Kyoto (1183), at Yashima on Shikoku, and then utterly in the land and sea battle of Dannoura, around the western Inland Sea, where they were led by Yoritomo's brother Minamoto Yoshitsune (1184).

Temujin (later Genghis Khan) began to conquer and absorb neighboring peoples, building his Mongol kingdom (1180-1190).

d. Taira Kiyomori (1118-1181), Japanese general who led Taira forces in the Hogen War (1156) and defeated the Minamoto family, becoming the dominant military leader of his time.

Minamoto Yoritomo became military dictator of Japan (r. 1185-1199), the first to hold the title of shogun.

b. Ogatai (Ögödei) Khan (ca. 1185-1241), Mongol ruler.

Muhammad of Ghor took Lahore (1186), also campaigning in the upper Ganges Valley (1187-1190).

Last definite record of the Norse visiting North America (1189).

Japanese dictator Minamoto Yoritomo assassinated his relations within the Minamoto clan, notably Minamoto Yoshitsune, Yoshiie, and Yoshinaka (1189).

d. Minamoto Yoshitsune (Ushiwaka) (1159-1189), Japanese general; he laid the basis for the government of his brother Yoritomo, who later assassinated him.

1190-1199

Captured returning from the Crusades, Richard I (the Lion-Hearted) was held captive in Austria (1192-1194) while his brother John ruled as regent in England; this was the background for the semilegendary tales of Robin Hood.

England's Richard I (the Lion-Hearted) was at war with France's Philip II (1194-1199), winning the key siege at Gisors, near Paris (1197); he was fatally wounded at Châlus, near Limoges (1199).

d. Richard I (1157-1199), English king (r. 1189-1199) known as Coeur de Lion (the Lion-Hearted), eldest son of Henry II and Eleanor of Aquitaine; he fought in the Third Crusade (1190-1192), helping to take Acre; he died of a wound suffered at Châlus (1199).

Almohad caliph Abu-Yusuf Ya'qub al-Mansour decisively defeated Alfonso VIII of Castile at the Battle of Alarcos, near Ciudad Real (1195).

d. Frederick I Barbarossa (Red Beard) (ca. 1123-1190), German emperor (r. 1152-1190) who fought in the Second and Third Crusades, during which he died on a river crossing.

Genoa took Bonifacio, establishing its power on Corsica (1195).

Under Kaloyan (r. 1197-1207), Bulgaria won territory variously from the Serbs, Hungarians, Byzantines, and Latin Crusader states.

1200-1209

Almohad forces took the Balearic Islands (1201).

At war with England's John I, France's Philip II took most of the English king's French domains, including Anjou, Brittany, Maine, Normandy, and Touraine, after the notable siege and capture of Château Gaillard and Rouen in Normandy (1202-1204).

Under Valdemar II the Danes expanded to take most of the Pomeranian coast (ca. 1203-1210).

Albigensian Crusade (1203-1226): French-born Englishman Simon de Montfort led an army against "heretics" in southern France, centered on Toulouse and Albi — in large part a battle between northern and southern French nobles; in the first campaign (1208-

Fourth Crusade (1202-1204): Crusaders from around Europe gathered at Venice; short of funds for their transport to Egypt, they agreed to retake the former Venetian territory of Zara from Hungary; they did so and were excommunicated by Pope Innocent for killing Christians. While some Crusaders, notably Simon de Montfort, headed toward Palestine, the rest turned toward Constantinople, ostensibly to place on the throne Alexius, son of the deposed Isaac II, who promised to turn the Byzantine Empire from Greek Orthodox to Roman Catholicism. Byzantines under Theodore Lascaris defended themselves successfully on land but yielded to the Venetian sea attack; the

Africa and Southwest Asia

Third Crusade: Using his effective crossbowmen, Frederick I Barbarossa took Iconium (Konya), in Anatolia (1190); he later drowned, and his son Frederick of Swabia lost two-thirds of his force before arriving at Acre.

Third Crusade: French king Philip II and English king Richard I (the Lion-Hearted) brought their Crusaders by sea to Sicily (1190), with Richard taking Cyprus before joining Philip's forces in besieging Acre (1191).

Teutonic Knights (originally Order of the Knights of the Hospital of St. Mary of the Teutons in Jerusalem) were founded at Acre, originally a charitable German hospital (1190) but soon becoming military (1198).

Third Crusade: Crusaders, now under Richard I, defeated Saladin's army and tightened the siege of Acre, which then fell (July 12, 1191); Philip II returned to France.

Third Crusade: En route to Ascalon, Richard I and the Crusaders were ambushed by Saladin at Arsouf, which Richard turned into a coordinated attack, routing the Turks (Sept. 7, 1191).

Third Crusade: After wintering at Ascalon, where the Assassins killed Conrad of Montferrat, the Crusaders pursued Saladin, who destroyed water and crops after him. Abandoning plans to besiege Jerusalem, Richard I made a treaty with Saladin, outlining special rights and privileges for Christian pilgrims to Jerusalem (1192), then headed toward Europe, where he was taken and imprisoned in Austria for two years.

d. Saladin (Salah-al din Yusuf ibn Ayyub) (ca. 1138-1193), Kurdish general and sultan of Egypt (r. 1174-1193), self-named "Saladin" (Honor of the Faith); he founded the Ayyubid dynasty, ruling from Cairo and later taking Syria and much of Iraq, launching a holy war against the Crusader states (1187-1192).

Expanding from Central Asia through Persia, Khwarezm conquered Mesopotamia (1194).

On what was intended as the Fourth Crusade (1197-1198), Henry VI, Holy Roman (German) Emperor and king of Sicily, sent an army of German Crusaders to the Holy Land; they took Beirut and other coastal towns (1198), but Henry died (1197) before he could join them.

Temujin expanded his Mongol Empire in east-central Asia (1190-1206), establishing its capital at Karakorum and proclaiming himself Genghis Khan (Supreme Emperor).

Southern India's Chalukya dynasty was overthrown by a Hindu alliance under Vira Bellala II of Hoysala, whose queen, Ummadevi, was an active general in the campaign (1190).

Under Jayavarman VII, the Khmer drove the Cham from Angkor, then took Champa and split it (1190), also expanding north and south.

Muhammad of Ghor's conquest of India was halted after his defeat by Prithviraja, raja of Delhi and Ajmer, in the first Battle of Tarain (Tirawari) (1191); he prevailed in the second battle (1192), killing Prithviraja.

Under a puppet ruler, Suryavarman, Champa was reunited and the Khmer driven out (1191-1192), although war continued.

Muhammad of Ghor took Delhi (1193), then delegated further Indian campaigns to general Qutb-ud-Din, who took Benares (1194) and then Badaun and Kannauj (1198-1199), also warring with the Rajpurs in Gujarat (1195-1198).

Genghis Khan and his Mongol forces successfully campaigned against the Kerait Mongols southwest of the Gobi Desert (1194).

d. Minamoto Yoritomo (1147-1199), Japanese shogun who created the military-dominated government so characteristic of Japan; his military successes were largely due to his brother Yoshitsune, whom he later assassinated.

Civil war sparked by Saladin's death (1193) was won by Abul Bakr Malik al-Adil, whose final victory came at Bilbeis, in Egypt (Jan. 1200).

Under King Sumanguru, Soso forces sacked Kumbi, once the capital of Ghana (1203), becoming dominant in the region.

In a civil war involving remnants of the Byzantine Empire, Theodore Lascaris of Nicaea defeated Alexius Comnenus of Trebizond and David Comnenus of Bithynia and Paphlagonia (1207-1211).

India's southern states, among them Yadava, Kakatiya, Pandya, and Hoysala, warred constantly (1200-1294).

Ikhtiya-ud-Din, a freebooting adventurer from Ghor, conquered Magadha and Bengal (1201-1203) but failed to take Tibet (1204-1205).

Ghor's general Qutb-ud-Din took Kalinja, defeating the Chandela (Candella) kingdom of Bundelkhand, in northern India (1202).

1200-1209 (cont.)

1213), the crusaders captured many cities, often killing their inhabitants, although Toulouse and Montauban remained untaken.

b. James I (1208-1276), king of Aragon and Catalonia (r. 1214-1276).

Venetians installed Isaac II and Alexius IV as coemperors, then left to await cash payment.

Fourth Crusade: Byzantines overthrew Venetian puppets Isaac II and Alexius IV, placing Alexius Ducas Mourtzouphlous on the throne; Venetians and Crusaders then attacked, took, and sacked Constantinople (Apr. 11-13, 1204), effectively ending the Byzantine Empire, although the Latin Empire of Constantinople continued.

At Adrianople (1205), Bulgarian king Kaloyan defeated the combined forces of Venetian doge Enrico Dandalo and Baldwin I, Latin emperor of Constantinople, who was taken and died a captive.

d. Enrico Dandolo (ca. 1120-1205), Venetian doge who led forces of the Fourth Crusade in taking Constantinople (1205), where he died.

Crusaders under Henry I defeated Bulgaria's King Boril at Philippopolis (Plovdiv) (1208).

1210-1219

Alfonso VIII of Castile and León capped a series of campaigns against the Almohads by winning Las Navas de Tolosa (1212), there aided by Affonso II of Portugal; he then took central Spain (1212).

Albigensian Crusade: Pedro of Aragon joined Raymond of Toulouse and the "heretic" forces being attacked by the Crusaders, but they were overwhelmed at the Battle of Muret (Sept. 12, 1213).

France's Philip II attempted to take Flanders but was prevented from doing so by an English victory in the sea battle of Damme (1213).

With German and Flemish allies, England's King John I tried to regain lost territory north of the Loire River in France, but he was decisively defeated at the Battle of Bouvines (1213-1214).

d. Alfonso VIII (1155-1214), ruler and general of Castile and León who led the fight against Spanish Muslims, notably at Las Navas de Tolosa (1212). Ferdinand III won a dynastic struggle (1214-1217) for the throne of Castile.

After running conflicts between King John I, brother and successor of Richard the Lion-Hearted, and England's nobility, John was forced to sign the Magna Carta (June 1215) at Runnymede, limiting his powers.

Nobles opposed to King John I tried to put Louis, the French dauphin, on the English throne (1215); in the civil war that followed, Scotland's King Alexander II reached near London before being defeated (1216); Louis and the rebels eventually lost in southern England after John's death (1216), in a land battle at Lincoln, and in a sea battle off Sandwich (both 1217). John was succeeded by Henry III (r. 1216-1272), then still a child.

Affonso II of Portugal, aided by Crusaders, defeated the Moors at Alcácer do Sol (1217), expanding southward.

Teutonic Knights, under the leadership of Hermann von Salza (1210-1239), moved from the Middle East to central Europe (1211), at first helping Andrew of Hungary fight off the Cuman Turks.

Theodore Ducas Angelus, ruler of a Byzantine remnant, expanded Epirus by taking much of Macedonia and Thrace (1214-1230).

Bulgaria's King Boril was besieged at Trnovo by Ivan Asen, who captured and replaced him (1217), becoming Ivan Asen II.

Africa and Southwest Asia

1200-1209 (cont.)

	After defeating Muhammad of Ghor at Andkhui, south of the Oxus River (1205), Mohammed, shah of Khwarezm, expanded into Afghanistan and Persia; Muhammad of Ghor then campaigned in India, putting down rebellions, notably in Rajputana, before being assassinated (1206).
	Mongols under Genghis Khan fought and came to dominate the Western Hsia in Kansu (1205-1209).
	Qutb-ud-Din, general from Ghor, renamed himself Aibak and founded the Sultanate of Delhi, becoming the first of the Slave (Mamluk) dynasty (1207); he was succeeded, after some turmoil, by his son-in-law Iltutmish (1210).
	Genghis Khan defeated his last main Mongol rivals, the Naiman, at the Irtysh River (1208); their leader, Kushlik (Gichluk), took refuge with the Kara Khitai.

1210-1219

The Beni Marin, a Berber people, took Morocco from the Almohads, whom they largely replaced with the Marinid dynasty, centered on Fez (1217-1258).	Developing the necessary siege craft, Genghis Khan's Mongols conquered China up to the Great Wall (1213), then defeated the main Chin army to take northern China, sacking Peking (1215).
Fifth Crusade (1218-1221): Crusaders from Europe gathered at Acre, joined by the Knights Hospitallers and Knights Templars and by forces from the Crusader states (1218). Led by John of Brienne, king of Jerusalem, Crusader forces sailed to Egypt, where northeast of Cairo they faced a Muslim army under Malik al-Kamil; Crusaders besieged Damietta, which fell after a year and a half (Nov. 1219); meanwhile, an Egyptian fleet was defeated on the Nile by the Genoans (1218).	b. Kublai (Khubilai; Kubla) Khan (1215-1294), Mongol ruler.
	Pushed out by Khwarezmian forces, refugees from Ghazni, led by Taj-ud-din Yildiz, invaded the Punjab and were defeated by Iltutmish, sultan of Delhi, at Taraori (1216).
	Genghis Khan's forces, led by general Chepe (Jebei), conquered the Kara Khitai under the Naiman Mongol Mushlik, who was executed (1217).
	Genghis and his sons — Juji, Jagatai, and Ogatai — led four armies westward against the empire of Khwarezm, which had been allied with the Kara Khitai (1218-1224).
	Khwarezmian forces under Mohammed Shah (Alaud-Din Mohammed) inconclusively fought a much smaller Mongol army under Juji and Chepe at Jand, in the Ferghana Valley (1219).

1210-1219 (cont.)

Albigensian Crusade: Simon de Montfort was killed near Toulouse (1218), but the attacks against "heretics" continued until 1226.

Danes under Valdemar II campaigned in Estonia (1219), building a fortress at Reval (Tallinn).

1220-1229

d. Philip II (Augustus) (1165-1223), French king (r. 1179-1223) who was best known for his sparring with England's Henry II, often acting through Henry's three sons, notably Richard the Lion-Hearted, Philip's ally in the Third Crusade (1189-1192) but rival in France, and Richard's younger brother John I.

Denmark's Valdemar II was captured (1223) and, after losing the Battle of Bornhöved (1227), was forced to give up his Estonian conquests.

Russians under Duke Jaroslav of Novgorod occupied parts of eastern Finland, introducing Russian Orthodox Christianity (1227-1229).

James I (the Conqueror) of Aragon retook the Balearic Islands (1229-1235) and Valencia (1233-1245).

b. Alexander Nevsky (of the Neva) (1220-1263), prince of Novgorod (r. 1236-1263).

Mstislav, prince of Kiev, refused Mongol peace offers, killed their ambassadors, and, with his Russian-Cuman army, attacked Chepe and Subotai's Mongol army at the Kalka River; the Russian-Cuman forces were utterly destroyed (1223). The Mongols then turned east to join Genghis Khan; Chepe died en route.

Latin Empire of Constantinople was defeated twice — at Poimanenon by John of Nicaea and at Serres by Theodore of Epirus, who also fought off John's attempt to take Thrace (1224).

As the Teutonic Knights grew more powerful, Andrew of Hungary banished them from his land (1224); they then established themselves in eastern Poland, centered at Thorn.

b. Charles I (Charles of Anjou) (1226-1285), king of Naples and Sicily (r. 1265-1285).

Italy was the battleground for wars between the German emperor Frederick II and Pope Gregory IX (1228-1229; 1240-1241), ending with Frederick's annexation of Tuscany.

After the Sixth Crusade, Frederick II returned to retake southern Italy from the papal armies (1229).

1210-1219 (cont.)

1220-1229

Fifth Crusade: Crusaders rejected Muslim offers to exchange Damietta for parts of the Holy Land and, with reinforcements from Europe, headed toward Cairo; they were decisively defeated by the Muslims, who also retook the Nile; cut off, the Crusaders were forced to give up Damietta, ending the Crusade (1221).

En route to Europe Chepe and Subotai took a Mongol army to Armenia and Azerbaijan (1221), meeting and defeating an army of Georgian Crusaders, defeating the Cumans at the Kuban River, taking Astrakhan, and then attacking Genoa's fortress Sudak, in the Crimea, before heading into the Ukraine (1222).

Soso under King Sumanguru conquered Mali (1224).

Sixth Crusade (1228-1229): German emperor Frederick II came to the Holy Land and, without fighting, negotiated with the Muslims for Nazareth, Bethlehem, and Jerusalem, with a connection to the coast, then proclaimed himself king of Jerusalem (1229).

Moving westward with their four armies, Mongols under Juji besieged Khojend in the Ferghana Valley; Jagatai and Ogatai besieged Otrar on the Syr (Jaxartes) River; Genghis Khan headed for the lower Syr at the Aral Sea; and Chepe took the Amu (Oxus) Valley into Transoxiana. On learning of all this, Mohammed Shah fled Khwarezm, apportioning his army in key fortresses, such as Samarkand, which the Mongols took and destroyed, killing many of the inhabitants, as they had at Khojend and Otrar; Bokhara surrendered but was destroyed (all 1220). While Genghis Khan and his generals completed the conquest of Khwarezm and Khorasan, Chepe and Subotai pursued Mohammed, who died at the Caspian Sea before they reached him (1221).

Under Jaya Parmesvaravarman II (r. 1220-1252), Champa continued its fight with Annam over border provinces.

Having raised a new army in Ghazni, Mohammed Shah's son Jellaluddin defeated a much smaller Mongol force at Pirvan (1221); the main Mongol force under Genghis Khan pursued Jellaluddin to the Indus River, where the Turks retreated after a hard fight; Jellaluddin escaped in a dramatic jump from a cliff into the river. Small Mongol forces raided widely in the Punjab but failed to find Jellaluddin, eventually withdrawing to Ghazni (1222-1224); denied refuge by the sultan of Delhi, Jellaluddin fled down the Indus and on into Persia.

In western Java rebels against the Kediri kingdom founded the state of Singosari (1222).

Genghis Khan attacked the Western Hsia in Kansu, in a battle on the frozen Yellow River, annihilating the Tangut forces, which suffered an estimated 300,000 dead (1226); Genghis Khan then attacked the Chin dynasty (1227), dying during the campaign, which was then halted.

d. Genghis Khan (Temujin; Chingghis; Jenghis) (1162-1227), Mongol ruler; one of the world's greatest conquerors, he forged

1220-1229 (cont.)

1230-1239

Ferdinand III of Castile campaigned with great success against the Moors, capturing Córdoba (1236), Seville (1248), and Jaén (1246) and leaving the Moors confined to Granada.

b. Edward I (1239-1307), English king (r. 1272-1307).

Bulgarians under Ivan Asen II defeated and captured Theodore of Epirus at Klokonitsa, on the Maritz River (1230).

Teutonic Knights under Hermann Balk began what would be a five-decade conquest of Prussia (1233-1283).

At Cortenuova, Germany's Frederick II defeated the Lombard League and the Guelph army of Milan (1237).

Mongol forces led by Mangu quickly conquered Cuman territories north of the Caucasus Mountains and the Black Sea (1237).

Mongol forces under Batu and Subotai invaded eastern Europe, defeating the Bulgarians (Dec. 1237) and then destroying the Russian principalities; at the Sil River, the Mongols annihilated the Russian army and killed its leader, Yuri II, grand prince of Vladimir (Mar. 4, 1238).

1240-1249

Norway's Haakon IV suppressed a revolt led by Jarl Skuli (1240).

England's Henry III invaded France but was repelled by Louis IX (Saint Louis) in the Battle of the Saintes (1242); Henry won most of Aquitaine and Toulouse (1242).

Birger Magnusson and his Swedish Crusaders campaigned in Finland and eastward, but their expansion was halted at the Neva River by Russian forces under Alexander of Novgorod, who was then called Nevsky (July 1240).

Mongols under Subotai attacked Kiev, which refused demands to surrender and was destroyed (Dec. 6, 1240).

Mongols under Subotai invaded central Europe. One army, under his grandson Kaidu, defeated four larger Polish armies, including that of Boleslav V of Poland at Cracow (Mar. 1241), and raided widely through Silesia, Lithuania, East Prussia, and Pomerania. At Leignitz (Wahlstatt) (Apr. 9, 1241), Kaidu's forces met and broke an army of Germans, Poles, and Teutonic Knights led by Prince Henry (the Pious) of Silesia. Now effectively controlling north-central Europe, Kaidu turned south to join the other Mongols.

Another Mongol army, under Ogatai's son Kadan, swept through Transylvania and the Hungarian plain (Apr. 1241). At the Sajo River (Apr. 11, 1241), they met and routed an army under Hungary's King Bela IV, ambushing the retreating forces and killing more than 40,000. The Mongols now controlled all of eastern Europe.

Preparing invasions of Austria, Germany, and Italy, the Mongols broke off (Dec. 1241) and returned to Mon-

1220-1229 (cont.)

a massive Asian empire; his adopted name, Genghis Khan, means Supreme Emperor. He was succeeded by Ogatai.

1230-1239

Shah Jellaluddin of Khwarezm was defeated by the Seljuks of Rum at Erzinjan (1230) and later was assassinated (1231).

Seljuk Turks fought off an invasion of Anatolia by Ayyubid forces (1231-1232).

Mongol forces took the rest of Persia, northern Mesopotamia, Azerbaijan, Georgia, and Armenia (1231-1236).

Under King Sundiata, Mali gained its independence from Soso (1235) and expanded.

Abu Zakariya led a successful rebellion against the Almohad dynasty in Tunisia, eastern Algeria, and Tripolitania, establishing the Hafsid dynasty (1236).

Rebels against Srivijayan rule in Malaya founded the kingdom of Ligor, under Dharmaraja Chandragam (ca. 1230).

Shah Jellaluddin, who had kept the western part of his Khwarezmian Empire after escaping from the Mongols, was defeated at Erzinjan (1230) by Ala ud-Din Kaikobad (Khaikobad), Seljuk sultan of Rum; this left open a path to western Asia for the Mongols.

Mongol forces conquered Korea (1231) and then the Chin Empire; under Subotai they besieged and finally took the capital, Pien Liang (1233), ending the dynasty (1231-1234), and shortly beginning a war with the Sung Empire for the rest of China.

Mongols led by Godan, son of Ogatai, took Tibet (1239).

1240-1249

Under Malik-al-Salih (r. 1240-1249), the Ayyubids retook much of Syria.

The Mongols established their dominance over Anatolia by defeating the Seljuk Turks at Kosedagh (1243).

Khwarezmian forces trying to outrun the Mongols took and sacked Jerusalem; allying themselves with the Egyptians, they defeated the Crusaders and their Muslim allies from Damascus at Gaza (1244); this sparked another Crusade.

Egypt's Mamelukes took Ascalon from the Crusaders (1247).

Seventh Crusade (1248-1254): France's King Louis IX (later Saint Louis) led the Crusaders to Egypt, again taking Damietta (1249), then marching on Cairo; they attempted a surprise attack at Mansura (Feb. 1250) but were badly defeated; later they were largely destroyed at Fariskur (Apr.); Louis was captured and later ransomed.

Abu Yahia Yarmorasen led the Zenata people against the Almohads, taking Tlemcen and establishing the new Ziyanid dynasty in western Algeria (1248).

Mongols raided in the Punjab, seizing Lahore (1241); more raids would follow over the decades.

d. Ogatai (Ögödei) Khan (ca. 1185-1241), Mongol ruler, Genghis Khan's third son and successor; his death (Dec.) may have saved Europe, as Mongol forces called off their offensive and returned to Karakorum to select a new khan.

Mongol offensives largely ended after the death of Ogatai (1241) during a four-year succession struggle, centered on his two eldest sons — Kuguk, eventually named khan (Jan. 1246), and Batu, named khan of eastern Europe and northwest Asia (the Khanate of the Golden Horde, with its capital at Sarai, on the Volga).

Under Parakamabahu II, the Sinhalese kingdom of Dambadeniya drove the Kalinga peoples from Ceylon (Sri Lanka), also fighting off a Malay invasion led by Chandrabanu (1242; 1258).

Mongols defeated the Seljuk Turks at Kosedagh, taking the remains of Khwarezm and also Anatolia (1243).

Franciscan monk John de Plano Carpini traveled as a European embassy to the

1240-1249 (cont.)

golia to elect a successor to Ogatai, whose death very likely saved Europe; on their way back east, the Mongols ravaged and effectively destroyed Serbia and Bulgaria.

Russian forces under Alexander Nevsky defeated the Teutonic Knights in a key battle on the ice of Lake Peipus (early Apr. 1242).

German ruler Frederick II invaded the Roman Campania and successfully fought the forces of Pope Innocent IV (1244-1247), who then supported rival claimants in civil wars (1247-1256) against Frederick and later his son Conrad IV.

After the Mongols withdrew, Bela IV resumed power in Hungary, fighting off an invasion by Frederick of Austria (1246).

John of Nicaea finally succeeded in conquering Macedonia and Thrace (1246).

1250-1259

Bulgarians under Michael Asen took Thrace and Macedonia (1254), but Theodore II Lascaris of Nicaea regained them after winning at Adrianople (1255).

Serbia lost Bosnia and Herzegovina to Hungary (1254).

As the Holy Roman Empire collapsed, Manfred, Conrad IV's half-brother, came to power in southern Italy (1255) and Sicily (1256), then campaigned widely and took most of Italy (1255-1265).

Ottocar II of Bohemia campaigned with the Teutonic Knights against the Prussians (1255).

Under Bereke (r. 1256-1263), Batu's brother, the Khanate of the Golden Horde raided the Balkans, Hungary, and Poland; Bereke was the first Mongol leader to accept Islam.

Mongols from the Golden Horde, led by Tulubaga and Nogai, raided into Silesia, taking and sacking Cracow, Sandomir, and Bythom (1259).

Byzantine troops took the fortress of Mistra on Greece's Peloponnesian coast (1259).

1240-1249 (cont.)

	Mongol camp on the Dnieper River, then on to Karakorum, south of Lake Baikal (1245).
	d. Subotai (Subodei) (ca. 1172-1245), Mongol general who was field commander of the troops who took much of eastern Europe (1237-1241).
	Dharmaraja Chandragam of Ligor, in Malaya, raided Ceylon (1247; 1270).
	Kuguk was leading a Mongol army toward Europe when he died (1248); Batu chose to remain in the west, while Mangu took the east. Other khanates were established, notably in Turkestan and Transoxiana, but these remained subordinate to the great khan for at least a century, establishing the Pax Mongolica, the only time in history (lasting until roughly 1307) when travelers (such as Marco Polo) could cross Eurasia with a single passport.

1250-1259

Mamelukes revolted against the Ayyubid dynasty, with Aidik coming to power (1250).	European envoy William de Rubruk (Rubruquis), from Flanders, traveled east to visit the Mongols' great khan, whom he said promised to concentrate on Muslims before again attacking Christian Europe (1252).
Hulagu Khan, founder of the Ilkhan Mongol dynasty, captured the Assassins' fortress at Alamut (1256), killing all its defenders and exterminating the Persian branch of the sect.	Long war between Champa and Annam ended when Champa's Jaya Parmesvaravarman II was killed during an invasion by King Tran Thaiton (1252).
Hulagu Khan and his Mongol forces took southern Mesopotamia, including Baghdad, ending the Abbasid Caliphate (1258). Ilkhan general Kitboga (Ket-Buka) took northern Syria (1258-1260), allied with Bohemund VI of Antioch against the Mamelukes.	Now led by Ogatai's nephews Mangu and Kublai, the Mongols took the Tai kingdom of Nanchao (Yunnan, Guizhou, and parts of Gaungzi) (1253-1256); many of the Tai then moved southwest into the Irrawaddy and Menam valleys, pushing ahead of them the Burmese, Mon, and Khmer peoples.
b. Osman (Othman) I (1258-1326), Turkish founder of the Ottoman Empire.	d. Batu Khan (?-1255), Mongol general who led the invasion of Russia and Europe (1235-1241); grandson of Genghis Khan, he founded the Khanate of the Golden Horde.
	Mangu led the Mongols in a series of victories against southern China's Sung dynasty (1257-1259), ending with his death.
	Mongols under general Sogatu invaded Annam (1257), driving the Cham into the mountains, where they became guerrillas.

1250-1259 (cont.)

1260-1269

b. Aymer de Valence, earl of Pembroke (ca. 1260-1324), English military commander.

England's Henry III faced a revolt of his barons (1263-1265), led by Simon de Montfort (son of the Albigensian Crusader), who decisively defeated him at Lewes (May 14, 1264), making Henry a puppet; Henry's son Prince Edward escaped and, with a new army, defeated Simon and his ally Llewellyn, prince of Wales, at Newport (July 8, 1265), driving them into Wales; Edward destroyed an army under Simon's son, Simon the Younger, at Kenilworth (Aug. 2, 1265), then trapped and crushed the elder Simon at Evesham (Aug. 4), effectively ending the revolt.

Scotland's Alexander III swept the Norse out of the Hebrides, winning the Battle of Largs (1263).

b. Philip IV (1268-1314), French king (r. 1285-1314).

Ottocar II of Bohemia defeated Hungary's Bela IV at Kressenbrunn (1260), taking Styria.

Nicaean forces under general Alexius Stragopulos captured Constantinople from the Latin emperor, then reestablishing the Byzantine Empire under Nicaea's King Michael VIII Paleologus (1261).

Now allied with Genoa, the Byzantines fought against the Latins and the Bulgarians in Greece, Thrace, Macedonia, and Epirus (1261-1265).

Bela IV of Hungary fought off a second Mongol invasion (1261).

d. Alexander Nevsky (1220-1263), prince of Novgorod (r. 1236-1263), known for his wars against Swedish Crusaders and Teutonic Knights; named Nevsky (of the Neva) for his victory at the Neva River (1240).

Venice won the upper hand in its long war with Genoa (1253-1299) with a victory at Trepani, near Sicily (1264).

Supported by Pope Urban IV against Manfred in the succession for southern Italy, Charles of Anjou invaded Italy, landing at Naples and Benevento (Feb. 26, 1266), defeating and killing Manfred, and becoming king of Naples.

Conradin, the last German of the Hohenstaufen line to claim southern Italy, led a Ghibelline army in taking Rome (July 1268) and invading southern Italy. He lost to Charles of Anjou at Tagliacozzo (Aug. 25, 1268) and was executed, leaving Charles as ruler of the Two Sicilies (Naples and Sicily).

1270-1279

b. William Wallace (ca. 1270-1305), Scottish partisan leader.

d. James I (1208-1276), king of Aragon and Catalonia (r. 1214-1276) called El Conquistador (the Conqueror) for his conquests of the Balearic Islands (1229-1235) and Valencia (1235-1238); also active in the Moorish War (1256-1276).

Ottocar II of Bohemia fought a losing war against Rudolph of Hapsburg (1274-1278) before being killed at Marchfeld (Durnkrut) (Aug. 26, 1278).

Africa and Southwest Asia

	1250-1259 (cont.)
	Mongols took Tonkin, including Hanoi (1257).
	1260-1269
At Ain Jalut, west of the Euphrates, near Nazareth, Mameluke forces under Kotuz routed a small Mongol army with some Crusader allies (1260); Mongol general Kitboga was killed.	Succeeding Mangu, Kublai Khan fought and won civil wars against his rivals (1260-1261), including his younger brother Arik-Buka and Ogatai's grandson Kaidu.
Mamelukes led by Baibars expanded at the expense of the Crusader states (1260-1268), finally taking Antioch (1268).	Several Hindu states, including Malwa and Gujarat, asserted their independence (ca. 1266-1287); the Mongols made numerous raids into northern India.
Inconclusive Mongol civil war was fought in the Caucasus Mountains between the Ilkhans under Hulagu Khan and the Khanate of the Golden Horde under Bereke, allied with the Mamelukes (1261-1262).	
	1270-1279
Eighth Crusade (1270): France's Louis IX and his brother Charles of Anjou invaded Tunisia and besieged Tunis; Louis and many of his troops died in an epidemic.	Using a Korean fleet, part of which had previously been lost in a storm, Mongols took the islands of Tsushima and Iki, then invaded Japan, at Hakata Bay (Ajkozaki), in northern Kyushu, but were easily driven off (1274).
In Ethiopia a rebellion ended the Zagwe dynasty; a new dynasty was founded by Yekuno Amlak (1270), who moved the capital to central Ethiopia.	Mongols under Bayan, grandson of Subotai, completed the conquest of Sung China (1276-1279), taking the capital, Hangchow (1276), and winning the decisive naval battle in the bay of Canton (1279), at which the Sung fleet was destroyed.
Under Yakub II, the Marinids campaigned in Algeria against the Ziyanids (1270-1286).	
Edward I of England campaigned with his Crusaders against the Muslims, at one point reaching Nazareth (1271-1272).	
Mamelukes under Baibars captured a great prize — the Knights of St. John's fortress-castle at Krak, near Tripoli, Lebanon (1271) — then destroyed the Syrian branch of the Assassins (1272).	d. Chang Shih-chieh (?-1279), Chinese admiral who commanded the last Sung fleet in a vain fight against Mongol conquest (1276-1279); he died at sea after losing the crucial battle at Canton bay.
Christian Maqurrah kingdom fell after continued raids by Muslim Mamelukes from Egypt (ca. 1275-ca. 1350).	

1270-1279 (cont.)

1280-1289

England's Edward I defeated and killed the Welsh prince Llewellyn at Radnor (1282) and went on to conquer Wales (1282-1284), thereafter adopting the Welsh longbow as a key English weapon.

Marinids from Morocco, led by Yakub II, campaigned with Alfonso X of Castile and León against his rebel son Sancho, who was briefly in control of Spain when Alfonso died (1284).

France's Philip III invaded Aragon but was held off (1284).

Teutonic Knights expanded to the Baltic Sea, cutting off Poland (1280).

Byzantine emperor Michael VIII Paleologus defeated the forces of Charles of Anjou at Berat, Albania, halting his campaign to take Constantinople (1281).

In the War of the Sicilian Vespers, Charles of the Two Sicilies faced a revolt on Sicily and a related invasion by Pedro of Aragon; Charles's fleet was defeated by Aragonese admiral Roger de Loria and his Catalan fleet off Messina (1283) and again off Naples (1284); he then lost Sicily.

d. Charles I (Charles of Anjou) (1226-1285), king of Naples and Sicily (r. 1265-1285) who defeated Hohenstaufen claimants of southern Italy (1266; 1268). He was succeeded by Charles II (r. 1285-1309), who was held captive by the Spanish (1284-1288).

1290-1299

After the death of Scotland's Alexander III (1290), a succession struggle ended with John de Baliol becoming king, with England as overlord.

Jews were expelled from England (1290).

Genoese explorers Doria and Vivaldo sailed westward from Europe into the Atlantic Ocean searching for India, but they never returned (1291).

Swedes under Torgil Knutsson campaigned in Karelia (eastern Finland) (1293), reviving war with Novgorod (1293-1323).

1270-1279 (cont.)

Burmese forces raided Kanngai, a Chinese satellite, but at Ngasaunggyan were defeated by a Mongol army one-third their size (1277), which then pursued them back into Burma to Bhamo.

The conquest of China completed, Kublai Khan founded the Yuan dynasty (1279), making his capital at Peking.

1280-1289

Charles of Anjou, king of the Two Sicilies, invaded Tunisia, defeating Muslim forces at Carthage (1280).

Ilkhan Mongols invaded Syria and, though supported by some small Crusader forces, were defeated at Homs by Mamelukes under Sultan Kala'un (1281).

Mamelukes under Sultan Kala'un took Tripoli from the Crusaders (1289).

In their second invasion of Japan (1281), the Mongols were again defeated, by Japanese military strategy, including raiding the fleet itself, and by a storm wrecking many of their ships; only a few invaders survived.

Mongols defeated the Burmese at Kaungsin, penetrated to Bhamo, and built fortified garrisons on the upper Irrawaddy River (1283).

Under Rama Khamheng (r. 1283-1317), the kingdom of Sukhot'ai expanded from its center in the upper Menam Valley to far south on the Malay Peninsula, conquering the kingdom of Ligor (ca. 1295), and to the Mekong River, near Luang Prabang.

Kublai Khan's son Togan brought Mongol reinforcements to Annam, taking Hanoi; they were then defeated by the Annamese and blocked from joining up with Sogatu's Mongol army, which was driven into Champa, where Sogatu was killed (1285).

Mongol forces under Ye-su Ti-mur, Kublai Khan's grandson, conquered Burma, including its capital, Pagan (1287).

Mongol forces again took Hanoi (1287), but the Annamese under King Tran Nhon-Ton halted the invasion, their last.

1290-1299

Mamelukes under Sultan Khalil Malik al-Ashraf, son of Kala'un, took Acre, the last Crusader stronghold in the East (1291). The Knights of St. John Hospitallers moved their headquarters to Cyprus.

In the continuing Venetian-Genoese war, the Genoese won at Alexandretta (1294), the eastern Mediterranean port, but lost their trading post of Galata, near Constantinople, after it was sacked by a Venetian fleet under admiral Morosini. The Genoese won at Curzola, in the Adriatic (1299).

Ilkhan Mongols under Ghazan Mahmud took Damascus and much of Syria, then retired (1299-1301).

With Mongol help, Prince Vijaya overthrew his father-in-law, Kertanagara, taking the throne of Singosari, in Java, then defeating the Mongols (1292-1293).

Jalal-ud-din Firuz Khalji, founder of the Afghan Khalji dynasty, fought off a Mongol invasion (1292).

b. Kitabatake Chikafusa (1293-1354), Japanese general.

Ala-ud-din Khalji took Muslim forces farther south in India than they had reached, beyond the Narbada River, taking and

1290-1299 (cont.)

England's Edward I campaigned against France's Philip IV (1294; 1296; 1297), maintaining his claim to Gascony, which was finally acknowledged by treaty (1303).

After Scotland's King John allied himself with France, England's Edward I invaded Scotland, sacking Berwick-upon-Tweed, defeating John at Dunbar and annexing Scotland (1296).

Scottish nobles under William Wallace revolted, defeating English forces under the earl of Warenne at Cambuskenneth Bridge (1297) and raiding widely in Northumbria and Durham; they lost to Edward I at Falkirk (1298), where the English first used the Welsh longbow on a large scale.

1300-1309

France again tried to take Flanders but was defeated at Courtrai (July 11, 1302), called the Battle of the Golden Spurs because the Flemish pikemen ripped the spurs off the boots of fallen French knights.

d. William Wallace (ca. 1270-1305), Scottish partisan leader during the Scottish-English wars; he was convicted of treason and executed (Aug. 23).

Scots again revolted against English rule, this time led by Robert Bruce, who lost to English forces under the earl of Pembroke at Methven (Ruthven) (June 19, 1306) and Dalry (Aug. 11) before winning at Loudon Hill (May 1307); as Robert I, he cleared English forces from most of Scotland (1307-1314), except Berwick, Dunbar, and Stirling.

Jews were arrested, attacked, and driven from France (1306).

d. Edward I (1239-1307), English king (r. 1272-1307) nicknamed "Longshanks"; noted for his campaigns against his uncle and sometime mentor Simon de Montfort, especially at Lewes (1264) and Newport (1265), and against Simon the Younger at Kenilworth (1265).

In Hungary a succession dispute led to civil war (1301-1308).

b. Stephen Dushan (Stephen Urosh IV) (1308-1355), king of Serbia (r. 1331-1355).

1310-1319

b. Edward III (1312-1377), English king (r. 1327-1377).

Austrian forces, invading Switzerland to confirm Hapsburg rule there, were repelled and destroyed at Morgarten (Nov. 15, 1315).

Africa and Southwest Asia

East, Central, and South Asia, the Pacific, and the Americas

	sacking the Yadava capital, Devagiri (1294); he later assassinated and replaced his uncle and mentor, Jalal-ud-din Firuz Khalji, the sultan of Delhi (1296).
	b. Kusunoki Masashige (1294-1336), Japanese general.
	d. Kublai (Khubilai; Kubla) Khan (1215-1294), Mongol ruler, grandson of Genghis Khan; he completed the conquest of the Sung Empire in China (1231-1279), establishing the Pax Mongolica.
	Vijaya and his son, Jayanagara, faced various revolts (from 1295), put down by Gaja Mada (1319), who as prime minister led Java in taking Bali, West Java, Madura, and other nearby islands and coastal colonies.
	Mongols raided in the Punjab (from 1297), but forces from Delhi, led by Ala-ud-din, repelled two attempts to reach Delhi (1299; 1303).
	Burmese deposed their Mongol puppet ruler in the Shan revolt (1299).

In their continuing war, Yusuf IV and the Marinids of Morocco besieged the Ziyanid capital of Tlemcen (1300-1307), in Algeria, until Yusuf's assassination.	Mongol invasion to retake Burma was stopped at the Shan city of Myinsaing (1300); paid off, the Mongols left for good.
Ilkhan Mongols invading Syria were defeated at Marj-as-Suffar by the Mamelukes (Apr. 20, 1303).	Sultan of Delhi, Ala-ud-din, retook Malwa and Gujarat (1300-1305) after bitter sieges at Ramthanbor (1301) and Chitor (1303), where defenders made final suicide attacks after reportedly burning their wives and children on a funeral pyre.
Knights Hospitallers captured Rhodes (1309), making it their new base, effectively a highly fortified independent state controlling the eastern Mediterranean.	b. Nitta Yoshisada (1301-1338), Japanese general.
	Ala-ud-din and his Delhi forces again fought off Mongol invasions (1305; 1306), the Mongols' last serious foray into India.
	b. Ashikaga Takauji (1305-1358), Japanese general and shogun.
	b. Ashikaga Tadayoshi (1306-1352), Japanese general and deputy shogun.
	Muslim forces from Delhi, under general Malik Kufar, took most of the Deccan, including Devagiri (1308), Warangal (1309-1310), Hoysala (1310), and Pandya (1311).

The pope dispatched a party of Dominican friars to East Africa (1316), the first of many seeking the mythical Christian leader Prester John.	In India's southern Deccan, Madura revolted to become an independent Muslim sultanate (1311).

1310-1319 (cont.)

Robert I (Robert Bruce) fought off Edward II's attempts to retake Scotland, dealing him a disaster at Bannockburn (1314).

d. Philip IV (1268-1314), French king (r. 1285-1314) nicknamed "Le Bel" (the Handsome), who fought against England and Flanders, winning decisively at Mons (1304).

Scottish forces under Edward Bruce, Robert's brother, successfully invaded Ireland (1316), with Edward becoming king before he was defeated and killed at Faughart (1318).

Scottish forces, which had been raiding widely in England (1314-1328), won the Battle of Myton (1319).

1320-1329

During civil war in England, Edward II defeated his opponents under the duke of Lancaster at Boroughbridge (1322).

Scots under Robert I defeated another invasion by England's Edward II at Byland (1322).

d. Aymer de Valence, earl of Pembroke (ca. 1260-1324), English military commander who defeated the Scots under Robert Bruce at Methven (1306), lost at Loudon Hill (1307), and commanded the rear guard at Bannockburn (1314).

Under Philip VI, the first of the Valois line, France won control of Flanders at the Battle of Cassel (1328).

Under the Peace of Northampton, the English recognized Scotland's independence (1329).

Lucca won a war with Florence (1320-1323).

Byzantine Empire was riven by civil war between an emperor and his grandson, both named Andronicus, which was finally won by the younger (1321-1328).

Aragon began its three-decade bid to oust Genoa and Pisa from Sardinia (1323).

First documentary evidence of guns in Europe, described in Florentine (1326) and English (ca. 1326) manuscripts.

Teutonic Knights, joined by John of Bohemia, campaigned against the Lithuanians (1328-1345).

1330-1339

At age 15, England's Edward III led a party of nobles in a successful revolt (1330) against the regency of his mother, Queen Isabella, and her lover, Roger Mortimer, who had killed Edward II (1327).

b. Edward, Prince of Wales (the Black Prince) (1330-1376), English general.

Pressing his claim for Scotland's throne, Edward de Baliol led an irregular army of English freebooters and Scottish exiles into Scotland, after a surprise night attack defeating Scottish forces under the earl of Mar at Dupplin Muir (1332); England's Edward III invaded Scotland, sharply defeating Scottish forces at Halidon Hill (1333); Scotland's David II took refuge in France.

Hundred Years' War (1337-1453): The long series of contests between the French and English was a rivalry with its roots in the feudal claims of English kings to French domains. France's Philip VI rejected English claims to French land (1337); England's Edward III proclaimed himself king of France (recognized by Ger-

Under Stephen Dechanski, Serbia conquered most of the Vardar Valley, notably defeating a Byzantine-Bulgarian army at Kustendil (Velbuzhde) (1330).

Swiss forces fought off a Burgundian invasion at Laupen (1339).

Africa and Southwest Asia

1310-1319 (cont.)

Under Abu-Said (r. 1316-1335), the Ilkhan Mongols fought the Khanate of the Golden Horde, under Uzbeg, primarily in the Caucasus Mountains but sometimes as far north as the Terek River (1316-1335).

Ottoman Turks under Osman I besieged and finally took Brusa, in northwest Anatolia (1317-1329), making it the capital of their new empire.

Annam conquered Champa (1312), but the two united to fight off an invasion by the Tai, under Rai Khamheng (1313), after which Champa again reasserted its primacy under Che Anan.

Civil war and disorder followed the death of Delhi's sultan, Ala-ud-din (1316), who was immediately succeeded by his general Malik Kufar.

d. Ala-ud-din Khalji (?-1316), Afghan-Indian ruler (r. 1296-1316) who deposed his uncle (1296), then conquered Gujarat (1297) and Rajasthan (1301-1312), several times beating off Mongol invaders.

b. Kitabatake Akiie (Akiiye) (1317-1338), Japanese general.

1320-1329

Under Mansa Musa, Mali became dominant in West Africa; his general Sagmandia (Saga-man-dir) took Songhai, including its capital at Gao (1325).

d. Osman (Othman) I (1258-1326), Turkish ruler who founded the Ottoman Empire, named after him.

Under Amda Tseyon, Ethiopia conquered Ifat, a Muslim state on the Red Sea (1328), and tried to protect Coptic Christians.

Ottoman Turks under Orkhan I defeated Andronicus III and his Byzantine forces at Maltepe (1329).

Aztec (Mexica) people settled in the Valley of Mexico, notably on two defensible islands, Tenochtitlán and Tlatilulco, in Lake Texcoco (ca. 1325), soon controlling the whole valley.

b. Imagawa Sadayo (Ryoshun) (1325-1420), Japanese general.

b. T'ai-tsu (Chu Yüan-chang) (1328-1398), Chinese emperor (r. 1368-1398).

Mongols from Transoxiana, led by Tarmarshirin, reached Delhi but were paid off by Sultan Mohammed bin Tughluk (1329).

b. Hosokawa Yoriyuki (1329-1392), Japanese general.

1330-1339

Ottoman Turks took the Byzantine territories of Nicaea (1331) and Nicomedia (1337).

Marinids under Ali V, Yusuf IV's successor, again besieged Tlemcen and finally took the Ziyanid capital (1335-1337).

Emperor Go Daigo II rebelled against rule by the Hojo clan; though briefly captured, Go Daigo escaped and was eventually victorious, but the civil war split Japan (1331-1333); among his key supporters were the samurais Kitabatake Chikafusa and Kusunoki Masashige, later joined by Hojo general Ashikaga Takauji, who helped take the Hojo capital, Kamakura.

Recently conquered Deccan territories rebelled against the sultan of Delhi (1331-1347).

Ashikaga Takauji revolted against Japanese emperor Go Daigo II, winning Minatogawa (1336) and beginning another long civil war (1336-1392); driving Go Daigo from the capital, Kyoto (1336), he installed

1330-1339 (cont.)

many's Emperor Louis IV) and raided France from bases in Flanders (1338-1339).

b. Charles V (1338-1380), French monarch (r. 1364-1380).

1340-1349

Hundred Years' War: Edward III's English fleet destroyed a French fleet off Sluys (June 24, 1340); Edward besieged Tournai but later agreed to a truce.

Alfonso XI of Castile and Affonso IV of Portugal crushed an army of Spanish and Moroccan Muslims at Rio Salado (Oct. 30, 1340), effectively ending Muslim threats to Christian Spain.

b. Henry Percy, first earl of Northumberland (1342-1408), English soldier.

Alfonso XI of Castile besieged and took Algeciras (1344), controlling the north side of the Strait of Gibraltar.

Hundred Years' War: England's Edward III campaigned in Brittany (1345).

Allied with France, David II returned to Scotland and invaded England, but he was defeated and captured at Neville's Cross (1346), ransomed only years later (1357).

Hundred Years' War: French forces under John, duke of Normandy, Philip VI's son, invaded Gascony, in southwest France, claimed by England through Aquitaine, a major Hundred Years' War battlefield (1346); they then besieged Aiguillon (Apr.-Aug. 1346).

Hundred Years' War: Edward III and an English army invaded northern France, landing at Cherbourg (July 1346) and taking Caen; learning that the French had raised the siege of Aiguillon, the English retreated north of the Seine and the Somme, leaving open a retreat to Flanders.

In the Byzantine Empire a succession struggle between John V and John Cantacuzene brought a new civil war, with Serbs and Turks sometimes brought in as allies; many parts of the empire were devastated (1341-1347).

Ottoman Turks made their first forays into Europe, on behalf of Byzantine claimant John Cantacuzene (1345).

Hungary's King Louis, son of Charles of Anjou, campaigned in Italy to maintain Angevin dominance in Naples (1347).

John VI (Cantacuzene) captured Constantinople (1347), bringing in Turks to help fight the Serbs.

Serbia's King Stephen Dushan (Stephen Urosh IV) conquered Macedonia, Albania, Thessaly, Epirus, Bulgaria, part of Bosnia (1349-1352), and part of the western bank of the Danube River, including Belgrade.

Africa and Southwest Asia

East, Central, and South Asia, the Pacific, and the Americas

	1330-1339 (cont.)
	a puppet emperor with himself as shogun, effectively military dictator (1338).
	d. Kusunoki Masashige (1294-1336), Japanese general who supported the restoration of Emperor Go Daigo II against the much larger Ashikaga army at Minatogawa (1336); he committed suicide to prevent being captured.
	In India two brothers, Harihara and Bukka, founded the Vijayanagar Empire around Mysore (1336).
	b. Tamerlane (Timur-e-lenk; Timur the Lame) (1336-1405), Central Asian ruler.
	Mohammed bin Tughluk, sultan of Delhi, campaigned in northern India and Tibet, losing an estimated 100,000 soldiers in his vain attempt to dominate the mountain peoples (1337).
	d. Kitabatake Akiie (Akiiye) (1317-1338), Japanese general killed at Ishizu during the Japanese civil wars.
	d. Nitta Yoshisada (1301-1338), Japanese general who supported Emperor Go Daigo II and died in battle.
	1340-1349
Portuguese explorer Malocello visited the Canary Islands (1340); the pope awarded them to Castile (1344).	Muslim governors in the Deccan revolted against Delhi (1345-1346), some uniting in the Bahmani Sultanate under Ala-ud-Din Bahman Shah, centered at Gulbarga (1347).
Weapons using gunpowder may have been first used in Africa at Algeciras (1342).	
Knights Hospitallers, aided by forces from Cyprus and Venice, took Smyrna from the Ottoman Turks (1344).	
The Hafsids of Tunisia fought off a Marinid invasion (1347).	

1340-1349 (cont.)

Hundred Years' War: In a field near Crécy-en-Ponthieu (Aug. 26, 1346), French armies under Philip VI and John, duke of Normandy, met English forces led by Edward III, his son Edward (the Black Prince), and the field general Warwick. Although the French army was three times as large as the English and included Genoese crossbowmen, the French made nothing of their advantage, sending successive waves of cavalry directly into a hail of arrows from powerful English and Welsh longbows; some 10,000 to 20,000 knights — "the flower of French chivalry," as well as Bohemia's King John — were slaughtered, while English losses totaled perhaps 200. After Crécy infantry once again became dominant in warfare. Weapons using gunpowder — essentially small cannons inaccurately shooting arrows — may have been first used at Crécy (perhaps earlier) but had no effect on the outcome.

Hundred Years' War: English forces besieged and took Calais (1346-1347); a truce followed, as both sides were stricken by the plague (the Black Death) (1347-1354).

Pedro IV of Aragon ended a civil war with his nobles at Eppila (1348).

1350-1359

In a sea battle off Winchelsea, England's Edward II defeated a Spanish naval expedition threatening cross-Channel communication with Calais (1350).

Pedro (the Cruel) fought his brother Henry of Trastamara for the throne of Castile (1350-1369), partly an extension of the Hundred Years' War, with the parties supported by England and France, respectively.

Hundred Years' War: After the failure of talks toward a permanent peace, English forces raided France. Edward II raided in the north; his son Edward (the Black Prince) raided in the center, from Bordeaux into Languedoc; and John of Gaunt, Edward's second son, raided from Brittany into Normandy (1356).

Hundred Years' War: French troops under King John (formerly duke of Normandy) met English troops under Edward (the Black Prince) at Poitiers (Sept. 19, 1356); the English also had heavy losses, but their archers again cut down the French cavalry, 2,500 of whom died, while a like number were captured, including King John. After this the French avoided open-field battles, usually remaining in fortifications.

French nobility under Charles (the Bad) of Navarre put down a peasant uprising north of Paris called The Jacquerie (1358).

b. Owen Glendower (Owain Glyndwyr) (1359?-1416?), Welsh leader.

Florence and Milan fought an inconclusive war for Tuscany (1351).

Again at war, Genoa decisively defeated Venice at Sapenza (1354), annihilating the Venetian fleet.

Ottoman Turks gained their first permanent foothold in Europe, at Gallipoli (1354).

John V retook Constantinople and again became emperor (1355).

Serbia's King Stephen Dushan took Adrianople (1355), dying as his army advanced on the Byzantine capital, Constantinople.

d. Stephen Dushan (Stephen Vrosh IV) (1308-1355), king of Serbia (r. 1331-1355) who created an empire.

Hungary's King Louis halted a Turkish invasion of the Balkans, in northern Bulgaria (1356).

After the death of Uzbeg (1359), the Khanate of the Golden Horde was wracked by civil war (1359-1379).

1340-1349 (cont.)

1350-1359

After deposing and replacing his father, Ali, the Marinid leader Faris I conquered the rest of Algeria (1351-1357) and Tunisia (1357), until being driven back by combined Ziyanid and Hafsid forces, who retook the key cities of Tunis and Tlemcen.

Ramadhipati (r. 1350-1369), founder of Ayuthia, conquered Sukhot'ai and other nearby territories; later regarded as the first king of Thailand (Siam), he also battled against the Tai state of Chiengmai and the Khmer of Cambodia.

d. Ko (Kono; Ko No) Moronao (?-1351), Japanese general during the civil wars.

d. Ashikaga Tadayoshi (1306-1352), Japanese general and deputy shogun to his older brother, Takauji, against whom he led an unsuccessful revolt; he was then captured and died in custody.

In Vietnam the Annamese blocked a Cham invasion of Hué province (1353).

d. Kitabatake Chikafusa (1293-1354), Japanese general who wrote the imperial history *Jinno Shotoki (Legitimate Succession of the Divine Sovereign)* (ca. 1338-39).

b. Ouchi Yoshihiro (1355-1399), Japanese general.

Red Turban army, led by Buddhist monk Chu Yüan-chang (later Emperor T'ai-Tsu), revolted against China's Mongol Yuan dynasty, taking Nanking (Nanjing) (1356).

Chinese rebel leader Chang Shih-ch'eng founded the kingdom of Wu in the lower Yangtze River valley, after taking Soochow and Hangchow (Hangzhou) (1356).

d. Ashikaga Takauji (1305-1358), Japanese general and shogun, older brother of Ashikaga Tadayoshi.

1360-1369

Hundred Years' War: In the Peace of Bretigny (Oct. 24, 1360), the French ransomed King John and recognized English claims to Calais, Ponthieu, and larger areas in southwest France, while the English dropped claims to Normandy; unemployed mercenaries raided throughout France for years.

Valdemar IV led Danish expansion, retaking Skåne (Scania) (1360) and then Gotland after defeating the Swedish at Visby (1361); he also defeated the Hanseatic League at Hälsingborg (1362).

Hundred Years' War: During a succession struggle in Brittany, the English besieged and took Auray, defeating a French relief army (1364).

Under Charles V (the Wise) (r. 1364-1380), the French reorganized their military, forming a permanent army and strengthening Paris's fortifications.

b. Henry Percy (1364-1403), English soldier known as Harry "Hotspur."

b. Henry IV (Henry of Lancaster; Bolingbroke) (1366?-1413), English king (r. 1399-1413).

b. Jean II le Meingre (Bouciquault; Boucicault) (ca. 1366-1421), marshal of France.

As part of Pedro's bid to regain the Castilian throne, Edward (the Black Prince) led an English army against French and Castilian armies under Bertrand Du Guesclin and Henry of Trastamara; the two sides met at Navarrette (Nájera), south of the Ebro River, where the English won, with heavy French and Spanish losses (1367).

Hundred Years' War: Open hostilities revived after a revolt in Gascony against the English overlord Edward (the Black Prince) was supported by France's King Charles V, who sent French troops under Bertrand Du Guesclin, constable of France (1368).

Danish expansion was checked by an alliance of the Hanseatic League, Mecklenburg, Holstein, Sweden, and others, forcing Valdemar IV into exile (1368); with the Treaty of Stralsund (1370), the Danes ceded Skåne to the Hanseatic League.

Edward (the Black Prince) quarreled with Pedro of Castile and left Spain; Pedro then met and was killed by his brother Henry of Trastamara at Moutiel, near Ciudad Real (1369).

Ottoman Turks took Adrianople (1365).

Crusaders under Amadeus of Savoy and Louis of Hungary briefly retook Gallipoli from the Ottoman Turks but were defeated near Vidin (1366).

Ottoman Turks conquered Bulgaria (1369-1372).

1370-1379

Hundred Years' War: Edward (the Black Prince) took and sacked Limoges, killing most of its inhabitants (1370).

Hundred Years' War: The English lost control of the French coast after their fleet was defeated by a combined French-Castilian fleet at the Battle of La Rochelle (1372).

Hundred Years' War: A truce mostly held (1375-1383), during which key figures died: Edward (the Black Prince) (1376), Edward III (1377), Charles V (1380), and Bertrand Du Guesclin (1380).

d. Edward, Prince of Wales (the Black Prince) (1330-1376), English general; son of Edward III, whom he served during the Hundred Years' War, most notably at Crécy (1346) and Poitiers (1356).

Ottoman Turks founded their Janissary Corps, Christian boys captured and raised to be elite Muslim troops (ca. 1370).

Ottoman Turks conquered Macedonia, defeating Serbians under Lazar I at Cernomen, on the Maritza River (1371).

Bosnian ruler Tvrtko I conquered western Serbia, including most of the Adriatic coast, naming himself king of Serbia and Bosnia (1376).

While the Byzantine Empire had yet another succession struggle (1376-1392), the Ottoman Turks took most of its domains.

Africa and Southwest Asia

East, Central, and South Asia, the Pacific, and the Americas

Africa and Southwest Asia	East, Central, and South Asia, the Pacific, and the Americas	
Peter I of Cyprus launched a new Crusade against Syria and Egypt (1365-1369), sacking Alexandria (1365).	Under Chu Yüan-chang the Red Turban army defeated rival rebel forces under Ch'en Yu-liang in a naval battle on Poyang Lake (1363).	

Korea's Wang dynasty under general Li Taijo finally drove the Mongols from the country (1364).

Shan leader Thadominbva founded a Shan-Burmese kingdom, centered on Ava, in the central Irrawaddy Valley (1365); it was soon at war with its various neighbors.

The Hindu Vijayanagar Empire retained its independence, despite several defeats by the Muslim Bahmani Sultanate (1367; 1377; 1398).

Red Turban forces under Chu Yüan-chang defeated the rival Wu army under Chang Shih-ch'eng, gaining control of the Yangtze Valley (1367).

d. Chang Shih-ch'eng (?-1367), Chinese rebel leader who founded the kingdom of Wu (1356); he committed suicide after defeat by other rebel forces.

Chu Yüan-chang and his Red Turban army defeated the Mongol (Yuan) dynasty at their capital, Peking (Beijing), renaming himself T'ai-tsu, emperor of the new Ming dynasty (1368).

Tamerlane (Timur the Lame) deposed and replaced the khan of the Jagatai Mongols, centered at Samarkand (1369).

New Ming emperor T'ai-tsu took eastern Mongolia (1369).

Under Bakku, the Hindu state of Vijayanagar conquered the Muslim sultanate of Madura (1370), becoming dominant in southern India.

Ayuthia's Boromoraja I put down a rebellion in Sukhot'ai (1371-1378); however, Chiengmai fought off his invasion at Sen Sanuk.

Ming emperor T'ai-Tsu conquered Szechuan (Sichuan) (1371) and Kansu (Gansu) (1372).

1370-1379 (cont.)

d. Edward III (1312-1377), English king (r. 1327-1377) who, by reviving a claim to the French throne, began the Hundred Years' War (1337-1453); he was succeeded by Richard II, son of Edward (the Black Prince).

b. John (Jan; Johan) Ziska (ca. 1376-1424), Bohemian Hussite general.

War of Chiogga (1378-1381): In the renewed Venetian-Genoese war, the Genoese won at Pola, although their admiral Luciano Doria was killed; his brother Pietro Doria captured Chiogga and blockaded Venice, but the Venetians under Vittorio Pisani blockaded and seized the Genoese fleet, ending Genoa's days as a maritime power.

Mamai won the long succession struggle for the Khanate of the Golden Horde, defeating Toktamish, who took refuge with Tamerlane (1379).

1380-1389

d. Charles V (1338-1380), French monarch (r. 1364-1380) called "Le Sage" (the Wise), active during the Hundred Years' War.

During the Peasants' Revolt (1381), some 100,000 rebels led by Wat Tyler and Jack Straw took London, threatening the throne but dispersing after some of their demands were met.

French forces put down a Flemish revolt led by Philip van Artevelde at Roosebeke (1382).

b. John Talbot, earl of Shrewsbury (ca. 1384-1453), English soldier.

Fending off Castilian forces with English help, Portugal, under John I of Aviz, won at Aljubarrota (1385), later making a formal alliance with England in the Treaty of Windsor (May 9, 1386).

Thomas, duke of Gloucester, led a rebellion against England's Richard II, whose supporters lost at Radcot Bridge (1387), leaving him in the control of his nobles.

Hundred Years' War: The English defeated a French-Castilian invasion fleet off Margate (1387); another truce followed.

b. Henry V (1387-1422), English king (r. 1413-1422).

Hundred Years' War: Earl James Douglas led a Scottish-French invasion of northern England, defeating the English under Henry Percy (Northumberland) at Otterburn (1388), where Douglas was killed.

After Albert of Mecklenburg rejected the conditions made when he was given the Swedish throne, nobles called in Margaret of Denmark, whose army defeated and captured Albert (1389); Margaret became regent (1389-1396).

Trying to reestablish control over the Khanate of the Golden Horde, Mamai was defeated at Kulikovo, on the upper Don River, by Russian allies under Prince Dmitri Donskoi of Moscow (1380). It was the first Russian victory over a Mongol force.

At the Kalka River, Mamai was defeated by his rival Toktamish, who then became khan of the Golden Horde (1380); he reconquered Russia (1381-1382), taking Moscow (Aug. 23, 1382) and killing many of its inhabitants.

As an ally of Genoa, Louis, Angevin king of Hungary, fought against Venice, which was forced to pay tribute and give up Dalmatia (1381).

Swiss forces fought off an invasion intended to establish Hapsburg dominance, crushing an army under Leopold II of Swabia at Sempach (July 9, 1386); after the Swiss also won at Näfels (1388), the Hapsburgs accepted Swiss independence (1394) within the Holy Roman (German) Empire.

b. János (John) Hunyadi (ca. 1387-1456), Hungarian general and national hero.

Ottoman Turks under Murad I and his son Bayazid effectively took control of the Balkans, at Kossovo (Field of the Blackbirds) (June 20, 1389), defeating a combined army of Serbs, Bulgarians, Bosnians, Wallachians, and Albanians under Lazar of Serbia, who was killed in the fighting, along with much of the Serbian nobility.

1390-1399

Widespread massacres of Jews in Castile caused many to convert (sometimes only outwardly) to Christianity (1391).

Hundred Years' War: England's Richard II and France's Charles VI made the Peace of Paris, intended to last for 30 years, confirming England's claim to Calais and Gascony, between Bayonne and Bordeaux (1396).

Margaret of Denmark's regency in Sweden (1389-1396) ended with the Union of Kalmar, in which Erik of Pomerania became, simul-

Pursuing his war against Toktamish, Tamerlane invaded Russia, defeating the Khanate of the Golden Horde at Kandurcha (Battle of the Steppes) (1391) before returning home.

Ottoman Turks led by Bayazid I besieged Constantinople, successfully defended by troops under French marshal Jean Bouciquault (1391-1399).

1370-1379 (cont.)

	Che Bong Nga of Champa invaded Annam, taking and sacking Hanoi (1371); he later fought off a counterattack, defeating Annam forces at Vijaya (1377) and killing Annamese king Tran Due-Ton.
	d. Kikuchi Takemitsu (?-1373), Japanese general during the civil wars.

1380-1389

Tamerlane conquered Persia, starting with Herat (1381), then Khorasan (1382-1385) and Fars, Iraq, Azerbaijan, and Armenia (1386-1387).	Tamerlane took Kashgar, then controlled eastern Turkestan (Jatah) (1380).
Toktamish and his Golden Horde invaded Azerbaijan, soon being driven out but triggering a war with his former protector, Tamerlane (1385).	Ming dynasty completed its conquest of China, taking Yunnan (1382).
	Invading Mongolia, the Chinese decisively defeated the Mongol (former Yuan dynasty) army at Bui Noir (Buyr Nuur) on the Orxon River and won at the Kerulen River, sweeping the Mongols from their capital, Karakorum (1388).
	Toktamish and his Golden Horde raided in Transoxiana in Tamerlane's absence, even threatening his capital of Samarkand (1388).
	Tamerlane defeated his former protégé Toktamish at the Battle of the Syr River (1389).

1390-1399

Armenia and Azerbaijan came under the control of the Black Sheep Turkomans, led by Kara Usuf (1390-1420).	Champa's soldier-king Che Bong Nga was killed at sea fighting Annamese and Chinese pirates (1390).
During a lull in the Hundred Years' War, the French and English joined forces under Prince Louis of Bourbon to besiege the port of Mahdia, in Tunisia, giving up after 61 days (1390).	Japan's long civil wars ended when Emperor Go Daigo II's successor abandoned his claim to the throne (1392).
Tamerlane suppressed a revolt in Persia, at Shiraz killing rebel leader Shah Mansur (1392), then conquered Mesopotamia, including Baghdad, and Geor-	

1390-1399 (cont.)

taneously, king of Denmark, Norway, and Sweden, including Finland.

After Richard II reclaimed the full power of the English throne (1397), various nobles rose against him, including his cousin Henry of Bolingbroke, who became King Henry IV after Richard's forced abdication (1399).

Again pursuing Toktamish and his Golden Horde, Tamerlane administered a crushing defeat at the Terek River (1395), then campaigned widely in southern Russia, killing and destroying, especially at Astrakhan and the capital, Sarai.

At the Vorskla River, near the Dnieper River, the Mongols of the Golden Horde defeated a combined army of Poles and Teutonic Knights, led by Lithuanian prince Vitov and refugee khan Toktamish (1396).

A new Crusade against the Ottoman Turks in the Balkans was smashed at Nicopolis (Nikopol), in Bulgaria (1396).

Ottoman Turks invaded Greece (1397).

Milan and Florence ended their long, inconclusive fight over Tuscany (1375-1398).

1400-1409

Scottish and French (Orleanist) troops under the earl of Douglas invaded England but were fought off by northern English forces under Henry (Harry "Hotspur") Percy, at Homildon Hill (Sept. 14, 1402).

With French (Orleanist) support, Owen Glendower revolted against English rule in Wales (1402-1409).

Hundred Years' War: French ships raided England's coast, especially the Channel ports, such as Plymouth (1403).

Northern English nobles led by the Percy family invaded central England, but before they could join forces with Welsh rebel Owen Glendower, they were defeated by Henry IV at Shrewsbury (July 21, 1403); Harry "Hotspur" was killed, and his father, the elder Henry Percy, surrendered.

d. Henry Percy (1364-1403), English soldier known as Harry "Hotspur," who with his father revolted against Henry IV and was killed at Shrewsbury.

b. Charles VII (1403-1461), French monarch called the Dauphin.

French forces landed in Wales to support Owen Glendower's rebellion, but to little effect, leaving within the year (1405).

In the Holy Roman (German) Empire, a four-way civil war (1400-1410) ended in the crowning of Sigismund of Luxembourg, king of Hungary, as the new emperor.

Milan, Venice, and Florence were variously at war (1402-1454).

Swiss troops defeated Savoy, taking the southern Alpine passes into northern Italy (1403-1416).

Florence conquered Pisa (1405-1406).

Hand-held firearms were used in Europe (by 1408).

gia (1393). He was then attacked by Toktamish, but he drove the Golden Horde back through the Caucasus Mountains (1393-1394).

As part of long-term warfare against Granada, the remaining Muslim corner of Spain, the Castilians raided and sacked Tetuán, in Morocco (1399).

Chaos in Korea ended when general Li Taijo deposed the Wang dynasty, founding his own (1392).

d. Hosokawa Yoriyuki (1329-1392), Japanese general who founded the Hosokawa line of counselors to the Ashikaga shoguns.

Tai forces from Ayuthia invaded and temporarily took much of western Cambodia (1394-1401).

d. T'ai-Tsu (Chu Yüan-chang) (1328-1398), Chinese emperor (r. 1368-1398) who, as leader of the Red Turban army (from 1355), conquered China and ejected the Mongols, founding the Ming dynasty. Civil war over the succession was won by Emperor Yung-lo (Ch'eng Tsu or Chu Ti) (r. 1398-1403).

Tamerlane's grandsons Pir-Mohammed and Mohammed Sultan led his first invasion of India, taking Multan, in the Punjab (spring 1398); Tamerlane himself quickly followed, defeating Mahmud Tughluk's Indian forces at Panipat (Dec. 1398), then taking Delhi and devastating northern India before leaving India forever (spring 1399).

d. Ouchi Yoshihiro (1355-1399), Japanese general who conducted the campaign that finally ended the civil wars (1335-1392); he died putting down yet another revolt.

In West Africa the city of Gao rebelled against Mali rule (ca. 1400).

Tamerlane crushed Mameluke forces at Aleppo (Oct. 30, 1400), then took Aleppo and Damascus, controlling Syria. After an uprising, Tamerlane retook Baghdad, punishing its inhabitants with a terrible massacre and destroying the city (1401).

Tamerlane invaded Anatolia (1402), defeating the Ottoman Turks (and some Serbian forces) under Bayazid I at Angora (Ankara), capturing Smyrna from the Knights Hospitallers, and being paid tribute by both Christians and Muslims.

Ethiopia's Christians sent ambassadors to Europe, seeking an alliance against Egypt's Mameluke Muslims; they went as far as Venice (1402; 1408).

Spanish forces took the Canary Islands (1402-1404).

Bayazid I's three sons fought each other for control of the Ottoman Empire (1403-1413), losing most of Turkey's European dominions in the process.

b. Constantine XI Paleologus (1404-1453), Byzantine emperor (r. 1449-1453).

Though embroiled in a civil war (1400-1407), Annam took northern Champa.

Under Minhkaung (r. 1401-1422), Burma's kingdom of Ava was variously at war with the Mon and Arakanese, but Ava failed to take Pegu.

Paramesvara, a refugee prince from Palembang, established an independent kingdom in Malacca (ca. 1402), controlling the vital strait.

In Burma, Ava and Arakan campaigned against each other (1404-1430), their conflict spurred by Razadarit of Pegu.

China's Muslim naval leader, Cheng Ho, invaded Sumatra, took Palembang, and exacted tribute from most of the Malay and Indonesian states (1405-1407); this was the first of a series of voyages that would take him to Africa and Arabia (1405-1433).

d. Tamerlane (Timur-e-lenk; Timur the Lame) (1336-1405), Central Asian ruler

1400-1409 (cont.)

Hundred Years' War: French forces, especially from Burgundy and Orléans, attacked English domains in France, notably Calais and Vienne (1406).

English forces captured Scotland's Prince James (1406), who later that year became King James I; he was held for 18 years.

Hundred Years' War: After Burgundians assassinated Louis, duke of Orléans, the two dukedoms were at war, with Count Bernard of Armagnac leading the Orleanist (Valois or Armagnac) faction (1407) and both sides seeking English support.

d. Henry Percy, first earl of Northumberland (1342-1408), English soldier who supported Henry Bolingbroke's deposing of Richard II; with his son Henry (Harry "Hotspur"), he later revolted against Henry IV; he was killed at Bramham Moor during yet another rebellion.

England's Henry IV finally suppressed the Welsh rebellion, taking Harlech, stronghold of Owen Glendower, who fled (1409).

1410-1419

At Harlaw, near Inveruris, Aberdeenshire, Scotland, the earl of Mar defeated an invasion force led by Donald, lord of the Isles, and northern English nobles (1411).

First documentary evidence of the matchlock, a device that lights gunpowder in a gun (1411).

b. Richard, duke of York (1411-1460), English general and statesman.

b. Joan of Arc (Jeanne d'Arc) (ca. 1412-1431), French general.

d. Henry IV (Henry of Lancaster; Bolingbroke) (1366?-1413), English king (r. 1399-1413) who deposed Richard II, founding the Lancastrian line (1399); his reign was marked by conflict, notably with Welsh patriot Owen Glendower and with the Percy family. He was succeeded by Henry V (r. 1413-1422).

England's Henry V suppressed a rebellion by the Lollards (1413-1414).

Hundred Years' War: After arranging for Burgundy's neutrality, Henry V led an English invasion of France, besieging and taking Harfleur (Aug. 13-Sept. 22, 1415).

Hundred Years' War: En route to Calais, Henry V's English army was met by French forces under Constable Charles d'Albret near the castle of Agincourt (Oct. 24, 1415); English longbowmen again cut down the cumbersomely armored French, with the loss of perhaps 5,000 knights, including d'Albret, the duke of Orléans, and marshal Jean Bouciquault; Henry then returned to England.

Hundred Years' War: English ships defeated a Genoese fleet supporting the French cause in the English Channel (1416).

Erik VII of Pomerania, ruler of Scandinavia, sought to wrest control of Schleswig from the count of Holstein (1416-1422).

Polish king Jagiello (Ladislas II) and his cousin Witowt, grand duke of Lithuania, combined forces to defeat the Teutonic Knights at Tannenberg (July 15, 1410); the First Peace of Thorn allowed the Teutonic Knights to keep much of their territory; Hussite John Ziska fought for the Poles.

Mohammed I (the Restorer) regained Turkish conquests in Europe (1413-1415), also taking Wallachia and expanding into Asia Minor.

Supported by Holy Roman Emperor and Hungarian king Sigismund, the Swiss took the Aargau region of Austria (1415).

Sultan Mohammed I's Turkish fleet off Gallipoli was annihilated by Venetians under doge Loredano (1416), as the Venetians battled the Turks for control of the Aegean Sea (1416-1453).

Hussite Wars (1419-1436) were triggered by Emperor Sigismund's execution of Bohemian nationalist and religious reformer John Hus (1415), regarded as a heretic, and more proximately by Sigismund's claim to the Bohemian throne. En route to their stronghold at Tabor, the Hussites under John Ziska fought off Catholic pursuers at Sudoner (1419). Sigismund besieged Prague (June 30-July 20), whose citizens called in the Hussites. Using the innovative technique of the *wagenburg*, the linking of artillery-equipped wagons into a fortress-ring, Ziska's Hussite forces defeated Sigismund at Prague (July 30), driving him from Bohemia.

Africa and Southwest Asia

who, from his capital at Samarkand, built an empire that included Persia, Turkey, Russia, and India; he took and sacked many great cities and destroyed Baghdad (1401); he died at Otrar, leading an invasion force toward China (1405).

In the conflict over India's central Deccan, the Muslim state of Bahmani, under Firuz Shah, dominated the Hindu kingdom of Vijayanagar, which paid it tribute (1406).

Chinese forces took Annam, ostensibly to restore order (1407).

In Thailand, Ayuthia, under Int'araja, invaded and took the northern kingdom of Chiengmai (1408) but failed to take the key cities P'ayao and Chiengmai (1411); the combatants probably did not use cannons, as some have suggested they did.

Chinese forces invaded and conquered Ceylon (Sri Lanka) (1408-1411).

Succession struggle in the Ottoman Empire eventually ended when Mohammed I killed Suleiman (1411) and Musa (1413).

Portuguese forces captured Ceuta, opposite Gibraltar (1415). Learning of the gold country south of the Sahara, Prince Henry (the Navigator) began to explore, sailing around Muslim-held North Africa, sending virtually annual expeditions southward (from 1415), and often raiding coastal settlements en route.

Ethiopia's Yeshaq I defeated Sultan S'adad-Din of Ifat, taking Zeila, on the Red Sea, near modern Djibouti (1415); Yeshaq also campaigned against Ethiopian Jews, called Falashas.

Chinese forces campaigned in Outer Mongolia (1410-1424).

After exploring the Indian Ocean coast to Hormuz (1412-1415), Chinese naval leader Cheng Ho led naval campaigns in the region, exacting tribute from most nations (1416-1424).

Burmese forces from Ava fought off a Shan invasion, led by the sawba (lord) of Shenwi (1413).

Delhi was taken by Khizar Khan, Tamerlane's governor of the Punjab, who founded the Sayyid dynasty (1414); the dynasty then contested the central Ganges Valley in a long series of conflicts with the Muslim state of Jaunpur (1414-1450).

Burmese forces from Ava, under Prince Minrekyawswa, invaded Pegu (1414-1415) but withdrew when the Shan invaded Ava (1415); in a second invasion of Pegu, Minrekyawswa was killed near the Irrawaddy River, and Burmese troops again withdrew (1416-1417).

Le Loi led an Annamese guerrilla war against Chinese occupation forces (1418-1427).

1410-1419 (cont.)

d. Owen Glendower (Owain Glyndwyr) (1359?-1416?), Welsh patriot who led a revolt against Henry IV's English rule (1402-1409).

Hundred Years' War: Henry V conquered Normandy (1417-1419), except for Mont-Saint-Michel, taking Rouen after a five-month siege (Sept. 1418-Jan. 1419).

Hundred Years' War: Allied with the English, the Burgundians took Paris (May 29, 1418), killing most Orléans and Armagnac leaders, except Charles, the Dauphin; John of Burgundy was later assassinated while negotiating with the Dauphin (Sept. 10, 1419).

1420-1429

Hundred Years' War: Henry V advanced on Paris, but the Burgundians arranged the Treaty of Troyes (May 21, 1420), which recognized Henry (not Charles, the Dauphin) as regent for and heir of the insane French king Charles VI, whose daughter Catherine he married.

Hundred Years' War: Henry V campaigned in northern France (1420-1422), establishing firm control and besieging and taking Meaux before becoming ill and dying; he was succeeded by his nine-month-old son, Henry VI, as king of England and (after Charles VI's death) France (1422), although Charles, the Dauphin, claimed the throne as Charles VII.

d. Jean II le Meingre (Bouciquault; Boucicault) (ca. 1366-1421), marshal of France.

d. Henry V (1387-1422), English king (r. 1413-1422) and eldest son of Henry IV; he was best known for leading the English in their victory at Agincourt (1415), a battle recorded not only in military annals but also in Shakespeare's play named for the young king. He was succeeded by his infant son Henry VI.

Hundred Years' War: As regent for Henry VI, John, duke of Bedford, campaigned for control in northern France (1422-1428), in the process losing Burgundian support.

Hundred Years' War: At Verneuil, John, duke of Bedford, and his English troops defeated French forces led by the duke of Alençon, who was captured, and Scots under John Stuart and Carl Archibald of Douglas, who was killed (1424).

Hundred Years' War: At St. James (near Avranches), English forces under John, duke of Bedford, defeated French troops led by constable Arthur de Richemont (1426).

Under Erik VII Scandinavia was at war with the Hanseatic League over Schleswig (1426-1435).

Diego de Sevilla discovered seven islands of the Azores (1427-1431), although some may have been known before him.

Hundred Years' War: Preparatory to invading across the Loire River into Charles, the Dauphin's territory, English forces under the earl of Salisbury besieged the river fort of Orléans (1428-1429); the defenders were led by Jean, count of Dunois, the "Bastard of Orléans."

b. Richard Neville, earl of Warwick (1428-1471), English general.

Holy Roman Emperor Sigismund lost Fruili to Venice (1420).

Hussite Wars: On Sigismund's return to Bohemia, Hussites under John Ziska again used the *wagenburg* to win victories at the battles of Lutitz and Kuttenburg (1421).

Defeated by Milan, Switzerland lost control of Bellinzona (1422).

Hussite Wars: Returning to Bohemia, Holy Roman Emperor Sigismund was defeated at Nebovid and Nemecky Brod (Jan. 1422) by Hussites under John Ziska, who was now blind.

Under Manuel II, the Byzantines fought off Murad II's Ottoman Turkish siege of Constantinople (1422).

Hussite Wars: Hussites under John Ziska made a failed invasion of Hungary (Sept.-Oct. 1423).

Hussite Wars: After Bohemia's Hussites split into warring factions, John Ziska led the Taborites to victory over the Utraquists at the battles of Horid and Strachov (1423).

Florence and Venice generally had the advantage in running battles with Milan (1423-1454).

Hussite Wars: In factional fighting, John Ziska and the Taborites defeated the Utraquists and Praguers at the battles of Skalic and Malesov (1424).

d. John (Jan; Johan) Ziska (ca. 1376-1424), Bohemian Hussite general who, despite losing both eyes in two separate battles, led troops in the early Hussite Wars; he died of the plague on the frontier.

Venice lost its coastal domains in Thessalonika, Albania, and Epirus to the Ottoman Turks (1425-1430).

Hussite Wars: Hussites under Prokop (the Great) fought off German invasions of Bohemia, winning the battles of Aussig (1426) and Tachau (1427). They then campaigned widely in Germany, Hungary, Misnia (Meissen), and Silesia (1427-1432).

Byzantines took Morea, on Greece's Peloponnesian peninsula, from the Franks (1428).

1410-1419 (cont.)

1420-1429

In West Africa, Takrur and Wolof successfully rebelled against Mali control (ca. 1420).

Black Sheep Turkomans of Armenia and Azerbaijan rebelled against the brief rule of the Timurids (Tamerlane's successors); under Kara Iskander, Kara Usuf's son, they expanded into northern Persia (1420-1435).

Mameluke forces from Egypt invaded Cyprus, initially taking the island but finally being driven off (1424-1426).

Castilian forces fought off Portuguese attempts to take the Canary Islands (1425).

An Ethiopian ambassador reached Venice (1427), seeking an alliance against the Muslims.

Vijayanagar briefly won control of India's central Deccan by defeating Bahmani's Firuz Shah at Pangul (1420).

d. Imagawa Sadayo (Ryoshun) (1325-1420), Japanese general who was one of the leading Ashikaga shoguns.

Though hard-pressed by their war with the Tai of Ayuthia (1421-1426), the Khmer of Angkor fought off Champa's invasion of the Mekong Delta.

Under Ahmad Shah, Bahmani regained control of India's central Deccan, defeating Vijayanagar (1423) and Warangal (1425).

Le Loi led Annamese rebel forces in besieging Hanoi, taking it from the Chinese occupation garrison (1427-1428), then making himself king (1431).

Aztec forces under Emperor Itzcoatl defeated the Tepanaca, earlier settlers of the Valley of Mexico (1428-1430).

1420-1429 (cont.)

Hundred Years' War: French forces led by Joan of Arc broke the English siege of Orléans (May 7, 1429); English forces withdrew into various garrisons in the Loire Valley, most of them also taken by Joan.

Hundred Years' War: At Patay (June 19, 1429), French forces led by Joan of Arc completed the reconquest of the Loire Valley, defeating English troops under John Fastolf (original for Shakespeare's Falstaff) and Lord John Talbot, who was captured.

Hundred Years' War: French troops under Joan of Arc took Troyes, Châlons, and Rheims (July 1429), where the Dauphin was crowned Charles VII; Charles then withdrew his support of Joan.

Hundred Years' War: With only a small force, Joan of Arc tried but failed to take Paris (Sept. 8, 1429).

1430-1439

Hundred Years' War: English-Burgundian forces captured Joan of Arc as she attempted to relieve their siege of Compiègne (May 23, 1430).

d. Joan of Arc (Jeanne d'Arc) (ca. 1412-1431), French general inspired by religious visions; called the "Maid of Orléans" for her relief of besieged Orléans (1429); captured at Compiègne, she was convicted of heresy and burned at the stake (May 30), not yet 20 years old; she was later "rehabilitated" by the Catholic Church and declared a saint (1920).

After a siege, the Hanseatic League took Schleswig (1432).

Hundred Years' War: At the Peace of Arras, the civil war between the Burgundians and Orléans-Armagnac supporters was settled, ending the Burgundian alliance with the English (Sept. 21, 1435).

Hundred Years' War: French forces retook Paris; after taking refuge in the Bastille, the English garrison troops surrendered (Apr. 1436).

Scotland's James I unsuccessfully tried to take Roxburgh from the English (1436).

Hussite Wars: In a new civil war among the Hussites, Taborites under Prokop the Great (a former Utraquist) and Prokop the Less (no relation) were defeated at Lipan by Utraquists and their aristocratic allies (1433-1434); both Prokops were killed.

Polish forces under regent Cardinal Olesnicki suppressed a Lithuanian rebellion supported by the Teutonic Knights (1435).

Alfonso V of Aragon conquered Naples (1435-1442).

Hussite Wars: These wars temporarily ended in Bohemia when the Hussites accepted a compromise bringing them back into the Catholic Church and acknowledged Sigismund as king (1436).

Zurich was at the center of a civil war involving various cantons and sometimes German and French interference (1436-1450).

A succession struggle in Hungary led to civil war, ended by the accession of Ladislas I (Ladislas III of Poland) (1439).

After Serbia, under George Brankovic, proclaimed its independence, the Ottoman Turks invaded, sweeping the Serbians from their new capital at Semendria (1439).

1440-1449

b. Edward IV (1442-1483), English king (r. 1461-1470; 1471-1483).

Hundred Years' War: The Truce of Tours brought five years of peace (1444).

France's Charles VII reformed the military, creating the first permanent European army since the Romans (1445-1449).

A struggle for power in Portugal ended when young Affonso V defeated and killed his uncle Peter at Alfarrobeira (1449).

Hundred Years' War: French forces retook most of Normandy from the English (1449-1450) and besieged English forces under the duke of Somerset at Caen.

---

b. Matthias I Corvinus (Mátyás Hunyadi) (1440-1490), king of Hungary (r. 1458-1490).

Now on the Christian-Muslim frontier in Europe, Hungarians under János Hunyadi defeated the Turks in several key battles at Semendria (1441), Hermannstadt (1442), the Iron Gates (1442), and most notably Snaim (Kustinitza) (1443); at Snaim, Sultan Murad II made a 10-year truce, also restoring independence for Serbia and Wallachia.

Albanians under Skanderbeg (George Castricata or Kastriotis) rebelled against Turkish rule (1443-1468), fighting off at least two Turkish invasions (1448; 1450).

1420-1429 (cont.)

1430-1439

Tuaregs took and sacked Timbuktu, in West Africa (1431).

b. Mohammed II Fatih (the Conquerer; Muhammed; Mehmet) (1432-1481), Ottoman Turk ruler (r. 1444-1446; 1451-1481).

After years of inching down Africa's west coast, Portuguese ships under Gil Eannes finally rounded Cape Bojador (Bulging Cape) (1433), within three years reaching beyond Muslim lands.

Muslim forces fought off a Portuguese invasion of Tangier (1437).

Boromoraja II of Ayuthia besieged and after seven months took Angkor before being repelled by Khmer forces (1430-1431).

Emperor Itzcoatl and his Aztec forces defeated the city of Xochimilco (1430-1433).

In his last Indian Ocean expedition, China's Cheng Ho sailed into the Red Sea, exacting tribute from Mecca (1431-1433).

After driving the Tai from Cambodia, the Khmer moved their capital from Angkor to Phnom Penh (1432).

The Chinese under general Wang Chi took the Shan states of northeast Burma (1438).

1440-1449

Under Ewaure the Great (r. ca. 1440-1480), Benin expanded in several directions in West Africa.

Portuguese ships that had sailed south of Muslim territory to West Africa returned with ten Black Africans, men and women, and began the enormous European expansion of the African slave trade (1441), for a time centered on Arguin Island, off Mauretania.

Knights of St. John Hospitallers fought off invasions of Rhodes by Mamelukes under Egyptian sultan Malik al-Zahir (1442-1444).

Portuguese ships under Nuõ Tristam reached the Senegal River (1444); another expedition under Dinis Dias rounded West Africa's Cape Verde (1445).

Though wracked by civil war (1441-1446), Champa made numerous unsuccessful raids into Annam.'

In Thailand, Chiengmai fought off invasions by Ayuthia under Boromoraja II (1442; 1448).

Under Ala-ud-din, Bahmani again defeated Vijayanagar, in India's central Deccan (1443).

Burmese forces from Ava fought off a Chinese invasion, killing general Wang Chi

1440-1449 (cont.)

Ignoring the truce with the Turks, Ladislas I and János Hunyadi led Hungarian and other forces in the last Crusade, invading Bulgaria; their allies the Venetians were to have kept the Turks from crossing into Europe, but they failed to do so; at Varna (1444) the Crusaders were routed and Ladislas was killed; the Turks then invaded Hungary (1445).

France's dauphin Louis (later King Louis XI) invaded Switzerland, at St. Jakob, near Basel, destroying a much smaller Swiss army but at such a heavy cost that he then withdrew (1444).

Byzantine forces under Constantine XI Paleologus invaded central Greece from Morea but were driven back by Turks under Sultan Murad II (1446).

Hungarians under regent-general János Hunyadi invaded Austria to bring the young king, Ladislas V, to Hungary (1446); German emperor Frederick III thereafter hampered Hungary's defense against the Turks.

Tartars (so called from *ta-ta*, the Chinese word for "nomads") invaded Russia (1447).

Francisco Sforza came to power after a civil war in Milan (1447-1450).

At the second Battle of Kossovo (1448), Turks under Sultan Murad II defeated a much smaller Hungarian force under János Hunyadi; both sides suffered extremely heavy losses; after this battle the Janissaries used guns instead of bows; Hungary also invaded Serbia (1449).

1450-1459

Hundred Years' War: At Formigny, near Bayeux, French forces under the count of Clermont crushed an English army under Thomas Kyriel and Matthew Gough, using cannon to batter the English longbowmen; almost all the longbowmen, nearly 4,000, were killed (Apr. 15, 1450).

Hundred Years' War: English forces surrendered at Caen (July 6, 1450) and Cherbourg (Aug. 12, 1450), England's last footholds in Normandy.

Jack Cade led a rebellion in Kent and Sussex, taking London and defeating royalist forces in an ambush at Seven Oaks before being swept from London (1450); although a general pardon was issued, Cade was later executed.

Hundred Years' War: French forces under Jean, count of Dunois, invaded Guyenne, taking Bordeaux (June 30, 1451) and Bayonne (Aug. 20).

Christian I Oldenburg, king of Denmark and Norway, fought with Sweden (1451-1457); although he deposed Charles VIII, he was rejected by the Swedes.

Hundred Years' War: Called in by Aquitaine, English forces under John Talbot, earl of Shrewsbury, landed in the Garonne Valley and were welcomed by Bordeaux (Oct. 1452).

Tartar invaders reached Moscow before being driven out by the Russians (1451).

Hussite Wars: George of Podebrad took Prague, establishing the Utraquists as the dominant Hussite sect in Bohemia (1452).

Polish–Teutonic Knights War (1454-1466): The Poles supported a Prussian revolt against the Teutonic Knights.

At Belgrade, János Hunyadi's Hungarian forces first defeated Sultan Mohammed II's Ottoman Turks on the Danube (July 14, 1456), then routed the Turkish army besieging the city (July 21-22); the Turks withdrew to Constantinople.

d. János (John) Hunyadi (ca. 1387-1456), Hungarian general and national hero for his leadership during numerous wars against the Turks; he died at Belgrade of the plague. His son Mátyás Hunyadi became Hungary's King Matthias I Corvinus.

Moscow's dominance was established with its victory, under Basil II, over Novgorod at Rusa (1456).

Ottoman Turks conquered and annexed Serbia (1459).

1440-1449 (cont.)

Genoese explorer Antonio Malfante reached south of the Sahara to the gold-trading centers of West Africa (ca. 1447).

Under Jehan Shah the Black Sheep Turkomans completed their conquest of north Persia, up to Herat (1448).

at Taguang (1445); they were unable to withstand another Chinese invasion (1446), after which King Narapati accepted Ming dominance.

Annam invaded Champa; took, lost, then retook the capital of Vijaya; then, under Le Thanh Ton, conquered the region south to Cape Varella (1446-1471), effectively ending the two nations' long conflict.

Under Montezuma I (r. 1449-1468), the Aztecs expanded, primarily south of Mexico City.

Oirat Mongols defeated the Chinese army on the northern frontier, capturing the Ming emperor Ying Tsung (1449).

1450-1459

Spanish forces fought off repeated Portuguese invasions of the Canary Islands (1450-1453).

Seeking an alliance against the Muslims, an Ethiopian ambassador reached Lisbon (1452).

Ottoman Turks under Mohammed II (the Conquerer) besieged and finally took shrunken Constantinople (Feb.-May 1453); its defenders included Genoese mercenaries under John Giustiniani, a Venetian fleet, and the last Byzantine emperor, Constantine XI Paleologus, who died battling to close a breach in the city's inner walls after massive bombardments and assaults; so ended the Roman and Byzantine Empires and Europeans' direct access to the East, as the Ottoman Empire continued expanding.

d. Constantine XI Paleologus (1404-1453), last Byzantine emperor (r. 1449-1453), killed in the fall of Constantinople (May 29).

Alvise da Cadamosto, a Venetian in Portuguese service, explored the Senegal and Gambia rivers and discovered the Cape Verde (Green Cape) Islands (1455-1457).

Norse settlers seem to have completely abandoned Greenland (by ca. 1450); however, Basques, Bretons, Gascons, and other Europeans apparently fished off North America and had temporary coastal settlements by then, keeping their routes secret.

After the Mongols released Ming emperor Ying Tsung (1450), a civil war erupted among various claimants to China's throne, including his brother Ching Ti; Ying Tsung eventually won (1457).

b. Francisco de Almeida (ca. 1450-1510), Portuguese admiral and viceroy of Portuguese India.

Civil war among the Mayans led to the destruction of Mayapan (1451); the nation collapsed, with people abandoning cities such as Chichén Itzá and Uxmal.

Bulal Lodi overthrew Delhi's Sayyid dynasty and founded the Lodi dynasty (1451).

1450-1459 (cont.)

b. Richard III (Richard of Gloucester) (1452-1485), English king (r. 1483-1485).

Hundred Years' War: John Talbot, earl of Shrewsbury, led English forces to raise the French siege of Castillon, but the English were cut apart and Shrewsbury was killed by French forces under Jean Bureau (July 17, 1453).

d. John Talbot, earl of Shrewsbury (ca. 1384-1453), English soldier late in the Hundred Years' War, notably at Patay (1429) and Castillon (1453), where he was killed.

Hundred Years' War: The 116-year war effectively ended with the French capture of Bordeaux (Oct. 19, 1453), leaving the English with only Calais.

b. Hernández Gonzalo de Córdoba (Gonsalvo de Cordova) (1453-1515), Spanish general.

Wars of the Roses (1455-1485): The long series of conflicts was triggered when Richard, duke of York, who had been protector during English king Henry VI's insanity (1454), was dismissed by Queen Margaret and the duke of Somerset, who effectively became dictators; Richard and his followers, including Richard Neville, earl of Warwick, revolted and at St. Albans (May 22, 1455) defeated the Lancastrians, killing Somerset; Richard then became dictator, controlling an incompetent Henry.

Scotland's James II raided Northumberland (1456).

b. Henry VII (Henry Tudor) (1457-1509), English king (r. 1485-1509).

Wars of the Roses: Yorkists led by the earl of Salisbury crushed the Lancastrians at Blore Heath, near Market Drayton (Sept. 3, 1459).

Wars of the Roses: Threatened in his castle by a Lancastrian army under Henry VI and Margaret, and abandoned by key supporters, Richard, duke of York, fled to Ireland; Warwick fled to Calais (Oct. 1459).

b. Maximilian I (1459-1519), king of Germany (r. 1486-1519) and Holy Roman Emperor (r. 1493-1519).

1460-1469

Wars of the Roses: Warwick and Edward (later Edward IV), son of Richard, duke of York, brought a small army to southeast England and were welcomed by London (June 1460).

Wars of the Roses: Yorkist forces under Warwick and Edward defeated Lancastrian forces heading toward London, at Northampton retaking King Henry VI (July 18, 1460).

Wars of the Roses: Lancastrians under Henry Beaufort, duke of Somerset, and Henry Percy, earl of Northumberland, defeated the Yorkists at Wakefield; Richard, duke of York, was killed (Dec. 1460).

d. Richard, duke of York (1411-1460), English general whose bid for power triggered the Wars of the Roses (1455-1485); although he died at Wakefield (1460), two of his sons later ruled England — his eldest as Edward IV and his fourth as Richard III.

Scotland's James II took Roxburgh from the English, although he was killed in the siege (1460).

Swiss forces took the region of Thurgau from Austria (1460).

Defeating a Genoese fleet, Turkish forces took control of the Aegean Sea, also conquering Morea (the Peloponnesian peninsula) (1461).

Polish–Teutonic Knights War: Poles under Casimir IV decisively defeated the Teutonic Knights at Puck (1462). Under the Second Peace of Thorn (1466), Poland gained Pomerania and the mouth of the Vistula River, giving it access to the Baltic; the Teutonic Knights kept Prussia but acknowledged the Poles as overlords.

Hussite Wars: Bohemia was again divided by civil war between Catholics and Hussites (1462-1471), who were declared heretics.

Ottoman Turk forces conquered and annexed Bosnia (1463).

1450-1459 (cont.)

d. Cheng Ho (?-1451), Chinese Muslim admiral who led seven great voyages into the Indian Ocean and adjacent waters (1405-1433).

In the virtually continual Ayuthian-Chiengmaian war in Thailand, Ayuthians captured the city of Chiengmai (1452) but were soon forced to withdraw.

b. Affonso de Albuquerque (1453-1515), Portuguese admiral and governor in the Indian Ocean.

In India Malwa's Mahmud I defeated Bahmani numerous times, taking its northern provinces (1457-1469).

1460-1469

White Sheep Turkomans, led by Uzun Hasan, attempted to expand from Persia into Anatolia but were halted by the Ottoman Turks (1461).

Ottoman Turks conquered Trebizond, on the Black Sea (1461), the last remnant of the Byzantine Empire.

Portuguese forces invaded Morocco, taking Tangier and Casablanca (1463-1476).

In West Africa, Songhai, under Sonni Ali Ber (Sunni Ali), fought a long war with Jenne (Djénné) (1466-1473).

Black Sheep Turkomans were defeated and Jehan Shah was killed by the White Sheep Turkomans under Uzun Hasan (1467), who also defeated the Timurids, killing their leader, Abu Said (1469).

b. Selim I (1467-1520), sultan of Turkey (r. 1512-1520).

In West Africa, Sonni Ali Ber and his Songhai forces drove the Tuareg from Timbuktu, sacking the city (1468).

The Portuguese sacked Casablanca (1468), destroying its pirate base.

Korea took the Tsushima Islands, longtime haven for pirates (1460).

At Doi Ba, in northern Thailand, Chiengmai's army decisively drove back Ayuthian forces (1463).

In Japan, the War of the Monks led to the defeat and destruction of the monastery of Honganji by the monks of Enryakui (1465).

b. Montezuma II (1466?-1520), last Aztec emperor of Mexico (r. 1502-1520).

In Japan, the region around Kyoto was ravaged by a civil war (1467-1477) within the Ashikaga family, originally sparked by the rivalry between Hosokawa Katsumoto and his father-in-law, Yamana Mochitoyo, both of whom died in the conflict (1473).

1460-1469 (cont.)

Under James III (r. 1460-1488), the Scottish recovered those parts of southern Scotland that had remained in English control.

b. Louis II de la Trémoille (1460-1525), French general.

b. Pedro, count of Oliveto Navarro (ca. 1460-1528), Spanish general.

Wars of the Roses: At Mortimer's Cross (Feb. 2, 1461), near Leominster, Yorkists under Edward crushed the Lancastrians, pursuing many and executing them, as the war took a more brutal turn.

Wars of the Roses: Margaret's Lancastrians defeated the Yorkists under Warwick at the second Battle of St. Albans (Feb. 17, 1461), recapturing King Henry VI and heading slowly toward London; they then retreated to Yorkshire on learning that Edward, duke of York, had proclaimed himself Edward IV.

Wars of the Roses: Edward and his Yorkist forces pursued the Lancastrians, routing them at Towton (Mar. 29, 1461), at which an estimated 28,000 soldiers were killed, perhaps 20,000 of them Lancastrians.

d. Charles VII (1403-1461), king of France (1422-1461), earlier called the Dauphin; best known for his use and abandonment of Joan of Arc (1429).

Wars of the Roses: Yorkists under Warwick's brother Lord Montague defeated the Lancastrians at Hedgeley Moor, near Wooler (Apr. 25, 1464), and again at Hexham, followed by many executions (May 15); Henry VI took refuge in a monastery but was later found and imprisoned in the Tower of London; Margaret and their son Edward fled to France.

France's Louis XI fought an inconclusive battle at Montlhéry against a rebellious group of nobles called the League of the Public Weal (July 13, 1465).

In the first "Cod War" (1468-1474), English forces fought at sea with the Danes and the Hanseatic League over fishing rights and trade off Iceland.

Wars of the Roses: Two Lancastrian rebellions in northern England were put down by the Yorkists under Warwick — at Edgecote, near Banbury (1469), and at "Lose-Coat" Field (1470), near Empington, in Rutlandshire; by now disaffected with Edward IV, Warwick fomented a third uprising to draw Edward north, then himself went to London, released Henry VI from the Tower of London, and restored him to the throne (Sep.-Oct. 1470); Edward fled to Flanders.

Hungarians under Matthias I Corvinus, János Hunyadi's son, launched minor campaigns against Turkey (1463; 1475).

b. Andrea Doria (1466-1560), Genoese naval leader.

Austrians invaded Switzerland during a civil war but were quickly driven out (1468).

With the death of Skanderbeg (1468), Albania's independence movement collapsed, and the country came under Turkish control; the Turks also controlled Venetian coastal holdings in Dalmatia and Croatia, from which they raided Venice.

b. Niccolò Machiavelli (1469-1527), Florentine statesman and political and military theorist.

1470-1479

Wars of the Roses: Edward IV returned to England with a largely mercenary army and defeated the Lancastrian army at Barnet (Apr. 14, 1471), killing Warwick; Queen Margaret and her son Edward tried to reach safety in Wales but were defeated by Edward IV at Tewkesbury (May 4); Prince Edward was killed, and King Henry VI was later murdered in the Tower of London.

d. Richard Neville, earl of Warwick (1428-1471), English general known as the "Kingmaker" for his support of the Yorkists, the Lancastrians during the Wars of the Roses; he was killed at Barnet (Apr. 14).

Turkish land and sea forces invaded Negroponte (Euboea) (1470), taking it from the Venetians.

Poland and Hungary were at war (1471-1478), each supporting a different claimant of the Bohemian throne — Casimir IV of Poland or Matthias I Corvinus of Hungary.

Ivan III (the Great) of Moscow conquered Novgorod (1471-1478).

Africa and Southwest Asia	East, Central, and South Asia, the Pacific, and the Americas	
1460-1469 (cont.)		
Under Baeda Maryam (r. 1468-1478) and Eskender (r. 1478-1494), Christian Ethiopia fought off Muslim attacks.	Under Axayactl (r. 1468-1481), the Aztecs campaigned both east and west of Mexico City, reaching the Gulf of Mexico and the Pacific Ocean.	
Sonni Ali Ber led Songhai forces against the Mossi peoples (1469-1470; 1478-1479; 1480), who had long been raiding the Niger Valley.	Under Mahmud Gawan, India's Muslim state of Bahmani revived, defeating and annexing various Hindu states between Gujarat and Goa (1469).	
1470-1479		
Portuguese ships under Ferñao Gomes, João de Santarem, and Pedro de Escolar reached what would be the Gold Coast (1470-1471), they would later found a trading fort at Elmina (São Jorge de Mina) (1482).	b. Sher Shah (Farid-ud-Din Sher Shah; Farid Khan) (ca. 1472-1545), Indian emperor (r. 1540-1545) of Afghan-Turkish descent.	
Spanish, Flemish, and English ships variously attacked Portugal's slave-trading centers at Arguin Island, off Mauretania; Elmina, on the Gold Coast; and Gato in Benin (from 1470s).	In the Valley of Mexico, two Aztec cities, Tenochtitlán and Tlatilulco, fought a bitter civil war, with Tlatilulco being crushed (1473).	
Spanish forces captured Melilla, in Morocco (1470).	Led by Mahmud Gawan, India's state of Bahmani defeated Vijayanagar and took	
Portuguese forces took Tangier, in Morocco, at the Strait of Gibraltar (1471).		
Fernando Po discovered the island off West Africa named for him (1472).		

1470-1479 (cont.)

At Brunkenberg (Oct. 10, 1471), Swedes under Sten Sture the Elder defeated Danish-Norwegian king Christian I Oldenburg, still after the Swedish Crown.

Charles the Bold, duke of Burgundy, invaded Normandy at the Île de France but was defeated at Beauvais (1471-1472).

The struggle over the Pyrenees (1472-1475) ended with Aragon controlling Catalonia and France taking Roussillon.

England's Edward IV invaded France but under the Treaty of Pic-quigny accepted cash for not fighting (1475).

Isabella, supported by her husband Ferdinand of Aragon, won a succession fight against a rival claimant, Joan, for the throne of Castile, the victory being ensured after the Portuguese forces sent by Joan's husband, Affonso V of Portugal, were defeated at Toro (1476).

After establishment of the Inquisition in Castile and Aragon (1478), many religious dissenters were persecuted and massacred, especially Jews and Muslims, including those who held their old beliefs while outwardly conforming; these groups were called Mar-ranos and Moriscos, respectively.

French forces under Louis XI invaded the Netherlands but were defeated by Hapsburg troops under archduke Maximilian at Guinegate (1479).

Swiss forces defeated Charles the Bold of Burgundy at Héricourt (Nov. 13, 1474); with their allies, the Haps-burgs and south Germans, the Swiss then took border regions of Switzerland and Alsace, including Granson, from Burgundy (1474-1475).

Moldavian forces under Stephen fought off a Turkish invasion (1475-1476).

b. Cesare Borgia, duke of Valentinois (1475-1507), Spanish-Italian general and statesman.

After retaking Granson (Feb. 1476), the Burgundians killed the entire Swiss force; a new Swiss army engi-neered a stunning defeat at Granson (Mar. 2) and again at Morat, near Bern, and Fribourg (June 22).

An army of Swiss and allied forces invaded Burgundy, defeating Charles the Bold's new army at Nancy, where Charles was killed (Jan. 5, 1477).

Hungary's King Matthias I Corvinus was at war with the German emperor Frederick III (1477-1485), be-sieging Vienna (1477).

Often supported by Tartars from Crimea, Russia fought an inconclusive war with Lithuania (1478-1489).

The Swiss won another war with Milan at Giornico (Dec. 28, 1478).

Venice made peace with the Ottoman Turks, ceding not only the territories they had won but also Scutari, which had held out (1479).

1480-1489

Muley Abu'l Hassan, king of Granada, invaded Christian Spain, triggering the final Muslim-Christian war in Iberia (1481).

Portugal's John II suppressed a revolt led by Ferdinand, of the powerful Braganza family (1481-1483).

b. Christian II (1481-1559), king of Denmark and Norway (1513-1523) and of Sweden (1520-1523).

English forces under Alexander, duke of Albany, and Richard, duke of Gloucester (later Richard III), invaded southern Scotland, retaking Berwick, seizing Edinburgh, and effectively winning con-trol of the country (1482), although they were later forced out.

In the fight against Granada, the forces of Ferdinand and Isabella of Castile and Aragon were ambushed and defeated at Loja (1482).

d. Edward IV (1442-1483), English king (r. 1461-1470; 1471-1483); son of Richard, duke of York, he became king during the Wars of the Roses. His successor was his 13-year-old son, Edward V, who with his younger brother were imprisoned and presumed killed in the Tower of London (ca. Aug. 1483).

Wars of the Roses: On Edward IV's death (1483), his brother Rich-ard of Gloucester became regent, then took the throne himself, as Richard III, suppressing a revolt by the duke of Buckingham,

Ottoman Turks invaded Italy, taking Otranto, on the Adriatic coast (1480), then withdrawing (1481).

Milan, Florence, and Naples allied themselves to keep Venice from taking Ferrara (1482-1484).

Turks conquered and annexed Herzegovina (1483).

Turks invaded Moldavia but made a truce and with-drew; massive Moldavian and Polish forces were not called on to fight (1484-1485).

Ivan III (the Great) of Moscow took Tver (1485); also variously at war with Lithuania, Viatka, and Kazan, he first took the title "czar of all the Russias."

The Hapsburgs were driven out of Austria, including Vienna, by Matthias I Corvinus and his Hungarians (1485), who won their war against German emperor Frederick III.

With the support of Florence, King Ferdinand I put down a revolt of nobles in Naples (1485-1486).

Hapsburg emperor Maximilian I founded the Lands-knechts, an imperial German army modeled on Swiss forces (1486).

Africa and Southwest Asia

1470-1479 (cont.)

Allied with the Venetians, the White Sheep Turkomans under Uzun Hasan invaded the Ottoman Turks in Anatolia but were driven back by Mohammed II at Erzinjan (1473).

Songhai finally defeated Jenne (1473).

The long struggle over the Canary Islands ends, with Spain keeping some inner islands, which it had settled, and Portugal the rest (1479).

Goa (1475); turning eastward, it then took the Hindu kingdom of Orissa and the nearby coast (1478).

At Zamacuyahuac, in Mexico, the Tarascans decisively defeated the Three-City League of Tenochtitlán, Tlacopan, and Texcoco (1478).

1480-1489

Nyatsimba, who took the name "Mwene Matapa" (Ravager of the Lands), founded the Matapa Empire between Africa's Zambezi and Limpopo rivers (ca. 1480).

Knights of St. John fought off a Turkish invasion of Rhodes; Mohammed II retired after heavy losses (1480-1481).

The Treaty of Alcacovas (1480) ended Portuguese control of the Canary Islands, awarding them to Castile.

An Ethiopian ambassador reached Rome (1481), seeking help against the Muslims.

d. Mohammed II Fatih (the Conqueror; Muhammed; Mehmet) (1432-1481), Ottoman ruler (r. 1444-1446; 1451-1481) who led the successful siege of Constantinople (1453), then took Serbia, Bosnia, and Greece (1456-1460), but failed to take Belgrade (1456).

Bayazid II won a brief civil war for the Turkish imperial throne, defeating his brother Djem, who took refuge in Rhodes (1481).

Portuguese ships under Diogo Cão reached the Zaire (Congo) River and Cape St. Augustine (1482-1484), then rounded capes Cross and Negro (1485-1486), still seeking the mythical Prester John for a Christian alliance.

Songhai forces under Sonni Ali Ber defeated Mossi raiders at the Battle of Kobi (1483), later campaigning against them again (1488).

India's Bahmani, led by Mahmud Gawan, again defeated Vijayanagar (1481); Vijayanagar and Orissa then combined forces against Bahmani, which eventually collapsed (1481-1500).

b. Babur (Zahir ud-din Muhammad) (1483-1530), Mogul ruler.

Under Ahuitzotol (r. 1486-1502), the Aztecs again campaigned east and west to both coasts, also expanding southward (1495-1498).

Delhi's Lodi dynasty finally conquered Jaunpur to control India's central Ganges Valley (1487).

1480-1489 (cont.)

apparently supported by Henry Tudor, earl of Richmond (head of the house of Lancaster).

Wars of the Roses: Landing at Milford Haven with an army of French mercenaries, Lancastrian leader Henry Tudor won key support in Wales and western England as he invaded central England, at Bosworth Field (Aug. 22, 1485), utterly defeating Yorkist forces and personally killing Richard, so ending the Wars of the Roses; as King Henry VII, he founded the Tudor line.

d. Richard III (Richard of Gloucester) (1452-1485), English king (r. 1483-1485) who engineered a route to the throne over several dead bodies; portrayed by Shakespeare as a consummate villain.

b. Hernán (Hernando; Fernando) Cortés (1485-1547), Spanish military leader.

Spanish Christian forces took Loja (1486) and besieged and captured Málaga (May-Aug. 1487), also taking the surrounding areas.

England's Henry VII put down two key revolts, one led by Lambert Simnel (1487) and the other by Perkin Warbeck (1488-1499).

Supported by the Tudors and the Hapsburgs, the dukes of Orléans and Brittany revolted against France's Charles VIII but were defeated at St.-Aubin-du-Cormier (1488); in the Netherlands, Hapsburg archduke Maximilian founded a permanent Dutch admiralty.

Spanish Christians took the strongholds of Baza and Almeria, isolating Granada (1489).

The no-longer-mighty Khanate of the Golden Horde invaded Poland and Lithuania (1487) but was decisively defeated at Zaslavl (1491).

1490-1499

b. Charles, count of Montpensier and duke of Bourbon (1490-1527), constable of France and imperial general.

Granada, the last Muslim stronghold in Spain, fell to the Christians after a long siege (Apr. 1491-Jan. 2, 1492); unconverted Jews were expelled from Spain.

b. Henry VIII (1491-1547), English king (r. 1509-1547).

b. Johann von Rantzau (1492-1565), Danish general.

Danish and Norwegian king Hans (John) I fought a war with Sweden (1493-1497), of which he also became king.

Jews who refused forcible conversion to Christianity were driven from Portugal (1496).

First record of the word *moschetto*, or "musket" (1499).

b. Albert von Hohenzollern (1490-1568), grand master of the Teutonic Knights and first duke of Prussia.

d. Matthias I Corvinus (Mátyás Hunyadi) (1440-1490), king of Hungary (r. 1458-1490) during wars with the Turks (1463; 1475), the Bohemian War (1468-78), and wars with Austria (1477-85); he was the son of national hero János Hunyadi.

Hapsburg emperor Maximilian I retook Vienna from the Hungarians (1491).

Aided by Crimean Tartars, Russia was again at war with Lithuania (1492-1503).

Hapsburg emperor Maximilian I fought off a Turkish invasion of Styria and Carniola (later Yugoslavia) (1492-1494), defeating the invaders at Villach (1492). He also put down a revolt in the Netherlands (1494).

Under Charles VIII the French invaded and took Naples (1494).

b. Suleiman I (the Magnificent) (ca. 1494-1566), Ottoman Turk sultan (r. 1520-1566), sometimes called Suleiman II.

Italian Wars (1495-1515): In the continuing contest for Italy, Spain intervened in Naples; its forces, under Hernández Gonzalo de Córdoba, were defeated at Seminara (1495).

b. Khair ed-Din (Barbarossa; Khizr) (ca. 1483-1546), Greek-Turkish admiral and North African ruler.

Portugal's Bartolomeu Dias was the first modern European sailor to round Africa's Cape of Good Hope (1487), reaching the Rio de Infante (probably the Great Fish River) before his sailors forced him to turn back.

Portugal's King John sent Pedro de Covilhão and Afonso de Paiva to India by way of Cairo, Aden, and Hormuz (1487); en route home from Calicut, Covilhão explored the East African coast as far south as the Zambezi River (1488).

Ottoman Turks fought off invasions of Adana and Tarsus by Egypt's Mamelukes (1487-1491).

White Sheep Turkomans, allied with Georgians, defeated and killed Haidar of the Turkoman Safawid dynasty in Azerbaijan (1488).

In West Africa, Sonni Ali Ber led the Songhai against the Fulani (1492), dying en route home; in the ensuing succession struggle, general Muhammad ibn abi Bakr Ture defeated Sonni Ali's son Sonni Baru at Anfao (Apr. 12, 1493), then ruled as Askia Muhammad (Mohammed I Askia).

d. Sonni Ali Ber (Sunni Ali) (?-1492), Songhai ruler (r. ca. 1464-1492) who conquered Timbuktu (1468) and Jenne (Djénné) (1473).

Portugal's Vasco da Gama was the first to sail around Africa to India and return (July 8, 1497-Aug. or Sept. 1499), opening Europe's route for colonization and conquest in the East; en route he visited various sites on Africa's east coast, including Mozambique and Mombasa, where he was not well received by Arab traders, and Melindi, where he employed a pilot to guide him to Calicut, India (May 1498). More than one-third of his crew died of scurvy, a major problem for centuries.

In West Africa, Songhai forces under Askia Muhammad defeated and conquered the Mossi of Yatenga (northern Burkina Faso, or Upper Volta) (1498-1502).

Turkoman Safawids under Ismail, son of Haidar, took Shirvan and Baku (1499-1500).

In a voyage financed by Ferdinand and Isabella of Spain (Aug. 3, 1492-Mar. 15, 1493), Christopher Columbus sailed south to the Canary Islands, then west to the Caribbean, landing in territory later known as the Americas, specifically the West Indies, named for his mistaken view that they were off east Asia; he first landed in the Bahamas (Oct. 12, 1492), on San Salvador (probably Watling Island), then Cuba and Hispaniola (Española; Santo Domingo), where he founded the post of Navidad, beginning the European conquest of the Americas.

On his second voyage to America, Columbus explored Dominica, Puerto Rico, parts of the Antilles, and Jamaica (1493); returning to Cuba and Hispaniola, he left his brother Bartholomew as governor.

The pope granted Spain exclusive rights to the American lands west of a specified line of demarcation, beyond the Azores and Cape Verde Islands (1493).

Japan was again wracked by decades of civil war after Hosokawa Masamoto deposed shogun Yoshitame (1493), instead installing a puppet.

1490-1499 (cont.)

Russia invaded Swedish-held Finland (1495; 1496), the second time reaching the Gulf of Bothnia; Swedes under Sten Sture took and sacked Ivangorod; the war was ended by a treaty (1497).

Moldavians under Stephen fought off separate invasions by Poles and Turks, both then recognizing Moldavia's independence (1497-1498).

After battles all along the Austrian-Swiss frontier, the Swiss defeated forces under Hapsburg emperor Maximilian I at Dornach (July 22, 1499); the Treaty of Basel gave them their independence.

After decisively defeating the Venetians at the first Battle of Lepanto (July 28, 1499), in the Gulf of Corinth, the Turks took numerous island and coastal possessions in the Aegean and Ionian seas.

1500-1509

b. Blaise de Lasseran-Massencome, seigneur of Monluc (Montluc) (1501?-1577), French marshal.

Unconverted Moors were driven from Castile (1502).

b. Christian III (1503-1559), king of Denmark and Norway (r. 1534-1559).

Hans (John) I, king of Denmark and Norway, fought with Sweden (1506-1513), attempting to reestablish the Union of Kalmar, with himself on the Swedish throne.

d. Henry VII (Henry Tudor) (1457-1509), English king (r. 1485-1509) crowned after his rival Richard III was killed at Bosworth Field (1485); by marrying Edward IV's daughter Elizabeth, he united the houses of Lancaster and York, ending the Wars of the Roses and founding the Tudor line. Henry VIII succeeded him as king of England (r. 1509-1547); he married Catherine of Aragon.

Italian Wars: Treaty of Granada (Nov. 11, 1500) partitioned Naples between France and Spain. Louis XII's French forces almost immediately reinvaded Italy, taking Milan and Naples, and Spanish forces under Hernández Gonzalo de Córdoba again contested the French advance. Córdoba withdrew from Naples (Aug. 1502) but returned with his heavily reinforced army to win the Battle of Cerignola (Apr. 21, 1503), notably aided by their use of harquebus (rifle) fire. Spanish forces again took Naples (May). Córdoba's forces decisively defeated the French at the Garigliano River (Dec. 29), then took Gaeta (Jan. 1, 1504), as French forces fled by sea. Under the Treaty of Blois (1505), defeated France withdrew its claim to Naples, now ruled by Spain.

Venetian-Turkish War: As the Ottoman Turks continued to attack Europe, a Turkish fleet again defeated the Venetian fleet at Lepanto, in the Gulf of Corinth (1500), while Turkish land forces moving west out of the Balkans attacked over the Alps into northern Italy.

Massive Russian imperial expansion east and south into Asia began. Russia took much of White Russia from

Africa and Southwest Asia

East, Central, and South Asia, the Pacific, and the Americas

Under the Treaty of Tordesillas (1494), Spain and Portugal moved the line that divided the Americas between them farther west.

John Cabot (Giovanni Caboto), a Genoan in English service, landed in North America, probably on Cape Breton Island and Newfoundland, establishing English claims to the land (1497); he was lost on a second voyage to North America (1498).

b. Mori Motonari (1497-1571), Japanese general.

On his third voyage to America, Columbus discovered Trinidad Island (July 31, 1498) and explored the South American coast down to the Orinoco River; after putting down a revolt in Hispaniola, he and his brother were returned to Spain, temporarily as prisoners, by the new governor Francisco de Bobadilla (1499).

Portuguese explorer Duarte Pacheco Pereira may have reached the South American coast (1498).

Alonso de Ojeda and Amerigo Vespucci led Spanish voyages exploring the Americas (May 1499-June 1500) from French Guiana to Cape St. Rogue, including the mouth of the Amazon River, then farther north; America may have been named for Vespucci.

Ismail of Persia attacked south and west against the Tartars, taking Baku (1500). His forces then took Azerbaijan, occupied Tabriz after winning the decisive Battle of Shurer (1501), and took control of all of Persia (1501-1510).

In East Africa, Abd Allah Jamma captured the kingdom of 'Alwah (ca. 1500).

Portuguese forces took and sacked Kilwa, Mombasa, and several other East African coastal cities (1505-1506).

Songhai forces led by Askia Muhammad expanded into Tuareg territory at Air (in modern Nigeria) (1506).

Songhai was at war with the peoples of the Niger Valley (1507).

Spanish forces took Oran and Mers El Kabir, on the North African coast (1509); seaborne invasion forces then took Oran, Bougie, and Tripoli (1509-1511).

Kazakhs, remnants of the Golden Horde, came to power in Turkestan and the Kirghiz steppe (ca. 1500).

Pedro Cabral landed on the South American coast and claimed what is now Brazil for Portugal, a claim quickly disputed by Spain (1500).

Ayuthia (Siam) and Chiengmai were at war (ca. 1500-1530).

Portuguese naval forces established fortified trading posts on the Indian coast (from 1500), most notably at Cochin (1503).

First African slaves were brought to Hispaniola (1501).

Uzbek forces expanding west in Central Asia took Herat, Khorasan, and Transoxiana (1501-1507).

Montezuma II became ruler of the Aztec Empire; Aztec power continued to grow (1502).

1500-1509 (cont.)

Lithuania (1501-1503) and, in alliance with the Crimean Tartars, defeated the Golden Horde (1502).

d. Cesare Borgia, duke of Valentinois (1475-1507), Spanish-Italian general and statesman; to Machiavelli he was a model Renaissance prince; he was killed at a siege of Viana (Mar. 12).

1510-1519

b. Edward Fiennes Clinton (1512-1585), English admiral.

James IV of Scotland went to war against England in support of his French allies (Aug. 11, 1513). Invading England, his army was defeated and he was killed at Flodden by English forces under Thomas Howard, with massive losses on both sides (Sept. 9, 1513). James V succeeded to the Scottish throne; the English-Scottish border war continued.

Christian II succeeded Hans (John) I as king of Denmark and Norway (1513), later also taking the Swedish Crown (1520).

Wheel lock was invented (ca. 1515).

d. Hernández Gonzalo de Córdoba (Gonsalvo de Cordova) (1453-1515), Spanish general who played a key role in driving the Moors from Granada; later, in the Italian Wars, he and his Spanish troops had great success in introducing firearms and new maneuvering tactics against heavy cavalry and pikemen.

b. Mary I (1516-1558), English queen (r. 1553-1558).

b. François de Lorraine, second duke of Guise (1519-1563), French general.

b. Gaspard II de Coligny (1519-1572), French general and admiral.

Russian forces took Pskov (1510), incorporating it into Russia.

Italian Wars: War of the Holy League (1510-1514) pitted Spain, Venice, the Papal States, and England against France and, in the early years, some German forces. French forces led by Gaston of Foix invaded and took much of northern Italy (1511-1512) and defeated Spanish forces at the Battle of Ravenna (Apr. 11, 1512); Austria and Switzerland's alliance with the Holy League forced French withdrawal from Italy. A renewed French invasion (May 1513) resulted in a French loss at Novara and subsequent flight back to France. English forces led by Henry VIII invaded France (June 1513), winning the Battle of Guinegate; the war ended indecisively with a series of short-lived peace agreements.

Hungarian peasant revolt failed, defeated by the forces of John Zapolya of Transylvania (1514).

Poland and Russia were at war; Russia took Smolensk (1514).

Italian Wars: Continuing to fight over Italy, Francis I of France led a 30,000-man army over the Alps into northern Italy (June 1515), meeting the Swiss at Marignano (Sept. 13-14), near Milan. Threatened by approaching Venetian forces on the second day of the battle, Swiss forces retreated in good order; the Swiss and French each lost an estimated 5,000 to 6,000 dead. The French then took Milan, with their control recognized under the Treaty of Noyon (Aug. 1516).

Africa and Southwest Asia

East, Central, and South Asia, the
Pacific, and the Americas

1500-1509 (cont.)

Portuguese forces led by Affonso de Albuquerque captured the key Persian Gulf trading island of Hormuz (1508) but were unable to hold it.

In an attempt to block Portuguese penetration, Indian naval forces and their allies defeated the small Portuguese Indian Ocean fleet off Chaul (1508).

Spanish forces took Puerto Rico from the Caribs (1508-1511).

b. Humayun (Na-sin-ud-Din Muhammad) (1508-1556), second Mogul emperor of India (r. 1530-1540; 1555-1556).

At Diu, Portuguese naval forces with superior weaponry destroyed a massive Egyptian-Arab Indian Ocean fleet, effectively removing opposition to the continuing Portuguese seaborne penetration of the area (Feb. 1509).

Sebastian Cabot, exploring the northern coast of North America, entered the strait that led to Hudson Bay (1509), establishing Britain's claim to the region.

1510-1519

Spanish forces captured the North African coastal city of Tripoli (1510).

Songhai forces led by Askia Muhammad took Diara (in modern Nigeria) (1512).

Selim I became Turkish sultan (1512).

Turkish forces numbering an estimated 60,000 and led by Selim I invaded Persia, defeating Persian defenders on the plains of Chaldiran (Aug. 23, 1515) and then taking Tabriz. Turkish forces also took much of Kurdistan.

Turkish armies numbering an estimated 40,000 and led by Selim I invaded Syria (July 1516), decisively defeating Mameluke forces at Merj-Dabik (Aug. 24); the Mamelukes retreated to Egypt.

Turkish forces led by Selim I invaded Egypt (Jan. 1517), defeating Mameluke forces at Ridanieh (Jan. 22) and quickly taking Cairo; Selim became caliph of Egypt, which passed into Turkish control, as did western Arabia.

Algerian rebels led by Khair ed-Din (Barbarossa) mounted a successful insurrection against occupying Spanish forces; Khair ed-Din became bey of Algiers (1518).

Portuguese ships began to appear on the south China coast (1510-1515) and became the first western European vessels to reach Canton (by 1514).

Persia and Uzbekistan were at war (1510). Persian forces took and held Herat and Khorasan, defeating the Uzbeks at Merv, where Uzbek leader Mohammed Shaibaini Khan died.

Portuguese forces took Goa (1510) and Malacca (1511).

d. Francisco de Almeida (ca. 1450-1510), Portuguese admiral and first viceroy to Portuguese India (1505), who was victorious at Diu (1509); en route home he was killed by Africans near Table Bay at the Cape of Good Hope.

Babur, his strength centered at Kabul, attacked Uzbeks in Transoxiana; his forces took Samarkand but were defeated at Ghazdivan, retreating to Kabul (1511-1512).

Spanish forces took Cuba (1511-1515).

In southern India, Vijayanagar defeated Bijapur (1512), beginning a period of dominance in the eastern Deccan.

1510-1519 (cont.)

b. Nicolo Dandolo (ca. 1515-1570), Venetian military leader.

At Wittenberg, Germany, Martin Luther published his Ninety-five Theses (Oct. 31, 1517), beginning the Protestant Reformation and setting the context for the massive religious wars that followed.

Russian forces took and annexed Riazan (1517).

d. Maximilian I (1459-1519), king of Germany (r. 1486-1519) and Holy Roman Emperor (r. 1493-1519) who brought Bohemia and Hungary into the empire, and laid the basis for Hapsburg dominance in the empire.

1520-1529

Henry VIII of England and Francis I of France allied themselves at the Field of the Cloth of Gold (June 7, 1520).

French forces attacked in Navarre (northern Spain), taking Pamplona and then retreating into southern France after their defeat at Equiroz (May-June 1521).

Christian II was driven from the Swedish throne by Gustav Vasa, who became Gustavus I, ending Scandinavia's Union of Kalmar (1523); Christian was deposed in Denmark and Norway by Frederick, duke of Holstein, whose forces, led by Johann von Rantzau, besieged and took Copenhagen (1523-1524).

d. Louis II de la Trémoille (1460-1525), French general who was killed at Pavia (Feb. 24).

b. Alvaro de Bazan, marquis of Santa Cruz (1526-1588), Spanish admiral.

d. Charles, count of Montpensier and duke of Bourbon (1490-1527), constable of France and imperial general.

A French-Swiss-Venetian army attacked Spanish forces in northern Italy (1521) but lost Milan to Spanish-German-Papal forces, then lost the decisive Battle of Bicocca (Apr. 27, 1522).

Crimean Tartar forces invaded Russia, threatening Moscow (1521).

Turkish forces led by Suleiman I continued their advance into Europe, invading Hungary (May 1521); besieged Belgrade surrendered (late Aug.).

Austrian-German forces took the offensive (spring 1524), defeating and scattering the French in northern Italy and attacking southern France (July), unsuccessfully besieging Marseilles and then fleeing back across the Alps, with French forces in pursuit (Oct. 1524). The French besieged Pavia (later Oct.) and were decisively defeated there (Feb. 24, 1525), with an estimated

Africa and Southwest Asia | East, Central, and South Asia, the Pacific, and the Americas

1510-1519 (cont.)

Juan Ponce de León landed in Florida, beginning the European conquest of North America (1513).

Portuguese forces established fortified posts in the Moluccas, the legendary Spice Islands (1513-1521), beginning the long contest for European supremacy in the East Indies (Indonesia).

Vasco Nuñez de Balboa reached the Pacific Ocean at Panama (1513).

Turning his attention to northern India, Babur began a series of raids into the Punjab (1515-1523).

Portuguese forces again took Hormuz (1515), this time holding the island.

d. Affonso de Albuquerque (1453-1515), Portuguese admiral and governor in the Indian Ocean who took Goa (1510) and Malacca (1511); he died at sea (Dec. 15).

Juan Díaz de Solis discovered the River Plate, in South America (1516).

Portuguese Indian Ocean forces built a fort at Colombo, Ceylon (Sri Lanka) (1518).

Spanish forces of 600, led by Hernán Cortés, attacked the Aztec Empire (Aug. 1519); at Tenochtitlán (Mexico City), emperor Montezuma initially received Cortés as the incarnation of the god Quetzalcoatl (Nov. 8), but Spanish forces later captured Montezuma (Dec.) and held him hostage.

Ferdinand Magellan launched the first round-the-world voyage, rounding Cape Horn and entering the Pacific (1519).

1520-1529

d. Selim I (1467-1520), sultan of Turkey (r. 1512-1520); he was succeeded by his son Suleiman I (r. 1523-1536).

Turkish forces numbering an estimated 100,000 landed on Rhodes (June 1522) and began the long siege of the Knights of St. John's Hospitallers fortress on the island. The fortress was finally taken (late Dec.); the remaining defenders evacuated under the surrender agreement.

With Turkish support, Muslims in Harar mounted a successful insurrection against Ethiopia (1523-1543).

Portuguese forces again took Mombasa (1523).

Turkish-Persian Wars (1526-1555): Persian forces attacked in Armenia and Mesopotamia, taking Baghdad and much of Syria.

Turkish government forces defeated Shi'ite insurrections against the Sunni Turkish regime in Anatolia (1526).

Songhai ruler Askia Muhammad was deposed by his son Askia Musa (1528).

Spanish forces put down an Aztec uprising in Mexico (June 30, 1520), killing Montezuma; with their anti-Aztec allies, they besieged and took Tenochtitlán again (Aug.-May 1521); they then took the entire Aztec Empire and much more.

d. Montezuma II (1466?-1520), last Aztec emperor of Mexico (r. 1502-1520), who initially received Cortés in peace (Nov. 8, 1519) but was later killed in fighting with Spanish forces (June 30).

Portuguese envoys reached Peking (ca. 1520-1522).

Ferdinand Magellan reached the Philippines; he was killed in a skirmish there (1521), but his crew — some of whom completed the round-the-world voyage —

1520-1529 (cont.)

d. Pedro, count of Oliveto Navarro (ca. 1460-1528), Spanish general who, after being captured at Ravenna (1512), entered French service; taken prisoner in Italy (1527), he died in Naples's Castel Nuovo.

8,000 casualties of the 20,000 engaged. Francis I of France was wounded and captured.

Lutheran peasant revolts failed in Germany (1524).

Albert von Hohenzollern, grand master of the Teutonic Knights, dissolved the order (Apr. 1525), proclaiming himself first duke of Prussia.

Francis I of France was freed under the Treaty of Madrid (Jan. 14, 1526), which cost defeated France all its Italian holdings and several French provinces, including Flanders and Burgundy. Once free, Francis resumed the war against the Holy Roman Empire, unsuccessfully attacking again in northern Italy and losing Milan (1526) and Genoa (1528).

Suleiman I led a Turkish invasion army numbering 70,000 to 80,000 into Hungary (Apr. 1526), meeting a Hungarian force less than half its size under Louis of Hungary on the plain of Mohács. The ensuing battle was a decisive victory for the Turks, who destroyed the defending Hungarian army, killing an estimated 15,000, including Louis, and scattering the remainder, which ceased to be an effective fighting force. Suleiman took control of Hungary, setting up a protectorate nominally ruled by John Zapolya of Transylvania.

A great cultural disaster occurred when troops of the Holy Roman Empire took and sacked Rome (May 6, 1527), in the process destroying many great works of art of the Italian Renaissance.

d. Niccolò Machiavelli (1469-1527), Florentine statesman and political and military theorist who is best known as author of *The Prince* (1513) and *The Art of War* (1520).

Turkish and Hungarian armies totaling 80,000 to 90,000 and led by Suleiman I moved toward Vienna (May 1529), took Buda (early Sept.), and unsuccessfully besieged Vienna (Sept.-Oct.). As cold weather approached, they broke off the siege and retreated, pursued by Austrian forces.

Treaty of Cambrai (1529) ended this phase of the long French–Holy Roman Empire wars, with the empire again in control of Italy and France largely restored to its previous borders.

claimed the islands for Spain (1522), beginning the conquest and long European occupation of the Philippines.

Spanish forces established armed outposts along the coast of northern South America (1521-1535).

b. Takeda (Harunobu) Shingen (1521-1573), Japanese military leader.

Spanish forces took southern Mexico and northern Central America (1522-1540).

b. Shibata Katsuie (1522-1583), Japanese general.

Giovanni Verrazano reached Newfoundland and Belle Isle (1524).

Spanish forces took much of northern Mexico, including part of the American Southwest (1524-1555).

Babur's forces took but could not hold Lahore, in the Punjab (1524). Babur again attacked northern India, with a force of no more than 10,000, taking the Punjab (1525).

Hernán Cortés led an expedition into Honduras (1524-1526).

Russian explorers and traders moved across the Amur River, penetrating Manchuria; Russian soldiers were not far behind. Manchu forces pushed them back across the Amur (1525-1526).

Babur's army decisively defeated a Delhi army of 30,000 to 40,000 at Panipat (Apr. 20, 1526); Sultan Ibrahim of Delhi and an estimated 15,000 died in the rout. Babur took Delhi (Apr. 26), becoming the first of the Mogul (Mughal) emperors of India.

Rama T'ibodi II and his Ayuthian (Siamese) forces defeated rival Tai forces from Chiengmai at the Battle of the Mewang River, near Lampang (ca. 1527).

Leading a force of no more than 20,000, Babur decisively defeated a massive Indian army of 90,000 to 100,000 at Khanua (Mar. 16, 1527).

Atahuallpa became ruler of the Inca Empire, succeeding Huayna Capac (1527).

Shan forces took most of northern Burma, sacking Ava (1527).

Babur conquered Bihar and Bengal; his forces won the decisive Battle of the Gogra River, near Patna (1528-1529).

Portuguese forces took Diu (1528).

1520-1529 (cont.)

1530-1539

Henry VIII established the Church of England (1530), a major step in the Protestant-Catholic realignment of Europe.

Christian II attempted to regain the throne of Denmark and Norway by force (1531) but was captured and imprisoned for life (1532).

Danish Civil War (1533-1536): Royalist forces, with the support of German and Holstein forces, installed Christian III (son of Frederick I) as king of Denmark after besieging and taking Malmö and Copenhagen (Apr. and July 1536).

b. Elizabeth I (1533-1603), English queen (r. 1558-1603).

b. William the Silent, count of Nassau and prince of Orange (1533-1584), Dutch general.

War between France and the Holy Roman Empire was inconclusive (1536-1538), with a largely failed French invasion of northern Italy, followed by unsuccessful imperial invasions of northern France. The Vatican mediated the Truce of Nice, which, meant to last ten years, lasted four.

b. Charles Howard, second Baron Howard of Effingham and first earl of Nottingham (1536-1604), English admiral.

Protestant-Catholic conflicts grew in Switzerland, as in much of northern Europe. Protestant Zurich was defeated by an alliance of Catholic Swiss cantons at the Battle of Kappel (Oct. 11, 1531).

Imperial forces led by Andrea Doria raided Turkish-held Morea (the Peloponnesian peninsula) (1532), taking Coron and triggering renewed Muslim-Christian contests in the Mediterranean (1532-1565).

Turkish forces again moved against Vienna but failed to reach it; after campaigning in southern Hungary, they returned home (1532).

Turkish admiral Khair ed-Din (Barbarossa) began a long series of Turkish attacks in the Mediterranean and North Africa, retaking Coron (1533).

Poland and Russia were at war (1534-1536).

Austrian forces invaded the Turkish-held portion of Hungary (Sept.-Dec. 1537); soon defeated, the Austrians fled, closely pursued by the Turks, who destroyed what remained of the invasion army, with an estimated 20,000 dead.

Turkey and Venice were at war; Khair ed-Din made seaborne raids on the Italian coast and took Venetian-held islands and coastal strongholds (1537-1538). The Turks, led by Suleiman I, unsuccessfully besieged Corfu (Aug.-Sept. 1537). Defeated Venice made peace with Turkey, ceding many Turkish-won territories (1539).

Turkish forces defeated an insurrection in Moldavia (1538).

Africa and Southwest Asia	East, Central, and South Asia, the Pacific, and the Americas

	b. Ch'i Chi-kuang (1528-1587), Chinese general and military theorist.
	Portuguese-held Malacca was attacked by Achenese Muslims, beginning the long Portuguese-Achenese conflict (1529).
	d. Rama T'ibodi II (?-1529), Siamese ruler (r. 1491-1529) who was on the throne when the Portuguese first arrived in Ayuthia (Siam).

1530-1539

Africa and Southwest Asia	East, Central, and South Asia, the Pacific, and the Americas
Knights of St. John Hospitallers took possession of the central Mediterranean island of Malta, given to them by Emperor Charles V (1530); it would be their stronghold until taken by Napoleon (1798).	b. Kikkawa Motoharu (1530-1586), Japanese general.
Turkish-Persian Wars: Persians retook Baghdad (Jan. 1534), lost in 1526; it would change hands several times.	d. Babur (Zahir ud-din Muhammad) (1483-1530), ruler who founded India's Mogul dynasty (1526); a descendant of Genghis Khan and Tamerlane, he was succeeded by his son Humayun.
Turkish-Persian Wars: Turks defeated Persian forces to take Tabriz, in Azerbaijan (July 1534); it also would change hands several times in the following two decades.	Mogul forces led by Humayun attacked Gujarat; after early successes they were driven out by the forces of Bahadur Shah (1531-1536).
Turkish naval forces under Khair ed-Din (Barbarossa) took Tunis (1534), but Spanish and Austrian forces recaptured it (1535) as Andrea Doria's Spanish fleet defeated Khair ed-Din's offshore.	A Spanish expedition of fewer than 200, led by Francisco Pizarro, attacked the Inca Empire (1532). Inca emperor Atahuallpa was seized at Cajamarca (Aug.) and held for ransom; it was paid, but he was murdered by the Spanish, who set up a puppet ruler. Pizarro's forces moved on Cuzco (1533), ultimately taking the city and the empire.
d. Askia Muhammad (Mohammed I Askia; Muhammad ibn abi Bakr Ture) (?-1538), Songhai general and emperor who expanded his empire at the expense of the Mossi, the Tuaregs, and the Bornu; he was deposed by his son (1528).	Jacques Cartier landed at Chaleur Bay, on the New Brunswick coast, beginning the French invasion and conquest of Canada (1534).
	b. Oda Nobunaga (1534-1582), Japanese general.
	Inca revolt in Peru was defeated by Spanish occupation forces (1535-1536).
	On his second voyage to North America, Jacques Cartier entered the St. Lawrence River, reaching the region of Quebec and Montreal (1535).
	Portuguese forces began their long series of small wars by which they would gradually take control of northern Java (1535).
	Spanish forces moved inland in Colombia, defeating the Chibchas near modern Bogotá (1536-1538).
	b. Toyotomi Hideyoshi (ca. 1536-1598), Japanese general.

1530-1539 (cont.)

1540-1549

English forces invaded Scotland, defeating Scottish forces at Solway Moss (Nov. 25, 1542).

b. Mary (Stuart) (1542-1587), queen of Scotland (r. 1542-1587) who inherited the throne at six days old on the death of her father, James V; she would be brought up in France, which would cause later problems with both the English and the Scots.

War came again to Europe after a French-Turkish alliance against the Holy Roman Empire (1542). French-Turkish naval forces sacked Nice (1543), while imperial forces unsuccessfully invaded northern France. English forces allied with the empire made a cross-Channel invasion at Calais (1544), ultimately taking Boulogne, as recognized by an English-French treaty (1546). Emperor Charles V made peace with France after a failed imperial invasion of France (1544).

b. Alessandro Farnese, duke of Parma (1545-1592), Italian general serving Spain.

b. Hugh O'Neill, third earl of Tyrone (ca. 1545-1616), Irish chief and general.

d. Henry VIII (1491-1547), English king (r. 1509-1547) of the Tudor line; best known for his six wives, his break with the Roman Catholic Church, and his children — Edward VI, Mary I, and Elizabeth I. His young son Edward succeeded him, with Edward Seymour, duke of Somerset, as lord protector (regent).

Somerset's English forces invaded Scotland and, with naval support, decisively defeated Scottish forces at the Battle of Pinkie, on the Firth of Forth (Sept. 10, 1547). Scottish casualties numbered more than 5,000, English in the hundreds. English troops occupied Edinburgh (1547).

d. Hernán (Hernando; Fernando) Cortés (1485-1547), Spanish military leader who led Spanish troops in the conquest of Mexico (1519-1521).

English forces led by John Dudley defeated a peasant revolt in Norfolk (1549).

b. Jan Zamojski (Zamoyski) (1541-1605), Polish general.

Turkish forces led by Suleiman I campaigned in Austria (Apr.-Sept. 1543). Turkey and Austria ended their hostilities, restoring their prewar shares of Hungary (1544).

Protestant insurrection in Germany (Schmalkaldic War) was defeated; Catholic forces scored a decisive victory at Mühlberg (Apr. 24, 1547).

b. John (Don Juan) of Austria (1547-1578), Spanish general and admiral.

1530-1539 (cont.)

Sher Khan, governor of Bihar, led a successful insurrection against Mogul emperor Humayun, defeating his forces at Chaunsha and Kanauj (1537); Humayun fled India (1537-1539). Sher Khan, now Sher Shah (r. 1539-1545), expanded the area of Delhi's control.

Portuguese-held Diu was unsuccessfully attacked by a Turkish fleet supported by Gujarati land forces (1538).

b. Maeda Toshiie (1538-1599), Japanese general.

Hernando de Soto began the conquest of Florida for Spain (1539).

1540-1549

Holy Roman Emperor Charles V led an invasion of Algiers (Sept. 1541), mounting a failed siege of the city. He lost 7,000 of the 21,000 in his invading army, then returned to Europe with the remainder.

Muslim forces under Admad Gran unsuccessfully besieged Kassala, in Ethiopia, which was relieved by Ethiopian and Portuguese allies (1543) led by Cristovao da Gama, son of Vasco da Gama.

d. Khair ed-Din (Barbarossa; Khizr) (ca. 1483-1546), Greek-Turkish admiral and North African ruler, originally a pirate nicknamed Barbarossa (Red Beard) who established himself in North Africa, becoming bey of Algiers (1518).

Francisco Vásquez de Coronado led an expedition north as far as New Mexico, capturing Zuni Pueblo (July 1540). His expedition, which reached the Grand Canyon, introduced the horse into North America, revolutionizing the lives of many Indian peoples (1540).

Spanish forces led by Pedro de Valdivia began the long attack on the Araucanian people of Chile (1540).

Exiled from India, Humayun took power in Afghanistan, defeating the forces of his brother Komran (1540).

Mongol forces increased their raids on western China (1540-1550).

Hernando de Soto's expedition reached the Mississippi River, bringing with it massive epidemics of culture-destroying diseases; he died of fever en route (1541).

Burmese king Tabinshwehti took the Mon kingdom of Pegu (1541).

Portuguese sailors reached Japan, the first of them on a Chinese junk blown off course (ca. 1542); their introduction of the musket revolutionized warfare in Japan.

Juan Cabrillo sailed north along the Pacific Coast of North America, from Navidad to Oregon (1542).

b. Akbar the Great (Abu-ul-Fath Jalal-uddin Mohammed Akbar) (1542-1605), Mogul Indian ruler (r. 1556-1605).

b. Tokugawa Ieyasu (1542-1616), Japanese general.

d. Sher Shah (Farid-ud-Din Sher Shah; Farid Khan) (ca. 1472-1545), Indian em-

1540-1549 (cont.)

1550-1559

French and Scottish troops forced an English withdrawal from Edinburgh and other occupied portions of Scotland (1550).

b. Charles IX Vasa (1550-1611), king of Sweden (r. 1604-1611).

b. Henri de Lorraine, third duke of Guise (1550-1588), French general.

b. Henry III (1551-1589), king of France (r. 1574-1589).

With the French invasion of Lorraine (Apr. 1552), France and the Holy Roman Empire were again at war.

In England a succession crisis arose on the death of Edward VI (r. 1547-1553). Lady Jane Grey, daughter of the duke of Northumberland (Warwick), took the throne but was deposed after nine days (July 6-19, 1553) and later executed. Edward's elder half-sister Mary raised an army and claimed the throne as Mary I. She reintroduced Catholicism to England and carried out the often-bloody persecution of Protestants. She married Philip II of Spain (1554), beginning a long conflict between Protestant England and Catholic Spain.

b. Henry IV (Henry of Navarre) (1553-1610), French king, first of the Bourbon line (r. 1589-1610); earlier Prince of Béarn and then Henry III, king of Navarre (r. 1572-1589).

English government forces defeated a rebellion led by Thomas Wyatt (1554).

b. Charles de Lorraine, duke of Mayenne (1554-1611), French general.

Philip II of Spain led Spanish and English forces (sent by his wife, Mary I of England) in an invasion of France (July-Aug. 1557), smashing French forces at St. Quentin (Aug. 10) and then taking the city by storm; he then withdrew, allowing the defeated French to recover and take the offensive. The war ended (1559) with French withdrawal from Italy, but the French kept several cities taken during the war, including Calais, Metz, and Verdun.

d. Mary I (1516-1558), English queen (r. 1553-1558), daughter of Henry VIII; she reimposed Roman Catholicism on her country, persecuting Protestants so harshly that she was called "Bloody Mary." She was succeeded by her younger half-sister Elizabeth I (r. 1558-1603).

Russian forces took Kazan and Astrakhan, conquering much of the Volga Valley (1552-1557).

As part of its war with the Holy Roman Empire, French forces again attacked Italy but were defeated at Marciano (Aug. 1553).

Poland and Russia were at war over disputed Livonia (1557-1571); Sweden and Denmark also participated in the war; Sweden ultimately occupied Estonia.

b. Johan Tserclaes (1559-1632), Flemish general primarily serving Bavaria.

1540-1549 (cont.)

peror (r. 1540-1545) of Afghan-Turkish descent who deposed and replaced Mogul emperor Humayun (1537); he was killed at the siege of Kalinjar. A succession crisis followed.

Spanish occupying forces put down a Mayan insurrection (1546).

Siamese forces defeated an invading Burmese army (1548).

Jesuit missionary Francis Xavier arrived in Japan, beginning Christian penetration of the country (1549).

1550-1559

Turkish forces took Tripoli, in Libya, from the Knights of St. John Hospitallers (1551).

Turkish-Persian Wars: Persian forces took Erzerum (1552); Suleiman I retook it during a major offensive into Persia, in which the Turks took and held much of Armenia, Georgia, and western Persia; the Turks continued to hold these territories under the Treaty of Amasia, which ended the long war (1555).

Japanese pirates attacked the Chinese coast with increasing force (1550-1560), besieging several cities, including Nanking (1555).

b. Date Masamune (1550-1600), Japanese general and daimyo.

Burmese king Bayinnaung (r. 1551-1581) unified Burma and conquered Laos, Ayuthia (Siam), and Chiengmai.

Humayun's Afghan forces invaded northern India, taking the Punjab and Delhi and restoring him to the Mogul throne.

French founded a settlement at Rio de Janeiro (1555); it was later destroyed by the Portuguese (1557).

d. Humayun (Na-sin-ud-Din Muhammad) (1508-1556), second Mogul emperor of India (r. 1530-1540; 1555-1556), who lost his kingdom to Sher Shah; son of Babur, he died accidentally soon after reoccupying Delhi. After his death a succession crisis again emerged.

Akbar, Humayun's son, resolved India's succession crisis by defeating the forces of Hindu general Hemu at the second Battle of Panipat (Nov. 5), becoming the Mogul emperor of India (r. 1556-1605).

d. Hemu (Vikramaditya) (?-1556), Afghan-Indian ruler, one of four main contenders for Sher Shah's empire (1545-1556); he was killed at Panipat.

Portuguese naval forces established a fortified center at Macao, on the south China coast (1557).

Portuguese forces attacked and took some coastal sections of Ceylon (Sri Lanka) (1557-1600).

1550-1559 (cont.)

d. Christian III (1503-1559), king of Denmark and Norway (r. 1534-1559), son of Frederick I.

d. Christian II (1481-1559), king of Denmark and Norway (r. 1513-1523) and of Sweden (r. 1520-1523) who lost his thrones when the Union of Kalmar ended; he was imprisoned (from 1532) after trying to regain them.

1560-1569

Aided by some English forces, Scottish forces protesting French influence on Mary, Queen of Scots, defeated the French at Leith (Feb. 1560). France withdrew from Scotland under the Treaty of Edinburgh (July 6). Mary, who had married France's Francis II (1558), returned to Scotland after his death (1560).

First Huguenot War (1562-1563): France began its long series of Protestant-Catholic Huguenot wars (Apr. 1562) with the insurrection that began after 650 Protestants were murdered at Vassy (Mar.) by the duke of Guise's Catholic forces. English forces sent by Elizabeth I intervened on the side of the Huguenots (Sept.), taking Le Havre. After the inconclusive Battle of Dreux (Dec.), the Peace of Aboise (Mar. 1563) restored the status quo; Catholic and Protestant French forces then attacked and defeated the English at Le Havre.

d. François de Lorraine, second duke of Guise (1519-1563), French general nicknamed "Le Balafré" (the Scarred) for the wounds he received at the siege of Boulogne (1544-1545); he was killed during the First Huguenot War.

d. Johann von Rantzau (1492-1565), Danish general who led the forces that deposed Christian II for Frederick I (1523), besieging and taking Copenhagen (1523-1524).

b. James I (1566-1625), king of England (r. 1603-1625); as James VI also king of Scotland (r. 1567-1625).

Second Huguenot War (1567-1568) began with a Huguenot insurrection against continuing Catholic persecution (Sept. 1567) and ended with the Peace of Longjumeau (Mar. 1568), which again promised religious tolerance. Peace last only a few months, with Catholic attacks beginning the Third Huguenot War.

Forces supporting Mary, Queen of Scots, were defeated by other Scottish forces at Carberry Hill (June 1567); Mary was imprisoned and forced to abdicate in favor of her son James VI of Scotland (later James I of England). After escaping from prison, Mary was again defeated, at the Battle of Langside (May 1568), by Scottish forces under James, earl of Moray, regent for James VI; she then fled into exile in England but was imprisoned by Elizabeth I.

Dutch War of Independence began with demonstrations by the Protestant Dutch against Catholic Spanish rule (1567-1568); William of Orange, who had fled to Germany, raised a revolutionary army (1568), which under his brother Louis was decisively defeated by the Spanish at Jemmingen (July 21, 1568), suffering an estimated 6,000 to 7,000 dead of 15,000 engaged. William commanded a failed invasion of Flanders (Oct. 1568), retreating to Germany.

Third Huguenot War (1568-1570): Although Catholic forces scored major victories at Jarnaca (Mar. 13, 1569) and Moncontour

d. Andrea Doria (1466-1560), Genoese naval leader in French and imperial service, most notably during the Turkish war against Khair ed-Din (Barbarossa).

Turkish forces unsuccessfully besieged Malta (May-Sept. 1565), retreating when Spanish forces relieved the island.

Suleiman I again led Turkish forces in an invasion of Austria (July 1566), besieging and taking Szigeth (Szigetvar) (Aug.-Sept.).

d. Suleiman I (the Magnificent) (ca. 1494-1566), Ottoman Turk sultan (r. 1520-1566), sometimes called Suleiman II, who greatly expanded the Ottoman Empire, taking Rhodes from the Knights of St. John's Hospitallers (1522) and parts of southeastern Europe, besieging Vienna (1529), and finally taking Hungary (1541); he died during the siege of Szigeth (Sept. 5).

d. Albert von Hohenzollern (1490-1568), grand master of the Teutonic Knights and (from Apr. 1525) first duke of Prussia.

Africa and Southwest Asia

East, Central, and South Asia, the Pacific, and the Americas

1550-1559 (cont.)

	Achenese forces unsuccessfully besieged Portuguese-held Malacca (1558).
	b. Nurhachi (Kundulun Khan) (1559-1626), Jurchen chief.

1560-1569

Turkish forces led by the bey of Algiers took Tunis from Spain (1569).	As pirates struck at Spanish shipping in the Caribbean with increasing intensity, Spain established a convoy system for the Atlantic crossing (1560), prefiguring the convoy system used by the Allies in two 20th-century world wars.
Turkish and Tartar forces attacked but failed to take Astrakhan from the Russians (1569).	Oda Nobunaga emerged as the most important of the Japanese military leaders, taking much of Honshu (1560-1568).
	Manchu forces began to raid northern China (1560-1570).
	Akbar began to expand Mogul control of India, taking Malwa (1562); after a long war (1562-1567), he also took Rajputana.
	b. Kato (Toranosuke) Kiyomasa (1562-1611), Japanese general.
	Burmese forces defeated and occupied Siam (1563-1584) and took but could not hold Laos (1564-1565).
	French founded the settlement of Fort Caroline on the St. Johns River, Florida (1564); it was later taken by the Spanish (1565).
	b. Ikeda Terumasa (1564-1613), Japanese general.
	Miguel López de Lagazpi found a practical route east across the Pacific Ocean from the Philippines to Panama, beginning the Manila trade; Spain then occupied the Philippines (1565).
	Muslim forces defeated Rama Raya, of the southern Indian Hindu kingdom of Vijayanagar, at the Battle of Talikot (1565).
	b. Samuel de Champlain (ca. 1567-1635), French soldier and explorer.
	Sultanate of Bantam expanded to take the rest of western Java (1568).
	b. Jahangir (Salim) (1569-1627), Mogul emperor (r. 1605-1627).

1560-1569 (cont.)

(Oct. 3, 1569), Protestant forces were strong enough to produce a stalemate; the Peace of St. Germain (Aug. 8, 1570) once again promised religious freedom to the Huguenots.

1570-1579

St. Bartholomew's Eve Massacre: Catholics killed thousands of Protestants overnight in Paris (Aug. 23-24, 1572), sparking the Fourth Huguenot War (1572-1574), in which Protestant forces set up a semiautonomous region in southwestern France.

d. Gaspard II de Coligny (1519-1572), French general and admiral who espoused religious toleration and the Huguenot cause; he died in the St. Bartholomew's Day Massacre (Aug. 23-24).

In spite of temporary setbacks, the Dutch insurrection against Spain grew; Dutch naval forces (the "Sea Beggars") were organized, and a massive insurrection took much of the country (1572), although Spanish forces took much back (1573), as the seesaw war continued.

Charles IX of France was succeeded by Henry III (r. 1574-1589). During Henry's reign there were three more outbreaks of civil war between Catholics and Protestants, all of them inconclusive.

England's Francis Drake began his round-the-world voyage (1577-1580).

b. Christian IV (1577-1648), king of Denmark and Norway (r. 1588-1648).

d. Blaise de Lasseran-Massencome, seigneur of Monluc (Montluc) (1501?-1577), marshal who led Catholic forces in the French religious wars.

b. Charles Créqui (Créquy) I, marquis of Créqui and duke of Lesdiguières (1578-1638), marshal of France.

Union of Utrecht united the northern Dutch provinces into a confederation (1579). Spanish forces led by Alessandro Farnese retook much of the country in the decade that followed.

Russian forces sacked Novgorod (1570).

d. Nicolo Dandolo (ca. 1515-1570), Venetian military leader.

Battle of Lepanto (Oct. 7, 1571): Venetian and Spanish fleets led by John (Don Juan) of Austria decisively defeated the main Turkish war fleet at Lepanto, in the Gulf of Corinth, ending the long, virtually unopposed Turkish drive west across the Mediterranean. Less than a quarter of the more than 200 Turkish ships survived, with an estimated 20,000 Turkish deaths and many thousands of other casualties. Allied losses included fewer than 15 ships and approximately 15,000 casualties, 7,000 of these dead.

Crimean Tartar forces took and sacked Moscow, vacating the city and retreating after the Russians defeated them at Molodi (1571-1572). A Volga Tartar revolt also was defeated (1572).

b. Maximilian I, duke of Bavaria (1573-1651), German elector (r. 1623-1651).

Poland and Russia were again at war over Livonia (1577-1582).

d. John (Don Juan) of Austria (1547-1578), Spanish general and admiral who commanded the Holy League fleet in its victory over the Turks at Lepanto (Oct. 7, 1571).

Russia lost Polotsk to Sweden after a Swedish victory at Wenden (1579).

1580-1589

d. William the Silent, count of Nassau and prince of Orange (1533-1584), Dutch general who helped lay the foundations for the modern Netherlands; he was assassinated in Delft (July 9).

Eighth Huguenot War (1585-1589) began when France's Henry III withdrew the government's promise of religious freedom for Protestants.

English-Scottish wars ended with the alliance of James VI of Scotland and Elizabeth I of England (1585).

Intervention by English forces under Robert Dudley (1585-1587) failed to keep Spanish forces from retaking most of the independent Dutch provinces.

b. Gonsalvo Fernandez de Córdoba, duke of Sesa (1585-1635), Spanish general.

In the 1580s Russian traders established posts as far east as the Amur River; Russian imperial expansion soon followed.

Spanish forces defeated the Portuguese at the Battle of Alcántara (Aug. 25, 1580), winning succession to the Portuguese crown for Philip II of Spain; Antonio de Crato fled into exile, in the early 1580s enlisting French support in two failed attempts to seize the Azores and later English support for a failed mainland invasion (1589).

b. Count Hans Georg of Arnim (1582?-1641), Saxon general.

1560-1569 (cont.)

1570-1579

Portuguese forces penetrated the Congo (1570).

Turkey and Venice were at war. Turkish invasion forces attacked disputed Cyprus (Jan. 1570) and besieged and took Nicosia (July-Sept.) and Famagusta (Sept. 1570-Aug. 1571). Turkish fleets raided into the western Mediterranean.

b. Abbas I (the Great) (1571-1629), shah of Persia (r. 1588-1629).

Spanish forces took Tunis from the Turks (Aug. 1572).

Tunis changed hands again, falling to Muslim forces under Ouloudj Ali of Algiers (Aug.-Sept. 1574).

Turkey and Persia were at war (1577-1590); Turkish forces took substantial portions of Luristan and Armenia.

Moroccan forces defending the Alcazar decisively defeated attacking Portuguese seaborne forces (1578).

Sebastian of Portugal led a failed attack on Morocco, dying in the Battle of Al Kasr al Kebir (1578).

Francis Drake made his first pirate raid on Spanish ships in the Caribbean (1570).

Spanish forces led by Miguel López de Lagazpi attacked the Philippines, advancing Spain's conquest of the islands (1570).

Tupac Amaru, "the last Inca," was captured and killed by Spanish forces (1571).

d. Mori Motonari (1497-1571), Japanese general.

Burmese forces again took but could not hold Laos (1572-1573).

Akbar's forces took Gujarat (1573).

Oda Nobunaga deposed shogun Ashikaga Yashiaki (1573).

d. Takeda (Harunobu) Shingen (1521-1573), Japanese general who was a key figure in the civil wars that preceded unification.

Besieged for four years by local forces on Ternate, the Portuguese garrison of the island's fortress surrendered (1574).

Akbar's forces took Bihar and Bengal (1574-1576), beginning a long, unsuccessful series of attacks in the Deccan (1576).

Francis Drake made his second pirate voyage to the Caribbean (1574).

b. Kobayakawa Hideaki (1577-1602), Japanese general.

1580-1589

Spanish forces occupied Ceuta, opposite Gibraltar (1580).

Turkish and Portuguese naval forces clashed off the coast of East Africa (1585); the Portuguese maintained their hold on the coastal cities.

Portuguese and Simba forces took and sacked Mombasa (1589).

Portuguese forces in Ceylon (Sri Lanka), attacking overland from Colombo, failed to take Kandy (1580).

Akbar's forces took Afghanistan (1581).

d. Oda Nobunaga (1534-1582), Japanese general, one of the great unifiers; outnumbered at his capital, Kyoto, surrounded, and about to be taken by the forces of general Akechi Mitsuhibi, he chose suicide rather than be captured (June 21).

After defeating the forces of general Mitsuhibi (1582), Toyotomi Hideyoshi succeeded Oda Nobunaga, taking control of much of central Japan (1582-1584) and

1580-1589 (cont.)

d. Edward Fiennes Clinton (1512-1585), English admiral.

Francis Drake took Cadiz from the sea, sacking the city (Apr. 19, 1587); he sacked Lisbon harbor on his way home to England.

d. Mary (Stuart) (1542-1587), queen of Scotland (r. 1542-1587); in exile, she was executed by the English (Feb. 8).

England was attacked by the massive 132-ship Spanish Armada (July 1588), in preparation since 1586, carrying an invasion army. In five days of running engagements with the English fleet off the south English coast (July 21-25), the Armada ran out of heavy ammunition and then retreated toward the French coast, anchoring off Calais. Attacked by the English (July 26-28) and still unable to secure heavy ammunition, the Spanish fleet headed north in disarray, sailing entirely around Britain to reach Spain. The voyage proved extraordinarily difficult; scores of ships and thousands of men were lost (Aug.-Sept.); less than half the original number of ships returned home.

d. Alvaro de Bazan, marquis of Santa Cruz (1526-1588), Spanish admiral who commanded the rear squadron at the Battle of Lepanto (1571); he planned and was to have commanded the Spanish Armada against England, but he died before it sailed.

d. Henri de Lorraine, third duke of Guise (1550-1588), French general during the Huguenot wars and later lieutenant general of France (1588); falling from favor, he was murdered by King Henry III's bodyguard.

d. Henry III (1551-1589), king of France (r. 1574-1589) during the religious wars; he was assassinated (Aug. 2). In the resulting succession crisis, Henry of Navarre emerged as Henry IV, the first Bourbon king of France; he fought a war against French Catholics and their Spanish allies (1589-1593) and then against Spain, winning a major victory at Arques (Nov. 1589).

b. Benjamin de Rohan Soubise (ca. 1589-1642); French Huguenot commander.

b. Albert Eusebius von Wallenstein, duke of Friedland and Mecklenburg and prince of Sagan (1583-1634), Bohemian-born general.

1590-1599

In his war against French Catholics and their Spanish allies, France's Henry IV (of Navarre) won a key victory at Ivry (Mar. 1590). Later proclaiming himself a Catholic (July 1593), he proceeded to unite Protestants and Catholics in France against the Spanish invader. The religious wars ended, for the time being, with the Edict of Nantes (Apr. 13, 1598), which again promised Protestant religious freedom; the Spanish war ended with the Treaty of Vervins (May 2, 1598).

The tide turned in Holland after the English defeat of the Spanish Armada. Dutch forces led by Maurice of Nassau (whose father, William the Silent, had been assassinated in 1584) went on the offensive, during the 1590s taking and holding all of Holland.

b. Robert Devereux, third earl of Essex (1591-1646), English general.

d. Alessandro Farnese, duke of Parma (1545-1592), Italian general who served Spain, most notably at Lepanto (1571).

Hugh O'Neill, earl of Tyrone, led the Tyrone Rebellion (1594-1603), scoring a victory over English forces on the Blackwater

Russia and Sweden were at war (1590-1593). Russian forces won desired outlets to the Baltic Sea and part of Finland.

b. Stanislaw (Alexander) Koniecpolski (1591-1646), Polish general.

Austria and Turkey resumed their long series of wars. At Sissek (June 20, 1593), invading Austrian forces destroyed the Turkish army in Bosnia; the Turks responded with attacks into Hungary (1594).

Polish forces defeated a Cossack insurrection in the Ukraine (1593).

b. Gottfried Heinrich Papenheim (1594-1632), German general.

Transylvanian forces led by Sigismund Bathory defeated a Turkish army at the Battle of Guirgevo (Oct. 28, 1595), part of a complex series of local wars that would lead to Transylvanian independence (1606).

eventually unifying the entire country (1584-1590).

d. Shibata Katsuie (1522-1583), Japanese general in the wars preceding unification and a supporter of Oda Nobunaga; after being defeated in 1583, he and his wife committed suicide.

Rapidly expanding to the Pacific, Russia annexed Siberia (1584).

Siamese insurrection led by Pra Naret defeated Burmese occupation forces, which evacuated Siam (1584-1587).

English expedition to the Caribbean led by Francis Drake took and sacked Hispaniola, Cartagena, and St. Augustine (1585-1586).

Akbar's forces took Kashmir, Sind, Orissa, and Baluchistan (1586-1595).

d. Kikkawa Motoharu (1530-1586), Japanese general during the wars preceding unification.

d. Ch'i Chi-kuang (1528-1587), Chinese general and military theorist noted for his *Practical Guide to Military Training* (1571).

Japan's Toyotomi Hideyoshi issued his Sword-Hunt Edict (1588), allowing swords to be worn only by samurai and daimyo, definitively establishing a hereditary military caste.

Moroccan forces with firearms invaded Songhai, destroying Gao, the Songhai capital, and taking and sacking Timbuktu (1591).

Portuguese forces completed Fort Jesus, Mombasa (1594).

Persia and Uzbekistan were at war, again contesting Khorasan, invaded by the Uzbeks. The war ended with Persia controlling most of Khorasan (1590-1598).

Pra Naret became King Narasuen of Siam (1590); Burma, Siam, Laos, Cambodia, and Chiengmai engaged in a series of wars for the balance of the century.

Japanese forces invaded Korea, taking Pusan (May 1592) and then Seoul and Pyongyang (June-July). At the Battle of the Yellow Sea (July), Yi Sun Shin led a Korean fleet, including his self-designed ironclad "turtle ships," to victory over the Japanese, sinking nearly 60 Japanese ships and introducing the use of ironclad vessels.

Laos won its independence from Burma (1592).

1590-1599 (cont.)

River, at Yellow Ford (Aug. 1598), and later besting the earl of Essex (1599-1600).

b. Gustavus Adolphus (Gustav II Adolf) (1594-1632), Swedish king (r. 1611-1632).

b. Maarten Harpertzoon van Tromp (1597-1653), Dutch admiral.

b. William Waller (ca. 1597-1668), English general.

b. César, duke of Choiseul and count of Plessis-Praslin (1598-1675), marshal of France.

A second Spanish seaborne invasion of England was frustrated by the weather and terminated before reaching England (1599).

b. Oliver Cromwell (1599-1658), English general and lord protector (1653-1658).

b. Robert Blake (1599-1657), English admiral.

Austrian forces invaded Turkish-held southern Hungary, as insurrections grew in several Turkish European provinces (1595). Turkish armies numbering an estimated 80,000 responded (1596), defeating a smaller Austrian army at Kerestes, near Erlau (Oct. 24-26, 1596), with losses exceeding 20,000 on each side.

b. Johan Banér (1596-1641), Swedish field marshal.

b. Prince Ottavio Piccolomini (ca. 1599-1656), Italian general and diplomat serving the Austrian Empire.

1600-1609

Dutch forces led by Maurice of Nassau met and defeated a Spanish army, then relieved besieged Nieuport (July 2, 1600).

b. Charles I (1600-1649), king of England, Scotland, and Ireland (r. 1625-1649).

Spanish and Irish forces took Kinsale but were defeated by the English at the decisive Battle of Kinsale, which spelled the effective end of the Tyrone Rebellion (1601).

b. David Leslie, Lord Newark (1601-1682), Scottish general.

b. Jean Baptiste Budes, count of Guébriant (1602-1643), marshal of France.

b. Lennart Torstensson, count of Ortola (1603-1651), Swedish field marshal.

d. Elizabeth I (1533-1603), English queen (r. 1558-1603), daughter of Henry VIII, last of the Tudor monarchs, and Anne Boleyn; she

Swedish-Polish War (1600-1611): Swedish forces attacked in the Baltic (1600), taking most of Livonia (Latvia) and Estonia; Polish forces continued to hold Riga, went on the offensive (1601), and retook most of both countries.

Swedish-Polish War: Swedish forces 14,000 strong, under Charles IX, attacked Polish-held Estonia but were defeated at Kircholm by a much smaller Polish army led by Jan Chodkiewicz (Sept. 27, 1604); the Swedes retreated after suffering heavy losses.

b. Bernhard, duke of Saxe-Weimar (1604-1639), general of Weimar.

b. Charles IV, duke of Lorraine and Bar (1604-1675), Austrian general.

1590-1599 (cont.)

b. Abahai (T'ai Tsung; Ch'ung Teh) (1592-1643), Manchu ruler (r. 1626-1643).

b. Hung Ch'eng-ch'ou (1593-1665), Chinese military and political leader.

Portuguese forces again failed to take Kandy (1594).

Dutch began their exploration and conquest of Indonesia; their first ships reached Sumatra, and their first treaty was made with Bantam, on Java (1596).

Japanese forces pressed northward in Korea (1597-1598), but at the sea battle of Chinhae Bay (Nov. 1598), the Koreans defeated the Japanese fleet, sinking half of their 400 ships; the rest returned to Japan.

d. Yi Sun Shin (?-1598), Korean admiral who fought off the Japanese invasion (1592-1598), using ironclad craft of his own design; a national hero, he was killed at Chinhae Bay (Nov. 18).

d. Toyotomi Hideyoshi (ca. 1536-1598), Japanese general who became the major power in Japan; he was succeeded by Tokugawa Ieyasu, who completed the unification of Japan.

After Toyotomi Hideyoshi's death and the Japanese fleet's defeat, the Japanese left Korea (Dec. 1598).

Spanish forces took Acoma Pueblo in North America's Southwest (1598).

d. Maeda Toshiie (1538-1599), Japanese general during the wars of unification who also directed the Korean campaign (1592-1598).

1600-1609

Turkish-Persian War (1602-1612): Persian forces led by Shah Abbas I took besieged Tabriz (Oct. 21, 1603) and went on to take Erivan, Shirvan, Kars, and much of the Caucasus, moving into Anatolia (1603-1604).

Turkish-Persian War: Persian forces led by Shah Abbas I decisively defeated a massive Turkish army led by Ahmed I at Sis (1606); Turkish losses reportedly included 20,000 dead. In the years that followed (1606-1612), the Persians went on to take much of Syria, Kurdistan, and Azerbaijan.

Druse and Kurdish rebels were defeated by Turkish forces in Syria (1606).

Japanese Civil War: At the Battle of Sekigahara (Oct. 1, 1600), the 72,000-strong forces of Tokugawa Ieyasu defeated and effectively destroyed the coalition army of the feudal nobles opposed to his rule; the coalition reportedly suffered losses of 40,000 of the 82,000 engaged.

d. Date Masamune (1550-1600), Japanese general and daimyo during the civil wars and invasion of Korea.

Dutch seaborne traders arrived in the Indian Ocean, notably on the Gujarat and Coromandel coasts of India, contesting Portuguese trading monopolies (from 1601).

1600-1609 (cont.)

presided over England's emergence as a world power, contesting with rivals from mainland Europe, most notably in the defeat of the Spanish Armada (1588). She was succeeded by James VI of Scotland, who ruled England as James I, first of the Stuart kings.

b. Louis XIII (1601-1643), king of France (r. 1610-1643).

Dutch forces lost Ostend to Spain after a three-year siege (1604).

d. Charles Howard, second Baron Howard of Effingham and first earl of Nottingham (1536-1604), admiral who commanded the English fleet against the Spanish Armada (1588); later lord lieutenant general of England, then lord high admiral.

Guy Fawkes and others were accused of conspiring to blow up the English Parliament and assassinate James I (1605); they were executed (1606).

Dutch naval forces defeated a Spanish fleet at Gibraltar (1607).

Anticipating arrest by English authorities, leaders of the Catholic Irish in Ulster fled abroad, in the Flight of the Earls (1607).

b. Michel (Michael) Adriaanszoon de Ruyter (1607-1676), Dutch admiral.

b. George Monck (Monk), duke of Albemarle (1608-1670), British general and admiral.

d. Jan Zamojski (Zamoyski) (1541-1605), Polish general who was deeply involved in Holy Roman Empire politics, becoming army commander in chief (1580).

Transylvania won its independence under the Treaty of Zsitva-Torok (Nov. 11, 1606).

Russo-Polish War (1609-1618): Polish forces besieged Smolensk (1609-1611).

b. Prince Raimondo Montecuccoli (1609-1680), Italian general serving Austria and military theorist.

Portuguese forces established a Burmese base at Syriam (1602).

d. Kobayakawa Hideaki (1577-1602), Japanese general; commander in chief in Korea, he changed sides at Sekigahara (1600), tipping the balance in favor of Tokugawa Ieyasu.

Tokugawa Ieyasu became shogun (1603), beginning the Tokugawa Shogunate, its capital at Edo (Tokyo). Persecution of Europeans increased, and the closing of Japan began.

Samuel de Champlain explored south on the St. Lawrence River to the Lichine Rapids, at what is now Montreal, claiming the area for France (1603).

French explorers and settlers founded The Habitation at Port Royal (Annapolis), Nova Scotia, the first French North American settlement (1605).

d. Akbar the Great (Abu-ul-Fath Jalal-ud-din Mohammed Akbar) (1542-1605), Mogul ruler (r. 1556-1605); son of Humayun, he expanded the Mogul Empire, fostering religious toleration. He was succeeded by his son Jahangir (r. 1605-1627).

Dutch forces attacked and took the Spice Islands (Moluccas) from the Portuguese, but the Portuguese held Malacca against Dutch attacks (1606-1607).

b. Chang Hsien-chung (1606-1647), Chinese rebel leader.

b. Li Tzu-ch'eng (1606-1645), Chinese rebel leader.

English settlers founded the Jamestown colony in Virginia (1607).

Portuguese forces unsuccessfully attacked Johore, on the southern tip of the Malay Peninsula, opposite modern Singapore (1607).

Burmese ruler Anaukpetlun retook much of southern Burma (1607-1613), including Prome (1607) and Toungoo (1610).

Mogul forces defeated an insurrection in Bengal (1607-1672).

Samuel de Champlain founded Quebec City (1608).

British ships arrived on the Indian coast (1608); William Hawkins of the British East India Company landed at Surat.

1600-1609 (cont.)

1610-1619

b. John Lawson (ca. 1610-1665), British admiral.

d. Henry IV (Henry of Navarre) (1553-1610), king of France (r. 1589-1610); earlier Prince of Béarn and then Henry III, king of Navarre (r. 1572-1589). During France's religious-civil wars, he commented, on converting to Catholicism (1593), "Paris is worth a Mass."

b. Henri de la Tour d'Auvergne, viscount of Turenne (1611-1675), marshal of France.

b. Henry Ireton (1611-1651), English general.

d. Charles de Lorraine, duke of Mayenne (1555-1611), French general and leader of the Catholic party after the assassination of his brothers Henry, duke of Guise, and Louis, cardinal of Lorraine; he raised the siege of Orléans and took Chartres (1589) but was then bested by Henry IV, notably at Arques (1589) and Ivry (1590).

d. Charles IX Vasa (1550-1611), king of Sweden (r. 1604-1611), active in wars against Poland.

b. James Graham, marquis of Montrose (1612-1650), Scottish general.

b. Thomas Fairfax, third Baron Fairfax of Cameron (1612-1671), English general.

b. Karl Gustav von Wrangel (1613-1676), Swedish marshal and admiral.

b. Friedrich Hermann (Frederic Armand) Schomberg (1615-1690), German-born English general and marshal of France.

Russo-Polish War: At Klushino, a 30,000-strong Russian-Swedish army attempting to relieve besieged Smolensk was defeated and dispersed by Polish forces led by Stanislas Zolkiewski (Sept. 1610). The Polish army then took and held Moscow.

Russo-Polish War: Smolensk surrendered. The people of Moscow successfully rose against Polish occupation forces, and the spreading insurrection forced Polish withdrawal from Russia (1611).

Russo-Swedish War (1613-1617): Russia unsuccessfully attacked Swedish-held Novgorod (1613).

Turkish-Polish War (1614-1621): After Polish Cossacks raided Turkish ports, and supported revolts against the Turks in Moldavia and Wallachia (Romania), the Turks and Tartars raided widely in the Polish Ukraine.

Polish-Swedish War (1617-1629): Swedish forces led by Gustavus Adolphus attacked Livonia, taking and holding part of the Baltic coast.

Russo-Swedish War: Swedish forces unsuccessfully besieged the Russian border fortress of Pskov, then withdrew (1617).

Thirty Years' War (1618-1648): This massive, multinational series of wars began as a Protestant-Catholic religious conflict in central Europe and ultimately engaged Germany, Austria, Bohemia, Spain, France, Sweden, Denmark, Holland, Poland, Italy, and several other European countries; it cost an estimated 8 mil-

1600-1609 (cont.)

On a Dutch East India Company expedition, Henry Hudson entered the mouth of the Hudson River, sailing some distance inland (1609).

1610-1619

Druse forces led by Fakhr-ad-Din mounted another insurrection against the Turks (1610-1613); defeated, Fakhr-ad-Din fled into exile.

Turkish-Persian War: Turkish forces unsuccessfully besieged Erivan (1616-1617).

Turkish-Persian War: Turkish forces again unsuccessfully attacked Persia, withdrawing after a treaty reestablished the status quo (1618).

b. Aurengzeb ('Alamgir; Muhi-ud-Din Muhammad) (1618-1707), Indian emperor (r. 1658-1707).

d. Kato (Toranosuke) Kiyomasa (1562-1611), Japanese general nicknamed "Kishokan" (Devil's General), active during the civil wars and Korean campaigns.

English warships defeated the Portuguese off the Gujarat coast, beginning the English armed penetration and conquest of India (1612); the British East India Company gained trading rights from the Moguls at Surat. Armed conflicts with the Portuguese continued as the English established bases on the Indian coast.

Dutch ships and settlers arrived at the mouth of the Hudson River, founding the New Netherlands colony (1612).

b. Dorgon (Dorgan) (1612-1650), Manchu general and ruler.

b. Wu San-kuei (1612-1678), Chinese general.

In the first major engagement of the long English-French contest for North America, English colonial forces destroyed Port Royal (Annapolis), Nova Scotia (1613).

Burmese forces led by Anaukpetlun expelled the Portuguese from their base on Syriam (1613).

1610-1619 (cont.)

d. Hugh O'Neill, third earl of Tyrone (ca. 1545-1616), Irish general during the Irish rebellions, especially the Tyrone Rebellion (1594-1603); he won at Yellow Ford (1598) but lost at Kinsale (1601); self-exiled, he died in Rome.

lion lives, more than 7 million of those civilians. The main human and material devastation occurred in Germany and Bohemia; large areas of both countries were blasted during the wars. War began in Bohemia, triggered by the Defenestration of Prague (May 22, 1618), the murder of two Austrian Catholic envoys by Bohemian Protestant leaders, who then formed a government and raised a Protestant army. In succeeding months Catholic Austria, joined by Spain and Bavaria, went to war against Protestant Bohemia, joined by Transylvania.

Thirty Years' War: Protestant forces invaded Austria (May 1619) but were forced to withdraw after their defeat at Zablat, in Bohemia (June 10, 1620).

Ferdinand II, a Catholic, became emperor of the Holy Roman Empire (Aug. 1619).

Frederick of the Palatinate became king of Protestant Bohemia (Aug. 1619).

b. Prince Rupert, Count Palatine of the Rhine and duke of Bavaria (1619-1682), Anglo-German general and admiral.

1620-1629

b. Louis II de Bourbon, prince of Condé (1621-1686), French general.

b. Charles X Gustavus (Gustav) (1622-1660), king of Sweden (r. 1654-1660).

Thirty Years' War: At Stadtlohn (Aug. 6, 1623), near the Dutch border, the Austrians decisively defeated the Protestant army, with an estimated 6,000 killed and 4,000 taken prisoner; the Protestant army ceased to be an effective fighting force (1623).

Thirty Years' War: Catholic France, at war with Spain, allied itself with the Protestants against Austria and its Catholic allies, converting the Thirty Years' War into a much wider and less religious conflict (1624). At Compiègne (June 10), France and Holland, soon to be joined by England, Sweden, Denmark, Savoy, and Venice, allied themselves against Spain, Austria, and their allies.

Turkish-Polish War: At Jassy Polish forces led by Stanislas Zolkiewski defeated Turkish and Tartar forces (Sept. 1620) but were themselves decisively defeated at Cecora, in Moldavia (Dec. 1620). The war ended with a truce following the major battle at Khotin (Sept. 22, 1621), which involved an estimated 100,000 to 200,000 Turks and 50,000 to 75,000 Poles. Low-level border warfare continued.

Thirty Years' War, Battle of White Mountain (Weisser Berg) (Nov. 8, 1620): Austrian forces decisively defeated and routed Bohemian forces, who lost an estimated 5,000 of the 15,000 engaged; Austrian casualties were fewer than 1,000. Austrians took and sacked Prague; they would hold Bohemia (Czechoslovakia) until the end of World War I.

Africa and Southwest Asia

1610-1619 (cont.)

Achenese forces sacked Johore (1613).

d. Ikeda Terumasa (1564-1613), Japanese general during the civil wars; he fought in the climactic Battle of Sekigahara (1600).

Dutch forces established Fort Nassau, toward the northern end of their area of penetration, near Albany (1614).

Japanese government forces besieged Osaka Castle (Dec. 1614-June 1615), then took it by storm, with massive losses on both sides, effectively ending the civil war.

Portuguese forces took the French colony on Maranhão Island, ending French penetration into Brazil (1615).

Allied Achenese and Johore forces made a failed attack on Portuguese-held Malacca (1616).

English traders of the British East India Company began trading with Persia, again coming into conflict with the Portuguese (1616).

d. Tokugawa Ieyasu (1542-1616), Japanese general who won at Sekigahara (1600), becoming shogun, the main power in Japan (1603).

Off Jask, Persia (1618), English naval forces defeated the Portuguese, beginning full English penetration of the Persian Gulf and northwestern Indian Ocean.

Manchu-Chinese War (1618-1659): Manchu forces began their long attack on China.

First African slaves were brought to Virginia and sold at Jamestown (1619).

1620-1629

Dutch forces took the Portuguese bases of Arguin and Goree, on the West African coast (1621). Portuguese-Dutch conflict in the area continued into the 1640s.

Osman II of Turkey (r. 1617-1621) was deposed by a Janissary revolt; he was briefly succeeded by Mustafa I, who was succeeded by Murad IV (r. 1623-1640).

Turkish-Persian War (1623-1628): Turkish forces attacked Persian forces in Mesopotamia, besieging Baghdad, which was relieved by Shah Abbas I (1625-1626).

France established St. Louis, its Senegal River base on the West African coast (1626).

d. Abbas I (the Great) (1571-1629), shah of Persia (r. 1588-1629) who fought the Ottoman Turks and invaded the Mogul Empire (1622-1623), capturing Kandahar and blocking the Portuguese from Hormuz (1622).

English settlers founded the Plymouth colony, in what would be Massachusetts (1620).

English seaborne forces, together with a Persian land force, took the Portuguese fortress at Hormuz (1621-1622); the main Portuguese base in the area then became Muscat.

Manchu-Chinese War: Manchu forces led by Nurhachi took Mukden, making it their capital (1621).

Powhatan forces attacked the Jamestown colony (Mar. 22, 1622), massacring more than 350 settlers and destroying more than 70 small settlements in Virginia. English

1620-1629 (cont.)

Thirty Years' War: Spanish forces 60,000 strong besieged and took the Dutch fortress of Breda; of its 9,000 defenders, 5,000 died (Aug. 1624-June 1625).

Responding to French Catholic repression, French Huguenots again mounted an insurrection but were decisively defeated. Their rebel fleet lost off La Rochelle (1625), which was then blockaded, first partially, then fully (1627); this was followed by a 14-month siege; two major English relief attempts also were defeated (1627; 1628). The city and its few remaining defenders finally surrendered (Oct. 29, 1628).

d. James I (1566-1625), king of England, Scotland, and Ireland (r. 1603-1625); as James VI, also king of Scotland (r. 1567-1625) who united the thrones; he was succeeded by Charles I.

b. François Henri de Montmorency-Boutteville, duke of Luxembourg (1628-1695), marshal of France.

As the long buildup to the English Revolution began, Charles I dissolved Parliament for the third time in four years, ruling alone (1629-1640).

b. Cornelis van Tromp (1629-1691), Dutch admiral.

b. François Créqui (Créquy), marquis of Créqui (1629-1687), marshal of France.

b. Niels Juel (Juul) (1629-1697), Danish admiral.

b. Frederick William (1620-1688), elector of Brandenburg (r. 1640-1688).

Thirty Years' War: Peter Ernst von Mansfield formed a new Protestant army in Germany; living off the land for want of any other source of supply, his was the first of many armies that would ravage Germany and several other countries in the next three decades (1621).

Polish-Swedish War: After a four-year truce, Swedish forces again attacked in the Baltic, taking Riga after a brief siege (Aug.-Sept. 1621).

Thirty Years' War: Bavarian and Spanish forces defeated the Protestant forces of George Frederick of Baden at Wimpfen (May 6, 1622) and those of Christian of Brunswick at Höchst (June 20); Protestant forces then retreated into Alsace and Lorraine. A Spanish army attacked allied Protestant Holland (Aug.); at Fleurus (Aug. 29) Spanish and combined Protestant forces fought to a draw, with Protestant forces then moving into East Friesland.

Polish-Swedish War: Attacking Swedish forces took Livonia and most of northern Prussia (1625-1626); Polish forces led by Alexander Koniecpolski mounted a counteroffensive.

Thirty Years' War: Denmark actively entered the war; an army led by Christian IV invaded Germany (July-Aug. 1625).

Thirty Years' War: France made peace with Austria (Mar. 1626).

Thirty Years' War: Peter Ernst von Mansfield's Protestant army was nearly destroyed by Wallenstein's Austrian forces at the Bridge of Dessau (Apr. 25, 1626), losing 4,000 dead and 4,000 captured of 12,000 engaged.

Thirty Years' War: At Lutter (Aug. 24-27, 1626), Austrian forces decisively defeated the Danes, who suffered massive losses.

Polish-Swedish War: At Tczew, attacking Polish forces were defeated by a reinforced Swedish army led by Gustavus Adolphus (May 1627).

Thirty Years' War: Danish forces, which had been pursued across the frontier into Holstein by Austrian forces, were defeated again at Wolgast (1628); Denmark was pushed out of the war (June 1629).

Polish-Swedish War: More than 30,000 Swedish troops advanced in Poland but then withdrew to Prussia as winter came on (1628).

Polish-Swedish War: The war ended with the Truce of Altmark (1629), which cost Poland part of northern Livonia and freed Gustavus Adolphus to enter the Thirty Years' War.

b. John (Jan) III Sobieski (1629-1696), king of Poland (r. 1674-1696).

Africa and Southwest Asia

forces defeated the Powhatans (1622-1625), massacring an estimated 1,000 Powhatans at Pamunkey.

Cambodia, a Siamese protectorate, declared its full independence; the Siamese attacked, were defeated, and withdrew (1622).

Manchu-Chinese War: Nurhachi's forces were defeated by a Ming army in western China, temporarily stopping the Manchu advance into China (1623).

Manchu forces took and held Inner Mongolia (1623-1633).

Dutch-Portuguese War: In Brazil Dutch forces took Bahia from the Portuguese (1624), who later retook it (1625).

b. Koxinga (Cheng Ch'eng-kung) (1624-1662), Chinese general and admiral.

d. Nurhachi (Kundulun Khan) (1559-1626), Jurchen chief who took much of Manchuria and China. He was succeeded by his son Abahai.

Manchu-Chinese War: Manchu forces took Korea, which then became a Manchu protectorate (1627).

d. Jahangir (Salim) (1569-1627), Mogul emperor (r. 1605-1627) whose name means "Conqueror of the World"; son of Akbar the Great, he was succeeded by Jahan (r. 1627-1658).

d. Anaukpetlun (?-1628), Burmese ruler (r. 1605-1628) who reunified Burma.

English forces took Quebec from the French (July 20, 1629).

Portuguese naval forces, with Indonesian allies, defeated the Achenese war fleet off Malacca (1629).

b. Charles II (1630-1685), king of England, Scotland, and Ireland (r. 1660-1685).

d. Gustavus Adolphus (Gustav II Adolf) (1594-1632), Swedish king (r. 1611-1632) called the "Lion of the North"; during the Polish wars and the Thirty Years' War, he introduced new types of military equipment, including three-pounder regimental guns, as well as new tactics stressing mobility, shock action, and combinations of arms.

b. James II (1633-1701), king of England, Scotland, and Ireland (r. 1685-1688).

b. Sebastien le Prestre de Vauban (1633-1707), French marshal.

Thirty Years' War: At Compiègne (Apr. 30, 1635), Sweden and Catholic France allied themselves against Austria and Spain; France quickly entered the war (May), invading Italy and the Spanish-held Netherlands.

Thirty Years' War: Spanish and Austrian forces unsuccessfully attacked parts of Germany and France (1636). In Germany, Swedish and allied forces defeated the Austrians at Wittstock (Oct. 4).

At La Sauvetat, in southern France, French troops decisively defeated the "croquant" rebels, with at least 1,000 casualties on each side (June 1, 1637).

b. François Louis de Rousselet, marquis of Châteaurenault (1637-1716), French admiral.

b. Nicholas Catinat (1637-1712), marshal of France.

d. Charles Créqui (Créquy) I, marquis of Créqui and duke of Lesdiguières (1578-1638), marshal of France during the Huguenot wars and the Thirty Years' War; he was killed by a cannonball at Brema.

Thirty Years' War, Battle of the Downs (Oct. 21, 1639); Dutch naval forces destroyed a large Spanish fleet off the English coast, sinking 51 and capturing 14 of the 77 Spanish ships; 7,000 Spanish sailors died; the Dutch lost 1 ship and 500 sailors.

First Bishops' War: Scottish insurgents successfully confronted English occupying forces, taking Edinburgh and stopping advancing English invasion forces; Charles I granted many of their demands, beginning a peace that lasted less than a year (1639-1640).

Thirty Years' War: Sweden actively entered the war (1630); a Swedish army of 13,000 led by King Gustavus Adolphus advanced into northern Germany, growing to approximately 40,000 as German Protestant forces joined it. Due to many innovations in weaponry, organization, and tactics, the Swedish army was the most advanced of its time, including lighter muskets, cartridges, lighter and more standardized artillery and gunnery training, and the orchestration of its musketeers, pikemen, regimental artillery, and artillery companies.

Thirty Years' War: Swedish and German forces took Frankfurt by storm (Apr. 13, 1631); Catholic troops soon took Magdeburg by storm (May 20). At Breitenfeld (Sept. 17), the Swedes and their Saxon allies decisively defeated and routed the Austrians, who lost more than 7,000 dead and 6,000 captured of 35,000 engaged. Protestant forces then took much of northern Germany and Bohemia.

Thirty Years' War: Swedish and Protestant German forces moved into southern Germany, defeating the Austrians at the Lech River (Apr. 15-16, 1632) and taking much of Bavaria. The two armies fought to a draw at Alte Veste, near Nuremberg (Sept. 3-4), and again at Lützen (Dec. 16), where Gustavus Adolphus was killed, changing the complexion of the war in Germany.

d. Johan Tserclaes (1559-1632), Flemish general primarily serving Bavaria, most notably at Lutter (1626), Magdeburg (1631), and Breitenfeld (1631); he was fatally wounded at the Lech River.

d. Gottfried Heinrich Papenheim (1594-1632), German general and cavalry commander at White Mountain (1620), Magdeburg (1631), and Lützen (1632), where he was fatally wounded.

Russo-Polish War (1632-1634): Russian forces 30,000 strong invaded Poland (Sept. 1632) and besieged Smolensk.

Russo-Polish War: Polish forces 40,000 strong, led by Ladislas IV, relieved besieged Smolensk (Sept. 1633), then besieged the former siege army, which surrendered six months later (1634).

After secret peace negotiations failed, Wallenstein proclaimed himself king of Bohemia (1633) but was later forced to flee (Feb. 24, 1634).

d. Albert Eusebius von Wallenstein, duke of Friedland and Mecklenburg and prince of Sagan (1583-1634), Bohemian-born general who led Austrian forces in the Thirty Years' War; after a failed coup in Bohemia, he was assassinated by imperial loyalist officers (Feb. 25).

Thirty Years' War: At Nördlingen (Sept. 6, 1634), Swedish forces in Germany were decisively defeated by an Austrian-Spanish army, suffering 16,000 casualties and captured of 25,000 engaged.

England established Kormantine, its first base on the West African coast (1631).

b. Abbas II (1632-1666), shah of Persia (r. 1642-1666).

Fakr-ad-Din returned from exile to continue the Druse insurrection; his forces were ultimately defeated by the Turks (1633), and he was executed.

Turkish-Persian War: A massive Turkish army led by Murad IV besieged and finally took Baghdad and much of Mesopotamia (1638).

Dutch forces in Brazil took Recife and then all of Pernambuco (1630), building a strong base in northeast Brazil in the two decades that followed.

Uzbek forces took Kandahar (1630).

Mogul forces took the Portuguese fort at Hooghly, on the Bay of Bengal (1631-1632).

England returned Quebec and other North American French settlements to France under a general peace treaty (1632).

Mogul forces took the Deccan states of Ahmadnagar, Golconda, and Bijapur (1633-1636).

Vietnamese Civil War (1633-1673): A long series of engagements pitted the north Vietnamese Trinh family and their Dutch allies against the south Vietnamese Nguyen family and their Portuguese allies.

Manchu-Chinese War: Manchu forces led by Abahai took Inner Mongolia; Manchu forces were then augmented by Mongols (1633).

Dutch and Kandyan forces captured Trincomalee, on Ceylon (Sri Lanka) (1633).

d. Samuel de Champlain (ca. 1567-1635), French soldier who explored northeastern North America, founding Quebec City (1608); he was commandant of New France (1612).

Pequot War (1636-1637): A small force of English colonists attacked and massacred Pequot Indians on Block Island (July 20, 1636); a brief war followed, in which the Pequots were defeated; the war ended with the massacre of an estimated 600 Pequots by fire (May 25, 1637) following a fight in which the colonists lost 2 dead.

Manchus established the Ch'ing dynasty in China, with its capital at Mukden (1636).

Manchu-Chinese War: Manchu forces again took Korea (1636-1637).

Manchu forces took control of the Amur River valley and adjacent areas (1636-1644).

Japanese government forces besieged Christian insurgents at Hara Castle (1637), massacring its defenders after their surrender. The Portuguese were expelled from Japan, and the country was closed to most outsiders; only the Dutch in Hirado and the Chinese in Nagasaki remained.

1630-1639 (cont.)

d. Bernhard, duke of Saxe-Weimar (1604-1639), general of Weimar during the Thirty Years' War.

1640-1649

Thirty Years' War: Off Cadiz, on Spain's Atlantic coast, the Spanish Cadiz Fleet was defeated by a French fleet (July 22, 1640).

Second Bishops' War: Scottish insurgents took the offensive, invading Northumberland after defeating government forces at Newburn (Aug. 28, 1640). Although the Treaty of Ripon (Nov.) brought peace, Scottish troops stayed on in northern England.

English Short Parliament met and was dissolved by Charles I when it refused to grant money for the war with Scotland. Charles called Parliament back into session, and it became the Long Parliament (1640-1660).

A Portuguese insurrection against Spanish occupying forces won independence (Nov.-Dec. 1640).

b. Hugh Mackay (ca. 1640-1692), Scottish general.

Catholics rebelled in Ireland, attacking and massacring Protestants throughout the island; in Ulster the rebellion was a civil war between Protestant and Catholic forces (1641-1649).

First English Civil War (1642-1646): Unable to resolve their differences, Parliament and Charles I went to war, both raising armies (June-Aug. 1642). At Edgehill (Oct. 23, 1642), royalist (Cavalier) forces defeated a parliamentary (Roundhead) army, which withdrew toward London, but the royalists were unable to take the city. More than a year of inconclusive fighting followed.

d. Benjamin de Rohan Soubise (ca. 1589-1642), French Huguenot commander who directed the defense of La Rochelle (1627-1628).

Thirty Years' War: Spanish forces invaded southern France (May 1643), besieging Rocroi, where they were met by a French relief force. In the ensuing battle (May 19), 15,000 of the 26,000 Spanish soldiers were killed or taken by the French, who suffered an estimated 8,000 casualties.

d. Louis XIII (1601-1643), king of France (r. 1610-1643); he was succeeded by Louis XIV (r. 1643-1715).

d. Jean Baptiste Budes, count of Guébriant (1602-1643), marshal of France during the Huguenot wars and Thirty Years' War, commanding the French Army of Germany; he died of wounds received during the siege of Rottweil, Württemberg.

First English Civil War: Scottish forces entered the war on Parliament's side, invading northern England with an army 18,000 strong (Jan. 1, 1644).

First English Civil War: At Marston Moor (July 2, 1644), a Roundhead army defeated Cavalier forces, which lost more than 5,000 of a total force of 18,000; Roundhead losses were approximately 2,000. Much of the north fell to the Roundheads, including York and Newcastle (July-Oct.).

d. Johan Banér (1596-1641), Swedish field marshal, chief of staff to Gustavus Adolphus and commander of the Swedish army in Germany.

d. Count Hans Georg of Arnim (1582?-1641), Saxon general who served in the Swedish, Saxon, and imperial armies.

Thirty Years' War: At the second Battle of Breitenfeld (Nov. 2, 1642), Swedish forces killed or captured nearly half of the 20,000-strong Austrian army.

b. Charles V (Charles Leopold), duke of Lorraine and Bar (1643-1690), Austrian general.

Thirty Years' War: The French retook Freiburg (Aug. 3-10, 1644), with the French and Bavarian armies losing almost half of their soldiers in the battle.

Turkish-Venetian War (1645-1670): Turkish seaborne forces numbering 50,000 attacked Crete (1645); Greeks on the island joined the Turks in the war against Venetian occupation forces. Besieged Canea fell to the Turks (June-Aug. 1645).

Turkish-Venetian War: Turkish forces on Crete took Retino (1646).

d. Stanislaw (Alexander) Koniecpolski (1591-1646), Polish general who became commander in chief of Polish forces (1632).

Thirty Years' War: The war concluded with the Treaty of Westphalia (Oct. 24, 1648), which recognized Protestant equality in Germany but was essentially a return to the status quo.

Cossack-Polish War (1648-1654): A massive uprising of Cossacks and Ukrainians in Polish-held Ukraine was led by Cossack leader Bogdan Chmielnicki, allied with the Crimean Tartars. During the war (especially 1648-1649), the atrocities committed by Chmielnicki's forces included the massacre of an estimated 150,000 to 200,000 Jews.

Turkish-Venetian War: Turkish forces on Crete began a long siege of Candia (1648-1669) but were unable to blockade the port; Venetian seaborne forces took Lemnos and Tenedos, beginning their long blockade of the Dardanelles (1648-1657).

Cossack-Polish War: Cossack-Tartar forces defeated a Polish army at Pilawce (1649).

Africa and Southwest Asia

East, Central, and South Asia, the Pacific, and the Americas

	1630-1639 (cont.)
	Swedish forces established Fort Christina, on the Delaware River (Mar. 1638).
	b. King Philip (Metacomet) (ca. 1639-1676), Wampanoag chief.
	1640-1649
Persian forces led by Shah Abbas II took Kandahar (1649). Turkish-Venetian War: A Turkish fleet was unable to break the Venetian blockade of the Dardanelles (1649).	England established its first military base in India at Fort St. George, near Madras; the fort was the headquarters of the British East India Company (1640).
	Dutch forces began a series of attacks on Portuguese Indian Ocean bases (1641-1663), taking Malacca, in Indonesia (1641).
	Algonquin forces attacked the Dutch in New Netherlands, then withdrew under pressure from the Dutch and Iroquois (1641-1645).
	Russian explorers and traders moving eastward reached the Pacific (1641).
	Russian forces defeated and annexed the territory of the Buryat Mongols, in the Lake Baikal region (1641-1652).
	Iroquois forces attacked the Hurons along the St. Lawrence River (1642), destroying many Huron towns and with them several French Jesuit missions.
	d. Abahai (T'ai Tsung; Ch'ung Teh) (1592-1643), Manchu ruler (r. 1626-1643) who conquered northern China, Mongolia, Korea, and the Amur River basin; he was succeeded by the child emperor Shun Chih (Fu-lin) (r. 1644-1661).
	Powhatan forces again attacked the Jamestown colony, massacring 400 (Apr. 18, 1644); English forces responded by massacring the entire Powhatan people.
	Manchu-Chinese War: The Ming capital of Peking (Beijing) was taken by rebel general Li Tzu-ch'eng (1644); he was then defeated by the Manchus, who themselves took Peking (May 26, 1644). At Yangchow Manchu forces led by Prince Dorgon defeated Ming forces, then took the new Ming capital of Nanking (1644).
	d. Li Tzu-ch'eng (1606-1645), Chinese rebel leader called "Ch'uang Wang" (Dashing King) who took Peking (1644) and later burned it on retreating; he was killed in a minor battle.
	Manchu-Chinese War: Manchu forces took Fukien (1645-1646).

1640-1649 (cont.)

First English Civil War: Cavalier forces in Cornwall defeated a Roundhead army at Lostwithiel (Sept. 2, 1644), forcing the surrender of 8,000 of the 10,000 Roundheads engaged.

b. François de Neufville, duke of Villeroi (1644-1730), marshal of France.

b. Godert (Godard) van Reede de Ginkel (1644-1703), Anglo-Dutch general.

b. Louis François, marquis and duke de Boufflers (1644-1711), marshal of France.

First English Civil War: Oliver Cromwell organized the highly professional Roundhead New Model Army (Jan.-Mar. 1645), taking it into the decisive battle of the war, at Naseby (June 14), where the Cavalier army of 9,000 lost 1,000 dead and 4,500 captured; Roundhead losses were negligible.

b. Pierre de Montesquiou d'Artagnan (1645-1725), marshal of France.

d. Robert Devereux, third earl of Essex (1591-1646), English general; his father, Elizabeth I's favorite, was executed for treason, but James I restored the family title and fortune; he was Charles I's second-in-command and headed the parliamentarian army (from July 1642), most notably at Edgehill (1642) and Lostwithiel (1644).

First English Civil War: Parliament imprisoned Charles I after he attempted to escape; negotiations between Charles and Parliament continued (1647).

d. Christian IV (1577-1648), king of Denmark and Norway (r. 1588-1648), active during the Thirty Years' War.

Thirty Years' War: Spain and Holland ended their war with the Treaty of Münster (Jan. 10, 1648). France and Spain remained at war.

Second English Civil War (1648-1651): Charles I, who had escaped to resume the civil war, led a rebellion against Parliament, this time in alliance with the Scottish Presbyterians, who had been Roundhead allies earlier in the decade. Insurrections in Wales and southern England were quickly defeated by Cromwell's forces (July-Aug. 1648). At the same time (July), a Scottish and Cavalier army of 24,000 invaded from the north; it was decisively defeated by Cromwell's 8,500-man New Model Army at Preston (Aug. 17-19).

War of the First Fronde (1648-1649): French Parlement led a rebellion against the effective rule of Cardinal Mazarin; the royalist army, led by Louis II de Bourbon, prince of Condé, besieged Paris and forced Parlement's capitulation (Mar. 1649).

d. Charles I (1600-1649), king of England, Scotland, and Ireland (r. 1625-1649) who lost his crown to Oliver Cromwell's Roundhead forces; he was beheaded in London (Jan. 30).

A 20,000-strong English Protestant army led by Cromwell arrived in Ireland (Sept. 1649) and systematically put down the insurrection there, committing considerable atrocities in the process (1649-1650). At Drogheda (Sept. 11, 1649), 3,000 to 4,000 Irish soldiers and civilians were massacred; at Wexford (Oct. 11, 1649), 2,000 to 3,500 were massacred; similar massacres occurred at several other locations.

1640-1649 (cont.)

Maratha insurrection in Bijapur established an independent Maratha state, led by Prince Sivaji (r. 1646-1680).

Mohawk forces raided north into French Canada on the St. Lawrence River, striking Montreal and as far north as Trois Rivières (1646).

Manchu-Chinese War: Manchu forces took Canton and much of south and southeastern China (1647-1648).

b. Nathaniel Bacon (1647-1676), English-American rebel.

d. Chang Hsien-chung (1606-1647), Chinese rebel leader who was temporarily allied with Li Tzu-ch'eng; captured after a defeat, he was executed by Manchu (Ch'ing) forces.

Portuguese forces defeated Dutch forces at the Guarapes Hills, near Recife, Brazil (Apr. 1648); the Dutch suffered an estimated 1,000 casualties of 4,500 engaged, with far fewer Portuguese losses. A year later the Portuguese again defeated the Dutch there, effectively deciding the Dutch-Portuguese war in Brazil.

d. Keng Chung-ming (?-1649), Manchuria-born Chinese general who originally served the Ming but defected to the Manchus; he committed suicide after accusations of collaboration with Ming forces.

1640-1649 (cont.)

b. James Scott, duke of Monmouth (1649-1685), British soldier and rebel.

1650-1659

Second English Civil War: Oliver Cromwell's New Model Army invaded Scotland and at Dunbar (Sept. 2, 1650) decisively defeated a much larger Scottish and royalist army, killing 3,000 and capturing 9,000, with negligible Roundhead losses.

d. James Graham, marquis of Montrose (1612-1650), Scottish general who became Scotland's lieutenant general (1644), defeating parliamentary forces at Inverlochy and Auldearn but losing at Philiphaugh (all 1645); returning from exile, he was captured and hung in Edinburgh by antiroyalists (May 20).

War of the Second Fronde (1650-1653): Many French nobles rebelled against the government of Louis XIV, dominated by Cardinal Mazarin. Frondist forces led by the viscount of Turenne were decisively defeated at Champ Blanc (Oct. 15, 1650).

b. John Churchill, first duke of Marlborough (1650-1722), British captain general.

b. William III (1650-1702), Dutch general, prince of Orange, and king of England, Scotland, and Ireland (r. 1689-1702).

b. Cloudesley (Clowdisley) Shovell (Shovel) (1650-1707), English admiral.

Second English Civil War: At Worcester (Sept. 2, 1651), Cromwell's New Model Army decisively and finally defeated Scottish and royalist forces, killing 2,000 and capturing 9,000 of 16,000 engaged.

d. Henry Ireton (1611-1651), English parliamentary general who signed King Charles I's execution warrant; he joined his father-in-law, Oliver Cromwell, in Ireland (1649-1650), remaining as governor general and commander in chief.

d. Lennart Torstensson, count of Ortola (1603-1651), Swedish field marshal during the Thirty Years' War, winning notably at the second Battle of Breitenfeld (1642).

War of the Second Fronde: At St.-Antoine (July 5, 1652), Henri de la Tour d'Auvergne, viscount of Turenne, now leading the royalist forces, decisively defeated the prince of Condé, now leading the Frondist forces and allied with Spain.

First Anglo-Dutch War (1652-1654): England won this first of three Anglo-Dutch wars, all generated by colonial and commercial competition, in a series of naval engagements, the key battles coming in 1653.

First Anglo-Dutch War: Off Beachy Head (Feb. 20-22, 1653), a British fleet of 70 warships attacked a Dutch fleet of 75 warships commanded by admiral Maarten van Tromp, escorting a convoy of 150 merchant ships. The Dutch lost 12 warships and 50 merchant ships; the British lost 6 warships.

First Anglo-Dutch War: At Gabbard Bank (June 2-3, 1653), the Dutch lost 17 ships and the British none.

First Anglo-Dutch War: At the decisive Battle of Scheveningen (July 31, 1653), the Dutch lost Admiral Tromp, 1,600 men, and 18

Cossack-Polish War: At Beresteczko (July 1651), Polish forces decisively defeated a massive Cossack-Tartar army led by Bogdan Chmielnicki, effectively ending the war, although Chmielnicki did not accept the peace.

d. Maximilian I, duke of Bavaria (1573-1651), German elector (r. 1623-1651) who personally commanded the Bavarian army.

Russo-Polish War (1654-1656): An estimated 100,000 Russian troops, led by Czar Alexis, attacked Lithuania (July 1654), besieged and took Smolensk (July-Oct.), and occupied Lithuania to the Berezina River. Smaller Russian forces attacked the Ukraine, taking Kiev.

First Northern War (1655-1660): Swedish forces totaling more than 30,000 invaded Poland; after a brief summer campaign, the Swedes, led by Charles X, captured Warsaw (Sept. 9). Brandenburg entered the war on its own (Oct.), taking West Prussia from defeated Poland; Charles then took both areas as a protectorate (Oct. 1655-Jan. 1656).

Russo-Polish War: Polish forces went on the offensive in Lithuania, defeating the Russians at Okhamatov (Jan. 1655); a Russian spring offensive took much of the rest of the country. Russian and allied Cossack forces, led by Bogdan Chmielnicki, took much of the Ukraine. Crimean Tartar forces, led by Khan Mahmet Girei, retook much of the Ukraine after defeating the Cossacks and capturing Chmielnicki at Zalozce.

b. Louis, margrave of Baden-Baden (1655-1707), Austrian field marshal.

First Northern War: Successful Polish uprisings against Swedish occupation forces drew John Casimir of Poland out of exile and Charles X and his army back to Poland; Charles was defeated by Polish forces at Sandomierz and retreated to Prussia, while Warsaw fell to Polish forces (June 1656). Swedish and Brandenburg forces moved back into Poland (late June), defeating John Casimir's forces and retaking Warsaw (July).

First Northern War: Russian forces led by Czar Alexis besieged Riga (July-Aug. 1656); reinforced Swedish forces sortied and defeated the more numerous Russians.

At Villmergen, Switzerland (Jan. 24, 1656), a Catholic army led by Christopher Pfyffer defeated Protestant forces, threatening but not destroying the Swiss union.

d. Prince Ottavio Piccolomini (ca. 1599-1656), Italian general in Austrian imperial service, most notably at Lützen (1632) and the relief of Prague (1648); he was

1640-1649 (cont.)

1650-1659

Dutch settlers arrived at the Cape of Good Hope, establishing a permanent settlement (1652); the Dutch began to move inland and north along the coast.

English naval forces bombarded Tunisian pirate installations at Porto Farino (1655).

Turkish-Venetian War: A second major Turkish attempt to break the Venetian blockade of the Dardanelles failed (1656).

Turkish-Venetian War: A third Turkish attempt to break the Venetian blockade of the Dardanelles resulted in a massive Venetian victory (1656); the Turks lost most of their war fleet, with an estimated 10,000 casualties.

Turkish-Venetian War: A fourth Turkish attempt to break the Venetian blockade of the Dardanelles succeeded; the Turks retook Tenedos and Lemnos, strongly moved into the Aegean, and reinforced and resupplied their army on Crete (1657).

Omani forces took the Portuguese base at Muscat (1650).

d. Dorgon (Dorgan) (1612-1650), Manchu general and ruler who established the Manchu dynasty in China, driving the Ming from Manchuria and then taking Peking (1644).

Russian forces reached the Amur River (1651) and with it the Chinese border, setting up fortified posts in the area and beginning their long Central Asian border conflict with the Chinese.

Dutch defeated a Chinese uprising on Taiwan (1652).

Chinese pirate admiral Koxinga, a Ming ally, took Amoy (1653), contesting Manchu power in eastern China (1653).

Besieged Recife surrendered to the Portuguese, ending Dutch penetration into Brazil (1654).

English forces took Jamaica (1654).

New England forces took Acadia from the French (1654), occupying it until 1670, when it was returned under Europe's Treaty of Breda.

b. Hsuan-Yeh (K'ang-Hsi) (1654-1722), Chinese emperor (r. 1661-1722), second in the Ch'ing dynasty.

Dutch forces attacked and took Sweden's Fort Christina, on the Delaware River (Sept. 1655).

Araucanian Indian forces in Chile destroyed a Spanish force of 300 to 400 at the Bueno River (1655).

Dutch forces took the Portuguese base at Colombo (1656).

Portuguese forces in Brazil successfully resisted Dutch attempts to resettle in Brazil (1657).

Koxinga's forces made a failed attack on Nanking (1657).

Ill and weakened Shah Jahan was deposed by his four sons; Aurangzeb emerged as Mogul emperor (r. 1658-1707).

Dutch forces took the Portuguese base at Negapatam (1658).

1650-1659 (cont.)

warships, 12 of these captured and 6 sunk. The English lost 2 warships.

d. Maarten Harpertzoon van Tromp (1597-1653), Dutch admiral who won at the Downs (1639); he was killed at Scheveningen (Aug. 10).

Oliver Cromwell dissolved the Rump Parliament and became lord protector of England (1653).

b. Duke Claude Louis Hector Villars (1653-1734), marshal of France.

b. Charles XI Vasa (1655-1697), king of Sweden (r. 1660-1697).

Swiss Catholic forces defeated Protestant forces at the first Battle of Villmergen (Jan. 24, 1656).

d. Robert Blake (1599-1657), English admiral; one of three "generals at sea" during the Second English Civil War (1648-1651).

War of the Second Fronde: French and British forces led by the viscount of Turenne defeated Spanish and English royalist forces under Don Juan of Austria at the decisive Battle of the Dunes (June 14, 1658); Turenne's army lost 400 and Don Juan's 6,000 (5,000 of these prisoners). Under the Peace of the Pyrenees (Nov. 1659), Spain lost Flanders and considerable disputed frontier territory.

d. Oliver Cromwell (1599-1658), English general during the civil wars and lord protector (1653-1658); he was succeeded by his son Richard Cromwell.

Richard Cromwell resigned as lord protector of England (1659); the Long Parliament reconvened and offered Charles II the throne.

involved in the ousting and murder of Wallenstein (1634) but failed to succeed him.

First Northern War: Russia, Denmark, and Austria entered the war against Sweden (spring 1657); Charles X withdrew from Poland, turning his attention to Denmark, which he invaded (July 1657) and defeated (Jan. 1658). Sweden attacked Denmark again in June 1658, besieging Copenhagen (July).

Transylvanian forces led by George Rakoczy II attacked southern Poland, taking Warsaw, but they were defeated by Crimean Tartar forces allied with the Turks; Rakoczy's forces were decimated during the pursuit into Transylvania (1657).

First Northern War: Dutch and English naval forces relieved besieged Copenhagen (Oct. 1658); the siege was later renewed.

First Northern War: Swedish forces consolidated their hold on the Gulf of Finland and the Latvian coast (1658).

Russo-Polish War (1658-1666): Russian forces attacked Lithuania, taking Vilna and much of the country (1658-1659). Russian forces attacking in the Ukraine were decisively defeated by Ukrainian forces at Konotop (1659).

First Northern War: Dutch naval forces again relieved Copenhagen (Feb. 1659).

First Northern War: Russian-Swedish truce (1659) recognized the status quo.

1660-1669

Charles II took the English throne (r. 1660-1685), beginning the Restoration.

d. Charles X Gustavus (Gustav) (1622-1660), king of Sweden (r. 1654-1660) during the Thirty Years' War and the First Northern War; he was succeeded by Charles XI (r. 1660-1697).

Spanish forces invaded Portugal (1661-1663) but were unable to retake the country, independent since 1640, and were decisively defeated at Villa Viciosa (June 1665). Spain recognized Portugal (1668).

Second Anglo-Dutch War (1665-1667): Off Lowestoft (June 3, 1665), the English battle fleet won a major victory over the Dutch, sinking or capturing 17 Dutch warships with 5,000 casualties to British losses of 2 ships and fewer than 1,000 casualties.

d. John Lawson (ca. 1610-1665), British admiral serving the parliamentary cause and later Charles II; he received fatal wounds at Lowestoft (1665).

Second Anglo-Dutch War: Dutch forces defeated an English fleet in four days of battle (June 1-4, 1666), sinking 4 and capturing 6 English warships, with 4,500 casualties and captured. The English fleet broke for home; the Dutch blockaded the Thames.

Russo-Polish War: Russian forces 60,000 strong were defeated at Lubar by a Ukrainian-Tartar army numbering 40,000 (1660). Bogdan Chmielnicki's Ukrainian army, allied with Russia, was decisively and finally defeated by Polish forces at Slobodyszcze; Chmielnicki then ended his war of independence.

b. Fedor Matveevich Apraksin (1661-1728), Russian admiral.

Turkish forces defeated remaining Transylvanian resistance at Nagyszollos (Jan. 22, 1662), completing their reconquest of the country.

Austro-Turkish War (1663-1664): Turkish forces inconclusively attacked Hungary (1663-1664); the Treaty of Vasvar (Aug. 1664) essentially restored the prewar status quo.

b. Eugène, prince of Savoy-Carignan (1663-1736), Austrian field marshal.

Russo-Polish War: The war ended with Poland and Russia partitioning the Ukraine at the Dnieper River (1667); Kiev and Smolensk went to Russia.

1650-1659 (cont.)

Manchu-Chinese War: After eight years of fighting, Manchu forces took southwestern China, completing their conquest of the country (1659).

1660-1669

English forces attacked the Dutch West African ports (Oct. 1663), taking Cape Coast Castle (1663) and St. Helena (1664); the Dutch took Kormantine (1665).

d. Abbas II (1632-1666), shah of Persia (r. 1642-1666) who, like his grandfather, Abbas I (the Great), invaded the Mogul Empire and took Kandahar (1649).

Manchu forces in Central Asia expelled Russian traders in the Amur region (1660).

Koxinga's forces took Taiwan from the Dutch and controlled much of the south China coast (1661-1662).

Siamese forces led by King Narai took Chiengmai from the Burmese (Mar. 1662).

d. Koxinga (Cheng Ch'eng-kung) (1624-1662), Chinese general and admiral; a Ming loyalist, he successfully campaigned against the Manchus.

Dutch forces took the Portuguese base at Cochin (1663).

Mogul forces took Assam (1663).

Maratha forces led by Sivaji took the Mogul port of Surat (1664).

Second Anglo-Dutch War: New Amsterdam, renamed New York, was taken by English seaborne forces (Sept. 7, 1664); the English also took Fort George.

1660-1669 (cont.)

Second Anglo-Dutch War: English naval forces broke the Dutch blockade of the Thames (July 25, 1666); in the Battle of the North Foreland, the English destroyed 20 Dutch warships with 7,000 casualties, 4,000 of these dead; the English lost 1 ship.

Second Anglo-Dutch War: A surprise naval raid brought Dutch warships into the Thames estuary and within 20 miles of London (June 1667).

Second Anglo-Dutch War: Treaty of Breda (July 21, 1667) ended the war, mainly a draw, although the English kept New Amsterdam (New York), in North America.

d. William Waller (ca. 1597-1668), English general who originally proposed the New Model Army; later disaffected and arrested, he helped negotiate Charles II's Restoration (1660).

Turkish-Venetian War: Candia fell after a 21-year siege (Sept. 6, 1669), effectively ending the war. Turkey took all but a Venetian toehold on Crete, Dalmatia, and Venice's Aegean islands.

1670-1679

d. George Monck (Monk), duke of Albemarle (1608-1670), British general and admiral who initially supported Charles I, then (after imprisonment in the Tower of London) served Oliver and Richard Cromwell.

d. Thomas Fairfax, third Baron Fairfax of Cameron (1612-1671), English general who was captain general (Feb. 1645) and prime organizer of the New Model Army, which he led at Naseby (1645).

Franco-Dutch War (1672-1678): France, England, and several German principalities jointly attacked the Netherlands (Mar. 1672); after William of Orange came to power (Aug. 27, 1672), Spain, Austria, and Brandenburg joined him in an anti-French alliance; England later left (1674) what became the Franco-Allied War.

Franco-Dutch War: French forces invaded the Netherlands; the Dutch broke their dikes to save Amsterdam (1672).

Third Anglo-Dutch War (1672-1674): This was part of a larger war that pitted Holland against France and several allied powers. At Sole Bay (May 28, 1672), a British fleet was defeated by the Dutch.

Third Anglo-Dutch War: At Schooneveld Channel, in the Netherlands (May 28, 1673), attacking British forces were defeated by Dutch counterattacks.

Franco-Allied War: French forces besieged and took Maastricht (June 29, 1673).

Third Anglo-Dutch War: England and Holland made peace with the Treaty of Westminster (Feb. 19, 1674).

Franco-Allied War: At Senef (Aug. 11, 1674), in the Netherlands, French forces led by the prince of Condé and Dutch forces led by William of Orange fought a major, inconclusive battle; the Dutch lost an estimated 14,000, including more than 5,000 prisoners, the French an estimated 6,000.

b. Philippe, duke of Orléans (1674-1723), French general.

d. Henri de la Tour d'Auvergne, viscount of Turenne (1611-1675), marshal of France who became marshal general (1660); he was killed at Nieder-Sasbach (July 27).

d. César, duke of Choiseul and count of Plessis-Praslin (1598-1675), marshal of France.

Don Cossack insurrection led by Stenka Razin took Tsaritsyn and Astrakhan and unsuccessfully besieged Simbirsk (1670).

Stenka Razin was captured and executed. Russian forces retook Astrakhan from the Don Cossacks (Aug. 1671), ending the insurrection.

Polish-Turkish War (1671-1677): Turkish forces claiming the Polish-held portion of the Ukraine, along with Ukrainian and Tartar allies, attacked Poland (1672) and in a summer campaign took Kamieniec and Lublin.

b. Peter I (the Great) (1672-1725), czar of Russia (r. 1682-1725).

Polish-Turkish War: Polish forces led by John III Sobieski decisively defeated a 30,000-strong Turkish army at Khotin (Nov. 11, 1673).

Franco-Allied War: In the Rhineland, the viscount of Turenne led French forces to victory at Sinsheim (June 16, 1674) and fought to a draw at Enzheim (Oct. 4).

Franco-Allied War: Turenne's forces won another engagement in Germany, at Turckheim (Jan. 5, 1675); he was killed in battle at Nieder-Sasbach (July 27), his army later retreating across the Rhine.

Polish-Turkish War: Turkish forces again invaded Poland; at Lwow (Lvov) they were defeated by John III Sobieski's Polish army, then retreated from most of Poland (1675).

d. Charles IV, duke of Lorraine and Bar (1604-1675), Austrian general during the Thirty Years' War.

French fleet sank six Dutch battleships off Palermo (June 12, 1676).

Polish-Turkish War: A massive Turkish army again attacked Poland, fighting to a draw with John III Sobieski's forces at Zorawno (Sept.-Oct. 1676). The war ended with the Treaty of Zorawno; Poland held the

1660-1669 (cont.)

d. Hung Ch'eng-ch'ou (1593-1665), Chinese leader and key Ming general who, after being captured, defected to become a Manchu general (1642) and eventually grand secretary in the resulting Ch'ing government.

Mogul forces took Chittagong (1666).

Bombay was founded by the English as one of a series of forts on the Indian coast (1667).

In Central America, English pirates led by Henry Morgan took and sacked Porto Bello (1668).

1670-1679

Ashanti forces led by Osei Tutu won independence from Denkyera; Tutu became the first king of Ashanti, establishing his capital at Kumasi (1670-1680).

British warships defeated an Algerian fleet off Cape Sparrel, sinking seven Algerian vessels (Sept. 1670).

French forces took the Dutch West African ports of Arguin and Goree (1677).

Maratha-Mogul War (1670-1674): Maratha forces led by Sivaji defeated Mogul occupying forces, gaining independence.

Henry Morgan's English pirates sacked Panama City (1671).

Third Anglo-Dutch War: Dutch seaborne forces retook New York and adjacent areas as far north as Albany (1672), but the Dutch returned the entire area to England under the Treaty of Westminster.

Torgut Mongol forces led by Ayuka Khan raided into European Russia (1672).

Vietnamese Civil War: After 40 years of fighting, 7 major campaigns, and the construction of 2 major defensive walls north of the Nguyen capital, Hué, the northern Trinh family and the southern Nguyen family partitioned Vietnam at the Linh River (1673).

Chinese general Wu San-kuei led the Revolt of the Three Feudatories (1673-1678), which effectively ended with his death.

Rajput insurrection against Mogul occupying forces was largely successful (1675-1679).

King Philip's War (1675-1676): New England colonies were at war with the Wampanoag people and their allies, led by the Wampanoag's King Philip (Metacomet); several English settlements were destroyed in the early fighting, with an estimated 600 lives lost. New England militia decimated the Wampanoags and their allies; the most notable massacre of noncombatants occurred when an entire walled Wampanoag village was burned with all the inhabitants, numbering 600 to 700, inside (Dec. 1675).

1670-1679 (cont.)

At sea, off Öland (June 1, 1676), a Danish and Dutch battle fleet sank three Swedish battleships.

d. Karl Gustav von Wrangel (1613-1676), Swedish marshal and admiral who commanded the Swedish army at Warsaw (1656).

d. Michel (Michael) Adriaanszoon de Ruyter (1607-1676), Dutch admiral during the Second and Third Anglo-Dutch Wars.

Ukraine, while Turkey took several areas in southern Poland.

At Lund (Dec. 3, 1676), Swedish forces allied with the French defeated Danish forces allied with the Dutch, at a cost of 3,000 Swedish casualties of 8,000 engaged and 5,000 Danish casualties of 8,000 engaged.

In Kioge Bay (June 30, 1677), a Danish fleet won a decisive victory over an opposing Swedish fleet, which lost 10 of its 25 battleships, 7 captured and 3 sunk, with 3,000 sailors captured and more than 1,000 casualties; no Danish ships were lost, and casualties were fewer than 500.

Imre Thokoly led a Hungarian insurrection against Austrian rule (1678), driving Austrian occupying forces out of much of western and northern Hungary and then, in alliance with Turkey, taking the rest of the country; the Austrian-Hungarian peace left only Transylvania to Austria (1682).

Nijmegen treaties between France and the Netherlands (Aug. 10, 1678), France and Spain (Sept. 10, 1678), France and Austria (Feb. 6, 1679), and France and Brandenburg (June 29, 1679) concluded the series of wars initiated by the French and English (1672), resulting in some French territorial and strategic gains.

Russo-Turkish War (1678-1681): Turkish forces attacked the eastern Ukraine (1678), ultimately withdrawing (1681).

1680-1689

b. Charles XII (1682-1718), king of Sweden (r. 1697-1718).

d. David Leslie, Lord Newark (1601-1682), Scottish general who fought alongside Oliver Cromwell in the First English Civil War, then commanded the Scottish-royalist army that lost to Cromwell at Worcester (1651); he was held in the Tower of London from then until the Restoration (May 1660).

French forces took Luxembourg (1684), holding it until 1697.

d. Charles II (1630-1685), king of England (r. 1660-1685); he was succeeded by James II (1685).

d. James Scott, duke of Monmouth (1649-1685), British soldier and natural son of Charles II; aiming to stop James, duke of York, a Catholic, from succeeding Charles II, he led Monmouth's Rebellion (1685), proclaiming himself king; defeated, he was captured, imprisoned in the Tower of London, and then beheaded (July 15).

d. Louis II de Bourbon, prince of Condé (1621-1686), French general best known for his victory at Rocroi (1643).

d. François Créqui (Créquy), marquis of Créqui (1629-1687), marshal of France.

Glorious Revolution: William of Orange accepted an invitation to become William III of England; he was the husband of Mary II of England, daughter of James II. After he landed in England (Nov. 1688), they became the Protestant corulers William and Mary (Feb. 13, 1689).

d. Prince Raimondo Montecuccoli (1609-1680), Italian general serving Austria; he was skilled in tactics and strategy, about which he wrote in several books (1650-1670), including *Delle Battaglie, Trattato della guerra, Dell'arte militare,* and *Aforismi dell'arte bellica.*

Strelsy (Russian palace guard) insurrection in Moscow installed Sophia as regent (r. 1682-1689).

d. Prince Rupert, Count Palatine of the Rhine and duke of Bavaria (1619-1682), Anglo-German general and admiral; King Charles I's general of the horse in the First English Civil War, notably at Edgehill (1642); he later served France, then England's Charles II.

Austro-Turkish War (1683): Turkish forces 150,000-200,000 strong, led by Mohammed IV, moved north from Adrianople to attack Austria (Mar. 1683). Their Hungarian allies made a failed attack in Slovakia. The Turks reached Austria (June) and besieged Vienna (July 14-Sept. 11). A 76,000-strong Polish-German-Austrian relief force led by John III Sobieski of Poland and Charles of Lorraine attacked (Sept. 12) and routed the Turkish army, with losses of an estimated 30,000. Pursuing allied forces took most of northern Hungary.

1670-1679 (cont.)

d. King Philip (Metacomet) (ca. 1639-1676), Wampanoag chief who died (Aug. 12, 1676) leading Native American forces during King Philip's War.

Bacon's Rebellion (1676-1677): Susquehannock forces raided across the Potomac River into Virginia (1676). Criticizing the colonial government's response as inadequate, Nathaniel Bacon led a small group of colonists against the Susquehannocks, massacring an estimated 100 friendly Occaneechees while doing so (May). Bacon then led a force of 300 against Jamestown, Virginia (Sept. 18), taking and burning the city. Troops sent from England defeated the rebels (1677), 23 of whom were executed.

d. Nathaniel Bacon (1647-1676), English-American rebel who led Bacon's Rebellion; he died of malaria.

d. Wu San-kuei (1612-1678), Chinese general who originally served the Ming, then the Manchu, and led the Revolt of the Three Feudatories (1673-1678).

1680-1689

French warships bombarded Algiers (Aug.-Sept. 1682).

French warships bombarded Algiers, Tunis, and Tripoli (1688).

Portuguese settlers founded Colonia, a stronghold on the River Plate (1680); it would figure in the Spanish-Portuguese dispute of the Banda Oriental (Uruguay), territory that both countries claimed.

Pueblo Indians under Popé mounted a successful insurrection against Spanish rule in Santa Fe, killing 400 people and forcing 2,200 Spanish survivors to retreat to El Paso (1680). Popé became dictator.

Dzungar forces led by Kaldan Khan conquered most of Kashgar, Yarkand, and Khotan from the Kirghiz and also expanded into Kazakh territory (ca. 1680-1688).

Manchu and Russian forces became engaged in a border war in the Amur region (1683-1685); the defeated Russians withdrew (1684), returning when the Manchu army withdrew (1685).

Mogul forces led by Aurangzeb campaigned in the Deccan, retaking Bijapur (1686) and Golconda (1687); in response,

1680-1689 (cont.)

War of the League of Augsburg (War of the Grand Alliance) (1688-1697): War began between France and the League of Augsburg, organized (1686) primarily by William of Orange as a counterweight to French strength in Europe. French forces attacked Germany (Sept. 25, 1688). England, now led by William III (of Orange), joined the anti-French alliance.

Ring and socket bayonet was invented, probably at Vauban (1688).

War of the League of Augsburg: At Walcourt (Aug. 25, 1689), allied forces in Flanders defeated a French army without great losses on either side.

Anglo-Irish War (1689-1691): Deposed English king James II led an Irish insurrection against British occupying forces; the Irish had French military support.

b. Ludwig Andreas von Khevenhüller, count of Aichelberg and Frankenburg (1683-1744), Austrian field marshal.

Turkish-Venetian War: Venetian forces in the Balkans retook Dalmatia and took much of southern Greece from the Turks (1685-1688).

Austro-Turkish War: Austrian forces took Buda after a two-month siege (Sept. 2, 1686).

Austro-Turkish War: At Harkány, Austrian forces led by Charles of Lorraine defeated a Turkish army, largely completing the Austrian conquest of Hungary and Transylvania (1687).

Austro-Turkish War: Austrian forces besieged and took Belgrade (Sept. 6, 1688), then went on to take much of Serbia.

d. Frederick William (1620-1688), elector of Brandenburg (r. 1640-1688); called the "Great Elector," he was involved in numerous wars with the Swedes; he founded the Prussian navy and strengthened the army.

b. Frederick William I (1688-1740), king of Prussia (r. 1713-1740).

1690-1699

War of the League of Augsburg: French forces led by François of Luxembourg decisively defeated allied forces under Frederick of Waldeck at Fleurus (July 1, 1690). French casualties totaled an estimated 6,000; of the 37,000 in the allied army, 6,000 died, 8,000 were captured, and 8,000 more suffered casualties. Off Beachy Head, nine days later (July 10), the French won a second major victory, defeating an Anglo-Dutch fleet. The allied fleet lost 12 of the 56 ships engaged; the French lost none.

Anglo-Irish War: The major battle of the war occurred at the Boyne River, approximately 40 miles northwest of Dublin (July 11, 1690). A 36,000-strong multinational Protestant army led by William III (of Orange) decisively defeated an Irish-French army of 26,000, deciding the fate of Ireland for 230 years. Afterward, tens of thousands of Catholic soldiers became "wild geese," joining those who had gone before them into foreign military service.

d. Friedrich Hermann (Frederic Armand) Schomberg (1615-1690), German-born general who served several countries, including France, Brandenburg, and Britain; he was killed at the Boyne River.

War of the League of Augsburg: French land forces continued on the offensive in the Netherlands, northern Italy, and Spain. The French took Mons by storm (Apr. 8, 1691), and French cavalry defeated the allied army at Leuze (Sept. 20).

Anglo-Irish War: At Aughrim (July 12, 1691), Protestant forces again defeated an Irish-French army, which suffered 7,000 casu-

Austro-Turkish War: Turkish forces retook Belgrade (Oct. 1690) and most of Serbia.

d. Charles V (Charles Leopold), duke of Lorraine and Bar (1643-1690), Austrian general.

Austro-Turkish War: At Szalánkemen (Aug. 19, 1691), Austrian forces defeated Turkish and Hungarian forces, which suffered heavy losses and retreated from Transylvania.

Turkish-Venetian War: Venetian seaborne forces took the island of Chios from the Turks (1691).

Russo-Turkish War: Russian land forces led by Peter I (the Great) attacked Turkish-held Azov, on the Black Sea, withdrawing in defeat after being unable to blockade the port (1695).

Russo-Turkish War: Having built a war fleet, Peter I again attacked Azov, taking the city from the Turks (July 28, 1696) after a siege by land and sea.

d. John (Jan) III Sobieski (1629-1696), king of Poland (r. 1674-1696); he was commander in chief of the Polish army (1668), then elected king; best known for relieving the Turkish siege of Vienna, personally leading the decisive cavalry charge (1683).

Austro-Turkish War: At Zenta (Sept. 11, 1697), Turkish invasion forces were decisively defeated by an Austrian army; the Turks suffered massive losses, in the

1680-1689 (cont.)

Africa and Southwest Asia	East, Central, and South Asia, the Pacific, and the Americas	
	Maratha forces mounted a long, low-level war against Mogul occupying forces.	
	In Bengal the British at Hooghly had running conflicts with Mogul forces (1686), spurring the British to build Fort William at modern Calcutta (1686).	
	Persian forces took Khiva, ruling it as a protectorate (1688).	
	King William's War (1689-1697), part of Europe's War of the League of Augsburg: In North America, this was largely a French-English frontier war, merging with continuing Iroquois attacks on the French and their Indian allies.	
	Leisler's Rebellion (1689-1691): Jacob Leisler led a successful anti-Catholic rebellion centered in New York, with the rebels declaring their allegiance to William and Mary; when Leisler refused to give up power, he was taken by British troops (Mar. 30, 1691) and executed (May 26).	
	Manchu-Russian border dispute on the Amur was resolved by Russian withdrawal from much of the region under the Treaty of Nerchinsk (1689).	

1690-1699

Africa and Southwest Asia	East, Central, and South Asia, the Pacific, and the Americas	
Omani forces besieged and took Mombasa from the Portuguese (Dec. 1698).	King William's War: New England forces took Port Royal, capital of French Acadia (May 1690), and made failed attacks on Montreal and Quebec (Oct.). French and Indian forces attacked northern English settlements from Maine to New York; English and Iroquois forces raided north into French Canada (1690-1697).	
	d. Popé (?-1690), Pueblo leader who organized a revolt against Spanish colonials near Santa Fe (1680); he was dictator until his death.	
	Spain reoccupied Santa Fe (1692).	
	b. Edward Braddock (1695-1755), English general.	
	Manchu forces defeated the Dzungar Mongols at Chao-Modo (1697), ending Dzungar raids into Mongolia.	

1690-1699 (cont.)

alties; Protestant losses were fewer than 1,000. Besieged Limerick fell on Oct. 13, 1691, ending the Anglo-Irish War.

d. Cornelis van Tromp (1629-1691), Dutch admiral during the Anglo-Dutch wars; his father was admiral Maarten van Tromp.

War of the League of Augsburg: Namur was besieged and taken by French forces led by Vauban (May 25-June 5, 1692).

War of the League of Augsburg: At La Hogue (Barfleur) (May 29-June 3, 1692), an Anglo-Dutch fleet decisively defeated a smaller French fleet, which lost 15 of its 44 battleships; the allies lost none. As a result of the engagement, the French called off their planned cross-Channel invasion of England.

War of the League of Augsburg: Allied forces led by William III (of Orange) unsuccessfully attacked the French at Steenkerke (July 24-Aug. 3, 1692), ultimately withdrawing after successful French counterattacks.

d. Hugh Mackay (ca. 1640-1692), Scottish general who became commander in chief in Scotland (1689), building Fort William at Inverlochy (1690); he was killed at Steenkerke.

War of the League of Augsburg: At Neerwinden (Landen) (July 29, 1693), allied forces of 50,000 led by William III (of Orange) were attacked by French forces of 80,000 led by the duke of Luxembourg, whose cavalry broke through the allied defensive line, turning retreat into rout. Allied losses totaled 19,000; French losses totaled 9,000.

War of the League of Augsburg: Allied forces led by William III (of Orange) besieged and took Namur (June-Sept. 1695).

d. François Henri de Montmorency-Boutteville, duke of Luxembourg (1628-1695), marshal of France who won at Neerwinden (1693).

War of the League of Augsburg: Treaty of Turin ended the war between France and Savoy, restoring the prewar status quo (June 1696).

b. Hermann Maurice, count of Saxe (1696-1750), German-born marshal of France.

War of the League of Augsburg ended with the Treaty of Ryswick (Oct. 1697), the combatants in the main restoring their earlier boundaries as set by the Nijmegen treaties (1678; 1679).

b. George, Lord Anson (1697-1762), British admiral.

d. Charles XI Vasa (1655-1697), king of Sweden (r. 1660-1697).

d. Niels Juel (Juul) (1629-1697), Danish admiral who commanded at Öland (1676).

20,000 to 30,000 range, while Austrian losses were fewer than 1,000. This battle effectively ended the war. Defeated Turkey ceded Hungary and Transylvania to Austria and substantial territory to Poland and Venice in the Treaty of Karlowitz (1699).

b. Hans Joachim von Zieten (1698-1786), Prussian general.

Russia, Denmark, Poland, and Saxony formed an anti-Swedish alliance (1698).

Strelsy (Russian palace guard) insurrection was defeated by government forces (1698); Peter I (the Great) deactivated the Strelsy.

1700 - 1993

Europe

Africa and Southwest Asia

Central, South and East Asia, and the Pacific

The Americas

1700

Great Northern War (1700-1721): A series of attacks by the anti-Swedish alliance began the long war. Denmark attacked and took Holstein, a Swedish protectorate (Apr.); a Polish-Saxon army attacked Livonia, besieging Riga (June); and Russian forces attacked Finland, besieging Narva (Aug.). Charles XII of Sweden responded by invading Denmark and quickly forcing that country out of the war (Aug.), with the return of Holstein. He then went to the relief of Narva (Nov. 20), destroying the Russian siege army of 40,000, which lost an estimated 8,000 and ceased to be an effective fighting force; Swedish losses were less than 2,000.

Supplied with European-made weapons, the Lunda kingdom rose in west-central Africa (ca. 1700).

Masai people began to move into what is now Kenya and Tanzania, pushing out the Bantu and other inhabitants (ca. 1700).

1701

Great Northern War: Swedish forces relieved besieged Riga (June 17). Charles XII then moved against Poland, defeating the allies at Dunamunde and taking much of Lithuania.

War of the Spanish Succession (1701-1714): France and several small allied states fought an anti-French alliance comprising Austria, England, the Netherlands, Prussia, and many smaller states.

d. James II (b. 1633), king of England, Scotland, and Ireland (r. 1685-1688), younger son of Charles I, who fought for the royalist cause from exile, then, on the Restoration (1660), became lord high admiral; he succeeded to the throne (1685) but lost it to William and Mary (1688), accepting defeat after his loss at the Boyne River (1690).

Forces from Oman took the East African port of Zanzibar from the Portuguese.

1702

Great Northern War: Russian forces moving toward the Baltic defeated opposing Swedish forces at Errestfer (Jan.) and reached the mouth of the Neva River, there founding St. Petersburg (May 1703).

Great Northern War: Swedish forces took Warsaw (May 14), then defeated an allied army at Klissow (July 2), with fewer than 1,000 Swedish casualties to 4,000 Polish and Saxon casualties and prisoners taken. Charles XII took Cracow (July).

War of the Spanish Succession: Allied forces 50,000 strong, led by John Churchill (after this named the duke of Marlborough), invaded the Spanish Netherlands (June); they took several French fortresses on the Meuse River (Sept.-Oct.).

War of the Spanish Succession: At Vigo Bay (Oct. 12), an Anglo-Dutch fleet defeated a French-Spanish squadron guarding a Spanish fleet carrying silver from the Americas, sinking or capturing all but 3 of 24 escort ships.

b. Thomas Arthur, count de Lally (d. 1766), French general.

d. William III (b. 1650), Dutch general, prince of Orange, and king of England, Scotland, and Ireland (r. 1689-1702) who, in England's Glorious Revolution (1688), was brought in to take the English throne with his wife, Mary Stuart; later defeated Catholic James II and his allies at the Boyne River (1690).

1703

War of the Spanish Succession: At Hochstadt, in the Danube Valley (Sept. 20), French forces 30,000 strong led by General Claude de Villars decisively defeated an Austrian army led by Hermann Styrum; 11,000 of 20,000 Austrians were casualties or prisoners, to French losses of 1,000.

Great Northern War: Swedish forces under Charles XII completed their conquest of Poland, installing Stanislas Leszczynski as puppet ruler (1704).

Janissaries, the elite Turkish guard, revolted, forcing the abdication of Ottoman emperor Sultan Mustafa II. He was succeeded by his brother Ahmed II (r. 1703-1730).

Central, South and East Asia, and the Pacific	The Americas
1700	
In India, Maratha fought to stay independent of Aurengzeb's Mogul Empire. Sikhs became a power in the Rajputana and Punjab regions of the Indian subcontinent (ca. 1700).	
1701	
French East India Company (Compagnie des Indes) established a new base at Calicut, India.	War of the Spanish Succession: French forces attacked Portuguese coastal settlements in Brazil.
1702	
	Queen Anne's War (1702-1713), part of Europe's War of the Spanish Succession: Carolinian militia and their Indian allies took and sacked Spanish St. Augustine (Dec.). War of the Spanish Succession: French forces temporarily took Colonia, Portugal's stronghold on the River Plate.
1703	
	Queen Anne's War (War of the Spanish Succession): French and Indian forces attacked New England frontier settlements (1703-1704); notable was the massacre at Deerfield, Massachusetts.

1703 (cont.)

Ferenc II Rákóczi led a Hungarian national uprising against Austria (1703-1711), gaining control of most of Hungary, but ultimately superior Austrian forces would wear down the rebels.

d. Godert (Godard) van Reede de Ginkel (b. 1644), Anglo-Dutch general who was a key lieutenant to William III (of Orange) during the Glorious Revolution (1688) and later at the Battle of the Boyne (1690), remaining in Ireland as commander in chief.

1704

War of the Spanish Succession: English seaborne forces took Gibraltar (July 24).

War of the Spanish Succession: At Blenheim, on the Danube (Aug. 13), English and Austrian forces led by the duke of Marlborough and Eugène, prince of Savoy, decisively defeated a French and Bavarian army led by Count Camille de Tallard and Maximilian I. Of 60,000 French and Bavarians, more than 38,000 were reportedly casualties or prisoners, with 12,000 allied casualties. Austria then took Bavaria.

War of the Spanish Succession: Off Málaga (Aug. 13), the main Anglo-Dutch and French war fleets fought to a draw, with heavy casualties but no ships sunk or captured.

Great Northern War: Russian forces retook Narva (Aug. 9).

1705

b. Edward, Baron Hawke (d. 1784), British admiral.

Turkish rule over Tunisia was effectively ended by Hussein ben Ali, who became bey of Tunis (r. 1705-1710).

1706

Great Northern War: At Fraustädt (Feb. 3), a Swedish army of 8,000 decisively defeated a 30,000-strong Polish-Saxon force. Swedish forces led by Charles XII attacked in Saxony (Aug.-Sept.), taking Leipzig. Defeated Poland left the war.

War of the Spanish Succession: At Ramillies, near Namur in the Netherlands (May 23), an allied army of 60,000 led by the duke of Marlborough attacked and routed an equally large French army led by Duke François of Villeroi, which suffered 15,000 casualties and prisoners taken, to allied casualties of less than 5,000. Marlborough then went on to take much of the Spanish Netherlands.

War of the Spanish Succession: In Italy French forces were defeated by Prince Eugène's allied army, with the decisive battle coming at Turin (Sept. 7), where the 60,000-strong French siege army was routed with more than 9,000 casualties and prisoners taken, to allied losses of 3,000 to 4,000.

1707

War of the Spanish Succession: At Almansa (Apr. 25), allied forces advancing on Madrid were defeated by French defending forces, suffering more than 7,000 casualties to considerably smaller French casualties before retreating.

Cossack-Russian War (1707-1708): Don Cossack forces of 5,000 to 10,000 led by Kondrati Bulavin were defeated by much larger Russian forces in a series of engagements (Oct. 1707-July 1708), with some Cossack strong points holding out (until Nov. 1708).

Central, South and East Asia, and the Pacific	The Americas	
1703 (cont.)		
1704		
Continuing their conquest of Java, Dutch forces used a succession crisis in Mataram to install a puppet ruler, also directly taking more of western Java and eastern Madura (1704-1705).	Queen Anne's War (War of the Spanish Succession): English and colonial forces attacked Acadia (Nova Scotia); they were repelled at Port Royal (later Annapolis) but took and razed the largest French Acadian settlement, Grand Pré. French forces and their Indian allies wiped out the English settlement of Bonavista, on Newfoundland.	
1705		
As the Dzungar-Chinese confrontation over Tibet grew, Chinese forces invaded Tibet, installing a puppet Dalai Lama.		
1706		
Dutch colonial forces defeated the forces of Surapati in northeastern Java, then taking the region (1706-1707).	Queen Anne's War (War of the Spanish Succession): Spanish-French forces unsuccessfully attacked Charleston, South Carolina.	
1707		
d. Aurengzeb ('Alamgir; Muhi-ud-Din Muhammad) (b. 1618), Indian emperor (r. 1658-1707) who with his brothers deposed his father, Shah Jahan; he expanded the Mogul Empire and revived active persecution of Hindus.	Queen Anne's War (War of the Spanish Succession): English and colonial forces again unsuccessfully attacked Port Royal, Acadia (Nova Scotia).	

1707 (cont.)

d. Cloudesley (Clowdisley) Shovell (Shovel) (b. 1650), English admiral who, after participating in the successful siege of Gibraltar (1704), became commander in chief of the Mediterranean; he was drowned when his ship sank off the Scilly Isles (Oct. 22).

d. Louis, margrave of Baden-Baden (b. 1655), Austrian field marshal, called "Türkenlouis" for his role in the Turkish War (1683-1699).

d. Sebastien le Prestre de Vauban (b. 1633), French marshal; a military engineer who introduced new, scientifically based siegecraft techniques, some involving a series of parallel trenches; designed and directed the building of new types of fortresses, using towers and bastions in new ways; and invented the socket bayonet.

1708

Great Northern War: A Swedish army of 45,000, led by Charles XII, crossed the Vistula River to attack Russia (Jan. 1). Russian forces did not massively engage, instead conducting a fighting retreat, coupled with a scorched earth policy. After wintering near Minsk and severely depleting their supplies, the Swedes advanced on Moscow, defeating the Russians in a series of small battles. A large Swedish supply wagon train was destroyed by its escorting army after its defeat at Lyesna, near the Dniester River (Oct.); the Swedes lost half of the 12,000-strong escorting army in the battle and subsequent flight to meet Charles. The Swedish army then endured the Russian winter.

War of the Spanish Succession: At Oudenarde, on the Scheldt River in Flanders (July 11), an 80,000-strong allied army led by the duke of Marlborough attacked the French Flanders army, of similar strength and led by Louis, duke of Vendôme. Ultimately, the French retreated, after suffering 15,000 casualties or prisoners taken; there were more than 7,000 allied casualties.

War of the Spanish Succession: Lille fell to the allies (Dec. 11).

Ferenc II Rákóczi's national uprising in Hungary effectively ended after the Austrians defeated his forces at Trencin (1711).

Algerian forces besieged and took Oran, an Algerian coastal city held by Spain since 1509.

1709

Great Northern War: Swedish and allied Cossack forces were decisively defeated by a much larger Russian army led by Peter the Great at Poltava (June 28). Suffering many more casualties than the Russians, the Swedes mounted a failed final assault against a Russian force 42,000 strong. Of the 31,000 Swedes and Cossacks, an estimated 7,000 were killed, 2,000 wounded, and 14,000 captured; Charles XII and fewer than 2,000 soldiers escaped into Turkey.

Great Northern War: Russian forces occupied Poland, restoring Augustus II to the throne, and took Livonia, Estonia, and other Swedish territories on the Baltic; Danish forces took Holstein, several areas in northern Germany, and part of southern Sweden.

War of the Spanish Succession: At Malplaquet in Flanders, near besieged Mons (Sept. 11), the French fought allied forces in a major, largely inconclusive battle that cost the duke of Marlborough's allied army more than 20,000 casualties of 90,000 engaged, 6,500 of these dead; French casualties were more than 12,000, some 4,500 of these dead.

War of the Spanish Succession: Besieged Mons fell to the allies (Oct. 26).

At Kandahar, Ghilzai Afghan rebel forces — largely Sunni Muslims led by Mir Vais — led a successful insurrection against Shia Persian rule, establishing an independent state.

Central, South and East Asia, and the Pacific	The Americas

1707 (cont.)

1708

At Agra, Aurengzeb's son Bahadur Shah defeated and killed the intended successor to the Mogul throne, his elder brother Muazim. Sahu was placed on the throne of Maratha, independent from the Moguls in all but name.	Queen Anne's War (War of the Spanish Succession): French forces took St. John's, Newfoundland. War of the Emboadas: The *emboadas*, new Portuguese immigrants to Brazil, waged a small-scale, inconclusive rising against the planter-dominated São Paulo government (1708-1709).

1709

1710

Great Northern War: At Helsingborg (Feb.), Swedish forces led by general Magnus Steinbock defeated the Danes in southern Sweden and then moved into northern Germany. Turkey entered the war against Russia.

In Tunisia, Ali Pasha overthrew and killed his uncle, Hussein ben Ali, making himself bey of Tunis (r. 1710-1756).

Turkey was at war with Russia (1710-1711), part of the Great Northern War.

1711

Great Northern War: A massive Turkish force trapped Russian forces 60,000 strong, led by Peter the Great, at the Pruth River; the Turks negotiated the return of Azov and some border concessions, then released the Russians (July). Turkey's war with Russia ended with the Treaty of Pruth.

b. Marriot Arbuthnot (Arbuthnott) (d. 1794), British admiral.

d. Louis François, marquis and duke de Boufflers (b. 1644), marshal of France.

Persians under Khusru Khan besieged Kandahar but were defeated by Mir Vais's Afghan rebel forces, with massive Persian losses; Khusru Khan was killed.

1712

Swiss Protestant forces numbering 8,000 defeated Catholic forces 12,000 strong at Villmergen (July 25).

b. Frederick II (the Great) (d. 1786), Prussian ruler (r. 1740-1786).

b. Louis-Joseph de Montcalm-Gozon, marquis of Montcalm (d. 1759), French general.

d. Nicholas Catinat (b. 1637), marshal of France who commanded the army in Italy (1690-1696).

In West Africa, Bambara forces under King Mamari Kulibali (r. 1712-1755) revived the kingdom of Segu; they ultimately took Timbuktu, Djénné, and Bamako.

1713

War of the Spanish Succession: Treaty of Utrecht resulted in territorial gains by England, including Gibraltar and various American territories, and by Savoy in Sicily and northern Italy.

1714

Great Northern War: Russian naval forces for the first time defeated the Swedes, at Gangut (Hanko or Hangö) (Aug. 5), breaking Swedish control of the Gulf of Finland. Russian land forces took Finland.

War of the Spanish Succession: Barcelona fell to the French (Sept. 11). Austria and France made peace, essentially maintaining the prewar status quo.

In Montenegro, insurrections against Turkish occupying forces failed.

Under Ahmed Pasha Karamanli, Tripolitania, in North Africa, effectively became independent from Turkey.

1715

In Scotland, in a rising called "The Fifteen" (Sept. 1715-Feb. 1716), Jacobites — supporters of the Stuart line — were quickly defeated by British govern-

Central, South and East Asia, and the Pacific	The Americas
1710	
Mogul leader Bahadur Shah campaigned against the Sikhs in India.	Queen Anne's War (War of the Spanish Succession): A 4,000-strong English and colonial army again attacked and this time took Port Royal, Acadia (Nova Scotia).
1711	
	Queen Anne's War (War of the Spanish Succession): English and colonial forces mounted a failed expedition against the French at Quebec and Montreal, losing more than 900 of the 5,000-strong force in a storm on the St. Lawrence River.
	Tuscarora War (1711-1713): In the Carolinas, the Tuscaroras fought colonial and allied, mainly Yamassee, forces (1711-1713).
	War of the Spanish Succession: French forces under Admiral René Duguay-Trouin took Rio de Janeiro from the Portuguese, then sacked the city.
1712	
Central and northern India were wracked by civil wars (1712-1719) after the death of Maratha's leader, Bahadur Shah; Balaji Visvanath Bhat became peshwa, the first of the hereditary prime ministers who were thereafter to rule Maratha, building a powerful confederacy as the Moguls weakened.	
1713	
During anarchy among the Moguls in Delhi, viceroy and general Asaf Jah (Chin Kilich Khan) regained control over most of India's Deccan, calling himself Nizam ul-Mulk.	Europe's Treaty of Utrecht largely brought an end to the War of the Spanish Succession, in America, Queen Anne's War. England gained Acadia (Nova Scotia), Newfoundland, and Hudson Bay.
	Tuscarora War: Conflict in the Carolinas ended with the massacre of more than 500 Tuscaroras in their burning village on Contentnea Creek (Mar. 13). The survivors moved north, joining the Iroquois Confederacy, centered on New York State.
1714	
In a Cambodian war of succession (1714-1716), Vietnamese and Laotian forces intervened on one side and the Siamese on the other, with the Siamese side ultimately winning the war.	
Manipur forces under Raja Gharib Newaz raided widely in Upper Burma (1714-1759).	
b. Alaungpaya (Alompra; Maung Aung Zeya) (d. 1760), Burmese monarch and general.	
1715	
	In the Carolinas, Yamassee and some Creek forces rose against the English colonists (1715-1718), with some early success.

Europe	Africa and Southwest Asia

1715 (cont.)

ment forces, with the decisive engagement coming at Preston, where the Jacobites surrendered (Nov. 14); James Edward, the "Old Pretender," landed in Scotland (Dec.) but quickly returned to France (Feb. 1716).

Turkish-Venetian War: Turkish forces besieged and took Venetian fortresses in Morea (the Peloponnesus) and Crete, then took the Aegean islands.

b. Charles de Rohan, prince of Soubise (d. 1787), marshal of France.

1716

At Peterwardein (Aug. 5), an Austrian army of more than 60,000 led by Prince Eugène decisively defeated a reportedly 150,000-strong Turkish army, which suffered 20,000 casualties to 5,000 Austrian casualties. The Austrians went on to besiege and take Timisoara (Oct. 14).

b. Baron Wilhelm von Knyphausen (d. 1800), Prussian general.

b. George, Viscount Sackville Germain (Lord George Germain) (d. 1785), British general.

d. François Louis de Rousselet, marquis of Châteaurenault (b. 1637), French admiral who lost at Vigo Bay (1702).

1717

Great Northern War: Swedish forces led by Charles XII attacked Danish-held Norway.

Austrian forces led by Prince Eugène besieged Turkish-held Belgrade (July), defeated a large Turkish relief army (Aug. 16), and took the city (Aug. 21).

b. Jeffrey Amherst (d. 1797), British field marshal.

At Herat, Abdali Afghans led by Asadullah Khan led a successful revolt against Persian rule, founding an independent state.

1718

War of the Quadruple Alliance (1718-1720): England, France, and the Netherlands formed an anti-Spanish alliance (Jan.); Spanish forces occupied Sardinia (Nov.).

War of the Quadruple Alliance: Spanish forces occupied Sicily (July). At Cape Passaro, off Syracuse (Aug. 11), a British fleet commanded by Admiral George Byng decisively defeated a Spanish war fleet, sinking or taking 20 of 29 Spanish ships. Austria joined the anti-Spanish alliance (Aug.), attacking the Spanish in Sicily and eventually taking Messina (Oct. 1719).

b. George Brydges Rodney (d. 1792), British admiral.

d. Charles XII (b. 1682), king of Sweden (r. 1697-1718) during the Great Northern War; killed in battle at Fredrikshald (Halden), near Oslo.

1719

Great Northern War: Under the Stockholm treaties (1719-1721), Denmark kept Schleswig and Prussia kept several Baltic coast areas taken during the war; other minor adjustments and indemnities were set; the prewar status quo was largely restored to Poland and Saxony.

War of the Quadruple Alliance: A 30,000-strong French army attacked northern Spain (Apr.), withdrawing when winter came (Nov.).

Attacking Persian forces numbering about 30,000 were defeated by much smaller Afghan forces at Herat (1719).

Central, South and East Asia, and the Pacific	The Americas	
1715 (cont.)		
	b. William Johnson (d. 1774), American political and military leader.	
1716		
Dzungar Mongol forces led by Chewanlaputan (Tsewang Araptan) attacked in Tibet, taking Lhasa, capturing the Dalai Lama, and decisively defeating a Chinese force sent to contest their conquest (1716-1718).	Carolina settlers and their Cherokee allies pushed the Yamassee and their Creek allies into Florida. Carolina settlers built fortifications along several rivers, including the Savannah, as protection against French and Spanish attackers (1716-1721).	
1717		
Russian forces expanding east into Central Asia were defeated at Khiva.		
1718		
	French and Spanish were at war on the Gulf Coast (1718-1720), especially in Florida and Texas, part of Europe's War of the Quadruple Alliance. b. Israel Putnam (d. 1790), American general.	
1719		
Civil war in the Mogul Empire ended when Mohammed Shah became emperor, with the support of Maratha and Nizam ul-Mulk. During another Mataram succession crisis, the Dutch seized much of the remainder of eastern and central Java (1719-1723).		

Europe	Africa and Southwest Asia

1720

War of the Quadruple Alliance: Treaty of The Hague ended the war; Austria took Sicily, and Savoy took Sardinia.

b. Thomas Gage (ca. 1720-1787), British general.

Mahmud Khan, son of Mir Vais, led an Afghan invasion of Persia, taking Kerman, but his forces were routed and pushed back to Kandahar.

After a period of civil war, Opuku Ware became leader of the Ashanti, in West Africa (r. ca. 1720-1750).

b. Agha Mohammed Khan (d. 1797), Persian general and ruler.

1721

Great Northern War: Under the Treaty of Nystad (Aug. 30), Russia kept much of the Swedish territory taken during the war, including Estonia, Livonia, and several other Baltic coast and island areas, but not Finland.

b. William Augustus, duke of Cumberland (d. 1765), British general.

Afghan forces under Mahmud Khan raided widely in the Persian region of Khorasan.

1722

b. François Joseph Paul de Grasse (d. 1788), French admiral.

b. John Burgoyne (d. 1792), British general.

d. John Churchill, first duke of Marlborough (b. 1650), British captain general and (with his wife, Sarah) a power at court; among his best-known victories are four in the War of the Spanish Succession: Blenheim (1704), Ramillies (1706), Oudenarde (1708), and Malplaquet (1709); he was an ancestor of Winston Churchill.

Afghan forces led by Mahmud Khan invaded Persia, again taking Kerman, then besieging and taking Isfahan (Mar.-Oct.); they then captured and ruled much of the country after Persia's shah abdicated, although the shah's son Tahmasp mounted an effective resistance.

1723

d. Philippe, duke of Orléans (b. 1674), French general during the War of the League of Augsburg and the War of the Spanish Succession; nephew of Louis XIV, he was regent for young Louis XV (1715-1723).

Ostensibly supporting Persia's Tahmasp, Russia took Resht and Baku; Turkey then took Tiflis, in Georgia.

1724

b. Guy Carleton (d. 1808), British general.

Russia and Turkey effectively partitioned northern and western Persia in the Treaty of Constantinople, with the Turks taking Tabriz, Hamadan, and Kerman.

King Agaja of Abomey took the Guinean port of Allada, founding the kingdom of Dahomey.

1725

b. Augustus, Viscount Keppel (d. 1786), British admiral.

b. Jean Baptiste Donatien de Vimeur, count of Rochambeau (d. 1807), marshal of France.

b. Pasquale Paoli (d. 1807), Corsican general.

In Isfahan, Mahmud Khan was killed, reportedly because he went mad; he was succeeded by his cousin Ashraf Shah.

Central, South and East Asia, and the Pacific	The Americas	
		1720
Chinese forces attacked Dzungaria, decisively defeating Dzungar forces and taking Turfan and Urumchi. Another Chinese force defeated the Dzungars in Tibet, installing a new Dalai Lama and leaving an occupation force at Lhasa. Low-level frontier war with the Dzungars continued.	French settlers built Fort Niagara, a stronghold on the lower Great Lakes. Spanish forces occupied Texas, seeking to block westward movement by the French out of Louisiana (1720-1722). b. Pontiac (ca. 1720-1769), Ottawa chief.	
		1721
Chinese occupation forces defeated a rising on Formosa (Taiwan).	In Paraguay, a Comunero insurrection led by José de Antiquera, governor of Asunción, established an independent state (1721-1726). b. Johann Kalb (Baron de Kalb) (d. 1780), German-born general serving in America.	
		1722
Peace of Astrakhan established Russian control over the Torgut peoples. b. Ahmad Shah Durani (Ahmad Khan Durr'ani) (ca. 1722-1772), Afghan chief and general. d. Hsuan-Yeh (K'ang-Hsi) (b. 1654), Chinese emperor (r. 1661-1722), second in the Ch'ing dynasty, who, after concluding the Treaty of Nerchinsk with the Russians (1689), took control of large areas of Mongolia and Tibet, against resistance from the Dzungar peoples.		
		1723
	Araucanian peoples mounted another failed rising against Spain in Chile.	
		1724
As the Mogul Empire began to fragment, Nizam ul-Mulk (Asaf Jah or Chin Kilich Khan) left Delhi to found the independent kingdom of Hyderabad (r. 1724-1748) in the Deccan.	In Paraguay, José de Antiquera and his Comuneros defeated troops from Buenos Aires, sent to put down their rebellion.	
		1725
	British forces on Jamaica unsuccessfully attacked the Maroons, former slaves living in the interior. British settlers built Fort Oswego on Lake Ontario, their stronghold on the lower Great Lakes.	

Europe	Africa and Southwest Asia

1725 (cont.)

Europe	Africa and Southwest Asia
b. Robert Clive, Baron Clive (d. 1772), British general and colonial administrator.	
d. Peter I (the Great) (b. 1672), czar of Russia (r. 1682-1725) who created the modern Russian state, building a strong army and navy modeled on Western styles; during the Great Northern War (1700-1721), he personally led Russian forces, most notably in defeating Charles XII of Sweden at Poltava (1709); he reportedly died from a chill caught while rescuing soldiers from an icy river.	
d. Pierre de Montesquiou d'Artagnan (b. 1645), marshal of France who was believed to be the model for the hero in Alexandre Dumas's 1844 novel *The Three Musketeers*.	

1726

Europe	Africa and Southwest Asia
b. Richard Howe (d. 1799), British admiral.	Afghans under Ashraf Shah defeated attacking Turkish forces at Isfahan.
	West African kingdom of Oyo defeated expanding Dahomey (ca. 1726-1730).

1727

Europe	Africa and Southwest Asia
b. James Wolfe (d. 1759), British general.	Hostilities in Persia ended with Turkey retaining seized frontier territories.
	In West Africa, King Agaja of Dahomey took Whydah, on the coast of Guinea.
	City-state of Pate made an alliance with the Portuguese against the Omanis, a power on the East African coast.

1728

Europe	Africa and Southwest Asia
b. Eyre Coote (d. 1783), British general.	Persian forces numbering 10,000 to 12,000, led by Tahmasp and general Nadir Kuli Beg, defeated a much larger Afghan army at Herat.
d. Fedor Matveevich Apraksin (b. 1661), Russian admiral who commanded the Baltic Fleet during the Great Northern War, later commanding on the Caspian Sea against the Persians (1722-1723).	Aided by Pate, Portuguese forces retook Mombasa from the Omanis.

1729

Europe	Africa and Southwest Asia
b. William Howe (d. 1814), British general.	Persian forces under Tahmasp and Nadir Kuli Beg defeated the Afghans in a series of battles, taking Isfahan.
b. Pierre André de Suffren Saint-Tropez (d. 1788), French vice admiral.	
b. Alexander Vasilievich Suvorov (d. 1800), Russian field marshal.	Rebels in Mombasa expelled the newly returned Portuguese; the city then fell back under Omani domination.
b. Jean-Baptiste Charles Hector d'Estaing (d. 1794), French admiral.	

1730

Europe	Africa and Southwest Asia
d. François de Neufville, duke of Villeroi (b. 1644), marshal of France who was decisively defeated at Ramillies (1706).	Persian forces again defeated the Afghans, at Zarghan, going on to retake all of Persia; the real power then rested with General Nadir Kuli Beg, not Shah Tahmasp.

Central, South and East Asia, and the Pacific	The Americas	
1725 (cont.)		
1726		
	Paraguayan rebel José de Antiquera was captured, but his Comunero insurrection continued with low-level guerrilla resistance until the mid-1730s. Spanish colonists settled Montevideo, in Banda Oriental (Uruguay), disputed territory also claimed by Portugal.	
1727		
Chinese occupation forces defeated a major insurrection in Tibet (1727-1728). Treaty of Kiakhta settled border disputes between China and Russia.	b. Artemis Ward (d. 1800), American general.	
1728		
After civil war in Tibet, China increased its forces there, exiling the Dalai Lama.	Low-level free slave insurrection occurred in Surinam, occasionally flaring into more substantial hostilities (from 1728). b. Horatio Gates (d. 1806), American general. b. Nicholas Herkimer (d. 1777), American general. b. John Butler (d. 1796), colonial Loyalist military leader.	
1729		
Chinese forces mounted a series of campaigns against the Dzungar Mongols in Tibet (1729-1735).		
1730		
	b. Baron Friedrich Wilhelm von Steuben (d. 1794), German general serving in America.	

1730 (cont.)

	Turkish-Persian War (1730-1735): When the Turks failed to return Persian territory, Nadir Kuli Beg's Persian forces defeated Turkish forces at Hamadan, also taking Azerbaijan and Iraq and besieging Erivan.
	In West Africa, Mamari Kulibali, king of Segu, blocked an invasion by the king of Kong (ca. 1730).

1731

Corsicans fought for independence from Genoa (ca. 1731-1768).	Turkish-Persian War: Lifting the siege of Erivan, Nadir Kuli Beg defeated an insurrection in Khorasan, besieging and taking Herat (1731-1732). After Nadir left, Tahmasp himself besieged Erivan.

1732

	Turkish-Persian War: A Turkish army relieved besieged Erivan, defeating Tahmasp's Persian forces in a second major battle at Hamadan, then retaking all territories lost to Nadir Kuli Beg and imposing a peace settlement on Tahmasp. On returning from Herat, Nadir deposed Tahmasp, replacing him with his own infant son, Abbas, and continuing the war.
	Spanish forces took back Oran from the Algerians.

1733

War of the Polish Succession (1733-1738): On the death of Augustus II of Poland (Feb.), war developed over the conflicting claims to the throne of French-backed Stanislas Leszczynski and Augustus III of Saxony, supported by Russia and Austria. After the election of Stanislas (Sept.), Russian and Saxon armies totaling 40,000 invaded Poland, took Warsaw, and put Augustus III on the throne; Stanislas fled to Danzig.	Turkish-Persian War: Nadir Kuli Beg's Persian forces attacked the Turks in Mesopotamia, besieging Baghdad. A Turkish relief army defeated the Persians at Karkuk and relieved Baghdad, but the reinforced Persians decisively defeated the Turks near Karkuk and took Baghdad.
b. Charles Joseph de Croix, count of Clerfayt (Clairfayt) (d. 1798), Austrian field marshal.	

1734

War of the Polish Succession: Besieged Danzig, refuge of Polish royal claimant Stanislas Leszczynski, fell to its Russian and Saxon attackers (June) when French relief forces were stopped.	Nadir Kuli Beg campaigned with his Persian forces in the Transcaucasus, but the Turkish army remained in a fortified camp.
War of the Polish Succession: French forces took Lorraine. French and Spanish forces attacked Sicily, Lombardy, and Naples, then fought an inconclusive campaign against the Austrians (1734-1735).	
d. Duke Claude Louis Hector Villars (b. 1653), marshal of France who commanded the main French army at Malplaquet, losing to the duke of Marlborough and Prince Eugène (1709); he later defeated Eugène, with whom he negotiated the Peace of Rastatt (1714).	

Central, South and East Asia, and the Pacific	The Americas
1730 (cont.)	
1731	
Russian forces defeated the Kazakhs (1730-1731), taking regions formerly controlled by Khiva and Bukhara.	
1732	
In Tibet, Chinese forces handed the Dzungars a major defeat.	b. Francis Marion (d. 1795), American general. b. George Washington (d. 1799), American general and first president of the United States (1789-1797).
1733	
	At St. Johns, in the Danish-held Virgin Islands, more than 200 Europeans were killed in a slave rising (Nov. 13). English settlers under James Oglethorpe began building forts in Georgia. b. Benjamin Lincoln (d. 1810), American general. b. Philip John Schuyler (d. 1804), American general.
1734	
	Danish and French troops massacred 1,000 Black inhabitants of St. Johns, in the Virgin Islands. b. Daniel Boone (d. 1820), American frontiersman and militia officer.

Europe	Africa and Southwest Asia

1735

Austro-Russian-Turkish War (1735-1739): Turkey was at war with Russia, which was later joined by Austria (Jan. 1737).

b. François Étienne Christophe Kellermann (d. 1820), French marshal of the empire.

b. John Jervis (d. 1823), British admiral.

Africa and Southwest Asia:
Turkish-Persian War: At Baghavand, near Kars, Nadir Kuli Beg's forces defeated a large Turkish army, effectively ending the war.

1736

Austro-Russian-Turkish War: Russian forces 60,000 strong invaded Turkey, with one army taking Azov and another attacking in the Crimea. Both forces withdrew after suffering heavy losses; the Crimean force was reportedly cut in half due to natural causes rather than combat. Crimean Tartar forces responded with massive raids on the Ukraine.

d. Eugène, prince of Savoy-Carignan (b. 1663), Austrian field marshal who served notably through numerous wars; he was allied with the duke of Marlborough at Blenheim (1704) and Malplaquet (1709).

Africa and Southwest Asia:
On the death of his son Abbas, Nadir Kuli Beg made himself shah of Persia (r. 1736-1747).

1737

Austro-Russian-Turkish War: Austrian forces attacked the Turks in the Balkans, taking much of Turkish Serbia, Bosnia, and Wallachia (Romania); they were then forced back by Turkish counteroffensives. Russian forces again took Turkish-held Azov and the Ukraine, and again withdrew.

1738

War of the Polish Succession ended with the Treaty of Vienna; Augustus III became king of Poland, and Stanislas, who had abdicated, became duke of Lorraine.

Austro-Russian-Turkish War: Again attacking south into Turkey, the Russians were defeated and forced to withdraw at Bendery, in Moldavia.

b. Charles Cornwallis (d. 1805), British general.

b. Henry Clinton (d. 1795), British general.

b. George Collier (d. 1795), British admiral.

Africa and Southwest Asia:
In West Africa, the kingdom of Oyo fought a long war against Dahomey (1738-1748).

1739

Austro-Russian-Turkish War: Turkish forces sharply defeated the Austrians at Kroszka, in southern Serbia, then besieged Belgrade. The fourth Russian offensive of the war brought a 70,000-strong Russian army victory over a larger Turkish force at Khotin (Stavuchany), in Moldavia; the Russians then took Jassy, the capital. Austria withdrew from the war with the Treaty of Belgrade (Sept. 18), losing the rest of Serbia and other Balkan territory to the Turks; the Russians also made peace, holding only Azov.

b. Prince Gregori Aleksandrovich Potemkin (d. 1791), Russian field marshal.

Central, South and East Asia, and the Pacific	The Americas

1735

	Spanish-Portuguese War (1735-1737), part of the War of the Polish Succession: Spanish forces took Colonia, in La Plata, later returning the town to Portugal (1737).
	b. Paul Revere (d. 1818), American militia commander.

1736

	At Oruro, in central Peru, Indian miners unsuccessfully rose against murderous conditions in the Portuguese-operated mines (1736-1737).
	b. Arthur St. Clair (d. 1818), American general.
	b. Daniel Morgan (d. 1802), American general.

1737

In India, Maratha forces defeated the main Mogul army at Delhi, then further expanded the area of Maratha control.	
Nadir Shah's Persian forces besieged Kandahar.	

1738

Kandahar fell to Nadir Shah's Persian forces, who also conquered Balkh and Baluchistan. They then took Ghazni and Kabul (Sept.) and attacked India, defeating Mogul forces at the Battle of the Khyber Pass and moving toward Delhi.	b. Ethan Allen (d. 1789), American soldier.
Manipuri forces led by Raja Gharib Newaz raided into Upper Burma, threatening Ava.	

1739

At Karnaj (Feb. 13), Persian forces led by Nadir Shah decisively defeated a Mogul army of 80,000, then took Delhi. A failed rising in Delhi the next day ended with a Persian massacre of thousands. Nadir's forces then took much of northern India, but he chose not to stay, instead returning to Persia with massive booty.	War of Jenkins's Ear (1739-1743), which would become part of the War of the Austrian Succession (1740-1748): The Spanish and English fought over Florida's boundaries. Jenkins was an English sea captain whose ear was allegedly severed by the Spanish, triggering the conflict. British forces led by Admiral Edward Vernon took Spanish-held Porto Bello.
Cambodian-Vietnamese War (1739-1749): Attacking Cambodian forces were defeated by the Vietnamese, who then attacked and defeated the Cambodians, taking more of the Mekong River basin.	
Maratha's Peshwa Bajo Rao wrested Bassein from Portugal; he soon assumed full power in Maratha (r. 1740-1761).	

1740

War of the Austrian Succession (1740-1748): A set of disputes over the succession to the Austrian throne became a widespread war involving all the main European states and their forces abroad. The war began with an attack on Silesia by the forces of Frederick the Great of Prussia (Dec. 16).

d. Frederick William I (b. 1688), king of Prussia (r. 1713-1740) during the Great Northern War and the War of the Spanish Succession.

Nadir Shah's Persian forces attacked and took Bukhara and Khiva from the Uzbeks.

1741

War of the Austrian Succession: Austrian forces invaded and took much of Silesia. Austrian and Prussian armies met at Mollwitz (Apr. 10), with the Austrians ultimately withdrawing after their apparently successful cavalry had been defeated by Prussian infantry. The Austrians had 4,000 to 5,000 casualties and prisoners taken, with a similar number of Prussian losses. In the following months, Bavaria, France, Saxony, Savoy, and Sweden joined Prussia, while England and the Netherlands joined Austria. Bavarian and French forces invaded Austria (July) and then Bohemia (Oct.), taking Prague in a nighttime attack (Nov.); Austrian forces invaded Bavaria (late Dec.).

Russo-Swedish War (1741-1743): Swedish forces attacked far more numerous Russian forces, miscalculating the impact of Russian involvement in the War of the Austrian Succession. At Wilmanstrand, a 10,000-strong Russian army defeated a Swedish army of 6,000, which suffered 3,300 casualties and 1,300 prisoners taken, losing in all more than two-thirds of its force.

Nadir Shah failed to suppress a rising of the Lesgians against Persian rule, only driving them into the mountains.

1742

War of the Austrian Succession: At Chotusitz (May 17), Frederick the Great's Prussian army of 28,000 defeated an Austrian army of the same size; the Prussians suffered almost 7,000 casualties, the Austrians 3,000, with more than 3,000 Austrians captured. Prussia left the war with the Austrian-Prussian Treaty of Breslau, which gave Silesia to Prussia (June 11).

Russo-Swedish War: Russian forces attacked Finland, trapping the Swedish army at Helsinki; the Swedes surrendered their entire force of 17,000, effectively ending the war. The peace settlement gave Russia more of Finland (1743).

b. Gebhard Leberecht von Blücher (d. 1819), Prussian field marshal.

b. Jean Mathieu Philibert Sérurier (d. 1819), French marshal of the empire.

1743

War of the Austrian Succession: Austrian forces invaded Bavaria (Apr.), defeating French and Bavarian forces at Braunau (May 9) and forcing their retreat to the Rhine. The French and Bavarians also retreated from Bohemia, losing Prague to Austria. A 40,000-strong allied army led by George II of England fought to a draw against a 30,000-strong French army at Dettingen (June 27).

b. Jacques Antoine Hippolyte, count of Guibert (d. 1790), French army officer and military theorist.

Turkey again invaded Persia, whose people were increasingly restive under Nadir Shah.

In West Africa, war continued between the kingdoms of Oyo and Dahomey.

Central, South and East Asia, and the Pacific	The Americas	
		1740
Successful Mon insurrection in Lower Burma (1740-1752) established an independent Mon state.	War of Jenkins's Ear: English forces took Chagres but made a failed attack on Cartagena. Colonial settlers under James Oglethorpe took two Spanish forts on the San Juan River but were driven back at St. Augustine. Yaqui rising in Sonora was defeated by Spanish-Mexican colonial forces (1740-1741). b. John Sullivan (d. 1795), American general.	
		1741
Vitus Bering, a Danish explorer in Russian service, discovered the Bering Strait.	War of Jenkins's Ear: English forces made a failed attack on Cuba. b. Benedict Arnold (d. 1801), American and British general.	
		1742
	War of Jenkins's Ear: English forces fought off a Spanish attack on St. Simons Island, off Georgia, in the Battle of the Bloody Swamp. b. Joseph Brant (Thayendanegea) (d. 1807), Mohawk chief. b. Nathanael Greene (d. 1786), American general.	
		1743
On Java, a Chinese insurrection was defeated by the Dutch (1740-1743), who then massacred thousands of Chinese. The Dutch then took the Javanese northern coast and the rest of Madura, also defeating a Madura independence rising (1743-1744).	War of Jenkins's Ear: Colonial forces led by James Oglethorpe failed in a second attack on St. Augustine.	

1744

War of the Austrian Succession: Off Toulon, British and French-Spanish war fleets fought to a draw, with the latter losing one battleship (Feb. 11).

War of the Austrian Succession: Prussia reentered the war, in alliance with France; Frederick the Great led an army of 80,000 into Bohemia, taking Prague (Sept. 6); faced with far larger Austrian and allied forces, the Prussians withdrew into Silesia.

War of the Austrian Succession: In Italy Sardinian forces led by Charles Emmanuel I failed to relieve besieged Cuneo, suffering a major defeat at Madonna del Olmon (Sept. 30).

d. Ludwig Andreas von Khevenhüller, count of Aichelberg and Frankenburg (b. 1683), Austrian field marshal who wrote several military textbooks.

1745

War of the Austrian Succession: Austrian forces invaded Bavaria, decisively defeated the Bavarians at Amberg (Jan. 7), and went on to take most of Bavaria, forcing Bavaria out of the war (Jan.-Mar.).

War of the Austrian Succession: Attacking allied forces of 50,000 coming to relieve besieged Tournai were defeated by a slightly larger French army at Fontenoy, in Flanders (May 10); the allies suffered huge losses when massed infantry were ordered to attack entrenched French positions across an open field. Allied losses were considerably larger than the 7,500 reported; the French reportedly suffered 7,200 casualties. After Fontenoy, the French took Tournai and much of the rest of Flanders and the northern Netherlands.

War of the Austrian Succession: At Hohenfriedberg (June 4), Frederick the Great's Prussian army quickly and decisively defeated an Austrian-Saxon army of 70,000, which lost more than 15,000, 3,000 of them dead; Prussian losses were fewer than 1,000.

War of the Austrian Succession: At Sohr (Sept. 30), Frederick's army, now numbering 18,000 and retreating into Silesia before larger allied forces, defeated an allied army of 39,000. In a series of battles during the months that followed, the Prussians scored several major victories, the last at Kesselsdorf (Dec. 14), which cost Austria more than 10,000 casualties and prisoners taken. The Treaty of Dresden essentially preserved the status quo prior to Prussia's reentry into the war.

Prince Charles Edward Stuart ("Bonnie Prince Charlie" or the "Young Pretender") returned from exile to lead a Jacobite insurrection in Scotland called "The Forty-Five" (1745-1746). His small Highland army of approximately 2,000 took Edinburgh (Sept. 17) and defeated a slightly larger British force at Prestonpan (Sept. 20). His forces, now 5,000 strong, then invaded northern England but did not pick up mass support or French assistance; they retreated to Scotland (Dec.), besieging Stirling.

b. Mikhail Ilarionovich Golenischev Kutuzov, prince of Smolensk (d. 1813), Russian field marshal.

Attacking Turkish forces were defeated by Nadir Shah's Persian army at Kars (Aug.); the Persians took Armenia.

1746

War of the Austrian Succession: In Italy Austrian and Sardinian forces defeated a French-Spanish army at Piacenza (June 16); the French and Spanish retreated to Genoa and then into southern France, fighting a strong holding action at Rottofredo (Aug. 12).

War of the Austrian Succession: French forces taking the Austrian Netherlands defeated allied forces at Raucoux, near Liège (Oct. 11); the French suffered 3,000 casualties and the allies 6,000.

In Mombasa, 'Ali ibn Uthman al-Mazrui led a successful rebellion against the Omanis, then also took Pemba; after his death later that year, the Omanis returned.

Central, South and East Asia, and the Pacific	The Americas
1744	
First Carnatic War (1744-1748), part of Europe's War of the Austrian Succession: Off Negapatam, on the southern Indian coast (July 25), a French fleet under Count Mahé de la Bourdonnais defeated British naval forces led by Commodore Edward Peyton. After British withdrawal, the French besieged and took the British base at Madras (Sept. 10).	King George's War (1744-1748), part of the War of the Austrian Succession: French forces unsuccessfully attacked Annapolis (formerly Port Royal), Nova Scotia.
1745	
	King George's War: British naval forces and a New England militia army of more than 4,000, under William Pepperell, besieged and took the French fortress of Louisbourg, on Cape Breton Island, Nova Scotia (May 30-June 16).
	b. Anthony Wayne (d. 1796), American general.
	b. John Barry (d. 1803), Irish-American naval officer.
1746	
French forces took the British base at Madras (Sept. 10), defeating the forces of Britain's ally Nawab Anwar-ud-din, of the Carnatic, at Madras (Sept. 21) and then again at St. Thomé (Nov.). French forces began a siege of British-held Fort St. George (Nov. 1746-Apr. 1748).	King George's War: French attack fleet was destroyed in a storm off Nova Scotia.
	b. Jean Jacques Dessalines (ca. 1746-1806), Haitian military and political leader.

Europe	Africa and Southwest Asia

1746 (cont.)

War of the Austrian Succession: Genoa successfully rose against Austrian occupation troops (Dec. 5-11); the city was quickly besieged by the Austrians.

Jacobite forces in Scotland were decisively defeated at Culloden Moor (Apr. 16) by English forces led by the duke of Cumberland; the Scottish army lost 1,000 dead, 1,000 taken prisoner, and many more casualties, of a total force of less than 5,000; the insurrection ended with the remaining army's dispersal. After the battle, the English instituted a reign of terror in Scotland. Charles Edward Stuart escaped to France.

b. Tadeusz (Thaddeus) Andrezj Bonawentura Kosciusko (d. 1817), Polish general.

1747

War of the Austrian Succession: Off Spain's Cape Finisterre (May 3), a British war fleet destroyed a French fleet escorting a Caribbean convoy, capturing all nine French battleships and several merchant ships, while suffering minor losses.

War of the Austrian Succession: French forces attacking Holland defeated allied forces at Lauffeld, near Maastricht (July 2).

War of the Austrian Succession: French forces relieved besieged Genoa (July).

War of the Austrian Succession: In a second naval engagement off Cape Finisterre (Oct. 14), the British captured six of nine French battleships, again with minor losses.

Turkey and Persia made peace, with Turkey returning territories taken over the previous two decades.

d. Nadir Kuli Beg (b. 1688), shah of Persia (r. 1736-1747) who was assassinated by his bodyguards; anarchy resulted in Persia.

1748

War of the Austrian Succession ended with the Treaty of Aix-la-Chapelle (Oct. 11), essentially restoring the prewar status quo.

b. Cuthbert Collingwood (d. 1810), British admiral.

1749

In West Africa, the kingdom of Oyo finally won its long war with Dahomey, thereafter receiving tribute from its former rival.

	1746 (cont.)

	1747

Afghan forces led by Ahmad Shah began a long series of raids into northern India, halted briefly at Sirkind.

Chinese forces campaigned along the Tibetan border (1747-1749).

Khiva reasserted its independence.

b. John Paul Jones (d. 1792), Scottish-born American naval officer.

b. Casimir (Kazimierz) Pulaski (d. 1779), Polish-born general serving America.

	1748

First Carnatic War: British forces withdrew from the failed siege of Pondicherry (Aug.-Oct.), on the southeastern Indian coast.

First Carnatic War: British-held Fort St. George, near Madras, was relieved by a British fleet after an 18-month French siege (Nov. 1746-Apr. 1748).

Under the European Treaty of Aix-la-Chapelle, Britain regained Madras.

War of the Austrian Succession: Off Havana, Cuba, a British Caribbean fleet sank one of seven Spanish battleships, with minor British losses, though it was an essentially drawn engagement (Oct. 12).

King George's War: Under Europe's Treaty of Aix-la-Chapelle, Louisbourg was returned to France in exchange for Madras, in India.

	1749

Javanese-Dutch War (1749-1757): Dutch occupation forces on Java, involved in another Mataram succession crisis, suffered early reverses, also facing an insurrection in western Java, but ultimately reasserted their control over the island.

Second Carnatic War (1749-1754): At Ambur, Marquis Charles de Bussy's French forces and their Indian allies defeated Nawab Anwar-ud-din, who died in the battle. The nawab's successor, Mohammed Ali, kept Trichinopoly, with British support.

Ahmad Shah's Afghan forces again campaigned against India.

Creole insurrection was put down in Venezuela.

Europe	Africa and Southwest Asia

1750

d. Hermann Maurice, count of Saxe (b. 1696), German-born general who was marshal of France; his notable victories included his nighttime capture of Prague (1741) and, during the War of the Austrian Succession, battles at Fontenoy, Tournai, Ostend, Brussels, Antwerp, Raucoux, and Lauffeld.

Karim Khan (r. 1750-1779) won control of Persia after the three-way succession struggle that followed the death of Nadir Shah.

Ali Bey emerged as the most powerful of the Mameluke contenders for the Egyptian throne, still nominally subject to the Ottoman Empire.

Tuaregs began a long series of invasions of West Africa (ca. 1750-ca. 1775), taking the central Niger Valley, centering on Timbuktu.

Leading a massive southward migration of the Bantu, the Xhosa reached the Keiskama River in southern Africa.

1751

1752

b. John Graves Simcoe (d. 1806), British general.

Under their new leader, Osei Kofo (r. 1752-1781), the Ashanti expanded at the expense of their neighbors.

1753

b. Louis Alexandre Berthier (d. 1815), marshal of France.

b. Lazare Nicolas Marguerite Carnot (d. 1823), French general.

b. Jean-Baptiste Kléber (d. 1800), French general.

Portugal retook Bissan, in what would be Portuguese Guinea.

Exiles from Bambara founded Kaarta, center of a new power in West Africa (ca. 1753).

1754

b. Bon Adrien Jeannot de Moncey, duke of Conegliano (d. 1842), French general.

b. Banastre Tarleton (d. 1833), British general.

b. Francis Rawdon-Hastings, earl of Moira (d. 1826), Irish-born British general.

Central, South and East Asia, and the Pacific	The Americas	
		1750
Chinese central government forces defeated an insurrection in Tibet.	b. Henry Knox (d. 1806), American general.	
		1751
In India's Carnatic, small English forces led by Robert Clive besieged and took Arcot, then successfully resisted a siege mounted by a substantial Indian army (Sept.-Nov.). Chinese forces took Lhasa, in Tibet.	François Macandel led a major slave insurrection on Haiti, building a guerrilla insurrection from mountain bases (1751-1758). b. Henry Dearborn (d. 1829), American general.	
		1752
Mon forces took Ava, ending Burma's Toungoo dynasty; the Mon capital was reestablished at Pegu. Burmese forces led by Alaungpaya began their campaign to regain Burma (1752-1757).	b. George Rogers Clark (d. 1818), American general. b. Walter Butler (ca. 1752-1781), colonial Loyalist military leader.	
		1753
In Burma, the British founded a post at Negrais. After its revolt effectively ended the Mogul dynasty, Maratha invaded the Punjab.		
		1754
Alaungpaya's forces retook most of Lower Burma from the Mons (1754-1755).	French and Indian War (1754-1763), which became part of the Seven Years' War (1756-1763): British colonial forces, led by Colonel George Washington, built Fort Necessity (Feb.-June), near France's Fort Duquesne (Pittsburgh). After a brief battle, Washington surrendered the fort to the French (July 3). War of the Seven Reductions (1754-1756): Spanish and Portuguese forces attacked the Jesuit missions (called reductions) in Guarani Indian territory in Paraguay; their second expedition destroyed all the missions, with thousands of Guarani casualties.	

Europe	Africa and Southwest Asia

1755

b. Francis Joseph Lefebvre, duke of Danzig (d. 1820), French marshal of the empire.

b. Gerhard Johann David von Scharnhorst (d. 1813), Prussian general.

d. Edward Braddock (b. 1695), British general.

West Africa's kingdom of Segu endured civil war (1755-1766) after the death of King Mamari Kulibali.

1756

In the run-up to the Seven Years' War, the French sent an expedition to British-held Minorca (Apr. 12), besieging the capital, Port Mahon. Off Minorca (May 20), a French battle fleet defeated a British fleet attempting to relieve besieged Port Mahon; Minorca fell (May 28).

Seven Years' War (1756-1763): In Europe a war by Austria, France, Russia, Sweden, and Saxony against Prussia and England (declared May 17); also a worldwide colonial war, merging with the French and Indian War in North America and the rest of the worldwide English-French contest. The war began in Europe with an attack by Frederick the Great's Prussian forces on Saxony (Aug. 29). The Prussians occupied Dresden, penned in the retreating Saxon forces on the Elbe River, and defeated an Austrian relief army at Lobositz; Saxony surrendered.

d. Ali Pasha (?-1756), bey of Tunis (r. 1710-1756) who killed and overthrew his predecessor and uncle, Hussein ben Ali.

1757

Seven Years' War: Frederick the Great's forces invaded Bohemia (Apr.); defeated an Austrian army before Prague (May 6), with casualties close to 14,000 for each side; and besieged the city.

Seven Years' War: At Kolin (June 18), Frederick's army of 34,000 was defeated, with more than 8,000 casualties and more than 5,000 prisoners taken, after attacking a 60,000-strong Austrian relief army, which had more than 8,000 casualties. Frederick lifted the siege of Prague and retreated into Germany, while allied forces totaling more than 400,000 began the attack on Prussia and Hanover.

Seven Years' War: At Hastenbeck (July 26), the duke of Cumberland's forces were defeated by the French and forced out of Hanover.

Seven Years' War: At Rossbach (Nov. 5), Frederick's army of 21,000 decisively defeated a French army twice its size, losing fewer than 600 to French casualties of 3,000 and 5,000 prisoners taken.

Seven Years' War: At Leuthen, near Breslau (Dec. 6), Frederick's army of 36,000 sharply defeated an Austrian army of 65,000, with Prussian casualties of more than 6,000 to Austrian casualties of 10,000 and 12,000 prisoners taken. Breslau then surrendered, with 17,000 more Austrians captured.

b. Marie Joseph Paul Yves Roch Gilbert du Motier, Marquis de Lafayette (La Fayette) (d. 1834), French general who also served in America.

b. Pierre François Charles Augereau, duke of Castiglione (d. 1816), French marshal of the empire.

Seven Years' War: British forces attacked and took French bases in Senegal.

In Morocco a period of turbulence ended when Sidi Mohammed (Mohammed XVI) came to the throne (r. 1757-1790).

Central, South and East Asia, and the Pacific	The Americas

1755

Chinese forces put down a revolt by Mongols in the Ili River valley (1755-1757).	French and Indian War: English colonial forces took forts St. John and Beausejour, then the whole coast of the Bay of Fundy (June); French settlers were exiled from Acadia (Nova Scotia), many going to Louisiana, a tale told poignantly in Longfellow's *Evangeline*.
	French and Indian War: A French and Indian force of 900 attacked and decisively defeated a British army of almost 2,000, led by General Edward Braddock (b. 1695), on the Monongahela River, near Fort Duquesne (July 9); Braddock and almost 1,000 of the British and colonials were killed.
	French and Indian War: At Lake George (New York), British colonial forces more than 3,000 strong defeated French forces numbering 2,000 (Sept. 8) but did not pursue them.

1756

Seven Years' War: Bengali forces under Nawab Suraja Dowla took British-held Calcutta (June); reportedly, more than 100 British prisoners died subsequently in a dungeon called the Black Hole of Calcutta.	French and Indian War: Reinforced French forces led by Louis Montcalm went over to the offensive, taking Oswego (New York), on Lake Ontario.
Alaungpaya's Burmese forces besieged and took the Mon stronghold of Syriam (1756-1757), allied with France.	b. Henry Lee (d. 1818), American officer.

1757

Seven Years' War: British forces under Robert Clive and Admiral Charles Watson took Calcutta (Jan. 2), rescuing survivors of the "Black Hole." Clive's British and Indian troops took Chandernagore (Mar. 23) and then at Plassey (June 23) defeated a much larger French-assisted Bengali army under Nawab Suraja Dowla, who was assassinated shortly after.	French and Indian War: Louis Montcalm's French forces took besieged Fort William Henry, on Lake George (Aug. 9); the English and their Indian allies, who had surrendered and were being allowed to retreat, were attacked by France's Indian allies, and many were killed; this is the background of James Fennimore Cooper's novel *The Last of the Mohicans*.
Afghan forces led by Ahmad Shah took Delhi.	French and Indian War: British expedition against France's fort at Louisbourg was abandoned after Britain's blockading force was blown apart during a storm.
Burmese forces under Alaungpaya completed their long drive to retake Burma from Mon occupying forces, besieging and taking the Mon capital of Pegu (1756-1757), effectively unifying Burma.	b. James Wilkinson (d. 1825), American general.

1758

Seven Years' War: At Zorndorf (Aug. 25), Prussian and Russian armies fought to a draw with huge losses on both sides. Of 36,000 Prussians, there were more than 11,000 casualties; of 44,000 Russians, there were more than 21,000 casualties.

Seven Years' War: At Hochkirch, in Saxony (Oct. 14), the Prussians were defeated by the allies, again suffering enormous losses: of 39,000 Prussians, more than 9,000 were casualties, with allied casualties totaling more than 7,500 of 80,000 engaged.

b. Horatio Nelson (d. 1805), British admiral.

b. André Masséna, duke of Rivoli and prince of Essling (d. 1817), French marshal of the empire.

1759

Seven Years' War: At Minden (Aug. 1), a German-British army of 43,000 suffered almost 3,000 casualties while defeating a French army of 60,000 that had more than 7,000 casualties.

Seven Years' War: At Kunersdorf, near Frankfurt (Aug. 12), Frederick the Great suffered his greatest loss, with his attacking army of 50,000 having more than 17,000 casualties and more than 1,000 captured; the allied army of 98,000 had almost 16,000 casualties.

Seven Years' War: Admiral Edward Hawke's British fleet, with negligible casualties, defeated the French fleet under Admiral Hubert de Conflans off Lagos, Portugal (Aug. 18); 2 French battleships were sunk and 3 captured. The rest fled to Quiberon Bay, Brittany, where the British decisively defeated them (Nov. 20), sinking or capturing 7 of 21 French battleships.

b. Johann David Ludwig Yorck von Wartenburg (d. 1830), Prussian field marshal.

d. James Wolfe (b. 1727), British general who led the daring assault up the cliffs below Quebec to the Plains of Abraham, there defeating the French under Louis Montcalm; he was killed during the battle.

d. Louis-Joseph de Montcalm-Gozon, marquis of Montcalm (b. 1712), French general who lost on the Plains of Abraham, in Quebec, where he was wounded and shortly died.

1760

Seven Years' War: At Leignitz (Aug. 15), Frederick the Great's Prussian army lost more than 3,000 to the Austrians, who lost more than 8,000; Frederick retreated before much larger allied forces.

Seven Years' War: At Torgau, near the Elbe River, the Prussians and Austrians fought essentially to a draw (Nov. 3); the Prussians suffered more than 13,000 casualties and 4,000 captured of an army of nearly 49,000; the allies had more than 4,000 casualties and 7,000 captured of an army of 52,000.

b. August Wilhelm Anton, Count Neithardt von Gneisenau (d. 1831), Prussian field marshal.

Migrating northward in southern Africa, the Boers crossed the Orange River.

Central, South and East Asia, and the Pacific	The Americas
	1758
Seven Years' War: French forces led by Thomas Lally besieged and took British Fort St. David, in southeastern India (Mar.-June).	French and Indian War: Seaborne British and colonial forces of 9,500 besieged the French fortress at Louisbourg, in Acadia (Nova Scotia) (June 2); the fort surrendered (July 27).
Seven Years' War: Off Fort St. David, in the Bay of Bengal (Apr. 29), British and French naval forces fought to a draw.	French and Indian War: British forces 12,000 strong besieged and failed to take Fort Ticonderoga by storm (July 8), then withdrew.
Seven Years' War: Off Negapatam (Aug. 3), British Indian Ocean naval forces defeated a French fleet.	French and Indian War: British and colonial forces moved west to attack Fort Duquesne (Pittsburgh); the French abandoned and demolished the fort (Nov.).
Seven Years' War: Lally's French forces besieged British-held Madras (Dec.).	French and Indian War: British colonial forces took Fort Frontenac (Kingston), on Lake Ontario.
Manchus continued to expand into Central Asia, taking Kashgar and the entire Tarim Basin (1758-1759) and establishing the province of Sinkiang.	Haitian rebel François Macandel was captured and executed; low-level guerrilla war continued and merged with the continuing Maroon insurrection.
Alaungpaya's Burmese army raided into Manipur.	
	1759
Seven Years' War: British seaborne forces under Francis Forde defeated the French in the naval battle of Masulipatam (Jan. 25), after which Lally lifted the siege of Madras (Feb.).	French and Indian War: British and colonial forces under General John Prideaux retook Oswego and took Fort Niagara (July 25), where Prideaux was killed.
Seven Years' War: Off Pondicherry (Sept. 10), the British and French Indian Ocean fleets again fought to a draw.	French and Indian War: A British and colonial force of 11,000, led by Jeffrey Amherst, took Ticonderoga and Crown Point (July).
Seven Years' War: British naval forces defeated a Dutch fleet, taking the Dutch port of Chinsura.	French and Indian War: British forces 9,000 strong, led by General James Wolfe, besieged Quebec (June 25); the fortress on the St. Lawrence River was defended by a garrison of 14,000, commanded by Louis Montcalm. Making a daring night assault up the cliffs to the Plains of Abraham, British regulars won the decisive battle for North America (Sept. 13); they withstood a single French volley, stopped the French militia with two volleys, and routed the French with an infantry charge. Both leaders died.
Alaungpaya's Burmese forces took Negrais, killing most of the English and Mon inhabitants of the post.	
	Seven Years' War: English West Indian forces took Guadeloupe (Apr.).
	1760
d. Alaungpaya (Alompra; Maung Aung Zeya) (b. 1714), Burmese monarch and general who gave himself the name Alaungpaya (Embryo Buddha). He died of wounds received during an unsuccessful invasion of Siam and siege of its capital, Ayuthia.	French and Indian War: French forces failed in their siege of Quebec (Apr.). British troops took Montreal in a three-pronged attack; the city surrendered (Sept. 8), ending French rule in Canada.
Seven Years' War: After defeating the French at Wandiwash (Jan. 22), the British besieged Pondicherry (Aug.).	Seven Years' War: English West Indian forces took Dominica.
	British forces defeated a slave rebellion on Jamaica, led by Tacky, who was ultimately killed, as were several hundred former slaves; fewer than 100 British colonists and soldiers died.
	Cherokee-British War (1760-1761): After the murder of 25 Cherokee hostages by the British (Feb.), a Carolina frontier war developed.

Europe	Africa and Southwest Asia

1761

Spanish forces attacked Portugal, taking Bragança and Almeida before being defeated by Portuguese and British forces (1761-1762).

b. Henry Shrapnel (d. 1842), British general.

b. Charles Pichegru (d. 1804), French general.

1762

Seven Years' War: Russia left the war with the Treaty of St. Petersburg, ending the conflict between Russia and Prussia (May 15); Sweden left the war with the Treaty of Hamburg (May 22).

b. Karageorge (George Petrovich; Djordje Petrovic) (d. 1817), Serbian general and independence leader.

b. Prince Jozef Antoni Poniatowski (d. 1813), Vienna-born Polish general and French marshal of the empire.

b. Jean-Baptiste Jourdan (d. 1833), French marshal of the empire.

d. George, Lord Anson (b. 1697), British admiral who commanded at Cape Finisterre (1747); he became first lord of the admiralty (1751-1756; 1757-1762) and is called the "Father of the British Navy."

1763

Seven Years' War: Austria and Prussia ended the war in Europe with the Treaty of Hubertusburg (Feb. 16), restoring the prewar status quo.

Seven Years' War: Treaty of Paris ended the colonial portion of the conflict, with Britain and Spain largely dividing North America between them. Britain became the dominant European power in India.

b. Frederick Augustus, duke of York and Albany (d. 1827), British field marshal.

b. Pierre Charles Jean Baptiste Silvestre de Villeneuve (d. 1806), French admiral.

b. Charles XIV (Jean Baptiste Jules Bernadotte) (d. 1844), king of Sweden and Norway (r. 1818-1844), previously marshal of France.

b. Guillaume Marie Anne Brune (d. 1815), French marshal of the empire.

b. (Jean) Victor (Marie) Moreau (d. 1813), French general.

Africa and Southwest Asia:

Seven Years' War: Under the Treaty of Paris, France regained Goree, but Britain retained other formerly French bases in Senegal.

1764

b. Laurent Gouvion Saint-Cyr (d. 1830), French marshal of the empire

b. William Sidney Smith (d. 1840), British admiral.

b. Claude, duke of Victor-Perrin (d. 1841), French marshal of the empire.

Africa and Southwest Asia:

Osei Kwadwo came to the Ashanti throne (r. 1764-1777).

1765

b. Jacques Étienne Joseph Alexandre Macdonald, duke of Taranto (d. 1840), French marshal of the empire.

b. Jean Baptiste Drouet d'Erlon (d. 1844), marshal of France.

b. Peter Ivanovich Bagration (d. 1812), Russian prince and general.

Africa and Southwest Asia:

ships attacked Larache and Salé, ...ting to halt the depredations of Bar-...irates based in North Africa.

Central, South and East Asia, and the Pacific	The Americas	
		1761
Seven Years' War: Besieged Pondicherry fell British (Jan. 15). At Panipat (Jan. 14), Ahmad Shah's Afghan a[...] 50,000 decisively defeated a Maratha army num[...] 70,000, reportedly with 20,000 Maratha casualti[...]	Cherokee-British War: British and colonial forces numbering almost 3,000 invaded Cherokee territory; the defeated Cherokees negotiated peace after at least 15 of their towns and villages were burned.	
		1762
Seven Years' War: British naval forces took Manila (Oct. 5).	Seven Years' War: British West Indian forces under Admiral George Rodney took Martinique (Feb. 12) and several smaller islands. Seven Years' War: British forces took besieged Morro Castle, at Havana, Cuba (July 30); the city then surrendered. Spanish-Portuguese War, part of the Seven Years' War: Spanish forces again took Colonia from the Portuguese but did not hold it.	
		1763
Bengali troops mutinied against the British at Patna (June 25), taking the city. British Indian forces attacked and defeated Bengali forces (early Sept.), retaking Patna (Nov.) and killing 2,000 of its 6,000 defenders. Under Europe's Treaty of Paris, France regained Pondicherry, but its French East India Company (Compagnie des Indes) was disbanded. Britain now became the dominant colonial power in India.	Pontiac's War: Ottawa chief Pontiac led an Indian coalition against the British in the Old Northwest (May-Oct.), destroying 9 of 11 British frontier forts; only the sieges of Fort Detroit and Fort Pitt failed. Reinforced British forces defeated the coalition in a series of small engagements. Under Europe's Treaty of Paris, ending the Seven Years' War, Britain took from France all of Canada and everything east of the Mississippi River except New Orleans, as well as the Lesser Antilles (except St. Lucia). Spain took New Orleans and western Louisiana and regained Havana, ceding to Britain Florida and all other Spanish North American territories. In the West Indies, France retained Martinique and Guadeloupe.	
		1764
Burmese forces under Alaungpaya's son Ksinbyushin attacked and took Manipur. General Maha Nawraha led a Burmese invasion of Siam (1764-1767), quickly taking much of the Malay Peninsula before being stalled at P'etchaburi by Siamese troops under P'ya Taksin, who then claimed the Siamese throne.	b. José Gervasio Artigas (d. 1850), Uruguayan general.	
		1765
Burmese-Chinese border war escalated into a massive Chinese invasion of Burma (1765-1769). Chinese forces took much of eastern Burma, but the Burmese mounted an effective guerrilla war against them.		

Europe	Africa and Southwest Asia

1765 (cont.)

d. William Augustus, duke of Cumberland (b. 1721), British general who crushed supporters of Prince Charles Edward Stuart ("Bonnie Prince Charlie") at Culloden Moor (1746), effectively ending the Jacobite rebellion; he was called the "Butcher Cumberland" or "Bloody Butcher" for his punishment of Jacobite sympathizers and repression of the Scottish Highlands clan system.

1766

b. Emmanuel, marquis of Grouchy (d. 1847), French marshal of the empire.

b. Robert Ross (d. 1814), British general.

d. Thomas Arthur, Count de Lally (b. 1702), French general who led the unsuccessful defense of besieged Pondicherry (1760-1761); the French tried and executed him for that failure.

Ali Bey was temporarily driven from Egypt but quickly returned.

Ngolo Diara became king of Segu, ending the civil war.

1767

b. Joachim Murat (d. 1815), French marshal and grand admiral of the empire.

b. Nicolas Charles Oudinot (d. 1847), French marshal of the empire.

Morocco signed a treaty acknowledging France's special status and agreeing to help halt pirate attacks on French ships.

1768

Russo-Turkish War (1768-1774): Russian forces attacked Georgia and the Balkans. A Russian army led by Peter Rumiantsev defeated the Turks on the Dniester River (Sept. 9), then took most of Wallachia and Moldavia, occupying Bucharest.

French army numbering 30,000 defeated Corsican independence forces (1768-1769) for Genoa, which then sold the island to France.

Rising of the Confederation of the Bar began in Poland (1768-1776).

b. Édouard Adolphe Casimir Joseph Mortier (d. 1835), French marshal of the empire.

b. Henry William Paget (d. 1854), English field marshal.

b. Jean-Baptiste Bessières (d. 1813), marshal of France.

b. Louis Lazare Hoche (d. 1797), French general.

b. William Carr Beresford (d. 1854), British general.

In Ethiopia, Mikael Sehul came to power in Tigre province, rebelling against King Iyasu II, whom he deposed and killed (1768-1769).

1769

French forces decisively defeated Corsican rebels at Ponte-Nuovo (May).

b. Napoleon I (Napoleon Bonaparte; Napoléone di Buoneparte) (d. 1821), French general and emperor.

b. Arthur Wellesley, duke of Wellington (d. 1852), British field marshal.

b. Nicolas Jean de Dieu Soult, duke of Dalmatia (d. 1851), marshal general of France.

Russo-Turkish War: Egyptian governor Ali Bey, in alliance with Russia, led an insurrection against the Turks (1769-1773); his forces took Cairo and moved east, taking much of Arabia, especially the Red Sea coast (1769-1770).

b. Mohammed Ali (d. 1849), Mameluke ruler of Egypt.

Central, South and East Asia, and the Pacific	The Americas	
1765 (cont.)		
1766		
First British-Mysore War (1766-1769): Haidar Ali of Mysore opposed British East India Company troops.		
1767		
First British-Mysore War: At Trincomalee, British forces defeated Mysore and Hyderabad armies led by Haidar Ali of Mysore (Sept. 24), with reported Mysore casualties of more than 4,000 and negligible British losses. Burmese forces defeated Siam, taking and destroying the capital, Ayuthia.	b. Andrew Jackson (d. 1845), American general and seventh president of the United States (1829-1837). b. Black Hawk (Ma-ka-tai-me-she-kia-kiak) (d. 1838), Sauk and Fox war chief.	
1768		
While Burma was occupied fighting the Chinese, Siamese forces retook much of central Siam (1767-1768).	b. Tecumseh (ca. 1768-1813), Shawnee chief.	
1769		
First British-Mysore War: War ended without British territorial gains. Unsuccessful Chinese invasion forces withdrew from Burma, having suffered heavy losses. Siam's P'ya Taksin failed in his bid to retake Chiengmai from the Burmese occupiers but remained on the Siamese throne.	d. Pontiac (b. ca. 1720), Ottawa chief who was a longtime French ally and the key figure in Pontiac's War (1763).	

1769 (cont.)

b. Jean Lannes, duke of Montebello and prince of Sievers (d. 1809), French marshal of the empire.

b. Michel Ney (d. 1815), marshal of France.

1770

Russo-Turkish War: Greek independence forces, aided by a Russian fleet, mounted an insurrection against the Turks in the Peloponnesus. Turkish forces defeated the Greeks and Russians (June).

Russo-Turkish War: At Chesme, near Chios in the Aegean (July 6), a Russian war fleet decisively defeated a Turkish fleet, sinking 12 battleships of 16 engaged, 11 of them with fire ships while the Turks were at anchor after the main direct battle had been completed.

Russo-Turkish War: At Karkal, in Moldavia (Aug.), Peter Rumiantsev's army decisively defeated a Turkish and Tartar army.

b. Dominique Joseph René Vandamme (d. 1830), French general.

b. Louis Gabriel Suchet (d. 1826), French marshal of the empire.

b. Louis Nicolas Davout, duke of Auerstädt and prince of Eckmühl (d. 1823), French marshal of the empire.

Abiodun assumed the throne of Oyo (r. ca. 1770-1789), ending civil strife.

Migrating northward in southern Africa, the Boers reached the area of Graaff-Reinet.

b. Dingiswayo (Godongwana) (ca. 1770-1818), Mtetwa (Bantu) chief.

1771

Russo-Turkish War: Russian forces took Crimea, later formally annexing it (1783).

b. Charles Louis John, archduke of Austria and duke of Teschen (Cieszyn) (d. 1847), Austrian field marshal.

b. Jean Andoche Junot, duke of Abrantes (d. 1813), French general.

b. Karl Philip, prince of Schwarzenberg (d. 1820), Austrian field marshal.

b. Hermann von Boyen (d. 1848), German field marshal.

Russo-Turkish War: With Russian support, Egyptian forces commanded by general Abu'l Dhahab attacked Syria, taking Damascus.

Ethiopian leader Mikael Sehul was defeated at the Battle of Sarbakussa but retained power; the conflict was observed and described by Scottish traveler James Bruce.

1772

Russia, Prussia, and Austria agreed on the first partition of Poland.

b. George Cockburn (d. 1853), British admiral.

b. Rowland Hill (d. 1842), British general.

d. Robert Clive, Baron Clive (b. 1725), British general and colonial administrator who, during the Bengal War, rescued prisoners from Calcutta's "Black Hole" and defeated the Bengals at Plassey (both 1757).

Russo-Turkish War: Egyptian general Abu'l Dhahab changed sides, attacking and taking Egypt for the Turks, while Egyptian leader Ali Bey fled (Apr. 8) to Acre, where he was resupplied by the Russians.

1773

Cossacks, Bashkirs, and other Central Asians led by Cossack Emelyan Pugachev mounted a major rising in southern Russia (1773-1774) but were repeatedly defeated by smaller Russian forces.

Russo-Turkish War: Ali Bey took Palestine and headed back toward Egypt; he was defeated and taken at Salihia, on the Sinai Peninsula (Apr.), dying later in the year.

Central, South and East Asia, and the Pacific	The Americas	
		1769 (cont.)
		1770
Burmese forces again attacked Manipur. Siamese forces invaded Cambodia (1770-1773).	Boston Massacre (Mar. 5): Five Americans, one of them African-American freedman Crispus Attucks, were killed when British troops fired on demonstrators at the Boston Customs House; part of the run-up to the American Revolution. b. William Clark (d. 1838), American army officer and explorer.	
		1771
Maratha and Mysore fought, without a decisive result. British forces founded a base at Penang, in Malaya.	Prefiguring the war to come, British forces of 1,000, with cannon, defeated a 2,000-strong, lightly armed American militia, the Regulators, at Alemance, North Carolina, with 200 American and fewer than 100 British casualties (May 16). Several Americans were later executed by the British, while many fled west, returning to fight in the American Revolution. Britain and Spain came near to war over their rival claims to the Falkland Islands.	
		1772
d. Ahmad Shah Durani (Ahmad Khan Durr'ani) (b. ca. 1722), Afghan chief and general who won at Panipat (1761).		
		1773
Siamese forces secured control of Cambodia. Vietnam was torn by civil war between the Trinh and Tay Son families.	Boston Tea Party (Dec. 16): Responding to the British Tea Act, Americans defiantly dumped British tea into Boston harbor, as the run-up to the American Revolution accelerated. b. William Henry Harrison (d. 1841), American soldier and ninth president of the United States (1841).	

Europe	Africa and Southwest Asia

1774

Russo-Turkish War: At Kozludzha (June), Russian forces defeated a major Turkish army; under the Treaty of Kuchuk Kainarji, the Turks ceded much strategic territory in Crimea and the Caucasus Mountains to the Russians, who also gained full access to the Black Sea.

Cossack rebel leader Emelyan Pugachev was taken (Aug.) and executed, ending the rising he had led.

b. Auguste Frederic Louis Viesse de Marmont, duke of Ragusa (d. 1852), French marshal of the empire.

1775

b. Antoine Charles Louis Lasalle (d. 1809), French general.

b. Thomas Cochrane, 10th earl of Dundonald (d. 1860), British admiral.

Still pressing north, the Boers fought with and enslaved or killed many black inhabitants of southern Africa, especially the Khoisa and the San (from ca. 1775).

Succession struggles flamed into civil war in Benin (ca. 1775).

1776

Rising by Polish nobles (Confederation of the Bar) under French command was defeated by Russian forces.

Muslim clerics created the Tukulor theocracy in Fouta-Toro, in north Senegal.

Central, South and East Asia, and the Pacific	The Americas	
1774		
British East India Company troops joined with their ally Shuju-ud-Dowla, the wazir of Oudh, to suppress a revolt of the Rohilla Afghans.	Lord Dunmore's War: Virginia governor John Murray, earl of Dunmore, sent colonial militia 2,000 to 3,000 strong against Indian coalition forces under Shawnee chief Cornstalk in Virginia and Kentucky. The Battle of Point Pleasant (Oct. 10) was the only substantial engagement of the war, which was given up by Cornstalk's greatly outnumbered forces. American militia units formed throughout the colonies as the Continental Congress met in Philadelphia (Sept.-Oct.); war was near. b. Meriwether Lewis (d. 1809), American army officer and explorer.	
1775		
Siamese forces under P'ya Taksin retook Chiengmai from Burma, unifying Siam.	American Revolution (1775-1783): British forces out of Boston moved on Lexington and Concord (Apr. 19); warned by Paul Revere and others, American militia met them; firefights ensued, and the British retreated to Boston, harassed by thousands of riflemen. American Revolution: An American force of 16,000 under Artemas Ward besieged Boston, fighting the first substantial engagement of the war, the Battle of Bunker Hill, actually fought at nearby Breed's Hill (June 17). American Revolution: Second Continental Congress at Philadelphia named George Washington head of the Continental Army (June 15); he took full command in Boston (July 3). American Revolution: Ethan Allen and his Green Mountain Boys took Ticonderoga (May 10); American forces under Benedict Arnold also took Crown Point (May 12), using the forts as bases for an attack on Canada (Aug.); Americans later took St. John (Nov. 2) and Montreal (Nov. 13), then made a failed attack on Quebec (Dec. 31). Frontiersman Daniel Boone led settlers through the Cumberland Gap in the Appalachian Mountains, founding the first permanent American settlements in Kentucky and beginning generations of bitter conflict with the Indians.	
1776		
Tay Son forces took Saigon. Siamese forces fought off Burmese attempts to retake Chiengmai.	American Revolution: British forces led by General William Howe evacuated besieged Boston by sea to Halifax, Nova Scotia (Mar. 17). American Revolution: Confronted by General John Burgoyne's newly arrived, 8,000-strong British army, American forces retreated from Canada (June). American Revolution: On July 4, 1776, at Independence Hall, Philadelphia, the American Declaration of Independence was proclaimed; with the French Declaration of the Rights of Man (1791), it became the ideological basis for successive waves of democratic revolutions throughout the world in the centuries that followed. American Revolution: Howe's British army of 32,000 landed on Staten Island (July 1), defeating the Americans on Long Island (Aug. 27) and driving them back toward Brooklyn Heights; George	

Europe	Africa and Southwest Asia

1776 (cont.)

1777

b. Alexander I (Aleksandr Pavlovich) (d. 1825), Russian czar (r. 1801-1825).	Sidi Mohammed (Mohammed XVI) ended slavery in Morocco.

1778

b. Edward Michael Pakenham (d. 1815), British general.	With the opening of British-French hostilities in the American Revolution, French forces took back their bases in Senegal from the British (1778-1779).

Central, South and East Asia, and the Pacific	The Americas	
	1776 (cont.)	
	Washington withdrew his army from Long Island, retreating before the pursuing British and losing battles at Kip's Bay, Harlem Heights, and White Plains (Sept.-Oct.). Fort Washington and Fort Lee fell (Nov.). The American army retreated south through New Jersey into Pennsylvania, losing most of its rear guard of 4,000 at Morristown. At Trenton (Dec. 26), American morale lifted after a surprise night crossing of the Delaware River and the capture of more than 1,000 Hessians. Washington's army then evaded much larger British forces at Trenton (Jan. 2, 1777), defeated a British force at Princeton the next day, and escaped.	
	Spanish forces took Colonia and much other disputed territory in Brazil and the Banda Oriental (1776-1777), keeping Colonia and the Banda Oriental by the terms of the Treaty of San Ildefonso.	
	b. Bernardo O'Higgins (d. 1842), Chilean general.	
	1777	
	American Revolution: Pursuing a three-pronged plan to take northern New York and sever New England from the rest of the new nation, British forces numbering 9,400, led by General John Burgoyne, moved south out of Canada and took Fort Ticonderoga (July 5), while 2,000 British and Indian troops under Colonel Barry St. Leger and Iroquois leader Joseph Brant attacked east in the Mohawk Valley. General William Howe moved no farther north than Bear Mountain, and British forces in the Mohawk Valley retreated after suffering heavy losses at Oriskany (Aug. 6). At Saratoga, surrounded by more than 20,000 Americans and running out of supplies, Burgoyne's whole force surrendered (Oct. 17) to American general Horatio Gates, providing the key American victory of the war.	
	American Revolution: In the mid-Atlantic region, William Howe led a seaborne landing of 18,000 at Chesapeake Bay, defeating George Washington's army on Brandywine Creek, with 1,000 American casualties (Sept. 11), then occupying Philadelphia. The British defeated the Americans again at Germantown, with more than 1,000 American casualties and prisoners taken (Oct. 4). The Americans retreated to Valley Forge, where they wintered; Baron Friedrich Wilhelm von Steuben helped train the colonial forces.	
	d. Nicholas Herkimer (b. 1728), American general who commanded Revolutionary forces at Oriskany; he died after amputation of a wounded leg (Aug. 16).	
	1778	
British Indian forces took the French bases at Pondicherry and Mahé. Siamese forces took Vientiane and controlled all of Laos.	American Revolution: The Americans signed a treaty with France (Feb. 6); France and England were at war (June 17). American Revolution: British forces, now 13,000 strong and commanded by Henry Clinton, evacuated Philadelphia (June 18), moving north to New York, with George Washington's army, of equal size, in pursuit. The armies fought an inconclusive engagement at Monmouth; the British then completed their move to New York. American Revolution: Admiral Jean-Baptiste d'Estaing's French fleet briefly blockaded New York but was damaged in a storm before joining with American forces for an attack on Newport (Aug. 11).	

1778 (cont.)

1779

American Revolution: Spain declared war on England (June 21).

b. Hugh Gough (d. 1869), British general.

First "Kaffir" War (1779-1781): In southern Africa, especially in Graaff-Reinet and Swellendam, Boer settlers moving east and north attacked the southward-migrating Bantu peoples they met; *Kaffir* was the Boer word for "black Bantu."

General Agha Mohammed led a revolt against Karim Khan, throwing Persia into civil war (1779-1794).

1780

b. Karl Maria von Clausewitz (d. 1831), Prussian general and military theorist.

Central, South and East Asia, and the Pacific	The Americas	
	1778 (cont.)	
	American Revolution: American captain John Paul Jones made several raids on British shipping off Britain and Ireland. In Quiberon Bay, he received the first salute of the U.S. flag by French ships (Feb. 14, 1778).	
	American Revolution: On the northwestern frontier, British and Indian forces attacked American settlements; massacres occurred in many locations, as at Cherry Valley (Nov. 11) by Walter Butler's Tory irregulars and Joseph Brant's Iroquois. American forces also conducted massacres, primarily of Indians in western Pennsylvania and western New York.	
	American Revolution: In the South, British forces took Savannah (Dec. 29).	
	b. José de San Martin (d. 1850), Latin American general.	
	1779	
First British-Maratha War (1779-1782): British forces were defeated in the Deccan (Jan.).	American Revolution: In the West, Americans under George Rogers Clark took Vincennes (Indiana) (Feb. 25), which would later give Americans a claim to the region between the Appalachian Mountains and the Mississippi River.	
	American Revolution: British forces captured Stony Point (New York) (May 31), but Americans under General Anthony Wayne retook it (July 15-16), reestablishing American control of the Hudson River at West Point. Major Henry "Lighthorse Harry" Lee took Paulus Hook (Aug. 19).	
	American Revolution: American and French forces led by Admiral Jean-Baptiste d'Estaing and General Casimir Pulaski unsuccessfully besieged Savannah (Sept.-Oct.).	
	d. Casimir (Kazimierz) Pulaski (b. 1747), Polish-born general who created and led a mixed cavalry-infantry American force (Pulaski's Legion); he was killed in a cavalry charge at Savannah.	
	American Revolution: In the *Bonhomme Richard,* John Paul Jones defeated the *Serapis* off England (Sept. 23), proclaiming, when asked to surrender, "I have not yet begun to fight!"	
	American Revolution: Admiral d'Estaing's French fleet took St. Vincent and Grenada in the West Indies.	
	American Revolution: Spanish forces took British bases on the Mississippi River, including Manchac, Baton Rouge, and Natchez.	
	b. Stephen Decatur (d. 1820), American naval officer.	
	b. Zebulon Montgomery Pike (d. 1813), American explorer and general.	
	1780	
First British-Maratha War: British forces took Maratha's fortresses at Ahmadabad and Gwalior.	American Revolution: British forces under Henry Clinton besieged and took Charleston, which surrendered with its garrison of 5,400 (Feb. 11-May 12). Strong American guerrilla opposition continued.	
Second British-Mysore War (1780-1783), also part of the British-French Indian and North American wars: Haidar Ali's Mysore forces, allied with France, decisively defeated a British army, took the Carnatic, and threatened Madras.	American Revolution: Spanish forces took Mobile (Mar.).	
	American Revolution: General Jean Baptiste de Rochambeau's French army landed at Newport (July 10) but was blocked by the British.	

Europe	Africa and Southwest Asia

1780 (cont.)

1781

b. Eugène de Beauharnais (d. 1824), French general and adopted son of Napoleon Bonaparte.

Europe	Africa and Southwest Asia

Central, South and East Asia, and the Pacific

The Americas

American Revolution: At Camden (Aug. 16), British forces under General Charles Cornwallis routed American forces under Horatio Gates.

d. Johann Kalb (Baron de Kalb) (b. 1721), German-born general who was second-in-command to the Marquis de Lafayette; he was killed at Camden.

American Revolution: Capture of British major John André (Sept. 23) revealed Benedict Arnold's intention to defect to the British and surrender West Point; André was hanged; Arnold fled to the British.

American Revolution: Americans blockaded the British in New York while suppressing mutinies in their own ranks (1780-1781).

American Revolution: At Kings Mountain, an American force of 1,400 decisively defeated a British force of 1,100, composed of colonial Loyalists (Oct. 7).

Tupac Amarú led a massive Indian insurrection in Peru (Nov.), his forces ultimately numbering an estimated 100,000.

Second British-Mysore War: The British defeated Haidar Ali's Mysore forces at Porto Novo, near Madras (June), and again at Pollilur (Aug.) and Sholingarth (Sept.).

American Revolution: At Cowpens, South Carolina (Jan. 17), Banastre Tarleton's British force of 1,100 lost more than 900 killed or captured to an American force of 1,000 led by General Daniel Morgan.

American Revolution: Spanish forces took the British Fort St. Joseph, on Lake Michigan (Jan.), and Fort St. George, near Pensacola (Mar.).

American Revolution: At Guilford Courthouse, North Carolina (Mar. 15), attacking British troops numbering fewer than 2,000 defeated an American force twice as large; General Charles Cornwallis, with diminishing forces, then retreated north into Virginia; after inconclusive spring operations, he moved his force of 7,000 into Yorktown. There, in the decisive and concluding battle of the American Revolution, he was trapped and besieged by an American-French force of 15,000 (Sept. 18), led by generals George Washington, Jean Baptiste de Rochambeau, and the Marquis de Lafayette. Meanwhile, in the two Battles of the Capes, a French fleet under Admiral François J. P. de Grasse had twice defeated the British fleet in Chesapeake Bay (Mar. 16; Sept. 5-9); the British fleet then retired to New York, leaving Cornwallis trapped at Yorktown. Cornwallis surrendered the British army (Oct. 19), effectively ending the Revolution.

Tupac Amarú's Peruvian Indian forces were defeated at Cuzco (Jan. 8); he and his family were executed by the Spanish after their capture (Apr.). His brothers continued to lead the insurrection until it ended (1783).

b. John Drake Sloat (d. 1867), American admiral.

d. Walter Butler (b. ca. 1752), American colonial leader who commanded Tory irregulars (Butler's Legion) during the Revolution; with Joseph Brant, he carried out the Cherry Valley Massacre (1778); son of John Butler, he was killed during a Mohawk Valley raid.

1782

b. Charles James Napier (d. 1853), British general.

1783

Russia formally annexed the Crimea, previously taken from Turkey.

d. Eyre Coote (b. 1728), British general called "Coote Bahadur" ("Brave Heart") in India, where he took Pondicherry (1760-1761), later becoming commander in chief (1769).

Under the Treaty of Paris, England split the Senegalese posts with France, which kept St. Louis.

b. Abbas Mirza (d. 1833), Persian general.

1784

b. Thomas Robert Bugeaud de la Piconnerie, duke of Isly (d. 1849), marshal of France.

d. Edward, Baron Hawke (b. 1705), British admiral during the War of the Austrian Succession and Seven Years' War; he was commander of the Channel Fleet (from 1759), then first lord of the admiralty (1766-1771).

Mikael Sehul was decisively defeated, leaving Ethiopia in a state of virtual anarchy called the "time of princes."

1785

Failed Romanian insurrection in Transylvania.

d. George, Viscount Sackville Germain (Lord George Germain) (b. 1716), British general who led the cavalry at the Battle of Minden (1759) and was court-martialed for his failure to follow orders; later secretary of state for the Colonies (1775).

Ottoman forces suppressed a revolt in Egypt (1785-1786).

Muscat forces took the East African port of Kilwa.

1786

d. Frederick II (the Great) (b. 1712), Prussian ruler (r. 1740-1786) and battle commander during numerous wars, including the War of the Austrian Succession, the Seven Years' War, and the War of the Bavarian Succession.

d. Augustus, Viscount Keppel (b. 1725), British admiral who led the Channel Fleet at Ushant (1778), surviving a subsequent court-martial to become first lord of the admiralty (1782-1783; 1783).

d. Hans Joachim von Zieten (b. 1698), Prussian general who, during the Seven Years' War, led the army after Breslau (1757).

1782

d. P'ya Taksin (Phaya Sin or Tashin) (?-1782), Siamese general and ruler of Chinese-Thai descent; he was killed during a revolt against his presumed insanity and unpopular rule. He was succeeded by General Chakri, who became King Rama I (r. 1782-1809), founding the new capital of Bangkok.

Kamahameha's forces completed their conquest and unification of the island of Hawaii.

Second British-Mysore War: French naval forces, commanded by Admiral Pierre de Suffren, took Trincomalee from the British (Aug. 30), then resupplied Haidar Ali's Mysore forces.

First British-Maratha War: War ended with the prewar status quo intact.

Bodawpaya, Alaungpaya's youngest son, took the Burmese throne after civil war.

American Revolution: Off Dominica, in the Caribbean, in the Battle of the Saints (Apr. 12), the British under George Rodney and Samuel Hood decisively defeated the French under François J. P. de Grasse, capturing 7 of 29 French battleships, with French casualties of almost 5,000 and 8,000 prisoners taken; there were more than 1,000 British casualties.

1783

Second British-Mysore War: After Haidar Ali's death and cessation of French aid, his son and successor, Tippoo, sued for peace.

Europe's Treaty of Versailles ended the American Revolution and, more generally, the English, French, and Spanish conflicts over the Americas (Jan. 20); Florida was given to Spain, the Bahamas to Britain.

b. Simón Bolívar (d. 1830), Latin American general and political activist.

1784

Siamese forces mounted a failed invasion of Vietnam.

Burmese forces took Arakan (1784-1785).

b. Zachary Taylor (d. 1850), American army officer and 12th president of the United States (1849-1850).

1785

Kamahameha's forces took Oahu, in the Hawaiian Islands.

Burmese forces invaded Siam (1785-1786), with little success, except for taking Tavoy and Tenasserim.

b. José Miguel Carrera (d. 1821), Chilean general.

Oliver Hazard Perry (d. 1819), American naval officer.

1786

Tay Son forces completed their conquest and reunification of Vietnam.

b. Winfield Scott (d. 1866), American general.

d. Nathanael Greene (b. 1742), American general during the Revolutionary War, both as a field commander and (from 1778) a quartermaster general.

1787

Europe	Africa and Southwest Asia
Russo-Austrian-Turkish War (1787-1792): Turkey was at war with Russia and its ally Austria. b. Henry George Wakelyn Smith (d. 1860), British general. d. Thomas Gage (b. ca. 1720), British general best known as commander in chief of British North American forces and governor of Massachusetts, recalled to Britain after losses at Concord and Bunker Hill (1775). d. Charles de Rohan, prince of Soubise (b. 1715), marshal of France during the War of the Austrian Succession and the Seven Years' War; he led the losing French forces at Rossbach (1757).	Britain took Sierre Leone. b. Shaka (Chaka) (ca. 1787-1828), Zulu king.

1788

Europe	Africa and Southwest Asia
Russo-Austrian-Turkish War: Turkish forces attacking in Crimea were defeated by Alexander Suvorov's Russian army. Russian forces attacked Moldavia, taking Chotin and Jassy and besieging Ochakov on the Black Sea. Montenegrins under Prince Peter rebelled against Turkey. Russo-Austrian-Turkish War: At Liman, near the mouth of the Dnieper River (June 17), Russian naval forces decisively defeated a Turkish fleet, sinking seven battleships and several smaller ships and capturing one battleship, with casualties of 3,000 and more than 1,000 prisoners taken. Russian losses were negligible. A Russian fleet commanded by John Paul Jones sank nine more Turkish ships at Ochakov (June 27). Swedish-Russian War (1788-1790): Swedish forces led by Gustavus III attacked Russian-occupied Finland, besieging Svataipol. b. Fitzroy James Henry Somerset Raglan (d. 1855), British field marshal. b. George Gordon, Lord Byron (d. 1824), British poet and fighter for Greek independence. d. François Joseph Paul de Grasse (b. 1722), French admiral who during the American Revolution, in the two Battles of the Capes (1781), led the French fleet that stopped British naval forces from relieving General Charles Cornwallis's army at Yorktown. d. Pierre André de Suffren Saint-Tropez (b. 1729), French vice admiral who served in the Indian Ocean during the Seven Years' War.	

1789

Europe	Africa and Southwest Asia
French Revolution began when Parisian citizens took the Bastille by storm (July 14). Russo-Austrian-Turkish War: Russian and Austrian armies attacked Moldavia, driving the Turks back to the Danube. Austrian forces defeated the Turks in Bosnia and took Belgrade. Insurrection in the Austrian-held Netherlands (Belgium) was defeated by Austrian occupation forces (1789-1790). Swedish-Russian War: At the first Battle of Svensksund (Aug. 24), Russian naval forces defeated a Swedish fleet, which lost 11 warships.	

Central, South and East Asia, and the Pacific	The Americas

1787

1788

Britain established the New South Wales penal colony in Australia, run by a military governor and the New South Wales Corps. Vietnamese forces defeated an invading Manchu army (1788-1789).	

1789

Third British-Mysore War (1789-1792): British forces led by Lord Cornwallis attacked Mysore.	Revolutionary War commander in chief George Washington became the first president of the United States; he would serve two terms (Apr. 30, 1789-Mar. 1797). Spain and Britain disputed the Pacific Northwest, with Spanish forces taking Nootka Island and several nearby British ships. d. Ethan Allen (b. 1738), American soldier during the Revolutionary War, leader of the Green Mountain Boys, who took Fort Ticonderoga (1775).

Europe	Africa and Southwest Asia

1790

Greek independence forces mounted a major insurrection against the Turks.

Swedish-Russian War: In Vyborg harbor (July 3), a Swedish fleet escorting a seaborne army was greatly damaged by an attacking Russian war fleet, losing 7 battleships and more than 60 other ships of all kinds.

Swedish-Russian War: At the second Battle of Svenskund (July 9), the Swedish fleet decisively defeated the Russians, who lost more than 60 ships, with more than 7,000 casualties. Swedish casualties were light, and 4 ships were lost.

b. Konstantinos Kanaris (d. 1877), Greek admiral.

d. Jacques Antoine Hippolyte, count of Guibert (b. 1743), French army officer best known for his works of military theory.

Under a new leader, Agonglo (r. 1789-1797), and supplied with European weapons, Dahomey fought against continued Oyo domination (from ca. 1790).

1791

Declaration of the Rights of Man was published as the preface to the French Constitution; with the American Declaration of Independence (1776), it became the ideological basis for successive waves of democratic revolutions throughout the world in the centuries that followed.

d. Prince Gregori Aleksandrovich Potemkin (b. 1739), Russian field marshal during the Russo-Turkish War (1768-1774) and the Russo-Austrian-Turkish War (1787-1792); dubbed prince of Tauris (Tabriz) by Catherine the Great (1787), he died en route to Jassy to negotiate peace terms (Oct. 16).

In North Africa, Spain gave up its attempts to hold Oran, still keeping some bases, including Ceuta and Melilla.

1792

French Revolution: French Republicans took the royal palace, the Tuileries, by storm (Aug. 10). The French National Convention ended the monarchy (Sept. 21).

War of the First Coalition (1792-1798): Austria and Prussia, quickly joined by Sardinia, declared an anti-French alliance and began to move against revolutionary France (Feb.); France responded by declaring war on Austria (Apr. 20). An allied army invaded France, moving through the Argonne toward Paris; it was met at Valmy by the French (Sept. 20) and retreated after a skirmish. French forces invaded northern Italy, took Mainz and Frankfurt in Germany, and defeated an Austrian army at Jemappes (Nov. 6), then taking Brussels. Allied forces counterattacked in Germany, retaking Frankfurt.

Russia and Prussia invaded Poland.

Russo-Austrian-Turkish War: Under the Treaty of Jassy (Jan.), defeated Turkey ceded to Russia much territory north of the Black Sea and east of the Dniester River, including the Black Sea port of Ochakov.

b. Colin Campbell, first Baron Clyde (d. 1863), British field marshal.

d. John Burgoyne (b. 1722), British general nicknamed "Gentleman Johnny," who lost to American forces at Saratoga (1777).

d. George Brydges Rodney (b. 1718), British admiral during the Seven Years' War and the American Revolution, taking Guadeloupe (1782), though the war had already been lost on land.

Struggle between Britain and France over Senegal flared during Europe's French revolutionary wars, with Britain making several failed attacks on St. Louis.

1793

War of the First Coalition: Louis XVI of France was executed (Jan. 21). England, Spain, and the Netherlands joined the anti-French alliance. The French Reign of Terror began (July). Powerful allied armies attacked the French,

In West Africa, the kingdom of Oyo, seeking slaves, attacked the state of Ife but was surprisingly defeated.

1790

In Ohio, Miami Indian forces decisively defeated an American force of 1,500, led by General Josiah Harmar, in a series of engagements (Oct. 8-22), with American casualties of almost 200.

d. Israel Putnam (b. 1718), American general who led Revolutionary War forces at Bunker Hill, issuing the famous order "Don't fire until you see the whites of their eyes."

1791

Third British-Mysore War: Mysore's capital, Bangalore, fell to Charles Cornwallis's British troops (Mar.); Tippoo's Mysore forces were defeated at Carigat (May) and besieged at Seringapatam.

Pierre Dominique Toussaint L'Ouverture led a massive slave insurrection on French-held Haiti; a rebellion of freed slaves and mulattoes also began.

On the Wabash River, in Indiana (Nov. 4), an Indian coalition army reportedly numbering 3,000 decisively defeated an American force of less than 1,000, with American casualties of 900.

1792

Third British-Mysore War: Mysore fortress at Seringapatam surrendered (Feb. 16), ending the war; the British took large territories from defeated Mysore.

Pierre Toussaint L'Ouverture's forces besieged Port-au-Prince; the French in the city and on the island were saved when France abolished slavery; Toussaint's forces then joined in the war against England.

b. Robert Patterson (d. 1881), American general.

d. John Paul Jones (b. 1747), Scottish-born American naval officer who, during the American Revolution, raided British shipping off North America and the British Isles, receiving the only naval gold medal awarded; he also received the first salute of the American flag (1778).

1793

b. Samuel (Sam) Houston (d. 1863), American military and political leader.

1793 (cont.)

defeating them at Neerwinden (Mar. 18), besieging Mainz and Dunkirk, taking Brussels, and advancing in northern France. French national conscription was instituted (Aug.), quickly creating massive, though untrained, French armies. The French defeated the English at Hondschoote, near Dunkirk (Sept. 8), the Dutch at Menin (Sept. 13), and the Austrians at Wattignies (Oct. 15); by year's end, they had pushed allied forces out of much of France. French republican forces besieged and took royalist and allied-held Toulon (Aug. 27-Dec. 19), although the allies destroyed 10 French battleships and many smaller ships at anchor. Artillery colonel Napoleon Bonaparte served notably at Toulon and was promoted to brigadier general.

Russia and Prussia made the second partition of Poland.

Second "Kaffir" War (1793-1795): Boers and Bantu fought inconclusively, as they would in several small wars over the following decades.

1794

War of the First Coalition: Allied armies again attacked northern France (spring) and were defeated at Courtrai (May 11) and Tourcoing (May 18), where both sides, 70,000 to 75,000 strong, suffered 3,000 to 4,000 casualties. The armies fought to a draw at Tournai (May 23). After French victories at Hooglede (June 17) and Fleurus (June 26), the French pursued the retreating allies to the sea, taking Belgium. French forces invaded Germany and Holland (Sept. and Oct.) and moved ahead in Italy.

War of the First Coalition: British forces took Corsica from the French (Aug. 10).

War of the First Coalition: Prefiguring the Atlantic convoy battles of a later day, a French convoy of 130 merchant ships carrying food from the United States reached Brest after its escorting war fleet engaged an intercepting British fleet 400 miles off Ushant; 1 French battleship was sunk and 6 captured.

Thaddeus Kosciusko led a Polish insurrection against foreign occupation forces. The insurgents defeated a 5,000-strong Russian army at Raclawice (Apr. 3) and took Warsaw (Apr. 17), fighting off a siege of the city by Russian and Prussian armies totaling 100,000. Ultimately, Russian forces defeated the insurgents in several battles (Sept.-Oct.); Kosciusko was wounded and taken at Maciejowitz (Oct. 10), and with him went the insurrection. Warsaw fell (Nov.), with tens of thousands of casualties.

d. Jean-Baptiste Charles Hector d'Estaing (b. 1729), French admiral during the Seven Years' War and the American Revolution; during the French Revolution, he was commander of the National Guard (1787) and admiral (1792), but he was guillotined in Paris during the Reign of Terror.

d. Marriot Arbuthnot (Arbuthnott) (b. 1711), British admiral during the Seven Years' War and American Revolution, later naval commander in chief in America (1779-1780).

Agha Mohammed emerged victorious from Persia's civil war (r. 1794-1797).

1795

War of the First Coalition: French forces took the Netherlands (Jan.-Mar.).

War of the First Coalition: Off Genoa (Mar. 13), a British fleet captured 2 French battleships of the 15 engaged; the French retreated. One British battleship of 13 was sunk in the battle.

War of the First Coalition: Prussia, Spain, Saxony, Hanover, and Hesse-Cassel left the war (Apr.-June). Inconclusive operations continued on the Rhine.

b. Henry Havelock (d. 1857), British general.

British forces took southern Africa (Sept.). The frontier regions of Graaff-Reinet and Swellendam had earlier declared their independence from central Capetown rule.

Agha Mohammed's Persian forces captured and annexed Georgia (1795-1796).

Central, South and East Asia, and the Pacific	The Americas	

1793 (cont.)

1794

	At Fallen Timbers, Ohio (Aug. 20), an American army of 3,000, led by Anthony Wayne, decisively defeated an Indian coalition army half its size, effectively ending the Indian-American war in the area. The defeated Indians were then pushed west, losing most of their land to American settlement.	
	b. Antonio López de Santa Anna (d. 1876), Mexican general.	
	b. Matthew Perry (d. 1858), American naval officer.	
	b. Stephen Watts Kearny (d. 1848), American general.	
	d. Baron Friedrich Wilhelm von Steuben (b. 1730), German general who, as inspector general of American troops, led the training of American soldiers at Valley Forge (1778).	

1795

British forces attacked and defeated the Dutch on Ceylon (Sri Lanka) (1795-1796), which it then annexed.	British forces on Jamaica again unsuccessfully attacked the Maroons, ultimately fighting to a standoff and granting the Maroons semiautonomy on the island.	
	Under Europe's Treaty of Basel, France gained Santo Domingo from Spain.	
	d. Francis Marion (b. 1732), American general nicknamed the "Swamp Fox" for his swamp-based guerrilla tactics against the British during the American Revolution.	

1795 (cont.)

d. Henry Clinton (b. 1738), British general who was commander in chief of British forces (1778-1782) during the American Revolution.

d. George Collier (b. 1738), British admiral during the American Revolution.

1796

Napoleonic Wars, War of the First Coalition: Napoleon Bonaparte became commander of French forces in Italy (Mar. 27). At Montenotte (Apr. 12), his forces went on the offensive and in less than two months drove Piedmont out of the war, took Milan and almost all of northern Italy, besieged Mantua, and drove Austrian forces into the Tyrol. At Lonato (Aug. 3), Bonaparte's army decisively defeated Austrian forces attacking south from the Tyrol west of Lake Garda. Two days later, at Castiglione, east of the lake, the French defeated a second Austrian army. Napoleon's forces defeated another Austrian relief attempt at Arcola (Nov. 17).

Napoleonic Wars, War of the First Coalition: A French spring offensive (June) sent two armies across the Rhine. At Amberg, in the north (Aug. 24), Austrian forces led by Archduke Charles defeated the French led by General Jean Jourdan; on the same day, a second French army, under Victor Moreau, defeated the Austrians at Friedberg, in Bavaria. At Würzburg (Sept. 3), the Austrians again defeated Jourdan's forces, forcing them back to the Rhine. Moreau's army in Bavaria disengaged and retreated.

Napoleonic Wars, War of the First Coalition: French seaborne forces 13,000 strong set off for an invasion of Ireland (Dec.); they encountered storms that frustrated the intended landing at Bantry Bay and turned back after the loss of 11 ships to weather and the British fleet.

Irish rising against British occupation forces (1796-1797) led by the United Irishmen failed after French seaborne invasion forces were unable to land in Ireland.

British forces suppressed the rebellion of Graaff-Reinet and Swellendam in southern Africa and occupied the Cape Colony.

1797

Napoleonic Wars, War of the First Coalition: After Napoleon Bonaparte's French army defeated Austrian relief forces at Rivoli (Jan. 14), besieged Mantua and its garrison of 16,000 surrendered (Feb. 2).

Napoleonic Wars, War of the First Coalition: Off Cape St. Vincent (Feb. 14), a British fleet captured 4 of 17 Spanish battleships, with almost 4,000 Spanish casualties and prisoners taken.

Napoleonic Wars, War of the First Coalition: Napoleon's forces crossed the Alps in pursuit of retreating Austrian forces (Mar. 10) and were at Leoben (Apr. 6), directly threatening Vienna, when Austria accepted his peace terms (Apr. 18). French armies were again attacking on the Rhine (Apr.) when the war ended.

Naval mutinies at Spithead, Nore, and other ports immobilized much of the British fleet (Apr.-Aug.).

Napoleonic Wars, War of the First Coalition: Off Camperdown, in Holland (Oct. 11), British naval forces captured 9 of 15 Dutch battleships, with more than 1,000 Dutch casualties and almost 4,000 prisoners taken; there were more than 1,000 British casualties.

Napoleonic Wars, War of the First Coalition: At Campo Formio (Oct. 17), the formal peace settlement ceded Belgium to France and created the northern Italian republic, effectively a French protectorate. Austria took Venice. Conflict continued in the Mediterranean, however.

d. Agha Mohammed Khan (b. 1720), Persian general and ruler; he was assassinated during another campaign against Georgia.

Central, South and East Asia, and the Pacific	The Americas	
1795 (cont.)		
	d. John Sullivan (b. 1740), American general who, during the Revolution, campaigned against Tory and Indian forces in Pennsylvania and New York (May-Nov. 1779).	
1796		
White Lotus Society rising in southern and southwestern China (1796-1804) was ultimately defeated by the Manchus.	b. James Bowie (d. 1836), American soldier.	
	d. Anthony Wayne (b. 1745), American general nicknamed "Mad Anthony," famed for his successful night assault on Stony Point (1779); he later fought in the Northwest (1794).	
	d. John Butler (b. 1728), colonial Loyalist leader who fought at Oriskany (1777) and led Tory irregulars (Butler's Rangers) against frontier settlements, notably at Wyoming Valley, Pennsylvania (1778), and Schoharie Valley, New York (1780); he was the father of Walter Butler.	
1797		
	Under Europe's War of the First Coalition, Spain gave Trinidad to Britain.	

1797 (cont.)

b. Ernst Eduard Vogel von Falckenstein (d. 1885), Prussian general.

d. Jeffrey Amherst (b. 1717), British field marshal who captured Louisbourg (1758), becoming commander in chief in America during the French and Indian War.

d. Louis Lazare Hoche (b. 1768), French general during the French revolutionary wars; he died of pneumonia shortly after being named commander in chief.

1798

French forces took Rome, setting up the Roman republic (Feb.), and Switzerland, founding the Helvetian republic.

United Irishmen, led by Wolfe Tone and Napper Tandy, again led a failed Irish rising against the British. After defeating a small British force at Ballymore, an Irish army marched on Dublin but was quickly defeated by British regulars. British forces stormed and took the rebel camp on Vinegar Hill (June 12), with 4,000 Irish casualties of 16,000 engaged. A small French seaborne force reached Ireland (late Aug.), surrendering in early September. A second French seaborne force was intercepted and defeated by a British squadron off Donegal (Oct. 12); with it was Wolfe Tone, who reportedly committed suicide while awaiting execution in Dublin.

Napoleonic Wars, War of the Second Coalition (1798-1802): Russia, England, Austria, Turkey, and several smaller armies formed a new anti-French alliance (Dec. 24).

d. Charles Joseph de Croix, count of Clerfayt (Clairfayt) (b. 1733), Austrian field marshal.

Napoleonic Wars, War of the Second Coalition: Napoleon Bonaparte led a 40,000-strong French army in a seaborne invasion of Egypt (May 19). Landing at Alexandria (July 1), the French took the city by storm the next day and moved on Cairo. They decisively defeated a 60,000-strong Egyptian army at the Battle of the Pyramids (July 21) and took Cairo the next day.

Napoleonic Wars, War of the Second Coalition: At Aboukir Bay, Egypt (Aug. 1), in the Battle of the Nile, a British war fleet commanded by Admiral Horatio Nelson surprised and destroyed a French war fleet; of 13 French battleships, 11 were sunk or captured, with more than 3,000 casualties and 3,000 prisoners taken; the British had fewer than 1,000 casualties.

Napoleonic Wars, War of the Second Coalition: Napoleon's forces took the island of Malta, ending the days of the Knights of St. John Hospitallers as a territorial power.

Persian forces attacked Afghanistan.

b. Andries (Andreas) Wilhelmus Jacobus Pretorius (d. 1853), Boer general and statesman.

1799

Napoleonic Wars, War of the Second Coalition: French forces attacked the allies in Italy, Germany, the Netherlands, and Switzerland. In Italy, French forces took Capua and then took Naples by storm (Jan. 24). In northern Italy, the French attack on Magnano failed (Apr. 5); an allied army of 70,000, led by Russian marshal Alexander Suvorov, decisively defeated Victor Moreau's 30,000-strong French army at Cassano (Apr. 27), taking Milan and Turin. Suvorov's forces defeated the French again at the Trebbia River (June 17-19) and a third time at Novi (Aug. 15). The remaining French forces retreated across the Alps after their defeat at Genoa (Nov. 4).

Napoleonic Wars, War of the Second Coalition: In Germany, French forces unsuccessfully attacked Stockach (Mar. 25), then retreated to the Rhine River, while in the Netherlands an inconclusive campaign ended with allied withdrawal. The Treaty of Alkmaar ended the French-Dutch portion of the war, essentially restoring the prewar status quo.

As southern Africa's frontier regions, especially Graaff-Reinet and Swellendam, still resisted Capetown control, the Xhosa and Hottentot also fought for independence, attacking settlers.

Central, South and East Asia, and the Pacific	The Americas	

1797 (cont.)

1798

New Persian shah, Fath Ali, invaded Afghanistan, beginning a long, inconclusive, debilitating conflict.

1799

Fourth British-Mysore War: British Indian forces again attacked Mysore, besieging and taking Seringapatam (May 4), then massacring a reported 6,000 of its remaining defenders, including Tippoo of Mysore. The British then took the country.

Ranjit Singh's forces began his battle to unite the Sikhs and control the Punjab (1799-1802).

d. George Washington (b. 1732), American general and first president of the United States (1789-1797); he was commander in chief of Revolutionary forces, leading them from Boston (1775) through Valley Forge to victory at Yorktown (1781).

Pierre Toussaint L'Ouverture's forces, led by Jean Jacques Dessalines, defeated the mulatto-led republic in southern Haiti, massacring thousands (1799-1800).

Europe	Africa and Southwest Asia
1799 (cont.)	
Napoleonic Wars, War of the Second Coalition: In Switzerland, early allied successes were replaced by a stalemate after a French victory at Zurich (Sept. 25), which cost the allies 8,000 casualties of 20,000 engaged. Napoleon Bonaparte became first consul of France (Nov. 9). d. Richard Howe (b. 1726), British admiral whose naval support during the American Revolution helped his younger brother, General William Howe, take New York; he was first lord of the admiralty (1783; 1783-1788) and came out of retirement to mediate the sailors' mutiny at Spithead (1797).	
1800	
Napoleonic Wars, War of the Second Coalition: Napoleon Bonaparte's army of 28,000 crossed the Alps (mid-May) and decisively defeated an Austrian army of 31,000 at Marengo (June 14); the Austrians suffered more than 9,000 casualties and 4,000 prisoners taken, the French almost 6,000 casualties. Napoleonic Wars, War of the Second Coalition: Allied forces continued to attack the remaining French in Italy, defeating them near Genoa and then besieging the city, which fell with its garrison of more than 11,000 (June 4). Napoleonic Wars, War of the Second Coalition: At Hohenlinden, near Munich (Dec. 3), Victor Moreau's French army of 55,000 to 60,000 decisively defeated a slightly smaller Austrian force at a cost of 4,000 French and more than 5,000 Austrian casualties; almost 7,000 Austrians were captured. Defeated Austria left the war (late Dec.). Besieged Valetta fell to Maltese insurgents and their British allies after a two-year siege (Sept. 1798-Sept. 1800). b. Helmuth Karl Bernhard von Moltke (d. 1891), German field marshal. d. Alexander Vasilievich Suvorov (b. 1729), Russian field marshal who took Warsaw (1794); during the War of the Second Coalition, he commanded the Austro-Russian army in Italy (1799). d. Baron Wilhelm von Knyphausen (b. 1716), Prussian general who was commander in chief of German mercenary troops (from 1777) during the American Revolution. d. Jean-Baptiste Kléber (b. 1753), French general during the French revolutionary wars, first in Europe, then commanding the Army of Egypt; he was assassinated in Cairo (June 14).	Napoleonic Wars: British forces captured Malta from the French; their control would be confirmed at war's end (1815). In East Africa, the kingdom of Buganda expanded to its greatest extent, taking the area of Budda (by ca. 1800).
1801	
Napoleonic Wars, War of the Second Coalition: At Copenhagen (Apr. 2), Horatio Nelson's British fleet entered the harbor and successfully attacked Danish warships and harbor installations.	Napoleonic Wars, War of the Second Coalition: In Egypt a British-Turkish seaborne army of 18,000 defeated Egyptian-French forces at Aboukir (Mar. 20), took Cairo (July), and then completed the reconquest of Egypt; French forces surrendered (Aug. 31). Tripolitan-American War (1801-1805): After the pasha of Tripoli declared war on the United States (May 14), American naval forces periodically interrupted some of the seaborne traffic at Tripoli in an unsuccessful attempt to blockade the port.

1799 (cont.)

1800

b. Franklin Buchanan (d. 1874), American Confederate (CSA) naval officer.

d. Artemas Ward (b. 1727), American general who initially directed Revolutionary forces at the siege of Boston (1775-1776), then for a time was ranked second only to George Washington.

1801

French general Victor Leclerc, with a force of almost 22,000, unsuccessfully attempted to reconquer Haiti, taking several coastal towns but not the interior.

b. David Glasgow Farragut (d. 1870), American admiral.

d. Benedict Arnold (b. 1741), American and British general, a key American commander during the Revolutionary War who became a British spy, fleeing after exposure; he died in London.

Europe	Africa and Southwest Asia

1802

Napoleonic Wars, War of the Second Coalition: The British-French portion of the war ended with the Treaty of Amiens (Mar. 27).

1803

Napoleonic Wars, French-British War (1803-1805): As the French gathered a cross-Channel invasion force, Britain blockaded the European mainland and attacked French concentrations in the North Sea ports. British forces first adopted the exploding canister shell named for its inventor, Henry Shrapnel. b. James Outram (d. 1863), British general.	Tripolitan-American War: The American frigate *Philadelphia* was captured off Tripoli and its crew held for ransom. French forces retook Tamatave, on Madagascar.

1804

Napoleon Bonaparte became French emperor (Dec. 2). Serbian national forces led by Karageorge (George Petrovich) successfully rose against the Turks (1804-1806). b. Claude É. Minié (d. 1879), French officer and weapons inventor. d. Charles Pichegru (b. 1761), French general during the French revolutionary wars, initially hailed as a hero, later deported for his role in the attempted coup of 18 Fructidor (Sept. 4, 1797); secretly returning to France, he was captured and strangled in prison, possibly a suicide (Apr. 5).	Fulani leader Usman dan Fodio led a jihad (holy war) (1804-1810), creating a substantial West African empire, including the Hausa city-states, much of northern Nigeria and northern Cameroons, and part of Benin. Russo-Persian War (1804-1813): Russian forces attacked Persia, unsuccessfully besieging Erivan. A long, small-scale war ensued. Tripolitan-American War: An American party led by Lieutenant Stephen Decatur burned the captured American ship *Philadelphia* in the harbor at Tripoli (Feb. 16).

1805

Napoleonic Wars, War of the Third Coalition (1805-1807): Britain, Austria, Russia, and Sweden formed another anti-French alliance. Austrian forces attacked in Bavaria and Italy (Sept. 2), as Napoleon Bonaparte's massive armies moved east. General Mack von Leiberich's Austrian army of 30,000, encircled at Ulm, surrendered (Oct. 17). French forces attacked Austria and took Vienna (Nov. 14). Napoleon, with an army of 73,000, turned north, meeting and destroying an allied army of 85,000 at Austerlitz (Dec. 2). Allied losses included 13,000 casualties and more than 10,000 prisoners taken, with French casualties at more than 8,000. Austria quickly and unconditionally surrendered (Dec. 4).	Tripolitan-American War: An American force of a little more than 100 took Derna (Apr.), in Tripoli, and was there besieged; the siege, the naval expedition, and the war ended when the United States ransomed the crew of the *Philadelphia*.

Central, South and East Asia, and the Pacific	The Americas

1802

Nguyen Anh took the Vietnamese throne as Gia Long, ruling from Hué, after long years of civil war (1773-1801).

In Maratha, civil war resulted when Holkar of Indore defeated the British-supported ruler, Baji Rao II, at Poona.

Ranjit Singh and his Sikh forces completed taking most of the Punjab.

In Haiti, rebel leader Pierre Toussaint L'Ouverture was taken while negotiating with the French and died in prison (1803); the war was continued by Jean Jacques Dessalines and Henri Christophe.

b. David Hunter (d. 1886), American general.

d. Daniel Morgan (b. 1736), American general who led 500 riflemen in the Corps of Rangers (Morgan's Rifles), serving notably at Saratoga (1777) and Cowpens (1781).

1803

British forces attacked inland on Ceylon (Sri Lanka), taking Kandy (Feb.) but then losing it to counterattacking Sinhalese forces (June).

Second British-Maratha War (1803-1805): In a contest for control of the Deccan, British forces led by Arthur Wellesley (later the duke of Wellington) invaded the Deccan against Holkar of Indore, who had deposed the ruler of Maratha; Wellesley's troops took Poona (Mar. 20) and Ahmadnagar (Aug. 11), decisively defeated Maratha forces at Assaye (Sept. 23) and Argaon (Nov. 28), then took Gawilarh (Dec. 15).

Second British-Maratha War: In Hindustan, British forces took Aligarh by storm (Sept. 4), defeated Maratha forces before Delhi and took the city (Sept. 16), and decisively defeated the Marathas at Laswari (Nov. 1).

French forces left Haiti (Nov.).

British seaborne forces took St. Lucia (June 21-23).

b. Albert Sidney Johnston (d. 1862), American Confederate (CSA) general.

b. Samuel Francis Du Pont (d. 1865), American admiral.

d. John Barry (b. 1745), Irish-American naval officer during the Revolutionary War.

1804

Second British-Maratha War: At Farrukhabad (Nov. 17), British forces defeated Holkar's Maratha forces; the British then took Indore.

British forces on Ceylon (Sri Lanka) again took Kandy and were again forced to evacuate the city.

At the New South Wales penal colony, a prisoners' revolt failed.

Jean Jacques Dessalines took power in Haiti; his forces quickly massacred all the Whites they could find on the island, numbering in the thousands.

British seaborne forces took the Dutch colony at Surinam (May 5).

b. Osceola (d. 1838), Seminole chief.

b. José Ballivian (d. 1852), Bolivian general.

d. Philip John Schuyler (b. 1733), American general who was one of General George Washington's four major generals in the Revolutionary War, organizing the initial invasion of Canada (1775) and helping defeat General John Burgoyne's offensive (1777).

1805

Second British-Maratha War: British forces unsuccessfully attempted to take Bhurtpore by storm, losing more than 3,000 in four attacks (Jan.-Apr.); pursued into the Punjab, Holkar and his Maratha forces surrendered at Amritsar (Dec.).

1805 (cont.)

Napoleonic Wars, War of the Third Coalition: In Italy, Austrian forces led by Archduke Charles were defeated by André Masséna's army at Caldiero (Oct. 30); the Austrians then retreated across the Alps.

Napoleonic Wars, War of the Third Coalition: Off Cape Trafalgar (Oct. 21), Horatio Nelson's British fleet won a decisive victory over a French-Spanish fleet, capturing 20 of 33 battleships in a five-hour battle that cost almost 7,000 French casualties and 7,000 prisoners taken, with British casualties at fewer than 2,000 but including Nelson.

d. Horatio Nelson (b. 1758), British admiral during the American Revolution, French revolutionary wars, and Napoleonic Wars, most notably at the Battle of the Nile (1798) and Trafalgar (1805), where he was fatally wounded.

Serbian independence forces led by Karageorge took Belgrade (Dec.).

b. Eduard von Clam-Gallas (d. 1891), Austrian general.

d. Charles Cornwallis (b. 1738), British general during the American Revolution who surrendered at Yorktown, Virginia (1781); he later served in India and was governor and commander in chief in Ireland (1797).

1806

Napoleonic Wars, War of the Third Coalition: Widening the war, Napoleon Bonaparte attacked Prussia (Oct. 8), moving toward Berlin. At Jena (Oct. 14), the French army of 95,000 to 100,000 routed a Prussian-Saxon army of 50,000, with 5,000 French casualties to 10,000 Prussian casualties and 15,000 prisoners taken. On the same day, at Auerstädt, the French defeated a second Prussian army of 50,000, which was routed with losses of 12,000 casualties and 3,000 captured, with French losses at 8,000. The French took Berlin (Oct. 24), as 50,000 more Prussians surrendered piecemeal (through Nov.). The French then moved into Poland, taking Warsaw (Nov. 30).

Russo-Turkish War (1806-1812): Russian forces attacked and held Wallachia and Moldavia.

Serbian independence was proclaimed (Dec.).

b. Ramón (Cabrera y Griño), count of Morella Cabrera (d. 1877), Spanish Carlist general.

d. Pierre Charles Jean Baptiste Silvestre de Villeneuve (b. 1763), French admiral who was defeated by Horatio Nelson at the Battle of the Nile (1798) and Trafalgar (1805).

d. John Graves Simcoe (b. 1752), British general who led the Queen's Rangers during the American Revolution.

Ashanti forces under King Osei Bonsu took the Gold Coast (1806-1807).

Napoleonic Wars: British seaborne forces attacked and took Capetown from the French and Dutch (Jan. 8).

1807

Napoleonic Wars, War of the Third Coalition: Russian forces numbering 100,000, led by Lévin Bennigsen, mounted a winter offensive against the French in Poland and East Prussia (Jan.). At Eylau (Feb. 8), Napoleon Bonaparte's forces met them in an inconclusive battle that cost 23,000 casualties of the 65,000 to 75,000 French and 22,000 of the 83,000 Russians and Prussians engaged.

Napoleonic Wars, War of the Third Coalition: Besieged Danzig fell to the French (Apr. 27).

Napoleonic Wars, War of the Third Coalition: At Friedland (June 14), Napoleon's army of 65,000 had more than 10,000 casualties in decisively defeating a Russian army of 60,000, which suffered 18,000 casualties. The French went

British forces took Alexandria, Egypt (Mar.), but were defeated at Rosetta (Apr.) and then left Egypt (Sept.) as Turkish governor Mohammed Ali's power grew.

Dingiswayo came to the throne of the Mtetwa Empire (r. ca. 1807-1818); in southeastern Africa, he quickly expanded against his neighbors.

British naval forces based themselves in the Gold Coast in increasing strength after Britain outlawed the slave trade in its own

1805 (cont.)

1806

Failed mutiny at Vellore by the Sepoys prefigured the Indian Army (Sepoy) Mutiny to come half a century later (1857-1858).

Another rising at the New South Wales penal colony was harshly put down by the ruling governor, Captain William Bligh.

d. Jean Jacques Dessalines (b. ca. 1746), Haitian leader who succeeded Pierre Toussaint L'Ouverture; self-declared lifetime governor general, he was killed during a revolt in Port-au-Prince (Oct. 17). Civil war followed (1806-1820) between the forces of Henri Christophe and those of Alexandre Pétion.

Napoleonic Wars: British forces took Buenos Aires (June 17) but were quickly defeated by local militia (Aug. 12).

Off Santo Domingo (Feb. 6), all five battleships of the French West Indian fleet were captured by a British force of six battleships.

d. Henry Knox (b. 1750), Revolutionary War general who founded the Academy Artillery School (1777) and became first commandant of its successor, West Point (1782); he was commander in chief (1782-1783) and secretary of war (1785-1794).

d. Horatio Gates (b. 1728), American general who commanded Revolutionary forces in New York (from Dec. 1776), most notably in defeating British forces at Saratoga (1777).

1807

British seaborne forces numbering 8,000 took Montevideo (July); they also occupied Buenos Aires but were forced to retreat.

Exploring overland west of the Mississippi River, Zebulon Pike was captured by Spanish colonists and imprisoned for a time in Santa Fe, New Mexico.

b. Robert Edward Lee (d. 1870), American Confederate (CSA) general.

b. Joseph Eggleston Johnston (d. 1891), American Confederate (CSA) general.

Europe	Africa and Southwest Asia

1807 (cont.)

on to take Tilsit (June 19), effectively ending the war. The Tilsit treaties with Russia and Prussia (July) gave Napoleon control of Poland and much of Germany.

Napoleonic Wars, War of the Third Coalition: A British fleet of 25 battleships, carrying an army of more than 20,000, attacked Copenhagen (Sept. 2-5); the city surrendered after heavy bombardment. The Danish fleet, which included 16 battleships, surrendered to the British.

Napoleonic Wars, Peninsular War (1807-1814): French forces of more than 20,000 attacked Portugal (Nov.), taking Lisbon (Nov. 30).

Russo-Turkish War: Off Lemnos, a Turkish war fleet lost three battleships in fighting a Russian fleet (June 30).

Britain withdrew from slave trading, the first European nation to do so.

b. Giuseppe Garibaldi (d. 1882), Italian military leader and revolutionary.

d. Jean Baptiste Donatien de Vimeur, count of Rochambeau (b. 1725), marshal of France who was lieutenant general of French forces in the American Revolution; his encirclement of Charles Cornwallis's British forces led to their surrender (1781) and the war's end.

d. Pasquale Paoli (b. 1725), Corsican general who led rebellions of his people against Genoa (ca. 1731-1768) and France (1768-1769).

territories (1807) and began to intercept slave-carrying ships of all nations (effective 1808).

1808

Napoleonic Wars, Peninsular War: French forces of more than 115,000 attacked Spain (Mar.), installing Joseph Bonaparte, Napoleon's brother, as puppet king. A massive insurrection began in Madrid (early May), quickly spreading throughout Spain and Portugal; regional regular armies also fought the French, forcing the surrender of a French army of 18,000 at Baylen, in Andalusia (June 20). British seaborne forces of 14,000, led by Arthur Wellesley (later duke of Wellington), landed near Lisbon (Aug. 1). Napoleon took personal command (Nov. 3); going on the offensive, the French quickly took all of northern Spain, including Madrid (Dec. 4), and forced a British retreat and evacuation by sea (Jan. 18), with almost 9,000 casualties in the 22,000 to 23,000 British force.

Russian forces attacked Finland (Feb.), which was evacuated by Swedish occupying forces (Dec.) and formally taken by Russia, along with the Aland Islands, under the Treaty of Frederikshavn.

b. Marie Edmé Patrice Maurice de MacMahon (d. 1893), marshal of France.

d. Guy Carleton (b. 1724), British general who served most notably at Louisbourg (1758), Havana (1762), and Quebec (1759; 1775); he was commander in chief in America (1782-1783) and three times governor of Canada.

Usman dan Fodio's Fulani forces attacked Kanem-Bornu, with early success against the forces of Mai Ahmad.

b. Abd-el-Kader (Abd-al-Kadir) (d. 1883), Algerian ruler.

1809

Napoleonic Wars, Peninsular War: French forces invaded Portugal, took Oporto (Mar. 29), and then lost it to Arthur Wellesley's British forces (May 12). The allies and French fought to a draw at Talavera (July 28), with French losses of more than 7,000 and British losses of more than 6,000; the allies then retreated to Portugal.

Napoleonic Wars, Austro-French War: Austrian forces of more than 200,000 attacked Bavaria (Apr. 9), while smaller forces attacked Italy (50,000) and Poland (40,000). In Italy, the Austrians defeated the French at Sacile (Apr. 16). In Bavaria, Napoleon Bonaparte defeated the Austrians at Abensberg (Apr. 19-20), Landeshut (Apr. 21), Eckmuth (Apr. 22), and Ratisbon (Apr. 23), with

Napoleonic Wars: British forces took the French base at St. Louis (Senegal).

Central, South and East Asia, and the Pacific	The Americas

	d. Joseph Brant (Thayendanegea) (b. 1742), Mohawk chief who was a longtime British ally, raiding Mohawk Valley settlements, as at Cherry Valley (1778); he and his people later settled in Canada.

1808

Rum Rebellion at the New South Wales penal colony caused the removal of Captain William Bligh as governor, disbandment of the New South Wales Corps, and the beginning of the sequence of events that would lead to the establishment of the Australian nation (Jan. 26). Dutch forces completed their conquest of western Java.	Spanish forces in Santo Domingo drove back rebel Haitian forces and retook the eastern part of the island (1808-1809). b. Jefferson Davis (d. 1889), American military and political leader and president of the Confederate States of America (CSA) (1861-1865).

1809

Treaty of Amritsar temporarily set a boundary on the Sutlej River between British and Ranjit Singh's Sikhs. d. Rama I (Chakri) (?-1809), Siamese general who deposed the supposedly insane monarch P'ya Taksin (1782), and took the throne himself (r. 1782-1809), founding a new and continuing dynasty and moving Thailand's capital to Bangkok.	British seaborne forces numbering almost 11,000 took French-held Martinique, taking more than 2,000 French prisoners (Jan.-Feb.). b. Abraham Lincoln (d. 1865), 16th president of the United States (1861-1865). d. Meriwether Lewis (b. 1774), American army officer and explorer who, with William Clark, explored the new Louisiana Territory all the way to the Pacific (1804-1806), becoming governor of the territory (1807-1809).

1809 (cont.)

total Austrian losses of 35,000 to 40,000 and French losses of 10,000 to 15,000. Napoleon then took Vienna (May 13), but at Aspern-Essling on the Danube, he encountered his first major defeat, withdrawing after losses of 22,000 to 24,000; Austrian losses were in the same range. Napoleon responded with a decisive victory over the Austrians at Wagram (July 5-6), at a cost of more than 33,000 French and 24,000 Austrian casualties; 18,000 Austrians were taken during or soon after the battle. Austria surrendered (July 10); the Treaty of Schönbrunn (Oct. 14) gave Napoleon control of substantial additional Austrian territories. After the Austrian defeat, the French again took full control of the Tyrol, which had risen against them (Apr.).

d. Jean Lannes, duke of Montebello and prince of Sievers (b. 1769), French marshal of the empire who died of wounds suffered at Aspern-Essling.

b. Baron Edwin von Manteuffel (d. 1885), Prussian field marshal.

d. Antoine Charles Louis Lasalle (b. 1775), French general who was an outstanding light cavalry commander.

1810

Napoleonic Wars, Peninsular War: French forces again invaded Portugal (July), pursuing retreating British forces under the duke of Wellington (formerly Arthur Wellesley); the French later withdrew (Oct.).

b. Karl Konstantin Albrecht Leonhard von Blumenthal (d. 1900), Prussian field marshal.

b. Robert Cornelis Napier (d. 1890), British field marshal.

d. Cuthbert Collingwood (b. 1748), British admiral who was second-in-command at the Battle of Trafalgar (1805), taking over after Horatio Nelson's death.

Napoleonic Wars: British forces took all French posts on Madagascar.

East African ports of Pate and Mombasa were defeated, and their power was broken, by nearby Lamu.

1811

Napoleonic Wars, Peninsular War: At Fuentes de Oñoro (May 5), André Masséna's French army of 48,000 fought to a draw with the duke of Wellington's British-Portuguese army of 37,000.

Napoleonic Wars, Peninsular War: At Albuera (May 16), Nicolas Jean de Dieu Soult's advancing French forces of 25,000 made a failed attempt to relieve besieged Badajoz, taking 6,000 casualties while being turned back by William Beresford's defending army of 32,000.

Napoleonic Wars, Peninsular War: Besieged Tarragona fell to the French (July 28), with 7,000 Spanish dead and 8,000 captured; there were 4,000 French casualties.

In Egypt Mohammed Ali's forces attacked and decisively defeated the remaining Mameluke forces throughout the country, killing most of the survivors, ending the Mamelukes as a military caste subsidiary to Turkey, and establishing an independent power (Mar.).

Egyptian-Arabian War (1811-1818): Mohammad Ali's forces attacked Wahhabi-held territories in Arabia, taking Mecca and

Central, South and East Asia, and the Pacific	The Americas	
1809 (cont.)		

		1810

Napoleonic Wars: British forces attacked the Dutch on Java, taking Batavia (Aug.); the defeated Dutch ceded Java and several other Indonesian territories to Britain (Sept.); all were returned after the end of the Napoleonic Wars (1816).

Napoleonic Wars: British naval forces took the French-held Indian Ocean islands of Mauritius and Réunion (Dec.).

Kamahameha's forces completed their conquest of the Hawaiian Islands.

Sikh forces led by Ranjit Singh attacked and took the remainder of the Punjab from the Afghans (1810-1820).

b. Tantia Topi (Tatya Tope; Ramchandra Panduroga) (ca. 1810-1859), Indian rebel leader.

Led by José Miguel Carrera and Bernardo O'Higgins, Chile declared itself an independent nation but was once again taken by Spain after a Spanish army defeated O'Higgins's forces at Rancagua (Oct. 7); he and his remaining forces fled to Argentina.

Argentina effectively won its independence from Spain, although formally it was still a Spanish colony.

Mexican War of Independence (1810-1823): Catholic priest Miguel Hidalgo y Costilla led a peasant revolution against Spain, threatening Mexico City, but was defeated by Spanish forces under General Félix Calleja.

American forces seized a Spanish fort at Baton Rouge, establishing West Florida; President James Madison then annexed the area (Oct. 27).

British seaborne forces numbering 7,000 took Guadeloupe (June 28).

b. Andrew Atkinson Humphreys (d. 1883), American general.

b. John Bankhead Magruder (d. 1871), American Confederate (CSA) general.

d. Benjamin Lincoln (b. 1733), American general who as George Washington's deputy formally accepted Britain's surrender at Yorktown (1781), then became secretary of war.

		1811

Arakanese led an ultimately failed insurrection against Burmese rule (1811-1815).

b. Tseng Kuo-feng (d. 1872), Chinese statesman and general.

Mexican War of Independence: At the Bridge of Calderón, on the approaches to Guadalajara (Jan. 17), the forces of Spanish general Félix Calleja decisively defeated Miguel Hidalgo's poorly armed forces, estimated at 80,000, reportedly with 10,000 rebel casualties. Hidalgo was captured and executed a month later. The conflict continued, largely as a guerrilla war in the countryside, led by Catholic priest José Maria Morelos.

Venezuela declared its independence from Spain (July 5), beginning its wars with that country.

Paraguay declared its independence from Spain (Aug. 14).

1811 (cont.)

Medina, as well as a substantial portion of the Red Sea coast of Arabia.

Usman dan Fodio's Fulani forces were defeated by those of Muhammad al-Kanami, coming to the aid of Mai Ahmad of Kanem-Bornu.

Religious leader Shehu Ahmadu Lobbo led an insurrection against the ruling Fulani in Macina, West Africa, founding a new state centered on Hamdallahi.

Dingiswayo brought the Buthelezi and other Zulu clans, including that led by Senzangakona, into his Mtetwa Empire (ca. 1811).

Continuing attacks by Boers drove the Xhosa beyond the Fish River.

1812

Napoleonic Wars, Franco-Russian War: Napoleon Bonaparte's Grand Army attacked Russia (June 23), crossing the Niemen River and advancing essentially unopposed. The Russians retreated, following a scorched earth policy; fought at Smolensk (Aug. 17-19), with 10,000 casualties on each side; and again retreated. At Borodino (Sept. 7), Mikhail Kutuzov's army turned to fight a major battle that cost the Russians 45,000 casualties of 120,000 engaged and the French 28,000 of 130,000 engaged. The French army of 95,000 took Moscow, which the retreating Russian garrison had set ablaze (Sept. 14). Without adequate supplies, the French left Moscow (Oct. 19), fought an inconclusive battle at Maloyaroslavets, and then embarked on a long, disastrous retreat. Finally, trapped crossing the Berezina River (Nov. 26-28), the French lost 30,000 of their estimated 50,000 men.

d. Peter Ivanovich Bagration (b. 1765), Russian prince and general who died of wounds suffered at Borodino (Sept. 7).

Napoleonic Wars, Peninsular War: The duke of Wellington's forces went on the offensive, taking Ciudad Rodrigo (Jan. 19) and Badajoz (Apr. 18) by storm. At Salamanca, Wellington's retreating army turned and defeated the pursuing French, at a cost of 5,000 allied and 6,000 French casualties, with 7,000 French prisoners taken. Madrid then fell to the allies (Aug. 12), who lost it later in the year as a French offensive drove Wellington's army back to Portugal.

Russo-Turkish War: The Treaty of Bucharest (May) awarded Bessarabia to Russia; Turkey continued to hold Moldavia and Wallachia.

Their war with Russia concluded, Turkish armies defeated Serbian independence forces, retaking the entire country (1812-1813).

Russo-Persian War: In the decisive battle of the war, Russian forces defeated Abbas Mirza's Persian army at Aslanduz, on the Aras River (Oct. 31), and went on to besiege and take the Black Sea fortress of Lenkoran, effectively ending the war.

1813

Napoleonic Wars: Napoleon Bonaparte, having raised a new army, attacked allied forces in Germany (Apr.). At Lützen (May 2), his army of 110,000 defeated an allied army of 73,000, breaking through Ludwig Wittgenstein's center but failing to exploit the opportunity. Both sides suffered massive losses, in the 15,000 to 20,000 range, and took similar losses at Bautzen (May 20-21), another French victory. A third major French victory came at Dresden (Aug. 26-27); French casualties were 10,000, but the allies retreated after suffering 38,000 casualties of 170,000 engaged. In the Battle of the Nations at Leipzig

Russo-Persian War: Russia took Georgia and other territories in the Caucasus Mountains from defeated Persia under the Treaty of Gulistan (Oct. 12).

1811 (cont.)

Rebels under José Artigas took control of the Banda Oriental (Uruguay), territory claimed by both Portugal and Spain.

American forces, led by Indiana Territory governor William Henry Harrison, moved with 1,000 militia against Prophetstown, headquarters of the Prophet, brother of Shawnee chief Tecumseh, leader of a major Indian coalition (Nov.). The Americans decisively defeated Indian forces at the Tippecanoe River (Nov. 8), then went on to burn Prophetstown. American settlers continued to push west in great numbers.

1812

Siamese forces occupied Cambodia, deposing Ang Chan and setting his brother Ang Snguon on the throne. Vietnam responded with a large army, and the Siamese withdrew; Ang Chan retook the throne, but with Cambodia now a Vietnamese protectorate.

b. Tso Tsung-t'ang (d. 1885), Chinese statesman and general.

War of 1812 (1812-1814): After the American declaration of war (June 19), a series of small-scale engagements generally favored the British on the Canadian-American border. British forces took Forts Mackinac (July 15), Dearborn (Aug. 15), and Detroit (Oct. 13), the latter surrendering without a fight to a much smaller Canadian and Indian force. At Queenston (Oct. 13), an attempted American invasion of Canada was repulsed, with 200 American casualties and almost 1,000 captured; British casualties were negligible. At sea the British blockaded the American coast, although the Americans won several single-ship engagements.

Spanish forces led by General Juan Monteverde defeated the Venezuelan revolutionary army, led by Francisco Miranda, which surrendered at La Victoria (July 12), effectively ending the first phase of the revolutionary war; Simón Bolívar and other revolutionary leaders fled abroad.

b. Cochise (ca. 1812-1874), Apache leader.

b. John Alexander McClernand (d. 1900), American general.

1813

War of 1812: American raiding forces took York (Toronto) (Apr. 27) and burned the public buildings of the city (May 8), then retreated.

d. Zebulon Montgomery Pike (b. 1779), American explorer and general who explored the Louisiana Territory, including Pikes Peak, named after him; he was fatally wounded leading American forces at York (Toronto).

1813 (cont.)

(Oct. 16-19), Napoleon was decisively defeated; his army of 200,000 suffered 38,000 casualties and 15,000 prisoners taken; the remainder retreated across the Rhine River, while the allies captured more than 100,000 French soldiers stranded in Germany. Leipzig cost the allies more than 53,000 casualties.

d. Gerhard Johann David von Scharnhorst (b. 1755), Prussian general who became minister of war and chief of the general staff (1808); he died of wounds suffered at Lützen.

d. (Jean) Victor (Marie) Moreau (b. 1763), French general who was killed in the Battle of Dresden (Aug. 27).

d. Prince Jozef Antoni Poniatowski (b. 1762), Vienna-born Polish general who led Polish forces in defending Warsaw (1794); later French marshal of the empire, commander of the First Polish Legion, and war minister of the Grand Duchy of Warsaw (1807), serving notably at Borodino (1812) and Leipzig, where he drowned under his horse (Oct. 19).

Napoleonic Wars, Peninsular War: Again on the offensive, the duke of Wellington's army took Madrid (May 17) and pursued the retreating French to the Ebro River; at Vittorio, his 70,000-man force decisively defeated a French army of 60,000, with more than 5,000 French casualties and more than 2,000 prisoners taken. Allied casualties were 6,000. The French armies fell back across the Pyrenees into southern France, pursued by Wellington's forces (early Oct.).

d. Mikhail Ilarionovich Golenischev Kutuzov, prince of Smolensk (b. 1745), Russian field marshal whose forces lost at Borodino (1812).

d. Jean Andoche Junot, duke of Abrantes (b. 1771), French general serving most notably in Portugal and Spain.

d. Jean-Baptiste Bessières (b. 1768), marshal of France; a cavalry commander killed in a skirmish at Rippach (May 1).

1814

Napoleonic Wars: Allied forces of more than 350,000 attacked France, defeating Napoleon Bonaparte's defending forces of 120,000 (Jan.-May), although Napoleon won several engagements in the course of the hopeless defense, including those at Brienne (Jan. 29), Champaubert (Feb. 10), Montereau (Feb. 18), and Rheims (Mar. 13). Paris surrendered (Mar. 31); Napoleon abdicated (Apr. 11) and was exiled to Elba. The Treaty of Paris (May 30) essentially restored the pre-1793 status quo.

Napoleonic Wars, Peninsular War: Allied seaborne forces landed and besieged Bayonne, France (Feb. 14). Wellington's advancing forces engaged the retreating French at Orthez (Feb. 27). The allies attacked Toulouse (Apr. 10), which the French then evacuated. Napoleon's first abdication ended the Peninsular War.

Holland withdrew from the slave trade.

d. Robert Ross (b. 1766), British general who led the forces that attacked and burned Washington, D.C. (Aug.).

d. William Howe (b. 1729), British general best known for his capture of New York (Forts Washington and Lee) (1776), with naval support from his brother Admiral Richard Howe.

A second Egyptian invasion force in Arabia was defeated by the Wahhabis.

Napoleonic Wars: Europe's Treaty of Paris ceded the Dutch Cape Colony to Britain, which had occupied the colony since 1806.

	War of 1812: American forces took Fort George (May 27), on the Niagara River, and then Fort Erie, which the British retook.

War of 1812: The USS *Chesapeake* lost a fight with the HMS *Shannon;* the Americans surrendered (June 1).

War of 1812, Creek-American War (1813-1814): Creek forces attacked and took Fort Mims, Alabama (Aug. 30), massacring more than 500 people. Tennessee and Georgia militia led by General Andrew Jackson and others responded with a series of attacks on Creek towns, burning several.

War of 1812, Battle of Lake Erie (Sept. 10): A small American flotilla under Captain Oliver Perry defeated and captured a British flotilla of six small vessels, clearing the way for the advance on Detroit, which was taken without opposition (Sept. 29). On the Thames River, near London, Ontario, American forces defeated a British and Indian force (Oct. 5), capturing almost 500 of the 1,000 engaged. Casualties on both sides were light, although British ally Tecumseh was killed in the battle.

d. Tecumseh (b. ca. 1768), Shawnee chief who fought against the Americans, dying alongside the British in the Battle of the Thames.

War of 1812: American forces attempting to move on Montreal were defeated in small-scale engagements at Chateaugay (Oct. 25) and Chrysler's Farm (Nov. 11); they then abandoned their project.

War of 1812: British and Indian forces took Fort Niagara (Dec. 18), then went on to take and burn Buffalo (Dec. 29-30).

Returning to Venezuela, Simón Bolívar's forces defeated Juan Monteverde's Spanish army in a series of battles, taking Caracas (Aug. 6) and besieging Monteverde at Puerto Cabello (Sept.).

b. David Dixon Porter (d. 1891), American admiral.

b. John Charles Frémont (d. 1890), American general and explorer.

British forces attacked Gurkha fortified towns in southern Nepal (1814-1815).

b. Hung Hsiu ch'üan (d. 1864), Chinese rebel leader.

War of 1812, Creek-American War: At Horseshoe Bend, on the Tallapoosa River (Mar. 27), Andrew Jackson's army of 2,000 decisively defeated the remaining Creek main force of 1,100 to 1,200, killing 600 to 700. The Americans then took most of the land of the decimated Creeks, an estimated 20 million acres.

War of 1812: American forces numbering more than 3,000 invaded Canada, taking Fort Erie (July 2-3). On the Chippewa River (July 5), they met and defeated a British-Canadian-Indian force of 2,000. At Lundy's Lane, near Niagara Falls (July 25), a British army of 3,000 defeated the Americans; the British pursued the retreating Americans back to Fort Erie, which they then besieged.

War of 1812: British seaborne forces routed American troops at Bladenburg (Aug. 24) and took Washington, D.C. (Aug. 24-25), burning many buildings in the city, including the White House and the Capitol.

War of 1812: The Napoleonic Wars completed, Britain strongly reinforced its North American forces. A British invasion army of 14,000 moved south out of Montreal (Aug. 31), meeting an American force of 4,500 at Plattsburgh, with a small British flotilla meet-

1814 (cont.)

1815

Napoleon Bonaparte returned to France from Elba (Mar. 1), took power, and remobilized the country. His new army attacked allied forces led by the duke of Wellington and Gebhard von Blücher in Belgium, fighting inconclusive but costly battles at Ligny and Quatre-Bras (June 16). Napoleon's final battle was at Waterloo (June 18), where his army of 71,000 met Wellington's army of 66,000 and Blücher's army of 45,000, which joined the battle later in the day. Ultimately, the French were unable to break through British lines, the full Prussian strength came onto the field, the British counterattacked, and the French broke and fled. Napoleon abdicated again (June 22) and was exiled to St. Helena. The Treaty of Paris (Nov. 20) imposed still more stringent terms on the French.

Poland's partition among Prussia, Russia, and Austria was reestablished by the Congress of Vienna.

France ended its involvement in the slave trade; other European countries gradually followed the lead of Britain, Holland, and France.

d. Michel Ney (b. 1769), marshal of France; in the fray from Neerwinden (1793) to Waterloo (1815), he commanded the rear guard during the retreat from Moscow (1812).

d. Joachim Murat (b. 1767), French marshal and grand admiral of the empire who became king of Naples (1808) but was eventually court-martialed and executed.

d. Louis Alexandre Berthier (b. 1753), marshal of France who served with Rochambeau (1780-1782) in America; later Napoleon Bonaparte's chief of staff, possibly assassinated after breaking with him.

American naval forces, led by Commodore Stephen Decatur, entered the harbor of Algiers (Mar. 3), without armed action forced release of any American prisoners, received promises that piracy would be ended, and sailed away (June 30). Tunis and Tripoli also promised to end piracy. Piracy continued.

Mohammed Ali put down a mutiny in Cairo, primarily by Albanians in his army.

1814 (cont.)

ing a small American flotilla on Lake Champlain (Sept. 11). The complete victory of the Americans on the lake caused the British land force to retreat to Montreal.

War of 1812: British seaborne forces unsuccessfully attacked Baltimore (Sept. 12-14). The failed British attack on Baltimore's Fort McHenry was the inspiration for Francis Scott Key's "The Star-Spangled Banner," which became America's national anthem.

The Treaty of Ghent (Dec. 24) ended the War of 1812, restoring the prewar status quo. But the British had mounted a major seaborne invasion of Louisiana with a force of 7,500 (Dec. 13). Neither side knowing about the war's end, the British attacked Andrew Jackson's fortified positions across an open field and were decisively defeated, with 2,100 casualties and 500 captured; American casualties totaled 13.

Heavily reinforced Spanish forces in Venezuela lost a series of battles to Simón Bolívar's forces but decisively defeated Bolívar at La Puerta (June 15), took Caracas (July 16), and again defeated his army at Aragua (Aug. 18), at a cost of 2,000 Spanish casualties of 10,000 engaged and most of the 3,000 in the rebel army. Bolívar then fled into exile.

Spain reestablished its control over Santo Domingo.

b. Joseph Hooker (d. 1879), American general.

b. Philip Kearny (d. 1862), American general.

1815

British forces again attacked and this time took and held Kandy, on Ceylon (Sri Lanka) (Feb.).

Mexican War of Independence: Reinforced Spanish and colonial forces defeated José Morelos's rebel forces in a series of small battles, capturing the rebel priest (Nov.) and executing him (Dec.). Low-level guerrilla war continued.

Nueva Granada (Colombia) was invaded by a Spanish and colonial army of 12,000, which besieged and took Cartagena (Sept.-Dec.).

b. George Gordon Meade (d. 1872), American general.

b. William Joseph Hardee (d. 1873), American Confederate (CSA) general.

Europe	Africa and Southwest Asia

1815 (cont.)

d. Edward Michael Pakenham (b. 1778), British general who was killed leading British forces against New Orleans after the War of 1812 had ended.

d. Guillaume Marie Anne Brune (b. 1763), French marshal of the empire.

1816

d. Pierre François Charles Augereau, duke of Castiglione (b. 1757), French marshal of the empire who was called "Child of the People" or "Proud Brigand"; he served during the French revolutionary wars and the Napoleonic Wars.	Napoleonic Wars: As part of the postwar settlements, Britain returned France's Senegalese installations. British and Dutch naval forces bombarded Algiers (Aug. 26); the Algerians released several thousand prisoners. A third Egyptian invasion of Arabia defeated the Wahhabis (1816-1818). After the death of his father, Senzangakona, Shaka took control of the Zulu army, developing new tactics, especially fighting in highly disciplined regimental formations (*impis*) and using short-bladed swords for close engagements.

1817

d. Tadeusz (Thaddeus) Andrezj Bonawentura Kosciusko (b. 1746), Polish general who helped build West Point during the American Revolution, later serving in Poland against Russian invaders (1792) and during the Polish insurrection (1794); using back pay from his American army service, he bought and freed American slaves, also freeing the serfs on his Polish property. d. André Masséna, duke of Rivoli and prince of Essling (b. 1758), French marshal of the empire whom the duke of Wellington regarded as Napoleon Bonaparte's finest field commander. d. Karageorge (George Petrovich; Djordje Petrovic) (b. 1762), Serbian general and independence leader called Kara ("Black") George, under whom irregulars briefly won freedom from the Turks; he was proclaimed leader of independent Serbia (1808-1813). He was assassinated (July 25).	Yoruba kingdom of Oyo essentially collapsed after its northernmost province was taken by the Fulani (ca. 1817).

1818

b. Franz Eduard Ivanovich Todleben (d. 1884), Russian general.	Zulu general Shaka took dictatorial power in Natal, conquering neighboring peoples (1818-1828). d. Dingiswayo (Godongwana) (b. ca. 1770), Mtetwa (Bantu) chief involved in clan warfare in Natal; he was in a civil war against his rival Zwide, of the Ndwandwe clan. Zulu-Ndwandwe War (1818-1819): After Dingiswayo's death, Shaka fought off an attack by Zwide of Ndwandwe at the Battle of Gqokli Hill. King Adandozan of Dahomey was overthrown and replaced by Gezo (r. 1818-1858); his kingdom, which had grown rich from trading captured slaves to Europeans,

Central, South and East Asia, and the Pacific	The Americas

1815 (cont.)

1816

Britain returned Java and other Indonesian regions to the Dutch after the Napoleonic Wars ended. After defeating the Gurkhas and reaching the Katmandu Valley, British forces effectively took control of Nepal. Persians invaded and briefly took Herat before being pushed back.	Spanish and colonial forces completed their reconquest of Nueva Granada (Colombia), taking Bogotá (May). Simón Bolívar returned to Venezuela (Dec.), again leading a largely unsuccessful insurrection against Spain (1816-1818). Argentina declared its independence (July 9). b. George Henry Thomas (d. 1870), American general.

1817

Third British-Maratha War (1817-1818): British forces decisively defeated Holkar's Maratha army at Mahidput (Dec. 21), effectively ending the Maratha wars. Dutch forces defeated a substantial insurrection in the Molucca Islands (May-Nov.).	Argentine and Chilean forces of almost 4,000, led by generals José de San Martin and Bernardo O'Higgins, crossed the Andes (Jan.), defeated Spanish and colonial forces at Chacabuco (Feb. 12), and then took Santiago (Feb. 15). First Seminole War: Negro Fort on the Apalachicola River, built and held by escaped slaves and Seminoles, was attacked by American land and riverborne forces, who destroyed the fort and killed almost all of its more than 300 defenders (July 27). b. Braxton Bragg (d. 1876), American Confederate (CSA) general.

1818

On Ceylon (Sri Lanka), an islandwide Sinhalese insurrection (1817-1818) against British rule was defeated. Third British-Maratha War: Maratha formally surrendered to the British (June 2). b. Feng Tzu-ts'ai (d. 1903), Chinese general.	At Cancha-Rayada (Mar. 16), José de San Martin's forces were defeated by Spanish and colonial forces; the revolutionary army won a decisive battle on the Maipo River (Apr. 5), with minor revolutionary casualties; Spanish casualties were 1,000 and more than 2,000 captured; Spanish forces then retreated to Peru. General Andrew Jackson led an American and Indian force of 5,000 in an invasion of Spanish-held Florida, attacking villages of Seminoles and escaped slaves, taking St. Marks, and ultimately occupying Florida. The United States took Florida from Spain under the Adams-Onis Treaty (Feb. 22, 1819). b. Pierre Gustave Toutant Beauregard (d. 1893), American Confederate (CSA) general. b. Wade Hampton (d. 1902), American Confederate (CSA) general.

Europe	Africa and Southwest Asia

1818 (cont.)

	was unusual in that women formed its elite royal guard. Under Ahmadu ibn Hammadi, the Fulani jihad state of Macina took Segu, Djénné, and Timbuktu. Boer forces again attacked the Xhosa.

1819

d. Gebhard Leberecht von Blücher (b. 1742), Prussian field marshal called "Alte Vorwärts" ("Old Forward"). d. Jean Mathieu Philibert Sérurier (b. 1742), French marshal of the empire.	Zulu-Ndwandwe War: Attempting to withdraw after a failed attack, Zwide's Ndwandwe forces were annihilated by Shaka's Zulu (May). This laid the basis for Shaka's Zulu Empire.

1820

Spanish Revolution (1820-1823): Colonel Rafael del Riego led a successful republican insurrection in Spain (Jan.), capturing Ferdinand VII. Portuguese democrats took power in a successful insurrection (Aug. 29), establishing a constitutional monarchy. General Guglielmo Pepe led an insurrection in Naples. d. Karl Philip, prince of Schwarzenberg (b. 1771), Austrian field marshal who became commander in chief of allied forces against France (1813); he was defeated at Dresden but won at Leipzig. He led the Army of Bohemia in the invasion of France (1814). d. François Étienne Christophe Kellermann (b. 1735), French marshal of the empire who commanded the Army of the Moselle at the Battle of Valmy (1792). d. Francis Joseph Lefebvre, duke of Danzig (b. 1755), French marshal of the empire.	Shaka's Zulu army began the period called the Mfecane (Crushing) (ca. 1820-1835), attacking and destroying, absorbing, or driving out neighboring peoples, mostly Bantu, with an estimated death toll of 1 million to 2 million. Mohammed Ali's Egyptian forces, led by his son Hussein, attacked in the Sudan (1820-1839); their conquests included much of the western coast of the Red Sea and extended south to Gondokoro (Equatoria).

1821

d. Napoleon I (Napoleon Bonaparte; Napoléone di Buoneparte) (b. 1769), French general and emperor, popularly called "Le Petit Caporal" ("The Little Corporal"), who came to prominence during the French Revolution and convulsed Europe with the Napoleonic Wars; exiled to Elba (1814), he returned to France but lost definitively at Waterloo (1815); he was exiled permanently to St. Helena, where he died, possibly of arsenic poisoning. Greek War of Independence (1821-1832): Greek forces took much of Morea (the Peloponnesus) and many Aegean islands from the Turks; the rising was	Turkish-Persian War (1821-1823): Persian forces led by Abbas Mirza attacked northern Turkey; at Erzurum the Persians defeated a Turkish army reportedly 50,000 strong; the Turks made a counterthrust in the south.

Central, South and East Asia, and the Pacific	The Americas	
1818 (cont.)		
	d. George Rogers Clark (b. 1752), American general active during Lord Dunmore's War (1774) and the Revolutionary War; his younger brother was explorer William Clark (of Lewis and Clark).	
	d. Paul Revere (b. 1735), American militia commander famed for his "midnight ride" from Boston to Lexington, Massachusetts, to warn patriots that the British were coming (Apr. 18-19, 1775).	
	d. Henry Lee (b. 1756), Revolutionary War officer nicknamed "Lighthorse Harry" who led a mixed corps of dragoons and light infantry (Lee's Legion); in the House of Representatives, he memorialized George Washington as "first in war, first in peace, and first in the hearts of his countrymen" (1799).	
	d. Arthur St. Clair (b. 1736), American general who evacuated his troops from Fort Ticonderoga (1777), preserving them for Saratoga, an action for which he was court-martialed and acquitted.	
1819		
Burma took Assam. Singapore was founded by Stamford Raffles. Ranjit Singh's Sikh forces conquered Kashmir.	Simón Bolívar's forces crossed the Andes into Nueva Granada (Colombia) (June-July). At Boyacá (Aug. 7), his army of 2,000 defeated a Spanish and colonial force of 3,000. b. William Starke Rosecrans (d. 1898), American general. d. Oliver Hazard Perry (b. 1785), American naval officer who defeated the British at Lake Erie (1813), reporting, "We have met the enemy and they are ours."	
1820		
After Burma took Assam, Assamese rebels mounted an insurrection against the Burmese, from centers in British-held Manipur (1820-1822).	Simón Bolívar's republican forces took Bogotá (spring); he then became the first president of the Colombian republic. Civil war ended in Haiti with the assassination of Henri Christophe; Jean Pierre Boyer became president. Brazil annexed the Banda Oriental (Uruguay) after defeating rebel leader José Artigas. b. William Tecumseh Sherman (d. 1891), American general. b. Horatio Gouverneur Wright (d. 1899), American general. d. Daniel Boone (b. 1734), American frontiersman and militia officer who opened the Cumberland Gap route beyond the Appalachians (1775). d. Stephen Decatur (b. 1779), American naval officer active in the War of 1812; he led a 10-ship squadron against Barbary pirates in the Mediterranean (1815).	
1821		
Siamese forces took Kedah, in Malaya. b. Shih Ta-k'ai (d. 1863), Chinese rebel general.	Mexican War of Independence: General Augustín Iturbide made an alliance with guerrilla forces and took Mexico City. Mexico became an independent nation (Feb. 24), with Iturbide as Emperor Augustín I (July 21). Simón Bolívar returned to Venezuela (Apr.), leading an army of 7,000 from Nueva Granada (Colombia). At Carabobo (June 25), his forces decisively defeated Spanish and colonial forces, winning Venezuelan independence, although hostilities continued.	

1821 (cont.)

accompanied by many massacres of Muslims by Greeks, most notably at Tripolitsa (Oct. 5), where 10,000 Turkish soldiers and civilians were reportedly killed after the fortress was taken.

Intervening Austrian forces at Rieti put down an insurrection in Naples (Mar.).

At Novara, Austrian forces joined royalist Sardinian forces to defeat Sardinian revolutionaries (Apr. 8).

John VI returned from Brazilian exile to take the throne of Portugal's new constitutional monarchy (July 4).

Greek forces defeated a Romanian rising (Mar.-June).

1822

Greek War of Independence: The Greeks declared their independence at Epidauros (Jan. 13). Turkish seaborne forces took Chios (June 18-19), massacring or enslaving most of its population of 20,000.

Greek War of Independence: Turkish forces unsuccessfully besieged Missolonghi (July 1822-Jan. 1823). Greek forces under Marco Bozzaris surprised and routed Turkish forces led by Mustai Pasha at the Battle of Karpenizi (Aug. 21).

Former slaves from America founded Monrovia, Liberia.

Sayyid Sa'id of Muscat, allied with Britain, expanded in East Africa (1822-1824), taking Pemba and threatening Mombasa, making repeated failed attacks.

1823

French forces intervened in Spain (Apr. 17); an army of 100,000 crossed the Pyrenees, took Madrid, and pursued and decisively defeated Rafael del Riego's forces near Cadiz, at the Trocadero (Aug. 31). Ferdinand VII again took the throne, until his death (1833).

Portuguese Civil Wars: Miguel, a son of John VI, made a failed attempt to take power (1823-1824).

d. John Jervis (b. 1735), British admiral of long service, most notably off Cape St. Vincent (1797); he became first lord of the admiralty (1801-1803) and admiral of the Channel Fleet (1806-1807).

d. Lazare Nicolas Marguerite Carnot (b. 1753), French general who directed military affairs as part of the Committee of Public Safety (from 1793) but went into exile in Switzerland (1797) until serving in the War Ministry under Napoleon Bonaparte (1800).

d. Louis Nicolas Davout, duke of Auerstädt and prince of Eckmühl (b. 1770), French marshal of the empire.

Turkish-Persian War ended with restoration of the prewar status quo.

1824

d. George Gordon, Lord Byron (b. 1788), British poet who died while fighting on the Greek side during their war of independence. His death spurred espousal of the Greek cause by many Europeans and would be a decisive element in the resolution of the conflict.

First British-Ashanti War (1824-1826): British and colonial forces disputed with the Ashanti for control of the Gold Coast.

British naval forces bombarded Algiers.

Central, South and East Asia, and the Pacific	The Americas

	1821 (cont.)
	Chilean seaborne forces led by José de San Martin invaded Peru, taking Lima (July). José Carrera briefly made himself dictator but was soon assassinated.
	d. José Miguel Carrera (b. 1785), Chilean general during the Napoleonic Wars and the Latin American wars of independence; briefly Chilean dictator, he was killed by his own forces (Sept. 4).
	b. James Longstreet (d. 1904), American Confederate (CSA) general.
	b. John Cabell Breckenridge (d. 1875), American Confederate (CSA) general.
	b. Nathan Bedford Forrest (d. 1877), American Confederate (CSA) general.

	1822
Burmese forces attacked Manipur but ultimately retreated into Burma after being engaged by British and Manipur forces.	Brazil became an independent nation (Sept. 7); Portuguese prince Dom Pedro became Emperor Pedro I (Dec. 1).
	At Pinchincha, Ecuador (May 24), General Antonio de Sucre's Venezuelan forces defeated Spanish and colonial forces defending Quito, then took the city.
	Jean Pierre Boyer's Haitian forces retook Santo Domingo from the Spanish.
	b. Ulysses Simpson (Hiram Ulysses) Grant (d. 1885), American general and 18th president of the United States (1869-1877).
	b. Red Cloud (Mahpiua Luta) (d. 1909), Oglala Sioux war chief.
	b. John Pope (d. 1892), American general.

	1823
First British-Burmese War (1823-1826): Burmese forces successfully attacked Bengal, threatening Chittagong. British Indian forces prepared for an attack on Burma.	Mexican War of Independence: Republican revolution in Mexico deposed Augustín I (Mar. 19).
b. Hung Ta-chüan (d. 1852), Chinese rebel general.	Portuguese forces evacuated Bahia by sea (July), returning to Portugal after Brazilian naval forces took their intended destinations elsewhere on the Brazilian coast.

	1824
First British-Burmese War: Indian and British forces invaded Arakan, taking Arakan City with negligible losses (Apr. 1), but retreated after being struck by an epidemic. Indian forces also attacked the Burmese in	At Ayacucho (Dec. 9), Antonio de Sucre's republican army of 7,000 decisively defeated José de La Serna's Spanish army of 10,000, with more than 1,000 republican casualties to more than 2,000 Spanish casualties and more than 2,000 captured, among them La Serna.

Europe	Africa and Southwest Asia

1824 (cont.)

d. Eugène de Beauharnais (b. 1781), French general; adopted son of and key aide to Napoleon Bonaparte, who made him viceroy of Italy (1805) and commander of the Army of Italy (1809).	Muscat ruler Sayyid Sa'id took control of the East African port of Pate.

1825

Decembrist Rising: Republican revolutionary forces numbering 3,000 were defeated by Czarist forces in Moscow (Dec. 14), effectively ending the insurrection. Greek War of Independence: Turkish forces again besieged and would this time take Missolonghi (May 1825-Apr. 1826). Greek War of Independence: Turkish forces, having reconquered most of Greece, moved on Athens, besieging the Acropolis (May-June); the Greeks surrendered (June 5). Egyptian seaborne forces retook much of Morea (the Peloponnesus) (Feb.). d. Alexander I (Aleksandr Pavlovich) (b. 1777), Russian czar (r. 1801-1825) during the Napoleonic Wars; he was in nominal command at Austerlitz (1805) and Leipzig (1813) and also expanded Russia into the Caucasus Mountains and the Balkans.	Russo-Persian War (1825-1828): Persian forces led by Abbas Mirza attacked the Russians in the Caucasus Mountains, with some early successes, besieging Tiflis. First British-Ashanti War: British and colonial forces were defeated on the Gold Coast by Ashanti forces. After years of failure (1818-1825), the French gave up their attempt to take Madagascar.

1826

Greek War of Independence: Besieged Missolonghi fell to the Turks. d. Louis Gabriel Suchet (b. 1770), French marshal of the empire; he was a key general in Spain, from which he eventually had to withdraw because of French losses elsewhere, being placed in command of the Army of the South. d. Francis Rawdon-Hastings, earl of Moira (b. 1754), Irish-born British general during the American Revolution and the French revolutionary wars; he later served in India and Malta, where he was governor and commander in chief.	Russo-Persian War: At Ganja (Sept. 26), Russian forces numbering 15,000, led by General Ivan Raskevich, went on the offensive, defeating Abbas Mirza's army of 15,000 in the decisive battle of the war. After a Janissary revolt in Constantinople, a reported 6,000 Janissaries were massacred (June 15-16). Muhammad al-Kanami came into full control in Bornu, with a puppet ruler.

1827

Greek War of Independence: In the harbor of Navarino (Oct. 20), an English-French-Russian war fleet destroyed a much weaker Turkish-Egyptian fleet at anchor, with minimal allied losses, effectively ending the war. The Treaty of London (May 7) recognized Greek independence. Portuguese Civil Wars: On the death of John VI, Miguel again tried to seize power, taking Lisbon; he was defeated by government forces supported by a British seaborne force of 5,000 and temporarily withdrew. b. Wilhelm von Tegetthoff (b. 1871), Austrian admiral.	Russo-Persian War: Ivan Paskevich's forces took Erivan by storm; Tabriz surrendered. The defeated Turks acknowledged the prewar status quo. France began a sustained attack on Algeria with a blockade of the port of Algiers. b. Frederick Augustus Thesiger, second Baron Chelmsford (d. 1905), British general.

Central, South and East Asia, and the Pacific	The Americas	

Assam and Bengal, forcing them back into Burma. A British-Indian army made seaborne landings at Rangoon, took the city without a battle (May 11), and was unsuccessfully besieged (May-Dec.). Malacca again came under English rule, exchanged by the Dutch (Mar. 17) for Benkgulen, on Sumatra. b. Li Hsiu-ch'eng (d. 1864), Chinese rebel general.	Spanish surrender came the next day. Sucre became the first president of the Bolivian republic. Mexican War of Independence: Mexican republic came into being (Oct. 4). b. Thomas Jonathan Jackson (d. 1863), American Confederate (CSA) general. b. Ambrose Everett Burnside (d. 1881), American general. b. Edmund Kirby Smith (d. 1893), American Confederate (CSA) general.	

1825

First British-Burmese War: British forces moved out of Rangoon, defeated the Burmese in a series of battles on the Irrawaddy River, and took Prome (Apr. 25), where they were besieged by Burmese forces during the monsoon season. The British decisively defeated the Burmese at Prome (Nov. 30-Dec. 2) and moved toward the Burmese capital of Ava. Major Javanese rising against the Dutch was defeated (1825-1830). b. Sher Ali Khan (d. 1879), Afghan ruler (r. 1863-1878).	Argentine-Brazilian War (1825-1828): Argentine forces invaded the Banda Oriental (Uruguay) in support of a Uruguayan insurrection against Brazilian rule (Dec.). Mexican forces defeated a Yaqui rising in Sonora (1825-1827). b. George Edward Pickett (d. 1875), American Confederate (CSA) general. b. Ambrose Powell Hill (d. 1865), American Confederate (CSA) general. b. John Hunt Morgan (d. 1864), American Confederate (CSA) general. d. James Wilkinson (b. 1757), Revolutionary War soldier who later became commander in chief of forces fighting Indians in the Northwest (1796).	

1826

First British-Burmese War: Britain took Arakan, Assam, and much of Tenasserim from defeated Burma (Feb.). Laotian-Siamese War (1826-1828): Laotian forces attacked Siam, threatening Bangkok, but they were thrown back by the Siamese. British forces again attacked Bhurtpore, this time taking the city by storm (Jan. 18). British colonists consolidated their holdings in Malaya as the Straits Settlement.	b. George Brinton McClellan (d. 1885), American general. b. Benjamin Henry Grierson (d. 1911), American general.	

1827

Laotian-Siamese War: Siamese forces attacked Laos, decisively defeated the Laotians at Nong-Bona-Lampon, on the Mekong River, and went on to take and destroy Vientiane. b. Takamori Saigo (d. 1877), Japanese field marshal.	At Ituzaingo (Feb. 20), joint Argentine-Uruguayan forces defeated a Brazilian army; each army of more than 8,000 lost fewer than 500. Peruvian forces attacked Bolivia and Ecuador.	

Europe	Africa and Southwest Asia

1827 (cont.)

d. Frederick Augustus, duke of York and Albany (b. 1763), British field marshal who became commander in chief (1798), focusing strongly on improving training for officers and infantry.	b. Cetshwayo (Cetewayo) (d. 1884), Zulu king (r. 1873-1879).

1828

Portuguese Civil Wars: Miguel took power in Portugal (July 7); infant Queen Maria went into Brazilian exile. Civil War began between the "Miguelites" and royalist forces, who were supported by England and France. Miguelite naval forces made a failed attempt to take the Azores (Aug.).	**First British-Ashanti War:** British forces decisively defeated an Ashanti army at Dodowah (Aug. 7), effectively taking control of several coastal areas.
Russo-Turkish War (1828-1829): Russian forces attacked the Balkans, besieging and taking Varna (Oct.), then besieging Silestra. In the Caucasus Mountains, the Russians took besieged Kars (July 5) and Akhaltikhe (Aug. 27).	Muscat ruler Sayyid Sa'id established a base at Zoazibar, in East Africa.
b. Prince Frederick Charles (d. 1885), Prussian field marshal.	Russo-Persian War ended with the Treaty of Turkomanchi (Feb. 22).
	d. Shaka (Chaka) (b. ca. 1787), Zulu leader whose highly effective shock tactics allowed for a Zulu expansion (1818-1828) so brutal that it became known as the Mfecane (Crushing); the illegitimate son of Zulu leader Senzangakona, he was assassinated (Sept. 28) by two half-brothers — Dingane, who succeeded him, and Mhlangana, who lost the succession struggle.

1829

Russo-Turkish War: Russian forces took Adrianople (Aug. 20) and threatened Constantinople; the war ended with Russian acquisition of eastern portions of the Black Sea coast and the mouth of the Danube.	Muscat ruler Sayyid Sa'id made a failed attack on Mombasa.
	French forces ineffectively bombed Tamatave, on Madagascar.

1830

Belgian War of Independence began with an insurrection against Dutch forces in Brussels (Aug. 25); Belgium then declared its independence (Oct. 4). Dutch forces attacked Brussels, taking its citadel (Oct. 27), but they could not take the city. Belgian independence was declared by the London Conference (Dec.), which dissolved the Kingdom of the Netherlands.	**French-Algerian War (1830-1847):** French seaborne forces numbering 37,000 to 38,000 attacked Algiers (June), defeated a defending force of 45,000, took the city (July 3), and then occupied much of coastal and some of inland Algeria. The long war of resistance that followed was led by Abd-el-Kader.
French Revolution of 1830 (July 28) deposed Charles X and established a new constitutional monarchy headed by Louis Philippe.	
Polish Revolution (1830-1831): Insurrection against Russian occupation forces began in Warsaw (Nov. 29) and grew into a full-scale revolution.	

1827 (cont.)

1828

Siam annexed Laos.

1829

Cuba-based Spanish forces mounted a failed invasion of Mexico, taking Tampico (Aug. 18). Mexican forces led by Antonio Santa Anna besieged and retook the city and the Spanish invasion force (Sept. 11).

Peruvian naval forces captured Guayaquil (Jan.); Bolivian and Ecuadorian forces defeated the Peruvian army at Tarqui (Feb. 27), then retook Guayaquil (Feb. 28).

b. Geronimo (Jerome; Goyathlay) (d. 1909), Chiricahua Apache leader.

b. George Crook (d. 1890), American general.

d. Henry Dearborn (b. 1751), American general active in the Revolutionary War and the War of 1812; as Thomas Jefferson's secretary of war, he founded Fort Dearborn (1803), which became Chicago.

1830

d. Simón Bolívar (b. 1783), Latin American general called "El Libertador" ("The Liberator"), a key leader in the fight for Latin American independence; after a stunning victory at Boyacá (Aug. 7, 1819), he took Bogotá and established the Republic of Nueva Granada (Colombia) (spring 1820); he wrote a constitution and sought a Pan-American union, but later, ill and disillusioned by dissension, he left for Europe.

Ecuador became an independent nation.

b. Porfirio Díaz (d. 1915), Mexican revolutionary general and dictator.

1830 (cont.)

Europe	Africa and Southwest Asia
d. Johann David Ludwig Yorck von Wartenburg (b. 1759), Prussian field marshal during the Napoleonic Wars, at first allied with Napoleon Bonaparte, later against him. d. Laurent Gouvion Saint-Cyr (b. 1764), French marshal of the empire who fell out of favor with Napoleon but was later restored; he became Louis XVIII's minister of war (1815; 1817-1819). d. Dominique Joseph René Vandamme (b. 1770), French general who served most notably at Austerlitz (1805).	

1831

Europe	Africa and Southwest Asia
Dutch forces numbering 50,000 attacked Belgium (Aug. 2), retaking most of the country. A French army of 63,000 intervened, driving the Dutch out of Belgium, except for Dutch forces besieged in Antwerp's citadel, which later surrendered (Dec.). Polish Revolution: At Grochow, near Warsaw, attacking Russian forces were forced to withdraw by defending Polish forces (Feb. 20); at Ostrolenka (May 26), the Poles retreated toward Warsaw after fighting to a draw. The Russians took Warsaw by storm (Sept. 8), ending the insurrection. b. Charles Jean Jacques Joseph Ardant du Picq (d. 1870), French army officer and military theorist. d. Karl Maria von Clausewitz (b. 1780), Prussian general noted for his writings on military theory, especially *Vom Kriege (On War)*, begun in 1819; he was director of the Allgemeine Kriegsschule (War College) in Berlin (1819). d. August Wilhelm Anton, Count Neithardt von Gneisenau (b. 1760), Prussian field marshal who was chief of staff to Gebhard von Blücher during the Waterloo campaign (1815).	b. Petrus Jacobus Joubert (d. 1900), Boer general.

1832

Europe	Africa and Southwest Asia
Portuguese Civil Wars: Royalist forces organized in England and led by Dom Pedro, Maria's father, took Oporto (July) and were there unsuccessfully besieged by Miguelite forces numbering 80,000 (1832-1833). b. Frederick Sleigh Roberts (d. 1914), British field marshal.	First Egyptian-Turkish War (1832-1833): Egyptian forces attacked and took Syria (May-July) and later defeated the Turks at Konya (Dec.), in Anatolia. b. Osman Nuri Pasha (d. 1900), Turkish general.

1833

Europe	Africa and Southwest Asia
First Carlist War (1833-1839): A Spanish civil war of succession followed the death of Ferdinand VII, between the government forces of regent Maria Christina for the infant Isabella, which drew substantial French, English, and Portuguese support, and those of Don Carlos, Ferdinand's brother. The conflict was largely a long guerrilla war that cost an estimated 120,000 lives, with the Carlists gaining strength until their disastrous attempt to take Madrid (1837). Portuguese Civil Wars: João Carlos de Saldanha's royalist forces made seaborne landings in Algarve (June), then campaigned successfully against the Miguelites in southern Portugal. Portuguese Civil Wars: Off Cape St. Vincent (July 5), a royalist Portuguese-British fleet commanded by Admiral Charles Napier defeated Miguelite forces, then took and held Lisbon.	Muscat ruler Sayyid Sa'id made another failed attack on Mombasa. d. Abbas Mirza (b. 1783), Persian general during wars against the Russians and the Turks, whom he defeated decisively at Erzurum (1821).

Central, South and East Asia, and the Pacific

The Americas

Central, South and East Asia, and the Pacific	The Americas	

1831

Siamese-Cambodian War (1831-1834): Siamese forces attacked Cambodia; after early successes in which the Siamese took much of the country, Vietnamese forces and Cambodian risings forced the Siamese out of Cambodia; the Vietnamese stayed, holding much of the country.

Nat Turner led a slave rebellion in Virginia; hundreds of slaves, including Turner, died during the rising and in the reign of terror that followed, as did more than 50 Whites.

b. Sitting Bull (Tatanka Yotanka) (ca. 1831-1890), Hunkpapa Sioux chief.

b. Philip Henry Sheridan (d. 1888), American general.

b. John Bell Hood (d. 1879), American Confederate (CSA) general.

1832

Black Hawk War: After being forced off their land, an Indian coalition led by Sauk and Fox chief Black Hawk went to war in Illinois and Wisconsin. Of a force numbering 600 to 900, an estimated 300 Indians died at the Battle of Bad Axe (Aug. 2), with minimal American casualties, effectively ending the war.

1833

b. James Ewell Brown (Jeb) Stuart (d. 1864), American Confederate (CSA) general.

Europe	Africa and Southwest Asia

1833 (cont.)

Britain, which had given up slave trading (1807), prohibited slavery in its entire empire.

b. Alfred von Schlieffen (d. 1913), Prussian general.

b. Charles George Gordon (d. 1885), British general.

b. Garnet Joseph Wolseley (d. 1913), British field marshal.

d. Banastre Tarleton (b. 1754), British general during the American Revolution, nicknamed "Bloody Ben" after the Battle of Camden (1780), when his troops bayoneted Americans trying to surrender.

d. Jean-Baptiste Jourdan (b. 1762), French marshal of the empire.

1834

Europe	Africa and Southwest Asia
Portuguese Civil Wars: João Carlos de Saldanha's royalist forces decisively defeated Miguel's forces at Santarém (May 16), ending the war. d. Marie Joseph Paul Yves Roch Gilbert du Motier, Marquis de Lafayette (La Fayette) (b. 1757), French general who served with distinction with the Americans during the Revolutionary War, playing a crucial role in the decisive siege of Yorktown (1781).	Boers in southern Africa intensified the development of their separatist movement (ca. 1834), partly reacting to Britain's ban on slavery. Boer attacks on the Xhosa continued, but the British forced them to return land just taken, restoring the status quo along the Fish River.

1835

Europe	Africa and Southwest Asia
b. George Stuart White (d. 1912), British field marshal. d. Édouard Adolphe Casimir Joseph Mortier (b. 1768), French marshal of the empire serving most notably at Dürrenstein (1805); he was killed by a bomb intended for King Louis Philippe, whom he was escorting on parade.	Turkish forces took Tripolitania (1835-1836). b. Samori Toure (ca. 1835-1900), Dioula war chief and ruler.

1836

Europe	Africa and Southwest Asia
Holland formally recognized Belgian independence (Apr. 19).	Boer Trek: In southern Africa 10,000 to 14,000 Trekboers and their slaves (called apprentices) migrated north out of the Cape Colony into the high veld. The Potgeiter and Cilliers parties together defeated much larger Matabele Zulu forces at Vegkop in the Transvaal (Oct. 19). French forces took Constantine, in eastern Algeria, by storm (Oct.).

Central, South and East Asia, and the Pacific	The Americas	
1833 (cont.)		
1834		
1835		
b. Tz'u Hsi (d. 1908), the dowager empress of China.	Texas War of Independence (1835-1836): American settlers mounted an insurrection against Mexican rule, winning early battles at Concepción (Oct.) and San Antonio (Dec.). Second Seminole War (1835-1843): American forces mounted a long guerrilla war against the Seminoles and escaped slaves of the Everglades, who resisted expropriation of their lands. The Seminoles were led by Osceola until his capture (1837), the Americans by generals Winfield Scott and Zachary Taylor. Samuel Colt was granted his first revolver patent, in England. b. William Rufus Shafter (d. 1906), American general.	
1836		
Persian forces led by Mohammed Shah attacked Afghanistan, moving through Khorasan toward Herat. b. Ch'en Yü-ch'eng (d. 1862), Chinese Taiping general. b. Sumiyoshi (Jungi) Kawamura (d. 1904), Japanese admiral. b. Takeaki (Buyo) Enomoto (d. 1908), Japanese admiral.	Texas War of Independence: At the Alamo, in San Antonio, a force of fewer than 200 Texans, led by Colonel William B. Travis, chose to die rather than surrender to a besieging Mexican army of 3,000, with artillery, led by Mexican president Antonio López de Santa Anna (Feb. 23-Mar. 6). Texas declared its independence (Mar. 2). At San Jacinto (Apr. 21), the main Texan army of fewer than 800, led by Sam Houston, decisively defeated the Mexicans, with more than 900 Mexican casualties and more than 700 captured, including Santa Anna, effectively ending the war. d. James Bowie (b. 1796), American soldier who fought for Texan independence, dying in the Mexican siege of the Alamo (Feb. 23-Mar. 6); the Bowie knife used in hunting was named after him. b. Joseph Wheeler (d. 1906), American general.	

Europe	Africa and Southwest Asia

1837

First Carlist War: Although the Carlists won a substantial victory at Huesca (May), they failed to take Madrid, and in the subsequent retreat to the Ebro River, they lost 13,000 of their 17,000 soldiers.

Russian forces took the besieged Murid fortress at Ahulgo, in Daghestan, with almost 3,000 Russian casualties, as a long Russian-Murid guerrilla war in the Caucasus Mountains intensified.

After repeated attacks (1822-1837), Muscat's Sayyid Sa'id took Mombasa.

1838

b. Henry Evelyn Wood (d. 1919), British field marshal.

b. Valeriano Weyler y Nicolau, marquis of Tenerife (d. 1930), Spanish general.

Durban Massacre: Boer negotiators led by Piet Retief were massacred by Dingane's Zulu forces in Natal (Feb.); the Zulu simultaneously attacked several thousand Trekboers who had just traversed the Drakensberg Mountains, with several hundred Boer casualties.

At the Blood River in southern Africa (Dec. 16), Andries Pretorius's small Boer force, equipped with guns and horses, defeated Dingane's large Zulu army, fighting on foot and without firearms; the Zulu lost 3,000; Boer losses were negligible.

1839

First Carlist War: Conflict formally ended with the Convention of Vergara (Aug. 31).

Second Egyptian-Turkish War (1839-1841): Turkish forces, with Prussian advisers, invaded Syria and were decisively defeated at Nezib (June 24). The Turkish fleet was surrendered to the Egyptians (July).

British forces took Aden, in Yemen, on the Red Sea route to India.

1840

In Spain General Baldomero Espartero led a successful revolt (1840-1843), forcing Queen Isabella II to flee the country.

d. Jacques Étienne Joseph Alexandre Macdonald, duke of Taranto (b. 1765), French marshal of the empire; he was the son of Nael Stephan Macdonald, a

Second Egyptian-Turkish War: British and Austrian naval forces intervened in favor of Turkey (Sept.); British forces took Beirut and Acre from the Egyptians (Sept.-Oct.).

Central, South and East Asia, and the Pacific	The Americas
	1837
Persian forces led by Mohammed Shah besieged Herat City (Nov. 23).	Louis Papineau led a failed French-Canadian rising against British rule in Quebec (Nov.). His forces were defeated by the British at St. Denis (Nov. 22).
	Second Seminole War: At Lake Okeechobee, in the Everglades, American forces led by Winfield Scott defeated a Seminole force, though not decisively; the guerrilla war continued.
	b. William Clarke Quantrill (d. 1865), American Confederate (CSA) guerrilla leader.
	b. George Dewey (d. 1917), American admiral.
	b. James Harrison Wilson (d. 1925), American general.
	b. Robert Frederick Hoke (d. 1912), American Confederate (CSA) general.
	b. Robert Gould Shaw (d. 1863), commander of the first African-American regiment, the 54th Massachusetts.
	1838
British East India Company's Bombay Army forced Mohammed Shah's Persian forces to lift a 10-month siege of Herat City (Sept. 28).	French seaborne forces took Veracruz (Apr. 16) and blockaded Mexico's Atlantic coast, withdrawing from both areas after satisfaction of French demands (1838-1839).
Mon independence forces mounted a failed rising against the Burmese.	d. Black Hawk (Ma-ka-tai-me-she-kia-kiak) (b. 1767), Sauk and Fox war chief whose people were largely destroyed after their defeat in the Black Hawk War (1832).
b. Aritomo Yamagata (d. 1922), Japanese field marshal.	d. Osceola (b. 1804), Seminole chief who led protests against being moved off Indian land to a reservation; he was captured and died in prison (Jan. 30).
	d. William Clark (b. 1770), American army officer and explorer who joined Meriwether Lewis in exploring North America to the Pacific coast (1803); he was the younger brother of George Rogers Clark.
	1839
First British-Afghan War (1839-1842): British forces numbering more than 15,000, led by John Keane, attacked out of India into Afghanistan, taking Ghazni (July 23) and Kabul (Aug. 7). Before leaving, they set up Shah Shuja as a puppet ruler, in place of his deposed older brother Dost Muhammad; they left a British garrison at Kabul.	At Yungay (Jan. 20), a Chilean army decisively defeated the joint armies of Bolivia and Peru, forcing the dissolution of the Peruvian Bolivian Confederation.
	b. George Armstrong Custer (d. 1876), American general.
	b. Nelson Appleton Miles (d. 1925), American general.
Chinese-British Opium War (1839-1842): British forces attacked China when the Chinese attempted to stop the British-sponsored opium trade at Canton. British naval forces defeated a Chinese fleet.	b. Winfield Scott Schley (d. 1909), American admiral.
	1840
Chinese-British Opium War: British naval forces defeated another Chinese fleet, then moved onshore.	Inconclusive Comanche-Texan border war was generated by the murders of 12 Comanche chiefs and other Comanches by the Texans while engaged in peace negotiations (Mar. 19).
	b. Chief Joseph (Hinmahton-Yahlaktit; Thunder-Rolling-Over-the-Mountains) (ca. 1840-1904), Nez Percé chief.

Europe	Africa and Southwest Asia

1840 (cont.)

Europe	Africa and Southwest Asia
Scottish Jacobite self-exiled in France after Charles Stuart's defeat at Culloden Moor (1746). d. William Sidney Smith (b. 1764), British admiral during the American Revolution, French revolutionary wars, and Napoleonic Wars, most notably in harassing French ships (1793-1796) and defending besieged Acre (1799).	West Africa's kingdom of Dahomey went into decline with the effective end of the slave trade that had made its fortune (ca. 1840). Zulu leader Dingane was forced to flee after being defeated by his brother (and successor) Mpande, who had allied himself with the Boers, ceding them southern Natal. Muscat ruler Sayyid Sa'id established his capital at Zanzibar.

1841

Europe	Africa and Southwest Asia
b. Georges Eugene Benjamin Clemenceau (d. 1929), French politician and wartime premier. b. Edward VII (d. 1910), king of Britain (r. 1901-1910). b. John Arbuthnot (d. 1920), British admiral. d. Claude, duke of Victor-Perrin (b. 1764), French marshal of the empire who commanded the rear guard in the retreat from Moscow (1812), later becoming minister of war.	Second Egyptian-Turkish War: Egyptian forces left Syria, returning that country to Turkey (Feb.).

1842

Europe	Africa and Southwest Asia
d. Bon Adrien Jeannot de Moncey, duke of Conegliano (b. 1754), French general during the French revolutionary wars and the Napoleonic Wars. d. Henry Shrapnel (b. 1761), British general who gave his name to the exploding canister shell he invented, first adopted by Britain (1803). d. Rowland Hill (b. 1772), British general during the French revolutionary wars and the Napoleonic Wars; he returned from a 10-year retirement to become commander in chief (1828-1842).	Boer settlers in Natal proclaimed the Republic of Natal. Britain responded with a force of 250, which took Port Natal and was there besieged by the Boers until seaborne relief forces relieved them, reestablishing British rule. French colonial forces expanded their area of control in West Africa, moving south from Senegal to take much of the Ivory Coast (1842-1843). b. Abdul Hamid II (d. 1918), Turkish ruler (r. 1876-1909).

1840 (cont.)

Central, South and East Asia, and the Pacific	The Americas	
	b. Alfred Thayer Mahan (d. 1914), American admiral and strategist.	
	b. Gall (Pizi) (ca. 1840-1894), Sioux war chief.	
	b. William Thomas Sampson (d. 1902), American admiral.	

1841

Chinese-British Opium War: British forces took the Bogue forts, on the Pearl River approaches to Canton (Feb. 16), and then Canton itself (May 24). Moving north on the coast, the British took Amoy (Aug. 26) and Ninghsien (Oct. 13). First British-Afghan War: Akbar Khan, son of Dost Muhammad, led a successful rising against British occupation forces of almost 4,000 at Kabul (Nov.); General William Elphinstone's surrendered British forces and civilians were promised safe conduct for their retreat into India. Siamese-Vietnamese War (1841-1843): Siam and Vietnam fought inconclusively over Cambodia, with the Siamese gaining tenuous control of much of the country.	Peruvian forces invaded Bolivia but were defeated by the Bolivians at Ingaví (Nov. 18); among the more than 500 Peruvian dead was president Augustín Gamarra. d. William Henry Harrison (b. 1773), American soldier and ninth president of the United States (1841), nicknamed "Old Tippecanoe" for his defeat of Tecumseh's forces at the Tippecanoe River (1811); he died after a month in office.	

1842

First British-Afghan War: British refugees, approximately 4,500 soldiers and 12,000 civilians, who had been promised safe conduct on their evacuation from Kabul to India, were massacred by Afghan forces in the Khyber Pass (Jan. 13); only a few survived. First British-Afghan War: British-held Ghazni fell to Afghan forces; Kandahar and Jellalabad were besieged. British forces relieved the besieged city of Jellalabad (Apr. 16) and again invaded Afghanistan, taking Kabul (Sept. 15) before retreating to India (Dec.). Chinese-British Opium War: British forces took Shanghai (June 19) and Ching-kiang (July 21). Under the Treaty of Nanking (Aug. 29), Britain took Hong Kong and a $20 million indemnity and required the Chinese to open concessionary "treaty ports" at Canton, Amoy, Foochow (Minhow), Ningpo, and Shanghai. The opium trade continued. b. Iwao Oyama (d. 1916), Japanese field marshal.	d. Bernardo O'Higgins (b. 1776), Chilean general who was a key figure in the gaining of Chilean independence; he became dictator (r. 1817-1823).	

Europe	Africa and Southwest Asia

1843

| In Spain, General Ramón Narváez led a successful counterrevolt (July-Aug.) against dictator Baldomero Espartero, who was forced to flee the country; Isabella II again took the throne. | After a failed Boer attack on the British port of Durban, the British occupied and annexed Natal. |

1844

| d. Jean Baptiste Drouet d'Erlon (b. 1765), marshal of France who commanded the center under Napoleon Bonaparte at Waterloo (1815).

d. Charles XIV (Jean Baptiste Jules Bernadotte) (b. 1763), king of Sweden and Norway (r. 1818-1844), previously marshal of France (1804) who later fought against Napoleon (1813). | On the Isly River, in Morocco (Aug. 14), French forces led by General Thomas Bugeaud decisively defeated Abd-el-Kader's Algerian forces, effectively ending major Algerian resistance.

Under the Treaty of Tangier (Sept. 10), the French left Morocco.

b. Muhammad Ahmad "The Mahdi" (al-Mahdi; Muhammad Ahmad ibn as-Sayyid 'Abd Allah) (d. 1885), Sudanese religious and military leader. |

1845

| | |

1846

| Guncotton (nitrocellulose) was invented by C. F. Schönbein.

b. Alexander von Kluck (d. 1934), German general.

b. Karl von Bülow (d. 1921), German general. | As Boer and British colonists continued to take Xhosa territory, British and Xhosa forces fought a sporadic war beyond the Keiskama River (1846-1847).

In Bornu, the puppet ruler (*mai*) unsuccessfully rebelled against the true ruler, 'Umar, who had succeeded his father, Muhammad al-Kanami.

b. Abdullah et Taaisha (Abdullah ibn-Mohammed) (d. 1899), Sudanese Dervish general and ruler. |

1843

British-Sind War: After British demanded much more control over Sind, Baluchi forces besieged the British residency at Hyderabad (Feb. 15). Relief forces defeated Baluchi forces twice, relieved the British (Mar.), and went on to take Sind (May-Aug.) against ineffective resistance.

First British-Maori War (1843-1848): In New Zealand the expropriation of native lands generated a five-year Maori guerrilla war against the British.

b. Maresuke Nogi (d. 1912), Japanese general.

Uruguayan Civil War (1843-1852): This civil war quickly became an international war, with the forces of Argentine dictator Juan Manuel de Rosas on the Blanco (White; Conservative) side and Colorado (Red; Liberal) forces aided by Brazil, France, England, and Paraguay. Montevideo was unsuccessfully besieged by an Argentine army (1843-1851).

Second Seminole War: Most of the remaining Seminoles were forcibly moved to Oklahoma after their defeat, ending the war; substantial numbers of Seminoles and escaped slaves remained in the Everglades and were never defeated.

1844

Santo Domingo won its independence from Haiti.

1845

First British-Sikh War (1845-1846): Continuing their conquest of India, British forces numbering 10,000 led by Hugh Gough met and defeated Lal Singh's Sikh army of an estimated 16,000 at Mudki (Dec. 18). At Ferozeshah (Dec. 21-22), attacking British forces again defeated the Sikhs, with the Sikhs suffering a reported 5,000 casualties and the British a reported 2,500 casualties.

United States annexed Texas, as requested by the Republic of Texas (Mar. 1). Mexico and the United States prepared for war.

Dominican forces unsuccessfully invaded Haiti (July).

b. Arthur MacArthur (d. 1912), American general.

d. Andrew Jackson (b. 1767), American general and seventh president of the United States (1829-1837), nicknamed "Old Hickory"; he served in the Revolutionary War and the War of 1812, most notably in defending New Orleans (1814).

1846

First British-Sikh War: British forces defeated a Sikh force at Aliwal (Jan. 28), then invaded the Punjab and decisively defeated the Sikhs at Sobraon (Feb. 10). The British then took Lahore, forcing the Punjab to become a British protectorate, though not yet effectively controlling the entire Punjab.

b. Yasukata Oku (d. 1930), Japanese field marshal.

Mexican-American War (1846-1848): An American army of 3,500, led by General Zachary Taylor, established Camp Texas (Brownsville), on the Rio Grande. War began with a cavalry skirmish; Mexican forces then besieged Camp Texas. At Palo Alto (May 8), an American force of 2,200 sharply defeated a Mexican army of 4,500; they did so again the next day, at Resaca de la Palma. Taylor's army moved south into Mexico (Aug.). At Monterey (Sept. 20-24), Taylor's army defeated another Mexican army.

Mexican-American War: American settlers revolted in California, led by John Charles Frémont (June). American forces of fewer than 1,500, led by General Stephen W. Kearny, moved overland through New Mexico and Arizona to take and hold California, while a force of fewer than 1,000 moved west through Chihuahua to take Saltillo. An American squadron under John Drake Sloat formally annexed California at Monterey. Frémont became governor (July).

1847

b. Paul von Hindenburg (d. 1934), German general.

b. Radomir Putnik (d. 1917), Serbian general.

d. Emmanuel, marquis of Grouchy (b. 1766), French marshal of the empire who became commander in chief of cavalry (1813); he was much criticized for failing to reinforce Napoleon Bonaparte at Waterloo (1815).

d. Nicolas Charles Oudinot (b. 1767), French marshal of the empire during the French revolutionary wars and the Napoleonic Wars; he later served Louis XVIII, refusing to join Napoleon at Waterloo.

d. Charles Louis John, archduke of Austria and duke of Teschen (Cieszyn) (b. 1771), Austrian field marshal during the French revolutionary wars and the Napoleonic Wars.

Abd-el-Kader surrendered (Dec. 23), but Algerian resistance to French rule continued.

Liberia became an independent nation (July 26).

1848

French Revolution of 1848 (Feb. 22-24): A republican rising forced the abdication of Louis Philippe; the monarchy was replaced by the Second Republic. A workers' rising in Paris was defeated by government forces (June 23-26). Prince Louis Napoleon Bonaparte was elected president of the republic (Dec. 20).

Insurrections grew throughout the Austrian Empire. A rising in Vienna (Mar. 13) forced the resignation of Prime Minister Klemens Metternich. In Hungary a successful national rising led by Lajos Kossuth (Apr. 10) brought a large measure of autonomy. But the Austrians defeated a Czech national rising (June), and Austrian forces then attacked Hungary (Sept.). Hungarian forces defeated the Austrians and invaded Austria (Oct.), but they were defeated at Vienna; a second democratic rising was defeated there by royalist forces. A republican rising in Romania was defeated by Turkish and Russian forces.

Italian Revolutions (1848-1849): Independence movements spread throughout Italy, beginning with Milan's "Five Days" (Mar. 18-22), a successful insurrection against Austrian occupying forces. Sardinia declared war on Austria (Mar. 22); Venice declared its independence (Mar. 26); Giuseppe Garibaldi organized a revolutionary army. At Custozza (July 24-25), Austrian forces led by Marshal Joseph Radetsky decisively defeated the Italian allies led by Charles Albert of Sardinia. Radetsky's army then besieged Venice and took Milan.

Liberal forces rose in Berlin (Mar. 15); Frederick William IV of Prussia responded with more liberal policies until royalist forces retook the city (Nov. 10), ending the brief democratic period.

Prussia took Schleswig-Holstein from Denmark.

b. Helmuth Johannes Ludwig von Moltke (d. 1916), German general and chief of staff (1906-1914).

b. Arthur James Balfour (d. 1930), British politician and diplomat.

d. Hermann von Boyen (b. 1771), German field marshal during the Napoleonic Wars.

Securing his power, Bornu's ruler al-Hajj 'Umar raised an army and equipped it with European weapons, in preparation for a jihad (holy war).

British forces under Harry Smith defeated Andries Pretorius's Boers at the Battle of Boomplaats (Aug. 29), forcing their retreat north of the Vaal River.

Mexican-American War: American land and sea forces under Stephen Kearny defeated Mexican forces at San Gabriel (Jan. 8) and the Battle of the Mesa (Jan. 9), occupying Los Angeles and completing the conquest of California.

Mexican-American War: At Buena Vista, in northern Mexico (Feb. 22-23), Zachary Taylor's army of fewer than 5,000 defeated Antonio López de Santa Anna's army of 15,000, with more than 700 American and more than 1,500 Mexican casualties.

Mexican-American War: An American seaborne army of 8,000 to 9,000, led by General Winfield Scott, took Veracruz and its garrison of 5,000 (Mar. 27), then moved inland. At Cerro Gordo (Apr. 18), the Americans decisively defeated Antonio López de Santa Anna's army of 12,000, with 1,000 Mexican casualties and 3,000 prisoners taken; American casualties were fewer than 500. Scott's forces attacked Mexico City (Aug.), winning major battles and suffering heavy losses at Churubusco (Aug. 20), Molino del Rey (Sept. 8), and Chapultepec (Sept. 13) before taking the city (Sept. 14).

Mayan insurrection began in southern Mexico; Mayan forces of more than 15,000 took Valladolid and Ichmul. The long, largely guerrilla war (1847-1900) would ultimately take more than 100,000 lives.

Second British-Sikh War (1848-1849): In the Punjab Sikh independence forces rose against British control; the British responded with an invasion army of an estimated 15,000.

b. Heihachiro Togo (d. 1934), Japanese admiral.

Under the Treaty of Guadalupe Hidalgo (Feb. 2), the United States took California and what is now the American Southwest from Mexico; Mexico also recognized the American annexation of Texas.

d. Stephen Watts Kearny (b. 1794), American general who during the Mexican-American War took New Mexico and then moved on to become American commander in California (1846).

1849

Italian Revolutions: The Roman republic was founded by Giuseppe Mazzini (Feb. 9) after a successful rising in the Papal States. At Novara (Mar. 23), Joseph Radetsky's Austrian forces again decisively defeated the Sardinians and their allies; Sardinia, no longer a factor in the war, surrendered to the Austrians (Aug.). French forces numbering 7,000 intervened in behalf of the pope (Apr.), besieging Rome, which surrendered (June 29). Giuseppe Garibaldi's forces were then dispersed by allied royalist forces.

Hungarian Revolution: Austrian forces took Budapest (Jan. 5). The Hungarian republic was formed, with Lajos Kossuth its first president. Hungarian forces defeated the Austrians in several engagements, driving them back into Austria. Russian and Austrian forces ultimately totaling more than 500,000 attacked Hungary from two directions (June 17); they defeated the Hungarians in several engagements, decisively at Segesvar (July 31) and Timosoara (Aug. 9), effectively ending the revolution.

b. Alfred von Tirpitz (d. 1930), German admiral.

b. August von Mackensen (d. 1945), German field marshal.

d. Thomas Robert Bugeaud de la Piconnerie, duke of Isly (b. 1784), marshal of France active during the Napoleonic Wars and the conquest of Algeria, most notably at the Isly River (1844).

d. Mohammed Ali (b. 1769), Mameluke ruler of Egypt; originally sent to Egypt by the Turks to fight Napoleon (1798), he became governor and then took complete control (1811).

1850

Under pressure from Sweden, Britain, Russia, and Austria, Prussia returned Schleswig-Holstein to Denmark.

b. Horatio Herbert Kitchener (d. 1916), British field marshal.

Eighth "Kaffir" War (1850-1853): British forces defeated a Xhosa uprising in southern Africa, as the long attack on the Xhosa continued.

Al-Hajj 'Umar led the last of the Fulani jihads (holy wars) in West Africa (1850-1864).

1851

Louis Napoleon Bonaparte took power by coup in France (Dec. 2-4).

b. Ferdinand Foch (d. 1929), French general.

d. Nicolas Jean de Dieu Soult, duke of Dalmatia (b. 1769), marshal general of France serving in the French revolutionary wars and the Napoleonic Wars; later minister of war (1830-1834).

1852

Turkish-Montenegrin War (1852-1853): Turkish forces attacked Montenegro but withdrew after military defeats and Austrian pressure.

b. Joseph Joffre (d. 1931), French general.

b. Franz Xavier Josef Conrad von Hüotzendorf (d. 1925), Austro-Hungarian field marshal.

b. John Denton Pinkstone French (d. 1925), British general.

d. Arthur Wellesley, duke of Wellington (b. 1769), British field marshal called the "Iron Duke" who gave Napoleon his final defeat at Waterloo (1815); he

Basuto forces defeated an invading British force of more than 2,000 at Belea Mountain (Dec. 20).

Central, South and East Asia, and the Pacific	The Americas	
		1849
Second British-Sikh War: At Chilianwala (Jan. 13), in the Punjab, the British were defeated by a Sikh army, retreating after suffering almost 3,000 casualties. Reinforced British forces defeated the Sikhs and their allies the Afghans, led by Dost Muhammad, at Gujarat (Feb. 21). Britain then annexed the Punjab. b. Hikonojo Kamimura (d. 1916), Japanese admiral. d. Akbar Khan (?-1849), Afghan general who led the forces besieging the British at Kabul, granting them safe passage but massacring them in the Khyber Pass (1841-1842).	Haitian forces unsuccessfully invaded the Dominican Republic (Mar.). b. Crazy Horse (Tashunca-Uitco) (ca. 1849-1877), Oglala Sioux war chief.	
		1850
Taiping Rebellion (1850-1864): Massive Chinese civil war that would ultimately cost an estimated 20 million lives, pitting the Taipings, led by Hung Hsiu-ch'üan (T'ien Wang, or "Heavenly King") against the ruling Manchus; it began in Kwangsi (Nov.) and in the following two years became a major insurrection. b. Kageaki Kawamura (d. 1926), Japanese field marshal. b. Hoshimichi Hasegawa (d. 1924), Japanese field marshal.	d. José de San Martin (b. 1778), Latin American general who was a key figure in the liberation of Spanish America; after taking Lima (1821), he proclaimed Peru's independence; in conflict with Simón Bolívar, he later resigned, dying in exile. d. Zachary Taylor (b. 1784), American army officer and 12th president of the United States (1849-1850), nicknamed "Old Rough and Ready"; he served in various wars, most notably during the Mexican-American War at Buena Vista (1847). d. José Gervasio Artigas (b. 1764), Uruguayan general in his country's wars of independence (1810-1820); called "Protector of the Free Peoples."	
		1851
Vietnamese under King Tu Duc began what would be a long series of conflicts with the French, both missionaries and military forces (1851-1857).		
		1852
Taiping Rebellion: Taiping forces took Wuchang (Jan. 12) and grew into a force of 500,000 as they approached Nanking, which they took by storm (Mar. 19) and made the Taiping capital. d. Hung Ta-chüan (b. 1823), Chinese rebel general who joined the Taiping Rebellion in 1851 and was appointed a king by its leader, Hung Hsiu-ch'üan; he was captured and executed.	Uruguayan Civil War: Allied forces decisively defeated Argentine forces at Monte Caseros (Feb. 23), with 600 allied and 1,500 Argentine casualties; 7,000 Argentine prisoners were taken. d. José Ballivian (b. 1804), Bolivian general who defeated the Peruvians at Ingaví (1841).	

1852 (cont.)

later became commander in chief (1827; 1842-1846) and prime minister (1828-1830).

d. Auguste Frederic Louis Viesse de Marmont, duke of Ragusa (b. 1774), French marshal of the empire who served during the French revolutionary wars and the Napoleonic Wars, primarily for Napoleon Bonaparte but at the end for the restored monarchy.

1853

Crimean War (1853-1856): Russian forces attacked Turkish-held Romania (July). Britain and France responded by sending fleets to Constantinople; Turkey declared war on Russia (Oct. 4). Turkish land forces defeated the Russians at Oltenitza, Romania (Nov. 4), while Russian naval forces defeated the Turks at Sinope (Nov. 30).

Britain introduced the Enfield rifle.

Turkish-Montenegrin War: Turkish forces again invaded Montenegro but again withdrew after military reverses and Austrian pressure.

b. Alexei Alexeevich Brusilov (d. 1926), Russian general.

b. Ian Standish Monteith Hamilton (d. 1947), British general.

d. Charles James Napier (b. 1782), British general during the Napoleonic Wars, the War of 1812, and the conquest of Sind (1842-1843), where he commanded British troops.

d. George Cockburn (b. 1772), British admiral who was naval commander of British operations against Washington, D.C. (1814).

b. Hussein Ibn Ali (d. 1931), king of the Hejaz and sharif of Mecca.

d. Andries (Andreas) Wilhelmus Jacobus Pretorius (b. 1798), Boer general and statesman who defeated the Zulu led by Dingane, notably at the Blood River (1838); he was one of four commandants general of the Transvaal; the city of Pretoria is named for him.

1854

Crimean War: British and French war fleets entered the Black Sea in support of Turkey (Jan.). Russian forces attacked the Turks in Bulgaria (Mar. 20). France and Britain declared war on Russia (Mar. 28).

Crimean War: Allied forces were transported to the Crimean Peninsula in a great convoy.

Crimean War: Allied seaborne forces numbering more than 55,000 attacked in the Crimea, landing north of Sevastopol (Sept. 13) and moving toward the city by land and sea. Allied and Russian forces met at the Alma River; the Russians retreated after a battle that cost 2,000 allied and 4,000 Russian casualties. The allies went on to besiege Sevastopol (Oct. 8).

Crimean War: At Balaklava (Oct. 25), Russian forces tried to break through to the rear of besieging British forces; during the battle British commanders ordered the "charge of the Light Brigade," a cavalry charge through artillery crossfire that was doomed before it was ordered.

Crimean War: At Inkerman (Nov. 5), the Russians unsuccessfully tried to drive a wedge between elements of the allied siege army, suffering casualties of 12,000 in the failed effort; the allies suffered more than 4,000 casualties.

Austrian forces occupied Romania (Aug. 1854-Mar. 1857).

Military junta led by generals Baldomero Espartero and Leopoldo O'Donnell took power in Spain (July).

b. Louis, prince of Battenberg (Louis Mountbatten) (d. 1921), British admiral.

In a Fulani jihad, Al-Hajj 'Umar and his forces took the Bambara kingdom of Kaarta and several other neighboring states.

Orange Free State was established (Feb. 17).

b. Christiaan Rudolph De Wet (d. 1922), Boer general.

1852 (cont.)

Second Burmese War (1852-1853): British forces attacked Burma; seaborne forces took Rangoon (Apr. 12), moved north that spring, and took Pegu and Prome (Oct.). The British then annexed southern Burma.

b. Gentaro Kodama (d. 1906), Japanese general.

b. Gonnohyoe (Gombë) Yamamoto (d. 1933), Japanese admiral.

1853

Taiping Rebellion: Taiping forces attacked west on the Yangtze River and north toward Peking (May). Early northern force successes took the Taipings no farther than Tientsin, but they did take the key city of Shanghai (Sept. 7), nearly splitting the country.

American commodore Matthew Perry took a four-vessel squadron into Tokyo Bay, ending Japan's self-imposed isolation (since 1637) and opening peaceful Japanese-U.S. trading relations, formalized in the Treaty of Kanagawa (Mar. 31, 1854).

1854

Taiping Rebellion: Manchu forces defeated the Taipings in Hunan, pursuing them east; Wuchang was retaken (Oct.), but the Taipings stopped the Manchu advance on Nanking.

Nien Rebellion (1854-1868): Allied with the Taipings, the Nien people of Anhwei and Hunan launched a massive insurrection against the Manchus.

Russians completed their conquest of the Syr River basin from the Persians (which began in 1849), whose power in Central Asia effectively ended.

b. Shichiro Kataoka (d. 1920), Japanese admiral.

Direct run-up to the American Civil War began after the Kansas-Nebraska Act repealed the Missouri Compromise of 1820; an undeclared war began between antislavery and proslavery forces in "Bleeding Kansas."

b. Victoriano Huerta (d. 1916), Mexican general.

Europe	Africa and Southwest Asia

1854 (cont.)

b. Pavel Karlovich Rennenkampf (d. 1918), Russian general.

d. Henry William Paget (b. 1768), British field marshal during the French revolutionary wars and the Napoleonic Wars; he lost a leg at Waterloo (1815).

d. William Carr Beresford (b. 1768), British general who reorganized the British army in Portugal (1809); he was a key commander in the Peninsular War.

1855

Crimean War: Allied forces unsuccessfully stormed Sevastopol (June 7), at a cost of 7,000 allied and 8,500 Russian casualties. The allies tried and failed again 10 days later (June 17-18). The Russians again unsuccessfully tried to breach siege lines (Aug. 16), at a cost of more than 8,000 casualties. Allied forces successfully stormed the fort (Sept. 8), at a cost of 23,000 casualties, 13,000 of them Russian and 10,000 allied. The Russians then withdrew.

Crimean War: Besieged Kars surrendered to the Russians (Nov. 26).

b. Magnus F. W. von Eberhardt (d. 1939), German general.

d. Fitzroy James Henry Somerset Raglan (b. 1788), British field marshal serving late in the Napoleonic Wars and the Crimean War, commanding the British Expeditionary Army of the East at the Alma River, Sevastopol, Balaklava, and Inkerman (all 1854).

1856

Crimean War: Treaty of Paris (Mar. 30) was signed at the Conference of Paris, restoring Russian and Turkish prewar borders, but with quasi-independent Romania under Turkey. The Black Sea and lower Danube River were neutralized and opened to merchant fleets of all countries.

b. Henri Philippe Pétain (d. 1951), French general and Nazi collaborator.

b. Robert Georges Nivelle (d. 1924), French general.

b. Grand Duke Nicholas (Nikolai Nikolaevich Romanov) (d. 1929), Russian general.

b. Louis Félix François Franchet D'Esperey (d. 1942), marshal of France.

b. Svetozar Borojevic (Boroevic) Edler von Bojna (d. 1920), Austro-Hungarian field marshal.

Republic of South Africa was established in the Transvaal, with Martin (Marthinus) Pretorius, eldest son of Andries Pretorius, as its first president (Dec. 16).

Zulu king Cetshwayo decisively defeated his half-brother Mbulazi's rival iziGgoza faction at the Battle of 'Ndondakusuka.

1857

b. Oskar von Hutier (d. 1934), German general.

b. Mikhail Vasilievich Alekseev (d. 1918), Russian general.

b. Otto von Below (d. 1944), German general.

b. Robert Stephenson Smyth Baden-Powell (d. 1941), British general and founder of the Boy Scouts.

b. Herbert Charles Onslow Plumer (d. 1932), British field marshal.

d. Henry Havelock (b. 1795), British general serving primarily in India, most notably at Lucknow, where he died.

Basuto forces led by King Mosheshu defeated an invading British force of almost 2,000 at Viervoet.

Central, South and East Asia, and the Pacific	The Americas	

1854 (cont.)

1855

Taiping Rebellion: Remaining Taiping northern forces surrendered (May).

In southwest China, the Miao people mounted a long, ultimately unsuccessful rising against the Manchus (1855-1872).

In Yunnan, the Muslim Panthays unsuccessfully rose against the Manchus (1855-1861).

b. Sotaro Misu (d. 1921), Japanese admiral.

Haitian forces numbering 30,000 invaded the Dominican Republic (Nov.) but were decisively defeated at Santomé and Cambronal (Dec. 22), then forced back into Haiti.

John Brown emerged as a leader of abolitionist forces in Kansas, as violence between proslavery and antislavery forces grew.

American adventurer William Walker briefly took power in Nicaragua (1855-1857) but was defeated by a Central American coalition that included Costa Rica, El Salvador, Honduras, and Guatemala.

American forces numbering 600 massacred Brulé Sioux villagers at Ash Hollow, Nebraska, with at least 150 dead or wounded of 250 total, many of them noncombatants (Sept.).

1856

Persian troops took Herat, in Afghanistan, an area treated by the British as though in their sphere of influence. Britain responded by declaring war on Persia (Nov. 1).

Taiping Rebellion: Shih Ta-k'ai led a Taiping army of 200,000 into Kwangsi and Szechuan, beginning the ultimately failed Taiping Long Expedition.

Second Opium War (1856-1860): Conflict began after the Chinese seized the British ship *Arrow* at Canton. The British bombarded the Chinese ports.

American forces in Texas began a long, inconclusive set of campaigns against the Comanches and Kiowas (1856-1860).

Proslavery protesters sacked Lawrence, Kansas (May 21); John Brown and his antislavery followers killed 5 on Pottawatomie Creek (May 24). The run-up to the American Civil War intensified throughout the country.

b. (Thomas) Woodrow Wilson (d. 1924), 28th president of the United States (1913-1921).

1857

British Indian army forces invaded Persia, forcing Persian withdrawal from Afghanistan (Apr.).

Indian-British War (Indian Army Mutiny or Sepoy Mutiny) (1857-1858): A wide-scale insurrection against British occupying forces in India was immediately triggered by British insistence on using a new cartridge greased with cow fat, which had to be bitten while loading and was therefore not religiously acceptable to Muslims and Hindus. Massacres of Europeans began at Meerut (May 10), then spread to Delhi and throughout India, as Indian troops and independence forces rose. Besieged Cawnpore fell (June 27); 200 were massacred after surrendering with a promise of safe conduct. In the same period, British forces massacred many hundreds, and probably thousands, of Indian

Mexican Civil War (1858-1861): Mexican Liberal president Benito Juárez was defeated by the Conservative forces of Félix Zuloaga and fled from Mexico City to Veracruz (Jan.); civil war spread throughout the country. Conservative forces decisively defeated the Liberals at Ahualalco (Oct. 29).

Defeated adventurer William Walker fled Nicaragua (May).

b. Hunter Liggett (d. 1935), American general.

b. Joseph Theodore Dickman (d. 1928), American general.

Europe	Africa and Southwest Asia

1857 (cont.)

1858

b. Horace Lockwood Smith-Dorrien (d. 1930), British general.	Basuto forces defeated the invading Boer forces of the Orange Free State.

1859

Austria-France/Piedmont War: Austrian forces invaded Piedmont (Apr. 29), retreating after losing battles at Montebello (May 20) and Palestro (May 30). Napoleon III led allied forces into Lombardy, defeating the Austrians at Magenta (June 4) and decisively at Solferino (June 24), with Austrian casualties of 22,000 of 120,000 engaged and allied casualties of 17,000 of the same number engaged. Defeated Austria ceded most of Lombardy to Piedmont.	France established a protectorate on the coast of Madagascar.
Spanish North African forces attacked Morocco (Oct.), expanding Spanish-occupied territory at Ceuta and winning other concessions and indemnities (1859-1860).	Russian forces took the Murid base at Gounib, in the Caucasus Mountains; Shamil surrendered, ending the long Russian-Murid guerrilla war.
French ironclad warship *Gloire* was launched, beginning a new era in naval warfare.	
b. John Rushworth Jellicoe (d. 1935), British admiral.	
b. Alexander Vasilievich Samsonov (d. ca. 1914), Russian general.	
b. Alfred Dreyfus (d. 1935), French army officer.	
b. Kaiser Wilhelm II (d. 1941), German emperor (r. 1888-1918).	

1860

Resorgimento (Wars of the Italian Reunification) (1860-1870): Failed risings in Naples were the first battles of the Resorgimento (Apr. 4).	Germany penetrated the coast of Cameroons.
Resorgimento: Giuseppe Garibaldi's "Thousand Redshirts" made a seaborne attack on Marsala, Sicily (May 11), picking up Sicilian strength as they advanced. Garibaldi's combined forces of 3,000 defeated a Neapolitan army of 4,000 at Calatafimi (May 15), took Palermo from much larger Neapolitan forces (May 27), and won another victory at Milazzo (July 20), completing their conquest of Sicily. Attacking across the Strait of Messina, they took Naples (Sept. 7). Piedmontese forces then invaded the Papal States (Sept. 10), defeating papal forces at Castelfidardo (Sept. 18).	

Central, South and East Asia, and the Pacific	The Americas	

prisoners. British forces retook Delhi by storm (Sept. 20), broke through siege lines to reinforce Lucknow (Sept. 25), and relieved and evacuated the British from Lucknow (Nov. 16-22).

Second Opium War: British and French forces took and then withdrew from China's Taku forts, near Tientsin (May). They later took Canton (Dec.).

1858

French forces began their campaign of conquest in southern Vietnam.

Indian-British War: British forces took Lucknow (Mar. 16) and besieged and took Jhansi (Mar. 21-Apr. 5), massacring an estimated 5,000 Indians, many of them noncombatants, after they had surrendered. The rani of Jhansi was killed at Gwalior (June 17-19). The British then instituted a reign of terror in northern India.

b. Hsu Shih-chang (d. 1939), Chinese general and politician, president of China (1918-1922).

b. Theodore Roosevelt (d. 1919), 26th president of the United States (1901-1909).

b. George Washington Goethals (d. 1928), American Army officer and engineer.

b. William Sowden Sims (d. 1936), American admiral.

d. Matthew Perry (b. 1794), American naval officer during several wars, most noted for his entry with a four-ship squadron into Tokyo Bay (1853), marking the reopening of Japan to the West.

1859

Second Opium War: British and French forces attacked and were defeated at the Taku forts, near Tientsin, China (June 25).

French forces took Saigon, in Vietnam.

b. Yüan Shih-k'ai (ca. 1859-1916), Chinese general.

d. Tantia Topi (Tatya Tope; Ramchandra Panduroga) (b. ca. 1810), Indian rebel leader during the Indian-British War (Sepoy Mutiny), aiding in the defense of the rani of Jhansi, in the siege of her fort (1858) and at Gwalior, where she was killed; he was captured and executed (Apr. 18).

John Brown and a small group of followers seized the federal arsenal at Harpers Ferry, Virginia (Oct. 16-18), but their hoped-for slave revolt did not eventuate; taken by Union forces under Robert E. Lee, Brown and six others were hanged. The run-up to the American Civil War was nearly over.

b. Venustiano Carranza (d. 1920), Mexican revolutionary leader.

b. Jonathan Edmund Browning (d. 1939), American arms inventor.

1860

Second Opium War: British and French seaborne forces totaling 18,000 took the Taku forts by storm (Aug. 21) and moved inland to take Peking (Sept. 26), where they looted and burned the Summer Palace. Britain took Kowloon, on the mainland opposite Hong Kong, and both countries took massive indemnities from China.

Taiping Rebellion: Taiping forces broke the Manchu siege of Nanking; a Taiping army moved against Shanghai (May). Taiping forces in Anhwei were defeated, retreating east.

Abraham Lincoln was elected 16th president of the United States (Nov. 6). South Carolina seceded from the Union (Dec. 20), precipitating civil war.

Mexican Civil War: Liberal forces decisively defeated the Conservative army at Calpulalpam (Dec. 20); Benito Juárez again took power.

American adventurer William Walker invaded Honduras with a small force; quickly defeated, he was executed by the Hondurans (Sept.).

1860 (cont.)

Resorgimento: Garibaldi's forces, including Piedmontese troops and warships, besieged Gaeta (Nov. 3).

b. Archibald James Murray (d. 1945), British general.

b. William Robert Robertson (d. 1933), British field marshal.

d. Henry George Wakelyn Smith (b. 1787), British general who served in various colonial wars, becoming governor of the Cape Colony (1847).

d. Thomas Cochrane, 10th earl of Dundonald (b. 1775), British admiral, active not only during the French revolutionary wars and the Napoleonic Wars but also the Greek and Latin American wars of independence.

1861

Resorgimento: Francis II of Naples surrendered at Gaeta (Feb. 13). The Kingdom of Italy was established (Mar. 17), with Victor Emmanuel as its first king.

Turkish-Montenegrin War: Turkish forces again invaded Montenegro, this time taking the country and turning it into a protectorate (1861-1862).

b. Douglas Haig (d. 1928), British field marshal.

b. Edmund Henry Hynman Allenby (d. 1936), British general.

b. Erich von Falkenhayn (d. 1922), German general.

1862

Resorgimento: Giuseppe Garibaldi's forces marched on Rome but were defeated (Aug. 29) by Italian army units.

b. Aristide Briand (d. 1932), French politician and internationalist.

b. Nicolai Nikolayevich Yudenich (d. 1933), Russian general.

b. Julian Hedworth George Byng (d. 1935), British field marshal.

b. Louis Botha (d. 1919), Boer general and first prime minister of the Union of South Africa.

Central, South and East Asia, and the Pacific	The Americas

1860 (cont.)

Second British-Maori War (1860-1872): This was an intensification of the existing low-level war between the British, continuing their conquest of New Zealand, and resisting Maori forces.	b. John Joseph "Blackjack" Pershing (d. 1948), American general. b. Leonard Wood (d. 1927), American general.

1861

Taiping Rebellion: Taiping forces numbering 250,000, led by Hsiu-ch'eng, took Hangchow (Dec. 29). French relief forces ended the 11-month Vietnamese siege of French-held Saigon (Mar. 1860-Feb. 1861). France annexed eastern portions of southern Vietnam. b. Koichiro Tachibana (d. 1929), Japanese general.	**American Civil War (1861-1865):** The Confederate States of America was formed at Montgomery, Alabama (Feb. 9), with Jefferson Davis its first president, as Mississippi, Florida, Alabama, Georgia, Louisiana, and Texas also seceded from the Union; Virginia, Arkansas, Tennessee, and North Carolina followed later in the year. Abraham Lincoln was inaugurated as president of the United States (Mar. 4). The Civil War began with Confederate forces under General Pierre Beauregard bombarding Fort Sumter, South Carolina (Apr. 12), which surrendered (Apr. 13). American Civil War: At Bull Run (Manassas), Virginia (July 21), the first major battle of the war, General Irvin McDowell's Union forces of 28,000 moving toward Richmond were routed by Beauregard's Confederate army of 32,000, with 1,500 Union and 2,000 Confederate casualties and 1,300 Union prisoners. Here Confederate general Thomas J. Jackson won the nickname "Stonewall," for his brigade's resistance to Union attacks. French, British, and Spanish forces occupied Veracruz (Dec. 17). The British and Spanish soon withdrew, but the French stayed on, intending to take Mexico while the United States was preoccupied with its Civil War. Apache-American guerrilla wars began in the American Southwest, while the long Apache-Mexican guerrilla wars continued in contiguous northern Mexico (1861-1886).

1862

Taiping Rebellion: Li Hsiu-ch'eng's Taiping army was unable to take Shanghai against Western mercenary and Manchu forces (Apr.-May). A Taiping-Nien army of 250,000 moved north against Peking but was defeated piecemeal by the Manchus (1862-1864). b. Ts'ao K'un (d. 1928), Chinese general. d. Ch'en Yü-ch'eng (b. 1836), Chinese Taiping general who, with Li Hsiu-ch'eng, raised the siege of Nanking (1860); he was later killed by imperial forces (May).	American Civil War: Ulysses S. Grant's Union forces took Fort Henry, then Fort Donelson, on the Cumberland River (Feb.), capturing its garrison of almost 15,000. American Civil War: Off Hampton Roads, Virginia (Mar. 8-9), the Confederate ironclad *Virginia* (*Merrimack*) sank two blockading Union wooden ships before being engaged by the ironclad *Monitor;* the two ironclads then fought to a draw, in an engagement that decisively changed naval warfare by making wooden warships obsolete. American Civil War: At Shiloh (Pittsburg Landing), on the Tennessee River (Apr. 6-7), Grant's army of 62,000 defeated Pierre Beauregard's army of 40,000 in one of the costliest battles of the war. Union casualties were more than 10,000, with almost 3,000 captured or missing; Confederate casualties were almost 10,000, with almost 1,000 captured or missing.

1862 (cont.)

d. Albert Sidney Johnston (b. 1803), American Confederate (CSA) general whose death at Shiloh (Apr. 6) was described by Jefferson Davis as "the turning point of our fate."

American Civil War: Union squadron under Commodore David Farragut moved up the Mississippi River (Mar.-Apr.), breaking through wooden barriers to take New Orleans (Apr. 24), then Baton Rouge and Natchez, but being turned back at Vicksburg (May 23).

American Civil War: In the Seven Days' Battles (June 25-July 1), George McClellan's Union army of more than 90,000, moving close to the Confederate capital of Richmond, was ultimately forced to withdraw by Robert E. Lee's slightly larger forces. Union losses in the campaign included almost 10,000 casualties and 6,000 captured or missing; Confederate casualties were more than 20,000, with fewer than 1,000 captured or missing.

American Civil War: At the second Battle of Bull Run (Manassas) (Aug. 29-30), which included the Battle of Chantilly (Sept. 1), John Pope's Union forces were sharply defeated by "Stonewall" Jackson's forces. Union losses were more than 16,000, Confederate losses more than 9,000.

d. Philip Kearny (b. 1814), American general who lost an arm at Churubusco (1847) during the Mexican-American War and later served in Napoleon III's Imperial Guard in the Austria-France/Piedmont War (1859), becoming the first American to win the French Legion of Honor; he was killed at Chantilly (Sept. 1).

American Civil War: Lee's 50,000-strong Confederate forces made their first invasion of the North (Sept. 4-9), taking Harpers Ferry and 15,000 prisoners (Sept. 15). At Antietam (Sharpsburg), Maryland (Sept. 17), Lee's army, now 45,000 strong, defeated McClellan's army of 87,000 in the worst single day of the war, costing almost 12,000 Union and more than 11,000 Confederate casualties.

American Civil War: At Fredericksburg (Dec. 13), Ambrose Burnside's Union army, now 106,000 strong, could not cross the Rappahannock River against Confederate resistance, suffering more than 12,000 casualties before withdrawing; Confederate losses were fewer than 5,000.

French forces numbering 6,000 moved on Mexico City (Apr.). They were defeated by Republican forces numbering 4,000 at Puebla (May 5), in the Battle of Cinco de Mayo, so named for the date.

Sioux-American War (1862-1865): Long-standing conflicts grew into war when Santee Sioux forces in Minnesota massacred several hundred settlers and attacked American towns and strong points in Minnesota and Iowa (Aug.). Responding American forces decisively defeated the Sioux at Wood Lake (Sept. 23), effectively ending the immediate conflict; American forces numbering more than 4,000 then campaigned widely against the Sioux in the Dakota Territory, with inconclusive results.

After the defeat of Apache guerrillas by California volunteers at Apache Pass, Arizona (July), Cochise took full command of the Apache forces.

Dr. Richard Gatling was granted a patent for his Gatling gun.

b. Edwin Burr Babbitt (d. 1939), American general.

1863

Russian forces defeated a Polish guerrilla insurrection (Jan. 1863-Apr. 1864).

b. Francis Ferdinand, Austrian archduke, heir to the throne; he and his wife would be assassinated by Bosnian terrorists at Sarajevo (June 28, 1914), sparking World War I.

b. Reinhard Scheer (d. 1928), German admiral.

b. Franz von Hipper (d. 1932), German admiral.

b. David Lloyd George (d. 1945), British prime minister.

d. Colin Campbell, first Baron Clyde (b. 1792), British field marshal who led the "Thin Red Line," the 93d Highlanders, at Balaklava (1854); he was commander in chief in India during the Indian-British War (Sepoy Mutiny) (1857).

d. James Outram (b. 1803), British general serving primarily in India who commanded the besieged British garrison at Lucknow (1857).

In a Fulani jihad, Al-Hajj 'Umar and his forces took Timbuktu but failed to take positions in Senegal; the war ended the following year (1864).

Central, South and East Asia, and the Pacific

The Americas

Taiping Rebellion: Manchu and Western (Ever Victorious Army) forces commanded by British officer Charles (thereafter "China") Gordon took Wuchang (July 29), then Soochow and other major cities, usually with massacres of thousands of those surrendering, including civilians. Another Taiping western expedition failed.

Taiping Rebellion: Shih Ta-k'ai's remaining Taiping forces were defeated and surrendered to the Manchus near the Tatu River, in Szechuan (May).

d. Shih Ta-k'ai (b. 1820), Chinese rebel general in the Taiping Rebellion who for a time ruled in Nanking as prime minister and commander in chief; after his defeat and surrender, he was executed at Chengdu.

Japanese Civil War (Meiji Restoration) (1863-1869) was a series of engagements between those who supported the Tokugawa shogunate and those who wished to replace it with a strong central government, nominally and spiritually led by a restored Meiji emperor but actually led by the Choshu and Satsuma clans.

Japanese shore batteries and Western warships exchanged fire at Shimonoseki (June).

French colonial forces forced Siam to withdraw its forces from Cambodia.

Besieged Herat fell to Afghan government forces (May 26).

British warships bombarded Kagoshima, Japan (Aug. 15-16), in a dispute over a British subject who had been killed.

Cambodia became a French protectorate.

Muslim Panthays in Yunnan again rose unsuccessfully against the Manchus (1863-1871).

American Civil War: Abraham Lincoln's Emancipation Proclamation (Jan. 1) freed all slaves in areas held by Confederate forces; as a direct result, former slaves joined Union forces in large numbers.

American Civil War: At Chancellorsville, on the Rappahannock River (May 1-6), Robert E. Lee's Confederate army of 61,000 decisively defeated Joseph Hooker's Union army of 97,000, with Union casualties of more than 11,000 and more than 6,000 captured or missing; Confederate casualties were almost 11,000.

d. Thomas Jonathan Jackson (b. 1824), American Confederate (CSA) general, nicknamed "Stonewall" for his defense at Bull Run (1861); he served notably in other key battles, including second Bull Run, Antietam, Fredericksburg, and finally Chancellorsville, where he was accidentally but fatally wounded by his own soldiers.

American Civil War: At Gettysburg, Pennsylvania (July 1-3), in the most decisive and costliest battle of the war, George Meade's Union army of 88,000 defeated Lee's Confederate forces of 75,000, which had crossed the Potomac River (mid-June) in the Confederacy's final invasion of the North. In three days of attack, Lee's forces were unable to break through or envelop Union lines. Their final attempt was Pickett's Charge, a hopeless direct attack by 15,000 men, led by General George E. Pickett's Virginia brigades, across an open field on foot, against entrenched troops with artillery; the charge cost 7,500 casualties. Lee broke off and retreated south (July 4). Southern losses included an estimated 23,000 casualties and 5,000 missing or captured, with Northern losses of 15,000 casualties and 5,000 missing or captured.

American Civil War: On the same day that Lee broke off at Gettysburg, Ulysses S. Grant's forces on the Mississippi River took the surrender of the 30,000-strong Confederate army at Vicksburg, splitting the Confederacy in two. Grant's forces had defeated Confederate armies in a series of battles on the approaches to Vicksburg (May-June) and besieged the fortress (May 19).

American Civil War: At Chickamauga Creek, near Chattanooga (Sept. 19-20), Braxton Bragg's Confederate army of 66,000 sharply defeated William Rosecrans's army of 58,000; after attacking Southern forces had split the Northern army, a rout was averted when the corps of General George Thomas (the "Rock of Chickamauga") held. Southern losses were more than 18,000, Northern losses more than 16,000. The Union army retreated into Chattanooga, where it was besieged (Sept.-Oct.) until relieved and reinforced by Grant (Oct.-Nov.). Grant's army of more than 60,000 defeated Bragg's siege army of 40,000 at Chattanooga (Nov. 25-27), with Union losses of almost 6,000 and Confederate losses of almost 7,000.

Proslavery irregulars under William Quantrill, nominally part of the Confederate army, sacked Lawrence, Kansas (Aug. 21), killing 150 noncombatants and burning much of the town. Quantrill's raiders, dressed as Union soldiers, also attacked Union soldiers at Baxter Springs, Kansas (Oct.), killing 100 of them.

Greatly reinforced, a French army of 30,000 besieged and took Puebla (May 17), then took Mexico City (June 7). Austrian archduke Maximilian became the French puppet emperor of Mexico (June 12). A nationwide guerrilla war of resistance began.

1863 (cont.)

1864

First Geneva Convention covered medical treatment and personnel.

Schleswig-Holstein War: Prussian forces, in alliance with Austria, attacked Schleswig-Holstein (Feb.) and took the province after light Danish resistance. Denmark ceded the province to Prussia and Austria (Aug. 1).

b. Henry Hughes Wilson (d. 1922), British field marshal.

Boer forces again attacked the Basuto, this time winning and taking large portions of their country (1864-1866).

1863 (cont.)

d. Robert Gould Shaw (b. 1837), commander of the first African-American regiment, the 54th Massachusetts; he died during their costly attempt to storm Fort Wagner, South Carolina.

d. Samuel (Sam) Houston (b. 1793), American leader whose victory over the Mexicans at San Jacinto and capture of Antonio López de Santa Anna there (Apr. 21, 1836), won the independence of Texas; later president of the republic, then senator and governor of the state, he lost his offices over his opposition to secession and the Confederacy.

1864

Taiping Rebellion: Hangchow fell to Manchu forces (Apr.). Hung Hsiu-ch'üan, the "Heavenly King," committed suicide (June 1); he was succeeded by his son T'ien Kuei-fu. Besieged Nanking, the Taiping capital, fell (July 19). Taiping resistance continued until 1866.

d. Hung Hsiu-ch'üan (b. 1814), Chinese rebel leader whose vision of a Heavenly Kingdom of Great Peace (T'ai-p'ing T'ien-kuo) inspired the Taiping Rebellion; facing capture by imperial forces besieging Nanking, he committed suicide (June 1).

d. Li Hsiu-ch'eng (b. 1824), Chinese rebel general who became commander in chief of the Taiping armies (1858), twice reaching the walls of Shanghai (1860; 1862); he was captured and executed (Aug. 7).

American Civil War: Signaling the approaching end of the Confederacy, Ulysses S. Grant's 120,000-strong Army of the Potomac attacked Robert E. Lee's 64,000-strong Army of Northern Virginia, crossing the Rapidan River (May 4); during the next seven weeks, Grant steadily moved south while both sides suffered enormous casualties in a war of attrition that greatly favored the better supplied and reinforced Union army. North and South fought major battles at the Wilderness (May 5-6), Spotsylvania (May 8-18), Cold Harbor (June 3-12), and Petersburg (June 15-18), then began the long, costly siege of Petersburg (June 19, 1864-Apr. 2, 1865). Grant's forces lost an estimated 66,000 and Lee's an estimated 35,000 during the campaign.

American Civil War: At Mobile Bay (Aug. 5), Admiral David Farragut's Union fleet defeated Confederate naval forces under Admiral Franklin Buchanan; after his leading ship, *Tecumseh*, was sunk by a mine, Farragut uttered his famous cry — "Damn the torpedoes!" — proceeding through the minefield.

American Civil War: William Tecumseh Sherman's army of almost 100,000 moved out of Chattanooga toward Atlanta (May 5), pushing a Confederate army of 60,000 back to Atlanta, despite a series of delaying actions. The Union army took Atlanta (Aug. 31). Sherman's army marched through Georgia, from Atlanta to the sea (Nov. 15-Dec. 8), leaving behind a 300-mile-long, 50-mile-wide band of devastation that cut Lee's forces in Virginia off from supplies and reinforcements from the south. The Union army besieged and took Savannah (Dec. 19-21), completing the campaign. In the same period, John B. Hood's Army of Tennessee, which had attacked north in an attempt to draw Sherman's forces away from Georgia, was destroyed by George H. Thomas's much stronger forces at Nashville (Dec. 15-16).

American Civil War: At Cedar Creek, in the Shenandoah Valley (Oct. 19), Philip Sheridan's much larger Union forces defeated Jubal Early's army of 18,000, ending the Confederate diversionary campaign in the valley (July-Oct.).

d. James Ewell Brown (Jeb) Stuart (b. 1833), American Confederate (CSA) general who carried out numerous raids on Union forces; he died (May 12) of wounds suffered fighting against Philip Sheridan at Yellow Tavern, Virginia.

d. John Hunt Morgan (b. 1825), American Confederate (CSA) general who led a series of raids (from spring 1862), generally in Tennessee and Kentucky, reaching near Cincinnati, Ohio, farther north than any other Confederate leader; relieved of command (1864), he was later killed by Union soldiers (Sept. 4).

Europe	Africa and Southwest Asia

1864 (cont.)

1865

b. George V (d. 1936), king of Britain (r. 1910-1936).

b. Erich Ludendorff (d. 1937), German general.

b. Frederick Rudolph Lambert, 10th earl of Cavan (d. 1946), British field marshal.

b. Edith Cavell (d. 1915), British nurse executed as a spy.

b. William Riddell Birdwood (d. 1951), British field marshal.

b. James Frederick Noel Birch (d. 1939), British general.

1866

Austro-Prussian War (Seven Weeks' War): Prussian forces attacked in Hanover, forcing the surrender of Hanover's army, despite the Hanoverian victory at Langensalza (June 28). Prussian armies totaling 220,000, attacking through southern Germany into Bohemia, met and decisively defeated a slightly smaller Austrian and Saxon army at Sadowa (Königgrätz) (July 3). Prussian losses were 9,000; Austrian and Saxon losses were more than 15,000, with 22,000 captured.

Central, South and East Asia, and the Pacific	The Americas

	At Sand Creek, Colorado (Nov. 29), American forces massacred at least 300 Cheyennes and Arapahos, most of them noncombatants. War of the Triple Alliance (Paraguayan War) (1864-1870): Paraguayan riverborne forces moved north on the Paraguay River (Dec. 14), invading and taking most of Brazil's Matto Grosso province.

1865

Bhutan War: British Indian army forces attacked Bhutan (Mar.), decisively defeating Bhutanese resistance forces at the Dewangiri Stockade (Apr. 1) and massacring more than 100 after their surrender.

Russian forces took Tashkent (June).

b. Henry George Chauvel (d. 1945), Australian general.

b. Tuan Ch'i-jui (d. 1936), Chinese warlord.

d. Seng-Kuo-Lin-Ch'in (?-1865), Mongol general serving China who defended Peking during the Taiping Rebellion, defeating Taiping generals Li K'ai-feng and Lin Feng-hsiang; he became commander in chief in the northeast (1858).

American Civil War: William Tecumseh Sherman's Union army of 60,000 moved north through the Carolinas, driving much weaker Confederate forces before it and aiming to link up with Ulysses S. Grant in Virginia (Jan.-Mar.). Before Petersburg, Philip Sheridan's Union cavalry made a breakthrough at Five Forks (Apr. 1), and Grant's main force then took Petersburg by storm (Apr. 2). Robert E. Lee's forces withdrew but were trapped at Appomattox Courthouse, where Lee surrendered to Grant (Apr. 9). Remaining Confederate forces surrendered (Apr.-May).

d. Ambrose Powell Hill (b. 1825), American Confederate (CSA) general who played key roles in several Civil War battles; he was wounded at Chancellorsville (1863) and killed at Petersburg (Apr. 2).

d. William Clarke Quantrill (b. 1837), American Confederate (CSA) guerrilla leader whose irregulars — sometimes outlaws — raided in Missouri and Kansas, most notably at Lawrence (Aug. 21, 1863); he was fatally wounded by Union troops in Kentucky.

With the conclusion of the American Civil War, the United States demanded French withdrawal from Mexico and concentrated troops on the Mexican border.

d. Abraham Lincoln (b. 1809), 16th president of the United States (1861-1865), commander in chief of federal forces to preserve the Union during the Civil War; he was assassinated by John Wilkes Booth at Ford's Theater, Washington, D.C., just five days after the war's end (shot Apr. 14; died Apr. 15). He was succeeded by Vice President Andrew Johnson.

War of the Triple Alliance: Paraguay's dictator, Francisco Solano López, declared war on Argentina (Mar. 18). Brazil, Uruguay, and Argentina allied themselves against Paraguay (May 1). Paraguayan forces moved across Argentina to attack Brazil's Rio Grande do Sul province (June 10). At Uruguaiana (Aug. 5), allied forces captured the entire invasion force of 5,500.

b. William Sidney Graves (d. 1940), American general.

d. Samuel Francis Du Pont (b. 1803), American admiral who served in the Mexican-American War and the Civil War.

1866

b. Sun Yat-sen (d. 1925), leader of the Chinese Revolution and founder of the Chinese republic.

b. Tetsutaro Sato (d. 1942), Japanese admiral and military theorist.

War of the Triple Alliance: Allied forces invaded Paraguay (Jan.). At Tuyuty (May 24), allied forces numbering 32,000 decisively defeated a Paraguayan army of 24,000, with 4,000 allied and 13,000 Paraguayan casualties. At Curupayty (Sept. 22), the allies suffered losses of 9,000, with negligible Paraguayan losses, in a failed assault on Paraguayan positions.

Red Cloud's War (1866-1868): In Wyoming and Montana, an Indian coalition led by Teton Sioux chief Red Cloud went to war

Europe	Africa and Southwest Asia
1866 (cont.)	
Austro-Italian War: Italy and Prussia became allies (May 12), and Italy declared war on Austria when the Austro-Prussian War began. An Austrian army of 80,000 invaded Italy, defeating a larger Italian army at Custozza (June 24), then withdrawing to Austria to meet the advancing Prussians. The Treaty of Vienna awarded Venetia to Italy. Turkish forces defeated a major insurrection on Crete (1866-1868). b. Emilio de Bono (d. 1944), Italian general. b. Hans von Seeckt (d. 1936), German general.	
1867	
Resorgimento: Giuseppe Garibaldi led an army of 4,000 in a failed invasion of Rome; at Mentana, his forces were decisively defeated by French and papal forces (Nov. 3). Alfred Nobel invented dynamite. b. Jósef Klemens Pilsudski (d. 1935), Polish general. b. Karl Gustaf Emil Mannerheim (d. 1951), Finnish general.	British forces numbering 13,000 conducted a punitive expedition against Abyssinia, took and destroyed Magdala, the capital (Apr. 10), and then withdrew from the country.
1868	
Military junta, led by General Francisco Serrano, deposed Isabella II of Spain (Sept.). b. Nicholas II (d. 1918), the last Russian czar (r. 1894-1917). b. Miklós Horthy (d. 1957), Hungarian dictator (r. 1920-1944).	
1869	
b. Neville Chamberlain (d. 1940), British prime minister (1937-1940). d. Hugh Gough (b. 1779), British general who commanded during the Chinese-British Opium War (1839-1842), then became commander in chief in India during the annexation of the Punjab.	
1870	
Franco-Prussian War (1870-1871): France declared war on Prussia (July 15). At Wiessenberg (Aug. 4), Prussian forces numbering 50,000 pushed back a French division. At Fröschwiller (Wörth) (Aug. 6), Crown Prince Friedrich William's army of more than 95,000 defeated Marie de MacMahon's French army	b. Jan Christian Smuts (d. 1950), South African Boer general and politician.

to hold their territory against American forces, besieging several new forts built along the Bozeman Trail and ultimately forcing their evacuation.

Napoleon III withdrew French troops from Mexico (1866-1867).

d. Winfield Scott (b. 1786), American general during the Mexican-American War, driving from Veracruz to Mexico City (1847), where he served as military governor; though retired during the Civil War, he developed the Union's Anaconda Plan for taking the Mississippi Valley and blockading the South.

War of the Triple Alliance: Allied forces continued to advance on Paraguay, taking Asunción (Dec. 31). Paraguay's dictator, Francisco Solano López, continued a low-level guerrilla war until his death (1870).

With French troop withdrawals completed, Maximilian's forces were unable to hold Mexico; he was captured on May 14 and executed on May 19. The Mexican republic was restored, with Benito Juárez as president.

b. Wilbur Wright (d. 1912), American pioneer of aviation.

b. Emily Greene Balch (d. 1961), American pacifist.

d. John Drake Sloat (b. 1781), American admiral who, arriving with a squadron at Monterey, formally annexed California to the United States (July 7, 1846).

Japanese Civil War (Meiji Restoration): At Toba-Fushimi (Jan.), the Japanese imperial army decisively defeated shogunate forces.

Russian forces took Samarkand (May).

b. Suzuki Kantaro (d. 1948), Japanese admiral.

Cuban insurrection against Spanish rule began. Ultimately, Spanish and Cuban colonial forces defeated the insurgents in a long war of attrition (1868-1878).

Red Cloud's War: The Teton-led Indian coalition forced American troops to give up their newly built forts on the Bozeman Trail, formally winning respite under the Treaty of Fort Laramie (Apr. 29).

b. Mark Lambert Bristol (d. 1939), American admiral.

b. Mohandas Karamchand "Mahatma" Gandhi (d. 1948), Indian political and spiritual leader.

b. Emilio Aguinaldo (d. 1964), Philippine independence leader.

French-Canadian Metí leader Louis Riel led an insurrection in Manitoba, took Fort Garry (Winnipeg), and became the first president of the revolutionary government.

In Haiti, two concurrent insurrections defeated the government forces of Sylvain Selnave; Port-au-Prince fell (Dec. 18).

b. Hans Anton Kundt (d. 1939), German commander serving in Bolivia.

Louis Riel's Metí insurrection was defeated by Canadian troops, with very few casualties on either side.

1870 (cont.)

of less than 50,000; MacMahon retreated, with the Prussians in pursuit. To the north, Prussian forces defeated Achille F. Bazaine's French army, which retreated toward Metz, failing to break out of the developing German encirclement after a battle at Vionville–Mars-La-Tour (Aug. 16), that cost almost 16,000 German and almost 14,000 French casualties. The Gravelotte-St. Privat battle (Aug. 18) cost more than 20,000 Prussian and more than 12,000 French casualties and trapped the French at Metz. MacMahon, bringing a force of 130,000 to relieve Bazaine, was instead trapped at Sedan, on the Meuse River; there Napoleon III surrendered his army of 83,000, which had already suffered 17,000 casualties and 21,000 prisoners taken (Sept. 1). The siege of Paris began (Sept. 19). The entire French army of 170,000 surrendered at Metz (Oct. 27).

Resorgimento: Italian government forces besieged and took Rome (Sept.), the papacy's French protectors having withdrawn because of the Franco-Prussian War. Completing the Resorgimento, Italy annexed Rome, which became the national capital.

b. Vladimir Illich Lenin (Vladimir Illich Ulyanov) (d. 1924), Bolshevik leader.

b. James Connolly (d. 1916), Irish Republican leader.

b. Alexander Stanhope Cobbe (d. 1931), British general.

b. Hubert de la Poer Gough (d. 1963), British general.

d. Charles Jean Jacques Joseph Ardant du Picq (b. 1831), French army officer and military theorist who wrote *Études sur le combat: combat antique et moderne* (published 1880).

1871

Franco-Prussian War: Besieged Paris surrendered (Jan. 28). The Treaty of Frankfurt (May 10) gave Germany Alsace and much of Lorraine, as well as a $1 billion indemnity.

Paris Commune took power (Mar. 18-May 28); French government troops led by Marshal Marie de MacMahon defeated the rising, attacking the Communards in a close engagement in Paris (May 21-28).

b. Karl Liebknecht (d. 1919), German communist leader.

b. Pietro Badoglio (d. 1956), Italian general.

b. Rosa Luxemburg (d. 1919), Polish socialist and German communist leader.

b. David Beatty (d. 1936), British admiral.

b. Ioannis Metaxas (d. 1941), Greek general and military dictator (1936-1941).

d. Wilhelm von Tegetthoff (b. 1827), Austrian admiral who, after service against Denmark (1864), commanded the Austrian Fleet in the Austro-Prussian War (1866).

1872

Third Carlist War (1872-1876): Carlos VII led an exile army into northern Spain; early defeats gave way to successful development of a 50,000-strong rebel force.

b. Maurice Gustave Gamelin (d. 1958), French general.

b. Anton Denikin (d. 1947), Russian general.

b. Haakon VII (d. 1957), king of Norway (r. 1905-1957).

1870 (cont.)

War of the Triple Alliance: Low-level guerrilla war against the allies effectively ended with the death in battle of Paraguay's dictator, Francisco Solano López (Mar. 1).

At the Blood River, in Montana (Jan. 23), the American cavalry massacred at least 170 Blackfoot villagers, all but a few of them noncombatants, with 1 American killed.

d. Robert Edward Lee (b. 1807), American Confederate (CSA) general who led Virginia and then Confederate forces, suffering a decisive defeat at Gettysburg (1863) and eventually surrendering at Appomattox Courthouse (1865).

d. David Glasgow Farragut (b. 1801), the American navy's first rear admiral (1862) and first vice admiral (1866), best known for his success at Mobile Bay (1864), where he shouted, "Damn the torpedoes! Full speed ahead!"

d. George Henry Thomas (b. 1816), American general called the "Rock of Chickamauga" for his defensive action there (Sept. 19-20, 1863).

1871

Cochise's Apache guerrillas were forced to give up their fight against American forces (Sept.).

b. Orville Wright (d. 1948), American aviation pioneer.

d. John Bankhead Magruder (b. 1810), American Confederate (CSA) general, nicknamed "Prince John"; he commanded Confederate forces in Virginia (1862) and then in Texas; later he served in Mexico under Emperor Maximilian I (1865-1869).

1872

d. Tseng Kuo-feng (b. 1811), Chinese statesman and general serving the imperial army during the Taiping Rebellion; he forged an army from Hunan militia forces (1852) and led the recapture of the Taiping capital of Nanking (1863-1864); he strongly supported the modernization of China.

Cochise's Apache forces negotiated a peace with the Americans; the Apaches then moved onto reservations.

d. George Gordon Meade (b. 1815), American general who commanded the Union's Army of the Potomac at Gettysburg (1863), Petersburg (1864), and Appomattox (1865).

1873

Third Carlist War: The first Spanish republic was formed. Carlist forces in northern Spain took Estella.

Second British-Ashanti War (1873-1874): Ashanti forces, claiming several coastal areas, attacked the Gold Coast.

1874

Third Carlist War: In Spain, Carlist forces lost strength after a constitutional monarchy was established, with Alfonso XII on the throne.

b. Winston Leonard Spencer Churchill (d. 1965), British prime minister.

b. Alexander Vasilievich Kolchak (d. 1920), Russian admiral and general.

Second British-Ashanti War: Ashanti forces withdrew from the Gold Coast after British forces attacked and burned Kamasi, the Ashanti capital (Feb.).

1875

Alfred Nobel invented ballistite, a smokeless gunpowder.

Turkish forces defeated risings in Bosnia and Herzegovina.

b. Karl Rudolph Gerd von Rundstedt (d. 1953), German field marshal.

Egyptian forces took several Abyssinian cities, including Massawa and Harar. John of Abyssinia ultimately responded with force, decisively defeating the Egyptians at Gundat (Nov. 13).

1876

Serbian-Turkish War: Serbia and Montenegro, with Russian support, declared war on Turkey (July), but both were quickly defeated. Serbian forces held advancing Turkish forces led by Suleiman Pasha at Alexinatz, on the approaches to Belgrade (Aug. 7-12), but they lost to the Turks at Djunis (Oct. 29). The war was overtaken by the Russo-Turkish conflict.

Turkish forces defeated risings in Bulgaria, massacring an estimated 15,000 near Philippolis (Apr.-Aug.).

Third Carlist War: Estella fell to Spanish government forces led by General Primo de Rivera; Carlos VII fled across the Pyrenees into exile.

Britain introduced its first torpedo boat, the *Lightning*.

b. Erich Raeder (d. 1960), German admiral.

b. Konrad Adenauer (d. 1967), German lawyer and politician.

b. Mata Hari (Margaretha Geertruida Zelle) (d. 1917), Dutch dancer executed as a spy.

Egyptian forces again invaded Abyssinia but were defeated at Gura (Mar. 7), ending their penetration into the area.

Abdul Hamid II took power in Turkey.

Central, South and East Asia, and the Pacific	The Americas	
		1873
Russian forces took Khiva (Aug.). b. Chang Tso-lin (d. 1928), Chinese warlord called "Tiger of the North" or "Old Marshal." b. Wu P'ei-fu (ca. 1873-1939), Chinese warlord.	b. Francisco Indalecio Madero (d. 1913), Mexican revolutionary and president. d. William Joseph Hardee (b. 1815), American Confederate (CSA) general who served primarily with the Army of Tennessee.	
		1874
Hanoi Incident: French forces took Hanoi; although they later evacuated the city, they annexed more of Vietnam.	d. Cochise (b. ca. 1812), Apache leader who fought the Americans (1861-1871), taking full command after the loss at Apache Pass, Arizona (July 1862). d. Franklin Buchanan (b. 1800), American Confederate (CSA) naval officer who led attacks on the federal blockade of Hampton Roads (1862) and later commanded Confederate naval forces at Mobile Bay (1864).	
		1875
b. Kenkichi Ueda (d. 1962), Japanese general. b. Syngman Rhee (d. 1965), first South Korean president (1948-1960).	After a gold strike, the American government reneged on existing treaties and threw open Sioux land in the Black Hills of the Dakotas to prospecting and mining. Many Sioux left their reservations, moving west into the Powder River country. American forces pursued them after they refused to return to their reservations. Yaqui and Mayan rising in Sonora (1875-1898) scored early successes but was ultimately defeated by Mexican forces in a long war of attrition. d. George Edward Pickett (b. 1825), American Confederate (CSA) general who led the disastrous Pickett's Charge against Union forces at Gettysburg (1863), losing three-quarters of his troops. d. John Cabell Breckenridge (b. 1821), American Confederate (CSA) general who led his troops to victory at New Market (1863), in the Shenandoah Valley.	
		1876
b. Mohammad Ali Jinnah (d. 1948), founder of Pakistan. b. Shigeru Honjo (d. 1945), Japanese general.	Sioux/Cheyenne-American War (1876-1877): Pursuing some thousands of Sioux who had refused to return to their reservations in the Dakotas after the American government had reneged on its treaties and thrown the Black Hills open to mining, American forces attacked Sioux villages in Montana. Sioux and Cheyenne forces numbering 3,000 to 6,000, led by chiefs Sitting Bull and Crazy Horse, responded. General George Crook's forces withdrew after an engagement at the Rosebud River (June 17), but General George Armstrong Custer, at the head of 220 of his 750-strong Seventh Cavalry, charged the entire Sioux and Cheyenne force at the Little Bighorn (June 25); he and his entire cavalry force died in battle. Most of the rest of Custer's command survived. d. George Armstrong Custer (b. 1839), American general nicknamed "Yellow Hair," who rashly attacked the whole Sioux-Cheyenne army at the Little Bighorn; he and all his troops were killed. In Mexico, Porfirío Díaz seized power by coup, ruling as dictator until he was overthrown (1911). d. Antonio López de Santa Anna (b. 1794), Mexican general who led the forces that besieged and took the Alamo (1836); he was	

1876 (cont.)

1877

Russo-Turkish War (1877-1878): With the Russian declaration of war (Apr. 24), Russian forces attacked and took Romania, which quickly declared its independence (May 21) and joined the Russian side. Russian forces crossed the Danube into Bulgaria (June 23), besieged and took Plevna (July-Dec.), and took Sofia (Dec.). In the Caucasus Mountains, the Russians besieged and took Kars by storm (Nov. 18), then besieged Erzurum.

b. Felix Edmundovich Dzerzhinsky (d. 1926), organizer and head of the Soviet secret police.

d. Konstantinos Kanaris (b. 1790), Greek admiral during the Greek War of Independence (1821-1832).

d. Ramón (Cabrera y Griño), count of Morella Cabrera (b. 1806), Spanish Carlist general who was called the "Tiger of Maestrazgo" for his savagery in that Valencian region.

Britain annexed the Transvaal (Apr. 12).

Ninth "Kaffir" War (1877-1878): Final Xhosa rising in South Africa was defeated by the British, and all remaining Xhosa lands were taken.

Belgium penetrated the Congo (1877-1885).

As Egypt's governor-general in Sudan (1877-1880), British general Charles Gordon led in suppressing the slave trade, earning the name "Gordon Pasha."

1878

Russo-Turkish War: At Senova (Jan. 8-9), Russian forces led by General Mikhail Sobelov decisively defeated a Turkish army of 36,000 and were threatening Constantinople when the war ended (Jan. 31). The Treaty of San Stefano (Mar. 3) brought the independence of Serbia, Montenegro, Romania, and Bulgaria, the last a Russian protectorate. Russia took Kars and several Turkish-Russian border regions.

After the Treaty of San Stefano gave Bosnia to Austria, Austrian forces defeated substantial Bosnian independence forces and occupied Bosnia and Herzegovina.

b. Peter Nikolayevich Wrangel (d. 1928), Russian general.

b. John Frederick Charles Fuller (d. 1964), British general and military theorist.

b. Roger Roland Charles Backhouse (d. 1939), British admiral.

b. Reza Shah Pahlevi (Reza Khan) (d. 1944), Iranian general and shah.

1879

b. Joseph Stalin (Joseph Vissarionovich Dzhugashvili) (d. 1953), Soviet dictator (r. 1928-1953).

b. Leon Trotsky (Lev Davidovich Bronstein) (d. 1940), Bolshevik leader.

b. Nancy Langhorne Astor (d. 1964), American-born British politician.

b. Simon Vasilievich Petlyura (d. 1926), Ukrainian nationalist leader.

d. Claude É. Minié (b. 1804), French officer who invented the minié ball (1849).

British-Zulu War: British forces attacked Zululand (Jan. 11). At Isandhlwana (Jan. 22), Zulu forces numbering 20,000, led by Cetshwayo, attacked and destroyed a British and colonial force of 1,800, with almost 1,400 British and Black African colonials dead; an estimated 2,000 Zulu died. Zulu forces also were successful at Hlobane (Mar. 28) and Kambula (Mar. 29), and they unsuccessfully besieged Eshowe (Jan.-

Central, South and East Asia, and the Pacific	The Americas	
1876 (cont.)		
	later captured by Sam Houston at San Jacinto. He then commanded Mexican forces during the Mexican-American War.	
	d. Braxton Bragg (b. 1817), American Confederate (CSA) general who led the Army of Tennessee (1862-1863), most notably at Chickamauga (1863) but lost decisively at Chattanooga (1863).	
1877		
Japanese government forces defeated a Satsuma clan insurrection at Kumamoto, on Kyushu (Feb.-Sept.). d. Takamori Saigo (b. 1827), Japanese field marshal who became commander in chief (1872) but later led the Satsuma Rebellion, dying on the field at the rebellion's end (Sept. 14). b. Sadao Araki (d. 1966), Japanese general.	Sioux/Cheyenne-American War: American forces defeated the Sioux and Cheyenne in a series of small actions. Crazy Horse surrendered after a defeat at Wolf Mountain (Jan. 6); Sitting Bull fled into Canada. d. Crazy Horse (Tashunca-Uitco) (b. ca. 1849), Oglala Sioux war chief whose allied forces annihilated Custer's federal troops at the Little Bighorn (1876); later captured, he was killed in a reported escape attempt. Forced off their land in Washington, the Nez Percé, led by Chief Joseph, attempted to reach asylum in Canada. The small Indian nation of fewer than 1,000 successfully conducted a fighting retreat of more than 2,000 miles but were ultimately captured in the Bear Paw Mountains, south of the Canadian border (Oct.). d. Nathan Bedford Forrest (b. 1821), American Confederate (CSA) general; an active raider, he became cavalry commander of the Army of Tennessee. He was a founder and the grand wizard of the original Ku Klux Klan.	
1878		
Second British-Afghan War (1878-1881): British forces led by Frederick Roberts invaded Afghanistan (Nov.), defeated Afghan forces led by Sher Ali at Peiwar Kotal (Dec. 2), and took Kabul. b. Iwane Matsui (d. 1948), Japanese general.	b. Ernest Joseph King (d. 1956), American admiral. b. Francisco "Pancho" Villa (Doroteo Arango) (d. 1923), Mexican revolutionary general.	
1879		
d. Sher Ali Khan (b. 1825), Afghan ruler (r. 1863-1878) who was defeated by British forces at Peiwar Kotal (1878); he was succeeded by his son Yakub Khan. Second British-Afghan War: After a rising in Kabul, in which the British resident (diplomatic agent) was killed, Frederick Roberts's British forces again took the city after defeating an Afghan army at Charasia (Oct. 6); Yakub Khan then abdicated, and his brother Ayub took power. An Afghan army reportedly numbering	War of the Pacific (1879-1884): Chile attacked Peru and Bolivia, aiming to control nitrate-producing areas in both countries. After several naval victories (May-Oct.), Chilean forces moved north up the coast to attack Peru and Bolivia. Apache chief Victorio led a band of fewer than 200 in a yearlong guerrilla war against Mexican and American forces, until he and much of his small force were found and killed by Mexican forces (Oct. 15). b. William "Billy" Mitchell (d. 1936), American officer.	

Europe	Africa and Southwest Asia

1879 (cont.)

	Apr.). Reinforced British and colonial forces again invaded Zululand (June), decisively defeating the Zulu at Ulundi, the Zulu capital (July 4), effectively ending the war. Cetshwayo was deposed.

1880

b. Ion Antonescu (d. 1946), Romanian fascist leader. b. Fedor von Bock (d. 1945), German general. b. Paul Hausser (d. 1972), German general. b. Werner von Fritsch (d. 1939), German general.	Boer Republic was organized; a brief war of independence began (Dec. 30). b. Ibn Saud (Abd al-Aziz Ibn Saud) (d. 1953), first Saudi Arabian king (r. 1932-1953). b. Vladimir Jabotinsky (d. 1940), Zionist leader.

1881

b. Eamon De Valera (d. 1975), Irish revolutionary. b. Alexander Fyodorovich Kerensky (d. 1970), Russian revolutionary. b. Walther von Brauchitsch (d. 1948), German general. b. Paul Ludwig Ewald von Kleist (d. 1954), German general. b. Erwin von Witsleben (d. 1944), German field marshal. b. Henry Maitland Wilson (d. 1964), British field marshal.	At Laing's Nek, in the Drakensberg Mountains of Natal, a Boer army of 2,000 defeated a British army of 1,400 (Jan. 28). At Majuba Hill (Feb. 27), the Boers again defeated the British, who then recognized the Boer Republic under the Treaty of Pretoria (Apr. 5). First Sudanese-Egyptian-British War (1881-1885): Sudanese Dervish forces, led by the Mahdi (Muhammad Ahmad), defeated a 2,000-strong Egyptian force, with more than 1,000 Egyptian casualties. French seaborne forces took Bizerte (Apr.), while army units moved across the Algerian border; Tunis quickly surrendered (May), becoming a French protectorate. b. Mustapha Kemal (Atatürk) (d. 1938), founder and first president of the Republic of Turkey (r. 1919-1938). b. Pasha Enver (d. 1922), Turkish general.

1882

b. Georgi Mikhailovich Dimitrov (d. 1949), Bulgarian communist leader. b. Wilhelm Keitel (d. 1946), German general. b. Hans Gunther von Kluge (d. 1944), German general. b. Clement Richard Attlee (d. 1967), British prime minister.	First Sudanese-Egyptian-British War: British seaborne forces numbering 25,000 landed at Ismailia, Egypt (July 11). At Tell el-Kebir (Sept. 13), the British attacked and routed an Egyptian army of 38,000, with 2,500 Egyptian and minimal British casualties.

Central, South and East Asia, and the Pacific	The Americas	
1879 (cont.)		
100,000 attacked and was defeated by the British at Sherpur (Dec. 23). Japan annexed the Ryukyu Islands, over Chinese protests. Russian forces besieged but failed to take Geok Tepe, in Central Asia. b. Hisaichi Terauchi (d. 1946), Japanese general.	b. Albert Einstein (d. 1955), German-Swiss-American physicist. d. Joseph Hooker (b. 1814), American general called "Fighting Joe," who rose to be commander of the Army of the Potomac; he was defeated at Chancellorsville (1863). d. John Bell Hood (b. 1831), American Confederate (CSA) general.	
1880		
Second British-Afghan War: At Kandahar (Sept. 1), Frederick Roberts's forces decisively defeated an Afghan army led by Ayub Khan, Yakub Khan's brother, effectively ending the British portion of the war. b. Hajime Sugiyama (d. 1945), Japanese field marshal.	War of the Pacific: At Tacna (May 26), Chilean forces numbering 14,000 defeated slightly smaller allied forces, with more than 2,000 Chilean and more than 3,000 allied casualties; the Chileans then took Tacna and Arica. b. Douglas MacArthur (d. 1964), American general. b. George Catlett Marshall (d. 1959), American general. b. Alvaro Obregón (d. 1928), Mexican general. b. Jeannette Pickering Rankin (d. 1973), American politician and pacifist.	
1881		
Second British-Afghan War: British forces withdrew from Afghanistan after placing British ally Abdur Rahman on the throne. Ayub Khan's forces attacked and took Kandahar (July 27) but were decisively defeated by Abdur Rahman's Afghan army (Sept. 22), finally ending the war. Russian forces took Geok Tepe by storm (Jan.).	War of the Pacific: At Chorillos (Jan. 13), on the approaches to Lima, a Chilean army of 24,000 defeated defending Peruvian forces of 18,000, with 3,000 Chilean and 9,000 Peruvian casualties. The Chileans then took Lima. The defeated allies ceded substantial territories and made other concessions to Chile. b. Walter Krueger (d. 1967), Prussian-born American general. d. Ambrose Everett Burnside (b. 1824), American general during the Civil War who became commander of the Army of the Potomac (Nov. 1862) but was replaced after his loss at Fredericksburg (Dec. 13, 1862). d. Robert Patterson (b. 1792), American general during the Mexican-American War and Civil War.	
1882		
Chinese and Japanese forces confronted each other in Korea (1882-1885), with the Japanese seeking to supplant the Chinese protectorate with their own. b. Feng Yu-hsiang (d. 1948), Chinese general.	b. Franklin Delano Roosevelt (d. 1945), 32d president of the United States (1933-1945). b. William Frederick Halsey, Jr. (d. 1959), American admiral. b. Holland McTyeire Smith (d. 1967), American Marine general.	

1882 (cont.)

d. Giuseppe Garibaldi (b. 1807), Italian military leader and revolutionary who was a key figure in the Italian Revolutions (1848-1849); he was forced into exile in America (1848-1854) before returning for the Resorgimento that won Italy's independence (1860-1870).

Ahmet Arabi's forces surrendered; Britain made Egypt a protectorate.

First Sudanese-Egyptian-British War: Mahdist forces defeated an Egyptian expeditionary force of 5,500 in the Sudan. The Mahdi's army besieged and took El Obeid (Nov. 1882-Jan. 1883).

Italy established a colony at Assab, Eritrea, beginning its penetration of Abyssinia.

b. Abdullah Ibn Hussein (d. 1951), first king of Transjordan (r. 1946-1951).

1883

Hiram Maxim was granted his first patent for the Maxim machine gun.

b. Benito Mussolini (d. 1945), Italian fascist head of state (1922-1945).

b. Semën Mikhailovich Budënny (d. 1973), Soviet general.

b. Alan Francis Brooke (Alanbrooke) (d. 1963), British field marshal.

b. Pierre Laval (d. 1945), French politician.

b. Alexandros Papagos (d. 1955), Greek field marshal and statesman.

b. Andrew Browne Cunningham (d. 1963), British admiral.

First Sudanese-Egyptian-British War: An Egyptian army of 11,000, commanded by British general William Hicks, was entirely destroyed, with few survivors, by Mahdist forces at Kashgal, in the southern Sudan; Sudanese casualties were minimal.

French forces attacked Madagascar, defeating government forces after bombarding Tamatave and Majunga, and forced acceptance of a French protectorate over the country (1883-1885).

b. Faisal (d. 1933), Arab general and first Iraqi king (r. 1921-1933).

b. Thomas Edward Lawrence, "Lawrence of Arabia" (d. 1935), British officer.

d. Abd-el-Kader (Abd-al-Kadir) (b. 1808), Algerian ruler who lost his country to French invaders (1847).

1884

b. Claude Auchinleck (d. 1981), British field marshal.

b. Eduard Benes (d. 1948), Czech independence leader.

b. Franz Halder (d. 1972), German general.

b. Mikhail Markovich Borodin (d. 1951), Russian communist adviser to China.

d. Franz Eduard Ivanovich Todleben (b. 1818), Russian general who commanded the fortress at Sevastopol (1854-1855), which fell only after he was wounded and evacuated; he later became commander in chief of the Russian army (1878).

First Sudanese-Egyptian-British War: General Charles Gordon arrived at Khartoum (Jan. 18), reportedly to direct the Egyptian withdrawal from the city. Khartoum was besieged by Mahdist forces (Feb. 1884-Jan. 1885).

First Sudanese-Egyptian-British War: On the Red Sea coast, Mahdist forces destroyed a British-led army of 3,500 at El Teb, with fewer than 1,000 survivors (Feb.). British regular army forces then sharply defeated Mahdist forces at El Teb (Feb. 29) and Tamai (Mar. 14), with a reported 4,000 Sudanese dead; the British then withdrew from the area as part of a general British and Egyptian withdrawal from the Sudan.

Germany established protectorates in Cameroons and Togoland.

Central, South and East Asia, and the Pacific	The Americas

1882 (cont.)

	b. Husband Edward Kimmel (d. 1968), American admiral.
	b. Robert Hutchings Goddard (d. 1945), American rocket pioneer.

1883

After new conflicts between the French and the Vietnamese, French forces took Hanoi and Hué; Vietnam became a French protectorate.	b. Emiliano Zapata (d. 1919), Mexican Indian revolutionary leader.
b. Yen Hsi-shan (d. 1960), Chinese warlord.	b. Getúlio Dornelles Vargas (d. 1954), Brazilian dictator and president.
	b. William Joseph "Wild Bill" Donovan (d. 1959), American intelligence officer.
	d. Andrew Atkinson Humphreys (b. 1810), American general during the Civil War, most notably at Antietam, Fredericksburg, Chancellorsville, and Gettysburg, becoming the Army of the Potomac's chief of staff (1863).

1884

Manchus successfully contested French expansion into northern Vietnam and southern China.	b. Harry S. Truman (d. 1972), 33d president of the United States (1945-1953).
Russian forces completed their conquest of the Muslim states of Central Asia, taking Merv.	b. (Anna) Eleanor Roosevelt (d. 1962), American political figure.
b. Hideki Tojo (d. 1948), Japanese general and prime minister.	b. Roger Nash Baldwin (d. 1981), American pacifist and civil libertarian.
b. Isoroku Yamamoto (d. 1943), Japanese admiral.	
b. Thomas Albert Blamey (d. 1951), Australian field marshal.	
b. Yasuji Okamura (d. 1966), Japanese general.	

1884 (cont.)

	b. Ismet İnönü (d. 1973), prime minister of Turkey (1938-1950; 1961-1965).
	d. Cetshwayo (Cetewayo) (b. 1827), Zulu king (r. 1873-1879) who defeated the rival iziGgoza faction at the Battle of 'Ndondakusuka (1856); he was deposed after losing the British-Zulu War (1879).

1885

Serbo-Bulgarian War (1885-1886): Serbian forces attacked Bulgaria (Nov.) but were sharply defeated at Slivnitza (Nov. 17-19); pursued by Bulgarian forces, they retreated into Serbia and were again defeated by the Bulgarians at Pirot (Nov. 26-27); Austrian intervention on behalf of the Serbs forced Bulgaria to accept a prewar status quo peace settlement.

b. Albert Kesselring (d. 1960), German general.

b. Mikhail Vasilyevich Frunz (d. 1925), Russian revolutionary general and military theorist.

d. Charles George Gordon (b. 1833), British general called "China" Gordon for his activities in the Second Opium War and Taiping Rebellion and "Gordon Pasha" for his work in the Sudan, especially suppressing the slave trade; he was killed by Mahdist troops on the steps of the governor's palace in Khartoum (Jan. 26).

d. Baron Edwin von Manteuffel (b. 1809), Prussian field marshal who rose to lead the Second Army during the Franco-Prussian War, commanding occupation forces in France (1871).

d. Ernst Eduard Vogel von Falckenstein (b. 1797), Prussian general; he was commander in chief for south Germany and later the Army of the Main during the Austro-Prussian War (1866).

d. Prince Frederick Charles (b. 1828), Prussian field marshal who commanded the First Army in the Austro-Prussian War (1866) and the Second Army in the Franco-Prussian War (1870-1871).

First Sudanese-Egyptian-British War: Besieged Khartoum fell to Mahdist forces (Jan. 26). General Charles Gordon and the entire remaining garrison were killed.

d. Muhammad Ahmad "The Mahdi" (al-Mahdi; Muhammad Ahmad ibn as-Sayyid 'Abd Allah) (b. 1844), Sudanese religious and military leader who claimed descent from Mohammed; he died of natural causes, possibly typhus.

Britain and Germany contested the East African coast, with Germany establishing a protectorate in Tanganyika.

British forces began an intermittent war against Arab slave traders in Africa's Nyasaland.

First Mandingo-French War (1885–1886): French forces attacked the Ivory Coast, defeating the forces of Samori and establishing a protectorate.

Long Belgian penetration into the Congo ended with the Belgian-controlled area becoming a Crown colony.

1886

b. Béla Kun (d. 1937), Hungarian communist leader.

b. Karl Barth (d. 1968), anti-Nazi Swiss Protestant minister.

b. Jan Masaryk (d. 1948), Czech foreign minister.

b. Ernst Thaelmann (d. 1944), German communist leader.

---

b. David Ben Gurion (David Green) (d. 1973), Zionist leader and first Israeli prime minister.

1887

b. Bernard Law Montgomery (d. 1976), British field marshal.

b. Wilhelm Canaris (d. 1945), German anti-Nazi intelligence officer.

An Italian force of 500 was destroyed by an Abyssinian force of 15,000 at Dogali; very few Italians escaped (Jan. 26).

	1884 (cont.)	

| | **1885** | |

Large-scale Vietnamese rising against the French was ultimately defeated (1885-1895).

Third Burmese War: British forces again attacked Burma; riverborne forces advanced north on the Irrawaddy River (Nov. 14), took Burmese surrender of the capital city, Ava, two weeks later, and annexed all of Burma.

Both China and Japan temporarily withdrew from Korea.

Under the Treaty of Tientsin, France and China largely returned to their prewar positions on the Vietnamese-Chinese frontier, although much border territory remained disputed.

b. Tomoyuki Yamashita (d. 1946), Japanese general.

d. Tso Tsung-t'ang (b. 1812), Chinese statesman and general credited with winning back Chekiang province from the Taiping rebels (1862).

French-Canadian Metí leader Louis Riel led a second insurrection, this one in Saskatchewan (Mar.-May), costing more than 100 Canadian and Cree lives. Canadian forces took Batoche, Riel's capital (May 12); soon captured, Riel was later executed.

b. Chester William Nimitz (d. 1966), American admiral.

b. George Smith Patton (d. 1945), American general.

b. Frank Jack Fletcher (d. 1973), American admiral.

b. Richmond Kelly Turner (d. 1961), American admiral.

d. Ulysses Simpson (Hiram Ulysses) Grant (b. 1822), American general and 18th president of the United States (1869-1877); during the Civil War, he commanded the Military Division of the Mississippi after his capture of Vicksburg (1863) and eventually took General Robert E. Lee's surrender at Appomattox Courthouse (Apr. 9, 1865).

d. George Brinton McClellan (b. 1826), American general who led and reorganized the Army of the Potomac (1861-1862); he was replaced for hesitating to move into action.

| | **1886** | |

b. Zhu De (d. 1976), Chinese communist general.

b. Hitoshi Imamura (d. 1968), Japanese general.

b. Jisaburo Ozawa (d. 1966), Japanese admiral.

b. Masakazu Kawabe (d. 1965), Japanese general.

b. Nobutake Kondo (d. 1953), Japanese admiral.

White Mountain Apache leader Geronimo surrendered to American forces led by General Nelson Miles, ending the Apache-American wars (Sept. 4).

b. Henry Harley "Hap" Arnold (d. 1950), American aviator and air general.

b. Raymond Ames Spruance (d. 1969), American admiral.

b. Robert Lawrence Eichelberger (d. 1961), American general.

d. David Hunter (b. 1802), American general who during the Civil War organized former slaves into the First South Carolina Regiment; he later led the commission trying the conspirators who assassinated Abraham Lincoln.

| | **1887** | |

Siamese forces attacked Laos, taking much of the eastern part of the country.

b. Alexander Archer Vandegrift (d. 1973), American Marine general.

Europe	Africa and Southwest Asia

1887 (cont.)

b. Fritz Erich von Manstein (d. 1973), German general.

b. Vidkun Quisling (d. 1945), Norwegian puppet leader.

In the Anglo-German contest for East Africa, Britain made Kenya a protectorate.

1888

b. Alexander I (d. 1934), Yugoslav ruler.

b. Heinz Guderian (d. 1954), German tank corps general.

German forces defeated an Arab rising in East Africa (1888-1890).

b. Nuri al Said (Nuri as-Said) (d. 1958), Iraqi general and prime minister.

1889

b. Adolf Hitler (d. 1945), German dictator (1933-1945).

b. Georges Bidault (d. 1983), French Resistance leader and later prime minister.

b. Vasili Konstantinovich Blücher (d. 1938), Soviet general.

b. Jean de Lattre de Tassigny (d. 1952), marshal of France.

Sudanese-Abyssinian War: Mahdist forces numbering 60,000 attacked Abyssinia (Jan.), defeating Abyssinian forces numbering 70,000 at Debra Sin. Abyssinian forces, reportedly numbering 90,000, decisively defeated the Mahdists at Metemma (Mar. 12), effectively ending the war.

1890

b. Charles André Joseph Marie De Gaulle (d. 1970), French general and politician.

b. Michael Collins (d. 1922), Irish revolutionary.

b. Friedrich von Paulus (d. 1957), German general.

b. Arthur William Tedder (d. 1967), British air marshal.

b. Vyacheslav Mikhailovich Molotov (d. 1986), Soviet diplomat.

b. Max Immelmann (d. 1916), German pilot.

b. Anthony Herman Gerard Fokker (d. 1939), Dutch airplane designer.

d. Robert Cornelis Napier (b. 1810), British field marshal born in Ceylon (Sri Lanka) who served primarily in India and China, rising to commander in chief in India (1870-1876).

France took much of Upper Niger from the Tukolor Empire (1890-1892).

Britain established a protectorate in Zanzibar.

b. Jomo Kenyatta (d. 1978), Kenyan independence leader.

Central, South and East Asia, and the Pacific	The Americas	
	1887 (cont.)	
b. Chiang Kai-shek (d. 1975), leader of the Republic of China. b. Yasuhiko Asaka (1887-?), Japanese general who commanded the Shanghai Expeditionary Army that committed notable atrocities during the Shanghai-Nanking campaign (Aug.-Dec. 1933), called the "Rape of Nanking." b. Chuichi Nagumo (d. 1944), Japanese naval air officer. b. Homma Masaharu (d. 1946), Japanese general.	b. Marc Andrew Mitscher (d. 1947), American admiral. b. Courtney Hicks Hodges (d. 1966), American general.	
	1888	
b. Haruyoshi Hyakutake (d. 1947), Japanese general. b. Heitaro Kimura (d. 1948), Japanese general.	b. John Foster Dulles (d. 1959), American diplomat. b. Theodore Stark Wilkinson (d. 1946), American admiral. b. Thomas Cassin Kinkaid (d. 1972), American admiral. b. William Hood Simpson (d. 1980), American general. b. Henry Duncan Graham Crerar (d. 1965), Canadian general. d. Philip Henry Sheridan (b. 1831), American general during the Civil War, notably in the Shenandoah Valley; he commanded federal forces during the Indian Wars, later becoming overall commanding general (1883), then general of the army (1888).	
	1889	
b. Jawaharlal Nehru (d. 1964), Indian independence leader and first prime minister (1947-1964). b. Hiroaki Abe (d. 1949), Japanese admiral. b. Masaki Honda (d. 1964), Japanese general. b. Tadayoshi Sano (d. 1945), Japanese general. b. Takeo Kurita (d. 1977), Japanese admiral.	b. Alexander McCarrell Patch, Jr. (d. 1945), American general. b. George Churchill Kenney (d. 1977), American Army Air Force general. b. Walton Harris Walker (d. 1950), American general. b. Igor Sikorsky (d. 1972), Russian-American helicopter inventor. d. Jefferson Davis (b. 1808), American military and political leader who became president of the Confederate States of America (CSA) (1861-1865).	
	1890	
b. Ho Chi Minh (Nguyen That Thanh) (d. 1969), Vietnamese communist leader. b. Ho Ying-ch'in (1890-?), Nationalist Chinese general who served as Chiang Kai-shek's minister of war and chief of the Supreme Staff (1930-1944). b. Kingoro Hashimoto (d. 1957), Japanese army officer. b. Yoshitsugo Saito (d. 1944), Japanese general.	At Wounded Knee Creek, on the Pine Ridge Sioux reservation in South Dakota (Dec. 29), an American Seventh Cavalry force of 500, with cannons, massacred a captive Sioux band of 350, consisting of 230 women and children and 120 men, many of the men noncombatants, after a single shot had been fired. Sioux casualties included 150 to 200 dead and 50 to 100 injured; American casualties of 73 included an undetermined number of those killed and wounded by "friendly fire," as the cavalry attacked while soldiers surrounding the camp were still firing on it. The massacre occurred during the "Ghost Dance Wars," while Sioux who had left their reservations were being forcibly returned to them. Those massacred at Wounded Knee were the main casualties of the "wars." b. Dwight David Eisenhower (d. 1969), American general and 34th president of the United States (1953-1961). b. Edward Vernon Rickenbacker (d. 1973), American air ace.	

1890 (cont.)

1891

Europe

b. Erwin Rommel ("Desert Fox") (d. 1944), German general.

b. Harold Rupert Leofric George Alexander (Alexander of Tunis) (d. 1969), British field marshal.

b. Karl Dönitz (Carl Doenitz) (d. 1980), German admiral.

b. William Joseph Slim (d. 1970), British general.

b. Fridolin R. T. von Senger und Etterlin (d. 1963), German general.

b. Walther Model (d. 1945), German field marshal.

d. Helmuth Karl Bernhard von Moltke (b. 1800), German field marshal and chief of the General Staff (1866) who orchestrated the campaigns of the Franco-Prussian War (1870-1871); Helmuth Johannes Ludwig von Moltke was his nephew.

d. Eduard von Clam-Gallas (b. 1805), Austrian general.

1892

Europe

b. Francisco Franco (d. 1975), Spanish general and fascist dictator (1939-1975).

b. Tito (Josip Broz) (d. 1980), Yugoslav communist and head of state (1945-1980).

b. Arthur Travers Harris (d. 1984), British air marshal.

b. Baron Manfred von Richthofen (d. 1918), German air ace.

b. Josef Dietrich (d. 1966), German general.

Africa and Southwest Asia

French forces defeated the army of Dahomey, which it then made a protectorate.

b. Abd el-Krim (d. 1963), Moroccan independence leader.

b. Haile Selassie I (Ras Tafari) (d. 1975), Ethiopian regent and king (r. 1916-1930) and emperor (r. 1930-1974).

Central, South and East Asia, and the Pacific	The Americas	
	1890 (cont.)	

	The Americas
	b. Claire Chennault (d. 1958), American air commander.
	b. Daniel Judson Callaghan (d. 1942), American admiral.
	b. Lewis Hyde Brereton (d. 1967), American Air Force general.
	b. John Porter Lucas (d. 1949), American general.
	b. Charles Horatio McMorris (d. 1954), American admiral.
	d. Sitting Bull (Tatanka Yotanka) (b. ca. 1831), Hunkpapa Sioux chief during the Sioux/Cheyenne-American War; he was spiritual leader, though not field commander, of the allies who annihilated Custer's troops at the Little Bighorn (1876).
	d. John Charles Frémont (b. 1813), American general who explored the American West, in California leading a revolt by American settlers (1846) before becoming governor.
	d. George Crook (b. 1829), American general called the "Grey Fox"; he was active during the Civil War and the Indian Wars.

	1891	

Central, South and East Asia, and the Pacific	The Americas
b. Fumimaro Konoe (d. 1945), Japanese prime minister.	In Chile, the reform government of José Manuel Balmaceda was toppled by an armed forces–backed insurrection after rebel forces won decisive victories at Concón (Aug. 21) and La Placilla (Aug. 27), with total government losses of more than 5,000 and 1,500 prisoners taken of fewer than 10,000 engaged. Insurgent losses totaled fewer than 3,000.
b. Li Tsung-jen (d. 1969), Nationalist Chinese general.	
b. Tadamichi Kuribayashi (d. 1945), Japanese general.	b. Rafael Leonidas Trujillo Molina (d. 1961), Dominican Republic dictator (1930-1961).
b. Takijiro Onishi (d. 1945), Japanese admiral.	b. Carl Spaatz (d. 1974), American Air Force general.
	b. Pedro Albizu Campos (d. 1965), Puerto Rican lawyer and Nationalist Party leader.
	d. William Tecumseh Sherman (b. 1820), American general who during the Civil War drove to Atlanta (1864) and then made his March to the Sea; famed for his comment "War is hell," he became general and commanding general of the army (1869-1883).
	d. Joseph Eggleston Johnston (b. 1807), American Confederate (CSA) general in command at first Bull Run (1861), later commanding the Army of Tennessee (from Dec. 1863) and eventually surrendering at Durham Station, North Carolina (1865).
	d. David Dixon Porter (b. 1813), American admiral who during the Civil War led a Union river force on the Mississippi; he later became superintendent of the Naval Academy (1865-1869).

	1892	

Central, South and East Asia, and the Pacific	The Americas
b. Amanullah Khan (d. 1960), king of Afghanistan (r. 1919-1928).	b. James Van Fleet (d. 1991), American general.
b. Raizo Tanaka (d. 1969), Japanese admiral.	d. John Pope (b. 1822), American general during the Mexican-American War and the Civil War; his forces were defeated at second Bull Run (1862).
b. Ch'ing-ling Soong, Madame Sun Yat-sen (d. 1981), Chinese independence leader.	

Europe	Africa and Southwest Asia

1893

b. Mikhail Nikolayevich Tukhachevsky (d. 1937), Soviet general.

b. Hermann Goering (d. 1946), Nazi leader.

b. Draza Mihajlovic (d. 1946), Yugoslav general.

b. Joachim von Ribbentrop (d. 1946), German diplomat.

d. Marie Edmé Patrice Maurice de MacMahon (b. 1808), marshal of France during the Franco-Prussian War; after surrendering at Sedan (1870), he commanded government forces against the Paris Commune, retaking Paris (1871).

Mahdist forces numbering 11,000 attacked Eritrea but were decisively defeated at Agordat by an Italian force of 2,000 (Dec. 21); the Mahdists then withdrew.

Third British-Ashanti War (1893-1894): British forces openly took Ashanti, establishing a protectorate.

In the Spanish-occupied portion of Morocco, Riff forces unsuccessfully besieged Melilla.

Britain established a protectorate in Uganda.

French forces took Jenne and Timbuktu.

b. Haj Amin al Husseini (d. 1974), Palestinian Arab leader, the grand mufti of Jerusalem.

1894

Massacres of Armenians by Turks in western Turkey killed an estimated 100,000 (1894-1896).

Alfred Dreyfus, a French army officer of Jewish ancestry, was convicted of leaking military secrets to the Germans, a case that became a cause célèbre; it later emerged that anti-Semitic bias had led to suppression of information about someone else's guilt.

b. Nikita Sergeyevich Khrushchev (d. 1971), Soviet premier (1958-1964).

b. Rudolph Hess (d. 1986), Nazi leader.

b. Paul René Fonck (d. 1953), French military pilot.

b. Juan Negrin (d. 1956), Spanish prime minister.

Second Mandingo-French War (1894-1895): Ivory Coast forces led by Samori defeated the French, ending their protectorate.

Mohandas "Mahatma" Gandhi founded the Natal Indian Congress.

1895

Successful insurrection on Crete, with Greek and other European assistance, forced Turkey to withdraw; the island became a Greek protectorate.

b. Semëon Konstantinovich Timoshenko (d. 1970), Soviet field marshal.

b. George VI (d. 1952), king of Britain (r. 1936-1952).

b. Folke Bernadotte (d. 1948), Swedish diplomat.

b. Hans Langsdorff (d. 1939), German naval commander.

b. Aleksander Mikhailovich Vasilevskii (d. 1977), marshal of the Soviet Union.

b. Arthur Coningham (d. 1948), British air marshal.

b. Dolores Ibarruri ("La Pasionaria") (d. 1991), Spanish communist party leader.

Abyssinian-Italian War (1895-1896): Italian forces unsuccessfully invaded Abyssinia. At Ambu Alagi (Dec. 17), an Italian force of almost 2,500 lost more than half its strength in a defeat by a much larger Abyssinian force.

Fourth British-Ashanti War (1895-1896): Britain tightened its control over the Ashanti.

French forces attacked Madagascar.

Central, South and East Asia, and the Pacific	The Americas

French colonial forces forced the Siamese out of eastern Laos, which became a French protectorate.

b. Mao Zedong (d. 1976), leader of the Chinese Communist Party and the People's Republic of China.

b. Shin'ichi Tanaka, Japanese general during World War II, notably in the northern Burma campaign (1943-1944).

b. Kotoku Sato (d. 1959), Japanese general.

b. Pai Ch'ung-hsi (d. 1966), Nationalist Chinese general.

b. Omar Bradley (d. 1981), American general.

b. Augusto César Sandino (d. 1934), Nicaraguan guerrilla general.

b. Dean Gooderham Acheson (d. 1971), American lawyer and diplomat.

d. Edmund Kirby Smith (b. 1824), American Confederate (CSA) general who after Vicksburg fell (1863) became isolated and ran the Trans-Mississippi area ("Kirby Smithdom") with autonomy; his was the last Confederate force to surrender, at Galveston, Texas (May 26, 1865).

d. Pierre Gustav Toutant Beauregard (b. 1818), American Confederate (CSA) general who led the attack on Fort Sumter (1861).

Chinese-Japanese War (1894-1895): The contest over control of Korea began with a Japanese naval attack on a Chinese troop transport off the Korean west coast (July 21). Both sides declared war (Aug. 1). Japanese forces numbering 20,000 attacked and took Pyongyang (Sept. 15), then moved across the Yalu River into Manchuria (Oct. 24-25). Japanese forces advanced slowly against stiffening Manchu resistance in Manchuria. A Japanese war fleet decisively defeated a Chinese fleet off the mouth of the Yalu (Sept. 17), sinking five Chinese ships; the remainder fled. Japanese forces took Port Arthur (Nov. 19).

Sun Yat-sen founded the Revive China Society in Hawaii, beginning the anti-Manchu movement that would lead to the 1911 Chinese Revolution.

b. Tadashi Hanaya (d. 1957), Japanese general.

b. William Avery "Billy" Bishop (d. 1956), Canadian pilot and air force commander.

d. Gall (Pizi) (b. ca. 1840), Sioux war chief who was an ally of Crazy Horse's in the annihilation of General George Armstrong Custer's troops at the Little Bighorn (1876).

Chinese-Japanese War: Japanese forces took the Chinese naval base at Weihaiwei by storm (Jan. 30-31), and combined land and sea attacks destroyed most of the Chinese naval squadron off Weihaiwei (Feb. 2-12).

Chinese-Japanese War: Japanese forces in Manchuria gained ground, threatening Peking (Feb.-Mar.). Defeated China ceded Formosa (Taiwan), the Pescadores, and Liaotung Peninsula to Japan; agreed to pay indemnities; and recognized a Japanese protectorate over Korea, all under the Treaty of Shimonoseki (Apr. 17). Japanese forces occupying Formosa encountered and defeated a major Taiwanese insurrection (Apr.-Oct.).

French forces finally succeeded in suppressing a major Vietnamese insurrection.

Cuban War of Independence (1895-1898): A countrywide insurrection against Spain began after José Martí's return from exile; although he was killed in battle (May 19), the insurrection grew into a guerrilla war that pitted an estimated 30,000 Cubans against 100,000 Spanish.

b. Juan Domingo Perón (d. 1974), Argentine politician.

b. Lazaro Cardenas Del Rio (d. 1970), president of Mexico (1934-1940).

b. Matthew Bunker Ridgway (d. 1993), American general.

b. Walter Bedell Smith (d. 1961), American general.

1895 (cont.)

1896

Europe	Africa and Southwest Asia
b. Georgi Konstantinovich Zhukov (d. 1974), Soviet general. b. Imre Nagy (d. 1958), Hungarian communist prime minister. b. Konstantin Konstantivoch Rokossovski (d. 1968), marshal of the Soviet Union. b. Trygve Halvdan Lie (d. 1968), Norwegian diplomat and first secretary-general of the United Nations (1946-1952). b. Klement Gottwald (d. 1953), Czech communist president.	Abyssinian-Italian War: At Adowa (Mar. 1), the Italian main force of almost 18,000 was destroyed by an Abyssinian force reportedly numbering 90,000, suffering almost 7,000 dead, 1,400 wounded, and 1,700 captured. Italy withdrew from Abyssinia. Second Sudanese-Egyptian-British War (1896-1898): British and Egyptian forces of 15,000, led by Horatio Kitchener, moved methodically up the Nile, taking Firdar (June 7) and Dongola (Sept. 21). After the surrender of Tananarive, France annexed Madagascar, but low-level resistance continued in the countryside for a decade.

1897

Europe	Africa and Southwest Asia
Greek-Turkish War (Apr. 17-May 19): The brief war saw a series of victories by Edhem Pasha's Turkish forces over Prince Constantine's Greek forces. b. Anthony Eden (d. 1977), British diplomat. b. Joseph Goebbels (d. 1945), Nazi propagandist. b. Baron Hasso von Manteuffel (d. 1978), German general. b. Hans Speidel (d. 1987), German general. b. Ivan Stepanovich Konev (d. 1973), Soviet general.	Second Sudanese-Egyptian-British War: Horatio Kitchener's forces defeated Mahdist forces at Abu Hamed and Berber. British forces took northern Nigeria (1897-1899). Theodor Herzl organized and became the first president of the Congress of Zionist Organizations, founding the Zionist movement. b. John Bagot Glubb (Glubb Pasha) (d. 1986), British officer and head of Jordan's Arab Legion.

1898

Europe	Africa and Southwest Asia
b. George Grivas (d. 1974), Greek Cypriot guerrilla leader.	Second Sudanese-Egyptian-British War: Horatio Kitchener's forces defeated a Dervish army at the confluence of the Atbara and Nile rivers (Apr. 8). Outside Omdurman (Sept. 2), Kitchener's army, now 26,000 strong, met and decisively defeated the main Dervish army of 40,000 to 50,000, led by Khalifa Abdullah; Dervish losses

Central, South and East Asia, and the Pacific	The Americas	
	1895 (cont.)	

b. Hu Tsung-nan (d. 1962), Nationalist Chinese general.

b. Tai Li (d. 1946), Nationalist Chinese general.

b. Ali Khan Liaquat (d. 1951), prime minister of Pakistan.

| | **1896** | |

Philippine War of Independence (1896-1898): Emilio Aguinaldo led a successful insurrection against Spanish rule, in progress when the Spanish-American War began (1898).

b. Chang Fa-k'uei (1896-?), Nationalist Chinese general who was originally a warlord.

b. Ho Long (He Long) (d. 1967), Communist Chinese marshal.

Cuban War of Independence: Spanish forces, commanded by General Valeriano Weyler, set up concentration camps in Cuba in which tens of thousands died; the insurrection continued.

b. Albert Coady Wedemeyer (d. 1990), American general.

b. Mark Wayne Clark (d. 1984), American general.

b. James "Jimmy" Harold Doolittle (d. 1993), American Army Air Corps general.

b. Arthur William Radford (d. 1973), American admiral.

b. Clifton Albert Furlow Sprague (d. 1955), American admiral.

b. Evans Fordyce Carlson (d. 1947), American general.

b. Forrest Percival Sherman (d. 1951), American admiral.

b. Ira Clarence Eaker (d. 1987), American Army Air Corps general.

b. Anastasio Somoza Garcia (d. 1956), Nicaraguan dictator.

| | **1897** | |

Pathan-British War (1897-1898): Small-scale border war on the Afghan-British frontier grew into a substantial conflict as Pathan forces attacked many British installations (July), taking the Khyber Pass (Aug.). A British autumn campaign took an army of 44,000 into Pathan-held mountain territory, with inconclusive results.

b. Subhas Chandra Bose (d. 1945), Indian revolutionary.

b. Lucius DuBignon Clay (d. 1978), American general.

b. Nathan Farragut Twining (d. 1982), American Air Force general.

| | **1898** | |

Spanish-American War: In Manila Bay (May 1), American admiral George Dewey's cruiser squadron attacked and sank a much weaker Spanish cruiser squadron consisting of four cruisers, three gunboats, and three other vessels. American seaborne forces landed at Cavite (June 30), Manila surrendered (Aug. 14). As the Philippines came to the United States under the Treaty of Paris (Dec. 10), the Philippine War of Inde-

Spanish-American War: The American battleship *Maine* exploded and sank in Havana harbor (Feb. 15), with a loss of 260 lives, generating massive American media attacks on Spain and a declaration of war (Apr. 25). An American war fleet blockaded Santiago de Cuba (May), while an American seaborne army of 17,000 attacked Santiago (July 1), taking by assault El Caney, San Juan Ridge, and Kettle Hill, where assault units included Theodore Roosevelt's Rough Riders. Attempting to break through the blockade, the

Europe	Africa and Southwest Asia

1898 (cont.)

	were reportedly 20,000, with 5,000 prisoners taken; British and Egyptian losses totaled less than 500.
	Third Mandingo-French War: French forces ultimately defeated Samori's Ivory Coast forces, fully taking the Ivory Coast.
	b. Albert John Luthuli (d. 1967), Zulu chief and head of the African National Congress (1952-1967).

1899

Alfred Dreyfus, French officer wrongly accused of treason (1894), was pardoned by the president of France; he was later fully cleared (1906).

b. Lavrenti Pavlovich Beria (d. 1953), head of the Soviet secret police.

Boer War (1899-1902): Republic of South Africa and Orange Free State forces attacked British South Africa (Oct. 12), besieging Mafeking (Oct. 13) and Kimberley (Oct. 15); their main force met General George White's British troops in several minor engagements, then trapped them at Ladysmith (Nov.). British relief forces were defeated at the Modder River (Nov. 28), Stormberg (Dec. 10), Magersfontein (Dec. 10-11), and Colenso (Dec. 15).

Second Sudanese-Egyptian-British War: After more than a year of pursuit, Khalifa Abdullah was killed at Umm Diwaikarat in Kordofan, in southern Sudan (Nov.).

d. Abdullah et Taaisha (Abdullah ibn-Mohammed) (b. 1846), Sudanese Dervish general with the title *khalifa* (caliph); he was the Muslim commander at the siege of Khartoum (1884-1885) and successor to the Mahdi; he was killed by British forces (Nov. 24).

Somali leader Mohammed ben Abdullah began a long guerrilla war (1899-1920) against Italian and British colonial forces in Somalia.

French forces defeated Rabah Zobeir of Chad, completing their conquest of Chad (1899-1900).

1900

W. E. B. Du Bois, heading a group of American and West Indian Black leaders, convened the anticolonial First Pan-African Congress in London; it was to grow into the Organization of African Unity (OAU).

First rigid dirigible, from then on called the zeppelin, was built by Ferdinand von Zeppelin.

Simms "war car," an experimental armored, armed, powered, wheeled vehicle, was introduced.

Boer War: Now under the overall command of Field Marshal Frederick Sleigh Roberts, British forces took Paardeberg (Feb. 18); relieved Kimberley (Feb. 15), Ladysmith (Feb. 28), and Mafeking (May 17-18); took Bloemfontein (Mar. 13); and invaded the Transvaal to capture Johannesburg (May 31) and Pretoria (June 5).

Central, South and East Asia, and the Pacific	**The Americas**	

pendence quickly became the Philippine-American War.

Pathan-British War: British forces recaptured the Khyber Pass (Mar.).

b. Zhou Enlai (d. 1976), Chinese Communist military leader and diplomat.

b. P'eng Te-huai (d. 1974), Chinese Communist general.

Spanish squadron in Santiago harbor was sunk by a much stronger American force (July 3). Santiago surrendered (July 17). American forces numbering 5,000 also invaded and largely took Puerto Rico (July 25-Aug. 13). Under the Treaty of Paris (Dec. 10), Spain left Cuba and the United States took Puerto Rico, Guam, and (paying Spain $20 million) the Philippines.

d. William Starke Rosecrans (b. 1819), American general during the Civil War; a field commander under Ulysses S. Grant, he was defeated at Chickamauga (1863) and relieved of command.

1899

Philippine-American War (1899-1905): New Philippine republic named Emilio Aguinaldo its first president (Jan. 23), as the Philippine-American War developed and spread throughout the country; General Arthur MacArthur (father of Douglas) was field commander of punitive American forces.

Widespread antiforeign and anti-Manchu riots broke out throughout China.

b. Norman Bethune (d. 1939), Canadian doctor serving in China.

Guerrilla Liberal-Conservative civil war in Colombia (War of the Thousand Days) (1899-1902) took tens of thousands of lives, ending in a Conservative victory.

b. Hoyt Sanford Vandenburg (d. 1954), American Air Force general.

b. Lyman L. Lemnitzer (d. 1988), American general.

d. Horatio Gouverneur Wright (b. 1820), American general who during the Civil War was captured as he helped destroy the Norfolk Navy Yard (1861); later released, he commanded in the field.

1900

Boxer Rebellion and Chinese-Foreign War: Boxer forces entered Peking and besieged the foreign legations (June). The Manchu dowager empress Tz'u Hsi joined them, declaring war against the foreign powers (June 21). Western relief forces took Tientsin by assault (July 23), set out for Peking (Aug. 4), lifted the siege, and took Peking (Aug. 14), which they then burned and looted.

Russian troops occupied Manchuria (Oct.); China surrendered to the Western forces.

d. John Alexander McClernand (b. 1812), American general noted for his feuds during the Civil War with his superior Ulysses S. Grant.

Europe	Africa and Southwest Asia

1900 (cont.)

b. Heinrich Himmler (d. 1945), German secret police (Gestapo) head and a leading mass murderer of the Nazi era.

b. Louis Montbatten (d. 1979), British naval officer.

d. Karl Konstantin Albrecht Leonhard von Blumenthal (b. 1810), Prussian field marshal during the Franco-Prussian War.

The conflict then became a guerrilla war, with no more major actions.

France took and held northern Sahara and Chad, the latter becoming a protectorate.

b. Ayatollah Ruhollah Khomeini (Ruhollah Kendi) (d. 1989), religious and political leader of Iran.

b. Camille Chamoun (d. 1987), Lebanese politician.

d. Osman Nuri Pasha (b. 1832), Turkish general best known for his command of Turkish troops besieged in Plavna (Pleven) by the Russians (1877); he was four times war minister.

d. Petrus Jacobus Joubert (b. 1831), Boer general during the Boer wars.

d. Samori Toure (b. ca. 1835), Dioula war chief and ruler who built a state east of the upper Niger River (from 1868), coming into conflict with the French, who eventually (1889-1898) drove him from the region; he died in exile.

1901

Romania and Bulgaria neared war over their antagonistic claims on Turkish-held Macedonia.

In the third and final British-Ashanti war, Ashanti forces besieged British-held Kumasi (Apr.-July) but were defeated by British-led colonial forces later in the year (Sept.-Nov.). Britain then declared the defeated nation a protectorate.

b. Mustafa al-Barzani (d. 1979), Kurdish independence leader.

1902

Macedonian independence forces, with Bulgarian support, mounted a major insurrection against the Turks. Bulgarian, Romanian, and Turkish tensions grew, but war was averted by Great Power intervention.

Boer forces surrendered to the British, with the Treaty of Vereeniging ending the Boer War (May 31).

Central, South and East Asia, and the Pacific	The Americas	

1900 (cont.)

Philippine army and guerrilla forces fought a losing war against American occupation troops ultimately numbering 90,000 to 100,000 throughout the Philippines.

1901

Boxer Protocol formally ended the Boxer Rebellion and Chinese-Foreign War; its very harsh terms included huge indemnities. The American portion of those indemnities was set aside by President Theodore Roosevelt for Chinese student scholarships in the United States, with the result that many leaders of the later Chinese republic would be American educated.

Japanese Black Dragon Society was founded; the right-wing imperialist group strongly influenced Japanese expansionist policies in east Asia and the Pacific.

Philippine-American War: Emilio Aguinaldo was captured (Mar. 23), effectively ending the war, although guerrilla actions continued (until 1906), as did a Moro Islamic insurrection (until 1905).

b. Hirohito (d. 1989), Japanese emperor (r. 1926-1989).

b. Sukarno (d. 1970), first president of Indonesia (1949-1966).

b. Chen (Ch'en) Yi (d. 1972), Chinese Communist marshal.

Anarchist Leon Czolgosz assassinated American president William McKinley (shot Sept. 6, died Sept. 16) at the Buffalo Pan-American Exposition; Czolgosz was quickly executed (Oct. 29). Vice President Theodore Roosevelt succeeded to the presidency.

b. Maxwell Davenport Taylor (d. 1987), American general.

b. Arleigh Albert Burke, American admiral whose bold high-speed operations in the South Pacific during World War II won him the nickname "Thirty-one Knot Burke."

b. Fulgencio Batista y Zaldívar (d. 1973), Cuban dictator (r. 1952-1959).

b. Thomas Dresser White (d. 1965), American Air Force general.

b. Enrico Fermi (d. 1954), Italian-American nuclear physicist.

1902

Britain and Japan signed mutual assistance pacts in Far Eastern matters, strengthening Japan's position vis-à-

American occupation troops left Cuba (May), but it remained a de facto American protectorate.

1902 (cont.)

Europe	Africa and Southwest Asia
b. Jacques Philippe Leclerc (d. 1947), French general. b. André Beaufre (d. 1973), French general and military theorist.	Ibn Saud's forces began to take control of southern Arabia's Nejd district, beginning the long Arabian Civil War (1902-1925). Portuguese forces defeated a major insurrection in Angola.

1903

Europe	Africa and Southwest Asia
An estimated 50,000 Russian Jews were murdered in a series of massive pogroms that began at Kishinev, Bessarabia (Moldova). The attacks, encouraged by the Russian government, did not appreciably moderate popular unrest and the onset of the 1905 revolution; instead, they strengthened the growing revolutionary movement, while also greatly multiplying emigration to America and spurring the development of Zionism. Vladimir Illich Lenin founded the Bolshevik wing of the Russian Social-Democratic Workers' Party. Turks defeated the Bulgarian insurrection in Turkish-held Macedonia.	Attacking British forces in Nigeria completed their conquest of Kano and Sokoto (1902-1903). French-Moroccan clashes on the Algerian-Moroccan border began substantial French penetration into Morocco. b. Habib Bourguiba, Tunisian independence leader (1934-1956) and first premier and then president of Tunisia (1956-1987).

1904

Europe	Africa and Southwest Asia
Radar (radio detecting and ranging), which was to figure so prominently in World War II, was first patented by German engineer Christian Hülsmeyer. Anglo-French Entente Cordiale (Apr. 8) settled several outstanding colonial disputes; it was part of the settling into two major European alliances that preceded World War I.	Herero-Hottentot insurrection in German-held Southwest Africa (Namibia) ultimately failed (1904-1908). The Germans also defeated revolts in Cameroons and German East Africa.

1905

Europe	Africa and Southwest Asia
On Bloody Sunday (Jan. 9), Czarist troops at the Winter Palace in St. Petersburg fired on unarmed petitioners, killing and wounding hundreds and generating a massive series of armed forces mutinies and demonstrations, which grew into a full-scale insurrection. Czar Nicholas II in his October Manifesto	Morocco Crisis: A French-German dispute flared after a German landing in Tangier in support of Morocco against France; this was essentially a German challenge to

Central, South and East Asia, and the Pacific	The Americas	

1902 (cont.)

vis Russia; part of the run-up to the Russo-Japanese War (1905).

b. Mistsuo Fuchida (d. 1976), Japanese naval air officer.

Dominican Republic became a de facto American protectorate.

British, German, and Italian warships blockaded Venezuelan ports in an attempt to force payment of Venezuelan international debts.

d. William Thomas Sampson (b. 1840), American admiral who commanded the North Atlantic Squadron during the Spanish-American War (1898), blockading Santiago de Cuba.

d. Wade Hampton (b. 1818), American Confederate (CSA) general who led the Army of Northern Virginia's cavalry corps (1864) and was Robert E. Lee's chief of cavalry at Petersburg (1865).

1903

British expedition led by Francis Younghusband fought its way from India to Lhasa, Tibet, forcing Tibet to agree to British territorial demands regarding the Indian-Tibetan border.

b. Orde Charles Wingate (d. 1944), Indian-born British soldier.

d. Feng Tzu-ts'ai (b. 1818), Chinese general during conflicts with the French (1883-1885).

Powered flight began, with the successful flight of Wilbur and Orville Wright's airplane *Flyer I* (the *Kitty Hawk*) at Kill Devil Hills, near Kitty Hawk, North Carolina (Dec. 17); a pivotal event in the history of humanity and warfare.

Successful Panamanian revolt against Colombian rule was sponsored by the United States, which sought to build the Panama Canal; the Republic of Panama formally became an independent nation (Nov. 3), although in fact it was an American protectorate.

American Guantánamo naval base was established in Cuba by the Cuban-American Treaty, which formally made Cuba an American protectorate.

b. Frank Dow Merrill (d. 1955), American general.

1904

Russo-Japanese War (1904-1905): Japanese naval forces began the war with a successful surprise torpedo attack on the Russian Far Eastern Fleet at anchor in Port Arthur (Feb. 8). The next day, Japanese warships attacked Russian ships at Chemulpo (Inchon), Korea; a week later (Feb. 17), Japanese forces made amphibious landings at Chemulpo and moved north to the Yalu River, defeating a Russian army (May 1) and then moving through Manchuria toward Port Arthur. Japanese forces in Manchuria defeated the Russians on the Moteinlung River, followed by several major autumn-winter battles that were indecisive but resulted in Russian withdrawal to Mukden, where the decisive land battle of the war would be fought.

b. Deng Xiaoping, undisputed Chinese government and Communist Party leader from the late 1970s.

d. Sumiyoshi (Jungi) Kawamura (b. 1836), Japanese admiral who (from 1872) helped build and shape the Japanese navy along Western lines, serving as navy minister (1878-1880; 1881-1885).

In Uruguay, the liberal Colorado government forces of president José Batlle de Ordóñez decisively defeated conservative Blanco rebels led by Aparicio Sarava (Jan.-Sept.).

b. David Monroe Shoup (d. 1983), American Marine general.

b. Ralph Johnson Bunche (d. 1971), African-American diplomat and United Nations negotiator.

d. Chief Joseph (Hinmahton-Yahlaktit; Thunder-Rolling-Over-the-Mountains) (b. ca. 1840), Nez Percé chief who withdrew from federal troops in a long fighting retreat toward Canada, eventually pronouncing, "I will fight no more forever" (Oct. 5, 1877).

d. James Longstreet (b. 1821), American Confederate (CSA) general who fought in key engagements from the first Battle of Bull Run (Manassas) (1861) to Appomattox (1865).

1905

Russo-Japanese War: Port Arthur surrendered (Jan. 2) after a seven-month siege had cost an estimated 60,000 Japanese and 30,000 Russian casualties.

Industrial Workers of the World (IWW) was founded in America; during World War I, the labor organization would be a focus of antiwar action until suppressed (1917).

1905 (cont.)

promised major reforms and a constitutional monarchy; a weakened revolution was then defeated by government forces. A major event of the revolution was the sailors' mutiny on the battleship *Potemkin,* theme of the classic 1925 Sergei Eisenstein film, *Potemkin.*

Successful insurrection finally won Cretan independence from Turkish rule.

Sinn Fein became a political party; it was to become the chief political vehicle of the Irish Republican revolutionary movement.

b. Dag Hammarskjöld (d. 1961), Swedish statesman who was the second secretary-general of the United Nations (1953-1961).

b. Wladyslaw Gomulka (d. 1982), Polish communist premier.

French colonial interests that was part of the run-up to World War I.

Unrest in Persia grew into low-level, uncoordinated antigovernment guerrilla actions.

d. Frederick Augustus Thesiger, second Baron Chelmsford (b. 1827), British general who led the first British invasion of Zululand (1879), including the notable defeat at Isandhlwana.

1906

Following the defeat of the 1905 revolution, Russian premier Pyotr Stolypin, newly appointed by Czar Nicholas II, instituted a nationwide reign of terror; the run-up to the crisis of 1917 continued.

Treason case against Alfred Dreyfus was formally reopened; he was cleared and reinstated in the French army.

b. Leonid Ilyich Brezhnev (d. 1982), Soviet politician.

b. Ivan Chernyakovsky (d. 1945), Soviet general.

b. Sergei Korolev (d. 1966), Soviet spacecraft designer.

Final Zulu insurrection in South Africa failed, at a cost of more than 2,000 Zulu dead of a force numbering an estimated 12,000.

The international Algeciras Conference ended the Morocco Crisis of 1905 in favor of the French.

Mohandas "Mahatma" Gandhi initiated his first satyagraha (nonviolence) campaign (1906-1913), in South Africa.

1907

Russia and Britain settled most of their Central Asian sphere-of-influence disputes, creating the Anglo-Russian Entente; part of the alliance-building process preceding World War I.

Geneva Convention amendments expanded the treaties to include naval warfare.

A rising in Turkish-held Moldavia (Romania) included anti-Jewish pogroms; it was defeated by the Turks.

b. Pierre Mendes-France (d. 1982), French politician.

b. Dietrich Bonhoeffer (d. 1945), German Protestant anti-Nazi minister.

French naval forces bombarded Casablanca, in northwest Morocco. The French took the city and after that much of the coast, then moved inland, continuing their piecemeal conquest of Morocco.

Central, South and East Asia, and the Pacific	The Americas

Russo-Japanese War, Battle of Mukden (Feb. 21-Mar. 10): This was the decisive and final major land battle of the war, in which the Japanese ultimately forced back the Russians at an estimated cost of 100,000 Russian and 70,000 Japanese casualties.

Russo-Japanese War, Battle of Tsushima: Having spent more than seven months sailing around the world to fight in the war, the Russian Baltic Fleet under Admiral Zinovy Rozhdestvenski met Vice Admiral Heihachiro Togo's Japanese navy at Tsushima; of its eight battleships, eight cruisers, and nine destroyers, only one cruiser and five destroyers escaped; the Russians had 10,000 casualties. Japanese losses included three torpedo boats and fewer than 1,000 casualties.

Russo-Japanese War: The war ended with the Treaty of Portsmouth (New Hampshire), mediated by American president Theodore Roosevelt; Japan took Port Arthur and half of Sakhalin Island; the Russians also withdrew from Manchuria and recognized Japan's influence in Korea.

1906

All-India Muslim League was founded; in the 1930s, led by Mohammad Ali Jinnah, it would become the central organization of the Pakistani independence movement.

India's Congress Party sharply protested the partition of Bengal and moved from a request for greater participation in British Indian political life to the much stronger demand for home rule, beginning the long process that would ultimately lead to independence.

d. Gentaro Kodama (b. 1852), Japanese general who was first commandant of Japan's Army Staff College (1887) and rose to become chief of staff (1891-1906) and army minister (1900-1902).

El Salvador and Honduras were at war with Guatemala (May-July); the brief war ended inconclusively.

American troops again occupied Cuba (1906-1909).

b. Hans Albrecht Bethe, German-Jewish-American physicist who became a key figure in the development of the atomic bomb; after the Hiroshima and Nagasaki bombings, he became a leading anti–nuclear weapons activist.

b. Curtis Emerson LeMay (d. 1990), American Army and Air Force officer.

d. Joseph Wheeler (b. 1836), American general nicknamed "Fightin' Joe" who fought for the Confederacy (CSA) during the Civil War, notably at Shiloh (1862), later serving in the Spanish-American War.

d. William Rufus Shafter (b. 1835), American general who accepted the surrender of Santiago de Cuba (1898).

1907

b. U Nu, Burmese independence leader; he was the first prime minister of independent Burma (1948-1958) until deposed by a military coup, then prime minister again (1960-1962) until deposed by the Ne Win military coup.

b. Mohammed Ayub Khan (d. 1974), Pakistani general.

b. Lin Biao (d. 1971), Chinese politician.

Nicaragua-Honduras War (Feb.-Dec.) ended with Nicaraguan occupation of the Honduran capital.

Igor Sikorsky and others built experimental helicopters.

b. Joaquin Balaguer, Dominican Republic diplomat and politician.

b. Lauris Norstad (d. 1988), American Air Force general.

b. François "Papa Doc" Duvalier (d. 1971), Haitian dictator.

Europe	Africa and Southwest Asia

1908

Austro-Hungary formally annexed Bosnia-Herzegovina, which it had long occupied; the annexation, directly rejecting Serbian territorial ambitions, came close to generating an Austro-Serbian war.	In Persia, Tabriz fell to rebel forces; government forces then besieged the city (1908-1909).

1909

b. Andrei Andreyevich Gromyko (d. 1989), Soviet foreign minister.	Russian forces intervening in Persia took Tabriz from rebel defenders (Mar.). Rebel forces defeated and deposed Shah Mohammed Ali, capturing Tehran (July); he was succeeded by his 12-year-old son, Sultan Ahmad. British exploitation of Iranian oil began.
	Turkish army mutineers took Constantinople but could not hold the city (Apr.). Young Turks took effective power, with army support deposing Abdul Hamid II, whom they replaced with Muhammad V, a figurehead ruler.
	Moroccan forces and Spanish occupation forces fought at Melilla, on the Mediterranean coast (July 7), beginning a series of inconclusive engagements in and around the city that ended in 1910.
	b. Kwame Nkrumah (d. 1972), Ghanaian independence leader who was the first president of Ghana (1960-1966).

1910

Insurrection in Portugal ended the Portuguese monarchy and established the first Portuguese republic.	Natal, the British Cape Colony, and the former Boer republics of the Transvaal and the Orange Free State joined to form the Union of South Africa.
Rising against Turkish rule began in Albania (Apr.-June); it was repressed by the Turks, but low-level guerrilla warfare continued until the outbreak of the First Balkan War.	
d. Edward VII (b. 1841), king of Britain (r. 1901-1910); he was succeeded by his younger brother George V.	

1911

Italy declared war on Turkey (Sept. 29), bombarding Preveza.	Morocco Crisis: In a challenge to France, Germany sent the gunboat *Panther* to the Moroccan port of Agadir. Britain backed
Russian premier Pyotr Stolypin was assassinated in Kiev — a major destabilizing factor as world war approached.	

1908

d. Tz'u Hsi (b. 1835), the dowager empress of China; she abdicated, dying later in the year; she had formally been regent but was the actual ruler of China during the final decades of the 19th century, presiding over the decline of the Manchus (Ch'ing dynasty) and the Boxer Rebellion and Chinese-Foreign War that began the 20th century. She was succeeded by child emperor Hsüan T'ung (Henry P'u Yi).

Dutch forces completed their conquest of Sumatra, in Indonesia, defeating the Sultan of Atjeh (Achin) after a long, low-level struggle.

b. Wang Zhen (d. 1993), Chinese Red Army general.

d. Takeaki (Buyo) Enomoto (b. 1836), Japanese admiral.

b. Lyndon Baines Johnson (d. 1973), 36th president of the United States (1963-1968).

b. Joseph Raymond McCarthy (d. 1957), American senator.

b. Salvador Allende Gossens (d. 1973), Chilean politician and president (1970-1973).

1909

b. U Thant (d. 1974), Burmese diplomat and third United Nations secretary-general (1961-1971).

Honduran Civil War (1909-1911): Former president Manuel Bonilla led this insurrection, which continued indecisively.

d. Geronimo (Jerome; Goyathlay) (b. 1829), Chiricahua Apache leader who raided settlements in Arizona and New Mexico, especially during the Indian Wars (1885-1886).

d. Red Cloud (Mahpiua Luta) (b. 1822), Oglala Sioux war chief who was the allied leader in Red Cloud's War (1866-1868) against federal invasion of Native American lands.

d. Winfield Scott Schley (b. 1839), American admiral in tactical command at Santiago de Cuba (1898) during the Spanish-American War.

1910

Andrew Carnegie founded the Carnegie Endowment for International Peace.

Mexican Revolution (1910-1920): After losing a contested election, dictator Porfirio Díaz arrested his opponent, Francisco Madero, who then escaped to the United States, there organizing an armed insurrection. An estimated 1 million died in the series of civil wars that followed.

1911

Risings against the Ch'ing dynasty began at Wuchang, in central China (Oct. 10), and quickly toppled the

Mexican Revolution: Francisco Madero's rebel forces in Chihuahua defeated the forces of Porforio Díaz at Ciudad Juárez, the decisive battle of the Mexican Revolution (May). The revolutionary move-

Europe	Africa and Southwest Asia

1911 (cont.)

b. Aleksei Ivanovich Radzievskiy (d. 1978), Russian general.

b. Klaus Fuchs (d. 1988), German-British atomic physicist and Soviet spy.

France, and a general European war threatened until the Germans withdrew.

Moroccan forces besieged French-occupied Fez; the siege was lifted a month later by a French relief force.

Russian forces occupied much of northern Persia, while British forces occupied much of southern Persia (Nov.).

Italo-Turkish War: Italian forces shelled and took Tripoli in Turkish-held Libya (Oct.).

1912

Italo-Turkish War: Italian forces took Libya, Rhodes, and the Dodecanese Islands; Turkey ceded them to Italy in the Treaty of Ouchy formally ending the war, in which airplanes were first used as bombers.

First Balkan War (1912-1913): Serbian, Greek, and Bulgarian Balkan League armies totaling 300,000 to 400,000 attacked Turkish forces almost as large in Macedonia and Thrace (Oct. 17).

First Balkan War: In the decisive Battle of Monastir (Nov. 5), Serbian forces broke through the center of opposing Turkish forces; defeat became a rout, and the Turkish army in the area ceased to be an effective fighting force, with an estimated 20,000 Turks dead or captured by the Serbs.

First Balkan War: The 20,000-strong Turkish garrison of Salonika surrendered to Greek forces without appreciable resistance (Nov. 9).

Vladimir Illich Lenin led the Bolshevik wing out of the Russian Social-Democratic Workers' Party to form the Russian Social-Democratic Workers' Party — Bolsheviks; five years later, the new party would take control of the Russian Revolution.

b. Kim (Harold Adrian Russell) Philby (d. 1988), British spy for the Soviet Union.

b. Wernher von Braun (d. 1977), German rocket expert.

b. Jacques Emile Soustelle (d. 1990), French Secret Army leader in Algeria.

d. George Stuart White (b. 1835), British field marshal best known as leader of the troops defending Ladysmith (1899-1900) during the Boer War.

Moroccan soldiers in the French Fez garrison mutinied (Apr. 17), could not take the city, and were defeated by a French relief column. Moroccan forces unsuccessfully assaulted the augmented French garrison (late May). France declared Morocco a French protectorate, while the war continued.

African National Congress (ANC) was founded in South Africa; it would become the chief vehicle of the South African freedom movement, originally nonviolent but moving to armed insurrection after the Sharpeville Massacre (1960).

First Balkan War: Bulgarian forces besieged Constantinople (Nov.-Dec.) but could not take the city; they withdrew after suffering substantial casualties.

1913

First Balkan War: The 60,000-strong Turkish garrison at Adrianople surrendered (Mar. 26). Balkan League forces took Scutari, Yannina, and much of the rest of European Turkey and were besieging Constantinople when the war ended. Under the Treaty of London, which formally ended the war (May 30), Turkey ceded most of its remaining European provinces to the Balkan League, and the new nation of Albania was created. Turkey kept the Gallipoli Peninsula.

Dissatisfied with the terms of the Treaty of London, Bulgaria attacked Serbia and Greece (June), beginning the Second Balkan War. Serbian and Greek forces counterattacked in early July and were joined by intervening Romanian

Young Turks openly took power by coup; the new government moved toward alliance with Germany, and German general Liman von Sanders was engaged to reorganize the Turkish army.

Boer War general James Hertzog founded South Africa's National Party.

b. Menachem Begin (d. 1992), Israeli prime minister (1977-1983).

1911 (cont.)

Manchus. Sun Yat-sen returned home to become provisional president of the new Republic of China.

Japan annexed Korea.

b. Ne Win (Maung Shu Maung), Burmese general who took power by coup (1958), relinquished power (1960), and took power again by coup (1962-1988), thereafter remaining a powerful supporter of the successful Burmese army coup (Sept. 1988).

ment soon split, with Emiliano Zapata and others contesting the rule of the Madero government.

Honduran Civil War: After a stalemate in the conflict, former president Manuel Bonilla, who had led the insurrection, was re-elected president (Oct.).

American aviator Glenn Hammond Curtiss invented the seaplane.

b. Ronald Wilson Reagan, 40th president of the United States (1981-1989).

d. Benjamin Henry Grierson (b. 1826), American general who served in the Civil War, later building the 10th (Negro) Cavalry (1866-1888) into a much-honored frontier mounted unit, which by building roads and telegraph lines helped open the American Southwest to new settlement.

1912

Child emperor Hsüan T'ung (Henry P'u Yi) abdicated (Feb. 12), formally ending the Ch'ing (Manchu) dynasty. Sun Yat-sen gave way to General Yüan Shih-k'ai, who had served the Manchus and became the first president of the Republic of China.

Outer Mongolia declared itself an independent nation (Nov. 3).

b. Vo Nguyen Giap, North Vietnamese commander at Dien Bien Phu and army commander in chief during the Vietnam War.

b. Kim Il Sung (Kim Jong Ju) (d. 1994), Communist dictator of the Democratic People's Republic of North Korea (1948-94).

d. Maresuke Nogi (b. 1843), German-trained Japanese general (1885-1886) who, as commander of Japan's Third Army, directed the successful siege of Russia's fortress at Port Arthur (1904-1905); he and his wife committed suicide when the Meiji emperor died (July 30).

American marines landed in Honduras (Jan.), establishing a de facto protectorate over the country.

American marines landed in Nicaragua (July), ostensibly to end civil war; they established a de facto protectorate over the country.

d. Arthur MacArthur (b. 1845), American general who led the main American field force against Emilio Aguinaldo's Philippine revolutionaries, becoming commanding general and military governor of the islands (1899); he was the father of Douglas MacArthur.

d. Wilbur Wright (b. 1867), American pioneer of powered flight.

d. Robert Frederick Hoke (b. 1837), American Confederate (CSA) general.

1913

In China Sun Yat-sen led a failed insurrection against the government of General Yüan Shih-k'ai, then fled to Japan.

b. Bao Dai (Nguyen Vinh Thuy), head of puppet Vietnamese governments for the French (1925-1940; 1949-1954) and the Japanese (1940-1945).

b. Le Duc Tho (Phan Dinh Khai) (d. 1990), North Vietnamese leader.

Mexican Revolution: Mexican president Francisco Indalecio Madero (b. 1873), leader of the Mexican Revolution, was assassinated by the forces of Victoriano Huerta, commander of the Mexico City garrison, who took power by coup (Feb.), then ruling as dictator.

b. Richard Milhous Nixon (d. 1994), 37th president of the United States (1969-1974), forced to resign after the Watergate scandal.

b. Gerald Rudolph Ford (Leslie King, Jr.), 38th president of the United States (1974-1977).

1913 (cont.)

and Turkish forces. A Bulgarian defeat and cease-fire came quickly (July 13), as did the Treaty of Bucharest (Aug. 10), which took from Bulgaria the territories gained in the First Balkan War.

Irish Volunteers was founded; led by Patrick Pearse, the armed Republican militia would be the main force in the Easter Rising of 1916 and the core of the Irish Republican Army during the Irish War of Independence (1919-1921).

Irish Citizen Army was founded by James Connolly and James Larkin; the small group was a secondary force in the Easter Rising of 1916.

Ulster Volunteers was founded; the Protestant Northern Ireland militia prepared for civil war in Ireland.

b. Klaus Barbie (d. 1992), Nazi war criminal.

b. Willy Brandt (Carl Herbert Frahm) (d. 1991), German chancellor.

d. Alfred von Schlieffen (b. 1833), Prussian general who became chief of the German general staff (1891); his plan for sweeping through Belgium to the sea was successfully followed by the Germans in World War II, after they departed from it during World War I.

d. Garnet Joseph Wolseley (b. 1833), British field marshal in colonial service who wrote the popular *Soldier's Pocket-Book* (1869); he arrived two days late to relieve Khartoum (1885); as commander in chief (from 1895), he directed British mobilization for the Boer War.

1914

World War I (1914-1918): This massive conflict was triggered by the assassination of Austro-Hungarian archduke Francis (Franz) Ferdinand (b. 1863), heir to the Austrian throne, at Sarajevo (June 28), by Bosnian nationalists armed by the Serbian nationalist Black Hand society.

The war began with Austrian attacks on Serbia, German attacks on France and the Low Countries, and Russian attacks on East Prussia. In the west, the Germans, pursuing the Schlieffen Plan, held the French in Alsace-Lorraine and the Ardennes, while the main German forces overran Belgium, broke through in France, and headed for the Channel ports and quick victory. The mistaken German turn toward Paris and the subsequent historic French victory on the Marne River saved France.

The war ultimately drew in France, the British Empire, Russia, the United States, Serbia, Italy, Belgium, Greece, Romania, Montenegro, Japan, and Portugal on the Allied side, with Germany, Austro-Hungary, Turkey, and Bulgaria on the Central Powers side. Estimated human costs were 8 million war dead of 65 million mobilized, 21 million wounded, and an estimated 6 million to 7 million civilian dead, including those killed in the Armenian Holocaust, but without adding those killed by famine and the massive influenza pandemic that followed the war.

World War I: German main western front forces quickly overran much of Belgium (Aug. 3-20), their first major victory coming with the surrender of the fortress of Liège (Aug. 16); they took Brussels (Aug. 20) and besieged the fortress of Antwerp, which surrendered (Oct. 9).

World War I, Battles of the Frontiers (Aug. 14-23): The first major French offensives of the war were turned back with massive losses at the battles of Alsace-Lorraine and the Ardennes, while the German main force pursued retreating Allied forces toward the Channel ports. French forces failed to stem the German advance at the Battle of the Sambre River (Aug. 22-23), as did

World War I: Turkey declared war on the Allies (Oct. 29), with Turkish and German warships shelling the Russian Black Sea coast, including Odessa and Sevastopol. Turkish forces invaded the Caucasus Mountains; the major Russo-Turkish battle at Sarikamish began (Dec. 29). British ships shelled Turkish shore positions in the Dardanelles, while British forces moved into Egypt in strength. British Indian army forces invaded Turkish-held Mesopotamia, taking Bahrain and Basra. British forces took several German African colonies, including German Southwest Africa (Namibia), Cameroons, and Togoland, but German defenses held in German East Africa.

In South Africa Boer War general Christiaan De Wet led a pro-German Boer insurrection that was quickly defeated by South African government forces led by Boer War general Louis Botha and Boer commando leader Jan Smuts (Sept. 1914-Feb. 1915).

b. Mohammad Zahir Shah, king of Afghanistan (r. 1933-1973).

b. Shapur Bakhtiar (d. 1990), premier of Iran.

Central, South and East Asia, and the Pacific	The Americas

1913 (cont.)

b. Jacobo Arbenz Guzmán (d. 1971), Guatemalan officer and president (1950-1954).

b. William Joseph Casey (d. 1987), American Central Intelligence Agency (CIA) director.

1914

World War I: Japan entered World War I on the Allied side (Aug. 23), besieging and taking the German-held China coast base of Tsingtao (Nov. 7). Japanese forces took several key German-held island groups, including the Marshalls, Marianas, and Caroline Islands; all would see major engagements during World War II.

British forces took Samoa and several other German-held Pacific island bases.

Sun Yat-sen founded the Chinese political party Kuomintang (National People's Party).

Mohandas "Mahatma" Gandhi returned to India from South Africa, becoming a practicing lawyer.

b. Jiang Qing (Chiang Ch'ing; Luan Shu-meng) (d. 1992), Chinese politician and actress.

American naval forces bombarded and briefly occupied Vera Cruz, Mexico, thereby preventing German guns shipped through the port from reaching Mexican dictator Victoriano Huerta.

Mexican Revolution: Huerta fled into exile (July), and the forces of Venustiano Carranza took Mexico City (Aug. 15). Civil war continued, with the forces of Emiliano Zapata and Francisco (Pancho) Villa arrayed against the Carranza government.

World War I: Germany's China Squadron, commanded by Admiral Maximilian von Spee and consisting of two heavy and three light cruisers, steamed across the Pacific, sank two British heavy cruisers off Chile's west coast at Coronel (Nov. 1), and then rounded Cape Horn into the South Atlantic, there meeting a British battle cruiser squadron off the Falkland Islands (Dec. 8). The German heavy cruisers *Scharnhorst* and *Gneisenau* and two light cruisers were sunk, with most of their crews; only the light cruiser *Dresden* escaped.

b. Creighton Williams Abrams, Jr. (d. 1974), American general.

b. William Childs Westmoreland, commander of American forces in Vietnam (1964-1968).

d. Alfred Thayer Mahan (b. 1840), American admiral and strategist noted for his influential works on naval history and strategy, originally lectures at the Naval War College, of which he was president.

1914 (cont.)

British and Belgian forces at the Battle of Mons (Aug. 23). At Le Cateau (Aug. 26-27), British forces retreating through Belgium held the advancing Germans briefly; at Guise, French forces counterattacked, stemming the German advance south for 36 hours, but were then forced to retreat (Aug. 29).

World War I, First Battle of the Marne (Sept. 4-9): German armies sweeping south and west to envelop and destroy Allied armies in France changed course and turned to take Paris; the historic error made it possible for the French, using their Paris reserves (called the "taxicab army" for the vehicles that carried them to battle) to envelop the German right flank and stop the main force. The Race to the Sea by both sides ensued, followed by four years of trench warfare that cost millions of lives. In this one battle, an estimated 240,000 to 260,000 Allied and 260,000 to 270,000 German soldiers died.

World War I: During the Race to the Sea (Sept. 15-Nov. 24), each side unsuccessfully attempted to outflank and envelop the other; the French failed at the Battle of the Aisne (Sept. 15-18) and then in Picardy and Artois; the Germans failed at Verdun, although they took and held the St.-Mihiel salient. Ultimately, both drives ended in Flanders, at the inconclusive battles of the Yser (Oct. 18-Nov. 30) and of Ypres (Oct. 30-Nov. 24), where the British stopped the German drive to the Channel ports. Further Allied offensives (Dec.) were stopped by the growing German fortification system, paralleled by that of the Allies.

World War I: On the eastern front, the Germans' Schlieffen Plan for a two-front war called for defense against much larger Russian forces, while the main German forces in the west took France and were then able to turn east against Russia. Russian strategy involved a strike directly at East Prussia and, to the south, against the Austrian-held portion of Poland. Russian forces went on the offensive in East Prussia (Aug. 17), moving toward a major confrontation at Tannenberg.

World War I, Battle of Tannenberg (Aug. 26-31): German forces in East Prussia, led by generals Paul von Hindenburg and Erich Ludendorff, decisively defeated General Alexander Samsonov's surrounded Russian Second Army, which lost an estimated 125,000 men; German losses were 10,000 to 15,000.

World War I, First Battle of the Masurian Lakes (Sept. 9-14): Following Tannenberg, the Russians suffered a second massive defeat in East Prussia, that of General Pavel Rennenkampf's Russian First Army by the armies of General von Hindenburg. The Russians lost 125,000 to 150,000, narrowly escaping the same kind of complete encirclement they had experienced at Tannenberg. German losses were in the 40,000 range.

World War I, Battle of Rava Ruska (Sept. 3-11): In Galicia, Austrian forces mounted an offensive (Aug. 23-Sept. 3), moving forward into Russian Poland; they were decisively defeated at Rava Ruska, then retreated to the Carpathian Mountains, leaving most of Galicia in Russian hands. Austrian and Russian losses in the brief campaign totaled an estimated 500,000.

World War I, Battle of Lodz (Nov. 11-25): Russian armies once again advanced toward Silesia and East Prussia but were stopped by German forces; the Russians turned back into Poland after suffering casualties of 90,000 to 100,000. Russian forces did not again seriously threaten Germany, although the massive two-front war continued to sap German military and economic strength.

World War I: On the Austro-Serbian front, Serbian forces defeated invading Austrian forces numbering 200,000 at the Battle of Jadar (Aug. 12-21), the first major engagement of the war between the Serbs and the Austrians.

World War I: Austrians launched a new offensive (Nov. 5-30), occupying Belgrade after Serbs evacuated it (Dec. 2).

World War I, Battle of Kolubra (Dec. 3-9): Serbian forces mounted a successful counteroffensive against pursuing Austrian forces, retaking Belgrade.

b. Abdul Karim Kassem (d. 1963), premier of Iraq.

1914 (cont.)

World War I: The sea war off the western European coast included a British-German cruiser squadron action at Heligoland Blight (Aug. 28) that cost the Germans four cruisers; a German submarine raid on the British Grand Fleet at Scapa Flow (Oct. 18); the loss of several British cruisers to submarines and of the battleship *Audacious* to a German mine (Oct. 27); and German cruiser bombardment of the British North Sea coast. The French lost the battleship *Jean Bart* to an Austrian submarine in the Mediterranean.

French socialist leader Jean Juares was assassinated by a French nationalist (July 31), considerably weakening socialist opposition to French involvement in the war.

b. Yuri Vladimirovich Andropov (d. 1984), leader of the Soviet Union (1982-1984).

d. Alexsander Vasilievich Samsonov (1859-ca. 1914), Russian general whose forces were overwhelmed at Tannenberg; he is believed to have died, possibly a suicide, during the retreat.

d. Frederick Sleigh Roberts (b. 1832), British field marshal who served in India, retaking Kabul (1879) and defeating Ayub Khan at Kandahar (1880), and in the Boer War; he later became commander in chief of India (1885) and then overall (1901-1904).

1915

World War I: On the western front, both sides were mired in costly, unproductive trench warfare, suffering massive losses while making no significant gains anywhere on the long line of fortifications from the mountains to the sea. The failed French offensive in Artois and Champagne continued, with French and German losses in the First Battle of Champagne (Dec. 20, 1914-Mar. 30, 1915) totaling more than 300,000.

World War I, Second Battle of Ypres (Apr. 22-May 25): Germans made a surprise attack, releasing poisonous chlorine gas, the first such use on the western front; despite initial successes, they were thrown back, failing in their attempt to break through the Allied lines, at a cost of more than 100,000 casualties, including 60,000 British, 10,000 of them dead.

World War I: Failed attacks by both sides continued throughout the balance of the year, most notably the British and French actions at Artois and Vimy Ridge (May) and the entirely wasted Allied autumn offensive (Sept. 25-Nov. 6). At the Second Battle of Champagne, the Third Battle of Artois, and Loos, Allied and German forces suffered a total of more than 750,000 casualties.

World War I: On the eastern front, the year began with massive German and Austrian offensives (Jan.-Mar.), commanded by General Paul von Hindenberg. The German main force advanced out of East Prussia in the Masurian Lakes region, while German and Austrian forces to the south advanced through the Carpathian Mountains toward the relief of Przemysl and Lemberg (Lvov) beyond.

World War I: At Bolimov, in central Poland, the Germans used large quantities of poison gas for the first time in warfare (Jan. 31); although weather conditions made the gas ineffective, the German action ushered in the use of chemical and biological warfare, with its threat to all life on earth. A more highly publicized German poison gas attack occurred at the Second Battle of Ypres (Apr. 22-May 25).

World War I, Second Battle of the Masurian Lakes (Feb. 7-21): Russian forces suffered a major defeat, with an estimated 100,000 to 110,000 casualties and the surrender of 90,000 soldiers, most of them from the encircled XX Corps.

World War I, Gallipoli Campaign (Feb. 1915-Jan. 1916): Failed Allied attack on Turkish forces in the Dardanelles and Gallipoli Peninsula cost 6 battleships and an estimated 250,000 Allied casualties, as Allied forces never broke out of their small beachheads; Turkish casualties were estimated to be approximately the same.

World War I: In the Caucasus Mountains, the Turks were decisively defeated by Russian forces at Sarikamish (Jan. 1-3), suffering an estimated 30,000 dead and 30,000 more casualties and desertions of an invading force of 80,000.

World War I: Turkish massacres of Armenians in Anatolia generated an Armenian insurrection. Armenian forces took Van (Apr.), joining advancing Russian forces there in late May. The Turks retook Van (Aug.); many Armenians fled north with the Russian army.

World War I: In Egypt, British forces stopped a Turkish attack across the Sinai toward Suez (Jan.-Feb.).

World War I: In Mesopotamia, British forces pushed up the Tigris River (spring) and then advanced on Kut (Aug.), where the Turks suffered more than 4,000 casualties before withdrawing to Ctesiphon (Sept. 27-28). The British then moved on Ctesiphon (Nov. 22-26), where they were defeated by the Turks, with more than 4,500 casualties,

1914 (cont.)

1915

Insurrection aborted President Yüan Shih-k'ai's move to take absolute power as emperor of a new Chinese dynasty; he disclaimed such intentions, largely defusing the insurrection (Dec. 1915-Mar. 1916).

b. Aung San (d. 1947), Burmese independence leader and prime minister.

Mexican Revolution: At Celaya (Apr.), the forces of President Venustiano Carranza, led by General Alvaro Obregón, won a decisive victory over the forces of Francisco (Pancho) Villa, who then retreated to northern Mexico and was no longer a major threat. Emiliano Zapata retreated south undefeated, maintaining his positions until his assassination (1919).

d. Porfirio Díaz (b. 1830), Mexican revolutionary general who seized power by coup (1876) and ruled as dictator until a new revolution forced him to resign (1911).

American marines invaded Haiti (July 3), openly taking full control of the island as an American protectorate.

b. Augusto Pinochet Ugarte, Chilean general and dictator (1973-1989).

1915 (cont.)

World War I: In the southern sector of the eastern front, Austrian forces failed to break through in Galicia; a Russian counteroffensive was equally unsuccessful. Besieged Przemysl was not relieved, surrendering with its garrison of 110,000 (Mar. 27).

World War I: The German-Austrian spring offensive in Poland had far greater success, assaulting the Russian Third Army (May 2) to begin the Gorlice-Tarnów Breakthrough and then rolling up and breaking through the whole Russian line in Galicia; pursuing forces retook Przemysl (June 3) and then took Lemberg (Lvov) (June 22), as the Russian front collapsed all the way to the Baltic. German and Austrian forces advanced 300 miles on the entire front, taking Warsaw (Aug. 7) and Vilna (Sept. 19); the long front did not stabilize until late autumn.

World War I: German, Austrian, and Bulgarian forces attacked Serbia (Oct. 6), quickly defeating the Serbian army, which retreated in disorder toward the Adriatic through Montenegro, where the survivors were evacuated to Corfu. Serbian casualties exceeded 100,000, with 160,000 prisoners taken.

World War I: Italy entered the war on the Allied side (May 23), beginning more than two years of costly Italian-Austrian stalemate on the Isonzo River; there would be 11 battles and 1 million casualties there before the first Austrian-German breakthrough at Caporetto (1917). Four battles were fought on the Isonzo line in 1915, all failed Italian assaults (June 23-July 7; July 18-Aug. 3; Oct. 18-Nov. 4; Nov. 10-Dec. 2).

World War I: Off Dogger Bank, a British battle cruiser squadron met and defeated a German battle cruiser squadron (Jan. 24), sinking the heavy cruiser *Blücher.*

World War I: At sea the Battle of the Atlantic began in earnest (Feb.), with massive German submarine attacks on Allied, and in some instances neutral, shipping. One very notable sinking was that of the British liner *Lusitania,* torpedoed without warning by a German submarine off the Irish coast (May 7); 1,198 people died, including 128 Americans, helping turn American sentiment in favor of the Allies. The British introduced the depth charge as an antisubmarine weapon.

World War I: German dirigible bombing attacks on Britain began (Jan. 19).

French inventor Paul Langevin developed sonar (sound navigation ranging).

Fokker warplane was the first to have its machine guns synchronized with its propeller.

British nurse Edith Cavell (b. 1865) was executed by the Germans as a spy (Oct. 7); she then became a British wartime martyr.

retreating back to Kut. Pursuing Turkish forces besieged Kut (early Dec.).

b. Moshe Dayan (d. 1981), Israeli general and politician.

b. Yitzhak Shamir (Yitzhak Yzernitzsky) (ca. 1915), Israeli politician, Stern Gang leader in the 1940s, twice foreign minister, and twice prime minister (1983-1984; 1986-1989).

1916

World War I: The year saw two massive, failed, extraordinarily costly attempts to break through opposing lines of fortifications on the western front. The Germans began a failed 10-month attack on the French fortress of Verdun (Feb.), which ultimately cost an estimated 1 million casualties. The British and French began a failed nearly 5-month attack on the Somme River in June, which cost an estimated more than 1.25 million casualties. Both sides attempted to turn their massive defeats into victories, claiming advances in a war of attrition, but the truth was far darker.

World War I, Battle of Verdun (Feb. 21-Dec. 18): The failed German assault and siege of the French fortress on the Meuse River cost an estimated 550,000 French and 450,000 German casualties. The Germans once again used chemical and biological warfare, introducing phosgene gas at Verdun (June), to some initial effect, but they failed to break the French line.

World War I: In the Armenian Holocaust, the Turkish government committed the mass murder of an estimated 1 million to 1.5 million Armenians, most of them dying due to disease and famine while in concentration camps in the Syrian Desert. Approximately 1 million more Armenians fled north with retreating Russian forces into what would later become Soviet Armenia.

World War I, Arab War of Independence (1916-1918): Beginning in the Arabian Hejaz, Hussein Ibn Ali, sharif of Mecca,

1916

World War I: China entered on the Allied side but without waging war on the Central Powers.

d. Yüan Shih-k'ai (b. ca. 1859), Chinese general and first president of the Republic of China (1912-1916); after his death, Sun Yat-sen returned to China.

d. Hikonojo Kamimura (b. 1849), Japanese admiral during the Russo-Japanese War, notably at Tsushima (1905).

d. Iwao Oyama (b. 1842), Japanese field marshal trained in France who led the Second Army in the successful siege of Port Arthur (Oct. 24-Nov. 19, 1895), also serving notably at Mukden (1905).

Mexican-American border war (1916-1917): After Pancho Villa's forces made a cross-border raid on Columbus, New Mexico (Mar. 15), American forces approximately 10,000 strong led by John J. Pershing invaded northern Mexico in a failed attempt to find Villa.

Woodrow Wilson won a second American term as president with the slogan "He kept us out of war."

American forces invaded and occupied the Dominican Republic, holding the country until 1924.

Ten were killed and many injured in the San Francisco Preparedness Day parade bombing (July 22). Antiwar labor leaders Thomas J. Mooney and Warren K. Billings were convicted of the crime;

World War I, Battle of the Somme (July 1-Nov. 13): The massive British-French assault on German positions in the Somme Valley cost an estimated 650,000 British, 195,000 French, and 420,000 German casualties; gained only eight miles in four and a half months; and totally failed. In their first assault (July 1), the British suffered more than 57,000 casualties, more than 19,000 of them dead. They later introduced tanks here (Sept. 13).

World War I, Battle of Lake Naroch (Mar. 18): Attacking Russian forces at Lake Naroch, in northern Poland, made no gains against strongly defended German positions, suffering an estimated 100,000 casualties to German losses of 20,000.

World War I: The Russian summer offensive in southern Poland — the Brusilov Offensive (June 4-Sept. 20), named after Russian general Alexei Brusilov — scored major successes against defending Austrian armies and took an estimated 400,000 prisoners. But German positions to the north held, and German counterattacks (June-July), bolstered by 18 divisions transferred from the western front, stopped the offensive; each side suffered an estimated 1 million casualties.

World War I: In Italy, the stalemate continued on the Isonzo River, with five more costly Italian attacks, all failing to break through Austrian defenses and with total Italian losses of more than 125,000 and Austrian losses of more than 65,000.

World War I: Austrian forces went on the offensive for the first time in Italy, in Trentino (May); at the Battle of Asiago (May 15-June 17), they made early gains but ultimately retreated to their former battle lines, at a cost of an estimated 105,000 Italian and 55,000 Austrian casualties.

World War I: In the Balkans, Bulgarian and German forces moved south in the Vardar Valley against Allied forces centered at Salonika (Aug. 17-27); they were then driven north by an Allied counteroffensive that took Monastir (Nov. 19), before coming to a halt.

World War I: Romania entered the war on the Allied side, declaring war on Germany and Austria (Aug. 27). Romanian forces attacked Austrian-held Transylvania, were thrown back by German defenders, and retreated before a German counteroffensive, ultimately suffering decisive defeat at the Battle of the Arges River (Dec. 1-4), followed by the fall of Bucharest (Dec. 6). Surviving Romanian forces fled north into Russia.

World War I, Battle of Jutland (May 31-June 1): In the only major naval battle of the war, the British Grand Fleet, led by 28 modern dreadnoughts under Admiral John Jellicoe, and the German High Seas Fleet, led by 16 dreadnoughts under Vice Admiral Reinhard Scheer, fought to a draw off Jutland; no dreadnoughts were lost, although the British lost 6 cruisers and 8 destroyers, while the Germans lost 1 battleship, 5 cruisers, and 5 destroyers. Reported casualties totaled 6,784 British and 3,039 Germans. The German fleet ultimately broke off and headed for home under cover of darkness, staying there for the balance of the war.

World War I: The Battle of the Atlantic continued and greatly expanded, with German submarines sinking more than 2.2 million tons of Allied shipping.

World War I: Sporadic zeppelin bombing raids on Britain continued, with little damage and no strategic effect.

Liberal Party leader David Lloyd George became British wartime coalition prime minister.

Easter Rising (Apr. 24-29): In five days, 5,000 British regulars, with artillery, defeated 1,500 to 2,000 inadequately armed Irish Volunteers and Irish Citizen Army rebels in Dublin, where the insurrection was confined. Fifteen leaders of the Easter Rising were later executed by the British, becoming the leading mar-

led a revolt against Turkish rule, aided by his son Faisal and British officer Thomas Edward Lawrence ("Lawrence of Arabia"). Arab forces attacked Medina, took Mecca, and joined the Allies (June 5).

World War I: After a relief column failed to reach Kut, the besieged city surrendered to the Turks (Apr. 29), with more than 8,000 Indian and British prisoners taken.

World War I: British and Indian forces in Mesopotamia went on the offensive, pushing north on the Tigris River (mid-Dec.).

World War I: Attacking Turkish forces in the Sinai (Aug. 3) were defeated at Rumani (Aug. 3), falling back toward Palestine.

World War I: Russian forces scored substantial victories in the Caucasus Mountains, taking Erzurum by assault (Feb. 13-16) and Trebizond (mid-Apr.). The Turkish summer offensive failed, with a major defeat at Erzinjan (late July), at a cost of more than 30,000 casualties.

Ethiopian Civil War (1916-1917): The conflict pitted Muslims against the Christian (Coptic) majority; Ras Tafari (later Haile Selassi I) emerged as Ethiopian regent.

b. P. W. (Pieter Willem) Botha, South African leader (1978-1989).

after a worldwide clemency campaign, Mooney's death sentence was commuted to life imprisonment; both were released in 1939.

d. Victoriano Huerta (b. 1854), Mexican general and dictator (r. 1913-1914).

1916 (cont.)

tyrs of the Irish War of Independence that loomed just ahead. Captured Republican leader Roger Casement, who had unsuccessfully tried to secure German support for the Rising, was executed for treason (Aug. 3).

b. Edward Heath, British prime minister.

d. James Connolly (b. 1870), leader of the Irish Citizen Army and an organizer of the failed Easter Rising (Apr. 24-29); he was executed in Dublin after the insurrection (May 12).

d. Horatio Herbert Kitchener (b. 1850), British field marshal of wide service who commanded British troops against Mahdist forces, including the Battle of Omdurman (1898), and during the Boer War; he died when the cruiser *Hampshire* was sunk by a mine off the Orkney Islands (June 5).

d. Helmuth Johannes Ludwig von Moltke (b. 1848), German general and World War I chief of staff until the German defeat at the First Battle of the Marne.

d. Max Immelmann (b. 1890), German pilot who was a leading innovator of air combat tactics, such as the rolling turn; he died when his airplane inexplicably broke up in flight.

1917

World War I: As the western front stalemate continued, German forces withdrew a short distance to the newly built Hindenburg Line (Feb. 23-Apr. 5).

World War I, Battle of Arras (Apr. 9-15): During a failed British-Canadian attack on Arras, preceding the Nivelle Offensive, Vimy Ridge was taken, with 11,000 Canadian casualties (Apr. 9), but the main German lines were not broken. Total casualties on both sides were an estimated 150,000.

World War I: The French launched the massive failed Nivelle Offensive (Apr. 16-20) in Champagne, with French forces in five days suffering 120,000 casualties of the 1.2 million thrown into the offensive. French general Robert Nivelle, the hero of Verdun, had strongly predicted victory; the quick and massive failure of the offensive triggered massive disaffection in the war-weary French army.

World War I: Following the failed Nivelle Offensive, massive mutinies (Apr.-May) immobilized much of the French army; the mutinies were suppressed, and 55 soldiers were executed.

World War I: One month after the disastrous Nivelle Offensive, British forces went on the offensive again in Flanders, first attacking German positions at Messines (June 7), at a cost of 17,000 British and 17,000 German casualties.

World War I: Third Battle of Ypres (Passchendaele) (July 31-Nov. 10): Large British forces and small French forces launched a massive, failed attack at Ypres, making a meaningless five-mile gain at Passchendaele.

World War I: Battle of Cambrai (Nov. 20-Dec. 3): The British attacked again, with a spearhead of 200 tanks leading a Third Army attack on the Hindenburg Line and achieving a modest but unsustained breakthrough; this was the first such use of massed tank action, which would play such a decisive role in World War II.

Russian Revolution (Jan.-Mar.): On the eastern front, army mutinies began and spread (Jan.), as did strikes and demonstrations throughout Russia, growing into a nationwide insurrection against Czar Nicholas II (Feb.); he abdicated (Mar. 15) and was succeeded by the Provisional Government, led by Prince Lvov and then Alexander Kerensky.

World War I: British forces defeated the Turks in the Sinai at Magruntein (Jan. 8-9), clearing the way for the attack on Palestine.

World War I: The Palestine campaign began with a failed British attack on Gaza (Mar. 26), which cost 4,000 British casualties; the second attack (Apr. 17) failed, with more than 6,000 casualties, while Turkish losses in both battles amounted to an estimated 4,000.

World War I: A successful British attack on Beersheeba (Oct. 31) forced Turkish evacuation of Gaza; pursuing British forces went on to take Jerusalem (Dec. 9).

World War I: In Mesopotamia attacking British forces again took Kut (Feb. 22-23), pursuing the defeated Turks to Baghdad, which fell after a failed Turkish stand (Mar. 11). The British fall offensive moved north into Mesopotamia against ineffective Turkish resistance.

British Balfour Declaration (Nov. 2) supported the concept of a Jewish homeland in Palestine as part of the basis of the post–World War I British mandate in Palestine.

b. Joshua Nkomo, head of the Zimbabwe African People's Union (ZAPU), one of two guerrilla armies fighting the Zimbabwe-Rhodesia Civil Wars (1971-1984).

b. Oliver Tambo (d. 1993), African National Congress (ANC) leader in South Africa.

Central, South and East Asia, and the Pacific

The Americas

Japanese forces took Vladivostock (Dec.), beginning their five-year participation in the Russian Civil War.

b. Indira Gandhi (d. 1984), Indian prime minister.

b. Park Chung Hee (d. 1979), South Korean general and dictator (1971-1979).

b. Ferdinand Edralin Marcos (d. 1989), Philippine soldier and dictator (1972-1986).

John J. Pershing's forces withdrew from Mexico without finding and engaging Pancho Villa (Feb.), ending the Mexican-American border war.

World War I: The United States broke off diplomatic relations with Germany (Feb. 3); President Woodrow Wilson asked Congress for a declaration of war on Germany (Apr. 2), which was passed (Apr. 6). American warships entered the Battle of the Atlantic, participating in the inauguration of the successful convoy system (May). American war production accelerated, and conscription began. General Pershing became commander of the American Expeditionary Force and quickly began to move American troops to Europe, with the First Division arriving in June.

American troops again took Cuba, suppressing a revolution then in progress; Cuba remained a de facto American protectorate.

A munitions ship caught fire in the harbor at Halifax, Nova Scotia (Dec. 6); it exploded, setting off huge onshore munitions stockpiles and killing 1,600 people.

Still opposed to the war, the entire leadership of the Industrial Workers of the World (IWW) was charged with sedition by the U.S. government; hundreds were imprisoned.

b. John Fitzgerald Kennedy (d. 1963), 35th president of the United States (1961-1963).

d. George Dewey (b. 1837), American admiral who led the successful night attack on the Spanish fleet at the Philippines' Manila Bay (1898); the rank "admiral of the navy" was created for him (1899).

1917 (cont.)

The Petrograd Soviet (Council) of Workers and Soldiers Deputies was organized (Mar.).

Vladimir Illich Lenin arrived at the Finland railway station in Petrograd (St. Petersburg, later Leningrad) (Apr. 6), his German safe conduct having allowed him to journey across Europe.

World War I: The Russians launched a final, failed Kerensky Offensive (July 1-19), named for the minister of war of the new Provisional Government. Russian forces led by General Alexei Brusilov achieved some penetration of German lines in the Lemberg (Lvov) region of Galicia, but German counterattacks quickly routed and scattered the remaining Russian armies, effectively ending the war on the eastern front. The Russo-German armistice was signed at Brest-Litovsk (Dec. 15).

October Revolution (Nov. 6-7; in the old calendar, Oct. 24): The Bolsheviks mounted a coup in Petrograd; Red Guard and army units commanded by Leon Trotsky quickly overthrew the Kerensky government, storming the lightly defended Provisional Government center at the Winter Palace. Bolshevik units took power in major cities throughout the country.
Russian Civil War (1917-1922) followed the October Revolution, beginning with heavy fighting in Ukraine. Red Army and Cossack forces fought in the Don Basin (Dec.); by May 1918 a nationwide civil war was in progress.

Republic of Finland declared its independence from Russia (Dec. 6), beginning the Finnish War of Independence (1917-1920).

World War I: On the Italian front, the stalemate continued through two more failed Italian offensives. The Tenth Battle of Isonzo (May 12-June 8) cost more than 150,000 Italian and more than 50,000 Austrian casualties; the Eleventh Battle cost almost 150,000 Italian and more than 55,000 Austrian casualties.

World War I, Battle of Caporetto (Oct. 24-Nov. 12): The stalemate ended when reinforced German and Austrian forces broke through on the Isonzo River, then pursued retreating, fragmented Italian forces to the Piave River, north of Venice, with 40,000 Italian casualties and 275,000 captured to 20,000 German and Austrian casualties.

World War I: Greece entered the war on the Allied side (June 27), its forces joining Allied forces centered at Salonika.

World War I: In the Battle of the Atlantic, German submarine attacks increased greatly, with Germany declaring unrestricted submarine warfare (Jan. 31), even though the action hastened American entry into the war (Apr. 6; against Austro-Hungary, Dec. 7); more than 6 million tons of Allied shipping were sunk. A belatedly introduced convoy system (May 10) sharply curtailed sinkings, making British survival possible. American ships, supplies, and armies began to flow into Britain and France.

dGeorges Clemenceau (the "Tiger") became French premier (Nov.). He would play a major role for the rest of the war and at the 1919 Paris Peace Conference.

d. Mata Hari (Margaretha Geertruida Zelle) (b. 1876), Dutch dancer who was executed as a spy by the French (Oct. 15).

d. Radomir Putnik (b. 1847), Serbian general in numerous Balkan wars who became chief of staff (1903), war minister (1904-1905; 1906-1908; 1912), and commander in chief (1912).

b. Abdullah Sallal (d. 1994), Yemeni general, founder and head of the Free Yemen Republic (1962-67).

Central, South and East Asia, and
the Pacific

The Americas

World War I: On the eastern front, Russia left the war with the Treaty of Brest-Litovsk (Mar. 3), which provided for massive territorial losses in western Russia and Ukraine and for the demobilization of Russian armies. For the new Soviet government, the treaty was a holding action; it was repudiated after the German defeat.

World War I: On the western front, German forces, greatly reinforced by troops transferred from the eastern front after Russia left the war, mounted a series of five massive, failed offensives aimed at winning the war, while American troops began to arrive on the western front in large numbers.

World War I, Somme Offensive (Mar. 21-Apr. 5): The Germans advanced 40 miles toward Paris and were stopped; they came close enough to shell Paris with "Big Bertha" siege artillery, but without significant effect.

World War I: The Germans launched the failed Lys Offensive (Apr. 9-29) in Flanders, the second of five major failed German offensives in 1918.

World War I, Battle of Cantigny (May 28-29): In the first American land engagement of the war, the First Division took and held the village of Cantigny.

World War I: German forces attacked on the Aisne River, advancing 20 miles to the Marne River, where they were repulsed. It was the third German offensive of the year (May 27-June 6). American forces fought their first substantial actions at Château-Thierry and Belleau Wood (May 30-June 17), where American Second and Third Division counterattacks forced German toops back across the Rhine.

World War I: The Germans launched the fourth of their five failed major offensives in 1918, the Noyon-Montdidier Offensive (June 9-13), with German troops attacking toward Paris but being quickly repulsed by French forces.

World War I: On the southern front, the last Austrian offensive of the war was stopped on the Piave River (June 22-23).

World War I, Second Battle of the Marne (July 15-Aug. 5): In the fifth and last failed German offensive of 1918, a strike across the Marne, in Champagne, was quickly defeated; the Allies then went over to the offensive for the rest of the war.

World War I: Allied forces attacked German forces at Amiens and then along most of the western front, forcing the Germans back to the Hindenburg Line (Aug. 8-Sept. 4).

World War I, St. Mihiel Offensive (Sept. 12-16): American and French troops attacked German forces in the St. Mihiel salient, straightening Allied lines in preparation for further Allied offensives.

World War I, Meuse-Argonne Offensive (Sept. 26-Nov. 11): German forces on the Meuse River and in the Argonne forest fell back before advancing American and French forces, which continued their pursuit until the Armistice.

World War I, Battle of the Vardar (Sept. 15-29): Allied forces routed the Bulgarian army; the war in the Balkans ended with the Allied-Bulgarian armistice (Sept. 29).

World War I: British forces breached the Hindenburg Line (Sept. 27), while Belgian forces took Ypres and fought their way east until the Armistice (Nov. 11).

World War I, Battle of Vittorio Veneto (Oct. 24-Nov. 4): Allied forces split and smashed the Austrian army, taking 300,000 prisoners in this last battle of the war on the Italian-Austrian front, which ended with the Austrian-Allied armistice (Nov. 4).

World War I: In the Battle of the Atlantic, more than 2.8 million tons of Allied shipping were sunk by German submarines during 1918.

World War I: As the Russian Civil War developed, Georgia, Armenia, and Azerbaijan all declared their independence (Apr.-May); none would survive the war.

World War I, Battle of Megiddo (Sept. 19-21): In the last major engagement of the war in the Middle East, British forces under General Edmund Allenby routed Turkish forces at Jaffa and pursued them east, taking Damascus, Homs, and Aleppo before the Turkish armistice.

World War I: As Turkish resistance collapsed, French naval forces took Beirut, Lebanon (Oct. 5).

World War I: With the Turkish war ending, British forces out of Baghdad quickly took the Mosul oil fields (Oct. 29), also taking Baku (Nov.).

World War I: Turkey left the war with an armistice (Oct. 30).

b. Ahmed Ben Bella, Algerian independence leader and army officer who was a cofounder of the Special Organization and the National Liberation Front (FLN); he became the first premier of Algeria (1962-1965), was imprisoned by his former colleagues (1965-1980), and then went into exile.

b. Nelson Rolihiahia Mandela, African National Congress (ANC) leader, a key figure in the South African movement who was long imprisoned (1962-1990), later becoming South Africa's president (1994-   ); his release was a precondition for the ending of the three-decade South African civil war.

b. Anwar Sadat (d. 1981), Egyptian independence leader and president (1970-1981).

b. Gamal Abdel Nasser (d. 1970), Egyptian officer and president (1956-1970).

d. Abdul Hamid II (b. 1842), Turkish ruler (r. 1876-1909) who harshly repressed dissidents and ethnic minorities; he was directly responsible for the late-1870s Armenian massacres in Constantinople and the much larger mid-1890s Armenian massacres.

Indian Congress Party increased its demand from home rule to full self-determination, taking a long step toward independence from Britain, which would come in 1947.

American forces landed in Siberia, joining the many other countries that had intervened against Bolshevik forces in the Russian Civil War (Aug.). Admiral Alexander Kolchak took control of White forces in Siberia.

Woodrow Wilson put forward his Fourteen Points, basis of the American program at the 1919 Paris Peace Conference (Jan. 8); they included formation of a League of Nations.

Among those imprisoned for their opposition to American participation in World War I were three-time Socialist Party presidential candidate Eugene V. Debs, who was sentenced to 10 years in prison (he was released in 1921), and Industrial Workers of the World (IWW) leader Bill Haywood, who in 1921 fled to the Soviet Union.

Haitian insurrection against American occupation forces failed.

b. George Scratchley Brown (d. 1978), American Air Force general.

1918 (cont.)

German Revolution: Refusing to sail out for a final, suicidal battle with the British Grand Fleet, sailors at the Kiel naval base revolted and seized their ships (Oct. 29). Demonstrations and open armed insurrection spread throughout the country, along with Soviet-style Workers' and Soldiers' Councils (early Nov.). Emperor Wilhelm II abdicated (Nov. 9), then fled to Holland; he was succeeded by Social Democrat Friedrich Ebert.

World War I: The Armistice ended the war on the western front (Nov. 11, at 11 A.M.).

World War I: The German High Seas Fleet finally steamed out of refuge, into the Firth of Forth and internment (Nov. 21).

Former Czech and Slovak prisoners, numbering 40,000 to 70,000, formed the Czech Legion and began to fight their way out of the Soviet Union via Siberia, in alliance with the White forces of Admiral Alexander Kolchak. White forces threatened Moscow.

Ukrainian forces led by Simon Petlyura proclaimed an independent Ukraine, and Ukrainian troops entered Galicia, in a failed attempt to establish a West Ukrainian Republic centered on Lemberg (Lvov).

British, French, and American forces took Murmansk (June 23) and occupied Archangel (Aug. 1-2), also supplying northern White forces in the Russian Civil War. French forces took Odessa, supplying White forces on the southern front. A small American expeditionary force operated in Siberia, as did substantial Japanese forces.

Finnish War of Independence: Finnish White Guard forces, aided by German forces, defeated Soviet and Finnish Red Guard forces, winning Finnish independence.

Latvian War of Independence (1918-1920): The Latvian declaration of independence (Nov. 18) led to the invasion by Soviet troops and began a three-way Latvian-Soviet-German war.

Lithuanian War of Independence (1918-1920): Soviet troops invaded Lithuania after the Lithuanian declaration of independence (Feb. 16) but retreated after defeat by the Germans, who then occupied the country.

Estonian War of Independence (1918-1919): Estonian forces, aided by British naval forces in the Baltic, defeated invading Soviet troops, winning Estonian independence.

Tomás Masaryk became the first president of the new Czechoslovak republic.

Yugoslavia, composed of Serbia, Montenegro, Croatia, Dalmatia, and Bosnia-Herzegovina, became an independent nation.

Sinn Fein, the political arm of the Irish Republican movement, won the Irish elections, forming a government that would in 1919 declare Irish independence.

d. Nicholas II (b. 1868), the last Russian emperor (r. 1894-1917); he was executed with his wife and family by the Bolsheviks at Yekaterinburg (Sverdlovsk) on July 16.

d. Baron Manfred von Richthofen (the "Red Baron") (b. 1892), foremost German World War I fighter pilot who shot down 80 Allied planes; leader of the first independent fighter wing, Jagdegschwader I (from June 26, 1917), he was killed in aerial combat over the Somme River by Canadian pilot Roy Brown.

d. Mikhail Vasilievich Alekseev (b. 1857), Russian general who rose to be army chief of staff (1915), later leader of the White Russian government (1918).

1918 (cont.)

d. Pavel Karlovich Rennenkampf (b. 1854), Russian general who led the First Army from the beginning of World War I, suffering a severe loss at the First Battle of the Masurian Lakes (1914); he was killed by the Bolsheviks.

1919

Paris Peace Conference established the League of Nations; although in existence until 1946, it had lost all relevance by the mid-1930s, during the run-up to World War II. The conference set territorial losses, divided the colonial possessions of the losers, and set German reparations, all specified in the Treaty of Versailles with Germany (June 28); many of the territorial concessions, as in the Rhineland, the Polish Corridor, and the Saar Valley, became issues exploited by Adolf Hitler during his rise to power and the subsequent run-up to World War II.

Irish War of Independence (1919-1921): A Republican guerrilla insurrection began with the declaration of independence of the Irish Republic (Jan. 21), which was not accepted by the British government or Irish Protestants and their military arm, the Ulster Volunteers. Eamon De Valera was the first president of the Irish Republic.

d. Rosa Luxemburg (b. 1871) and Karl Liebnecht (b. 1871), German communists of the Spartacist League who led the Spartacist Revolt (Jan.), an insurrection against Germany's Social-Democratic government. The rebels were easily defeated by the government in alliance with the army, using the Freikorps militia, which captured and murdered them both (Jan. 15).

German communist insurgents founded the Bavarian Communist Republic (Apr.); it was quickly defeated by German Freikorps forces.

German Workers' Party, forerunner of the Nazi Party (Nationalist Socialist German Workers' Party), was founded. Adolf Hitler joined the party (1920) and became its leader (1921).

Communist-led insurrection in Hungary established the Hungarian Socialist Republic, led by Béla Kun (Mar.-Aug.). Hungarian troops invaded Czechoslovakia (Mar. 28). Romania intervened, invading Hungary (Apr. 10); the Romanian army occupied Budapest and smashed the new government (Aug. 4); Kun fled into exile.

Lithuanian War of Independence: Following the Armistice, German forces withdrew from Lithuania, and Soviet troops again invaded, occupying Vilna (Jan.). Poland, which also claimed Vilna, was drawn into the war, and Soviet forces were defeated, with Polish forces reoccupying Vilna (Apr.).

Latvian War of Independence: Soviet troops took Riga (Jan.), as fighting continued; German forces withdrew (Nov.) after the Treaty of Versailles.

Russian Civil War: Red forces captured Kiev (Feb. 3), later recaptured by Anton Denikin's White forces (Sept. 2) but changing hands again (Dec. 17) after a Red offensive. White forces went on the offensive in the east and northwest as well, but without lasting success. By year's end, Denikin's forces had been pushed south to the Black Sea.

Treaty of Saint-Germain (Sept. 10): Austro-Hungary was dismembered, with much territory going to Czechoslovakia, Poland, Yugoslavia, Italy, and Romania. The Hapsburg monarchy was ended, a republic was established, and reparations were set.

Treaty of Neuilly (Nov. 27): The postwar peace treaty with German ally Bulgaria set major territorial losses and reparations and sharply cut Bulgarian armed forces.

Afghan king Habibullah Khan was assassinated (Feb.); he was succeeded by his son Amanullah Khan, as Afghanistan, formerly a British protectorate, became an independent state.

Afghan-British War (May): Brief jihad (holy war) declared by Afghan king Amanullah Khan, whose forces invaded India but were quickly defeated and pursued by British Indian forces with air support. A low-level guerrilla border war continued after the Afghan defeat.

Arabian Civil War: The forces of Ibn Saud and those of the Hashemite king of Arabia, Hussein Ibn Ali, fought in the Hejaz (western Arabia) (1919-1925).

Arab leader Faisal had been promised Syria by the British, but the French — who by a covert postwar agreement succeeded the British in Syria — did not keep the promise; fighting between Arab and French forces began (Dec.).

Greek forces established a base in Smyrna (May), anticipating that they would take the area as part of the postwar settlement process; this occurred by the terms of the Treaty of Sèvres (1920). Unopposed, Greek forces moved into Anatolia and Thrace.

Following the Turkish collapse, Armenia rebelled; resurgent Turkish forces recaptured Armenia (autumn), taking Kars (Oct. 21) and once again massacring large numbers of Armenians.

b. Muhammed Reza Shah Pahlevi (d. 1980), the last shah of Iran (r. 1941-1979).

b. Moïse Kapenda Tshombe (d. 1969), Congolese politician and prime minister.

d. Louis Botha (b. 1862), Boer War guerrilla general, Transvaal premier (1907-1910), and first premier of the Union of South Africa (1910-1919).

Central, South and East Asia, and the Pacific	The Americas	
		1918 (cont.)
	1919	

Mohandas "Mahatma" Gandhi initiated his first satyagraha (nonviolence) campaign in India (Feb.).

Amritsar Massacre (Apr. 13): At least 379 Indians were killed and 1,200 wounded at Amritsar, in the Punjab, when British troops under General Reginald Dyer fired on an estimated 10,000 unarmed demonstrators, trapped in an open plaza called the Jillianwalla Bagh, which had only one exit.

May 4th Movement: China-wide demonstrations against the pro-Japanese Treaty of Versailles began with student demonstrations in Peking (May 4); from this movement would come many leaders of both sides in the Chinese Civil War.

In Russia, the Bolsheviks counterattacked Alexander Kolchak's White troops, retaking Ekaterinburg (Jan. 27); Kolchak's troops were driven back into Siberia, losing Omsk (Nov. 14); as White resistance in Siberia faltered, Kolchak fled.

With the Russian Civil War taking almost all of Russia's attention, Chinese forces reoccupied Outer Mongolia (Oct.).

British forces defeated a Masud insurrection in Waziristan (Feb.).

Women's International League for Peace and Freedom, a peace and disarmament-oriented organization, was founded; its leaders included Jane Addams and Emily Greene Balch.

d. Theodore Roosevelt (b. 1858), 26th president of the United States (1901-1909); as colonel of the Rough Riders, he led the charge up San Juan's Kettle Hill during the Spanish-American War (1898).

d. Emiliano Zapata (b. 1883), Mexican Indian revolutionary leader; he was assassinated.

1919 (cont.)

Communist International (Comintern, Third International) was founded. The Soviet-initiated organization of the communist parties of the world was largely a Soviet foreign policy vehicle (1919-1943).

Benito Mussolini founded the first Italian fascist organization.

Pacifists founded the International Fellowship of Reconciliation (IFOR).

Italian writer Gabriele D'Annunzio led a private army that took and held disputed Fiume (Sept.) until Italian forces retook the city (Dec.).

d. Henry Evelyn Wood (b. 1838), British field marshal in colonial service, most notably during India's Sepoy Mutiny (1857-1858) and in Egypt, becoming general of the Egyptian army (1884-1886).

1920

Russian Civil War: Bolshevik forces defeated Alexander Kolchak's White armies in Siberia and Peter Wrangel's White army in the Crimea but were defeated in Latvia, Lithuania, Estonia, and Finland, with all four countries winning their independence. Wrangel's White forces, defeated in southern Russia, were evacuated by the British to Constantinople (Nov.).

Soviet-Polish War: Polish and Ukrainian forces attacked Soviet forces in eastern Poland and the Ukraine (Apr. 25); the Poles quickly took Kiev, while the Ukrainians, led by Simon Petlyura, conducted massive anti-Jewish pogroms in the Ukraine. Counterattacking Soviet forces, led by Mikhail Tukhachevsky, neared Warsaw in late July and were decisively defeated in the Battle of Warsaw (Aug. 16-25). Polish forces pursued fleeing Bolshevik forces east into southern Russia as far as Minsk, with little opposition until the armistice (Oct. 12). National borders were defined by the Treaty of Riga (Mar. 18, 1921).

Freikorps forces led by Wolfgang Kapp briefly seized control of the German government by coup in the Kapp Putsch, but they could not hold power in the face of army and popular opposition.

Having defeated Béla Kun's communist government, Hungarian regent Miklós Horthy did not allow the king to return, instead taking power and becoming dictator of Hungary (r. 1920-1944).

Treaty of Trianon (June 4) settled Allied World War I claims against Hungary, which lost territory and paid reparations.

Treaty of Dorpat established Finnish and Estonian independence (Oct.).

Latvian War of Independence: Soviet forces withdrew (Jan.); the Treaty of Riga (Aug. 11) recognized Latvian independence.

Lithuanian independence was established by the Treaty of Moscow (July).

Storm Troopers (SA) were founded by Ernst Roehm; the Nazi Party street-fighting and terrorist organization would play a major role in the Nazi seizure of power.

Yugoslav-Italian Treaty of Rapallo (Nov. 12) made disputed Fiume a free city.

d. Alexander Vasilievich Kolchak (b. 1874), Russian Black Sea Fleet admiral who became commander of the Siberian White armies during the Russian Civil War; he was executed by the Bolsheviks after his capture.

d. John Arbuthnot (b. 1841), British admiral; Britain's first sea lord (1904), who introduced the "all-big-gun" battleship, such as the famous HMS *Dreadnought* (1906), and the battle cruiser (1909); he returned from retirement to succeed Prince Louis of Battenberg as first sea lord (1914).

In Syria fighting between French occupying forces and Faisal's Arab army continued; the French took Damascus (July), and Faisal fled the country.

Arab forces in Iraq also sought independence, unsuccessfully rising against British occupation forces (July).

Allied forces occupied Constantinople (Mar.). A new Turkish provisional government was established by nationalist forces (Apr. 23), headed by Mustapha Kemal (Atatürk), and moved toward confrontation with Greek and other Allied forces in Turkey.

The post–World War I Treaty of Sèvres (Aug. 10) dismembered Turkey, in Europe leaving it only Constantinople; created several new nations, including Armenia; promised independence to Kurdistan; and internationalized the Dardanelles. The Turkish provisional government refused to accept the treaty.

Soviet forces attacking via the Caspian Sea invaded northern Persia (May), taking Enzeli and Resht.

Palestinian Jews organized the paramilitary Haganah, which would later become the core of the Israeli army.

The former German Southwest Africa became Namibia, a League of Nations mandate administered by South Africa.

b. Mohammed Siad Barre, Somali general and dictator (r. 1969-1991).

b. Eduardo Mondlane (d. 1969), Mozambican independence leader.

Russian Civil War: Siberian White army commander Alexander Kolchak was captured and killed by Soviet forces; under czarist Russia, he had been admiral of the Black Sea Fleet.

White Russian forces occupied Outer Mongolia, retaking Urga (July).

Ch'en Tu-hsiu and Li Ta-chao founded the Chinese Communist Party (May).

Mohandas "Mahatma" Gandhi initiated a massive Indian satyagraha (nonviolence) movement in support of Indian independence; he was later imprisoned (1922-1924).

b. Mujibur Rahman (d. 1975); first president of Bangladesh (1970-1975).

d. Shichiro Kataoka (b. 1854), Japanese admiral who served at Tsushima (1905).

Mexican general Alvaro Obregón led a successful insurrection against Venustiano Carranza's government; after his forces assassinated Carranza (b. 1859), Obregón succeeded him as president, then ending the long civil war.

While still imprisoned for opposing World War I, Socialist Party candidate Eugene V. Debs won more than 900,000 votes in the presidential election.

b. Javier Pérez de Cuéllar, Peruvian diplomat and fifth secretary-general of the United Nations (1982-1992), who played a major role in mediating the Iran-Iraq War and the civil wars in Angola, Cambodia, and El Salvador.

1920 (cont.)

d. Svetozar Borojevic (Boroevic) Edler von Bojna (b. 1856), Austro-Hungarian field marshal who commanded the Third Army at Gorlice-Tarnów, taking over the Fifth Army on the Italian front, notably at the Isonzo and Piave Rivers; not allowed to return to his Croatian home, he died in exile.

1921

Irish War of Independence: A cease-fire in Ireland (July 11) led to a peace agreement that established the north-south partition of Ireland into the Irish Free State and Northern Ireland.

Irish Civil War (1921-1922): Irish Republican Army militants who refused to accept the terms of the Irish War of Independence peace agreement, with its partition of Ireland, rebelled and were defeated by the new Irish Free State government, then began the long guerrilla war in Northern Ireland.

Benito Mussolini became a member of the Italian parliament. Fascist para-military Blackshirts engaged in terrorist street fighting as part of the run-up to the Fascist seizure of power.

Kronstadt Rebellion (Mar.): Bolshevik sailors at the Kronstadt naval base, near Leningrad (St. Petersburg), mounted an armed insurrection against the Bolshevik government; the rebellion was quickly suppressed by army units led by Leon Trotsky and General Mikhail Tukhachevsky.

b. Alexander Dubcek (d. 1992), Czechoslovak communist, later democratic, leader.

d. Karl von Bülow (b. 1846), German general who commanded Germany's Second Army early in World War I, most notably at the Battle of the Marne (1914).

d. Louis, prince of Battenberg (Louis Mountbatten) (b. 1854), British admiral, born Prince Alexander of Hesse; a naturalized British citizen, married to Queen Victoria's granddaughter, he was forced to resign as first sea lord (1914) because of anti-German feelings, adopting the Anglicized name Mountbatten; his son was Louis Mountbatten.

Rif War (1921-1926): Abd el-Krim led a Moroccan guerrilla war of independence against joint Spanish-French colonial forces. At the Battle of Anual (July), Moroccan forces ambushed and destroyed a Spanish army of 20,000, killing 12,000 and capturing most of the remainder.

Greek-Turkish War: Greek forces pushed east out of Smyrna, granted them by the Treaty of Sèvres, into western Turkey, contested by Turkish forces led by Mustapha Kemal (Atatürk). Stopped twice at Inönü (Jan.; Mar.), they resumed their offensive (July), winning a very costly victory at Eskisehir (July 17) and falling back after suffering a defeat at the Sakkaria River (Aug. 24-Sept. 16).

General Reza Khan (Reza Shah Pahlevi), commander of the Cossack Brigade, seized power in Persia (Iran), deposing Ahmad Shah, and took full control of the country.

In Palestine, David Ben Gurion became the first secretary-general of the Histadrut, the Palestine Jewish labor organization. British occupying forces appointed Palestinian Arab leader Haj Amin al Husseini as grand mufti of Jerusalem. Arab-Jewish riots claimed more than 20 lives.

After the French expelled Faisal from Syria, the British placed him on the throne of Iraq, declaring it a protectorate.

b. Jean Bédel Bokassa, Central African Republic dictator (r. 1966-1979).

1922

Fascist Party Blackshirts marched on Rome (Oct. 24), unopposed by the Italian army or King Victor Emmanuel III; Benito Mussolini took power as premier (Oct. 31).

Japanese forces, which had intervened against the Bolsheviks, withdrew from Siberia, ending the Russian Civil War.

Following the Irish Civil War, the Irish Free State was formally established; it became the Republic of Ireland in 1937.

The Treaty of Rapallo established normal relations between the Soviet Union and Germany, which became the first major power to recognize the Soviet Union.

Greek-Turkish War: Mustapha Kemal's strong counteroffensive defeated and routed the Greeks (Aug.), who fled back to Smyrna; the pursuing Turks took the city (Sept.) and massacred tens of thousands of soldiers and noncombatants.

British forces defeated an insurrection in occupied Kurdistan (1922-1924), later granting some Kurdish autonomy in northern Iraq.

b. Augustinho Neto (d. 1979), Angolan independence leader.

1920 (cont.)

1921

Soviet and Mongolian forces invaded Mongolia, defeating White Russian forces (June-July); Mongolia became a de facto Soviet protectorate.

First Congress of the Chinese Communist Party met in Shanghai (July).

Japanese prime minister Hara Takashi (Hara Kei) was killed by a right-wing assassin; this was one of many assassinations that would help destabilize Japan and ultimately lead the country to militarism, fascism, and World War II.

b. Suharto, Indonesian general and president (1966-   ).

d. Sotaro Misu (b. 1855), Japanese admiral who was nicknamed the "One-Eyed Dragon" after losing an eye at Tsushima (1905).

Panama–Costa Rica border war was contained after U.S. political intervention (Feb.-Mar.).

Pacifist War Resisters' International was founded.

b. David C. Jones, American Air Force general who served in World War II, the Korean War, and the Vietnam War, becoming chairman of the Joint Chiefs of Staff (1978-1982).

b. Daniel Berrigan, American Catholic priest and leading anti–Vietnam War activist.

b. Virgilio Barco Vargas, president of Colombia (1985-1990) whose incumbency would be marked by continuing civil war with leftist revolutionaries and sharp conflict with international drug cartels; he was allied with the United States against the latter.

1922

Sun Yat-sen, relying heavily on the advice of his Soviet advisers, reorganized the Kuomintang along authoritarian Bolshevik lines, as the run-up to the Chinese Civil War proceeded.

Japanese forces withdrew from Siberia, ending the Russian Civil War.

b. Norodom Sihanouk, Cambodian king (r. 1941-1955; 1993-   ), prime minister (1955-1960), and president (1960-1970); a central figure in modern Cambodian history.

Washington Conference focused on east Asian political stability and naval disarmament (Nov. 1921-Feb. 1922); participating were Britain, China, France, Japan, Italy, Belgium, the Netherlands, Portugal, and the United States. Various treaties resulted, including one guaranteeing China's territories; another mutually guaranteeing British, French, Japanese, and U.S. lands in the Pacific; and a moratorium on building capital ships. Long-term successes were limited.

American troops were withdrawn from the Rhineland.

1922 (cont.)

d. Michael Collins (b. 1890), Irish intelligence head during the Irish War of Independence (1919-1921) and commander of Irish Free State forces during the Irish Civil War (1921-1922); he was killed in an insurgent ambush (Aug. 22).

d. Erich von Falkenhayn (b. 1861), head of the German general staff (1914-1916) from after the First Battle of the Marne through the siege of Verdun.

d. Henry Hughes Wilson (b. 1864), British field marshal who during World War I was the key liaison officer linking the British with their French allies.

b. Yitzhak Rabin, Israeli general, army chief of staff (1964-1968), and prime minister (1974-1977; 1992-   ).

d. Christiaan Rudolph De Wet (b. 1854), Boer general during the South African wars with the English, who became commandant general of Free State forces (1900).

d. Pasha Enver (b. 1881), Turkish general during the Balkan Wars, most notably in the recapture of Edirne (1913); during World War I, he was minister of war and effective commander in chief.

1923

Adolf Hitler's Nazi Party mounted the failed Beer Hall Putsch (Nov. 8-11), an attempted coup in Bavaria; Hitler wrote the first volume of *Mein Kampf* during a year in prison, emerging as a German national figure; this began the long run-up to Nazi power and World War II.

The French and British occupied the Ruhr Valley after German nonpayment of World War I reparations set by the Treaty of Versailles.

General Miguel Primo de Rivera took power in Spain by coup following an army revolt in Barcelona.

Guerrilla insurrection in Bulgaria (1923-1925) followed the assassination of Agrarian Party prime minister Alexander Stamboliyski.

Italian forces in Libya began their eight-year campaign of extermination (1923-1931) against the Senussi people, led by Omar Mukhtar.

After deposing the final Ottoman ruler of Turkey, Mustapha Kemal became the first president of the Turkish republic and pushed through the vastly different Treaty of Lausanne (July 24), replacing the less favorable Treaty of Sèvres (1920); Turkey kept Turkish Armenia, Turkish Kurdistan, several lesser territories, and control of the Dardenelles (by terms of the accompanying Straits Convention).

1924

Italian Fascists assassinated anti-Fascist Giacomo Matteotti, a leading Italian Socialist member of parliament.

d. Vladimir Illich Lenin (Vladimir Illich Ulyanov) (b. 1870), Russian revolutionary; founder of the Bolshevik Party; and leader of the Bolshevik Revolution of 1917, the Soviet Union, and world communism.

d. Robert Georges Nivelle (b. 1856), French general who was victorious at Verdun (1916); he was relieved of major command after his massive, failed Nivelle Offensive (1917).

Arabian Civil War: Ibn Saud's forces took Mecca (Oct. 13).

Boer War general James Hertzog, a right-wing Afrikaaner, became National Party prime minister of South Africa (1924-1929).

b. Robert Gabriel Mugabe, a founder of the Zimbabwe African National Union (ZANU) (1963), a leader of the guerrilla war of independence, and first prime minister of the Republic of Zimbabwe (1980-   ).

b. Apollo Milton Obote, first prime minister of the Republic of Uganda (1962); dictator of Uganda (1966-1971) until deposed by Idi Amin, then again (1979-1985) until deposed by coup.

b. Israel Tal, Israeli general known as "Talik," an armored force commander and key strategist of long service in the Israeli Defense Ministry.

Central, South and East Asia, and the Pacific	The Americas	

1922 (cont.)

d. Aritomo Yamagata (b. 1838), Japanese field marshal who was founder and first chief of the Army General Staff, a key figure in creating a German-style military organization largely free of civilian control; he also served as prime minister (1890; 1898-1900) and army minister (1894-1895).

1923

Sun Yat-sen founded the Whampoa Military Academy, training ground for most Kuomintang and some Communist military officers, and he began to organize the Northern Expedition against the warlords.

b. Nguyen Van Thieu, South Vietnamese general and president (1967-1975).

b. Henry Alfred Kissinger, who, while President Richard M. Nixon's national security adviser, was chief American Vietnam War peace negotiator; he was corecipient of the 1973 Nobel Peace Prize and later secretary of state (1973-1978).

d. Francisco "Pancho" Villa (Doroteo Arango) (b. 1878), Mexican revolutionary general who was assassinated three years after retiring.

1924

Mongolian People's Republic was founded, formally creating the Soviet-dominated, nominally independent Mongolian state (Nov.).

b. Mohammad Zia Ul-Haq (d. 1988), Pakistani general and dictator (1977-1988).

d. Yoshimichi Hasegawa (b. 1850), Japanese field marshal who rose to be commander of the Korea Garrison Army (1904-1908) and army chief of staff (1912-1915).

A military revolt at São Paulo, Brazil, was defeated by government forces (July-Aug.), who also defeated the forces of Luis Carlos Prestes in the south. Prestes then led a force of 2,000 on the long march of the Prestes Column, ultimately reaching asylum in Bolivia.

American forces withdrew from the Dominican Republic, but the country continued to be a de facto American protectorate.

b. James Earl "Jimmy" Carter, Jr., 39th president of the United States (1977-1981) and later international mediator.

b. George Herbert Walker Bush, 41st president of the United States (1989-1993), following two terms as vice president; he was a key figure in the final stages of the Cold War and in the Persian Gulf War.

d. (Thomas) Woodrow Wilson (b. 1856), 28th president of the United States (1913-1921), through World War I and his failed effort to bring the United States into the League of Nations.

1925

The use of poison gas in warfare was outlawed by the Geneva Protocol, part of the League of Nations Arms Traffic Convention; the United States was not a signatory, ratification was slow in coming, and the prohibition was never successfully enforced.

League of Nations mediation temporarily settled the crisis posed by Greek-Bulgarian border clashes (Oct. 21).

Hitler published the second volume of *Mein Kampf*.

Paul von Hindenburg, the Prussian general who became Germany's leading figure during World War I, became president of the Weimar Republic.

Germany made substantial reparations payments to France and Britain.

Treaty of Locarno (Oct. 5-16), actually a group of treaties provided for continuing demilitarization of the Rhineland; Germany's borders with Belgium and France were to remain as set by the Treaty of Versailles. The Locarno treaties were repudiated by Germany in 1936, on reoccupation of the Rhineland.

b. Margaret Roberts Thatcher, British prime minister (1979-1990).

d. Franz Xavier Josef Conrad von Hüotzendorf (b. 1852), Austro-Hungarian field marshal during World War I.

d. John Denton Pinkstone French (b. 1852), British general who led the British Expeditionary Force (BEF) in France at the outbreak of World War I (1914); he was later replaced by General Douglas Haig (1915).

d. Mikhail Vasilyevich Frunze (b. 1885), Russian general who was a professional revolutionary beginning in 1905; he was best known for his activities in the Russian Civil War and writings such as *Lenin and the Red Army* (1925).

Their promised independence unrealized, Kurdish forces rebelled unsuccessfully in Turkey, beginning the long, multination guerrilla wars in the area that were continuing in the mid-1990s.

Rif War: Attacking Moroccan forces destroyed many French blockhouses and threatened Fez; combined French-Spanish forces numbering 200,000 began a final offensive against the much smaller Moroccan forces (Sept.).

Druse insurrection in southern Syria (1925-1927) met with early success, as French forces withdrew (July); Druse forces took Damascus (Dec.).

Reza Khan of Iran became shah, head of the new house of Pahlevi.

b. Idi Amin, Ugandan president and dictator (1971-1979); he was deposed by a successful insurrection and accompanying Tanzanian invasion (1979).

b. Holden Alvaro Roberto, Angolan independence leader and head of the National Front for the Liberation of Angola (FNLA).

1926

Army insurrection in Portugal ended the first Portuguese republic.

Joseph Stalin took the major share of power in the Soviet Union, removing Grigori Zinoviev, Lev Kamenev, and several other Bolshevik leaders from positions of power.

Polish general Jósef Pilsudski took power in a military coup (May 12-14), ruling Poland effectively as dictator until his death (1935).

d. Alexsei Alexseevich Brusilov (b. 1853), Russian general who orchestrated two key World War I attacks — the Brusilov Offensive (1916) and the Kerensky (Second Brusilov) Offensive (1917).

d. Simon Vasilievich Petlyura (b. 1879), Ukrainian nationalist who was the leader of Ukrainian forces during the Russian Civil War (1917-1922) and the Soviet-Polish War (1920); organizer of pogroms that murdered tens of thousands of Jews, he was assassinated in Paris (May 26).

d. Felix Edmundovich Dzerzhinsky (b. 1877), organizer and head of the Soviet secret police.

Rif War: Pursuing French and Spanish forces forced the surrender of Abd el-Krim's guerrilla army, ending the war.

1925

May 30th Movement: China-wide demonstrations (1925-1926) were generated after British troops killed 12 Chinese demonstrators in Shanghai (May 30); unrest grew after 50 Whampoa Military Academy cadets were killed in an armed engagement with British and French forces (June 23).

d. Sun Yat-sen (b. 1866), leader of the Chinese revolutionary movement (1894-1911), provisional president of the new Chinese republic (1911-1912), and chief organizer of the Kuomintang; called "Father of the Chinese Republic."

American military aviator William "Billy" Mitchell, an advocate of air power, publicly criticized the armed forces after the loss of the dirigible *Shenandoah* and was court-martialed and cashiered. He was not silenced, continuing his criticism and predicting an attack like that made by the Japanese on Pearl Harbor (1941). Mitchell was later recognized as a prophet and was posthumously awarded a medal by Congress (1946).

In Nicaragua's civil war, Liberals fought Conservatives, who were aided by intervening American forces.

b. Anastasio Somoza Debayle (d. 1980), Nicaraguan general and dictator (1963-1979).

b. Robert Francis Kennedy (d. 1968), American politician.

d. Nelson Appleton Miles (b. 1839), American general who during the Civil War was wounded at Fredericksburg (1862) and Chancellorsville (1863); later he was the jailer for Confederate president Jefferson Davis and commanded the Fifth Infantry in the West.

d. James Harrison Wilson (b. 1837), American general; a topographical engineer, he served in the Civil War, Spanish-American War, and Boxer Rebellion, in the relief of Peking (June-Aug. 1900).

1926

Northern Expedition (1926-1928): Kuomintang and allied Communist forces commanded by Chiang Kai-shek drove north out of Canton against the warlords, capturing Hankow, Nanking, and Shanghai in the first main phase of the campaign to unify China under the republic.

Hirohito became emperor of Japan.

d. Kageaki Kawamura (b. 1850), Japanese field marshal who commanded the Army of the Yalu at Mukden (1905).

American physicist and rocketry pioneer Robert Hutchings Goddard launched the first liquid-propellant rocket (Mar. 16), a major event in the history of space flight.

Catholic insurrection in Mexico (1926-1929) followed government restrictions placed on the Catholic Church; the "Cristero" rising was defeated by government forces.

b. Fidel Castro Ruz, leader of the Cuban Revolution and dictator of Cuba (1959-   ).

Europe	Africa and Southwest Asia

1927

| Expansionist fascist Italy established a protectorate over Albania by the terms of the Treaty of Tirana. | French forces with armor and air support finally defeated Druse rebels in southern Syria.

b. Houari Boumedienne (Mohammed Boukharouba) (d. 1978), Algerian independence leader. |

1928

| Under the Kellogg-Briand Pact (Aug. 27), 62 nations declared their intent to renounce war as an instrument of national policy; the pact was a practical nullity, as rising fascism and militarism brought about a new world war.

Joseph Stalin began the purges that would culminate in a great reign of terror and millions of deaths in the Soviet Union; he also introduced his first five-year plan (1928-1932), which developed a countrywide attack on Soviet family farmers (kulaks).

d. Douglas Haig (b. 1861), commander of British forces in France (1915-1918) who suffered enormous losses during the years of trench warfare, as infantry again and again unsuccessfully attacked entrenched German machine-gun positions, as on the Somme (1916) and at Passchendaele (Third Battle of Ypres) (1917).

d. Peter Nikolayevich Wrangel (b. 1878), Russian general who was commander of the White armies in southern Russia (from 1920).

d. Reinhard Scheer (b. 1863), German admiral who commanded the High Seas Fleet at Jutland (1916), thereafter remaining blockaded. | Previously regent, Ras Tafari took power by coup in Ethiopia, proclaiming himself King Haile Selassie I.

b. Hafez al Assad, Syrian air force officer and Ba'ath Party leader who took power by coup (1970), becoming president and sole ruler of Syria (1971).

b. Mohammed Hosni Mubarak, Egyptian air general who succeeded assassinated Anwar Sadat as Egyptian president (1981-).

b. Mangosuthu Gatsha Buthelezi, South African Zulu leader who was a key figure in the African National Congress (ANC)–Inkatha civil war of the 1980s and early 1990s.

b. Ariel Sharon, Israeli officer and politician; a cabinet-level official in the conservative governments of the 1980s; as defense minister (1981-1982), he was a key figure in the Israeli invasion of Lebanon. |

1929

| Geneva Convention amendments expanded the treaties to include the treatment of prisoners of war. | Arab-Jewish riots in Palestine claimed more than 200 lives. |

Central, South and East Asia, and
the Pacific

The Americas

Chinese Civil War (1927-1949) began with the Shanghai Massacre (Apr. 12). Kuomintang army forces led by Chiang Kai-shek attacked their Communist allies in Shanghai and several other cities, executing 5,000 to 6,000 of those captured.

Chinese Civil War: In the Nanchang Uprising (Aug.), the first major Kuomintang-Communist engagement of the war, Communist forces under Zhu De (Chu Teh) were defeated, withdrawing to the Ching-kang Mountains of western Kiangsi.

Chinese Civil War: Mao Zedong led the Autumn Harvest Uprisings, a series of failed rural rebellions in the Yangtze River valley (Sept.), signaling his later turn toward the rural-based strategy that would ultimately win China.

Chinese Civil War, Canton Commune (Dec. 11-15): Communist rising in Canton was suppressed.

Manchurian warlord Chang Tso-lin was defeated by Kuomintang forces moving into north China and Manchuria.

Chiang Kai-shek married Mei-ling Soong (Madame Chiang Kai-shek); her sister Ch'ing-Ling Soong (Madame Sun Yat-sen) broke with Chiang's Kuomintang forces after the Shanghai Massacre.

After a truce in the Nicaraguan Civil War, Liberal forces led by Augusto César Sandino retreated into the mountains, mounting a guerrilla insurrection against the Conservative government and the American marine occupation force. His chief opponent was National Guard head Anastasio Somoza Garcia, later his murderer and Nicaraguan dictator.

d. Leonard Wood (b. 1860), American general who fostered civilian training camps for military preparedness, called the Plattsburgh Idea after the main camp in Plattsburgh, New York (1915).

d. Chang Tso-lin (b. 1873), Manchurian warlord nicknamed "Tiger of the North" or "Old Marshal"; he was assassinated by Japanese agents, and succeeded by his son Chang Hsüeh-liang, who allied himself with the Kuomintang.

Kuomintang forces driving north crossed the Yellow River, defeated the northern warlords, and took Peking (June), completing the Northern Expedition.

b. Pol Pot (Tol Saut; Saloth Sar), Khmer Rouge organizer and general secretary of the Communist Party of Kampuchea (Cambodia) (1963); leader of the Khmer Rouge through the Cambodian Civil War and bearer of primary responsibility for the Cambodian Holocaust, which killed 1 million to 3 million of his own people.

b. Zulfikar Ali Bhutto (d. 1979), prime minister of Pakistan.

d. ds'ao K'un (b. 1862), Chinese general during the Revolution and Civil War.

b. Che Guevara (Ernesto Guevara de la Serna) (d. 1967), guerrilla general and a leader of the Cuban Revolution (1956-1959).

d. Alvaro Obregón (b. 1880), Mexican Revolution general who took power by coup in 1920; he was president of Mexico at the time of his assassination.

d. George Washington Goethals (b. 1858), American Army officer who was chief engineer on the Panama Canal (Mar. 1907-Aug. 1914).

d. Joseph Theodore Dickman (b. 1857), American general whose Third Infantry Division fought notably at Château-Thierry and against the German Marne Offensive (both 1918).

Soviet forces invaded Manchuria in support of Soviet claims to the disputed Chinese Eastern Railway; they

The unfinished business of the Mexican Revolution generated another short-lived, failed rebellion (Mar.-Apr.), this one led by general Gonzálo Escobar in Sonora.

1929 (cont.)

The Italian government and the Vatican signed the Lateran Treaty, establishing Catholicism as the Italian state religion and recognizing Vatican sovereignty in the Vatican City State; in return, the Vatican recognized Benito Mussolini's government, legitimizing Italian fascism.

Leon Trotsky was expelled from the Soviet Union, going into exile (Jan.).

d. Georges Eugene Benjamin Clemenceau (b. 1841), French politician, twice premier (1906-1909; 1917-1920), and a key figure during the final year of the war and at the Paris Peace Conference.

d. Ferdinand Foch (b. 1851), French World War I general who was a key figure at the First Battle of the Marne and chief of staff from 1917.

d. Grand Duke Nicholas (Nikolai Nikolaevich Romanov) (b. 1856), Russian general who was the nephew of Czar Alexander II; he was commander in chief (Aug. 1914) until personally replaced by Czar Nicholas II (Sept. 1915), then commanded in the Caucasus Mountains.

Muslim Brotherhood, a Sunni fundamentalist and terrorist-oriented organization, was founded, centered in Egypt.

b. Sam Nujoma, first president of the Southwest Africa People's Organization of Namibia (SWAPO) (1959) and first president of the independent Namibia (1990-).

b. Yasir Arafat, leader of the Palestine Liberation Organization (PLO) (from 1969).

1930

London Naval Conference (Jan.-Apr.) set by treaty several limitations on American, Japanese, British, French, and Italian naval armaments; to run six years, it was never effectively enforced and became essentially a dead letter after Japan's invasion of Manchuria (1931).

French and British forces evacuated the Rhineland, leaving it a demilitarized zone, as provided by the Locarno treaties of 1925.

d. Alfred von Tirpitz (b. 1849), German admiral who was naval chief of staff before World War I.

d. Arthur James Balfour (b. 1848), British politician and diplomat; his Balfour Declaration (1917) played a major role in the development of a Jewish homeland in Palestine.

d. Horace Lockwood Smith-Dorrien (b. 1858), British general serving in the colonial wars and World War I, in France and German East Africa.

d. Valeriano Weyler y Nicolau, marquis of Tenerife (b. 1838), Spanish general who as captain-general of Cuba (1896-1897) dealt so harshly with rebels that Spain recalled him; he later served as minister of war (1901-1902; 1905; 1906-1907).

Kurdish independence forces mounted a failed insurrection in Iran (June-July). A more protracted Kurdish insurrection, led by Sheikh Mahmud, was mounted in Iraq (Sept.); it was defeated by the new Iraqi government, with British military assistance (Apr. 1931).

Iraq formally became an independent nation (Nov.), though still a de facto British protectorate; Nuri al-Said was prime minister (1930-1958).

David Ben Gurion founded the socialist Mapai Party in Palestine.

Dervish rebellion in Turkey was quickly defeated by the Mustapha Kemal government (Dec.).

b. Mohammed Gaafar al-Nimeiry, Sudanese officer who took power by coup (1969), set up an Islamic fundamentalist government, and ruled until he was himself deposed by coup (1985).

b. Mobutu Sese Seko (Joseph Désiré Mobuto), president of Zaire (1965-).

1931

Alfonso XIII of Spain was deposed by Republican forces (Apr. 14); the new government was headed by Alcalá Zamora, and the run-up to the Spanish Civil War began.

Greek-Bulgarian border clashes (Jan.-Feb.) again drew League of Nations mediation.

b. Mikhail Sergeyevich Gorbachev, leader of the Soviet Union (1985-1991), architect of *perestroika* (economic restructuring) and *glasnost* (openness), and a key figure in ending the Cold War, and with it many regional conflicts.

Italian forces in Libya defeated, captured, and executed Omar Mukhtar, ending the desert war with the Senussi (1923-1931) that had cost at least 50,000 lives, most of them imprisoned Senussi civilians.

Irgun Zvai Leumi (National Military Organization) was founded in Jerusalem; led by Avraham Tehomi, it advocated armed Jewish insurrection against British rule and war against Palestinian Arabs.

Central, South and East Asia, and the Pacific	The Americas

1929 (cont.)

withdrew after Chinese acceptance of the Soviet position regarding the railway.

Afghanistan was split by civil war between the forces of Habibullah Ghazi, who took Kabul (Jan.), and those of Mohammed Nadir Khan, who took Kabul and executed Ghazi (Oct.); Nadir Khan then ruled as Nadir Shah.

Led by Jawaharlal Nehru, the Indian Congress Party changed its main demand from self-determination to full independence.

d. Koichiro Tachibana (b. 1861), Japanese general who commanded the Kwangtung Army (1919-1921) and the Vladivostok Expeditionary Army in its withdrawal from Siberia (1921-1922).

The American stock market crash (Oct.) set in motion many of the forces that would bring the Great Depression, fascism, and World War II.

b. Martin Luther King, Jr. (d. 1968), American civil rights and nonviolence leader.

1930

Chinese Civil War: In the Battle of Ch'angsha (July), Kuomintang forces decisively defeated Communist attempts to take Ch'angsha and several other central Chinese cities, forcing Communist forces to flee into the mountains of western Kiangsi, there developing the Kiangsi Soviet.

Japanese prime minister Hamaguchi Osachi was shot by a right-wing assassin, dying in 1931; part of the run-up to Japanese militarism, facism, and World War II.

Mohandas "Mahatma" Gandhi led an all-India anti–salt tax satyagraha (nonviolence) campaign.

d. Yasukata Oku (b. 1846), Japanese field marshal who commanded the Second Army during the Russo-Japanese War, most notably at Mukden (1905); later he was army chief of staff (1906-1912).

Rafael Leonidas Trujillo Molina took power in the Dominican Republic; he ruled as dictator for 31 years (1930-1961) until deposed by revolution.

Getúlio Vargas lost the Brazilian presidential election; he charged electoral fraud and seized power by military coup (Oct.), ruling as dictator until deposed by another coup (1945).

b. James A. Baker III, American politician long associated with presidents Ronald Reagan and George Bush; he was Reagan's chief of staff (1981-1985) and treasury secretary (1985-1988); then Bush's secretary of state (1989-1993).

1931

Mukden Incident (Sept. 18-19): Japan's Kwangtung Army seized Mukden, China, on a pretext, charging that Japan planned to blow up the railroad serving the city; the Japanese then went on to take all of Manchuria, renaming it Manchukuo, which they held until the end of World War II; a major event in the run-up to Japanese militarism, fascism, and World War II.

Chinese Civil War: Kuomintang forces again attacked Communist positions in Kiangsi, in the second and third "antibandit" campaigns.

Harold C. Urey discovered deuterium, a hydrogen isotope that is a basic element in heavy water, used in nuclear reactors and as a hydrogen bomb energy source.

1931 (cont.)

b. Boris Nikolayevich Yeltsin, president of Russia (1990-   ) who as opposition leader faced down a right-wing coup attempt against Mikhail Gorbachev (1991), whom he later replaced.

d. Joseph Joffre (b. 1852), French commander at the First Battle of the Marne (1914) and French commander in chief (Dec. 1915-Dec. 1916).

d. Alexander Stanhope Cobbe (b. 1870), British general during World War I, serving in France, India, and Mesopotamia.

d. Hussein Ibn Ali (b. 1853), leader of the 1916 Arab War of Independence against the Turks, sharif of Mecca, and king of the Hejaz until his defeat by Ibn Saud in the Arabian Civil War. He was the father of Faisal I of Iraq and Abdullah Ibn Hussein of Transjordan.

1932

World Disarmament Conference (1932-1934) began at Geneva; it was very quickly overtaken by events, as Adolf Hitler came to power in Germany and Japan continued to prepare for war in Asia; it adjourned in 1934 without progress, a new arms race already under way.

Failed Spanish right-wing military insurrection led by General José Sanjurjo was largely confined to Seville, as the run-up to the Spanish Civil War continued.

Antonio de Oliveira Salazar became the fascist dictator of Portugal.

d. Aristide Briand (b. 1862), 11-term French premier and often foreign minister; he was the chief organizer of the Locarno (1925) and Kellogg-Briand (1928) treaties, key supporter of the League of Nations, and recipient of the 1926 Nobel Peace Prize.

d. Franz von Hipper (b. 1863), German admiral who led Germany's squadron of battle cruisers at Jutland; appointed commander of the High Seas Fleet (Aug. 1918), his forces mutinied against his order for a final sortie (Nov. 1918).

d. Herbert Charles Onslow Plumer (b. 1857), British field marshal who served in Africa; during World War I he had responsibility for the Allied attack called the Third Battle of Ypres (Passchendaele) (1917), later commanding the Second Army.

Kurdish independence forces renewed their rising in Iraq (Apr.-June); British warplanes and Iraqi ground forces defeated the Kurds.

1933

The Nazi period began in Germany, as fascist dictator Adolf Hitler took power (Feb. 28). Nazi attacks on German dissidents and Jews began, as did rearmament; Germany quickly started on the road to World War II, to the 6 million dead of the Jewish Holocaust, and to the deaths of an estimated 60 million more, large numbers of them Germans who had supported Hitler during the years of Nazi power.

The German concentration camp at Buchenwald, near Weimar, was established; the death camp would be the site of many "medical experiments" that were in actuality Nazi crimes against humanity.

"This House will not fight for King and Country" was the pacifist Oxford Pledge, taken by Britain's Oxford Union; it was soon superseded by antifascism as the great cause of the day; some of those who took the pledge died fighting for the Spanish republic only a few years later; most went to war in 1939, only six years later.

Ibn Saud granted Standard Oil the first Arabian oil concession, beginning the process that would make the oil fields of the Middle East some of the world's greatest prizes and the source of contention among the great powers for much of the rest of the century.

b. Samora Machel (d. 1986), Mozambican president (1975-1986).

d. Faisal (b. 1883), commander of Arab forces during the Arab War of Independence against Turkish rule (1916-1918) and first king of Iraq (r. 1921-1933).

Central, South and East Asia, and the Pacific	The Americas	

1932

Battle of Shanghai (Jan. 28-Mar. 8): After a nationwide Chinese boycott of Japanese goods began, protesting the Japanese conquest of Manchuria, Japanese forces landed at Shanghai. They were held on their beachheads by the Chinese 19th Route Army (until late Feb.), but then broke through; the defeated Chinese ended their boycott as a condition of Japanese withdrawal.

Hsüan T'ung (Henry P'u Yi), who as a child had been the last Manchu (Ch'ing) emperor of China (1908-1912), was installed by the Japanese as the puppet ruler of Manchuria (Manchukuo).

Takuma Dan, Japanese *zaibatsu* (industrial organization) leader who headed Mitsui, was murdered by right-wing assassins, as the Japanese military took control of Japan.

Japanese prime minister Inukai Tsuyohi, who opposed the seizure of Manchuria and growing control of the military, was assassinated by a group of right-wing naval officers; this marked the end of pre–World War II Japanese democracy and the triumph of militarism and fascism.

While in a British Indian prison, **Mohandas "Mahatma" Gandhi** began his lifelong campaign on behalf of the Harijans (Children of God; Untouchables).

Chaco War (1932-1935): Bolivia and Paraguay contested control of the Chaco region, Bolivia wanting an outlet to the sea via the Paraguay River. Paraguay's early successes were reversed by strengthened Bolivian forces, which won much of the region (by June).

The **"Bonus Marchers"** — World War I veterans demanding federal bonuses — were attacked in Washington, D.C., by regular army forces in divisional strength and with tanks, commanded by General Douglas MacArthur, as ordered by President Herbert Hoover. MacArthur dispersed the veterans and burned the squatter camps they had built.

In Brazil, **São Paulo** rose against the Getúlio Vargas dictatorship, fielding a Paulista army of 40,000 to 50,000; but the city rose alone and was successfully besieged and taken by larger and better-equipped government forces.

1933

Chinese Civil War: The fourth Kuomintang "antibandit" campaign against the Kiangsi Soviet (Apr.-June) failed; the fifth (Dec. 1933-Sept. 1934) defeated and almost encircled Communist forces.

Japanese forces invaded Jehol, in Inner Mongolia, claiming it as part of Manchuria (Jan.-Mar.); the Chinese were forced to withdraw from Tientsin.

Nadir Shah of Afghanistan was assassinated (Nov. 8); his son Mohammad Zahir Shah succeeded him, beginning a reign that would end 40 years later with the 1973 revolution.

b. **Corazon Cojuangco Aquino**, leader of the Philippine Revolution (1986) and subsequently president of the Philippines (1986-1992).

President Franklin Delano Roosevelt took office (Mar. 4), four days after Adolf Hitler took power in Germany, and began the New Deal era, a period in which he faced the twin specters of the Great Depression at home and the rise of fascism and war abroad.

In sharp reversals of policy, the new Roosevelt administration recognized the Soviet Union and introduced the Good Neighbor Policy, rejecting an imperial role in Latin America for the United States.

1933 (cont.)

Armed anarchist risings in Barcelona (Jan.-Feb.) and several other cities were defeated by the Republican government; left-right polarization developed further in Spain.

d. Nicolai Nikolayevich Yudenich (b. 1862), Russian general who was commander of the northwest White Russian armies during the Russian Civil War.

d. William Robert Robertson (b. 1860), British field marshal during World War I who commanded the British occupying forces in the Rhineland (1919-1920).

1934

Joseph Stalin began the Soviet Great Purge (1934-1939), a reign of terror that would result in millions of deaths and that left his country without much of its military leadership in 1941. Stalin used as his excuse to start the purge the assassination of Leningrad Communist Party leader Sergei Kirov, probably ordered by Stalin himself.

Blood Purge (Night of the Long Knives) (June 29-30): Nazi mass murders of Ernst Roehm and the rest of the Storm Trooper (SA) leadership, as well as other out-of-favor Nazis, was ordered by Adolf Hitler as the end of a power struggle between the SA leaders and their SS (*Schutzstaffel;* Blackshirts) opponents.

Austrian chancellor Engelbert Dollfuss dissolved opposition political parties and repressed a Social Democratic–led rebellion, becoming the fascist dictator of Austria — for a while; he was assassinated by Austrian Nazis during a failed coup attempt (July 25).

French fascists used the "Stavisky affair" to develop large anti-Jewish riots, in a failed attempt to destroy the government and, with it, the Third Republic. Serge Stavisky, a Russian Jew and French financier, had committed suicide when accused of bond fraud.

d. Paul von Hindenburg (b. 1847), German World War I general who was victorious at Tannenberg; he also was eastern front commander in chief, German general staff chief (from 1916), and president of the Weimar Republic (1925-1933), until the Nazis he brought into his government took power.

d. Alexander I (b. 1888), Yugoslav ruler who was assassinated by Croatian nationalists in Marseilles, France (Oct. 9).

d. Alexander von Kluck (b. 1846), German general who commanded the First Army, at the far right of the planned sweep across the lowlands to the sea; his turn toward Paris, after German losses at Guise, allowed the Allies to stop the Germans at the Marne River (1914), one of the key events of World War I; after being injured at the front (1915), he retired (1916).

d. Oskar von Hutier (b. 1857), German general who led the Eighth Army on the Russian front, where he was the first to use intense bombardment followed by infiltration of small battle groups, later called Hutier tactics (Sept. 11-21, 1917).

In a prelude to the coming Ethiopian-Italian War, troops of both nations fought in an engagement on the Ethiopian-Italian Somaliland border (Dec. 5).

b. Jonas Savimbi, founder of the National Union for the Total Independence of Angola (UNITA) (1966).

b. Yakubu Gowon, Nigerian general who was head of state during the Nigeria-Biafra Civil War (1967-1970); deposed by coup (1975), he went into exile.

1935

German rearmament was fully under way; Germany repudiated the disarmament portions of the Treaty of Versailles (Mar. 16), making Nazi intentions very clear.

Saar Valley once again became part of Germany, after its population voted overwhelmingly for return to Germany in the plebiscite called for by the Treaty of Versailles.

Ethiopian-Italian War (Oct. 1935-May 1936): Italian forces with armor, artillery, and air support invaded and quickly defeated the poorly equipped Ethiopian army, accompanying their conquest with unopposed terror bombing, while the League of Nations and the western democ-

d. Gonnohyoe (Gombë) Yamamoto (b. 1852), Japanese admiral primarily responsible for building the Japanese navy (from ca. 1892) and obtaining for it parity with the army; he became navy minister (1898-1906) and prime minister (1913-1914; 1923).

Chinese Civil War, Long March (1934-1935): Chinese Communist forces, defeated in Kiangsi, retreated north and west 2,500 to 3,000 miles through mountainous country to Shensi; in battle with Kuomintang forces as they retreated, the Communists suffered 150,000 to 170,000 casualties and defections of the approximately 200,000 who started from Kiangsi; most Communist leaders who later took power (1949) were on this journey, including Zhu De, Mao Zedong, and Zhou Enlai.

d. Heihachiro Togo (b. 1848), Japanese admiral who, as overall commander of the Japanese fleet, orchestrated the victory at Tsushima (1905) so decisively as to effectively end the Russo-Japanese War; he became chief of the Navy General Staff (1905-1909).

d. Augusto César Sandino (b. 1893), Nicaraguan guerrilla general who was murdered by government forces while negotiating a cease-fire. He led Liberal forces during the civil war (1926-1927) and guerrillas fighting American occupation forces and the Conservative government (1927-1933); he continued to fight government forces after American withdrawal (1933). Later Nicaraguan revolutionaries called themselves "Sandinistas" after him.

In line with America's new Good Neighbor Policy, American marines were withdrawn from Haiti (Aug. 6).

Chinese Civil War: After the Long March, the Chinese Communists made their headquarters at Yenan, in Shensi, as they settled into a decade of guerrilla war against the Japanese and sometimes against the Kuomintang as well.

The U.S. Neutrality Act prohibited the provision of arms or loans to warring parties and stated that Americans sailing on their ships would not be under American protection.

Greatly reinforced Paraguayan forces defeated Bolivian forces, substantially ending the Chaco War (June).

1935 (cont.)

Anti-Jewish terror mounted in Germany with passage of the Nazi Nuremberg Laws (decrees); the Holocaust drew closer.

In a sharp reversal of policy occasioned by Soviet fear of the rise of fascism, the worldwide communist policy of a "United Front against fascism" was introduced in a speech by Bulgarian Comintern leader Georgi Dimitrov. The worldwide communist embrace of previously reviled liberals and socialists lasted only four years, until the 1939 Nazi-Soviet Pact, but it would be reintroduced two years after that, when Germany attacked the Soviet Union.

The United States, Great Britain, Japan, France, and Italy failed to make any meaningful progress at the London Naval Conference, although a treaty was signed by Britain, France, and the United States. The new arms race accelerated.

Eduard Benes became president of Czechoslovakia; he would resign after the Munich Agreement (1938).

The first practical aircraft-detecting radar was developed by Scottish physicist Robert Alexander Watson-Watt; with other technical developments, it would give the British a decided edge in the Battle of Britain.

In Greece a military coup restored George II to the throne.

d. Jósef Klemens Pilsudski (b. 1867), Polish general and independence movement leader; he was commander in chief during the Soviet-Polish War (1920) and dictator of Poland (1926-1935).

d. Alfred Dreyfus (b. 1859), French army officer of Jewish ancestry who was convicted of treason (1894); a cause célèbre resulted, and he was later pardoned (1899), then cleared (1906).

d. John Rushworth Jellicoe (b. 1859), British admiral who was commander in chief of the Home Fleet (from 1914), personally leading the fleet at Jutland (1916), then becoming first sea lord (1916-1917).

d. Julian Hedworth George Byng (b. 1862), British field marshal who commanded the Canadian Corps in Flanders, most notably in taking Vimy Ridge (1917).

racies listened to repeated pleas from King Haile Selassie I and failed to take any significant action to stop the war.

b. Hussein I, king of Jordan (r. 1953-   ), a relative moderate in Middle Eastern affairs.

d. Thomas Edward Lawrence ("Lawrence of Arabia") (b. 1883), British officer who was adviser to Faisal during the Arab War of Independence against the Turks during World War I.

1936

German troops reoccupied the Rhineland without opposition from Britain and France (Mar. 7), abrogating the Treaty of Versailles and the Locarno treaties; a major Nazi victory in the run-up to World War II.

Spanish Civil War (1936-1939): Armed forces insurrections led by fascist general Francisco Franco began (July 18), as 12 mainland and 5 Moroccan garrisons revolted. Fascist forces quickly captured much of southern Spain (July-Aug.), taking Badajoz (Aug. 15), and began the long siege of Madrid (Nov. 1936-Mar. 1939). Germany and Italy supplied substantial air and land forces and munitions to the fascists, while the Soviet Union aided the Republican side on a much smaller scale; the Soviets also organized the International Brigades, composed of anti-fascist volunteers drawn from many countries, only some of these communists. International Brigade units began to arrive in Spain in October, going into action at Madrid (Nov.). Anarchist-organized volunteer forces from many countries also fought on the Republican side. The war was widely regarded as in part a fascist "rehearsal" for World War II.

The first of the Moscow "show trials" began (1936; 1937; 1938), with old-line Bolsheviks, military leaders, and other leading Soviet citizens confessing their nonexistent crimes against the state; part of the Great Purge (1934-1939).

Ioannis Metaxas, Greek World War I commander in chief, became premier (Apr.); he took power as dictator (Aug.), ruling until his death (1941).

Ethiopian-Italian War: The capital, Addis Abbaba, fell (May), effectively ending the war; King Haile Selassi I went into exile. Italy annexed Ethiopia, which was occupied by Italian forces until Axis defeat in World War II.

Arab Revolt (1936-1939): Arabs in Palestine mounted a six-month general strike that grew into a failed guerrilla war against British occupation that was simultaneously an Arab-Jewish civil war.

Lebanese Maronite Christian Phalange Party was organized, led by Pierre Gemayel.

1935 (cont.)

b. Abimeal Guzmán Reynoso, Peruvian philosophy professor and revolutionary leader, head of the Maoist-oriented Shining Path (Sendoro Luminoso) (1970-   ).

d. Hunter Liggett (b. 1857), American general who during World War I replaced John J. Pershing as commander of the First Army (1918).

1936

February Coup (Feb. 26-28): Right-wing Japanese army officers, leading 1,400 First Division soldiers, rebelled in Tokyo, assassinating many government leaders, including finance minister Korekiyo Taka-hashi; although quickly defeated, with many of its leaders executed, the revolt was a milestone on the path to Japanese fascism and World War II.

Xian Incident (Dec. 12-25): At Xian (Sian) to lead an anti-Communist offensive, Chiang Kai-shek was held by his erstwhile ally, Manchurian warlord Chang Hsüeh-liang, until he agreed to negotiate a truce and join with Communist forces in a concerted anti-Japa-nese front; Chiang did so, and the truce held, although Chang Hsüeh-liang spent the following decades under house arrest.

d. Tuan Ch'i-jui (b. 1865), Chinese warlord who was the first war minister and several times premier or president of the Chinese republic.

United States and the other major democracies pursued an arms embargo policy toward Republican Spain, while Germany and Italy directly intervened on the fascist side.

d. William "Billy" Mitchell (b. 1879), American officer whose championing of air power over the armed services' resistance led to his court-martial for insubordination (1925); the first American officer to fly over enemy lines (May 1918), he correctly foresaw the potential of strategic bombardment and massive air strikes and was later honored for his vision.

d. William Sowden Sims (b. 1858), American admiral during World War I who introduced the British-developed method of continuous firing for greater speed and accuracy; he commanded U.S. naval forces in European waters (1917).

1936 (cont.)

France outlawed the Croix de Feu (Cross of Fire) and several other fascist and monarchist organizations that during the interwar period, and climaxing in the early 1930s, had carried massive demonstrations into street fighting aimed at bringing down French democracy; part of the run-up to World War II.

Germany and Japan signed the Anti-Comintern Pact (Nov. 25), pledging mutual assistance against the countries of the Communist International; Japan did not keep its pledge after the Germany invasion of the Soviet Union (1941). Italy joined the pact in 1937.

d. George V (b. 1865), king of Britain (r. 1910-1936); he was briefly succeeded by Edward VIII, who then abdicated (Dec. 1936), succeeded by his younger brother George VI.

d. Edmund Henry Hynman Allenby (b. 1861), British general who was commander of British Middle East forces during World War I (from 1917), taking Palestine and Syria.

d. David Beatty (b. 1871), British admiral who commanded the battle cruisers and the Fifth Battle Squadron of battleships at the Battle of Jutland (1916).

d. Hans von Seeckt (b. 1866), German general and, briefly, last chief of the general staff (July 7-15, 1919); later a Nazi sympathizer; as adviser to Chiang Kai-shek (May 1934), he sparked modernization of the Chinese army and repression of the Communists, which indirectly triggered the Long March.

1937

Spanish Civil War: International Brigade units fought at the siege of Madrid. The American Abraham Lincoln Battalion saw its first action at the Battle of Jarama, near Madrid (Feb. 17); of 450 soldiers, 120 were killed and 175 wounded. Francisco Franco's forces, with Italian troops, took Málaga (Feb. 8), but two Italian divisions were destroyed at Guadalajara, near Madrid (mid-Mar.).

Spanish Civil War: Heavy German terror-bombing attack on the defenseless and nonmilitary northern Spanish city of Guernica (Apr. 25) generated worldwide protest and was the theme of Pablo Picasso's landmark painting *Guernica*.

Spanish Civil War: In Barcelona fighting broke out between communist and anarchist Spanish Republican forces (May 3-7); the Republican government sent in forces that defeated the anarchists, with an estimated 400 to 1,000 deaths and 2,000 to 4,000 other casualties on both sides.

Spanish Civil War: Republican forces mounted a failed offensive in Aragon (Aug.-Sept.) and won a victory at Teruel (Dec. 1937-Feb. 1938) but could not hold the city.

Irish Republican leader Eamon De Valera became prime minister of Ireland.

d. Mikhail Nikolayevich Tukhachevsky (b. 1893), Soviet chief of staff during the Russian Civil War; he was a key military strategist and builder of the modern Red Army. He was executed on false treason charges in Moscow (June 11) during Stalin's Great Purge, as were most of the Soviet officer corps, leaving the Soviet armed forces very nearly leaderless to face the German attack (1941).

d. Erich Ludendorff (b. 1865), German World War I general who was chief of staff to General Paul von Hindenburg on the eastern front (1914-1915), then quartermaster general.

d. Bela Kun (b. 1886), Hungarian communist leader.

As the Arab Revolt continued and grew in Palestine, the British Peel Commission recommended the partition of that country between Arabs and Jews. Support for Palestinian Arabs grew in other Arab countries.

b. Saddam Hussein, president and dictator of Iraq (1971-   ), whose invasion of Iran (1980) triggered the Iran-Iraq War, and whose invasion of Kuwait (1990) sparked the Persian Gulf War.

1938

Anschluss: Nazi forces marched into and annexed Austria without internal or external opposition (Mar. 12); a key event in the run-up to World War II.

b. Kasdi Merbah (Abdallah Khalaf; d. 1993), Algerian opposition leader and former prime minister.

1936 (cont.)

1937

Sino-Japanese War (1937-1945) began with the Marco Polo Bridge Incident (July 7), a battle between Chinese and Japanese troops at the Marco Polo Bridge, near Peking. The planned Japanese invasion of China followed; during the rest of the year, Japanese forces took Peking, Shanghai, Nanking, and most of the north China plain; the Chinese capital was moved to Hankow.

Sino-Japanese War, Battle of Shanghai (Aug. 8-Nov. 8): Invading Japanese forces were held on their beachheads until massive Japanese reinforcements forced Chinese retreat.

Sino-Japanese War: Communist Eighth Route Army forces ambushed and defeated a Japanese division in the Battle of P'inghsingkuan (Sept. 25); though of little military significance, this boosted Chinese morale.

Sino-Japanese War: In the Panay Incident (Dec. 12), Japanese planes bombed and sank the American gunboat *Panay* in the Yangtze River, near Nanking, also bombing several other Western warships in the river; part of the run-up to World War II.

Sino-Japanese War: After the fall of Nanking, China (Dec. 13), the Japanese army committed such a wave of extraordinarily brutal atrocities that they were condemned worldwide as the "Rape of Nanking."

b. Colin Luther Powell, American general who served during the Vietnam War, eventually becoming chairman of the Joint Chiefs of Staff (1989-1993), the first African-American to hold that post.

1938

Sino-Japanese War: Japanese forces continued to advance, somewhat impeded by a Chinese victory at Taierchwang (Apr.) but going on to take Süchow and

Treaty of Buenos Aires, formally ending the Chaco War (1932-1935), awarded most of the Chaco region to Paraguay but left Bolivia with its desired outlet to the sea (July).

1938 (cont.)

Munich Agreement (Sept. 29-30): In a decisive event in the run-up to World War II, France and Britain agreed to German annexation of much of northern Czechoslovakia (the Sudetenland) without the consent of the Czechs. Prime Minister Neville Chamberlain told the British people that the capitulation had guaranteed "peace for our time." However, Germany quickly followed up by seizing all of Czechoslovakia (Mar. 1939).

Spanish Civil War: In the Battle of the Ebro (July-Aug.), Francisco Franco's Nationalist summer offensive failed to take Barcelona; a Republican counteroffensive also failed, with an estimated 70,000 Republican casualties, losses that fatally weakened Republican forces; the next Nationalist winter offensive (Jan.-Feb.) would effectively end the war.

On Crystal Night (Kristallnacht, Nov. 9-10), so named for the broken glass on the streets of Germany, German fascists attacked Jews throughout the country, smashing the windows of Jewish homes, businesses, and places of worship; thousands died, and an estimated 30,000 more Jews were imprisoned.

b. Bernt Carlsson (d. 1988), Swedish diplomat and United Nations peace negotiator.

d. Vasili Konstantinovich Blücher (b. 1889), Soviet general who as "Galen" was Soviet military adviser to Chiang Kai-shek (1924-1927), later commanding the Soviet Far Eastern Army; executed during the Great Purge, he was later "posthumously rehabilitated" (1957).

d. Mustapha Kemal (Atatürk) (b. 1881), Turkish officer, commander of Turkish forces at Gallipoli during World War I and during the following Greek-Turkish War, and commander of the revolutionary forces that ended the Ottoman Empire (1923) and established the Turkish republic; he was the first president of the republic (1919-1938), changing his name from Mustapha Kemal to Atatürk (Father of the Turks).

1939

Spanish Civil War: Barcelona fell (Jan. 26), and major elements of the loyalist army fled into French internment, ending large-scale Republican resistance in northern Spain. France and Britain recognized Francisco Franco's government (Feb. 27). Madrid and Valencia surrendered (Mar. 28), ending the war.

The final run-up to World War II continued. Germany took the rest of Czechoslovakia (Mar. 10-16), directly annexing Bohemia and Moravia, with Slovakia left as a puppet state; Britain and France did not act, although Neville Chamberlain then saw that he had been entirely mistaken at Munich (1938).

Germany annexed Memel, the Lithuanian seacoast city taken from it after World War I (Mar. 23).

Germany attempted to annex the Baltic seaport and free city of Danzig (Gdansk) and the Polish Corridor (late Mar.), but Britain and France committed themselves to come to the aid of Poland if it was attacked (Mar. 31). Not yet ready for war, the Germans withdrew.

Italy annexed Albania (Apr. 7), essentially an Italian protectorate since 1927. The threat to neighboring countries was clear; Britain and France guaranteed the independence of Romania and Greece (Apr. 13).

Germany and Italy signed the "Pact of Steel," a 10-year military and political agreement (May 22).

The surprise Nazi-Soviet Pact (German-Soviet Nonaggression Pact) (Aug. 23-24) cleared the way for the German attack on Poland. It provided for the German-Soviet partition of Poland and contained a secret agreement providing a German sphere of influence in Lithuania and Soviet spheres of influence in Finland, Latvia, Estonia, and Bessarabia.

World War II (1939-1945): War began (Sept. 1), with an invasion of Poland by three German army groups totaling 60 divisions and 1 million to 1.25 million men, commanded by generals Walther von Brauchitsch, Fedor von Bock, and Gerd von Rundstedt; they were led by armored formations using the new blitzkrieg tactics, with armor pushing through and bypassing fixed defensive posi-

St. James Conference on Palestine was aborted in London when Arabs and Jews could not even agree on the terms of face-to-face meetings. The British government issued — and both sides rejected — a White Paper (May) calling for the independence of Palestine within 10 years, limiting current Jewish land purchases in Palestine, and limiting Jewish immigration into Palestine. As the European war unfolded, and with it the prospect of the Middle East once again becoming a theater of war, the 3-year Arab Revolt in Palestine waned; the guerrilla war then became a series of skirmishes and bombings conducted by both sides.

Haj Amin al Husseini, grand mufti of Jerusalem, went to Iraq, beginning the long association with the Nazis that would take him to Germany during World War II.

World War II: Pro-Nazi South African National Party prime minister James Hertzog resigned after unsuccessfully opposing entry into World War II; he was succeeded by Jan Smuts, who then took South Africa into the war on the Allied side.

British officer John Bagot Glubb (Glubb Pasha) took command of Jordan's army, the Arab Legion.

b. Joaquim Alberto Chissanó, Mozambican guerrilla general and president (1986-   ).

1938 (cont.)

Kaifeng (May-June). The Japanese offensive in north-central China was stopped for two months by Chinese breaching of the Yellow River dikes (June), which also caused massive damage on the Yellow River floodplain. Japanese seaborne forces took Canton (Oct.), completing their conquest of the entire south China coast. Hankow fell after very heavy resistance (Oct.); the Chinese capital was moved to Chungking in southwest China. Communist forces fought an anti-Japanese guerrilla war in north China.

At disputed Changkufeng Hill, on the Siberian-Manchurian border, Japanese forces made a protracted, unsuccessful assault on Soviet positions.

b. Manuel Antonio Noriega, Panamanian general and dictator (1982-1989); deposed by the 1989 American invasion of Panama and then imprisoned in the United States on drug trade charges.

1939

The Japanese Kwangtung Army, then occupying Manchuria, attacked Soviet and Mongolian forces holding disputed territory along the Khalkin River (May). The Japanese attacked in divisional strength (15,000 to 20,000); three Soviet and Mongolian divisions, including several armored brigades, in all numbering 60,000 to 70,000 and commanded by General Georgi Zhukov, successfully counterattacked, reoccupying and holding the disputed territory. Their elite forces badly beaten, the Japanese withdrew, ending the undeclared war (Sept.).

Sino-Japanese War: Japanese bombings of Chungking and other Chinese cities caused tens of thousands of casualties.

Sino-Japanese War: The 700-mile Burma Road opened, from Lashio, Burma, to Kunming, China; it was built by the Chinese republic to carry supplies arriving at Rangoon and sent on by train to Lashio.

Sino-Japanese War: Japanese forces captured Hainan Island (Feb.), going on to take most of the remaining Chinese ports; the Chinese Republic centered on Chungking was supplied along the Burma Road and from Haiphong, then in French Indochina.

Sino-Japanese War: On the ground in China, the Japanese offensive stalled after early spring gains. Chinese republican resistance hardened, rather than collapsing, and Communist resistance in northern China strengthened.

After their border war defeat by Soviet and Mongolian forces and their lack of progress in China, the Japanese

Western scientists laid the foundation for the development of the atomic bomb, as war threatened in Europe. In America, Niels Bohr, John Wheeler, and others worked with fission occurring in uranium-235 (U-235). Hans Bethe proposed that the energy of the sun and stars came from nuclear fusion, an understanding basic to the later development of the hydrogen bomb.

Refugee Italian Nobel Prize winner Enrico Fermi, who would in 1942 create the first chain reaction, learned of German atomic experiments and pressed for America to develop an atomic bomb before the Germans could do so. At the request of Fermi and others, Albert Einstein wrote to President Franklin D. Roosevelt (Aug. 2), calling the atomic bomb feasible and urging its development; his letter began the series of events and body of research that would eventuate in the atomic bomb.

Convinced after the Munich Agreement (1938) that world war was coming, Roosevelt moved the United States into large-scale rearmament, asking Congress (Jan. 4) for $552 million in defense appropriations and getting $549 million. He announced that he had authorized the sale of airplanes to France (Jan. 27). The aircraft carrier *Wasp* was launched (Apr. 4), and the War Department ordered 571 warplanes (late Apr.). The United States also repudiated its 1911 trade treaty with Japan, somewhat cutting the flow of vital war materials to that country.

Roosevelt demanded assurances from Germany and Italy that they would not attack 31 named nations (Apr. 15); no assurances were forthcoming.

World War II: General George Marshall was appointed chief of staff of the U.S. Army (Apr. 27) and began to organize the run-up to American participation in the war, including cooperation, much of it covert, with his British counterparts.

tions. The ground attack was accompanied by powerful air attacks, using 1,400 to 1,600 warplanes, which caught and destroyed most of the small Polish air force on the ground. Cracow fell (Sept. 6), as did Brest-Litovsk (Sept. 17). In the Battle of Warsaw, German armor besieged the city, which held out for three weeks (Sept. 8-27). The Hel naval base on the Baltic fell (Oct. 1), and so did the last major pocket of resistance, at Kock (Oct. 5). Some smaller pockets of resistance held out until early November.

World War II: Britain and France called for German withdrawal from Poland and, that failing, declared war on Germany (Sept. 3); they were quickly joined by Australia, New Zealand, and Canada, early members of what would become a huge worldwide alliance against fascism. Britain and France made no serious move to send aid to Poland, however, and did not attack light German forces in the west. Italy declared itself neutral.

World War II: Soviet troops invaded Poland from the east (Sept. 17), taking part of the country; German forces met them at the partition line specified by the Nazi-Soviet Pact. The pact was then amended (Sept. 28), giving Germany more of Poland and ceding Lithuania to the Soviet Union. Soviet forces invaded and took Latvia, Lithuania, and Estonia (Oct. 10).

World War II: The Battle of the Atlantic began. By year's end, German submarines had sunk more than 250 ships, beginning with the torpedoing of the passenger ship *Athenia*, sunk without warning by the German submarine *U-30* off Ireland (Sept. 3) on the same day Britain declared war; 112 people died. Other notable sinkings were those of the British aircraft carrier *Courageous* (Sept. 17), with 515 dead, and the British battleship *Royal Oak*, sunk by the German submarine *U-47* in the harbor of Scapa Flow (Oct. 14), with 786 dead. The German battleship *Deutschland* and the heavy cruisers *Scharnhorst* and *Gneisenau* also raided in the North Atlantic, as did the pocket battleship *Graf Spee*.

Finnish-Soviet War (1939-1940): War began (Nov. 30) after Finland refused Soviet demands for military bases. Soviet bombers attacked Helsinki and Viipuri, and ground forces numbering approximately 1 million invaded Finland by land and sea. In heavy early fighting, the Finns held the Soviets on all fronts, inflicting large losses at the Mannerheim Line, repulsing amphibious attacks on Finland's southern coast, and stopping attacking Soviet forces in the north after a brief early advance.

Finnish-Soviet War: At the Battle of Suomussalmi (Dec. 1939-Jan. 1940), Finnish forces defeated much more numerous Soviet forces; in heavy fighting, the Red Army lost 25,000 to 30,000 men, most of two divisions, with Finnish losses of fewer than 1,000.

World War II: On the western front, the French army and a British expeditionary force, which would number 400,000 by May 1940, sat out the year on the Maginot Line, with only light French probing attacks in the Saar Valley, beginning the "Phony War" period.

Lise Meitner, a German scientist exiled by the Nazis, published the first report describing the splitting of the uranium atom, naming it *nuclear fission.* Jean Frederic Joliot-Curie first recognized the possibility of a chain reaction in the nuclear fission of uranium, one of the series of discoveries that would lead to the development of the atom bomb (1945); along with others, he and his wife, co–Nobel Prize winner Irène Joliot-Curie, explored the possibility of producing a chain reaction, until war came; then the Joliot-Curies stayed on in France to fight in the Resistance, hiding their store of uranium and smuggling their store of precious heavy water out of the country for safety.

d. Werner von Fritsch (b. 1880), German general and chief of staff (1934-1938); he was killed in action at the Battle of Warsaw (Sept. 22).

d. Roger Roland Charles Backhouse (b. 1878), British admiral, first sea lord, and chief of the naval staff (Feb. 1938-July 1939).

turned decisively toward the invasion of Indochina and the coming war in the Pacific.

At Tientsin, the British concession was blockaded by Japanese forces (June 14); ultimately, the British gave up several Chinese in sanctuary and made other concessions.

Isoroku Yamamoto was appointed commander in chief of the Japanese fleet and began preparations for the invasion of Indochina and the coming war in the Pacific.

d. Wu P'ei-fu (b. ca. 1873), chief warlord of northern and central China in the early 1920s until he was defeated by rival warlord Chang Tso-lin (1924), then finished off by the Kuomintang during its Northern Expedition (1926).

d. Norman Bethune (b. 1899), Canadian doctor who was a battlefront surgeon with Chinese Communist forces (1937-1939), dying at the front; he became a revolutionary hero in the Chinese Communist pantheon.

d. Hsu Shih-chang (b. 1858), Chinese general and politician; president of China (1918-1922).

World War II: Roosevelt formally declared U.S. neutrality in the European war then in progress (Sept. 5) but hastened rearmament.

World War II: Arms exports were authorized by the Neutrality Act of 1939 (Nov. 4), and the United States began openly selling arms to the Allies.

Japanese naval officer and diplomat Kichisaburo Nomura became ambassador to the United States.

In Peru, a military coup failed (Feb.); coup leader General Antonio Rodríguez was killed during the action.

In Chile, General Ariosto Herrera and Carlos Ibánez led a failed coup attempt (Aug.).

World War II, Battle of the River Plate (Dec. 13): Three British cruisers caught up with the German pocket battleship *Graf Spee* at the mouth of the River Plate; the German ship had been raiding in the Atlantic and Indian Oceans (from early Sept.). The *Graf Spee* disabled the heavy cruiser *Exeter* and severely damaged two light cruisers, but was itself damaged and forced to make port in Montevideo, Uruguay. Ultimately, the *Graf Spee* was scuttled by its crew outside the harbor.

d. Germán Busch (b. 1904), Bolivian general, president, and dictator for several months before his suicide.

d. Edwin Burr Babbitt (b. 1862), American general.

d. Hans Anton Kundt (b. 1869), German commander of Bolivian forces during the Chaco War.

d. Jonathan Edmund Browning (b. 1859), American arms inventor.

d. Mark Lambert Bristol (b. 1868), American admiral.

1939 (cont.)

d. Hans Langsdorff (b. 1894), commander of the *Graf Spee,* who was interned in Argentina after sinking his ship on orders from Berlin; he committed suicide (Dec. 20).

d. Anthony Herman Gerard Fokker (b. 1890), Dutch airplane designer and manufacturer who supplied the German air force with fighter planes during World War I.

d. James Frederick Noel Birch (b. 1865), British general.

d. Magnus F. W. von Eberhardt (b. 1855), German general.

1940

Finnish-Soviet War: A new Soviet offensive breached the Mannerheim Line (Feb.); unable to resist further, the Finns gave up (Mar.), granting the Soviet Union the bases that had been the original cause of the war.

World War II, Battle of Norway (Apr.-June): German forces attacked Norway (Apr. 9), landing on both coasts, taking Oslo (Apr. 10), and easily defeating Norwegian forces, who had no air cover. Allied forces landed near Trondheim and Narvik (Oct. 15), but without significant air support; they took Narvik (May) but were forced to withdraw (June 8-9).

World War II: German forces took Denmark, meeting very little opposition (Apr. 9). Notably, unlike most other defeated countries, the Danes would protect the Jews in their country from capture, smuggling many of them abroad to neutral Sweden.

World War II, Katyn Massacre: In the Soviet-occupied portion of Poland, in the Katyn Forest, Soviet troops murdered an estimated 10,000 Polish prisoners, including most of the Polish officer corps. The Soviets blamed the massacre on the Germans until the advent of the new noncommunist Russian government (1990).

World War II, Battle of Flanders (May 10-June 4): German forces took France and the Low Countries in the battle, which began with the German invasion of Belgium, Holland, and northern France. The Maginot Line, which did not go from the Alps to the sea, as had the World War I battle line, proved no obstacle at all to mobile German forces with air superiority and armored spearheads using blitzkrieg tactics.

World War II: German forces took Holland in four days (May 10-14), pushing on through unsuccessful Dutch and French resistance even though the Dutch flooded the countryside by breaching their dikes; the Dutch surrendered (May 14).

World War II: German aircraft bombed and destroyed much of Rotterdam (May 13), a Dutch nonmilitary target; the terror bombing was aimed at destroying the Allied will to resist the German drive into France and the Low Countries.

World War II, Battle of Ardennes (May 12-15): In the decisive battle of the early war in the west, German armored forces, preceded by dive-bombers, broke through ineffective French opposition near Sedan, in a strategic move much like that of 1870. The German panzers crossed the Meuse River (May 12) and in the three days that followed smashed and split opposing French armies, then swiftly drove to the Channel ports.

World War II: In his first address to Britain's House of Commons as prime minister (May 13), Winston Churchill gave an inspiring speech, saying, "I have nothing to offer but blood, toil, tears, and sweat." He had succeeded Neville Chamberlain, who had resigned.

World War II: After the fall of France, French naval forces in Africa became a source of British concern. British naval forces sank three French battleships and other warships anchored at Oran, Algeria, rather than let the vessels fall into German hands (July 4). British naval forces also attacked French warships at Mers-el-Kebir, Algeria, after French refusal either to join the Allies or to sink or disable their own ships (July 3-4). French naval forces at Alexandria put themselves out of action.

World War II: British and Free French forces made a failed assault by sea on Dakar, in French West Africa (now Senegal) (Sept. 22-25), but were turned back by the Vichy French garrison.

World War II, Western Desert Campaign (Dec. 9, 1940-Feb. 7, 1941): The British-Italian conflict in North Africa began with a British victory over Italian forces four times their size at Sidi Barrani; the Italians were routed, and 38,000 prisoners were taken (Dec. 9). Pursuing British forces took Bardia and Tobruk (early Jan.), with an unconditional surrender of Italian forces following (Feb. 7). The final Italian prisoner count was 130,000, with fewer than 2,000 British casualties.

In Palestine, Abraham Stern founded the terrorist Stern Gang (Lehi; Fighters for the Freedom of Israel); Stern was killed by British forces (1942), but his organization continued.

d. Vladimir Jabotinsky (b. 1880), founder of the Zionist Revisionist movement, whose ideology was basic to the terrorist Irgun Zvai Leumi.

1939 (cont.)

1940

Mohammad Ali Jinnah, head of India's Muslim League, made a historic break with the Indian independence movement, demanding the establishment of an independent Islamic state of Pakistan; this began a sequence of events that led to the catastrophic partition of India and decades of war and cold war between Pakistan and India.

Sino-Japanese War: Japanese forces made a decisive turn south and away from war with the Soviet Union, taking Indochina (Sept.) and then attacking unconquered areas of China from the south. In north and central China, the war became largely a stalemate. Communist forces continued their anti-Japanese war in the north, mounting large numbers of guerrilla attacks (late summer-early autumn), collectively called the Hundred Regiments Offensive.

Wang Tsing-wei, a former aide to Sun Yat-sen and in the 1930s president of the Kuomintang, was installed (Mar.) as head of the Nanking-based Japanese puppet government.

American president Franklin Roosevelt was elected to an unprecedented third term, winning a landslide victory over Republican Wendell Willkie (Nov.). In a radio broadcast (Dec. 29), he said, "We must be the great arsenal of democracy."

World War II: In a "destroyers-for-bases" swap, the United States covertly gave Britain 50 badly needed destroyers, ostensibly in return for British bases in the Americas (Sept.). The American destroyers immediately entered the Battle of the Atlantic.

Plutonium, an essential element in atomic weapons and nuclear reactors, was discovered by Glenn Seaborg and his colleagues. Enrico Fermi later demonstrated how to produce it (1942).

Congress passed the Alien Registration Act (Smith Act), requiring all aliens to register and be fingerprinted; the act, which also declared illegal membership in any organization advocating the overthrow of the government, was used during the war against some dissenters and again after the war to prosecute suspected American communists.

As war loomed, Congress passed the Selective Service Act (Sept. 16); it was the first peacetime conscription act in American history.

The United States placed an embargo on scrap iron and steel shipments to Japan (Sept.), as the unlimited nature of Japanese aggressive plans became evident; war with Japan drew near.

Benjamin Oliver Davis became the first African-American general in the American army.

d. William Sidney Graves (b. 1865), American general who commanded American forces in Vladivostok and Siberia (Aug. 1918-Apr. 1920).

1940 (cont.)

World War II: The German XIX Panzer Corps reached the Atlantic coast near Abbeville (May 21), thereby splitting Allied forces and making their remaining positions in France and the Low Countries untenable. The Belgian army surrendered (May 28).

World War II: At Dunkirk (May 28-June 4), British naval forces and a flotilla of large and small ships evacuated the British Expeditionary Force of 220,000, approximately 130,000 French, and small numbers of Belgian troops, ferrying them from France to Britain.

World War II, Battle of France (June 5-25): German mopping-up actions in France followed the allied defeat in the Battle of Flanders and the Dunkirk evacuation; Paris, an open city, fell (June 14), and France surrendered (June 21; effective June 25).

World War II: After the fall of France, the London-based Free French government-in-exile was formed, led by Charles De Gaulle (June).

World War II: After France fell, the German puppet Vichy government was set up to rule "unoccupied France," led by collaborators Philippe Pétain (the World War I general) and (from Apr. 1942) Pierre Laval.

World War II: Italy entered the war as a German ally (June 10). Italian bombers attacked Malta (June 11), beginning the long, unsuccessful Axis siege of the Mediterranean island. Benito Mussolini prepared for the invasion of Greece and for an African campaign aimed at seizing the Suez Canal.

World War II: Soviet forces formally took Bessarabia and northern Bukovina (June 26-28), with no opposition.

World War II, Battle of Britain (Aug.-Oct.): In a sustained series of air battles, the Royal Air Force (RAF) defeated massive German air attacks aimed at achieving supremacy over the English Channel and Britain, an essential element of Adolf Hitler's British invasion plans (Operation Sea Lion). Although severely damaged, with a loss of more than 900 planes, the RAF won decisively, destroying more than 1,700 German planes and frustrating the invasion. Of the RAF, Winston Churchill said, "Never, in the field of human conflict, was so much owed by so many to so few." The defeated Luftwaffe then began the Blitz (Nov. 1940-May 1941), the ultimately ineffectual terror bombing of British cities, which would kill an estimated 43,000 noncombatants. Stopped in the west, Hitler turned east.

World War II: The British began night bombing raids on Berlin (Aug. 24), largely as a morale boost.

World War II: German forces took Romania's Ploesti oil fields, of great importance to the German war machine (Oct. 8).

World War II: In a supersecret system code-named Ultra, British cryptographers broke the code of the German "Enigma" machine, which Germany believed throughout the war was unbreakable; Polish scientists had smuggled early versions of the Enigma machine to safety before their country fell (1939), giving the Allies a notable advantage.

World War II: In an action code-named Moonlight Sonata, German terror bombers struck at Coventry (Nov. 14-15); the destroyed city became a rallying point for British resistance to the Germans. Not until many years after the war would it be revealed that the British knew (through their Ultra code-breaking system) of the attack but dared not show their knowledge.

World War II, Battle of the Atlantic: German submarines, supplemented by German surface raiders, sank scores of Allied freighters totaling several million tons, even though the convoy system was in operation.

World War II: German-Japanese-Italian Tripartite Pact (Sept. 27) formally established their alliance.

World War II: Romanian fascist Ion Antonescu took power, bringing Romania into the war as a German ally.

World War II: Italian forces concentrated in Albania attacked Greece (Oct. 28) and were quickly defeated; a Greek counteroffensive (Nov.) forced the Italians back into Albania, with the pursuing Greeks inflicting massive losses.

British troops based in North Africa occupied Crete (Oct. 30).

British carrier-based bombers sank three Italian battleships and damaged other Italian warships at Taranto, Italy (Nov. 11), with the loss of only two British bombers.

d. Leon Trotsky (Lev Davidovich Bronstein) (b. 1879), Bolshevik leader, commander in chief of communist forces during the October Revolution, and founder and commander in chief of the Red Army during the Russian Civil War; expelled from the Communist Party and Soviet Union after unsuccessfully opposing the rise of Joseph Stalin, he was assassinated by Soviet agents in Mexico City (Aug. 20).

d. Neville Chamberlain (b. 1869), British prime minister (1937-1940) whose policy of appeasement, most notably at Munich (1938), contributed to the rise of Adolf Hitler and the onset of World War II.

World War II, Battle of Cape Matapan (Mar. 28): The British Mediterranean Fleet decisively defeated Italian naval forces, which lost the heavy cruiser *Pola*, two other cruisers, and four destroyers; the battleship *Vittorio Veneto* suffered major damage.

World War II: German forces invaded Yugoslavia (Apr. 6) and took the country in less than two weeks with minimal losses. Zagreb was taken (Apr. 10), as were Belgrade (Apr. 12) and Sarajevo (Apr. 15), with Yugoslav surrender following (Apr. 17). Yugoslav casualties were in the 50,000 to 100,000 range, with 250,000 to 300,000 prisoners taken, while German losses were fewer than 1,000. Yugoslav guerrilla resistance movements began quickly, with communist-led Partisan forces led by Tito (Josip Broz) and Chetnik forces led by Draza Mihajlovic fighting the Axis forces and often each other as well.

World War II: German forces invaded Greece (Apr. 6) and quickly took the country, despite the presence of substantial British forces. The Greek army surrendered (Apr. 17), having suffered 50,000 to 70,000 casualties, with an estimated 250,000 prisoners taken. British forces of 43,000 were evacuated by sea; there were 12,000 British casualties. German casualties were 4,000 to 5,000.

World War II: Nazi leader Rudolph Hess parachuted into Britain (May) to propose an Anglo-German peace and an anti-Soviet alliance. Hess was imprisoned, convicted a war criminal at Nuremberg (1946), and died at Spandau Prison (1986).

World War II: A massive German airborne invasion, the first such major airborne attack ever made, took Crete (May 20-31). Surviving British forces were

World War II: British forces attacked and destroyed much larger Italian forces in East Africa. Invading Ethiopia and Eritrea from the Sudan, South African and colonial forces defeated Italian forces at Agordat (Jan.) and pushed to the sea, taking Massawa (early Apr.). Invading from Kenya, South African and colonial forces took Mogadishu and Harar, then Addis Abbaba (Apr. 4); Italian East African forces surrendered (May 18). The British took more than 50,000 Italian prisoners in the brief campaign, with losses of fewer than 500.

World War II: British forces invaded Syria (June 8), quickly taking Damascus (June 21), after which Vichy French Syrian forces surrendered (July).

World War II: The German Africa Korps, led by General Erwin Rommel and with substantial air support, arrived in Libya (late Mar.), immediately taking German and Italian forces into a protracted North African offensive. Rommel took El Agheila (Mar. 24) and initiated an ultimately failed six-month siege of the fortress of Tobruk (Apr.-Dec.). A brief British counteroffensive was stopped (mid-June). British forces went on the offensive (Nov. 18), pushing the Germans back to El Agheila (by year's end).

Central, South and East Asia, and
the Pacific

The Americas

New Fourth Army Incident (Jan. 6): Kuomintang forces breached the Communist-Kuomintang anti-Japanese truce, attacking and destroying the headquarters of the Communist New Fourth Army, with thousands of Communist casualties; the truce held, but it was clear that civil war would quickly resume if the Japanese threat lessened.

Hideki Tojo became premier of Japan (Oct. 17).

World War II: At Pearl Harbor (Dec. 7), on Oahu, Hawaii, 360 Japanese carrier-based aircraft, from an attack force that put to sea November 25, surprised the American Pacific Fleet at anchor and American aircraft on the ground, sinking 3 battleships, capsizing 1, and disabling 4 more, while also sinking many other vessels, destroying more than 250 aircraft, and causing more than 5,000 casualties; Japanese losses were minimal. All three major American carriers — the *Lexington, Saratoga,* and *Enterprise* — were at sea and undamaged, surviving to destroy the Japanese carrier fleet at Midway six months later (June 4-6, 1942) in the most decisive naval battle of World War II.

World War II, Battle of the Philippines (Dec. 1941-May 1942): Despite the warning of Pearl Harbor, most American aircraft were destroyed on the ground at Clark Field (Dec. 8); Japanese amphibious landings began (Dec. 10), followed by main force landings on Luzon (from Dec. 22). Manila surrendered (Dec. 26), as Japanese forces pursued American and Philippine forces south to Bataan.

In his State of the Union speech, Franklin Roosevelt put forth the Four Freedoms: freedom of speech and expression, freedom of worship, freedom from want, and freedom from fear of war (Jan. 6).

World War II: The American Lend-Lease Act (Mar. 11) authorized President Roosevelt to send massive American aid to Britain, the Soviet Union, and other Allied countries. All Japanese assets in the United States were frozen (July 26). The immense American war production effort continued to develop, going all-out after the Japanese attack on Pearl Harbor (Dec. 7).

World War II: The American destroyer *Reuben James* was torpedoed in the North Atlantic while on convoy duty (Oct. 31); it was the first American warship sunk in World War II, before the United States entered the war.

World War II: After the Japanese attack on Pearl Harbor, Hawaii (Dec. 7), the United States declared war on Japan (Dec. 8). In support of their Japanese ally, Germany and Italy declared war on the United States (Dec. 11).

Victor Paz Estenssoro founded the Nationalist Revolutionary Movement Party in Bolivia.

World War II: Roosevelt and Winston Churchill's Arcadia Conference (Dec. 1941-Jan. 1942), held in Washington, set the war in the West as the highest priority, with the Pacific war to be largely defensive for the present; the conference also established the Combined Chiefs of Staff. As a practical matter, American war production quickly became so massive as to be able to supply the war in the West, the Russians, and the Pacific war.

1941 (cont.)

evacuated by sea after suffering more than 17,000 casualties to German losses of fewer than 6,000.

World War II: In an operation code-named Barbarossa, German forces invaded the Soviet Union (June 22), overwhelming frontier forces; by July, on the central front, the Germans took Minsk, Smolensk, and almost 400,000 prisoners, more than 4,000 tanks, and massive ordnance. On the southern front, they took Kiev and threatened Sevastopol, taking 650,000 more prisoners and at least as much armor and artillery. In the north, they began the long, unsuccessful siege of Leningrad, which would eventually be relieved (1944) after an estimated 750,000 to 1 million people had died.

World War II: At Vyazma (Sept. 30-Oct. 7), advancing German Army Group Center forces took more than 600,000 more Soviet prisoners.

World War II: In the Battle of Moscow (Nov.-Dec.), German forces neared the city (Oct.), regrouped, and attacked, penetrating into Moscow's suburbs, after which Semën Budënny was replaced by Semën Timoshenko as Soviet commander. Moscow held, greatly aided by the arrival of major forces from the Soviet far east (Nov.), led by Georgi Zhukov; a successful Soviet counteroffensive then began (Dec. 6).

World War II: On the southern front in Russia, the German advance stalled at Rostov, where Soviet counterattacks pushed back attacking German armor (Nov. 15).

World War II: German attacks intensified in the Battle of the Atlantic, with submarines often attacking Allied convoys in "wolf packs" of 10 to 20 vessels. German surface raiders continued to be active, as were long-range bombers based in Norway and Denmark. Fighters from the first British escort carrier, the *Audacity,* began to combat the German bombers effectively (Sept.), and many escort carriers later went into action.

World War II: The German battleship *Bismarck,* pursued by British ships, sank the battle cruiser *Hood,* damaged the battleship *Prince of Wales* in Denmark Strait (May 24), and was itself damaged. Pursuing British ships found the *Bismarck* (May 26), sinking it two days later (May 28).

World War II: German submarines attacking an Atlantic convoy sank the British aircraft carrier *Ark Royal* (Nov.).

d. Kaiser Wilhelm II (b. 1859), German emperor (r. 1888-1918) who abdicated and fled to Holland after the German Revolution (1918).

d. Ioannis Metaxas (b. 1871), Greek general and military dictator (r. Aug. 1936-Jan. 1941).

d. Robert Stephenson Smyth Baden-Powell (b. 1857), British general and founder of the Boy Scouts; he commanded British forces at besieged Mafeking (1899-1900) during the Boer War.

Jewish forces in Palestine organized the Palmach, a commando strike force that would play a major role during the Israeli War of Independence (1948-1949); some Palmach units fought beside British forces in the Middle East.

World War II: The Allies forced the abdication of Reza Shah Pahlevi after he refused to enter World War II on their side; he was succeeded by his son Muhammed Reza Shah Pahlevi, who reigned until 1979.

1942

World War II: With the United States in the war and American industrial strength quickly turned to war production, American ships, armaments, supplies, and fighting strength began to pour into Britain, while massive armaments and supplies also went to the Soviet Union via Murmansk and Archangel. American and British forces began the long buildup to the invasion of Europe, although there were sharp disagreements as to whether 1943 would see a cross-Channel assault or strikes into Europe from the Mediterranean.

World War II: British commandos raided St. Nazaire on the French coast, suffering heavy losses while damaging the waterfront area.

World War II: At El Agheila, General Erwin Rommel's forces went on the offensive (Jan. 21), breaking through British Eighth Army defensive positions and forcing a British retreat to the Bir Hacheim–Gazala British defensive line. There Rommel successfully attacked again; the Battle of Bir Hacheim (May 28-June 13) became the beginning of a long British retreat into Egypt. Tobruk and its garrison of 33,000 fell (June 21), as the Germans pursued the

Central, South and East Asia, and the Pacific	The Americas

World War II: Japanese bombers struck Wake Island (Dec. 8); the first Japanese amphibious attack failed (Dec. 11), but the second took the lightly garrisoned island (Dec. 23).

World War II: Japanese forces began a bombardment of Hong Kong (Dec. 8), landed (Dec. 18), and quickly defeated the British defenders, who surrendered (Dec. 25).

World War II, Battle of Malaya (Dec. 1941-Jan. 1942): Japanese forces invaded northern Malaya (Dec. 8) and moved south toward Singapore.

World War II: Japanese forces took Guam (Dec. 10).

World War II: Japanese land-based aircraft easily sank the British battleship *Prince of Wales* and the battle cruiser *Repulse,* both operating off the coast of Malaya without air support (Dec. 10).

Ho Chi Minh organized the League for the Independence of Vietnam (Vietminh).

Norodom Sihanouk became king of Cambodia (r. 1941-1955).

World War II: Franklin Roosevelt and Winston Churchill, meeting off Newfoundland, put forward the Atlantic Charter, affirming joint world peace, freedom, and self-determination as war aims (Aug. 9-12). Much of the language in the statement was later included in the United Nations Charter.

b. Oscar Arias Sánchez, Costa Rican president in the mid-1980s; he was a major contributor to peace in the area and winner of the 1987 Nobel Peace Prize.

World War II, Battle of the Philippines: American forces on Bataan surrendered (Apr. 9), as did besieged Corregidor (May 6), while guerrilla warfare continued. After the surrender of Corregidor, Japanese forces captured and brutally mistreated American and Philippine soldiers, many of them wounded and ill, on a long march to their prison camps, many of them dying en route; this was the Bataan Death March, a war crime later prosecuted.

World War II: Americans began to develop the Manhattan Project (1942-1945), their massive effort to build the first atomic bomb. In a historic breakthrough that ushered in the nuclear age, physicist Enrico Fermi and his Manhattan Project group, working in a squash court at the University of Chicago, took the key step in the development of the atomic bomb: creating the first chain reaction in the first nuclear reactor (Dec. 2).

World War II: Under America's Executive Order 9066 (Feb. 19), 110,000 Pacific Coast Japanese-Americans were interned in concentration camps; official apology for the act came only in 1976.

1942 (cont.)

World War II: Following up on their victory at Moscow, Soviet forces went on the offensive (Jan.) on the whole eastern front, advancing but not breaking through and rolling up defending German forces. The answering German spring offensive reversed most Soviet gains, and in the south German forces reached and besieged Sevastopol.

World War II: Massive British night bombing of Cologne used 1,000 planes for the first time.

World War II: Nazi Gestapo head Reinhard Heydrich (Heydrich the Hangman) was assassinated in Czechoslovakia; in reprisal, the Germans destroyed the entire village of Lidice, murdered all the men over 16, and sent the rest of its 1,200 people to concentration camps.

World War II: American air attacks on "Fortress Europe" began (July), growing throughout the year as massive American air strength began to build up in Britain.

World War II: In German summer offensives (late June), Army Group South moved on the Don Basin and toward the Caucasus Mountains. Sevastopol was taken by assault (July 2); Veronezh fell on July 6; Rostov fell on July 23.

World War II: Canadian and British forces made a failed cross-Channel attack on Dieppe (Aug. 19), withdrawing with more than 3,000 casualties out of a force of 6,000.

World War II, Battle of Stalingrad (Aug. 23, 1942-Feb. 2, 1943): Protracted house-to-house infantry combat between attacking German Sixth Army forces and Soviet defenders stalled the German summer offensive advance on the southern front for three months, while Soviet forces built up on the German flanks; when the massive Soviet counteroffensive began (Nov. 19), a pincers movement trapped 250,000 to 300,000 Germans, with the survivors surrendering (Feb. 2, 1943). This was the pivotal battle of the war on the eastern front.

World War II: Despite the sinking of more than 1 million tons of Allied shipping during the year, American and British naval and air forces began to win the Battle of the Atlantic, as American war production continued to surge and huge quantities of American war materials reached the Soviet Union and Britain, while the German submarine fleet diminished.

World War II: Operation Bodyguard, a group of deceptions aimed at misleading the Germans as to Allied European invasion plans, began (1942-1944).

World War II: Mass executions began at Auschwitz-Birkenau (Oświecim), a German concentration camp complex in Poland; at least 2 million people, most of them Jews from Poland and the Soviet Union, were murdered there by the Germans (1942-1944).

d. Louis Félix François Franchet D'Esperey (b. 1856), marshal of France who was active during World War I, especially at the Battles of the Frontiers (1914), as well as at Charleroi, Guise, and the Marne.

British to a new defensive line at Adam Halfa. Rommel's forces attacked again at Adam Halfa (Aug.) but were unable to break through.

World War II, Battle of El Alamein (Oct. 23-Nov. 4): Allied forces, now led by British general Bernard Montgomery, went on the offensive in Egypt, decisively defeating Rommel's forces, with estimated German and Italian losses of more than 90,000 and reported Allied losses of 13,000. Montgomery's forces slowly pursued the retreating Axis forces, which were able to withdraw in good order despite fuel and ammunition shortages.

World War II: British forces assaulted and took Madagascar from Vichy French forces (Sept.-Nov.).

World War II: In Operation Torch (Nov. 8-11), American troops made successful amphibious landings at Casablanca, Oran, and Algiers, overcoming light Vichy French resistance in all three locations. Allied forces then moved swiftly to take the main German North African base at Tunis but were stopped by its defenders.

World War II: French naval officer and Nazi collaborator Jean François Darlan, who had shifted sides once again after his capture by Allied forces in North Africa, was assassinated (Dec. 24).

b. Muammar al-Qaddafi, Libyan head of state who seized power by coup (1969).

d. Chris Hani (Martin Thembisile Hani; b. 1942), General Secretary of the South African Communist Party.

World War II, Battle of Malaya: Japanese forces completed their conquest of Malaya, facing Singapore (Jan. 31).

World War II, Battle of Singapore (Feb. 8-15): Japanese forces, with air cover, attacked Singapore, whose fortifications faced the sea, from the Malayan mainland across the Strait of Johore (Feb. 8), quickly taking the heavily fortified city; its garrison of 70,000 surrendered after the Japanese captured the city's water supply (Feb. 15).

World War II: Japanese forces invaded Burma (Jan. 12), defeated British-led forces at Moulmein (Jan.) and on the Sittang River (Feb.), and took Lashio (Apr.) and Mandalay (May 1); defending forces retreated to Imphal, in Bengal (Bangladesh), and Chinese forces sent to aid the British retreated to Yunnan. The Japanese capture of Lashio closed the Burma Road until 1944, with the Chinese Republic then being supplied by an American air route (over the "hump") to Kunming (from June).

World War II: Japanese seaborne invasions (Jan.-Mar.) took Indonesia, then the Dutch East Indies, with strong Dutch resistance coming only on Java (Feb.-Mar.), but without air support. At the Battle of the Java Sea (Feb. 27), Japanese forces destroyed most of the small Dutch-American naval force that opposed their drive south. Dutch forces in the East Indies surrendered (Mar. 9).

World War II: In the Indian Ocean, Japanese carrier-based aircraft sank several British ships at Trincomalee and Colombo, including an aircraft carrier and two cruisers (Apr.).

World War II: American carrier-based B-25s led by Lieutenant Colonel James Doolittle bombed Tokyo and other Japanese cities (Apr. 18).

World War II: Japanese forces attacked New Guinea, taking New Britain, the Solomons, and substantial portions of Papua (Jan.-Mar.), then threatening Port Moresby (by Sept.). Their offensive was badly damaged by their loss in the Coral Sea (May).

World War II, Battle of the Coral Sea (May 7-8): In the first American-Japanese aircraft carrier battle of the Pacific war, both American carriers (*Lexington* and *Yorktown*) were damaged, and one of two Japanese carriers (*Shoho*) was sunk. The Japanese broke off their planned landings at Port Moresby, in southern Papua.

World War II, Battle of Midway (June 4-6): In a decisive American naval victory off Midway Island, the three surviving American aircraft carriers and a small supporting force surprised the main Japanese battle fleet under Admiral Isoroku Yamamoto, including all four of Japan's major aircraft carriers and nine battleships; the Americans under rear admirals Raymond A. Spruance and Frank J. Fletcher sank all four Japanese carriers and lost only one, the *Yorktown*. With no remaining air cover, the Japanese fleet went home, the

World War II: With the United States in the war, part of the Battle of the Atlantic shifted to the American Atlantic coast, where German submarines sank scores of American ships. American naval and air attacks on the submarines became far more effective as the year went on, and by autumn the main body of German submarines off North America had shifted their attention to the Caribbean and South Atlantic.

World War II: The bazooka was invented; the antitank rocket, used heavily for the rest of the war, was the precursor of the modern rocket launcher.

d. Daniel Judson Callaghan (b. 1890), American admiral called "Fighting Dan" or the "Fighting Admiral"; he was killed in action off Lunga Point, Guadalcanal (Nov. 12-13).

1942 (cont.)

1943

Europe

World War II: Friedrich Paulus and the 93,000 survivors of the encircled German Sixth Army surrendered to Soviet forces at Stalingrad (Feb. 2); a massive Soviet winter offensive destroyed Germany's ability to return to the offensive, although the Soviet capture of Kharkov was reversed by a German counterattack that retook the city (Mar. 14).

World War II: In the Warsaw Ghetto rising (Apr.-May), the city's remaining 60,000 Jews mounted an insurrection after the Germans had sent 400,000 to 450,000 of the city's Jewish population to death camps and gas chambers; this was essentially a decision to take a few of the Germans with them, rather than a military decision, for Warsaw's Jews knew that they had no chance to win and very little chance of surviving the mass murders that would — and did — follow.

World War II: Allied bombers began the "shuttle bombing" of Europe, with bombers from Britain refueling in North Africa for their return runs (June 20).

World War II, Battle of the Atlantic: Early in the year, German submarine wolf packs effectively attacked Allied supply convoys, but the tide began to turn in the spring, as combined Allied naval and air forces cut into German submarine fleet strength. In June American "hunter-killer" task forces — carriers accompanied by destroyer groups — began to score decisive victories over the wolf packs, and many convoys were able to make the Atlantic crossing without losses.

World War II, Battle of Kursk (July 1943): The final German offensive on the eastern front failed when it quickly ran into a massive Soviet counteroffensive; Soviet armor and artillery, with air superiority, overcame a German force that included 17 mechanized divisions. In this largest armored battle of the war, 3,000 German tanks and 1,400 planes were destroyed — massive losses that were irreplaceable. Although Soviet losses were similar, they were from a much larger store of armaments and also were replaceable.

World War II, Invasion of Sicily (July 9-Aug. 17): Allied forces led by generals George Patton and Bernard Montgomery quickly moved inland after establishing southeastern coast beachheads (July 9). Axis counterattacks were unsuc-

Africa and Southwest Asia

World War II, Casablanca Conference (Jan. 14-23): Franklin Roosevelt and Winston Churchill called for unconditional surrender and further planned the invasion of southern and western Europe, with massive flows of supplies to the Soviet Union and the Pacific war as well, all made possible by American war production.

World War II, North African Campaign: American forces in Tunisia suffered heavy losses when German armor successfully attacked Allied troops at the Kasserine Pass (Feb. 14-22). General Erwin Rommel, facing much superior Allied forces, was unable to exploit the victory and soon withdrew to his original defensive line at Mareth. Two weeks later (Mar. 6), Rommel's attack at Mareth was thrown back. Allied forces successfully took the offensive at Mareth (Mar. 20) and a month later (Apr. 22) began their final North African offensive. Bizerte and Tunis fell (May 7), and in the following week remaining German and Italian North African forces surrendered, ending the war in that theater, with 275,000 prisoners taken.

Menachem Begin became leader of the Israeli terrorist Irgun Zvai Leumi (National Military Organization), which was engaged in a campaign against the British in Palestine.

World War II: At the first Cairo Conference (Nov. 22-26), Roosevelt, Churchill,

tide of the war turned, and the Americans were able to begin the long, uninterrupted offensive that would take them across the Pacific.

World War II, Battle of Guadalcanal (Aug. 1942-Feb. 1943): American seaborne invasion forces landed on Guadalcanal (Aug. 7), capturing the airport; a Japanese counterattack on the airport (Bloody Ridge) failed (mid-Sept.), as did other attacks (late Oct.), as American forces built up their strength. Off Guadalcanal, Japanese naval forces attempting to reinforce and supply their troops on the island were defeated in a three-day battle (Nov. 12-15).

Rather than supporting the anti-Japanese war, Indian Congress Party leaders, including Mohandas "Mahatma" Gandhi and Jawaharlal Nehru, demanded that the British leave India and were imprisoned.

d. Tetsutaro Sato (b. 1866), Japanese admiral and military theorist; a key advocate of a powerful Japanese navy, he wrote several highly influential texts, some calling for expansion southward into the East Indies.

World War II and Sino-Japanese War: With Allied air dominance becoming apparent throughout the war in east Asia and the Pacific, Japanese forces in China mounted offensives aimed at Allied airfields in China, continuing to attack them (1943-early 1945). Japanese occupation forces in China did not otherwise press forward, as Japan was engaged in a far-flung war that was severely straining its resources, facing an American enemy so strong as to be able to mount a massive Pacific war while focusing its main effort in the European theater. In China the war became a three-way matter, with Kuomintang forces blockading Communist-held areas in north China in the continuing Chinese Civil War, while both sides fought the Japanese.

World War II: Heavily reinforced American forces on Guadalcanal went on the offensive (Jan. 10) and took the island (early Feb.); surviving Japanese forces were evacuated by sea.

World War II, Battle of the Bismarck Sea (Mar. 2-4): Americans attacked a Japanese convoy, sinking all eight transports and four of eight destroyers, with minimal American losses.

World War II, Battle of New Georgia (July-Aug.): American army and marine forces in divisional strength attacked New Georgia, the main Japanese base in the Solomon Islands, capturing the island in two months of very difficult jungle fighting.

World War II: American marines attacked and took most of Bougainville Island, in the Solomons (Nov.), ultimately taking the whole island (1944).

World War II, Battle of Tarawa (Nov. 20-24): American marines made a very costly attack on heavily forti-

World War II, Manhattan Project: J. Robert Oppenheimer's group began to design and build the atomic bomb at Los Alamos, New Mexico. Fissionable uranium began to be produced at the Oak Ridge, Tennessee, atomic fuel plant.

World War II: At the Quebec Conference (Aug. 14-24), Franklin Roosevelt and Winston Churchill decided to adopt the American plan for the cross-Channel invasion of Europe, rather than an expanded invasion of Churchill's "soft underbelly" of Europe. May 1, 1944, was set as the target date for the invasion.

b. Robert D'Aubisson Arrieta (d. 1991), Salvadoran soldier and politician.

1943 (cont.)

cessful, and Allied forces moved north. Patton's forces took western Sicily and joined Montgomery's forces for the assault on Messina, which fell (Aug. 17) after the Germans withdrew to the mainland, evacuating more than 100,000.

World War II: Benito Mussolini was deposed by his own Fascist Grand Council (July 24) and imprisoned. He was then restored to office by the Germans, as head of a puppet Italian government, while the Germans took over direction of all Axis forces in Italy.

World War II: Massive Allied air raids on Hamburg (July 26-29) destroyed much of the city, generating firestorms; an estimated 50,000 people died.

World War II: Allied bombers operating from North African bases made long-range attacks on the Romanian Ploesti oil fields (Aug. 1).

World War II: Allied planes bombed the German V-1 and V-2 rocket development base at Peenemunde, delaying the introduction of the terror weapons (Aug. 17-18).

World War II: Allied forces from Sicily made amphibious landings on the southernmost tip of the Italian mainland (Sept. 3), then moved north. Troops landing farther north at Salerno (Sept. 9) were pinned down on their beachheads until relieved from the south (Sept. 18). Combined Allied forces then took southern Italy and faced German forces on the Gustav Line (late Nov.).

World War II: Italy signed an armistice with the Allies (Sept. 7); Germany continued the war in Italy.

World War II: Allied bombing raids on Berlin intensified (Nov.).

World War II: Attacking Soviet armies recaptured Kiev and Smolensk and crossed the Dnieper River (Dec.), then mounted a powerful winter offensive.

b. Lech Walesa, Polish labor leader, founder of the Solidarity trade union movement (1980), and president of Poland (1990-   ).

and Chiang Kai-shek made plans for the Pacific war.

World War II: At the Tehran Conference (Nov. 28-Dec. 1), the first Roosevelt–Churchill–Joseph Stalin summit meeting, the leaders made many major decisions, including the projected May 1944 date for the invasion of Europe, the founding of the United Nations, the timing of the entry of the Soviet Union into the Pacific war, and many postwar territorial and political matters.

World War II: At the second Cairo Conference (Dec. 3-7), Roosevelt and Churchill planned the coming invasion of Europe.

1944

World War II: Although German submarine action continued, heightening late in the year, the Allies had won the long Battle of the Atlantic. They continued to attack the German submarine fleet while transporting more than 1 million Americans to Britain in preparation for the coming invasion, along with huge amounts of armaments and supplies to Britain and the Soviet Union.

World War II, Battle of Korsun (Jan.-Feb.): German forces on the Dnieper River were encircled and partially destroyed during the Russian winter offensive, losing most of two army corps, with an estimated 100,000 casualties. Advancing Soviet forces took Odessa (Apr. 10) and much of the Ukraine.

World War II: Besieged Leningrad was relieved by advancing Soviet forces (Jan. 15-19).

World War II: Allied seaborne forces landed at Anzio, south of Rome and north of the Gustav Line (Jan. 22); there they were pinned down on a small beachhead for three months. After breaching the Gustav Line and breaking out of the Anzio beachhead (May), they joined in pursuing the Germans retreating north in Italy. Attacking forces took the previously impregnable Monte Cassino (June 18).

World War II: "Fortitude" was the code name for the last of the Operation Bodyguard deceptions, a rather successful attempt to convince the Germans that the coming Normandy invasion would be at the Pas de Calais.

World War II: Sevastopol fell to attacking Soviet forces (May 19); the German garrison was evacuated by sea.

Founding meeting of the Arab League (League of Arab States) was attended by representatives of the Palestinian Arabs, Egypt, Saudi Arabia, Iraq, Jordan (then Transjordan), Syria, Lebanon, and Yemen (Sept.).

Stern Gang terrorists assassinated British Middle East colonial administrator Lord Moyne at Cairo.

d. Reza Shah Pahlevi (Reza Khan) (b. 1878), Iranian general who seized power (1921) and became shah (1925); founder of the new house of Pahlevi, he was the father of Muhammed Reza Shah Pahlevi.

1943 (cont.)

fied Betio Island, in the Tarawa Atoll; almost 1,000 marines died of 3,000 casualties, and more than 4,500 Japanese died, as most chose to fight to the death.

World War II: In Burma, British long-range Chindit raids on Japanese-held territory had no effect on the stalemate; Japanese attacks also failed to penetrate into northern India.

d. Isoroku Yamamoto (b. 1884), Japanese admiral, fleet commander (1939-1943), chief planner of the attack on Pearl Harbor (Dec. 7, 1941) that began the war in the Pacific, and losing commander at Midway (June 4-6, 1942); he was killed when his airplane was shot down by American fighters over the Solomon Islands (Apr. 18).

1944

World War II: Pursuing the Japanese across the Pacific, island by island, American forces landed on Kwajalein Atoll (Feb. 1) and in a single week defeated its Japanese defenders and took the island; almost all in the 8,000-strong Japanese garrison fought to the death; American losses were small.

World War II, Battle of Eniwetok (Feb. 17-21): Much larger American forces defeated the 2,000-strong Japanese garrison of Eniwetok and the Parry Islands; the Japanese fought to the death.

World War II: American forces landed on Saipan (June 15) and engaged in close combat (until July 9) with 25,000 to 30,000 defenders, most of whom fought to the death and some of whom committed suicide rather than surrender. There were more than 3,000 American dead among 16,000 casualties.

World War II, Battle of the Philippine Sea (June 19-20): During the invasion of Saipan, American naval forces won a massive victory, which cost Japan 3 aircraft carriers and 450 aircraft and pilots, with American losses of fewer than 100 aircraft.

World War II, Battle of New Guinea (Apr.-July): Allied forces attacked the Japanese in western New Guinea,

World War II: Bretton Woods (New Hampshire) Conference set up the International Bank for Reconstruction and Development and the International Monetary Fund, as well as other postwar financial structures (July).

World War II: At the Dumbarton Oaks Conference in Washington, D.C., American, British, Soviet, and Chinese representatives planned the form and main processes of the United Nations (Aug.-Oct.).

At Port Chicago, near San Francisco, a massive explosion of munitions ships killed 322 people.

World War II: At another Quebec Conference (Sept. 12-16), Franklin Roosevelt and Winston Churchill discussed the postwar occupation of Germany, the future of Eastern Europe, and several other postwar matters, as well as some aspects of what was then thought to be the coming invasion of Japan.

1944 (cont.)

World War II: Soviet forces breached the Mannerheim Line (June), then took Viipuri and much of eastern Finland, resulting in a cease-fire (Sept. 4).

World War II: Rome, declared an open city, fell to Allied troops driving north (June 4).

World War II: First German V-1 flying bomb struck England (June 13).

World War II, Normandy Invasion (D-Day; June 6): In Operation Overlord, Allied forces, carried and supported by a fleet of 5,000 ships and thousands of aircraft, landed on five beaches in Normandy (designated Utah, Omaha, Juno, Sword, and Gold), encountering substantial German opposition only on Omaha Beach; three airborne divisions were dropped inland. All beaches were secured by nightfall, and Allied forces moved inland. Allied forces in France built to 1 million (June-July). After taking Cherbourg (June 27), Allied forces broke through the German line at Avranches (Aug. 1), advancing to the Seine (late Aug.) and liberating Paris (Aug. 25), which German general Hans Speidel refused to destroy, as Adolf Hitler had ordered.

World War II: On the eastern front, massive Soviet armies, with armor and air superiority, drove the retreating Germans west. The German Army Group Center suffered a huge defeat early in the summer offensive, losing more than 500,000 in casualties and prisoners and a reported 2,000 tanks to Georgi Zhukov's attacking armies. Minsk was taken (July 3), as the Soviets moved into Poland all the way to the Vistula River, stopping just short of Warsaw.

World War II, Warsaw Rising (Aug.-Oct.): With powerful Russian forces just across the Vistula, Polish partisan forces in Warsaw rose against the German garrison in support of what was thought to be the impending Soviet attack. But the Soviet forces did not move, and the reinforced German garrison massacred the lightly armed partisans, as well as tens of thousands of noncombatants. Polish surrender came (Oct. 2).

World War II: At the Potsdam Conference (July-Aug.), the Allies met to discuss the future of Germany, dealing with many postwar questions, including occupation policies and the Nuremberg Trials.

World War II: A failed "officers' plot" to assassinate Adolf Hitler (July 20) was attempted by Colonel Klaus von Stauffenberg; many arrests and executions followed.

World War II: Soviet armies attacked Romania (Aug.-Sept.); Romanian forces soon surrendered, some changing sides, and the Romanian government surrendered (Aug. 23). German forces continued to retreat; Bucharest fell (Sept. 1).

World War II: In Operation Anvil-Dragoon, seaborne Allied forces invaded southern France (Aug. 15); French forces then quickly took Marseilles and Toulon, taking 45,000 to 50,000 prisoners; American forces pursued retreating German forces in the Rhône Valley, taking more than 30,000 prisoners (Sept.).

World War II: German V-2 rocket attacks on Paris and London began (Sept. 8).

World War II: British forces took Brussels (Sept. 3) and Antwerp (Sept. 4). Allied forces pursued the retreating Germans to the Siegfried Line and prepared for the coming attack into Germany.

World War II, Battle of Arnhem (Sept. 17): The British bridgehead across the Meuse River ended in retreat and the loss of 7,000 of 9,000 British forces; it was part of Operation Market Garden.

World War II: Advancing Soviet forces defeated German forces in Latvia and pursued them into East Prussia, taking Gdansk and most of the Baltic coast, while the German navy evacuated an estimated 1.5 million Germans from those areas (Oct. 1944-May 1945).

taking Hollandia (Apr.), and at the other Japanese bases on the island (by July); Japanese forces waged a jungle guerrilla war until the Japanese surrender (Aug. 1945).

World War II, Battle of Guam (July-Aug.): American seaborne forces took Guam in two weeks of close fighting; most of the 10,000 Japanese defenders fought to the death.

World War II, Battle of Leyte (Oct.-Dec.): American forces invaded Leyte (Oct. 22), moved inland in divisional strength, and then completed the reconquest of the island (late Dec.).

World War II, Battle of Leyte Gulf (Oct. 24-25): While American forces moved inland on Leyte, massive American naval forces destroyed much of the remainder of the Japanese navy in the largest naval battle of the Pacific war. Japanese losses included 4 aircraft carriers, 3 battleships, an estimated 500 airplanes, and many other ships, while American losses were light.

Sino-Japanese War: Japanese forces in east China mounted a successful offensive (May), taking Ch'ang-sha (June 19) and Hengyang (Aug. 9), then taking seven airfields, their main early objective. Kuomintang forces blocked their attempt to take the Chinese capital of Chungking.

World War II: In Burma British and Chinese forces mounted a series of inconclusive offensives in northern Burma, including a second wave of Chindit raids (Mar.-May). The Japanese 15th Army attacked across the Chindwin River from Burma into India (Mar.), besieging Imphal and Kohima. They retreated back into Burma after the relief of Kohima (Apr.) and Imphal (June). British forces in central Burma went on the offensive (Nov.).

b. Rajiv Gandhi (d. 1992), Indian prime minister who was the son of Indira Gandhi and the grandson of Jawaharlal Nehru.

d. Chuichi Nagumo (b. 1887), naval air officer, commander of Japan's First Air Fleet, and director of the attack on Pearl Harbor (1941) and of the lost Japanese carrier fleet at Midway (1942); he committed suicide (July).

d. Yoshitsugo Saito (b. 1890), Japanese general who led the defense against the American invasion of Saipan, at the end committing suicide.

d. Orde Charles Wingate (b. 1903), Indian-born British general who, as adviser to the Jewish Settlement Police in Palestine (1936-1939), provided training in guerrilla warfare; he later led Chindit forces against Japanese-held Burma (1944); he died in an air crash in Assam (Mar. 25).

1944 (cont.)

World War II: Soviet forces took Belgrade (Oct. 20), crossed the Danube (late Nov.), and besieged Budapest.

World War II: American First Army forces breached the Siegfried Line, pouring through to take Aachen, the first large German city to be taken by Allied forces in World War II (Oct. 20).

World War II: British bombers sank the German battleship *Tirpitz* while it was docked undergoing repairs at Tromsö (Nov. 12).

World War II: French armored forces operating in the Alsace (Nov. 16-Dec. 15) took Strasbourg (Nov. 23).

World War II, Battle of the Bulge (Battle of the Ardennes) (Dec. 1944-Jan. 1945): Germans made a massive, last-throw, 25-division counteroffensive in the Ardennes, pushing the Americans back, creating a 50-mile-deep salient (bulge), but not creating an exploitable breach in the western front. Surrounded American forces at Bastogne were relieved (Dec. 26), while defeated German forces, their reserves exhausted, began retreating from the salient (early Jan.), as Allied forces continued the pursuit to the Rhine.

World War II, Malmédy Massacre (Dec. 17): German SS troops murdered 86 American war prisoners at Malmédy during the Battle of the Bulge.

World War II, Battle of Bastogne (Dec. 19, 1944-Jan. 2, 1945): Germans made a failed attack on the American 82d Airborne and 101st Airborne divisions, holding Bastogne during the Battle of the Bulge; the Americans were relieved by George Patton's Third Army (Dec. 26) and began the long pursuit to the Rhine a week later. At Bastogne, confronted with a German surrender ultimatum, American general Anthony C. McAuliffe responded, "Nuts!"

World War II: Allied bombers extended their "shuttle bombing" of Europe, with bombers from Britain making the round-trip to Soviet bases and back.

World War II: The first German military jet, a Messerschmidt, was flown in action.

d. Erwin Rommel (the "Desert Fox") (b. 1891), German World War II commander in chief in North Africa and then in western Europe during the Normandy invasion. He approved of the failed attempt to assassinate Adolf Hitler and, under sentence of death, committed suicide, although his complicity was unannounced and he was treated as a war hero.

d. Hans Gunther von Kluge (b. 1882), German western front commander who committed suicide after having been relieved of command as a suspected participant in the failed Hitler assassination attempt.

d. Klaus Schenck von Stauffenberg (b. 1907), German colonel whose assassination attempt at Rastenburg, East Prussia, failed when his bomb detonated but did not kill Hitler; he was executed (July 20).

d. Ernst Thaelmann (b. 1886), German communist leader who was murdered by his Nazi captors at Buchenwald.

d. Emilio de Bono (b. 1866), Italian general who was a key figure in the march on Rome and Benito Mussolini's rise to power (1922); he was arrested, tried, and executed.

d. Erwin von Witsleben (b. 1881), German field marshal, commander of the First Army in Poland and then France, and commander in chief of Army Group West in France (1941-1942); he was revealed as part of the failed conspiracy against Hitler, convicted of treason, and hanged (Aug. 8).

d. Otto von Below (b. 1857), German general in World War I with many field commands, most notably at the Second Battle of the Masurian Lakes (1915) and Caporetto (1917).

1945

World War II: On the eastern front, massive Soviet armies made a final, sustained attack on Germany (from Jan.) until the German surrender, at a cost of at least 1 million German casualties. Georgi Zhukov's Soviet forces reached the Oder River (Jan. 31), and his and Konstantin Rokossovski's forces then turned north, trapping opposing German armies estimated at 500,000 against the Baltic; these and more than 1 million civilians were evacuated by sea. To the south, advancing Soviet forces took Budapest (Feb. 13) and Vienna (Apr. 15), then met American forces in the Danube Valley.

World War II: On the western front, Allied forces with air and armor superiority pushed outmatched German forces back to the Rhine, while Allied bombers destroyed what was left of Germany's industrial strength. Allied bombing raids on Dresden (Feb. 13-14) created a firestorm that destroyed most of the city, leaving an estimated 100,000 dead and several hundred thousand injured.

World War II: American forces driving into Germany took the Ludendorff Bridge over the Rhine at Remagen (Mar. 7) before it could be destroyed by the retreating Germans, establishing an unexpectedly easy bridgehead over the Rhine and speeding the invasion of Germany. General George Patton's American Fifth Division crossed the Rhine (Mar. 22), with British and American forces crossing at several locations in the following four days. German resistance in the west largely ceased (Apr.), with the surrender of more than 300,000 in the Ruhr Valley (Apr. 14-18) and the surrender of German forces in much of western Europe (by early May).

World War II: In Italy, Allied forces breached the Gothic Line (Apr. 9-20), took Bologna (Apr. 21), and quickly took northern Italy against disintegrating German and Italian resistance. The Germans unconditionally surrendered in Italy (Apr. 29; formally on May 2).

World War II: Soviet forces reached Berlin (Apr. 22), taking the city in hand-to-hand fighting (ended May 2).

d. Adolf Hitler (b. 1889), German Nazi Party head (from 1921) and Nazi dictator (1933-1945); a mass murderer who was directly responsible for the deaths of tens of millions, he was also a very poor military leader who ignored the advice of his own rather competent generals and took his country into a disastrous multifront war against a massive worldwide alliance. Hitler and Eva Braun committed suicide in his Berlin command bunker (Apr. 30).

World War II ended in the west (May 7) with the unconditional surrender of Germany, effective midnight, May 8, which then became V-E Day. The document of surrender was signed at Reims, France, by Admiral Hans von Friedeburg and General Alfred Jodl, who surrendered to Lieutenant General Walter Bedell Smith, Dwight D. Eisenhower's chief of staff. A second surrender, this time to Soviet general Georgi Zhukov and British general Arthur Tedder, occurred in Berlin (May 8).

Nuremberg Trials (Nov. 1945-Oct. 1946): War crimes trials of leading Nazis resulted in death sentences for Hans Frank, Wilhelm Frick, Hermann Goering, Alfred Jodl, Ernst Kaltenbrunner, Wilhelm Keitel, Joachim von Ribbentrop, Alfred Rosenberg, Fritz Sauckel, Arthur Seyss-Inquart, and Julius Streicher. Goering committed suicide; the others were executed. Three defendants were acquitted and seven imprisoned.

d. Benito Mussolini (b. 1883), founder of Italian fascism (1919) and head of the fascist Italian state (1922-1945); he was captured and killed by Italian partisans while in flight (Apr. 28).

d. Heinrich Himmler (b. 1900), Nazi leader, head of the SS (*Schutzstaffel;* Blackshirts), creator of the Gestapo, operator of the German concentration camp system in which 10 million to 26 million people were murdered, and head of the Waffen SS (Combat Blackshirts); he committed suicide (May 23).

World War II: At the Yalta Conference (Feb. 4-11), their second meeting, Franklin Roosevelt, Winston Churchill, and Joseph Stalin met to discuss the shape of the postwar world, focusing largely on establishing a Soviet sphere of influence in Eastern Europe; Stalin also would keep large portions of Poland seized in 1939. In return, Stalin again promised to declare war on Japan once the war with Germany was concluded.

Soviet forces moved into northern Iran, in support of a Tudeh Party insurrection that took control of the area. Strong American pressure on the Soviet government brought troop withdrawals (May). Iranian government forces completed their reconquest of the north (Dec.).

W. E. B. Du Bois, Jomo Kenyatta, Kwame Nkrumah, and many other Black leaders convened the Sixth Pan-African Congress at Manchester, England; a key event in the development of the massive anticolonial movement that would sweep Africa after World War II.

The long guerrilla war for Kenyan independence began.

The Arab League was formally established (Mar.).

World War II, Battle of the Philippines (Jan.-Aug.): American amphibious landings began in northern Luzon (Jan. 9); the invasion forces then moved south, with landings near Manila (Jan. 30). Manila fell (early Feb.), as did Bataan and Corregidor (late Feb.); remaining Japanese forces then went over to guerrilla warfare from mountain bases on Luzon and Mindanao until the end of the war.

World War II, Battle of Iwo Jima (Feb. 19-Mar. 16): American marines made an amphibious assault on the heavily defended island (Feb. 19), taking Mount Suribachi (Feb. 23). It took three more weeks to complete the action, as most of the 22,000 to 25,000 Japanese defenders fought to the death. American losses included almost 7,000 dead and 18,000 other casualties.

World War II: American B-29s firebombed Tokyo (Mar. 9-10); more than 80,000 people died in a firestorm similar to those in Germany that had engulfed Dresden and Hamburg.

World War II, Battle of Okinawa (Apr. 1-June 22): American forces made unopposed amphibious landings (Apr. 1), then a major attack on heavily fortified Japanese positions. Most of the 130,000 to 140,000 defenders fought to the death, with 12,000 American dead of 50,000 casualties. Japanese losses included an estimated 3,000 planes and pilots, many of them kamikazes (suicide bombers), and the *Yamoto*, the last Japanese superbattleship.

Sino-Japanese War: Early in the year, Japanese forces mounted new offensives in southeast and central China; weakened by their losses elsewhere, they were unable to sustain their attacks, and Chinese forces were on the offensive as the war ended.

World War II: British-led forces in Burma attacked Japanese forces on the Irrawaddy River (Jan.-Feb.); drew them into battle; executed a planned encirclement (Mar.); took Meiktila, Mandalay, and Rangoon (May); and were pursuing the slowly retreating Japanese toward Thailand when the war ended.

World War II, Hiroshima (8:15 A.M., Aug. 6): The American B-26 bomber *Enola Gay* dropped the first atomic bomb used in warfare on Hiroshima, on Honshu Island, directly or very soon afterward killing an estimated 70,000 to 80,000 people and destroying the city; 75,000 to 125,000 more died in the years that followed. The event ushered in the age that still calls into question the survival of humanity and all other life on earth.

World War II, Nagasaki (9:30 A.M., Aug. 9): An American B-29 dropped the second atomic bomb used in warfare on Nagasaki, on Japan's Kyushu Island, immediately killing 40,000 to 70,000 people, injuring as many more, and destroying much of the city; 50,000 to 100,000 more died of radiation, cancer, and other

d. Franklin Delano Roosevelt (b. 1882), 32d president of the United States (1933-1945), through the Great Depression and all but a few months of World War II; he died at Warm Springs, Georgia (Apr. 12), during his unprecedented fourth term in office. He was succeeded by Vice President Harry S. Truman.

World War II: Code-named Trinity, the first atomic bomb was exploded at Alamogordo, New Mexico (July 16). Work went forward on the atomic bombs that would be dropped on Hiroshima and Nagasaki.

San Francisco Conference (Apr. 25-June 25) founded the United Nations and established its charter, which was signed by the 51 original members on June 26, effective October 24.

Brazilian dictator Getúlio Vargas was deposed by military coup.

b. Daniel Ortega Saavedra, Nicaraguan Sandinista guerrilla leader and president of Nicaragua (1985-1990).

d. Robert Hutchings Goddard (b. 1882), American rocketry pioneer, a major figure in the history of space flight who launched the first liquid-propellant rocket (1926).

d. George Smith Patton (b. 1885), American World War II general; a controversial officer, he lost his command after playing a major role in North Africa and Sicily; he was Third Army commander during the European campaign, and his forces relieved Bastogne during the Battle of the Bulge.

d. Alexander McCarrell Patch, Jr. (b. 1889), American general who during World War II relieved Guadalcanal (1942), later commanding the Seventh Army in Europe (1944), most notably in invading southern France.

1945 (cont.)

d. Joseph Goebbels (b. 1897), Nazi propaganda minister; a war criminal, he committed suicide, murdering his wife and six children as well (May 1).

d. Fedor von Bock (b. 1880), German general in both world wars; he was commander of occupation forces in Austria and Czechoslovakia in the late 1930s and of major forces in the attacks on Poland, France, and the Soviet Union, including the failed German Army Group Center attack on Moscow (1941).

d. Ivan Chernyakovsky (b. 1906), Soviet general commanding major forces pursuing the Germans from western Russia into Germany (1944-1945); he died in battle (Feb.).

d. Pierre Laval (b. 1883), French premier (1931; 1935; 1942-1944) who was head of the collaborationist Vichy government; he was executed for treason (Oct. 15).

d. David Lloyd George (b. 1863), British World War I coalition prime minister (1916-1922) and a key figure at the Paris Peace Conference (1919).

d. Wilhelm Canaris (b. 1887), German naval officer, head of armed forces intelligence in World War II, and anti-Nazi underground leader; arrested after the unsuccessful attempt to assassinate Hitler in 1944, he was executed by the Gestapo (Apr.).

d. Dietrich Bonhoeffer (b. 1907), German Protestant anti-Nazi minister who was murdered in a Nazi concentration camp.

d. Vidkun Quisling (b. 1887), World War II Norwegian puppet leader whose name became synonymous with *traitor;* he was executed for treason.

d. Archibald James Murray (b. 1860), British general during the Boer War and World War I; chief of the British Expeditionary Force General Staff (1914), he later commanded British forces in Egypt (1915).

d. August von Mackensen (b. 1849), German field marshal who was a key World War I field commander on the eastern front, most notably at Lodz (1914) and Gorlice-Tarnów (1915); he took Lemberg (Lvov), Brest-Litovsk, and Belgrade (all 1915), as well as Bucharest (1916).

d. Walther Model (b. 1891), German field marshal; a Hitler loyalist, he led the Ninth Army (1942-1944) in Russia and later directed the German offensive in the Ardennes (1945); trapped, he surrendered his troops but shot himself (Apr. 21).

bomb-related injuries within a few years, and others continue to die.

Soviet-Japanese War (Aug. 9-14): The Soviet Union declared war on Japan, and in four days Soviet forces destroyed the Japanese Kwangtung Army and took most of Manchuria; they were moving across the Yalu River into Korea (Aug. 14) when Japan surrendered to the Allies.

World War II: The Japanese cease-fire (Aug. 15; called V-J Day) signaled the end of the war in the Pacific theater; the formal Japanese surrender was signed aboard the American battleship *Missouri* in Tokyo harbor (Sept. 2).

Chinese Civil War: Following the Japanese surrender, Communist Chinese forces occupied much of formerly Japanese-occupied north China (Aug.). American marines (53,000) occupied Peking and many strategic north Chinese centers (Sept.), as the civil war resumed and Kuomintang-Communist fighting became general (Nov.).

Republic of Indonesia was proclaimed by independence leaders (Aug. 17); the four-year Indonesian War of Independence (1945-1949) began. Dutch and British forces occupied Indonesia (Oct.), taking Surabaya (Nov.), while Indonesian forces went over to a guerrilla war.

d. Hajime Sugiyama (b. 1880), Japanese field marshal who, as army minister (1937-1938), commander of the North China Area Army (1938-1939), and chief of the general staff (1940-1944), was a major architect of Japan's role in World War II; he committed suicide at its surrender.

d. Takijiro Onishi (b. 1891), Japanese admiral who rose to command the First Air Fleet (Oct. 1944), orchestrating the first kamikaze assaults against U.S. naval units at Leyte Gulf (1944); he committed suicide after the emperor surrendered (Aug. 15).

d. Shigeru Honjo (b. 1876), Japanese general who led Japan's Kwangtung Army in its conquest of Manchuria (1931-1932); he committed suicide at Japan's surrender.

d. Tadamichi Kuribayashi (b. 1891), Japanese general who directed the defense of Iwo Jima, toward the end of which he was killed.

d. Tadayoshi Sano (b. 1889), Japanese general during World War II, most notably at Sumatra (1942) and Guadalcanal (1942-1943).

d. Fumimaro Konoe (b. 1891), Japanese pre–World War II prime minister; he committed suicide while awaiting his war crimes trial.

d. Subhas Chandra Bose (b. 1897), Indian revolutionary; during World War II, he was commander of the Japanese-sponsored Indian National Army that fought against the Allies.

1945 (cont.)

1946

Greek Civil War (1946-1949): Greek communist forces operating out of neighboring communist countries and led by General Markos Vafiades, went on the offensive (May), taking much of northern Greece and contesting government forces throughout the country.

An attempted military coup in Portugal failed to depose Antonio de Oliveira Salazar.

Albania became a one-party communist state ruled by Enver Hoxha; as the Socialist People's Republic of Albania, it became part of the Soviet bloc (until 1957).

d. Hermann Goering (b. 1893), Nazi leader, second only to Adolf Hitler; a war criminal, he committed suicide in his cell (Oct. 15) while awaiting execution after his conviction at the Nuremberg Trials.

d. Joachim von Ribbentrop (b. 1893), German diplomat and Nazi war criminal who was executed after the Nuremberg Trials (Oct. 16).

d. Wilhelm Keitel (b. 1882), German general and key military adviser to Adolf Hitler; he was executed after having been found guilty of war crimes at the Nuremberg Trials.

d. Draza Mihajlovic (b. 1893), Yugoslav World War II general who was head of the proroyalist, anti-Nazi Chetnik guerrilla forces (1941-1946); his forces also fought the communist guerrilla army led by Tito. Mihajlovic was captured and executed by Tito's forces.

d. Ion Antonescu (b. 1880), Romanian fascist leader (1940-1944) who was executed by the Romanian government.

d. Frederick Rudolph Lambert, 10th earl of Cavan (b. 1865), British field marshal active during World War I, most notably at the First and Third Battles of Ypres (1914; 1917) and the Somme; he later headed the Imperial General Staff (1922-1926).

King David Hotel bombing (July 22): Irgun Zvai Leumi terrorists, commanded by Menachem Begin, bombed the British office wing of Jerusalem's King David Hotel, killing 91 people, 17 of them Jews. Among other Irgun terrorist actions was the bombing of the British Embassy in Rome.

Under Mustafa al-Barzani, Kurdish republican forces, with Soviet backing, set up a post–World War II Kurdish republic in northern Iran but were defeated by Iranian forces; the republic dissolved, but guerrilla warfare continued.

Jordan (Hashemite Kingdom of Jordan) became an independent state (May 25).

Syria (Syrian Arab Republic) became an independent state.

1945 (cont.)

d. Henry George Chauvel (b. 1865), Australian general who commanded the then-new Desert Mounted Corps in World War I, most notably in their breakthrough at Megiddo (Sept. 19-20, 1918).

1946

American atomic bomb tests began on Bikini Atoll, in the Marshall Islands. Two atomic bombs were exploded in the air over the lagoon (July 1 and July 25), the first of 70 such tests at Bikini and Eniwetok.

Chinese Civil War: General George C. Marshall's attempt to mediate the Chinese Civil War resulted in a temporary truce (Jan.), but that did not hold. Kuomintang forces took much of north China, with substantial American assistance, but American supplies stopped (July), and as American marines began to withdraw from China, the tide began to turn in favor of the Communists.

Soviet forces withdrew from Manchuria (Mar.-May).

Indochina War (Vietnamese War of Independence; 1946-1954): A guerrilla insurgency became a full-scale war between France and the Democratic Republic of Vietnam, led by its first president, Ho Chi Minh (Nguyen That Thanh).

Republic of Indonesia was established on a limited basis by the Cheribon Agreement, with continued Dutch dominance. The guerrilla war of independence continued, with an Islamic insurgency making the war a three-way conflict.

Full-scale Hindu-Muslim conflict broke out in India as partition and the creation of independent India and Pakistan approached.

Republic of the Philippines became an independent nation (July 4). Communist-led Hukbalahap guerrillas in the Philippines went from anti-Japanese warfare to a prolonged antigovernment insurgency (1946-1954), taking much of rural central Luzon.

d. Homma Masaharu (b. 1887), Japanese general who was the commander of invasion forces on the Philippines (1941-1942); he was executed as a war criminal for atrocities against prisoners.

d. Tomoyuki Yamashita (b. 1885), Japanese general who was commander in Southeast Asia (1941-1942) and the Philippines (1944); he was executed as a war criminal.

d. Hisaichi Terauchi (b. 1879), Japanese general who was army minister (1936-1937) during the run-up to World War II, commanding the North China Area Army (1937-1938), then the Southern Army (1941-1945), and directing all Japanese army operations in Southeast Asia.

d. Tai Li (b. 1895), Nationalist Chinese general who was chief of the Kuomintang intelligence and secret police

Winston Churchill coined the phrase *iron curtain* to describe the Soviet bloc in his speech at Westminster College, Fulton, Missouri (Mar. 5); his talk was a centerpiece of the quickly developing Cold War.

United Nations General Assembly convened for its first meeting (Jan. 10); Trygve Lie of Norway was the first UN secretary-general (1946-1952).

Emily Greene Balch, a founder and first secretary of the Women's International League for Peace and Freedom (1919), was a Nobel Peace Prize corecipient, with John R. Mott.

Haitian president Élie Lescot was deposed by a military coup (Jan. 11); he was succeeded by Dumarsais Estimé.

Former Argentine minister of war Juan Perón became president; much influenced by his wife Maria Eva "Evita" until her death (1952), he was effectively dictator of Argentina until deposed by coup (1955).

b. Karen Gay Silkwood (d. 1974), American atomic plant worker.

d. Theodore Stark Wilkinson (b. 1888), American admiral who, as deputy commander of the South Pacific Force, directed landings through Leyte Gulf (1944) and Luzon (1945), as well as in Japan (Sept. 1945).

Europe	Africa and Southwest Asia

1946 (cont.)

1947

Greek Civil War: Greek government forces began to contain communist forces, as massive American and British aid and substantial numbers of military advisers poured into Greece.

In Hungary, the Communist Party took full control, backed by Soviet occupation troops; Mátyas Rákosi became premier of the Communist-controlled government.

European communist parties, dominated by the Soviet Union, formed the Cominform (Communist Information Bureau) (1947-1956); the organization fell into disuse as an instrument of Soviet control after Joseph Stalin's death (1953).

Yugoslav forces deployed at disputed Trieste were stopped by American occupation forces in Italy (Sept.). Allied occupation forces completed their withdrawal from Italy, leaving forces at Trieste (Dec. 14).

d. Anton Denikin (b. 1872), general of the White armies on the Don River during the Russian Civil War.

d. Jacques Philippe Leclerc (b. 1902), World War II Free French general who led the French Second Armored Division into Paris (1944).

d. Ian Standish Monteith Hamilton (b. 1853), British World War I general who was commander in chief of the Mediterranean (1910) and of Britain's Home Defense Army (1914) before directing the ill-fated landings at Gallipoli (1915); refusing to withdraw, he was dismissed and recalled.

Plans for the partition of Palestine went forward; the United Nations recommended partition into Arab and Jewish states, and British withdrawal was scheduled for October 1, 1948. Palestinian Arabs and their supporters in the Arab world did not accept this resolution of the Palestine question, and full-scale war seemed probable as guerrilla war grew in Palestine.

Anticolonial movements began to accelerate in many countries. In Madagascar a failed rebellion against the French cost an estimated 10,000 Malagasy and 1,000 French casualties (Jan.-Apr.).

Ba'ath Party (Arab Socialist Renaissance Party) was formally organized as a political party, having existed as a socialist, pan-Arab movement from the mid-1930s.

1948

As the Cold War threatened to break into armed conflict, Soviet forces blockaded West Berlin (June 22); in response, a massive Allied airlift supplied the city until the blockade was lifted (May 1949).

Czech democracy was destroyed in a bloodless coup backed by the presence of Soviet military power in Eastern Europe.

d. Eduard Benes (b. 1884), Czech independence leader who was the first Czech foreign minister (1918-1935) and president of Czechoslovakia (1935-1938; 1945-1948); he resigned after the communist takeover (1948).

d. Jan Masaryk (b. 1886), Czech foreign minister (1945-1948) who was the son of Tomás Masaryk; after the communist coup (1948), he stayed in office, in opposition, but a few weeks later he fell or was pushed from a window in Prague (Mar. 10).

Greek Civil War: Greek government forces went on the offensive, pushing back communist forces, who were increasingly short of arms and supplies as the Yugoslav-Soviet breach developed and worsened.

Israeli Irgun Zvai Leumi and Stern Gang forces massacred the 254 Palestinian Arab inhabitants of the village of Deir Yasin, near Jerusalem (Apr. 9); most of those killed were noncombatants.

Israeli War of Independence (First Arab-Israeli War) (May 1948-Jan. 1949): Arab-Israeli civil war broke out in Palestine (Jan.) as British forces prepared to leave, with massive Arab flight in progress (by early May). The British withdrew (May 14), the independent state of Israel was established, and Syrian, Lebanese, Iraqi, Jordanian, and Egyptian forces invaded Israel (May 14-15); Egyptian forces advancing along the coast came within 25 miles of Tel Aviv before being thrown back. Israeli

1946 (cont.)

services, reporting directly to Chiang Kai-shek (from 1938).

1947

Hindu-Muslim rioting and mass murder intensified with the partition of British India into the new nations of India and Pakistan (Aug. 15); 500,000 to 1 million people died, and internal migrations totaled 10 million to 18 million.

Kashmir War (1947-1949): The raja of Kashmir, a Hindu, attached Kashmir to India during the partition of India, generating a Muslim insurgency in Kashmir that quickly grew into an undeclared war involving substantial elements of the Indian and Pakistani armed forces.

Chinese Civil War: Although Communist and Kuomintang forces were stalemated in Manchuria, Communist forces decisively moved to the offensive and away from guerrilla actions into positional warfare, by year's end holding much of the countryside.

Field Marshal Luang Pibul Songgram took power in Thailand by coup.

Vietminh forces besieged Hué (Jan.-Feb.) but failed to take the city.

d. Aung San (b. 1915), Burmese prime minister who was assassinated with five members of his cabinet (July 19); he was the father of Daw Aung San Suu Kyi.

d. Haruyoshi Hyakutake (b. 1888), Japanese general who led the prolonged, ultimately unsuccessful attempt to hold Guadalcanal (1943).

American president Harry S. Truman announced the Truman Doctrine (Mar. 12), stating American opposition to communism worldwide, while asking Congress for massive aid to Greece and Turkey; a major step in the development of the Cold War.

American secretary of state George C. Marshall developed the Marshall Plan, a massive American aid program aimed at rebuilding postwar Europe and at the same time strengthening anticommunist European governments; a major Cold War strategem.

George Frost Kennan, writing as Mr. X in *Foreign Affairs*, authored the policy of "containment" of the Soviet Union, which became the basic American Cold War stance.

Central Intelligence Agency (CIA) was authorized by the U.S. National Security Act, succeeding the World War II Office of Strategic Services (OSS).

Paraguayan Civil War (Mar. 30-Aug. 20): Rebel forces led by former president Rafael Franco were decisively defeated by the government forces of President Higinio Morinigo at the Battle of Asunción (Aug. 20), ending the war.

Ecuador's president José Maria Velasco Ibarra was deposed by coup; he was succeeded by Colonel Carlos Mancheno (Aug. 23).

d. Marc Andrew Mitscher (b. 1887), American World War II admiral who was commander of the *Hornet* at Midway and later of the Fast Carrier Task Force.

d. Evans Fordyce Carlson (b. 1896), American general whose Second Marine Raider Battalion (Carlson's Raiders), trained using Chinese techniques, carried out daring raids, often behind enemy lines, as at Guadalcanal (Nov.-Dec. 1942); he was severely wounded at Saipan (1944).

1948

Chinese Civil War: Communist forces won a series of major victories over Kuomintang forces, effectively bringing the war to a close, except for mopping-up actions.

Chinese Civil War, Battle of Mukden-Chinchow (Oct. 27-30): Kuomintang armies in Manchuria were decisively defeated by pursuing Communist forces; the Kuomintang armies ceased to exist as fighting forces. Mukden fell (Nov. 1).

Chinese Civil War, Battle of Hwai Hai (Battle of Süchow) (Nov. 1948-Jan. 1949): Last and most decisive major battle of the war, involving approximately 500,000 on each side; attacking Communist field armies destroyed the Kuomintang Seventh Army Group and pursued the fleeing Second Army Group; Kuomintang losses were an estimated 250,000.

Colombian Civil War (La Violencia) (1948-1958): The massive Liberal-Conservative guerrilla war was fought mainly in the countryside and cost an estimated 200,000 to 300,000 lives and uncounted other casualties; it was never fully resolved, with guerrilla insurgency continuing through the early 1990s.

In testimony before the House Un-American Activities Committee (HUAC), Whittaker Chambers accused American diplomat Alger Hiss of being a communist spy.

Costa Rican insurrection led by José Figueres Ferrer restored the legally elected government of Otilio Ulate Blanco (Apr.).

Jamaica's President José Bustamante was deposed by coup (Oct.); he was succeeded by General Manuel Odria, who ruled until 1956.

d. John Joseph "Blackjack" Pershing (b. 1860), American general who was the commander of American expeditionary forces in Mex-

1948 (cont.)

d. Walther von Brauchitsch (b. 1881), German field marshal who, as commander in chief (1938-1941), planned the attacks on Poland, France, the Balkans, and Russia; he was relieved for advising that Moscow could not be taken.

d. Arthur Coningham (b. 1895), British air marshal nicknamed "Maori"; he organized and commanded the multinational Second Tactical Air Force for the Normandy landings (1944).

forces ultimately defeated their Arab opponents in all but the Jerusalem sector, where Jordan's Arab Legion took and held most of the city.

Israeli Stern Gang terrorists assassinated Swedish diplomat and United Nations chief Palestine peace mediator Folke Bernadotte (b. 1895). He was succeeded by Ralph Bunche.

In South Africa, National Party leader Daniel Malan took power, quickly introducing the racist apartheid system that would tear South African society apart and generate a decades-long civil war.

Menachem Begin founded the Israeli Herut Party.

d. Mohandas Karamchand "Mahatma" Gandhi (b. 1869), leading figure in the Indian independence movement and the foremost worldwide advocate of nonviolence; he was assassinated by a Hindu extremist in New Delhi (Jan. 30).

Burma became an independent state (Jan. 4); its first prime minister was U Nu. Multiple insurrections developed, as several communist and ethnic minority insurgencies challenged the new government; together they are often described as the Burmese Civil War (1948-   ), which continued on into the 1990s.

Malayan Civil War (1948-1960): Communist-led Chinese-Malayan forces began the Malayan insurrection, centered in the Irrawaddy Delta (Mar.); British occupation forces declared a state of emergency (June), as the conflict escalated. British-Malayan forces ultimately won the long guerrilla war, from which an independent Malaya emerged.

Dutch forces took Jogjakarta; Indonesian guerrillas continued their war of independence.

Democratic People's Republic of Korea (North Korea) became an independent state (Sept. 9).

Republic of Korea (South Korea) became an independent nation, led by Syngman Rhee (1948-1960). Insurrections in several South Korean cities failed.

Indian government forces took Hyderabad (Sept.) after its ruler, Nizam, refused attachment to India during the partition.

Karen War of Independence began in Burma (1948-1950).

d. Hideki Tojo (b. 1884), Japanese general, Kwangtung army chief of staff, and Japanese prime minister (from Oct. 1941 until his resignation in 1944); he was hanged as a war criminal.

d. Mohammad Ali Jinnah (b. 1876), Muslim League leader who became the founder of Pakistan.

d. Feng Yu-hsiang (b. 1882), Chinese general known as the "Christian General"; a powerful northern warlord in the 1920s, he was decisively defeated by the Kuomintang (1930).

d. Heitaro Kimura (b. 1888), Japanese general who commanded the Burma Area Army after its defeat at Imphal and Kohima (1944); he was executed for the mistreatment of Allied prisoners during construction of the Thailand-Burma railroad.

d. Iwane Matsui (b. 1878), Japanese general who led the campaigns to take Shanghai and Nanking (1937); he was commander of Japanese forces in China during the atrocities known as the Rape of Nanking, for which he was tried, convicted, and executed.

d. Suzuki Kantaro (b. 1868), Japanese admiral who was a key torpedo expert rising to chief of the Navy Gen-

ico (1916-1917) and France (1917-1918); he was the first American General of the Armies (1919).

d. Orville Wright (b. 1871), American aviation pioneer.

1948 (cont.)

1949

With the explosion of the first Soviet atomic bomb, the American nuclear monopoly ended, and the long, terror-filled Soviet-American stalemate of the Cold War began.

In a major Cold War development, the North Atlantic Treaty was signed (Apr. 4), and the North Atlantic Treaty Organization (NATO) was formed (Sept. 17). Its original members were Belgium, Canada, Denmark, France, Iceland, Italy, Luxembourg, the Netherlands, Norway, Portugal, the United Kingdom, and the United States. Germany, Greece, Spain, and Turkey joined later.

Greek Civil War: The war effectively ended when government forces took Mount Grammos, although a low-level guerrilla conflict continued. Without their previous bases and sources of supply in Yugoslavia and Albania, communist forces were unable to sustain a substantial campaign.

Postwar partition of Germany was completed. The Federal Republic of Germany (West Germany) became an independent nation (May), as did the German Democratic Republic (East Germany) (Oct.).

Geneva Convention amendments expanded the treaties to include the treatment of civilians and those involved in civil wars.

American-born World War II Nazi propagandist Axis Sally (Mildred Gillars) was convicted of treason and sentenced to a 12-year prison term.

d. Georgi Mikhailovich Dimitrov (b. 1882), Bulgarian Communist Comintern head (1935-1943) and postwar Bulgarian prime minister (1946-1949).

Israeli War of Independence (First Arab-Israeli War): The Egyptian-Israeli ceasefire (Jan. 7) ended the shooting war, but no peace treaty resulted; an estimated 1 million Arab refugees had fled their homes, and a decades-long set of Arab-Israeli wars and guerrilla actions had begun.

Armed clashes began between Algerians demanding independence and French colonial forces (May), as independence forces gathered and anticolonial actions developed throughout Africa.

1950

German-British atomic physicist Klaus Fuchs, head of the physics department at Britain's Harwell atomic energy installation, was exposed as a Soviet spy; he was imprisoned until 1959.

Walter Ulbricht became secretary-general of the ruling Socialist Unity Party and leader of East Germany (1950-1971).

South Africa enacted the Suppression of Communism Act, the legal basis for the creation of the South African police state.

d. Jan Christian Smuts (b. 1870), South African Boer War general, World War I commander of Allied East African forces, and twice prime minister of South Africa (1919-1924; 1939-1948).

Central, South and East Asia, and the Pacific	The Americas	

eral Staff; named prime minister (Apr. 1945), he initially said he would fight to the end.

1949

Chinese Civil War: Communist forces took Peking (Jan. 22), Nanking (Apr. 22), and the balance of China's major cities during the rest of the year, as opposing Kuomintang forces ceased to exist, with massive numbers going over to the Communist side. The People's Republic of China formally came into being (Oct. 1). Chiang Kai-shek's government fled to Formosa (Taiwan) (Dec.).

Kashmir War: India and Pakistan ended their two-year undeclared war in Kashmir with a United Nations–mediated cease-fire and the partition of Kashmir along existing battle lines (Jan. 1).

Indonesian War of Independence: A Dutch-Indonesian cease-fire ended the war (May 7); Dutch withdrawal followed (Dec.). Independence leader Sukarno became the first president of the new country.

Government of Thai ruler Luang Pibul Songgram defeated an attempted armed forces insurrection (Feb.).

Laos became an independent nation.

d. Hiroaki Abe (b. 1889), Japanese admiral who commanded the Eighth Cruiser Division in Japan's Pearl Harbor Strike Force (1941).

Remaining American troops were withdrawn from China (Feb.). A U.S. State Department White Paper announced a cutoff of military aid to the Nationalist government (Aug.), criticized that government for endemic corruption, and charged that it bore great responsibility for the Communist victory in the Chinese Civil War.

d. John Porter Lucas (b. 1890), American general during World War II; he was replaced after being blocked by the Germans at Anzio, in southern Italy (1944).

1950

Korean War (1950-1953): North Korean forces made a surprise attack on South Korea (June 25), quickly driving south to take the South Korean capital of Seoul. The United States and the United Nations quickly intervened (June 30), establishing a Korea-wide front (Aug.-Sept.), then making divisional-strength landings at Inchon, 150 miles to the north. Linking up with allied forces breaking out from the south, combined forces retook Seoul and took Pyongyang, then moved toward the Yalu River, which forms the Korean-Chinese border. Massive Chinese Red Army forces intervened; a main force of 180,000 routed allied forces (Nov. 25) and pursued them to a defensive line north of Seoul (Dec.), while more than 100,000 troops and as many civilians were evacuated by sea at Hungnam.

Indochina War: French forces withdrew to the Red River delta after substantial early defeats by Vietnamese independence forces in the north and in the Mekong Delta.

Laotian Civil War (1950-1973): The long civil war began with formation of the communist Pathet Lao army and clashes between Pathet Lao and Royal Laotian Army forces.

Pedro Albizu Campos led a failed uprising in Puerto Rico, which was quickly defeated by the island's National Guard (Oct. 30). Nationalists Oscar Collazo and Griselio Torresola attacked Blair House (Nov. 1), in Washington, D.C., in a failed attempt to assassinate American president Harry S. Truman. Torresola and a guard were killed in the attack; Collazo's life sentence was later commuted (1979).

Haitian president Dumarsais Estimé was deposed by military coup (Apr.); he was succeeded by Colonel Paul Magloire.

Congress overrode Harry S. Truman's presidential veto to pass the McCarthy-era anticommunist McCarran Internal Security Act.

Alger Hiss was convicted of perjury and imprisoned for almost four years.

Owen Lattimore, who had been falsely accused by Senator Joseph McCarthy of being a Soviet spy, was cleared by a Senate committee.

d. Henry Harley "Hap" Arnold (b. 1886), American general, World War II Army Air Corps commander.

d. Walton Harris Walker (b. 1889), American general who was an armor commander serving in World Wars I and II in Europe and in the Korean War, commanding the Eighth Army under General Douglas MacArthur; he was killed in an accident near the 38th parallel (Dec. 23).

1950 (cont.)

1951

British Soviet spies Guy Burgess and Donald MacLean escaped to the Soviet Union.

d. Henri Philippe Pétain (b. 1856), French general who was the hero of Verdun (1916), commander in chief (1917-1918), marshal of France (1918), Rif War commander (1925-1926), premier (from June 16, 1940), and head of the collaborationist Vichy government; after the war, his death sentence was commuted to life imprisonment by Charles De Gaulle.

d. Karl Gustaf Emil Mannerheim (b. 1867), commander in chief of White forces during the Finnish War of Independence and the Finnish-Soviet War (1939-1940), for whom the Mannerheim Line was named; later president of Finland (1944-1946).

d. Mikhail Markovich Borodin (b. 1884), Russian communist, an old-line Bolshevik, who was chief Comintern adviser to Sun Yat-sen and the Chinese Nationalists (1923-1927); having survived the purges of the 1930s, Borodin was arrested in Joseph Stalin's 1949 anti-Jewish purge and died in a Siberian prison.

d. William Riddell Birdwood (b. 1865), British field marshal; commander of ANZAC (Australian–New Zealand Army Corps) troops during World War I, notably in the Gallipoli landings (1915), he led the evacuation of Anglo-French troops from Gallipoli (1916).

In Iran the National Front Party took power, led by Mohammed Mossadeq, who quickly nationalized the oil industry and instituted major social changes.

d. Abdullah Ibn Hussein (b. 1882), emir and first king of Transjordan (r. 1946-1951); he was assassinated (July 20); his son, who became Hussein I, succeeded him.

1952

On Cyprus self-determination movement forces led by Colonel George Grivas and encouraged by the island's Greek Orthodox archbishop Makarios III began a guerrilla war for *enosis* (union with Greece) against British occupying forces, together with terrorist attacks on the island's Turkish minority (1952-1959).

Soviet Committee of State Security (KGB) was formed; this main Soviet espionage and counterespionage organization was the successor of the Cheka and OGPU (United State Political Administration).

North Atlantic Treaty Organization (NATO), formed under the 1949 North Atlantic Treaty, was reorganized and centralized.

d. George VI (b. 1895), king of Britain (r. 1936-1952) during World War II, when he and his wife, Elizabeth Bowes-Lyon, were important patriotic symbols; he was succeeded by his elder daughter, Elizabeth II.

Egyptian Revolution (June 23): Gamal Abdel Nasser led a coup that deposed Farouk I and established the Egyptian republic; its first premier was General Mohammed Naguib.

Mau Mau Uprising (1952-1956): Kenya's largely Kikuyu Mau Mau Society mounted a failed full-scale guerrilla war of independence against British colonial forces. During the rising, Jomo Kenyatta was arrested; held until 1961, he would emerge to become the first president of independent Kenya.

Central, South and East Asia, and the Pacific

The Americas

Chinese forces took Tibet, encountering little armed opposition. Although the Dalai Lama stayed on as a figurehead ruler, low-level guerrilla resistance began.	
Burmese government forces recaptured much of central Burma from Karen insurgents, as the Karen War of Independence failed, becoming a long guerrilla insurgency.	
Democratic insurrection in Nepal was defeated by government forces (Nov.).	
Republic of Indonesia was formally established (Aug. 15).	

Korean War: An estimated 500,000 Chinese and North Koreans mounted an offensive (Jan. 1) that took Seoul but then faltered; counterattacking allied forces retook Seoul (Mar. 14). General Douglas MacArthur was dismissed by American president Harry S. Truman (Apr. 11) after publicly demanding the right to bomb Chinese targets in Manchuria. United Nations forces ultimately established a new front north of Seoul. Off-and-on peace negotiations began in July and settled down at Panmunjon (Nov. 12); peace would come in 1953.	American atmospheric nuclear weapons tests began at the Nevada Test Site, approximately 75 miles northwest of Las Vegas; more than 100 aboveground nuclear device tests were conducted (1951-1958). The resulting radioactive fallout contaminated hundreds of square miles downwind, inhabited by more than 100,000 people, causing massive radiation damage and death. Those downwind were never warned of the hazards or evacuated.
Indochina War: Vietnamese independence forces grew stronger, linking up with Pathet Lao and Khmer Rouge guerrilla armies; French control was confined to the cities and some fortified bases. French recognition of the Bao Dai Vietnamese government had no effect.	Nationalist Revolutionary Movement Party head Victor Paz Estenssoro was elected to the Bolivian presidency, but a military coup led by General Hugo Ballívian prevented him from taking office.
d. Thomas Albert Blamey (b. 1884), Australia's first field marshal, who commanded ANZAC (Australian–New Zealand Army Corps) troops in the Middle East, became the Australian army's commander in chief (1942), and directed Allied land forces in their offensives, starting in New Guinea (1942).	Ethel Greenglass Rosenberg and Julius Rosenberg were convicted of spying for the Soviet Union and sentenced to death by Judge Irving R. Kaufman, generating a failed worldwide campaign for their release.
	Argentine dictator Juan Perón defeated an attempted military coup (Sept.).
d. Ali Khan Liaquat (b. 1895), first prime minister of Pakistan, who was assassinated while in office.	Panamanian president Arnulfo Arias was deposed by coup; he was succeeded by Vice President Alcibiades Arosmena (May).
	d. Forrest Percival Sherman (b. 1896), American admiral who during World War II helped plan key operations in the Pacific, including those in the Marianas, at Iwo Jima, and at Okinawa.

Britain exploded its first atomic bomb, on the Monte Bello Islands, off the western coast of Australia (Oct. 3), becoming the third member of the "nuclear club" and foreshadowing the nuclear proliferation of later decades.	In Bolivia, Nationalist Revolutionary Movement Party head Victor Paz Estenssoro became president (Apr. 16) after an insurrection (Apr. 8-11) that deposed General Hugo Ballívian and his military supporters; casualty estimates included 2,000 to 3,000 dead and several thousand wounded.
British occupation forces began a major successful campaign against insurgent forces in Malaysia (Feb.).	Former Cuban president Fulgencio Batista y Zaldívar seized power by coup, and ruled as dictator until he fled from the forces of Fidel Castro (Jan. 1, 1959).

1952 (cont.)

d. Jean de Lattre de Tassigny (b. 1889), marshal of France who commanded the French First Army from St.-Tropez through to Germany (1944-1945); he later assumed command in Indochina (1950).

Camille Chamoun, leader of Lebanon's Maronite Christian community, took power in a coup that toppled the Muslim-led government of Bishara al-Khouri.

Guerrilla war of independence against the French began in Tunisia, led by Habib Bourguiba.

First United Nations condemnation of the South African system of apartheid.

British forces intervened on behalf of Muscat and Oman against Saudi Arabian forces that had taken the disputed Buraimi Oasis (Oct.).

1953

d. Joseph Stalin (Joseph Vissarionovich Dzhugashvili) (b. 1879), Soviet communist dictator (1928-1953) who used the Communist Party apparatus to take power, then built a police state that ultimately cost the lives of tens of millions, through purges, famine, disease, and vulnerability to Nazi attack. His death (Mar. 5) began a power struggle over the succession and signaled the beginning of a Soviet "thaw" — a relaxation of internal tensions and loosening of tight secret police and bureaucratic controls, along with the release of tens of thousands of prisoners.

d. Lavrenti Pavlovich Beria (b. 1899), Soviet secret police head who tried to take control of the Soviet Union during the power struggle that followed Stalin's death; he was probably murdered by his opponents.

Antigovernment rioting broke out in East Berlin and throughout East Germany (June 16-17); Soviet occupation forces quickly moved against the rioters.

Yugoslav forces clashed with Italian, American, and British forces at disputed Trieste (Aug. 29-31). Tensions abated with a settlement (Dec. 5) that provided for the pullback of both sides and the evacuation of the Americans and British.

d. Karl Rudolph Gerd von Rundstedt (b. 1875), German World War II field marshal, army group commander during the Battle of France and on the eastern front, and commander in chief of western European forces opposing the Allied invasion.

d. Klement Gottwald (b. 1896), first president of communist Czechoslovakia (1948-1956).

d. Paul René Fonck (b. 1894), French military pilot who was the Allies' greatest ace in World War I, shooting down his 75th and final plane on November 1, 1918.

Iran's Mossadeq government defeated an American- and British-backed coup; Muhammed Reza Shah Pahlevi fled into exile (Aug.). Three days later, a military coup deposed the government, and the shah returned. Mohammed Mossadeq was imprisoned for three years, then held under house arrest until his death (1967).

Druze rising in Syria was defeated by Syrian government forces (Dec. 1953-Feb. 1954).

d. Ibn Saud (Abd al-Aziz Ibn Saud) (b. 1880), victor in the Arabian Civil War (1925) and first king of Saudi Arabia (r. 1932-1953).

1954

Soviet military deliberately exploded an atomic bomb, of power similar to that used at Hiroshima, in the air near approximately 45,000 of their own soldiers and many thousands of civilians near Totskoye, in the southern Urals (Sept. 14); the soldiers were then filmed during daylong exercises in the blast zone, with little or no protective clothing, even gas masks being impossible to use in the 115°F heat. Although women, children, and some men had been evacuated from Totskoye itself, more than a million people lived in the two nearest cities, within 100 miles. The number of people who died directly because of the explosion is not known; however, only a reported 1,000 of the soldiers were still alive 40 years later when the secret Soviet film was used in a

Algerian National Liberation Front (FLN) was founded (Nov.); it would later become the single party in independent Algeria.

Algerian War of Independence (1954-1962) began with an insurrection against French rule by FLN forces operating out of Tunisia (Nov. 1), who successfully fought 400,000 to 500,000 French troops; Algerian independence would ultimately be negotiated by Charles De Gaulle.

Central, South and East Asia, and the Pacific	The Americas	
		1952 (cont.)

1953

Korean War: Hostilities resumed in June, but a lasting armistice agreement was achieved at Panmunjon (July 27); the cease-fire line became the border between the two Koreas.	Fidel Castro led a failed insurrectionary attack on Cuba's Moncada barracks (July 26); he was captured and released in an amnesty two years later; his revolutionary movement became known as the July 26 Movement.	
British nuclear weapons tests began at the Maralinga, Australia, test range; they would continue until 1963.	In an extraordinary McCarthy era development, nuclear physicist J. Robert Oppenheimer, a central figure in the development of the Hiroshima and Nagasaki atomic bombs, was denied security clearance after being accused of disloyalty, an action later repudiated by the American government.	
d. Nobutake Kondo (b. 1886), Japanese admiral who commanded the Japanese Second Fleet that destroyed Britain's Force Z (1941), later leading the naval offensive at Guadalcanal.	Colombia's commander in chief Gustavo Rojas Pinilla seized power by coup, ruling as dictator (1953-1957).	
	Ethel Greenglass Rosenberg and Julius Rosenberg were executed as spies by the U.S. government.	
	Swedish diplomat Dag Hammarskjöld became the second secretary-general of the United Nations (1953-1961).	
	British forces deposed Guyana's elected prime minister, Cheddi Jagan, head of the left-oriented People's Progressive Party (Oct.).	

1954

First American hydrogen bomb was successfully tested, at Eniwetok Atoll (Nov. 1).	Long-range intercontinental ballistic missiles (ICBMs) were developed by the United States, each capable of carrying one or more nuclear warheads; these became the key instruments of potentially humanity-destroying nuclear war.	
Indochina War: In the decisive action of the Indochina War, north Vietnamese forces besieged Dien Bien Phu, a French fortress town on the Laotian-Vietnamese border, which fell (Mar.-May); the surrender of its garrison of 16,000 effectively ended the war.	d. Enrico Fermi (b. 1901), Italian-American nuclear physicist whose work included the creation of the world's first chain reaction and first nuclear reactor (1942); this was a central event in the development of the atomic bomb and the dawn of the terror-filled nuclear age.	
French–North Vietnamese Geneva Accords on Vietnam (July) formally ended the Indochina War, pro-		

1954 (cont.)

Finnish documentary. The event was kept secret until revealed in the Soviet newspaper *Pravda* (Oct. 1991), after the Cold War ended.

d. Heinz Guderian (b. 1888), German tank corps general whose forces spearheaded the invasion of Poland (1939) and made the breakthrough at Sedan (1940).

d. Paul Ludwig Ewald von Kleist (b. 1881), German armored forces general who was commander of the panzer forces that broke through at Sedan (1940) and of panzer armies during the invasion of the Soviet Union; he died in a Soviet prison.

Gamal Abdel Nasser, who had effectively ruled Egypt since the 1952 revolution, formally became premier.

Sudan gained autonomy from British-Egyptian rule.

1955

Nikita Khrushchev took full power as premier of the Soviet Union after defeating Georgi Malenkov in an internal power struggle.

American president Dwight D. Eisenhower and Soviet premier Khrushchev met at the Geneva Summit, the first post–World War II superpower meeting (July).

Warsaw Pact (Warsaw Treaty Organization), a military alliance of Soviet bloc countries set up to parallel NATO, was formed; its members were Bulgaria, Czechoslovakia, the German Democratic Republic, Hungary, Poland, Romania, and the Soviet Union.

d. Alexandros Papagos (b. 1883), Greek general who was commander in chief (1940); interned after surrendering to the Germans (1941), he was later reappointed commander in chief (1949) and defeated the communists, becoming field marshal and later prime minister (1952).

In the Sudan, civil war began between the Muslim-dominated government of the north and the Christian and animist Black Africans of the south; the war continued, though sometimes as a low-level guerrilla insurgency, into the mid-1990s.

Saudi Arabian forces were driven from the disputed Buraimi Oasis by British forces aiding rival claimants Muscat and Oman (Oct. 26).

1956

In his "secret speech" to the 20th Congress of the Soviet Communist Party (Feb.), Soviet premier Nikita Khrushchev exposed the massive crimes of Joseph Stalin, generating a greater "thaw" in the Soviet Union and also triggering

Sinai-Suez War (Second Arab-Israeli War) (Oct. 29-Nov. 6): Gamal Abdel Nasser nationalized the Suez Canal (July 26); an impasse developed, generating a British-

vided for French withdrawal, and partitioned the country into North and South Vietnam, generating the long civil war that followed.

Vietnamese Civil War (1954-1975): Civil war began as a North Vietnamese–supplied guerrilla insurrection in South Vietnam; in the 1960s it would merge with the Vietnam War.

Government forces, with American aid, defeated the main Hukbalahap guerrilla forces in the Philippines, but a low-level communist-led insurgency continued, merging with a new communist-led insurgency that grew in the 1960s and continued into the 1990s.

Low-level Pathet Lao insurgency against the newly independent Laotian government began to grow (1954-1959).

British occupying forces in Malaysia announced the withdrawal of the leadership of the insurrection to Indonesia, signaling a British victory.

Substantial insurrection in Tibet was defeated by Chinese occupying forces.

Thirty-six days of televised Army-McCarthy hearings (Apr.-May) exposed and disgraced witch-hunting American senator Joseph McCarthy, resulting in Senate censure (Dec.) and the beginning of the end of the McCarthy era.

In Guatemala, the elected government of Jacobo Arbenz Guzmán was accused by the American government of being communist dominated. With American aid, Arbenz was deposed by a military coup led by Carlos Castillo Armas (June). A decades-long guerrilla civil war began.

The American submarine Nautilus, the world's first nuclear submarine, was launched.

Paraguay's armed forces commander in chief Alfredo Stroessner seized power by military coup, then ruled as dictator until he was himself overthrown by military coup (1989).

d. Getúlio Dornelles Vargas (b. 1883), Brazilian dictator (1930-1945) and elected president (1950-1954); he committed suicide rather than accede to army demands for his resignation.

d. Hoyt Sanford Vandenburg (b. 1899), American Air Force general during World War II who became head of the Central Intelligence Group (June 1946), forerunner of the Central Intelligence Agency (CIA), then Air Force chief of staff during the Berlin Airlift and Korean War.

d. Charles Horatio McMorris (b. 1890), American admiral during World War II who later commanded the Fourth Fleet (1946).

At the Bandung (Indonesia) Conference, 29 loosely associated nations, most of them African and Asian, declared their neutrality in the Cold War, focusing instead on colonialism and racism (Apr.).

Ngo Dinh Diem became military dictator of South Vietnam.

American president Dwight D. Eisenhower and Soviet premier Nikita Khrushchev met in Geneva for a week (July); their first superpower summit yielded no specific results but began a long dialogue in what came to be called the "spirit of Geneva." Earlier in the year (Jan.), American secretary of state John Foster Dulles put forward the concept of "massive retaliation" in a nuclear war.

d. Albert Einstein (b. 1879), German-Swiss-American physicist who was a leading figure in the history of humanity. A devoted internationalist, pacifist, and anti-Nazi during the interwar period, Einstein urged President Franklin Delano Roosevelt to develop the atomic bomb during World War II before the Nazis could do so, then after the war urged that all nuclear arms be banned.

Argentine president Juan Perón was deposed by military coup; fleeing into exile, he was succeeded by General Eduardo Leonardi.

d. Clifton Albert Furlow Sprague (b. 1896), American admiral whose unit was vital in forcing the Japanese retreat at Leyte Gulf (1944).

d. Frank Dow Merrill (b. 1903), American general during World War II who commanded troops reopening the Burma Road (1944).

French forces completed their withdrawal from Indochina. As North Vietnamese forces began to win the North-South civil war, the United States replaced France as chief South Vietnamese patron; hundreds of

Cuban Revolution (1956-1959): A small band of Cuban revolutionaries, led by Fidel Castro, landed in Cuba (Dec. 2); quickly defeated by government forces, they fled into the Sierra Maestra, there mounting the guerrilla insurgency that would win the country.

1956 (cont.)

huge defections within the world communist movement, coupled with armed revolts and demonstrations in the captive nations of Eastern Europe.

Poznan Riots (June): More than 50 people were killed by Soviet troops suppressing massive riots in Poznan, Poland; one of the earliest of the wave of riots that swept Eastern Europe after Khrushchev's secret speech on the crimes of Stalin.

Hungarian Revolution: The insurrection began in Budapest (Oct. 23); a new government headed by Imre Nagy took power (Oct. 24), as Soviet troops withdrew. Nagy instituted major reforms, freed Cardinal Mindzenty, and announced withdrawal from the Warsaw Pact. Communist Party head János Kádár broke with Nagy, forming a rival government (Nov. 1). Soviet forces returned (Nov. 4) and quickly smashed lightly armed Hungarian forces, capturing Nagy, whom they later executed (1958); 100,000 to 200,000 people fled into exile.

Polish October: Massive Polish demonstrations (Oct.) toppled the hard-line communist government, bringing a somewhat reformist government led by Wladyslaw Gomulka; part of the unrest that swept the Soviet bloc in the wake of Khrushchev's secret speech and the Soviet thaw.

Makarios III, Greek Orthodox archbishop of Cyprus and leader of the Cypriot self-determination movement, was exiled to the Seychelles by British occupation forces.

d. Pietro Badoglio (b. 1871), Italian general who was commander in chief of Italian forces in the Ethiopian-Italian War (1935-1936) and again in 1940; he succeeded Benito Mussolini as Italian premier (1943).

d. Juan Negrín (b. 1894), the last prime minister of the Spanish republic.

French-Israeli agreement to seize the canal. Israeli paratroops and armor attacked Egypt (Oct. 29), pursuing retreating Egyptian troops in the Sinai and taking Sharm el-Sheikh (Nov. 5). British-French bombing of the canal area began (Oct. 30), and Port Said was attacked by paratroops (Nov. 5) and seaborne forces (Nov. 6). All three countries were forced to withdraw when the United States opposed the invasion; a United Nations peacekeeping force occupied the Suez Canal area until 1967.

National Liberation Front (FLN) forces took their guerrilla war of independence into Algiers.

Winning the struggle for independence from France, Tunisia became an independent state, the Republic of Tunisia (Mar. 20), led by its first president, Habib Bourguiba (1956-1987).

Popular Movement for the Liberation of Angola (MPLA) was founded, beginning the independence campaign in Portuguese-held Angola that would grow into the Angolan War of Independence (1961-1974).

Republic of Sudan became a fully independent nation (Jan. 1).

Morocco became an independent nation (Mar. 2).

1957

Soviet Union developed its own long-range intercontinental ballistic missiles (ICBMs), making the possibility of a humanity-destroying Soviet-American nuclear war seem very close.

Britain exploded its first hydrogen bomb (May 15).

At Chelyabinsk, near Kyshtym in the Urals, a nuclear accident caused an unreported number of deaths and thousands of casualties, contaminating hundreds of square miles; it was a Soviet state secret for decades.

A major nuclear accident occurred at the British Sellafield (Windscale) nuclear installation; the large radioactive cloud released contaminated large areas in Britain and caused an undetermined number of deaths in later years. The event was a British government secret for decades.

Albania left the Soviet bloc, becoming an independent communist state leaning toward China.

Government forces subdued rioters in Warsaw (Oct. 3).

Soviet general Vasili Konstantinovich Blücher, executed in 1938 during the Great Purge, was "posthumously rehabilitated."

d. Friedrich von Paulus (b. 1890), German Sixth Army commander at Stalingrad who ultimately surrendered the remnants of his army (1943).

d. Miklós Horthy (b. 1868), Hungarian dictator (1920-1944).

In Oman, recently restored sultan Said bin Taimur, aided by the British, suppressed a revolt led by the previously exiled imam of Oman (July-Aug.).

Spanish Morocco's territory of Ifni was invaded by Moroccan irregulars, who were then driven out by Spanish troops (Nov.-Dec.), although Ifni was later ceded to Morocco (Apr. 1, 1958).

French forces clashed with Tunisian troops near the Algerian border (May 26-June 7), incidents that would continue sporadically until Algerian independence (1962).

Border incidents (Oct.-Nov.) raised the level of tension between Syria and Turkey.

Ghana became an independent republic, led by Kwame Nkrumah (Mar. 6).

Central, South and East Asia, and the Pacific

The Americas

American military advisers formally took over the training of South Vietnamese forces, beginning the sequence of involvements that would result in the Vietnam War.

Tamil-Sinhalese conflicts escalated in Ceylon (Sri Lanka), as Tamil demonstrators demanded recognition of their language and culture.

Chinese forces invaded Burma, clashing with Burmese troops and taking disputed territory in northern Burma.

d. Anastasio Somoza Garcia (b. 1896), dictator of Nicaragua; he was assassinated and succeeded by his son Luis Anastasio Somoza Debayle, who also ruled as dictator (1956-1963).

d. Ernest Joseph King (b. 1878), World War II American Fleet commander in chief and chief of naval operations, Franklin Delano Roosevelt's chief naval adviser.

d. William Avery "Billy" Bishop (b. 1894), a leading Allied fighter pilot who shot down 72 German airplanes during World War I; he became a Canadian air marshal (1938) and was Canadian air force commander during World War II.

Indonesia claimed West Irian (Netherlands New Guinea), beginning a diplomatic and low-level military campaign against Dutch occupation forces on the island.

Tunku Abdul Rahman became the first prime minister of independent Malaysia.

d. Kingoro Hashimoto (b. 1890), Japanese army officer who was involved in a failed military coup (Feb. 26-28, 1936), then recalled for service with the start of war in China (1937); he was convicted as a war criminal.

d. Tadashi Hanaya (b. 1894), Japanese general during World War II; he had been involved in the "incident" (Sept. 18-19, 1931) providing the pretext for Japan's takeover of Manchuria.

President Dwight D. Eisenhower put forth the Cold War Eisenhower Doctrine (Jan. 5), emphasizing direct American military confrontation with the Soviet Union and promising American support, including direct armed intervention, on the behalf of any Middle Eastern countries attacked by the Soviet Union or its clients and allies.

François "Papa Doc" Duvalier won election as president of Haiti, then instituted a reign of terror administered by his Tonton Macoute secret police, becoming dictator until his death (1971).

d. Joseph Raymond McCarthy (b. 1908), American senator whose witch-hunting activities buttressed hard-line attitudes during the early years of the Cold War; his name characterized the era, as *McCarthyism* became a synonym for *witch-hunting*.

1957 (cont.)

d. Haakon VII (b. 1872), king of Norway (r. 1905-1957) who during World War II led his country's government-in-exile.

1958

Charles De Gaulle became premier of France, then quickly and successfully moved to defeat an impending civil war over the issue of Algeria; he developed a new constitutional basis for the French republic.

British Campaign for Nuclear Disarmament (CND) was founded; it was originally chaired by Bertrand Russell.

d. Imre Nagy (b. 1896), Hungarian communist prime minister (1953-1955; 1956) and leader of the Hungarian Revolution; he was imprisoned in 1956 and later executed.

d. Maurice Gustave Gamelin (b. 1872), French commander in chief (from 1935) whose defensive strategy and leadership failure greatly contributed to the German victory in the west; he was relieved of command (late May 1940) and later imprisoned during the war (1943-1945).

Lebanese Civil War: Arab and leftist Christian factions mounted an armed insurrection against the Maronite Christian government of Camille Chamoun; America intervened (July 15), with forces ultimately totaling 14,000. They were withdrawn (late Oct.) after a peace agreement that allowed Chamoun to serve the rest of his term but not to run for reelection.

In Algiers, French officers revolted, led by General Jacques Massu; France's Fourth Republic fell, as civil war threatened. The revolt was put down by Charles De Gaulle, heading France's Fifth Republic, who also offered self-determination to Algeria and released some captured National Liberation Front (FLN) leaders.

In the Battle of the Frontiers, Algerian rebels operating out of Tunisia fought against French forces over the Algerian-Tunisian border; rebels crossing from Tunisia encountered border minefields and high-voltage fences, backed by French troops. The FLN set up a provisional government-in-exile, headquartered in Tunis (Sept.).

In Iraq, General Abdul Karim Kassem led a successful army revolt (July 14), over-throwing the monarchy and killing King Faisal II.

d. Nuri al Said (Nuri as-Said) (b. 1888), Iraqi general active in various Arab nationalist movements; he was prime minister (1930-1958) until his assassination during an army coup.

Egypt and Syria formally joined to form the United Arab Republic, but the union was in name only and was later dissolved (1961).

General Ibraham Abboud took power by coup in Sudan (Nov. 17).

Republic of Guinea was founded; Ahmed Sékou Touré was the first president of the one-party state (1958-1984).

People's Republic of the Congo became an autonomous state.

Republic of Niger, a former French colony, became an independent state (Aug. 3).

1958

Burmese prime minister U Nu was deposed by an army coup; the succeeding caretaker government was headed by General Ne Win.

Inconclusive Thai-Cambodian border clashes took place over disputed territory (Nov.).

Fidel Castro's small guerrilla army came out of the Sierra Maestra (Oct.) and in less than three months took Cuba, against negligible resistance from the forces of the Batista government.

In Venezuela, the military dictatorship of Marcos Pérez Jiménez was overthrown by an insurrection with the support of the military (Jan.); the election of Romúlo Betancourt (Dec.) began a long period of constitutional democracy.

d. Claire Chennault (b. 1890), American air officer who became Chiang Kai-shek's air adviser (1937), organized the Flying Tigers (1941), and commanded American air forces in China (1942-1945).

Europe	Africa and Southwest Asia

1959

Charles De Gaulle became president of the new French Fifth Republic, then moved to stabilize the French economy and bring the war in Algeria to a close.

Makarios III (Michael Khristodoulou Mouskos) became the first president of independent Cyprus, as the ongoing guerrilla civil war escalated into a full-scale civil war that threatened to draw in Greece and Turkey; a cease-fire was negotiated (Mar. 13).

Republic of Upper Volta, a former French colony, became independent; it would later be renamed Burkina Faso (1984).

Fatah (al-Fatah), the Palestine Liberation Movement, was founded; it was led by Yasir Arafat.

In Iraq, government forces defeated an attempted army revolt in Mosul (Mar.) and a major rebellion mounted by a coalition of antigovernment forces centered on Kirkuk (July).

In Belgian-administered Rwanda, the Hutu majority successfully rose against the governing Tutsi minority. Hutu majority rule was legitimized in the elections of 1960 and 1961.

Southwest Africa People's Organization of Namibia (SWAPO) was founded as an independence organization seeking power by legal means; its armed insurrection would begin later (1966).

1960

France became a member of the "nuclear club," exploding its first atomic bomb at Reggane, in Algeria (Feb. 13).

U-2 incident: Soviet forces shot down an American U-2 reconnaissance plane in Soviet airspace, capturing its pilot, Francis Gary Powers (May 1). Powers was imprisoned as a spy and later exchanged for Soviet spy Rudolph Abel (Feb. 1962).

d. Albert Kesselring (b. 1885), German World War II air general who was commander of German forces during the Allied conquest of Italy and on the western front as the war ended; he was imprisoned for war crimes (1946-1952).

d. Erich Raeder (b. 1876), German grand admiral and commander in chief until relieved of command (1943).

Congo (later Zaire) became an independent nation (June 30) and immediately plunged into a series of related civil wars (1960-1967). The first of these came only 11 days after independence: Moïse Tshombe, supported by Belgian troops and industrialists, announced the secession of Katanga (July 11); President Joseph Kasavubu asked for a United Nations peacekeeping force, which was approved by the Security Council (July 14) and would stay until 1964.

Colonel Mobutu Sese Seko (Joseph Mobutu), Congolese army chief of staff, seized effective control of the new government (Sept.), unseating Congolese prime minister Patrice Lumumba, who then established a Soviet-backed secessionist government at Stanleyville.

Sharpeville Massacre (Mar. 21): South African police opened fire on unarmed demonstrators at Sharpeville, near Johannesburg, killing 67, with 200 more casualties. This was a major event in the development of the long South African guerrilla war, as it decisively moved the African National Congress (ANC) away from nonviolence and into armed action, and as South Africa's isolation from the world community deepened. The massacre generated a British Commonwealth condemnation of apartheid.

Antarctic Treaty (Dec.) provided that the area south of 60 degrees south latitude would become a nuclear test- and waste-free demilitarized zone and a multinational laboratory; signatories were the United States, the Soviet Union, Great Britain, France, Japan, Argentina, Chile, Australia, New Zealand, South Africa, Norway, and Belgium; 29 other nations later signed.

North Vietnamese forces opened the Ho Chi Minh Trail, a supply and troop transport route through Laos and Cambodia to South Vietnam.

Following a failed Tibetan insurrection against the Chinese (Mar.), the Dalai Lama, Tibetan religious and political leader, fled to exile in northern India, from there continuing to lead the Tibetan independence movement.

Air America, a U.S. Central Intelligence Agency (CIA) air force, began covert operations in Southeast Asia.

d. Kotoku Sato (b. 1893), Japanese general who was charged but never tried for his refusal to carry out a second attack against the British at Imphal and Kohima, the first (1944) having been so costly a failure.

Fulgencio Batista fled Cuba (Jan. 1); Fidel Castro's forces occupied Havana (Jan. 8). Castro then began the process of turning Cuba into a one-party state and consolidating his dictatorship.

d. George Catlett Marshall (b. 1880), American army chief of staff (1939-1945) who was a five-star general and General of the Army (from 1944); as secretary of state (1947-1949), he developed the Marshall Plan (1947).

d. John Foster Dulles (b. 1888), American diplomat who was a major Cold War figure as secretary of state (1953-1959); his negotiating style included taking the world to the "brink" of war; he developed the doctrine of "massive retaliation" by the use of nuclear weapons.

d. William Frederick Halsey, Jr. (b. 1882), American World War II aircraft carrier commander (1941), South Pacific commander (1942-1944), and Third Fleet commander (1944-1945).

d. William Joseph "Wild Bill" Donovan (b. 1883), American intelligence officer who during World War II organized and headed the Office of Strategic Services (OSS) (1942-1945), predecessor of the Central Intelligence Agency (CIA).

Kong Le seized power in Laos by coup; the continuing Pathet Lao insurgency became a full-scale guerrilla civil war, as American forces threatened to intervene on the government side.

Chinese and Indian forces skirmished over disputed territory on their border in the Himalayas, as their dispute escalated.

Mohammed Ayub Khan became chief martial law administrator in Pakistan, then took power as dictator (Oct.).

d. Yen Hsi-shan (b. 1883), Chinese warlord.

d. Amanullah Khan (b. 1892), king of Afghanistan (r. 1919-1928); he initiated and was defeated in the brief Afghan-British War (May 1919).

Senator John Fitzgerald Kennedy was elected 35th president of the United States.

Nicaraguan rebels invading from Costa Rica were defeated by government troops (Nov. 11-15).

El Salvador's elected president José Maria Lemus was deposed by a military coup and succeeded by Colonel César Yanes Urias (Oct. 26), beginning the long period of guerrilla insurgency that grew into the civil war of the 1980s.

Quebec Liberal premier Jean Lesage led in the formation of the Quebec separatist movement, which began to move toward armed guerrilla action against the Canadian government.

German SS officer and leading Nazi war criminal Adolf Eichmann was captured by Israeli agents in Buenos Aires.

1960 (cont.)

Europe	Africa and Southwest Asia
	French colonists' revolt in Algeria was put down by the French army (Jan.-Feb.).
	French nuclear testing began at Reggane, in Algeria (Feb.).
	Kurdish republican forces in Iraq, led by Mustafa al-Barzani, began another long war of independence, which ended (1970) when they were promised autonomy and began again when the promise was not kept.
	Ethiopian Imperial Guards attempted to take power by coup (Dec. 13-17), taking control of Addis Abbaba while Emperor Haile Selassie I was abroad; they were defeated by government forces (Dec.).
	Somalia became an independent nation (July 1). Border clashes with neighboring Ethiopia quickly followed (Aug.).
	Central African Republic, formerly part of French Equatorial Africa, became an independent nation (Aug. 13), led by President David Dacko.
	Chad became an independent nation (Aug. 11), led by President N'Garta (François) Tombalbaye.
	Federal Republic of Nigeria became an independent nation (Oct. 1).

1961

Europe	Africa and Southwest Asia
East Germany built the Berlin Wall overnight (Aug. 12), closing the border between East and West Berlin and creating the most prominent symbol of the Cold War; its later coming down (1989) decisively signaled the end of the Cold War.	Congo (Zaire) Civil War: United Nations peacekeeping forces in Katanga were defeated by Katanga forces, bolstered by South African and European mercenaries (Sept.). Greatly reinforced UN forces numbering more than 6,000 defeated the Katanga army, taking Elizabethville (Dec.).
Amnesty International was founded; the London-based organization would gain major attention for the plight of the world's political prisoners.	Soviet-backed Congolese leader Patrice Lumumba, first prime minister of the Congo (Zaire) (1960), was captured and murdered in prison by the insurgent Katanga government.
Republic of Cyprus was formed, led by archbishop Makarios III (Mar. 13).	
d. Dag Hammarskjöld (b. 1905), Swedish diplomat, second secretary-general of the United Nations (1953-1961), and key UN peace negotiator; he died in an airplane crash while trying to negotiate peace in the Congo and was posthumously awarded the 1961 Nobel Peace Prize.	Angolan War of Independence (1961-1975): Portuguese control was contested by the Soviet-backed Popular Movement for the Liberation of Angola (MLPA), the National Front for the Liberation of Angola (FNLA) (from 1962), and the National Union for the Total Independence of Angola (UNITA) (from 1966).
	French general Raoul Salan led a failed army revolt in Algeria (July) and then fled abroad, continuing to direct increasing ter-

1960 (cont.)

1961

American president John F. Kennedy promised direct American military aid to support the South Vietnamese government, sending General Maxwell D. Taylor to Vietnam and increasing the number of American advisers and the volume of supplies.

A cease-fire agreement was negotiated in the Laotian Civil War (Apr.), but the fragile cease-fire was soon broken, and American forces prepared to intervene directly.

In South Korea, General Park Chung Hee took power by coup (May 16).

Indian government forces seized Portuguese-occupied Goa, meeting negligible resistance (Dec. 18).

Bay of Pigs Battle (Apr. 17): In a failed amphibious attack, Cuban exile forces numbering 1,200 to 1,500 landed at Cuba's Bahia de los Cochinos (Bay of Pigs) with American arms and transport, but without promised air support or the popular insurrection they had expected. They were quickly defeated and captured by Cuban forces, suffering 90 dead; most of those captured were later traded for food and medical supplies.

In Nicaragua, Sandinista guerrillas, with Cuban support, began the long, low-level guerrilla war against the Luis Anastasio Somoza Debayle government that would in the late 1970s grow into a full-scale, decade-long civil war.

Burmese diplomat U Thant became the third secretary-general of the United Nations (1961-1971).

In Ecuador, the elected government of president José Maria Velasco Ibarra was deposed by coup (Nov.); he was succeeded by Carlos Julio Arosemena Monroy, who was himself deposed (1963).

d. Rafael Leonidas Trujillo Molina (b. 1891), Dominican Republic dictator (1930-1961) who was assassinated by a group of army officers; his death began a period of factional struggle that led to civil war (1965-1966).

1961 (cont.)

rorist Secret Army Organization (OAS) attacks on the French and Algerian governments, turning the Algerian War of Independence into a three-way war in Algeria and a right-wing guerrilla insurrection in France.

Following the Sharpeville Massacre (1960), the African National Congress (ANC) began three decades of guerrilla warfare in South Africa.

Oil-rich Kuwait became an independent nation (June 19) and immediately became a target for several of its larger neighbors. British forces were augmented in the Persian Gulf (Dec.), deterring planned Iraqi annexation of Kuwait.

During a Moroccan-French dispute, French troops took Bizerte (July).

After a coup in Syria, Egypt and Syria formally dissolved their United Arab Republic union, although Egypt kept the name until 1971.

1962

As Portuguese colonial insurrections grew, disaffection increased at home; a Portuguese troop revolt was quickly put down (Jan. 1).

Algerian War of Independence: A cease-fire between the National Liberation Front (FLN) and the Charles De Gaulle government was negotiated at Evian-les-Bains, France (Mar.). The Secret Army Organization (OAS) continued its terrorist campaign in France and Algeria until the FLN-OAS truce (June 17). Algeria became an independent nation (July 3); its first premier was FLN leader Ahmed Ben Bella.

Yemeni Civil War (1962-1970): A republican insurrection established the Free Yemen Republic (Sept.); the civil war began, with the monarchy supported by Saudi Arabia and the republicans supported by Egypt, which sent 60,000 to 80,000 troops into Yemen.

Rwanda Civil War (1962-1963): Former Tutsi leaders of Rwanda, deposed by Hutu electoral victories, made a failed attempt to seize power in the new Republic of Rwanda.

Ethiopia moved to negate promised autonomy for Eritrea and instead take full control of it, generating a powerful guerrilla resistance movement; the long Ethiopian-Eritrean wars began.

Nazi war criminal Adolf Eichmann was executed in Israel (Apr.); he had been cap-

1961 (cont.)

d. Emily Greene Balch (b. 1867), American pacifist, a founder and first secretary of the Women's International League for Peace and Freedom (1919), and corecipient of the 1946 Nobel Peace Prize.

d. Walter Bedell Smith (b. 1895), American general who, as chief of staff for General Dwight D. Eisenhower (Sept. 1942) and then for Supreme Headquarters, Allied Expeditionary Force (SHAEF) (Jan. 1944), was a key planner for the invasion of Europe and signed the surrender agreements of both Italy and Germany; he was second director of the Central Intelligence Agency (CIA) (Sept. 1950).

d. Richmond Kelly Turner (b. 1885), American admiral during World War II who became commander of the South Pacific and later all Pacific amphibious forces, planning and directing landing operations; at war's end, he was planning the invasion of Japan.

d. Robert Lawrence Eichelberger (b. 1886), American general who commanded the Eighth Army in the Pacific, directing the retaking of Clark Field and Manila in the Philippines (Feb.-Mar. 1945).

1962

Geneva peace agreement halted the Laotian Civil War, but only temporarily; fighting resumed later in the year, entwined with the war in neighboring Vietnam; North Vietnamese forces joined Pathet Lao forces in battle and used Laotian supply routes; America gave supplies and air combat support to Laotian government forces.

Burmese General Ne Win (Maung Shu Maung), who had been head of the caretaker government (1958) and then relinquished power, took power by coup. He would hold power openly until 1988, then play a major covert role.

Chinese frontier troops defeated Indian forces in a brief border war (Oct.-Nov.), taking and holding disputed territory; the Chinese declared a cease-fire (Nov. 21).

Indonesian forces sponsored a guerrilla campaign against Dutch occupation forces on Netherlands New Guinea (Feb.). The Dutch withdrew from New Guinea (Aug.).

Indonesia sponsored an insurrection in Brunei, which was defeated by British forces (Dec.).

d. Hu Tsung-nan (b. 1895), Nationalist Chinese general who played a key role in Chiang Kai-shek's Kuomintang forces from the mid-1930s to their final defeat by the Communists (1949), then retreated to Taiwan.

d. Kenkichi Ueda (b. 1875), Japanese general who was a key commander at Shanghai (1932), later command-

In the Cuban Missile Crisis (Oct. 22-Dec. 2), superpower confrontation came very close to generating thermonuclear war. In response to a major Soviet weapons buildup in Cuba, including missile sites and heavy bombers, American president John F. Kennedy formally announced a blockade of Cuba (Oct. 22), calling for the removal of all offensive weapons and further stating that any nuclear attack from Cuba on any Western Hemisphere nation would be considered a Soviet attack on the United States, which would then go to war. American plans to invade Cuba went forward, while Soviet armed forces went on maximum alert (Oct. 23). Unconditional Soviet withdrawal of missiles and bombers quickly followed.

Francis Gary Powers, captured when his U-2 reconnaissance plane was shot down (1960), was swapped for Soviet spy Rudolph Abel.

d. (Anna) Eleanor Roosevelt (b. 1884), wife and key associate of American president Franklin Delano Roosevelt during the Great Depression and World War II; while American delegate to the United Nations (1945-1952), she was primarily responsible for passage of the United Nations Declaration of Human Rights.

1962 (cont.)

tured by Israeli agents in Buenos Aires, Argentina (1960).

Mozambican National Liberation Front (Frelimo) was founded by Eduardo Mondlane; it would become the single party of independent Mozambique (1975).

Angolan War of Independence: National Front for the Liberation of Angola (FNLA) was founded, led by Holden Roberto; one of the three guerrilla armies, it would be destroyed by rival forces during the war.

Republic of Uganda became an independent nation (Oct. 9).

South African revolutionary Nelson Mandela, a leader of the African National Congress (ANC), was convicted of sabotage and imprisoned for what the government intended to be a life sentence.

1963

Cyprus Civil War (1963-1964): Low-level communist fighting became full-scale civil war as Greek-Turkish armed confrontations spread over the island (Dec.).

British intelligence operative Kim Philby, a Soviet mole, fled to the Soviet Union, there continuing his work for Soviet intelligence.

d. Andrew Browne Cunningham (b. 1883), British admiral who became commander in chief of Allied naval forces in the Mediterranean (1942).

d. Alan Francis Brooke (Alanbrooke) (b. 1883), British field marshal who commanded the II Corps of the British Expeditionary Force at Dunkirk (1940).

d. Fridolin R. T. von Senger und Etterlin (b. 1891), German general who led the troops defending Monte Cassino (1943-1944).

d. Hubert de la Poer Gough (b. 1870), British general during World War I, most notably in the Race to the Sea (1914) as cavalry corps commander; he led the new Fifth Army (from 1916) at the Somme (1916; 1918) and the Third Battle of Ypres (1917).

Following the failed Tutsi revolt in Rwanda, the Hutu-dominated government massacred 10,000 to 15,000 Tutsis; an estimated 200,000 Tutsis fled into exile (1963-1964).

Jomo Kenyatta became the first prime minister of the new Republic of Kenya (Aug. 15), becoming first president in 1964.

Congo (Zaire) Civil War: Further reinforced United Nations forces in Katanga decisively defeated the remaining Katanga forces (Dec. 15, 1963-Jan. 15, 1964); Moïse Tshombe fled into exile, ending the Katanga phase of the civil war.

Ba'ath Party (Arab Socialist Renaissance Party) took power by coup in Syria.

Guinea-Bissau War of Independence (1963-1974): African Party for the Independence of Guinea and Cape Verde (PAIGC), led by Amilcar Cabral, began an armed insurrection against Portugal.

Organization of African Unity (OAU) was formed by the independent African nations.

In Togo, President Sylvanus Olympio was assassinated in a successful military coup.

In Dahomey, President Hubert Maga was deposed by coup (Oct. 28); he was succeeded by General Christophe Soglo.

In the Congo (Zaire), President Fulbert Youlou was deposed by coup; he was succeeded by Alphonse Massamba-Debat.

ing the Korea Army (1934-1935) and Kwangtung Army (1935-1939) until being dismissed over internal dissension.

1963

South Vietnamese dictator Ngo Dinh Diem was deposed in an American-backed military coup (Nov. 1); he and his brother Ngo Dinh Nhu, head of the secret police, were murdered the next day. A military junta headed by General Duong Van Minh took power, operating a provisional government headed by Nguyen Ngoc Tho, which was recognized by the United States, by this time deeply involved in the civil war.

Pol Pot (Tol Saut; Saloth Sar) became head of the communist insurrection in Cambodia as general secretary of the Communist Party of Kampuchea; he accelerated development of the Khmer Rouge army, which would ultimately take Cambodia.

d. John Fitzgerald Kennedy (b. 1917), 35th president of the United States (1961-1963); he was assassinated in Dallas, Texas (Nov. 22), by Lee Harvey Oswald and possibly others. He was succeeded by Vice President Lyndon Baines Johnson.

American-Soviet Hot Line Agreement set up a direct emergency line between the leaders of the two powers in an attempt to minimize the danger of nuclear war.

Soviet-American-British Nuclear Test Ban Treaty banned atmospheric, underwater, and outer space testing of nuclear weapons, but permitted underground testing.

North American early warning radar system was set up to detect possible incoming Soviet missiles.

Federation for the Liberation of Quebec engaged in a series of bombings and other acts of terrorism, largely in Montreal.

In the Dominican Republic, the elected government of Juan Bosch was overthrown by a military coup.

Anastasio Somoza Debayle, commander of Nicaragua's National Guard, succeeded his brother Luis Anastasio Somoza Debayle as dictator, ruling until he was deposed (1979).

In Honduras, the government of elected president Ramón Villeda Morales was deposed by coup; he was succeeded by Colonel Osvaldo Lopez Arellano.

1963 (cont.)

	d. Abd el-Krim (b. 1892), Moroccan independence leader in the Rif War (1921-1926). Imprisoned afterward by the French on Réunion Island in the Indian Ocean, he escaped while en route to France (1947), finding asylum in Cairo. d. Abdul Karim Kassem (b. 1914), Iraqi premier who was killed during an army coup; Kassem had taken power in an earlier coup (1958).

1964

Cyprus Civil War: United Nations mediation and a peacekeeping force brought a truce (Mar.), but Turkish air attacks (Aug. 7-9) nearly generated a Greek-Turkish war; the UN was able to mediate a cease-fire.

d. Henry Maitland Wilson (b. 1881), British field marshal who during World War II commanded British expeditionary forces in Greece, Iraq, and Syria, then replaced Dwight D. Eisenhower as Allied commander in chief of the Mediterranean (1944).

d. John Frederick Charles Fuller (b. 1878), British general and military theorist who was most noted as the first chief general staff officer of the Tank Corps (1916), introducing tactics used successfully at Cambrai (1917); he later wrote books and articles on military affairs.

d. Nancy Langhorne Astor (b. 1879), American-born British right-wing politician who was a leader of the proappeasement Cliveden Set in the 1930s; she was the first woman member of Britain's Parliament (1919-1945).

In the Congo (Zaire), remaining United Nations peacekeeping forces left (June 30). A new insurrection led by Christophe Gbenye took much of the northeastern Congo, with Soviet and Cuban support. Moïse Tshombe returned to the Congo, as did many White mercenaries, now fighting for the Congolese government. Gbenye's forces took European hostages; approximately 1,650 of these were rescued by a Belgian battalion air-dropped into Stanleyville by American planes (Nov. 25-27).

Mozambique War of Independence (1964-1974): A guerrilla war against Portuguese rule, fought by the Mozambique National Liberation Front (Frelimo); independence came after the overthrow of Antonio de Oliveira Salazar's government by coup in Portugal (Apr. 1974).

Palestine Liberation Organization (PLO) was founded.

Zambia, formerly Northern Rhodesia, became an independent nation (Oct. 24); its first president was Kenneth Kuanda.

Intermittent Somali-Ethiopian border clashes continued, while the guerrilla war in Eritrea intensified.

In newly independent Zanzibar (1963), Black Africans successfully rebelled against the long-dominant Arab minority, which controlled the new government (Jan.).

1965

d. Winston Leonard Spencer Churchill (b. 1874), British politician, writer, and speaker; he was first lord of the admiralty (1911-1915; 1939); twice prime minister (1940-1945; 1951-1953), most notably during World War II; and a key figure in the development of the Cold War.

Cease-fire temporarily ended the shooting in the Yemeni Civil War; it would resume in 1968. Substantial Egyptian forces remained in Yemen.

Central, South and East Asia, and the Pacific

The Americas

1964

Tonkin Gulf Incident: North Vietnamese torpedo boats reportedly made two sets of attacks on American vessels in the Gulf of Tonkin, off Vietnam (Aug. 2; Aug. 4). It was the basis for the Tonkin Gulf Resolution, committing major American forces to the Vietnam War, though some critics later questioned the facts. By year's end, 20,000 to 25,000 American troops and hundreds of American warplanes were in Vietnam.

General Nguyen Kanh took power in South Vietnam by coup.

Nuclear weapons proliferation continued; China became the fifth member of the "nuclear club," beginning its atomic bomb testing program in the Lop Nor desert.

Low-level border war continued and escalated along the Thai-Cambodian border.

d. Jawaharlal Nehru (b. 1889), leader of India's Congress Party, longtime associate of Mohandas "Mahatma" Gandhi, and first prime minister of independent India (1947-1964); father of Indira Gandhi, grandfather of Rajiv Gandhi, and brother of Madame Vijaya Pandit.

d. Emilio Aguinaldo (b. 1869), leader of the Philippine revolt against Spanish rule (1896-1898), first president of the Philippine republic (Jan. 23, 1899), and leader of Philippine forces during the Philippine-American War (1899-1905), although he declared American allegiance after his capture (1901).

d. Masaki Honda (b. 1889), Japanese general who led Japan's 33d Army in northern Burma (1944).

Tonkin Gulf Resolution (Aug. 7): American congressional resolution, passed in the House unanimously and in the Senate with only two dissenting votes, authorized President Lyndon B. Johnson to take the United States into the undeclared Vietnam War, which he immediately did. The authorization was granted after reported North Vietnamese torpedo boat attacks on two American naval vessels in the Gulf of Tonkin; the reports were later the subject of great controversy.

In Brazil, the legitimate government of President João Goulart was overthrown by an armed forces coup (Mar.); he was succeeded by Marshal Humberto de Alencar Castello Branco, who quickly instituted an authoritarian government.

Nobel Peace Prize was awarded to Martin Luther King, Jr., leader of the American civil rights movement and worldwide proponent of nonviolence.

In Bolivia, the elected government of President Victor Paz Estenssoro was deposed by a military coup mounted by Vice President René Barrientos Ortuño, who then became copresident of a military government with General Alfredo Ovando Candía (Nov.).

d. Douglas MacArthur (b. 1880), World War II commander of the Philippines and southwest Pacific, five-star general, and United Nations Korean War commander until dismissed (Apr. 1951); he was the son of Arthur MacArthur.

1965

Vietnam War (1965-1973): Full American participation in the war began (Feb.), with heavy American bombing of North Vietnam and the mining of Haiphong and other harbors, along with the commitment of massive ground forces. Battalion-strength troop arrivals began

Dominican Republic Civil War (Apr. 1965-June 1966): An insurrection against the Dominican Republic's military government was directed at restoring the elected government of Juan Bosch, which had been deposed by military coup (1963). Charges of communist influence brought 21,000 American troops to the side of the

1965 (cont.)

	Fatah (Palestine Liberation Movement) began a guerrilla war against Israel, striking from bases in surrounding Arab countries.

Fatah (Palestine Liberation Movement) began a guerrilla war against Israel, striking from bases in surrounding Arab countries.

General Mobutu Sese Seko (Joseph Mobutu) formally took power (Nov. 25) in the Congo (Zaire), deposing President Joseph Kasavubu.

Southern Rhodesia (later Zimbabwe), a White-dominated British African colony under attack from Britain and the Commonwealth for its racist policies, declared itself the independent nation of Rhodesia (Nov.).

Ethiopian-Eritrean conflict grew into a full-scale guerrilla war for Eritrean independence (1965-1991).

1966

d. Sergei Korolev (b. 1906), Soviet spacecraft designer and rocket fuel developer; a central figure in humanity's exploration of space.

d. Josef Dietrich (b. 1892), German general who organized and led the Nazi headquarters guard (Leibstandarte Adolf Hitler) (1933), most notably on the Night of the Long Knives (June 29-30, 1934); he commanded the Sixth SS Panzer Army (from Oct. 1944) in the Ardennes offensive and the Malmédy Massacre; he was later imprisoned for war crimes.

Namibian War of Independence (1966-1988): Guerrilla war of independence led by the Southwest Africa People's Organization of Namibia (SWAPO) began, with Angolan, Soviet, and Cuban assistance, against South African occupying forces.

National Union for the Total Independence of Angola (UNITA) was founded by Jonas Savimbi, one of the three guerrilla armies that fought the Angolan War of Independence (1961-1975); UNITA and Savimbi would go on to fight the Angolan Civil War (1975-   ).

General Joseph Ankrah took power by coup in Ghana, deposing President Kwame Nkrumah, one of the historic leaders of the African anticolonial movement.

Jean Bédel Bokassa led a military coup in the Central African Republic, deposing President David Dacko and taking power himself as dictator (Jan. 1).

Insurgency grew in Chad, ultimately leading to the long Chad Civil War (1975-

(Mar.), and the decision to commit hundreds of thousands of troops was made later (July). By year's end, more than 150,000 American troops were in Vietnam.

Vietnam War, Battle of Ia Drang (Oct.-Nov.): First large-scale (regimental-strength) battle between American and North Vietnamese forces took place in the Ia Drang Valley, near the Cambodian border.

South Vietnamese air general Nguyen Cao Ky took power by coup.

India-Pakistan War: Low-level border skirmishing led to a divisional-strength Pakistani armored attack across the Kashmir cease-fire line (Sept. 1) and the bombing of Indian airfields. India contained the Pakistani thrust and attacked in the Punjab (Sept. 6). A United Nations–mediated cease-fire (Sept. 27) ended hostilities.

Failed Communist Party of Indonesia coup generated army and militia mass murder of 200,000 to 300,000 people, including many noncommunists, and the arrest of tens of thousands more, many of them murdered in prison.

d. Syngman Rhee (b. 1875), first president of South Korea (1948-1960); he was head of state during the Korean War.

d. Masakazu Kawabe (b. 1886), Japanese general who during World War II commanded the Burma Area Army (1943-1944) and led the Indian offensive blocked at Imphal and Kohima (1944).

Dominican military; some of these were later withdrawn as Organization of American States (OAS) peacekeeping forces arrived.

d. Pedro Albizu Campos (b. 1891), Puerto Rican lawyer and Nationalist Party leader; an advocate of armed insurrection, he was much imprisoned (1936-1943; 1950-1953; 1954-1964).

d. Thomas Dresser White (b. 1901), American Air Force general who served during World War II, most notably in the Philippines, New Guinea, and Borneo; as Air Force chief of staff (1957-1961), he oversaw development of the American strategic missile program.

d. Henry Duncan Graham Crerar (b. 1888), Canadian World War II general in command of substantial Canadian and other forces invading southern Germany.

Vietnam War: Massive American commitment to the war grew, as did opposition to the war at home; by year's end, more than 400,000 Americans, including secret forces, were directly involved in the war in Southeast Asia. American and South Vietnamese forces unsuccessfully attempted to secure Saigon, their headquarters city, while Viet Cong forces operated freely out of the Iron Triangle, a major guerrilla base only 25 miles from the city, as they would throughout the war. Viet Cong forces continued to fight a guerrilla war, as American and South Vietnamese forces tried to interdict their supply lines and defeat their operations in the north, the central highlands, on the coast, and in the Mekong Delta. American warplanes attacked North Vietnam, also beginning to attack supply lines through Cambodia.

Cultural Revolution (Great Proletarian Cultural Revolution) (1966-ca. 1971): Chinese Communist leader Mao Zedong instituted a campaign and a set of purges designed to make China an entirely classless society; the movement's main instruments were irregulars called the Red Guards, who attacked "revisionist" elements in the Party, with disastrous effects on the country's society and culture.

Dominican Republic Civil War: Guerrilla actions continued until the election (June), in which Joaquin Balaguer defeated Juan Bosch. Balaguer restored constitutional government, and the war ended.

Huey Newton and Bobby Seale organized the American Black Panther Party, which engaged in several defensive and offensive armed actions against law enforcement authorities through the early 1970s.

Che Guevara arrived in Bolivia (Nov.) and developed a small mountain-based guerrilla movement, apparently hoping to repeat the Cuban experience.

d. Chester William Nimitz (b. 1885), commander of the American Pacific fleet from after Pearl Harbor through the end of World War II; he was Fleet Admiral of by far the world's largest and most powerful navy.

d. Courtney Hicks Hodges (b. 1887), American general who led the First Army across northern France, including the first troops to enter Paris (Aug. 1944) and to cross the Siegfried Line (Oct. 1944), as well as those that took the Ludendorff Bridge across the Rhine at Remagen (Mar. 7, 1945).

1966 (cont.)

1987). The insurgent Chad National Liberation Front (Frolinat) was founded.

General Johnson Aguyi-Ironsi took power by coup in Nigeria (Jan.). His military government was deposed by a second army coup, which brought Yakubu Gowon to power (July).

Prime Minister Milton Obote openly took dictatorial power in Uganda as president, abolishing the constitution.

1967

Greek army colonels George Papadopoulos and Stylianos Pattakos led a successful military coup (Apr. 21); "the colonels" held power for seven years (1967-1974).

Cyprus was informally partitioned between its warring Greek and Turkish populations.

d. Arthur William Tedder (b. 1890), British air marshal who was World War II commander of Allied air forces in the Mediterranean and then in western and southern Europe, playing a key role in planning the Normandy invasion and commanding tactical forces (1944). On behalf of Dwight D. Eisenhower, he signed the German surrender document in Berlin (1945); he was later chief of the British air staff (1946-1950).

d. Clement Richard Attlee (b. 1882), British Labour Party leader (1935-1955) who strongly opposed fascism and its appeasers before World War II; he became postwar Labour prime minister (1945-1951) and played a major role in Britain's withdrawal from empire.

d. Konrad Adenauer (b. 1876), German lawyer and politician, post–World War II leader of the Christian Democratic Union, and first chancellor of the Federal Republic of Germany (1949-1963).

Six-Day War (Third Arab-Israeli War) (June 5-10): As the entire Middle East prepared for a new war, Israeli forces mounted surprise air strikes that destroyed most of the Egyptian, Jordanian, and Syrian air forces on the ground and severely damaged the Iraqi air force. In just six days, Israeli ground forces, with massive and unopposed air support, took the Sinai Peninsula from Egypt, the rest of Jerusalem and the West Bank from Jordan, and the Golan Heights from Syria, decisively defeating all three opposing armies. Israeli forces continued to occupy all territories taken; no peace treaty followed.

Egyptian troops were withdrawn from Yemen after the Six-Day War (Third Arab-Israeli War).

Nigeria-Biafra Civil War (1967-1970): In Nigeria, the largely Ibo-populated eastern region of Biafra seceded (May 20), generating civil war with the Muslim-dominated Nigerian government. Deaths numbered 1.5 million to 2 million, most of them children and other noncombatants who died of starvation and disease, as a worldwide relief effort largely failed because the government refused to admit relief workers and supplies.

1966 (cont.)

French nuclear weapons testing began at Moruroa Atoll, in the South Pacific, 750 miles southeast of Tahiti.

Full Indian withdrawal from Pakistan came after the Indian-Pakistani Tashkent Agreement (Jan. 19).

d. Sadao Araki (b. 1877), Japanese general known for his radical nationalism and idolized by like-minded young officers who undertook an abortive rebellion (Feb. 1936); he was a key adviser to Prime Minister Hideki Tojo early in World War II.

d. Yasuji Okamura (b. 1884), Japanese general who commanded the North China Area Army (1941-1944), with the policy "Kill all, burn all, take all." Later he led the Chinese Expeditionary Army in the offensive in southern China (1944).

d. Jisaburo Ozawa (b. 1886), Japanese admiral who, as commander of the First Mobile Fleet and the Third Fleet, led Japanese forces in the battles of the Philippine Sea and Leyte Gulf (both 1944).

d. Pai Ch'ung-hsi (b. 1893), Nationalist Chinese general who led the Chinese reoccupation of Manchuria after World War II (1945-1946), later becoming war minister (1946).

1967

Vietnam War: Successful North Vietnamese and Viet Cong guerrilla war continued, as American and South Vietnamese forces pursued elusive guerrillas, mined rivers, and failed to interdict supply lines in South Vietnam, Laos, and Cambodia. By year's end, American forces numbered nearly 500,000.

Nguyen Van Thieu was elected president of South Vietnam (Sept.).

Chinese hydrogen bomb testing began in the Lop Nor desert.

Noncommunist Southeast Asian nations formed the Association of Southeast Asian Nations (ASEAN).

d. Ho Long (He Long) (b. 1896), Chinese Communist marshal, who died under persecution by the Red Guards.

American president Lyndon Baines Johnson and Soviet premier Aleksei N. Kosygin held the Glassboro Summit, a two-day meeting at Glassboro, New Jersey (June); some progress toward a nuclear nonproliferation treaty was reported.

Because of Vietnam War setbacks, President Johnson decided not to seek reelection.

d. Che Guevara (Ernesto Guevara de la Serna) (b. 1928), Argentine-born Cuban Revolution guerrilla leader (1956-1959); he was killed by the Bolivian military after his capture (Oct. 7) while leading a guerrilla insurrection.

d. Lewis Hyde Brereton (b. 1890), American Air Force commander in the Philippines, most of whose planes were destroyed on the ground at Clark Field (Dec. 8, 1941); he later led the First Allied Airborne Army in Europe during their defeat in Operation Market Garden (1944).

d. Holland McTyeire Smith (b. 1882), American Marine general during World War II who planned and directed several key Pacific operations, including Saipan and Guam (1944) and Iwo Jima and Okinawa (1945).

d. Walter Krueger (b. 1881), Prussian-born American general; a strategy expert who rose to command of the Sixth Army in the southwest Pacific (Jan. 1943), he directed landings at Leyte, Mindoro, and Luzon, as Americans retook the Philippines.

1967 (cont.)

Europe	Africa and Southwest Asia
	Failed revolt in Katanga was joined by some mercenaries; it was defeated by Congolese (Zaire) government forces, which also used mercenaries. An invasion of exiles from bases in Rwanda also failed.

Process of destabilization began in Lebanon, with Palestinian commandos raiding Israel from Lebanese bases and Israeli armed response into Lebanon.

South Yemen became an independent nation (Nov. 30).

d. Albert John Luthuli (b. 1898), head of the African National Congress (ANC) (1952-1967); the Zulu chief, leader of the South African nonviolence movement, received the 1960 Nobel Peace Prize. Oliver Tambo succeeded him as head of the ANC. |

1968

Europe	Africa and Southwest Asia
Prague Spring (Jan.-Aug.): Led by Czech Communist Party reformer Alexander Dubcek, the Czech government instituted major democratic reforms. Czechoslovakia was then invaded and taken by an estimated 400,000 Soviet bloc troops (Aug. 20), bringing the Prague Spring to an end.

In an attempt to justify the Soviet invasion of Czechoslovakia, Leonid Brezhnev announced the Brezhnev Doctrine, stating that the Soviet Union was justified in intervening in the affairs of any other communist state in which the communist system was threatened (Sept. 26).

The Baader-Meinhof Group (Red Army Faction), an anarchist-terrorist guerrilla group, began a long series of bombings, murders, and robberies in West Germany (1968-1972). Chief organizer Andreas Baader was captured and imprisoned, but he escaped with the help of journalist Ulrike Meinhof, who then joined him.

d. Konstantin Konstantivoch Rokossovski (b. 1896), marshal of the Soviet Union who served in the Red Army during the Russian Civil War and became a key Soviet commander, holding off the German offensive at Moscow (1941) and decisively defeating the Germans at Stalingrad (1942-1943).

d. Trygve Halvdan Lie (b. 1896), Norwegian diplomat and first secretary-general of the United Nations (1946-1952).

d. Karl Barth (b. 1886), Swiss Protestant minister who became a leading anti-Nazi in the 1930s and was a notable post–World War II peace activist. | Ba'ath Party (Arab Socialist Renaissance Party) took power by coup in Iraq (July); Ahmed Hassan al Bakr became president (until 1979), although Saddam Hussein was de facto dictator (from 1971).

Palestine Liberation Organization (PLO) terrorists struck Israel repeatedly, mainly from bases in Jordan. Israel responded with military incursions into Jordan, sometimes also skirmishing with Jordanian army units.

Nigeria-Biafra Civil War: Government forces, with control of the air, drove deep into Biafra, as famine and disease killed hundreds of thousands of Biafran civilians.

Yemeni Civil War resumed (Feb.), with Southern Yemen entering the war on the Yemeni side and Saudi Arabia again supporting the monarchy.

Conflict between Arab and Black African forces in Chad continued. An Arab insurrection in the north was defeated by the Chadian government with the help of French troops (June).

In Muscat and Oman, government forces defeated an insurrection mounted by a faction within the governing National Liberation Front (May).

In Mali, President Mobido Keita was deposed by coup; he was succeeded by military officer Moussa Traore (Dec.). |

1967 (cont.)

1968

Vietnam War, Tet Offensive (Jan.-Feb.): North Vietnamese forces mounted an offensive throughout South Vietnam, including attacks on the American Embassy in Saigon. A military failure, the offensive was a major political success for the North Vietnamese, demonstrating that American government estimates of progress in the war had been overly optimistic and that there was no "light at the end of the tunnel." American public opinion turned decisively against continuation of the war.

Vietnam War, My Lai Massacre (Mar. 16): The mass murder of approximately 150 unarmed civilians, most of them women, children, and old men, by a platoon of the American Division, was commanded by Lieutenant William L. Calley, Jr., at the hamlet of My Lai, in Quang Tri province; it was part of a larger body of atrocities committed by American forces in the area at the time. Calley was the only one convicted; he was later paroled (Mar. 1974).

Vietnam War: Combined impact of the Tet Offensive and the My Lai Massacre forced American reconsideration of the war. Although major and largely unsuccessful American–South Vietnamese operations were mounted, the main American emphasis turned to peace negotiations, which opened in Paris (May 10). Outgoing president Lyndon Johnson ordered cessation of all attacks on North Vietnam (Oct. 31). By year's end, American forces in Southeast Asia numbered at least 550,000.

Bikini Atoll in the Marshall Islands was declared clear of atomic weapons test contamination, and its residents were allowed to return to their homes; they would be evacuated again (1978), in a reversal of this evaluation.

North Korean forces seized the USS *Pueblo* and its 83-man crew in the Sea of Japan (Jan. 23); 82 surviving crew members were released 11 months later.

Nuclear Nonproliferation Treaty was negotiated; it was ultimately signed by more than 100 nations, including the United States and the Soviet Union, though not by France or China, which had nuclear weapons, or by several other nations in the process of developing them.

Republican Richard M. Nixon defeated Vice President Hubert H. Humphrey, becoming the 37th president of the United States (1969-1974).

Catholic priests Daniel and Philip Berrigan led a group of American anti–Vietnam War protesters in a draft card burning at a Maryland draft board office; some were tried and convicted as the "Catonsville Nine." Anti–Vietnam War demonstrations throughout the United States grew larger after the failed Tet Offensive.

In Peru, the elected government of President Fernando Belaunde Terry was deposed by coup; he was succeeded by General Juan Velasco Alvarado.

d. Martin Luther King, Jr. (b. 1929), leader of the American civil rights movement and worldwide leader of the nonviolence movement, who was awarded the Nobel Peace Prize (1964); he was assassinated by James Earl Ray in Memphis, Tennessee (Apr. 4).

d. Robert Francis Kennedy (b. 1925), American politician, brother of President John Fitzgerald Kennedy; he was shot by Sirhan Sirhan in Los Angeles (June 5; died June 6) while campaigning for the Democratic presidential nomination.

d. Husband Edward Kimmel (b. 1882), commander of the American Pacific Fleet at Pearl Harbor (Dec. 7, 1941); he was relieved of his command after the terrible losses there.

1968 (cont.)

1969

Northern Ireland Civil War (1969-): Provisional Irish Republican Army (Provisionals) split off from the Irish Republican Army (IRA), as massive Catholic demonstrations built in Northern Ireland; a long terrorist guerrilla insurgency began. British forces were sent to Northern Ireland (Aug.), soon growing into a divisional-strength long-term occupying force.

d. Harold Rupert Leofric George Alexander (Alexander of Tunis) (b. 1891), British field marshal who commanded at Dunkirk (1940), in Burma (1942), and in the Middle East and Italian theaters (from 1942); he directed the invasion of Italy (1943-1944), becoming supreme allied commander of Mediterranean forces (1944).

Nigeria-Biafra Civil War: Biafran forces went on the offensive (Mar.) but failed to reach the sea. A Nigerian government offensive (June-Dec.) took much of the rest of Biafra. A worldwide Biafran relief effort failed because the Nigerian government still blocked relief supplies intended for Biafran civilians, who died of famine and disease by the hundreds of thousands.

Iran and Iraq disputed control of the Shatt al Arab waterway, their border troops clashing repeatedly.

Fatah (Palestine Liberation Movement) joined with the parallel Palestine Liberation Organization (PLO), led by Yasir Arafat, as the Israeli-PLO guerrilla war intensified. PLO development of bases in Lebanon brought Lebanese-PLO engagements, but the PLO was able to operate out of southern Lebanon.

Muammar al-Qaddafi seized power in Libya by coup, establishing one-party dictatorial rule.

General Mohammed Siad Barre seized power by coup in Somalia (r. 1969-1991).

George Habash founded the Popular Front for the Liberation of Palestine, a hard-line terrorist organization.

Colonel Mohammed Gafaar al-Nimeiry took power by coup in Sudan, deposing Prime Minister Mohammed Ahmed Mahgoub.

d. Eduardo Mondlane (b. 1920), founder of the Mozambique National Liberation Front (Frelimo) (1962) and leader of Frelimo guerrilla forces during the Mozambique War of Independence (1964-1969); he was assassinated by the Portuguese.

d. Moïse Kapenda Tshombe (b. 1919), leader of secessionist Katanga (1960) who fled abroad (1963) after defeat by United Nations forces and later was Congolese (Zairean) prime minister (1964-1965).

d. Hitoshi Imamura (b. 1886), Japanese general who led the invasion of Java (1942) but failed to retake Guadalcanal from the Americans (1942-1943).

Vietnam War: American and allied forces engaged in the war reached a high of at least 700,000, as North Vietnamese pressure continued, American bombing intensified, peace negotiations proceeded, and American withdrawal began. President Richard M. Nixon announced troop withdrawals (May); they began (June), while American bombing intensified, with bombing of North Vietnam resuming (June 5).

Vietnam War: American forces in regimental strength assaulted and took fortified North Vietnamese positions near the Laotian border, at "Hamburger Hill" (May). The hill was retaken by the North Vietnamese (June).

Vietnam War: Heavy American secret bombing of North Vietnamese and Khmer Rouge forces in Cambodia began (1969-1973).

Cambodian Civil War (1969-1975): A communist Khmer Rouge (Red Khmers) guerrilla insurgency began against the neutralist Norodom Sihanouk government, then against the Lon Nol government, which received massive American aid.

Guerrilla New People's Army was founded by the Communist Party of the Philippines–Marxist-Leninist and developed the long communist insurrection in progress into a full-scale guerrilla war.

Chinese-Soviet armed clashes intensified on the Manchurian-Soviet border (Mar.).

d. Ho Chi Minh (Nguyen That Thanh) (b. 1890), Vietnamese communist leader who was the first president of the Democratic Republic of Vietnam (1945-1969); he led his country through the Indochina War (1946-1954) and the early years of the Vietnam War.

d. Li Tsung-jen (b. 1891), Nationalist Chinese general who was a key Kuomintang leader, briefly succeeding Chiang Kai-shek as president of Nationalist China (1949).

d. Raizo Tanaka (b. 1892), Japanese admiral who served in such key 1942 battles as Java Sea, Midway, eastern Solomons, and Guadalcanal.

American president Richard M. Nixon unilaterally renounced the use of biological weapons and the first use of chemical weapons by the United States.

Massive anti–Vietnam War demonstrations continued in the United States, as President Richard Nixon and Henry Kissinger, his foreign affairs adviser, began the four-year process of negotiating a withdrawal while still waging war.

October Crisis: Quebec Liberation Front terrorists engaged in bombing, kidnapping, and murder, including the murder of Quebec labor minister Pierre La Porte; the Canadian government responded with mass arrests and sent army units into Montreal.

El Salvador and Honduras fought a brief border war (June 24-28), which was successfully mediated by the Organization of American States (OAS).

d. Dwight David Eisenhower (b. 1890), World War II Allied supreme commander in Europe (1943) and General of the Army (1944), who planned the Normandy invasion and the defeat of Germany; later army chief of staff (1945-1948), supreme commander of NATO (1951-1952), and 34th president of the United States (1953-1961).

d. Raymond Ames Spruance (b. 1886), American admiral who was a key commander of American forces at the decisive Battle of Midway (1942) and of substantial naval forces during the balance of the war.

1970

Europe	Africa and Southwest Asia
Renewed antigovernment activities in Poland (Dec. 15-20) cost 300 to 400 lives and brought down Wladyslaw Gomulka's government; unrest continued, although the new government of Edward Gierek promised reforms. d. Charles André Joseph Marie De Gaulle (b. 1890), head of Free French forces during World War II, postwar premier of France, and president of the Fifth Republic (1959-1969). d. William Joseph Slim (b. 1891), British general who was commander in the Burma theater (1942-1945); his Fourteenth Army defeated Japanese forces in Burma. d. Alexander Fyodorovich Kerensky (b. 1881), head of the Russian Provisional Government (1917) after the overthrow of the Czar; he went into exile after the Bolsheviks' October Revolution (1917). d. Semën Konstantinovich Timoshenko (b. 1895), Soviet field marshal who was commander of Soviet forces from 1940, during the Finnish-Soviet War and the early years of World War II.	d. Gamal Abdel Nasser (b. 1918), organizer of the military coup (1952) that deposed Farouk I and established the republic; president of Egypt (1956-1970), he was succeeded by Anwar Sadat. Jordanian forces defeated invading Syrian forces and their Palestine Liberation Organization (PLO) allies in northern Jordan, then decisively defeated and expelled PLO forces in Jordan. After the PLO's expulsion from Jordan, Yasir Arafat moved PLO headquarters to Lebanon, greatly expanding guerrilla attacks on Israel, drawing intensified Israeli armed response, and further destabilizing Lebanon. Biafra surrendered (Jan. 12); the destroyed country had suffered an estimated 2 million dead, most of them civilians. Low-level border war continued between Iran and Iraq. An Iranian-supported coup in Iraq failed. General Hafez al Assad, at the head of a Ba'ath Party faction, took power by coup in Syria (Nov.). Yemeni Civil War ended with the establishment of a republic.

1971

Europe	Africa and Southwest Asia
d. Nikita Sergeyevich Khrushchev (b. 1894), Soviet leader (from 1955) and premier (1958-1964), notable for his secret speech (1956) exposing the crimes of the Stalin era and for his role in the Cuban Missile Crisis (1962).	Zimbabwe-Rhodesia Civil War (1971-1984) began as a low-level guerrilla war, with Zimbabwe African National Union (ZANU) and Zimbabwe African People's Union (ZAPU) forces making cross-border attacks into Rhodesia from neighboring countries. Saddam Hussein took full power in Iraq, becoming de facto dictator. Jordanian forces expelled remaining Palestine Liberation Organization (PLO) forces from Jordan; PLO concentration continued in Lebanon. Armed forces chief of staff Idi Amin seized power by coup in Uganda, deposing Milton Obote and beginning an eight-year reign of terror. Iranian troops seized several disputed Persian Gulf islands (Nov.). Bahrain became an independent nation, ruled by Sheikh Salman ibn Hamad Al Khalifa. United Arab Emirates were established, consisting of Abu Dhabi, Sharjah, Ajman, Umm al Qaiwain, Fujairah, and Dubai.

Vietnam War, Cambodian Incursion (Apr.-June): American and South Vietnamese forces invaded Cambodia; they were forced to withdraw because the move generated even more massive American antiwar protests at home. Peace negotiations slowly continued, as did American withdrawal. At year's end, American and allied forces numbered approximately 400,000. North Vietnamese and Viet Cong forces continued to hold and strengthen their positions in South Vietnam.

Cambodian leader Norodom Sihanouk was deposed in a coup led by Lon Nol, ultimately going into exile in Beijing. Lon Nol became head of state, while Khmer Rouge power grew.

In Pakistan, the Awami League, led by Sheikh Mujibur Rahman, won an electoral victory (Dec.); the Pakistani military government refused to recognize the election results, generating a huge civil disobedience campaign in East Pakistan and the outlawing of the Awami League, as the run-up to the Bangladesh War of Independence began.

d. Sukarno (b. 1901), leader of the Indonesian War of Independence and first president of Indonesia (1949-1966).

Salvador Allende Gossens was elected president of Chile, beginning the sequence of events that would result in a right-wing coup (1973).

Canadian troops and police brought the terrorist "October Crisis" in Quebec to a close; the question of Quebec remained the central problem facing the nation.

Abimeal Guzmán Reynoso founded the Peruvian Maoist-oriented Shining Path (Sendoro Luminoso), which would become a substantial guerrilla movement (from ca. 1980).

d. Lazaro Cardenas Del Rio (b. 1895), Mexican general and left-oriented reformer who as president of Mexico (1934-1940) focused on carrying through the promises of the Mexican Revolution, especially in regard to land redistribution.

Bangladesh War of Independence (Mar.-Dec.): Mujibur Rahman declared East Pakistan independent (Mar. 26) and was imprisoned as the insurrection began. Insurgent forces were defeated in six weeks, with tens of thousands dead; 6 million to 10 million refugees fled to India, as guerrilla war continued from Indian bases. Rahman was freed and became the first prime minister of independent Bangladesh after Indian victory in the India-Pakistan War (Dec.).

India-Pakistan War: Pakistani forces bombed Indian airfields and made ground attacks in Kashmir (Dec. 3). India, then supporting Bangladesh independence forces, responded with a massive and sucessful invasion of East Pakistan, taking Dacca and 90,000 prisoners (Dec. 5) and mounting a successful counteroffensive in Kashmir. Bangladeshi independence was proclaimed (Dec. 16); a cease-fire took effect (Dec. 17).

Zulfikar Ali Bhutto founded the Pakistan People's Party.

Vietnam War: American troop withdrawals accelerated; by year's end, American and allied forces numbered approximately 200,000. During the year, South Vietnamese forces struck into Laos and Cambodia. American planes bombed North Vietnam (late Dec.).

American-Soviet Nuclear Accidents Agreement was signed in a further attempt to prevent a misunderstanding that could lead to nuclear war.

In the Seabed Non-nuclearization Treaty, the Soviet Union and the United States agreed not to set nuclear weapons on or under the ocean floor.

United Nations ratified the Biological Warfare Ban Treaty, supplementing the 1925 Geneva Protocol on chemical and biological warfare.

In Bolivia, an armed forces military coup overthrew the government of General Juan José Torres; he was succeeded by Colonel Hugo Banzer Suárez (Aug.).

d. Ralph Johnson Bunche (b. 1904), African-American diplomat who became chief United Nations mediator in the First Arab-Israeli War (1948) after the assassination of Folke Bernadotte; he was awarded the 1950 Nobel Peace Prize.

d. Dean Gooderham Acheson (b. 1893), American lawyer and diplomat, secretary of state (1949-1953) in the Truman administration, and a key early Cold War figure.

d. Jacobo Arbenz Guzmán (b. 1913), Guatemalan officer and president (1950-1954) who fled into exile after American-backed forces deposed him.

1971 (cont.)

1972

Northern Ireland Civil War: Conflict grew even more bitter and intense. On "Bloody Sunday" (Jan. 30), British troops killed 13 unarmed Catholic demonstrators in Londonderry. Guerrilla actions grew, and direct British rule over Northern Ireland was reimposed (Mar.).

Islamic Black September terrorists murdered two Israeli athletes at the Munich Olympics, taking nine more as hostages; all nine were killed during a rescue attempt, as were five terrorists.

West German terrorists Andreas Baader and Ulrike Meinhof were captured and imprisoned.

d. Paul Hausser (b. 1880), German general who created and led the Waffen SS (Combat Blackshirts [*Schutzstaffel*]) (1936) and new I SS Panzer Corps (1941); after the war he successfully sought veteran status for the SS equal to that for the regular army.

d. Franz Halder (b. 1884), German general who was chief of staff (1938-1942); he was imprisoned (1944) after the failed Hitler assassination attempt.

In Burundi, a Hutu rebellion failed; it was followed by the massacre of an estimated 100,000 to 250,000 Hutus by the Tutsi-dominated Burundi armed forces.

Sudanese Civil War seemed concluded, with promises of full autonomy for the Christian and animist Black African south; the promises were not fully kept, and low-level guerrilla war continued.

d. Kwame Nkrumah (b. 1909), Ghanaian independence leader, Gold Coast prime minister (1951-1957), and prime minister (1957-1960) and first president of Ghana (1960-1966) until deposed by coup.

1973

Greek dictator George Papadopoulos was toppled by a military coup led by General Demetrios Ioannides (Nov. 25); he was replaced by General Phaidon Gizikis.

b. Fritz Erich von Manstein (b. 1887), German World War II general in command of substantial forces on the western and eastern fronts; he took Sevastopol but failed to take Leningrad or relieve Friedrich von Paulus at Stalingrad; he was relieved of command (1944).

d. Semën Mikhailovich Budënny (b. 1883), Russian Civil War cavalry general and incompetent World War II Soviet southwestern sector commander who lost Kiev and an estimated 1 million prisoners to the Germans.

d. André Beaufre (b. 1902), French general and military theorist who was a key proponent of French nuclear forces (Force de Frappe).

d. Ivan Stepanovich Konev (b. 1897), Soviet World War II general who was commander of Soviet forces at Moscow, Kursk, and Berlin.

Yom Kippur War (Fourth Arab-Israeli War; October War) (Oct. 6-24): On the Jewish holy day of Yom Kippur, Egyptian, Syrian, Iraqi, and Jordanian forces surprised and pushed back Israeli forces on the Suez Canal and Golan Heights, with substantial Israeli losses. Israeli forces, with air dominance, quickly counterattacked, bombing Syria at will, and were poised to take Damascus (Oct. 12). Israeli divisions attacked across the canal (Oct. 16) and were ready to destroy the Egyptian Third Army (Oct. 24), but an American ultimatum (Oct. 24) stopped direct Soviet intervention on behalf of Egypt; a United Nations–sponsored cease-fire ended the war (Oct. 27) and sent UN peacekeeping forces to the Suez Canal and Golan Heights.

Afghanistan became a republic after King Mohammad Zahir Shah (r. 1933-1973) was

In Sri Lanka, a People's Liberation Front insurrection was defeated by the Bandaranaike government (Apr.-June); a low-level guerrilla insurgency continued.

d. Lin Biao (b. 1907), Chinese Communist leader; Mao Zedong's heir apparent, he was reported by the Chinese government to have attempted a failed coup and died in a plane crash while fleeing into exile.

Thai prime minister General Thanom Kittikachorn took power by coup.

d. François "Papa Doc" Duvalier (b. 1907), Haitian dictator (1957-1971); he was succeeded by his son Jean Claude ("Baby Doc"), who ruled until he was deposed (1986).

Vietnam War: Troop withdrawals continued; by year's end, American and allied troops numbered fewer than 50,000. North Vietnamese forces continued to strengthen, going over partially to positional warfare in the Easter Offensive, which, though largely failed, did succeed in taking Quang Tri City, in northern South Vietnam (Apr.). The city was retaken by the South Vietnamese, with American air support (Sept.). Peace negotiations continued. President Richard Nixon ordered the heavy "Christmas bombing" of Hanoi and Haiphong and the mining of North Vietnamese harbors (beginning Dec. 18).

Cambodian Civil War came near its close, as Khmer Rouge forces besieged and bombarded Phnom Penh.

Ferdinand Marcos took dictatorial power in the Philippines, imprisoning Benigno Aquino and other Liberal Party leaders and imposing martial law.

d. Chen (Ch'en) Yi (b. 1901), Chinese Communist marshal serving most notably during the Chinese Civil War.

American-Soviet Strategic Arms Limitation Agreements of 1972 (SALT I) set limits on the use of antiballistic missile (ABMs) and suspended additional deployment of intercontinental ballistic missiles (ICBMs) for five years.

Austrian diplomat Kurt Waldheim became the fourth secretary-general of the United Nations (1972-1982).

In Ecuador, the military deposed the elected government of President José Maria Velasco Ibarra (Feb.); he was succeeded by General Guillermo Rodriguez Lara.

d. Harry S. Truman (b. 1884), 33d president of the United States (1945-1953), who succeeded to the presidency on the death of Franklin Delano Roosevelt (Apr. 12, 1945); that summer he authorized the atomic bombing of Hiroshima and Nagasaki.

d. Igor Sikorsky (b. 1889), Russian-American inventor who developed the modern helicopter.

d. Thomas Cassin Kinkaid (b. 1888), American admiral who served in the Pacific during World War II, most notably at Coral Sea and Midway (1942) and the retaking of the Philippines (1944-1945).

Vietnam War: Paris Peace Accords on Vietnam (Jan. 27), negotiated by Henry Kissinger and Le Duc Tho, provided for American withdrawal, return of American prisoners of war, and a North-South truce ending the Vietnam War. The last American forces left Vietnam (Mar. 29). American warplanes continued to attack Khmer Rouge forces in Cambodia until forced to stop by a congressional resolution (June; effective Aug. 14). The Vietnamese and Cambodian Civil Wars continued. The Vietnam War cost an estimated 50,000 allied and 200,000 South Vietnamese battle-related deaths; 160,000 other allied casualties and more than 5,000 prisoners of war or missing in action; and 500,000 South Vietnamese wounded. North Vietnamese and guerrilla casualties were unavailable, as were massive civilian casualties throughout Vietnam, Laos, and Cambodia.

Cease-fire in the Laotian Civil War was called (Feb.); it was followed by a coalition government, which ruled until Pathet Lao takeover (1975).

Chilean military forces, led by General Augusto Pinochet and with the assistance of the U.S. Central Intelligence Agency (CIA), mounted a military coup against the elected government of President Salvador Allende (b. 1908), who was killed during the coup, probably by Pinochet's forces. The new military government imposed martial law and engaged in a reign of terror, in which tens of thousands died.

Uruguayan army forces, taking over internal security functions, defeated the long guerrilla insurrection by the Tuparamos (National Liberation Front). Some Tuparamos later returned from exile (1984), forming a new, legal political party (1985).

Washington Summit (June) between American president Richard Nixon and Soviet premier Leonid Brezhnev continued the dialogue between the two superpowers, in this instance with hardly perceptible specific results.

Returning from exile, Juan Perón again became president of Argentina (1973-1974); his second wife, Isabel, was his vice president.

1973 (cont.)

deposed by a coup led by his former prime minister and cousin Sardar Mohammed Daud Khan.

Western Sahara Polisario (Popular Front for the Liberation of Saguia el Hamra and Rio de Oro) was founded.

d. David Ben Gurion (David Green) (b. 1886), Israeli socialist labor leader and politician, leader of the Israeli independence movement (1935-1948), and first Israeli prime minister (1948-1953; 1955-1963).

d. Ismet Inönü (b. 1884), prime minister of Turkey (1938-1950; 1961-1965).

1974

In a bloodless coup, the Portuguese Armed Forces Movement ended the dictatorship in Portugal, instituting democracy and freeing the overseas colonies, many of them in a state of armed insurrection. General Antonio Spinola became the first president of the new democracy, holding the post until he resigned (Sept.).

Turkish forces invaded and took much of northern Cyprus, partitioning the island and forming the Turkish Republic of Northern Cyprus (July-Aug.).

Democracy was reestablished in Greece when the military government that had replaced the Papadopoulos dictatorship (1973) peacefully relinquished power to former premier Constantine Karamanlis.

At the Moscow Summit (June), American president Richard Nixon and Soviet premier Leonid Brezhnev continued to discuss détente between the two superpowers.

Valéry Giscard d'Estaing became president of France (1974-1981).

Helmut Schmidt became chancellor of West Germany (1974-1982).

d. Georgi Konstantinovich Zhukov (b. 1896), Soviet general who was Far Eastern Army commander in the late 1930s, defeating Japan's Kwangtung Army (1939); his arrival in Moscow (1941) helped save the city; as Soviet chief of staff, he accepted the German surrender in Berlin (1945).

d. George Grivas (b. 1898), Greek Cypriot guerrilla commander (1955-1959).

An army coup led by Haile Mariam Mengistu deposed Emperor Haile Selassie I of Ethiopia.

Ethiopian-Eritrean War grew even more intense as the Soviet-backed Ethiopian government made a series of failed attempts to smash Eritrean resistance.

Kurdish guerrilla war of independence resumed when Iraq refused to grant the Kurds promised autonomy.

Republic of Guinea-Bissau, formerly Portuguese Guinea, became an independent nation (Sept. 10) after a long guerrilla war of independence (1963-1974); Luis de Almeida Cabral was the first president.

d. Haj Amin al Husseini (b. 1893), grand mufti of Jerusalem (1921-1974), Palestinian Arab nationalist leader during the interwar period, and Nazi ally during World War II.

1975

d. Francisco Franco (b. 1892), Spanish general, leader of insurgent forces during the Spanish Civil War (1936-1939), and Spanish fascist dictator (1939-1975). With his death, the Spanish monarchy was restored, and Juan Carlos became king of Spain, then swiftly moving to reestablish democracy.

Portuguese forces left Angola (Nov. 10); Popular Movement for the Liberation of Angola (MPLA) leader Augustinho Neto announced the formation of the Soviet-

1973 (cont.)

d. Lyndon Baines Johnson (b. 1908), 36th president of the United States (1963-1968), who succeeded to the presidency at the death of John Fitzgerald Kennedy.

d. Edward Vernon Rickenbacker (b. 1890), America's top World War I air ace, who shot down 26 enemy planes over France.

d. Frank Jack Fletcher (b. 1885), American admiral who commanded U.S. carrier task forces at the battles of the Coral Sea and Midway (both 1942).

d. Arthur William Radford (b. 1896), American admiral who served during World War II, notably at Iwo Jima and Okinawa (both 1945), later becoming commander in chief of the Pacific Fleet (1949) and chairman of the Joint Chiefs of Staff (1953-1957).

d. Alexander Archer Vandegrift (b. 1887), American Marine general who served during World War II, leading the first American amphibious offensives, at Tulagi and Guadalcanal (1942).

d. Fulgencio Batista y Zaldívar (b. 1901), Cuban president (1940-1944) and dictator (1952-1959).

d. Jeannette Pickering Rankin (b. 1880), American politician and pacifist; the first woman to be elected to the House of Representatives (1917-1919; 1941-1943), she was the only person in the House to vote against both world wars.

1974

Vietnamese Civil War: North and South Vietnamese forces clashed repeatedly, despite a cease-fire (since June 1973), as the North Vietnamese prepared for their final offensive.

Cambodian Civil War: Khmer Rouge forces controlled much of Cambodia and prepared to take Phnom Penh and end the war.

d. Mohammed Ayub Khan (b. 1907), Pakistani army commander in chief (1951-1960) and military dictator of Pakistan (1960-1969).

d. U Thant (b. 1909), Burmese diplomat and third United Nations secretary-general (1961-1971).

d. P'eng Te-huai (b. 1898), a leading Chinese Communist general in the Chinese Civil War and commander in chief during the Korean War.

U.S. Senate ratified the 1925 Geneva Protocol, banning the use of chemical and biological warfare, and the 1972 Biological Warfare Ban Treaty supplementing the protocol.

d. Carl Spaatz (b. 1891), American general, commander of the American air forces in western Europe (1944) and in the Pacific (1945) until the Japanese surrender.

d. Creighton Williams Abrams, Jr. (b. 1914), American general who served in Vietnam as head of operations during the Tet Offensive (1968), then as overall commander (1968) and army chief of staff (1972).

d. Juan Domingo Perón (b. 1895), Argentine president and then dictator (1946-1955), later elected president again (1973-1974). He was succeeded by his wife, Vice President Isabel Perón (July 1).

d. Karen Gay Silkwood (b. 1946), American atomic plant worker who died under suspicious circumstances while working to expose safety hazards.

1975

Vietnamese Civil War: North Vietnamese forces mounted their final offensive in South Vietnam, taking Hué (Mar. 25) and Danang (Apr. 1). South Vietnam surrendered (Apr. 30). As North Vietnamese troops

The ban on producing and stockpiling biological and chemical weapons, under the Biological Warfare Ban Treaty, ratified by the United Nations in 1972 and the United States in 1974, went into effect (Mar. 26).

1975 (cont.)

d. Eamon De Valera (b. 1881), leader of losing Irish Republican forces in the Irish Civil War (1921-1922), founder of Ireland's Fianna Fail Party (1926), and long-term Irish prime minister (1937-1948; 1951-1954; 1957-1959) and president (1959-1973).

The Portuguese government defeated attempted coups from the right (Mar. 11) and from the left (Nov. 25-28), the latter a substantial air force rebellion.

Soviet dissident Andrei Sakharov won the Nobel Peace Prize.

backed People's Republic of Angola (Nov. 11), with himself as president, cutting out the National Front for the Liberation of Angola (FNLA) and the National Union for the Total Independence of Angola (UNITA), his partners in the war of independence against the Portuguese. Both of those organizations immediately went to war, beginning the Angolan Civil War (1975-   ).

Lebanese Civil War (1975-1991): Heavy fighting between Phalange Christian militia and Palestine Liberation Organization (PLO) forces began in Beirut, quickly drawing in other militias and becoming a chaotic, full-scale civil war.

President N'Garta (François) Tombalbaye of Chad was assassinated during an attempted coup, beginning the Chad Civil War (1975-1987). Libyan forces intervened on the side of northern forces; the French and several Black African governments supported southern forces.

Zimbabwe African National Union (ZANU) and Zimbabwe African People's Union (ZAPU) attacks from bases in Zambia and Mozambique drew a cross-border response from Rhodesian forces, as the civil war in Rhodesia grew into a full-scale conflict.

Mauritian troops invaded and took Southern Sahara (Dec. 10).

Moroccan troops invaded West Sahara (Dec. 11); war began over the disputed area when the Moroccans were attacked by Polisario (Popular Front for the Liberation of Saguia el Hamra and Rio de Oro) guerrilla forces.

General Muritala Rufai Mohammed took power in Nigeria by coup (July), deposing General Yakubu Gowon.

Desmond Mpilo Tutu became the first Black Anglican dean of Johannesburg and the general secretary of the South African Council of Churches, further emerging as a leader of the South African freedom movement and proponent of nonviolence.

d. Haile Selassie I (Ras Tafari) (b. 1892), Ethiopian politician, regent and king (r. 1916-1930), and emperor (r. 1930-1974), who was on the world stage during his unsuccessful appeals to the League of Nations after the Italian invasion of his country (1935). He was deposed by military coup (1974).

approached Saigon, approximately 7,000 Americans and Vietnamese were evacuated by air, including more than 2,000 from the American Embassy in Saigon.

Cambodian Civil War: Phnom Penh fell to the Khmer Rouge (Apr. 16); the Cambodian government surrendered, ending the Cambodian Civil War. In power, the Khmer Rouge, led by Pol Pot, instituted a genocidal reign of terror — the Cambodian Holocaust — in which an estimated 1 million to 3 million Cambodians died. A low-level border war with Vietnam began, which would later escalate into a full-scale conflict.

Pathet Lao forces broke the Laotian cease-fire (Apr.), and a new cease-fire recognized their control of Vientiane (May 23); they completed their conquest of the country (Aug.).

Mayaguez Incident (May 12-14): After the seizure of the American merchant ship *Mayaguez* in international waters off Cambodia, American armed forces attacked Cambodian targets and mounted a rescue attempt; the Cambodians released the ship's crew while the attack was under way.

Indonesia seized and annexed East Timor (Nov. 29).

d. Chiang Kai-shek (b. 1887), Chinese officer, commander of Kuomintang forces (from 1926), and undisputed leader of the Republic of China (1937-1975); he fled to Taiwan after the communist victory.

d. Mujibur Rahman (b. 1920), first president of Bangladesh (1970-1975); he was assassinated with his wife and five children during a failed army coup (Aug. 15).

American secretary of state Henry Kissinger engaged in "shuttle diplomacy," a long series of trips aimed at furthering the cause of Middle East peace.

Cuba became deeply involved in African affairs, sending troops in divisional strength to Angola, then a Soviet client.

1976

West German terrorist Ulrike Meinhof was found dead in her prison cell, having allegedly committed suicide; mass demonstrations charging police murder followed.

Portuguese democratic leader Mario Lopez Soares became prime minister of Portugal, beginning a period of stability.

d. Bernard Law Montgomery (b. 1887), British field marshal; he was Eighth Army commander at El Alamein (1942), defeating Erwin Rommel's forces in North Africa, and commander of British forces in Sicily and Italy, at Normandy, and during the European campaign that followed.

Syrian forces intervened in the continuing civil war in Lebanon (Apr.), later forcing a partial cease-fire in the north (Oct.-Nov.), although heavy, multifaction fighting continued in the south, as did Palestine Liberation Organization (PLO) raids into Israel and Israeli armed response.

South African police killed more than 600 people and injured thousands more as rioting broke out in Soweto and spread throughout the country, after the government unsuccessfully attempted to impose the use of Afrikaans as an official language in all South African schools.

In Zambia, rival Zimbabwe African National Union (ZANU) and Zimbabwe African People's Union (ZAPU) forces joined in a Patriotic Front, pursuing a unified guerrilla war in Rhodesia, although armed clashes between ZANU and ZAPU forces still occurred.

Spain withdrew from the western Sahara; a long three-way war began, with the Polisario-founded Saharan Arab Democratic Republic, Morocco, and Mauritania all claiming the area.

Airborne Israeli commandos rescued 98 Jewish hostages held by hijackers at Entebbe airport, in Uganda, with the loss of 3 lives (July 4).

1977

Further strengthening his hold on power, Leonid Brezhnev became general secretary of the Communist Party and president of the Soviet Union; the Cold War and its many accompanying regional conflicts continued.

West German terrorist Andreas Baader and two other imprisoned members of the Baader-Meinhof Group were found dead in prison, allegedly having committed suicide.

Amnesty International won the Nobel Peace Prize.

d. Anthony Eden (b. 1897), three-time British foreign secretary and prime minister during the Suez crisis (1956), which forced him from power.

d. Wernher von Braun (b. 1912), German rocket expert; during World War II, he was head of research on the Nazi V-I and V-2 terror bombs; during the Cold War, he transferred his work to the United States, becoming a key developer of American missile and space programs.

d. Aleksander Mikhailovich Vasilevskii (b. 1895), marshal of the Soviet Union who became chief of the general staff; he orchestrated the defense of Stalingrad (1942) and succeeding offensives, later becoming minister for war (1950-1953).

Somali-Ethiopian War (1977-1978): Somali forces invaded the disputed Ogaden region of Ethiopia (July) and unsuccessfully besieged Harar (Sept.). Soviet clients themselves, they were opposed by Soviet and Cuban forces, who chose to support their Ethiopian clients in war. In response, the Somalis broke with the Soviets (Nov.).

Ethiopian-Eritrean War: Eritrean forces scored major victories against Ethiopia and its Cuban and Soviet allies, taking much of northern Eritrea and besieging Massawa (Jan.-Aug.).

Haile Mariam Mengistu, leader of the coup that had deposed Ethiopian emperor Haile Selassie I (1974), emerged as dictator of the one-party Ethiopian state (1977-1991).

Egypt and Libya fought several border engagements (July).

West German commandos successfully rescued 86 hijacked Lufthansa passengers

Central, South and East Asia, and the Pacific

The Americas

d. Mao Zedong (b. 1893), leader of the Chinese Communist Party during the long Chinese Civil War and leader of the People's Republic of China (1949-1976).

Jiang Qing (Mao Zedong's widow), Zhang Chunqiao, Wang Hongwen, and Yao Wenhuan — all former leaders of China's Cultural Revolution — were arrested and subsequently convicted as the "Gang of Four" for plotting a post-Mao coup.

Admiral Sangad Chaloryu took power by coup in Thailand (Oct. 8).

d. Zhou Enlai (b. 1898), Chinese Communist leader; second only to Mao Zedong, he was the first premier, chief diplomat, and world spokesperson of the People's Republic of China (1949-1976).

d. Zhu De (b. 1886), Chinese Communist general who was the founder and commander of China's Red Army (1926-1954).

d. Mistsuo Fuchida (b. 1902), Japanese naval air officer who commanded Japanese forces in the air attack on Pearl Harbor (Dec. 7, 1941), personally directing the first wave of attack planes; after the war, he moved to the United States, becoming a citizen (1966).

Argentine president Isabel (Maria Estela) Perón, widow of Juan Perón, was deposed by an armed forces coup (Mar. 24). The new military government, initially headed by General Jorge Rafael Videla, instituted a campaign of state terrorism against all dissidents — the "dirty war" that saw the murders of tens of thousands, called the *desaparacios* (disappeareds).

Chilean secret police agents murdered former Salvador Allende government official Orlando Letelier del Solar in Washington, D.C. (Sept. 21).

As the Cambodian Holocaust continued, denounced by Vietnam and many other nations, Vietnam and Cambodia fought an increasingly heated border war.

General Mohammad Zia Ul-Haq took power in Pakistan after an army coup, overthrowing the government of Zulfikar Ali Bhutto, who was later executed (1979).

In Bangladesh, President Ziaur Rahman's forces defeated a military coup attempt.

d. Takeo Kurita (b. 1889), Japanese admiral during World War II, serving most notably at Midway (1942) and Leyte Gulf (1944).

d. George Churchill Kenney (b. 1889), American Army Air Forces general during World Wars I and II who rose to head the Pacific Air Command (1945-1946) and the Strategic Air Command (1946-1948).

1977 (cont.)

being held by the Baader-Meinhof Group at Mogadishu, Somalia (Oct. 18).

Lebanon's Druse Muslim leader Kamal Jumblat was assassinated (Mar.).

In the Central African Republic, Jean Bédel Bokassa proclaimed himself Emperor Bokassa I (Sept. 20).

1978

Italian Red Brigades terrorists expanded their activities; their most prominent victim was former Italian prime minister Aldo Moro.

d. Aleksei Ivanovich Radzievskiy (b. 1911), Russian general during World War II; a cavalry-trained tank commander, he served from Moscow to the final advance on Berlin.

d. Baron Hasso von Manteuffel (b. 1897), German general who commanded the Fifth Panzer Army during the German counteroffensive in the Ardennes (Nov.-Dec. 1944), blocked at Bastogne.

Egypt and Israel signed the Camp David Accords (Sept. 17), a landmark agreement looking forward to a peace treaty and normalization of relations; signed by Egypt's Anwar Sadat and Israel's Menachem Begin, the agreement was sponsored by American president Jimmy Carter.

Ethiopian-Eritrean War: Cuban and Ethiopian troops relieved besieged Harar (Feb.) and recaptured much of northern Eritrea. The Ethiopian summer offensive took most urban areas but again failed to smash Eritrean rebel forces, which retreated to rural areas and later re-emerged to retake most of the country; the long war of attrition continued, with more than 1 million civilian victims.

Israeli forces invaded southern Lebanon (Mar.), setting up a Christian Lebanese buffer zone before withdrawing (June). Throughout Lebanon, factional fighting intensified, continuing into the early 1980s.

Somali-Ethiopian War: Ethiopian, Cuban, and Soviet forces relieved Harar (Feb.) and decisively defeated the Somalis at the Battle of Diredawa-Jijiga (Mar. 2-5); the Somalis sued for peace (Mar. 8) and then withdrew from the Ogaden.

As massive demonstrations made Iran impossible to govern, the government of Muhammed Reza Shah Pahlevi faltered; he named prodemocracy leader Shahpur Bakhtiar premier (Dec. 25), but revolution was just ahead.

d. Houari Boumedienne (Mohammed Boukharouba) (b. 1927), Algerian National Liberation Front (FLN) military leader and dictator of Algeria (1965-1978).

d. Jomo Kenyatta (b. 1890), leader of the Kenyan independence movement (1946-

1978

Vietnamese-Cambodian border war escalated into a full-scale Vietnamese invasion of Cambodia. Vietnamese forces quickly defeated the Khmer Rouge army, which fled west toward the Thai border, there beginning a long guerrilla war against the Vietnamese and their Cambodian allies.

Afghan Civil War (1978-   ): Afghan president Sardar Mohammed Daud Khan, leader of the successful insurrection against the Afghan monarchy (1973), was assassinated during the military coup that deposed him (Apr.). Civil war followed; Mujaheddin forces took most of the country in the following 18 months.

Bikini Atoll in the Marshall Islands was evacuated after a decade of reoccupancy by its residents when reassessment indicated continuing massive fallout contamination on the site.

Nicaraguan Revolution and Civil War (1978-1988): Sandinista guerrilla forces grew in strength, went over to positional war against government forces, and forced Anastasio Somoza Debayle to flee into exile (July 17), taking power (July 19). With American support, elements of the Nicaraguan army then moved into guerrilla warfare against the new government, becoming the Contras (Againsts).

At Jonestown, Guyana, American congressman Leo Ryan and four others in his investigative party were murdered by followers of People's Temple cult leader Warren "Jim" Jones. Jones and 909 of his followers then died, most of them suicides, the others murdered.

d. Lucius DuBignon Clay (b. 1897), American general who was commander of U.S. forces in Europe and military governor (1947-1949), organizing the Berlin Airlift (June 24, 1948-May 12, 1949).

d. George Scratchley Brown (b. 1918), American Air Force general who became chairman of the Joint Chiefs of Staff (1974-1978).

1978 (cont.)

1963) and first president of the Kenyan republic (1964-1978).

1979

American president Jimmy Carter and Soviet premier Leonid Brezhnev signed the Strategic Arms Limitation Agreement (SALT II) at the Vienna Summit (June). The Soviet-American agreement limited the numbers of intercontinental ballistic missiles (ICBMs), multiple independently targetable reentry vehicles (MIRVs), and missile launchers.

Despite some government concessions, Basque separatists intensified their long terrorist campaign in northern Spain.

Margaret Thatcher, leader of the Conservative Party, became Britain's first woman prime minister, ultimately the longest-serving prime minister of the 20th century (1979-1990); she strongly pursued the Cold War abroad and instituted major right-leaning domestic changes.

British art historian Anthony Blunt was revealed to have been a Soviet spy, part of Kim Philby's Cambridge-originated network. He had been secretly pardoned (1964) in return for his cooperation after being discovered, but he was later publicly stripped of his honors.

Campaign for Nuclear Disarmament (CND) mounted a strong campaign against the deployment of American Cruise missiles in Britain.

d. Louis Mountbatten (b. 1900), British naval officer who was the commander of combined British forces (1942-1943), Allied Southeast Asia commander (1943-1946), and the last British viceroy of India; great-grandson of Queen Victoria and son of Louis Mountbatten (Prince Louis of Battenberg), he was assassinated by the Irish Republican Army off the coast of Ireland (Aug. 28).

Anwar Sadat and Menachem Begin signed an Egyptian-Israeli peace treaty (Mar. 26) normalizing relations and providing for Israeli withdrawal from the Sinai Peninsula.

Iranian Revolution: Muhammed Reza Shah Pahlevi of Iran fled abroad (Jan. 16) after massive demonstrations and the loss of army support destabilized his government. Ayatollah Ruhollah Khomeini returned from exile (Feb. 1) and seized power in Iran (Feb. 11), setting up a fundamentalist Shi'ite Islamic state.

Iran seized 66 Americans at the American Embassy in Tehran (Nov. 4) and held 52 of them for 444 days, while the Iranian government won several concessions from the United States, in the process severely harming the prestige of the United States and the political career of President Jimmy Carter. The hostages were released on the day President Ronald Reagan took office (Jan. 20, 1981).

Uganda-Tanzania War and Ugandan Civil War: Tanzanian forces invaded Uganda, defeated Idi Amin and his Libyan allies, and took Kampala (Apr. 11). An election reinstalled President Milton Obote, who instituted yet another reign of terror and generated a civil war won by the National Resistance Army forces of Yoweri Musaveni.

Libyan forces unsuccessfully invaded Chad; they were withdrawn after their defeat by French and Chadian forces.

Ian Smith's Rhodesian government relinquished power; Bishop Abel Muzorewa's succeeding government was not accepted by the Zimbabwe African National Union (ZANU) and the Zimbabwe African People's Union (ZAPU).

Angolan Civil War: Holden Roberto's National Front for the Liberation of Angola (FNLA) was completely defeated by the Popular Movement for the Liberation of Angola (MPLA) and its Cuban and Soviet allies.

In the Central African Republic, Jean Bédel Bokassa (Emperor Bokassa I) was

1979

Afghan-Soviet War (1979-1989) began when Soviet forces intervened in the Afghan Civil War, mounting divisional-strength airborne and land attacks that took Kabul (Dec. 25). After Afghan premier Hafizullah Amin died during the invasion, the Soviets installed Karmal Babrak in his place. Soviet troops numbering an estimated 130,000, with massive air and armor support, proved unable to defeat the Mujaheddin resistance fighters in the years that followed.

Vietnamese forces completed their conquest of Cambodia, taking Phnom Penh (Jan. 6) and establishing a puppet Cambodian government. The Cambodian Holocaust ended.

Divisional-strength Chinese forces invaded northern Vietnam, beginning a brief border war (Feb.-Mar.), then withdrew.

d. Park Chung Hee (b. 1917), South Korean general who seized power by coup (1961) and then was openly dictator (1971-1979); he was assassinated by the head of his own Central Intelligence Agency (Oct. 26).

d. Zulfikar Ali Bhutto (b. 1928), founder of the Pakistan People's Party and prime minister of Pakistan (Mar.-July 1977). He was executed on a false murder charge by the military government of General Mohammad Zia Ul-Haq, which had deposed him (1977). Bhutto's daughter, Benazir, became prime minister in 1988.

Soviet-American Strategic Arms Limitation Agreement (SALT II) limited the numbers of intercontinental ballistic missiles (ICBMs), multiple independently targetable reentry vehicles (MIRVs), and missile launchers.

Guerrilla insurgency in El Salvador grew into full-scale civil war, with massive American aid to the government and some Nicaraguan aid to the rebels. Terrorism grew as well, as Archbishop Oscar Romero was assassinated (Mar. 24).

Nicaraguan Civil War continued to be a full-scale conflict, with roles reversed after the Sandinista victory, as American-backed former government forces (Contras) in the north and dissident Sandinistas in the south continued to fight the new government.

Three Mile Island (Pennsylvania) nuclear accident (Mar. 28) came very close to creating a catastrophic reactor meltdown, greatly increasing public fear of nuclear energy.

Maurice Bishop led a military coup in Grenada, establishing a Marxist-oriented government (Mar.).

1979 (cont.)

deposed by the forces of David Dacko, with French army assistance.

Lieutenant Jerry Rawlings led a coup that deposed the Akuffo government in Ghana.

d. Augustinho Neto (b. 1922), leader of the MPLA during the long guerrilla Angolan War of Independence (1961-1975) and first president of the People's Republic of Angola (1975-1979).

d. Mustafa al-Barzani (b. 1901), leader of the Kurdish independence movement in Iraq and Iran, commander of the armed forces of the Kurdish republic (1946) in northern Iran, and leader of the Kurdish insurrection in Iraq.

1980

In the wake of the successful Gdansk Lenin Shipyard strike (Aug. 14-30), the Polish trade union Solidarity was formed (Sept. 18); led by Lech Walesa, it quickly grew into a 10-million-strong labor confederation and leading force in the Polish independence movement.

Basque independence movement terrorism intensified in Spain, despite government concessions that fell short of full independence.

d. Tito (Josip Broz) (b. 1892), Yugoslav Communist Party leader (from 1937), World War II partisan leader, and head of state (1945-1980), who broke with Joseph Stalin (1948) and pulled out of the Soviet bloc. With his death, and as fear of Soviet intervention receded, suppressed ethnic tensions began to surface once again in Yugoslavia.

d. Karl Dönitz (Carl Doenitz) (b. 1891), German admiral, commander of the submarine fleet during World War II, and Hitler's naval commander in chief (from 1943); chancellor after Hitler's death, he negotiated Germany's surrender (May 7, 1945); convicted of war crimes, he served 10 years in prison (1945-1956).

Iran-Iraq War (1980-1988): Iraq attacked Iran (Sept.), claiming the entire Shatt al Arab waterway in violation of a 1975 treaty; attacking forces captured Khorramshahr. The long war would cost more than 1 million lives.

British-supervised elections in Rhodesia resulted in a Zimbabwe African National Union (ZANU) government led by Robert Mugabe, the first government of independent Zimbabwe. Fighting between ZANU and Zimbabwe African People's Union (ZAPU) forces intensified and then gradually tapered off as the new government took hold and negotiations for a ZANU-ZAPU merger continued. The two groups merged in 1987.

Operation Desert One: American forces mounted a failed effort to rescue the hostages held in Iran (Apr. 24-25).

Ugandan Civil War (1979-   ): Yoweri Musaveni repudiated the December 1979 peace agreement, reopening what then became a long, unsettled civil war.

Sudanese Civil War intensified, as the government openly reneged on some of its previous promises of full autonomy for the south.

In Liberia, Samuel K. Doe took power by coup, deposing President William R. Tolbert (Apr. 12).

Military coup led by Joao Bernardo Viera deposed President Luis Cabral of the Republic of Guinea-Bissau (Nov. 13).

Central, South and East Asia, and the Pacific

The Americas

1980

Afghan-Soviet War: American president Jimmy Carter responded to the Soviet invasion of Afghanistan by stopping grain shipments to the Soviet Union, withdrawing American participation in the Moscow Olympics, and beginning a massive flow of military aid through Pakistan to Afghan forces. Resistance intensified in Afghanistan, and Soviet-Pakistani border incidents developed, as Pakistan became the main Afghan insurgent base and the home of 2 million to 3 million refugees.

Thai-Laotian border engagements intensified, as did Thai-Vietnamese conflicts on the Cambodian-Laotian border.

France tested a neutron bomb in the South Pacific (June).

In El Salvador, the civil war continued. Former president Carlos Romero mounted a failed military coup (May). Christian Democratic moderate José Napoleon Duarte was appointed to the presidency by the military (Dec.). Terrorism mounted, as right-wing death squads increased their activities. Four American nuns were murdered by death squads (Dec. 3), attracting international condemnation.

Led by Abimeal Guzmán Reynoso, the Maoist-oriented Shining Path (Sendoro Luminoso) moved toward armed insurgency in Peru, becoming a substantial guerrilla force, especially in the southern provinces, but also in poor urban areas.

d. Anastasio Somoza Debayle (b. 1925), Nicaraguan general and dictator (r. 1963-1979); he was assassinated at Asunción, Paraguay (Sept. 17).

d. William Hood Simpson (b. 1888), American general who led the Ninth Army through the Siegfried Line and across the Rhine to the Elbe (1945).

1980 (cont.)

	Peacekeeping forces sent by several neighboring African nations failed to bring an end to the Chad Civil War.
	General Kenan Evren led a military coup and took power in Turkey (Sept.).
	d. Muhammed Reza Shah Pahlevi (b. 1919), the last shah of Iran (r. 1941-1979), son of Reza Shah Pahlevi; he was forced to flee after the Iranian Revolution (1979).

1981

In a failed military coup attempt (Feb. 23-26), intended to restore the monarchy to full control, the Spanish cabinet and 350 legislators were captured and held hostage (Feb. 23); but King Juan Carlos did not take power, instead holding the army for the government and defeating the coup. During the year, Basque terrorist operations in northern Spain drew government troop deployments.	d. Anwar Sadat (b. 1918), Egyptian president (1970-1981) who made peace with Israel (1979); assassinated by Islamic fundamentalists in Cairo (Oct. 6), he was succeeded by Hosni Mubarak.
Responding to strong Soviet pressure, the Polish government outlawed Solidarity, which continued to operate underground (Dec.).	In Ghana, Jerry Rawlings dissolved the democratic government, taking power by coup and ruling as dictator.
Soviet-American negotiations on the reduction of medium-range nuclear missiles began in Geneva.	Libyan forces again invaded Chad (Jan.), intervening in the continuing civil war. Most Libyan forces were withdrawn late in the year, replaced by Organization of African Unity (OAU) peacekeeping forces.
American general James L. Dozier was kidnapped and held by Italian terrorists (Dec. 17, 1981-Jan. 28, 1982); he was freed by Italian police.	American-Libyan tensions continued to grow; two American warplanes shot down two Libyan planes over the Mediterranean (Aug. 19).
d. Claude Auchinleck (b. 1884), British officer in both world wars; a field marshal, he became British Middle Eastern commander (1941) and later in World War II British Indian commander.	Israeli bombers attacked and destroyed an Iraqi nuclear reactor (June 7).
	Remaining Tanzanian troops were withdrawn from Uganda (June).
	Small band of mercenaries made a failed coup attempt in the Seychelles (Nov.).
	South African forces attacked African National Congress (ANC) bases in Mozambique.
	d. Moshe Dayan (b. 1915), Israeli soldier, commander of Israeli forces during the Sinai-Suez War (1956), and later a cabinet-level official.

1982

Strategic Arms Reduction Treaty (START) negotiations began between the United States and the Soviet Union (June 29).	Iran-Iraq War: Iranian forces moving to the offensive regained lost territory, retaking Khorramshahr. Iraq sued for peace (May), but Iran instead unsuccessfully invaded Iraq; a stalemate and war of attrition developed after mid-1982, with huge losses as both sides engaged in World War I–style trench warfare, increased by
d. Leonid Ilyich Brezhnev (b. 1906), Soviet politician who was a leading figure from the early 1970s, Communist Party general secretary, and Soviet president (1977-1982).	
Yuri Andropov became Soviet Communist Party general secretary and leader of the Soviet Union.	

1980 (cont.)

1981

Afghan-Soviet War: Soviet forces drove the Mujaheddin into the mountains but could not take the country; a massive guerrilla war developed in the years that followed.

Sri Lankan Civil War (1981-   ): Tamil-Sinhalese ethnic civil war began, generated by unmet minority Tamil United Liberation Front demands for an autonomous Tamil state.

In Bangladesh, President Ziaur Rahman was killed in a failed coup attempt; he was succeeded by Vice President Abdus Sattar.

d. Ch'ing-ling Soong, Madame Sun Yat-sen (b. 1892), wife of Chinese republican leader Sun Yat-sen; she was a leading symbol of the Chinese Revolution in Communist China.

Death squads continued activity in El Salvador, as the guerrilla civil war continued; the deaths of several more Americans attracted international attention; they were a few of the tens of thousands of deaths suffered by both sides in the escalating war.

Worldwide movement to "freeze" nuclear weapons at current levels began; it was initiated at the 31st Pugwash, Canada, meeting of scientists and antiwar activists (Sept.).

Ecuadoran-Peruvian border war flared briefly (Jan. 28-Feb. 2); it was quickly and effectively mediated by the Organization of American States (OAS).

d. Omar Bradley (b. 1893), American general; First Army commander at Normandy and commander of the 12th Army Group, the largest field command force ever (both 1944); first chairman of the Joint Chiefs of Staff (1949-1953); and General of the Army (1950).

d. Roger Nash Baldwin (b. 1884), American pacifist who became director of the American Union Against Militarism during World War I and was imprisoned as a conscientious objector (1918). He was a founder and first director (1920-1950) of the American Civil Liberties Union (ACLU).

1982

Sikh separatist campaigns intensified in the Punjab, as did Hindu-Muslim confrontations, with rioting at Amritsar and other cities (May).

In Burma multiple low-level insurrections expanded, despite new joint Burmese-Thai campaigns against Burmese Communist Party, Karen, and insurgent forces.

Falklands (Malvinas) War (Apr. 2-June 14): Argentine forces took the disputed Falkland Islands (Malvinas) (Apr. 2), British-occupied since 1833. A British task force, using American bases en route for refueling and resupply, invaded the islands (late Apr.) and retook them in less than a month; the Argentine forces surrendered (June 14). Substantial Argentine losses included the cruiser *General Belgrano* (May 2). The Argentine military government collapsed after the war, beginning a new period in Argentine history.

1982 (cont.)

d. Pierre Mendes-France (b. 1907), French socialist politician and premier (1954-1955); he opposed and in office quickly ended the Indochina War.

d. Wladyslaw Gomulka (b. 1905), Polish communist leader who became premier (1956-1970).

Iran's "human wave" infantry attacks. The Kurdish insurgency in northern Iraq intensified, with Iranian military and supply support.

Israeli forces invaded Lebanon (June), quickly drove to Beirut, and encircled Palestine Liberation Organization (PLO) and Syrian forces in West Beirut, while also driving Syrian forces into the Bekaa Valley. PLO and Syrian forces withdrew from Beirut (Aug.) after a U.S.-negotiated agreement, monitored by a United Nations peacekeeping force.

Lebanese president-elect Bashir Gemayel was assassinated (Sept. 14); he was succeeded by his brother Amin Gemayel.

Sabra and Shatilla Massacres (Sept. 16-18): Lebanese Maronite Christian Phalange militia murdered 400 or more people at the Sabra and Shatilla Palestinian refugee camps in Beirut, while Israeli troops in the area stood by, causing worldwide charges of Israeli complicity.

Central African Republic military coup toppled the democratic government led by David Dacko; the succeeding one-party government was led by General André-Dieudonne Kolingba.

South African government forces attacked African National Congress (ANC) refugee centers in Lesotho (Dec.).

Thousands died in heavy fighting as Syrian forces defeated a Muslim Brotherhood insurrection at Hama (Feb.).

Chad Civil War: Forces of Hissen Habre temporarily took power after defeating Chad National Liberation Front (Frolinat) forces led by Goukouni Oueddi.

1983

In Yugoslavia Muslim separatist movements grew in Bosnia and Herzegovina, as did Serbian nationalism. Albanian nationalists in Kossovo mounted an increasingly effective campaign, including acts of terrorism.

Irish Republican Army (IRA) guerrillas committed a series of terrorist acts in England and Northern Ireland, including the bombing of Harrod's department store in London, which killed six people (Dec. 17).

d. Georges Bidault (b. 1889), French World War II Resistance leader (1943-1944) and twice prime minister (1946; 1949-1950). A leader of resistance to Algerian independence, he was in exile from France for several years (1962-1968).

Lebanese Civil War: Israeli forces withdrew from Beirut. American naval and marine forces were drawn into the Druse–Lebanese army confrontation in Beirut (Sept.-Oct.). Palestine Liberation Organization (PLO) forces in Tripoli were evacuated by sea after their defeat by Syrian-backed Lebanese army forces (Oct.). Factional fighting continued throughout the country.

Thai forces attacked drug-dealing Khun Sa's Shan United Army in northern Thailand.

General Hossein Mohammed Ershad seized power by coup in Bangladesh.

Nuclear freeze proponents mounted an anti–nuclear weapons demonstration in New York's Central Park that drew an estimated 500,000 to 1 million people.

Peruvian diplomat Javier Pérez de Cuéllar became the fifth secretary-general of the United Nations (1982-1992).

Manuel Antonio Noriega became the head of the Panamanian armed forces and de facto dictator of Panama, while continuing to be involved with American intelligence and drug trafficking.

d. Nathan Farragut Twining (b. 1897), American Air Force general who directed American air forces in the Pacific (from 1942), Allied air forces in the Mediterranean (from 1944), and the bombing of Japan (1945), including the atomic bomb missions; he was later chairman of the Joint Chiefs of Staff (1957-1960).

Returning from exile, Philippine opposition leader Benigno Aquino was assassinated as he stepped off an airplane (Aug.). His killing, probably by government agents, generated massive public opposition to Ferdinand Marcos's dictatorship and would make it possible for his widow, Corazon Aquino, to lead her country into the Philippine Revolution.

Soviet warplanes shot down Korean Air Lines Flight 007, which had strayed into Soviet airspace over the Sea of Japan (Sept. 1), killing all 269 people aboard.

President Chun Doo Hwan of South Korea, 4 members of his cabinet, and 13 other South Korean officials were

Grenadan leader Maurice Bishop was deposed (Oct. 13) and assassinated by intraparty opponents (Oct. 19). American forces invaded Grenada (Oct. 25) and within three days took the lightly defended island, establishing a new government.

President Ronald Reagan's administration developed the Strategic Defense Initiative (SDI, or "Star Wars") nuclear defense theory and convinced the U.S. Congress to pour massive resources into the project.

Following the lost Falklands War, Raúl Alfonsin Foulkes became the new president of Argentina, quickly moving to restore democracy and the economy.

1983 (cont.)

Arab guerrilla suicide bombers in Beirut drove trucks loaded with explosives into the barracks of American and French peacekeeping forces, killing 241 Americans and 58 French (Oct. 23).

Iran-Iraq War: Protracted Iranian offensives failed to break the stalemate that had developed in a conflict that was being conducted along trench warfare lines; Iraqi bombing attacks led to a massive blowout at the Nowruz oil field in the Persian Gulf, causing an ecological disaster.

Chad Civil War: Regrouping after their 1982 defeat, Chad National Liberation Front (Frolinat) forces went on the offensive, soon assisted by Libyan troops, taking much of northern Chad. French forces intervened (Aug.), forcing a cease-fire and peace talks.

In Sudan, guerrilla activity intensified in the south after the Muslim northern government of President Mohammed Gaafar al-Nimeiry moved to impose hard-line Islamic law on the whole country. By year's end, rebel forces controlled much of the countryside in the south.

South African troops attacked Southwest Africa People's Organization of Namibia (SWAPO) positions in southern Angola; South African warplanes bombed African National Congress (ANC) locations near Maputo, Mozambique.

Yitzhak Shamir succeeded Menachem Begin as the hard-line conservative prime minister of Israel (1983-1984).

General Mohammed Buhari took power by coup in Nigeria, deposing President Shehu Shagari.

1984

d. Yuri Vladimirovich Andropov (b. 1914), Soviet KGB head (1967-1982) and leader of the Soviet Union (1982-1984). He was briefly succeeded by Konstantin Chernenko (1911-1985).

d. Arthur Travers Harris (b. 1892), British air marshal nicknamed "Bomber" Harris for his use of area bombing of Nazi Germany after he became chief of Bomber Command (1942).

Iranian-supported Muslim terrorists in Lebanon began to take increasing numbers of Western hostages, gaining massive publicity and some substantial concessions in the years that followed, including the more than 2,000 American TOW missiles shipped to Iran (1985-1986) during the secret and controversial Iran-Contra arms-for-hostages negotiations.

Multinational peacekeeping forces were withdrawn from Beirut (Feb.-Mar.).

American Central Intelligence Agency (CIA) Beirut station chief William Buckley was kidnapped by terrorists (Mar. 16),

1983 (cont.)

killed by a bomb during a state visit to Burma, probably by North Korean agents (Oct. 9).

d. David Monroe Shoup (b. 1904), American Marine general during World War II, most notably at Tarawa (1943) and Saipan and Tinian (1944).

1984

Indian army forces assaulted and took the Sikh Golden Temple, killing Sikh fundamentalist leader Jarnail Singh Bhindranwale and an estimated 1,000 armed Sikh irregulars, who were using the temple as headquarters for their insurrection in the Punjab, which continued and intensified.

d. Indira Gandhi (b. 1917), Indian prime minister who was assassinated by two Sikh members of her personal guard (Oct. 31); she was succeeded by her son Rajiv Gandhi. After her assassination, a wave of anti-Sikh and anti-Muslim rioting swept India.

In El Salvador José Napoleon Duarte was elected to the presidency (May), but the election was boycotted by insurgent forces. Against considerable odds, he continued his attempts to negotiate a peace settlement. Although death squad activity continued, he attempted to curb it. Five National Guardsmen accused of the 1980 murders of four nuns were tried and convicted of murder (May).

Carl Sagan and others developed the "nuclear winter" theory, publishing *Long-Term Biological Consequences of Nuclear War.*

d. Mark Wayne Clark (b. 1896), American general who was Fifth Army commander in Italy during World War II and commander of United Nations forces in Korea (1952-1953).

1984 (cont.)

becoming a Lebanon hostage; he was tortured and later murdered (1985).

Iran-Iraq War: Further Iranian offensives failed to achieve a breakthrough, although the attacking Iranians used poison gas, as they would for the balance of the war. Iraq also used chemical weapons in the war and against Iraqi dissidents, most notably the Kurds.

South African forces began a limited withdrawal from Angola. South Africa and the Southwest Africa People's Organization of Namibia (SWAPO) negotiated a truce in Namibia, and South Africa and Mozambique agreed to withdraw support for cross-border guerrillas in both countries.

Libya and France agreed to withdraw their armed forces from Chad, and French forces did withdraw; Libyan forces remained on both sides of the Chad border, however, and the civil war continued.

Ethiopian-Eritrean War: As the stalemated war continued, famine and disease took hundreds of thousands of lives; in some periods, both sides refused to let international relief shipments reach intended recipients.

1985

Mikhail Sergeyevich Gorbachev became general secretary of the Soviet Communist Party and leader of the Soviet Union (Mar.); he began the processes that would transform the Soviet Union and the late-20th-century world, including the onset of massive internal Soviet reforms, the end of the Cold War and many regional conflicts (though the beginning of others), the end of the Soviet bloc, and the end of the Soviet Union.

Soviet premier Gorbachev and American president Ronald Reagan had their first summit meeting, at Geneva (Nov.), beginning the sequence of Soviet-American summit meetings and events that would end the Cold War.

An Air India 747 exploded in midair over the Irish Sea, killing 329 people, probably due to a terrorist bomb.

General Abdul Rahman Siwar el-Dahab took power by coup in Sudan (Apr. 6), imposing even harsher Muslim rule on the Christian and animist south. The civil war intensified, becoming a full-scale southern guerrilla war for independence, accompanied by massive starvation and disease that by the early 1990s had cost an estimated 1 million to 2 million lives; millions more emigrated to escape the war.

Iran-Iraq War: Still stalemated, both sides mounted militarily ineffective terror missile attacks on each other's cities.

Israeli planes bombed Palestine Liberation Organization (PLO) headquarters in Tunis (Oct. 1).

Islamic terrorists hijacked an Athens-to-Rome TWA flight, flew to Beirut, demanded the release of 700 Muslim prisoners, and murdered a passenger, U.S. navy diver Robert Stethem. Ultimately, passengers and crew were released, as were 300 Muslim prisoners. The hijackers escaped into Beirut, although one was later arrested in Nigeria (1993) and brought to the United States for trial.

French agents sank the Greenpeace antinuclear ship *Rainbow Warrior* in Auckland harbor, generating a major dispute between France and New Zealand; two French agents were ultimately convicted of manslaughter in the death of a photographer on board.

Vietnamese forces in Cambodia attacked Khmer Rouge bases on both sides of the Cambodian-Thai border, generating a series of engagements with Thai border forces.

Sikh terrorist actions continued in the Punjab and throughout India; nearly 100 people died in a coordinated set of bombings at Delhi and several other cities (May 10).

In Burma, Karen forces mounted several major terrorist actions, including a Rangoon-Mandalay train bombing (July 14) that killed more than 60 people. Government antiinsurgent campaigns were largely ineffective.

Manoon Roopkachorn led a failed coup attempt in Thailand (Sept. 9).

Haitian Revolution (1985-1986): Large, unchecked demonstrations, coupled with American and French pressure, destabilized the government of dictator Jean Claude Duvalier (Nov.-Dec.).

Iran-Contra Affair: American president Ronald Reagan's administration's attempts to sell arms to Iran in return for the release of the Lebanon hostages began; proceeds from such sales were used illegally to arm the Nicaraguan Contras.

In Colombia, M-19 guerrilla forces took more than 300 hostages at the Palace of Justice in Bogotá (Nov. 9); 95 of them were killed, including 11 Supreme Court justices, when the Colombian military took the building by storm.

Daniel Ortega Saavedra became president of the Sandinista government of Nicaragua.

1985 (cont.)

Lebanon hostage William Buckley, Beirut Central Intelligence Agency (CIA) station chief, was murdered by his Muslim terrorist captors. Journalist Terry Anderson had been taken earlier in the year (Mar. 15); he would be the longest held of the American hostages in Lebanon, not released until 1991.

Off the coast of Egypt, Palestinian terrorists seized the Italian cruise ship *Achille Lauro*, holding its more than 400 passengers and crew hostage (Oct. 7); they killed disabled American passenger Leon Klinghoffer (Oct. 8). After releasing the ship, the terrorists were taken when American planes forced down their escape plane (Oct. 10).

As South Africa became increasingly self-isolated and internal disorders mounted, President P. W. Botha declared a nationwide state of emergency (Mar. 7). Bowing to world and American opinion, the U.S. government applied economic sanctions to South Africa (July 31).

General Ibrahim Bagangida took power by coup in Nigeria (Aug. 17), promising a quick return to democratic government.

General Tito Okello took power by coup in Uganda, deposing President Milton Obote (July 27-29).

1986

At the Reykjavik Summit (Oct.), their second meeting, President Reagan and Premier Gorbachev failed to agree on limiting America's Strategic Defense Initiative (SDI, or "Star Wars").

Nuclear disaster at Chernobyl's Pripyat nuclear plant, near Kiev in the Ukraine (Apr. 26-May 1), resulted from a long-feared core meltdown, accompanied by an explosion and fire; it killed hundreds in the immediate area within a few days, injured and sickened tens of thousands more, and contaminated hundreds of square miles, ultimately forcing the long-term evacuation of 300,000. The immense nuclear cloud spread over Europe and then the entire Northern Hemisphere. The long-term death toll is unknown.

d. Vyacheslav Mikhailovich Molotov (b. 1890), a key Soviet foreign policy spokesperson (1939-1953) until the death of Joseph Stalin, later going out of power (1957).

d. Rudolph Hess (b. 1894), Nazi leader who flew to Britain to propose peace with Germany and an alliance against the Soviet Union (1941); convicted at Nuremberg as a war criminal (1946), he died at Spandau Prison.

Ugandan Civil War: Yoweri Musaveni's forces took Kampala (Jan. 17), and he became president of Uganda (Jan. 29). The civil war continued, with defeated government forces now becoming insurgent guerrillas.

South Yemen Civil War (Jan.): Assassins used by President Ali Nasser Mohammed al-Hasani murdered several leaders of a dissident faction of the ruling Socialist Party at a cabinet meeting, generating a week of factional fighting in which an estimated 4,000 died; al-Hasani's faction was defeated, and he fled into exile.

Libyan-American relations worsened. American warplanes and ships carried out air and sea attacks at Tripoli and Benghazi, their targets including the home and headquarters of Libyan president Muammar al-Qaddafi.

Iran-Iraq War: Although the frontline stalemate essentially continued, Iranian forces were able to take the Faw Peninsula (July). But Iranian forces were weakening, and

Central, South and East Asia, and the Pacific	The Americas

Philippine Revolution (Feb.): Massive demonstrations followed the Philippine election (Feb. 7), in which incumbent Ferdinand Marcos attempted to falsify the results, denying the election of Corazon Aquino. Civil war was averted when Marcos resigned under armed forces and American pressure.

Afghan-Soviet War: Soviet premier Mikhail Gorbachev began to negotiate Soviet withdrawal from Afghanistan. After Babrak Karmal was deposed by coup, Mohammed Najibullah took office as Soviet puppet ruler of Afghanistan.

Iran-Contra Affair: The Reagan administration's arms-for-hostages sales to Iran and the illegal arming of Nicaraguan Contras were exposed (Oct.); the scandal generated enormous publicity. Oliver North was fired from his White House national security post, and John Poindexter resigned as national security adviser (Nov. 25), as congressional and legal investigations started.

Haitian Revolution: As demonstrations grew and American and French pressure intensified, the government of dictator Jean Claude Duvalier fell; he fled Haiti (Feb. 7), and a period of instability followed.

Newly elected Costa Rican president Oscar Arias Sánchez convened a Latin American peace-seeking summit immediately following his inauguration.

1986 (cont.)

Europe	Africa and Southwest Asia
	Iraqi forces went more and more on the offensive as the year closed.
	In Chad attacking Libyan forces were turned back by Chad National Liberation Front (Frolinat) and French forces.
	Guerrilla general Joaquim Alberto Chissanó became president of Mozambique.
	Border skirmishes continued between South Africa and some of its neighbors; South African air and ground forces attacked targets in Botswana, Zambia, and Zimbabwe (May).
	d. Samora Machel (b. 1933), Mozambican guerrilla general who became the first president of independent Mozambique (1975-1986).
	d. John Bagot Glubb (Glubb Pasha) (b. 1897), British officer who developed and commanded Jordan's Arab Legion (1939-1956).

1987

Europe	Africa and Southwest Asia
Brought to trial four years after his capture in Bolivia (1983), Nazi war criminal Klaus Barbie, the "Butcher of Lyon," was sentenced to life imprisonment in France.	Chad Civil War: Southern Chadian forces mounted a counteroffensive, moving north to take the Ouadi Doum Libyan air base (Mar. 22) and the Faya-Largeau Libyan base and weapons depots, then went on into southern Libya, forcing the Libyans to seek a truce.
d. Hans Speidel (b. 1897), German general who refused orders to destroy Paris (Aug. 25, 1944); imprisoned, he escaped into hiding; he also joined conspiracies to overthrow Hitler; he later commanded all NATO forces in central Europe (1957-1963).	A surprise Iraqi missile attack in the Persian Gulf killed 37 sailors aboard the USS *Stark* (May 17); the Iraqi apology for the action was accepted.
	Hundreds of Iranian pilgrims, some of them pro-Khomeini activists, died in a battle with Saudi Arabian police at Mecca's Grand Mosque (July 1).
	d. Camille Chamoun (b. 1900), Lebanese politician who was president (1952-1958).

1986 (cont.)

1987

Sri Lankan Civil War: Government forces attacked and took Tamil-controlled Jaffna (June). The Indian government attempted to negotiate a settlement that favored the Tamils, were rebuffed by them, and ultimately committed divisional-strength peacekeeping forces to Sri Lanka.

Lieutenant Colonel Sitiveni Rabuka took power by coup in Fiji, establishing a military government.

As civil war grew in the Punjab, India imposed direct central government rule on the province.

New Zealand declared its territorial waters a nuclear-free zone.

In a historic move indicating that the Cold War was ending, American president Ronald Reagan and Soviet premier Mikhail Gorbachev signed the landmark Intermediate Nuclear Forces (INF) Treaty at the Washington Summit, for the first time agreeing to destroy a whole class of nuclear weapons (Dec. 8).

"Arias Plan" of Costa Rican president Oscar Arias Sánchez provided a basis for resolution of the Nicaraguan Civil War; he was awarded the Nobel Peace Prize.

Aldo Rico led a small-scale Argentine army insurgency at Monte Caseras barracks, near Buenos Aires, that was defeated by government forces (Apr. 19).

d. Maxwell Davenport Taylor (b. 1901), American general who was commander of the 101st Airborne in Normandy, the Eighth Army in Korea (1953), and all Far East forces (1954); as chairman of the Joint Chiefs of Staff (1962-1964), he championed the "flexible response" strategy.

d. William Joseph Casey (b. 1913), director of the Central Intelligence Agency (CIA), while under investigation for his possible role in the Iran-Contra Affair. He had resigned his CIA post (Feb. 2) due to illness.

d. Ira Clarence Eaker (b. 1896), American Army Air Corps general who led the first American heavy bombing raid over Nazi-occupied Europe, at Rouen (Aug. 17, 1942), and directed shuttle-bombing raids out of Italy as commander of Mediterranean Allied Air Forces (from Jan. 1944).

Meeting again at Moscow (May), Premier Mikhail Gorbachev and President Ronald Reagan further developed the entirely changed post–Cold War American-Soviet relationship, focusing on the settlement of regional conflicts and the signing and exchanging of several sets of documents, including the formal documents of the Intermediate Nuclear Forces (INF) Treaty, on which they had agreed in Washington in 1987.

Northern Ireland Civil War: Irish Republican Army (IRA) terrorist bombings and murders continued, as in the car bomb killing of 6 British soldiers (June 15); the death of 8 British soldiers and injury of 28 civilians in a Belfast bus bombing (Aug. 20); and the sequence of Protestant and IRA killings that followed the killing of 3 IRA men in Gibraltar by the British (Mar. 6).

A Pan Am 747 exploded over Lockerbie, Scotland, killing 259 people on board and 11 on the ground; Islamic terrorists from Libya were later held responsible for placing the bomb on the plane.

d. Bernt Carlsson (b. 1938), Swedish diplomat and United Nations peace negotiator in southern Africa; he died in the Lockerbie aircraft bombing (Dec. 21).

d. Kim (Harold Adrian Russell) Philby (b. 1912), British spy for the Soviet Union from the mid-1930s until he fled to the Soviet Union (1963).

d. Klaus Fuchs (b. 1911), German-British atomic physicist who was a Soviet spy (1943-1950); he was imprisoned (1950-1959) and thereafter was a key Soviet bloc nuclear scientist.

Iran-Iraq War: United Nations secretary-general Javier Pérez de Cuéllar mediated an Iran-Iraq cease-fire (Aug. 20); Geneva peace negotiations followed. Iraqi forces then moved against Kurdish insurgents, using chemical warfare to kill tens of thousands, most of them civilians, and creating hundreds of thousands of refugees.

Afghan-Soviet War: Withdrawal of Soviet troops from Afghanistan was formally agreed on at Geneva (Apr. 14).

Angolan Civil War: Angola, Cuba, and South Africa reached a set of agreements providing for the staged withdrawal of Cuban troops from Angola, the ending of South African aid to the National Union for the Total Independence of Angola (UNITA), and the independence of Namibia. UNITA was not a party to the agreement. South African forces withdrew from Namibia pursuant to the peace agreement.

Palestinian Intifada (Uprising) began on the Israeli-occupied West Bank of the Jordan River and the Gaza Strip, as hundreds of rock-throwing Palestinian teenagers facing heavily armed Israeli troops drew world attention.

Lieutenant Colonel William Higgins, American head of the United Nations Lebanon truce team, was kidnapped and murdered by Muslim terrorists.

An Iranian civilian airliner carrying 290 passengers was shot down over the Strait of Hormuz by a surface-to-air missile fired from the cruiser USS *Vincennes,* the Americans having mistaken it for an attacking warplane (July 3). All aboard were killed.

Azerbaijan-Armenian War (1988-   ) began, converting the long-standing dispute over the Armenian Nagorno-Karabakh enclave within Azerbaijan into a shooting war; the conflict grew despite Soviet peace-keeping intervention.

Insurrection against the Mohammed Siad Barre government began in Somalia (May).

Failed Hutu rebellion against the Tutsi-dominated government of Burundi was followed by the massacre of an estimated 5,000 or more Hutus by the Burundi armed forces.

Antigovernment riots in Algeria cost more than 500 lives (Oct.).

Burmese Spring (Mar.-Sept.): Massive demonstrations ultimately forced the resignation of military dictator Ne Win (July 23); U Nu announced formation of a provisional democratic government (Sept. 18). But a new armed forces dictatorship headed by General Saw Maung, a Ne Win associate, quickly took power, violently suppressing all dissent, with hundreds of deaths. Human rights leader Daw Aung San Suu Kyi was placed under house arrest by the dictatorship.

Sri Lankan Civil War: Indian forces numbering at least 50,000 began unsuccessful armed actions against the Tamil Liberation Tigers.

Afghan-Soviet War: Soviet troop withdrawals began (May).

Kanak independence movement forces and French forces clashed in New Caledonia; French commandos later freed several hostages held by the guerrillas.

d. Mohammad Zia Ul-Haq (b. 1924), Pakistani general who seized power by coup (1977) and ruled as military dictator (1977-1988) until his death in a plane crash (Aug. 17). He was succeeded by Benazir Bhutto, the daughter of Zulfikar Ali Bhutto, his predecessor, who had been executed.

In pursuit of retreating Contra forces, Nicaraguan government forces entered Honduras (Mar. 16-17) and were engaged by Honduran forces. The Nicaraguans withdrew. A cease-fire (Mar. 24) effectively ended the Nicaraguan Civil War.

After being decisively rejected by Chilean voters in a plebiscite (Oct. 5), General Augusto Pinochet agreed to end his military dictatorship and scheduled free elections.

Lieutenant General Prosper Avril led a coup that deposed Haitian president Henri Namphy (Sept. 17), who had deposed President Leslie Manigat three months earlier (June).

In Argentina, Aldo Rico escaped and led another rebellion at Monte Caseras barracks (Jan. 16-18), which was also defeated by government forces.

d. Lauris Norstad (b. 1907), American Air Force general who planned the two missions to drop atomic bombs on Japan (Aug. 6 and 9, 1945); he later commanded all NATO forces in Europe.

d. Lyman L. Lemnitzer (b. 1899), American general during World War II in the Mediterranean theater (Dec. 1944), becoming chairman of the Joint Chiefs of Staff (1960-1962).

1989

Romanian Revolution (Dec. 16-28): Romanian government forces attacked prodemocracy protestors at Timosaura, Transylvania (Dec. 16), and massacred hundreds the next day, triggering the revolution. Police fired on demonstrators at Bucharest (Dec. 21), and armed insurrection began (Dec. 22), which immediately became a nationwide civil war, with the army joining the revolution and quickly defeating government internal security forces. Dictator Nicolae Ceausescu (b. 1919) and his wife and coruler, Elena (b. 1918), were captured (Dec. 22) and executed by the new National Salvation Front government (Dec. 25).

New reform movements emerged in Czechoslovakia, led by figures such as 1968's Prague Spring leader Alexander Dubcek and longtime, much-imprisoned dissident playwright Vaclav Havel. After enormous rallies in Bratislava and Prague (Nov. 23-24), a new democratic government emerged, with Havel as the first president (Dec. 29) and Dubcek chairman of the parliament.

d. Andrei Andreyevich Gromyko (b. 1909), Soviet foreign minister (1957-1985) and chief Soviet diplomat through much of the Cold War.

Armenian and Azerbaijani forces intensified their war over Nagorno-Karabakh; divisional-strength Soviet peacekeeping intervention failed.

Ethiopian-Eritrean War: Eritrean and Tigrean joint forces took Axum; Ethiopian troops withdrew from Tigre.

Liberian Civil War (1989-   ): Charles Taylor led an exile force into Liberia, beginning a major insurrection (Dec.).

Lebanese Civil War: Lebanese army forces commanded by General Michel Aoun attacked Muslim forces in Beirut, as the civil war once again intensified (Mar.-Dec.).

Skirmishes continued between American and Libyan forces; two Libyan fighters were shot down by American planes over the Mediterranean (Jan. 4).

Free elections were held in Namibia (Nov.), with the Southwest Africa People's Organization of Namibia (SWAPO) winning a majority.

d. Ayatollah Ruhollah Khomeini (Ruhollah Kendi) (b. 1900), Iranian fundamentalist Shi'ite cleric who was long exiled (1963-1979) before becoming Iran's religious and political leader (1979-1989). He was succeeded by Ali Akbar Hashemi Rafsanjani.

1990

Mikhail Gorbachev, who won the 1990 Nobel Peace Prize, continued to press his program of economic and political reform in the Soviet Union, increasingly contested by Boris Yeltsin, who became Russian Federation president (May). The dismemberment of the Soviet Union became a clear possibility, as independence movements grew in the Baltic states and ethnic tensions increased in many areas. Latvia declared its independence (May 4).

Soviet troops began to withdraw from the newly freed countries of Eastern Europe. Warsaw Pact member countries withdrew from the alliance.

Slovenia declared its independence from Yugoslavia (Dec. 22), beginning the sequence of events that would lead to the dismemberment of that country, accompanied by a series of communal wars.

Antigovernment demonstrations grew in Albania; the right to emigrate was won (June), and a multiparty system began to emerge.

Lech Walesa was elected president of Poland.

d. Jacques Emile Soustelle (b. 1912), French Secret Army leader during the Algerian War of Independence.

Persian Gulf War (1990-1991): Saddam Hussein's Iraqi forces attacked and quickly took Kuwait (Aug. 2). American president George Bush immediately responded with a massive American and allied buildup in the Persian Gulf and Saudi Arabia, while the United Nations condemned the Iraqi action and demanded withdrawal.

In South Africa, Nelson Mandela was released by the government of Frederik Willem de Klerk (Feb. 11), beginning a new period in the country's history. Agreements between the African National Congress (ANC) and the South African government (Aug. 7) provided for a cease-fire, the release of many more political prisoners, and the beginning of the end of the apartheid system, all looking forward to the emergence of a multiracial state.

Ethiopian-Eritrean War: Eritrean forces took besieged Massawa, as the long war turned decisively against the Ethiopians.

Central, South and East Asia, and the Pacific

The Americas

Chinese student demonstrations began in Beijing (formerly Peking) and spread into massive prodemocracy demonstrations involving millions of students and others, focusing on a long student occupation of Beijing's Tiananmen Square. As the world watched and condemned, Chinese troops attacked students evacuating the square (June 4), killing hundreds; this was the beginning of a reign of terror against dissidents throughout the country.

Afghan-Soviet War: Soviet withdrawal from Afghanistan was completed (Feb. 15). The Afghan Civil War continued.

As the Soviet Union began to disintegrate, conflicts broke out in many areas. Rival Sunni and Shi'ite Muslim forces fought in Uzbekistan (June), as did Uzbeks and Kirghiz in Kirghizia (June).

Sri Lankan Civil War: Indian forces withdrew from Sri Lanka (Aug. 1989-Mar. 1990); the civil war continued.

President Corazon Aquino's forces defeated a substantial armed forces insurrection in Manila and several other locations (Dec. 1-9), assisted by the support and presence — but not the participation — of American forces.

d. Ferdinand Edralin Marcos (b. 1917), Philippine soldier, elected but increasingly repressive president (1965-1972) and dictator (1972-1986); he was deposed by the Philippine Revolution.

d. Hirohito (b. 1901), emperor of Japan (r. 1926-1989) during World War II.

Nicaraguan Civil War: The Tesoro Beach Accords (Feb. 14), mediated by the presidents of Costa Rica, El Salvador, Guatemala, and Honduras, provided for peace, free elections, democratic reforms, and the dissolution of Contra forces in Nicaragua.

Civil war continued in El Salvador; rebel forces demonstrated their strength with attacks in San Salvador, the capital (Nov.-Dec.).

In Panama, an attempted army coup against the Manuel Noriega government failed (Oct. 3). American forces numbering more than 22,000 attacked and took Panama, with fewer than 250 casualties; Panamanian losses were in the 1,000 to 2,000 range (Dec. 20-24).

In Paraguay, General Andres Rodriguez seized power by military coup (Feb. 2-3), overthrowing the 35-year rule of dictator Alfredo Stroessner.

As civil war grew in Assam, India instituted direct central government rule of the province. Muslim-Hindu civil war also spread in Kashmir and several other northern provinces, expressed as a series of separatist movements, often aided by Pakistan.

Philippine colonel Alexander Noble led a small-scale army rebellion on Mindanao (Oct. 4) but surrendered after government planes bombed his positions (Oct. 5).

Yielding to popular pressure, after more than 60 people were killed by government forces, King Birendra Bir Bakram Shah Deva established a multiparty democracy in Nepal.

d. Le Duc Tho (Phan Dinh Khai) (b. 1913), chief North Vietnamese peace negotiator in the early 1970s who refused a Nobel Peace Prize awarded jointly to him and Henry Kissinger.

Panamanian general Manuel Noriega, who had taken refuge in the Vatican Embassy, surrendered (Jan. 3) and was removed to the United States for trial, maintaining that he was a political prisoner.

Jean-Bertrand Aristide, a liberal Catholic priest, was elected president of Haiti (Dec. 17).

d. Curtis Emerson LeMay (b. 1906), American Army and Air Force officer; a key figure in the development of strategic air bombing during World War II, he became head of the Strategic Air Command (SAC) (1948-1957) and the Air Force (1961-1964); during the Vietnam War, he advocated using "all available means," including nuclear weapons.

d. Albert Coady Wedemeyer (b. 1896), American general who served primarily on the general staff during World War II, replacing Joseph Stilwell in China as commander and chief of staff to Chiang Kai-shek (Oct. 1944).

1990 (cont.)

Somali revolutionary forces joined in a common front against Mohammed Siad Barre, taking much of the country; the Battle of Mogadishu began (Dec.).

Syrian army and Lebanese Christian Phalangist militia forces defeated General Michel Aoun's Lebanese army, forcing Aoun out of power (Sept.-Oct.).

Southwest Africa People's Organization of Namibia (SWAPO) leader Sam Nujoma became the first president of free Namibia (Mar. 21).

Liberian Civil War: The forces of Charles Taylor, Prince Johnson, and President Samuel Doe fought a three-way war for the country. Doe was killed (Sept. 10). An international West African force took control of Monrovia (Aug.) and negotiated a cease-fire (Nov.) that did not hold; the war continued.

d. Shapur Bakhtiar (b. 1914), former Iranian premier; he was assassinated by an Iranian agent while in exile in Paris.

1991

While on holiday in Crimea, Soviet premier Mikhail Gorbachev was arrested by the right-wing communist State of Emergency Committee (Aug. 19), which proclaimed a seizure of power. Gorbachev refused to resign; Russian president Boris Yeltsin, with massive popular support, successfully resisted the coup, gathering hundreds of thousands at the Russian Federation White House. Air force and military units throughout the country refused to join the coup, and capital district paratroops and armor sent against the White House instead deployed themselves in defense of the government, dooming the coup, which disintegrated (Aug. 21). In the momentum created by the situation, the Gorbachev government and the Soviet Union also disintegrated, as Yeltsin took power in Russia. The Soviet Union ceased to exist (Dec.), and many new nations soon came into being. Civil war spread in Georgia; Armenia and Azerbaijan went to war over the Armenian enclave of Nagorno-Karabakh.

Yugoslavia disintegrated; Croatia and Slovenia declared their independence (June 25). Slovenian independence was only lightly challenged by Serbian armed action, but Serbia and Croatia went to war, with Serbian forces taking approximately one-third of Croatia.

Nazi rioting spread in Germany, as neo-Nazis generated antiforeign riots, focusing largely on Turkish immigrants in Germany; the riots were sharply opposed by many Germans, who mounted massive anti-Nazi demonstrations.

Irish Republican Army (IRA) guerrilla forces made a mortar attack on the British prime minister's residence at 10 Downing Street (Feb. 7) and conducted a series of bombings in London.

The Warsaw Pact nations decided to dissolve the Cold War organization (effective Mar. 31).

d. Dolores Ibarruri (b. 1895), Spanish Communist Party leader who was called "La Pasionaria" during the Spanish Civil War by Republican forces.

Persian Gulf War, Operation Desert Storm (Jan. 17-Feb. 28): Allied air and naval forces attacked Iraq (Jan. 17-Feb. 24), quickly destroying or grounding the Iraqi air force and severely damaging Iraqi air defense and missile delivery capabilities, but only partly destroying Iraq's mobile SCUD missile forces. The allied ground attack (Operation Desert Sabre) (Feb. 24-28) was a quick, massive armored envelopment that destroyed the effectiveness of the Republican Guard and armored reserves, coupled with a frontal attack in Kuwait that quickly broke through the Iraqi defensive line. Iraq suffered at least 30,000 dead and 70,000 other casualties; 60,000 to 65,000 Iraqi prisoners were taken. Allied losses were fewer than 1,000. Whether by design or inadvertence, allied forces did not pursue the defeated Iraqis, leaving Saddam Hussein in power in Iraq, with enough air and armor to defeat his internal enemies.

Somali revolutionary forces took Mogadishu, as Mohammed Siad Barre fled into exile (Jan.); no viable government emerged, as factional fighting began in much of the country, with some factions blocking humanitarian food and medical supplies

1990 (cont.)

1991

Cambodian Civil War: Treaty of Paris (Oct. 23) provided for an immediate cease-fire, the return home of an estimated 350,000 refugees, a major United Nations peacekeeping presence in Cambodia during the transition to multiparty democracy, and free elections in 1993.

Civil war continued in several north Indian states, including the Punjab, Kashmir, and Assam.

General Sunthorn Kongsompong took power by coup in Thailand (Feb. 23).

In Haiti a military coup against the newly elected Jean-Bertrand Aristide failed (Jan.), but he was deposed by an army coup (Sept. 29-30) and fled abroad, as attempts to negotiate a return to democracy began.

Panamanian general Manuel Noriega was convicted on a variety of charges in Florida (Apr. 9) and sentenced to a 40-year prison term; he was later classified by the court as a political prisoner.

d. James Van Fleet (b. 1892), American general who was American forces commander in Korea (1951).

d. Robert D'Aubisson Arrieta (b. 1943), right-wing Salvadoran soldier and politician.

1991 (cont.)

d. Willy Brandt (Carl Herbert Frahm) (b. 1913), German socialist politician who was mayor of West Berlin (1957-1966) and West German foreign minister (1966-1969) and chancellor (1969-1974).

aimed at ending the mass starvation and disease that had drawn world attention.

In South Africa, the war between adherents of the African National Congress (ANC) and the Zulu organization Inkatha intensified, considerably impeding the progress of ANC-government negotiations.

Ethiopian-Eritrean War: As the Ethiopian army dissolved before allied attacks, Haile Miriam Mengistu resigned and fled the country (May 21); rebel forces took Addis Abbaba, ending the long, complex series of wars.

Kurdish forces in northern Iraq revived their war of independence, taking Kirkuk, while a major Iranian-supported Shi'ite insurrection grew in southern Iraq. Both insurrections were crushed by Iraqi forces. Kurdish forces also struck out of northern Iraq into Turkey, generating cross-border responses by Turkish forces.

Ali Aref Bourhan led an unsuccessful coup attempt in Djibouti (Jan. 8-9).

Journalist Terry Anderson, longest held of the American hostages in Lebanon, was released by his Muslim terrorist captors (Dec. 4) after 2,454 days, nearly 7 years.

1992

Serbian forces went to war with secessionist Bosnia and Herzegovina (Mar. 3); fighting quickly spread, as Serbian forces besieged Sarajevo and other Muslim-held areas, taking more than two-thirds of the country. Croatian forces attacked Bosnia and Herzegovina (July), attempting to take a partly Croatian-populated area in the western portion of the country. Serbian forces practiced the policy of "ethnic cleansing," reminiscent of genocidal German actions in Yugoslavia and many other nations during World War II. The United Nations attempted, with little success, to bring relief supplies to civilian populations and imposed sanctions on Serbia, declaring it an aggressor.

Former Soviet foreign minister Eduard Shevardnadze became head of state in his native Georgia (Mar.), as the Georgian civil war intensified. His government survived an attempted coup by followers of former president Zviad Gamsak-jurdia in Tbilisi (June 24); joint Russian-Georgian peacekeeping forces were placed on the South Ossetian-Georgian border. But the war in Abkhazia grew, as rebel forces, with Russian "volunteers" and weapons, took most of the province.

Russian president Boris Yeltsin sent forces into Moldova and Georgia, and he refused to move troops out of the Baltic countries as scheduled. In Moldova, secessionist forces aided by Russia took much of the partly Russian western portion of the country.

d. Alexander Dubcek (b. 1921), Czechoslovak Communist Party leader who began the democratic Prague Spring (Jan. 1968) and later came out of obscurity to help lead the new, successful democratic movement (1989), becoming chairman of parliament.

Heavy fighting resumed in Angola (Oct. 30) after Jonas Savimbi and the National Union for the Total Independence of Angola (UNITA) refused to accept the validity of the electoral win of José Eduardo Dos Santos and the Popular Movement for the Liberation of Angola (MPLA). Neither side had really given up its weapons as provided in the 1991 peace agreement, and a United Nations–sponsored truce (Nov.) was not destined to hold.

American forces entered Somalia on a humanitarian mission and with United Nations approval (Dec.); they were quickly drawn into the Somali civil war.

Mozambican president Joaquim Chissanó and Mozambique National Resistance (Renamo) leader Afonso Dhlakama signed a cease-fire agreement in Rome (Aug. 7), ending the 16-year civil war; a formal peace treaty followed (Oct. 4).

Supported by Iran, fundamentalist Islamic Sudanese government forces pressed their attack on southern Sudan, held by the People's Liberation Army, sharply limiting the

1992

Cambodian Civil War: Khmer Rouge forces refused to adhere to the terms of the 1991 peace agreement, attacking twice in central Cambodia (Mar.; June); they also refused to disarm and to enter demobilization camps. They began to take groups of United Nations peacekeepers as hostages (Nov.-Dec.).

Fundamentalist Hindus destroyed the Babri Mosque in Ayodha, Uttar Pradesh (Dec. 6), triggering nationwide Hindu-Muslim rioting in which at least 1,000 people died. Separatist forces continued to wage guerrilla civil wars in Kashmir, Jammu, Andhra Pradesh, and the Punjab.

Thai troops fired on tens of thousands of demonstrators in Bangkok, killing hundreds (May 17).

d. Jiang Qing (Chiang Ch'ing; Luan Shu-meng) (b. 1914), Chinese actress who became Mao Zedong's third wife; a major political figure during the Cultural Revolution, she was later convicted of crimes against the state as leader of the "Gang of Four"; she died in prison, reportedly a suicide.

d. Rajiv Gandhi (b. 1944), Indian prime minister (1984-1989) who was assassinated while campaigning in southern India; he was the son of Indira Gandhi and the grandson of Jawaharlal Nehru.

President Alberto Fujimori, with army support, dissolved Peru's democratic institutions and took power as dictator (Apr. 5). The armed guerrilla insurgency of the Shining Path (Sendoro Luminoso) continued, although its leader, Abimeal Guzmán Reynoso, was captured (Sept. 12).

Guerrilla attacks intensified in Colombia, as Guerzas Armadas Revolucionarios (FARC) and Ejército de Liberación Nacional (ELN) forces continued their long insurgency after peace talks broke down (Mar.).

President Alfredo Cristiani Burchard of El Salvador negotiated a peace treaty with the Farabundi Marti National Liberation Front (FMLN), ending the long civil war (Jan. 6). A cease-fire was called (Feb. 1).

In Venezuela, two attempted military coups failed (Jan. 3-4; Nov. 27).

At a Washington summit meeting (June 16-17), Russian president Boris Yeltsin and American president George Bush agreed on major nuclear arsenal reductions.

1992 (cont.)

flow of international relief supplies to millions of starving people. These included hundreds of thousands, most of them Christians and animists, who had been driven out of Khartoum into the desert.

Liberian Civil War: Fighting intensified, as West African peacekeeping forces on the Sierra Leone border failed to keep opposing forces apart and then fought against Charles Taylor's forces, which had besieged Monrovia (Nov.-Dec.).

Yitzhak Rabin became Israeli prime minister and revived the stalled Middle East peace talks (Aug.), making considerable progress, although the Intifada continued, and the Israelis expelled more than 400 fundamentalists late in the year, which temporarily halted the talks.

Cross-border attacks in northern Israel and Lebanon intensified between Israeli forces and Hezbollah, the Iranian-influenced Shi'ite Muslim Lebanese militias.

In Egypt, guerrilla attacks by fundamentalists increased, as terrorists in southern Egypt attacked tourists and bombed historic sites; the government responded with riot police, troops, and increased prosecutions.

Guerrilla warfare began in Algeria after the army forces canceled scheduled elections (Jan.), imprisoned several thousand Islamic Front (FIS) activists, and banned the FIS. President Muhammad Boudiaf was assassinated (June 29).

Iraqi forces attacked Shi'ite populations in southern Iraq (Apr.-Dec.).

Turkish border forces and Iraq-based Kurdish forces repeatedly clashed.

Two coup attempts failed in Chad (Feb.; May), as the long civil war continued.

d. Menachem Begin (b. 1913), Israeli leader, head of the terrorist Irgun Zvai Leumi (from 1943), founder of the right-wing Herut Party (1948), and Likud Party prime minister (1977-1983).

1993

Russian Insurrection: The dispute between President Boris Yeltsin and conservative forces in Parliament, led by Vice President Alexandr Rutskoi and parliamentary speaker Ruslan Khasbulatov, grew into an armed confrontation. More than 5,000 Parliament supporters in Moscow went over to armed insurrection (Oct. 3), opening automatic weapons fire on the police while breaking through riot police formations to gather before the Russian White House. Rutskoi urged

Inkatha-African National Congress warfare continued in South Africa, as did rightwing terrorism aimed at disrupting progress toward multiracial democracy. ANC military forces, back from exile, organized effective resistance to Inkatha

Central, South and East Asia, and the Pacific	The Americas	

1992 (cont.)

1993

Hindu-Muslim clashes continued throughout India in the wake of the Hindu fundamentalist destruction of the historic Ayodhya mosque (Dec. 1992). Armed clashes occurred in Kashmir, Jammu, and the north-eastern states, requiring divisional-strength government security force action in affected areas. After a

Colombian Civil War: Fugitive Medellin drug cartel leader Pablo Escobar was killed by government forces (early Dec.), but the long civil war continued, with rebel coalition Simon Bolivar Liberation Front guerrillas beginning a new series of hit-and-run attacks, bombings, and assassinations (late Sept.).

the rebels to form up into military units and take the Moscow broadcasting center, the mayor's office, and the Kremlin; rebel forces, led by previously organized cadres, stormed and took the mayor's office and attempted to take the broadcasting center. But there was no active armed forces support for the rebellion, and the next day (Oct. 4), Russian armored and airborne forces surrounded, shelled, and took the White House, forcing the surrender of rebel forces, whose leaders were arrested but later released, in an amnesty proclaimed by the next Russian parliament, while the very fragile Yeltsin government continued to rule Russia.

Civil war continued in the former Yugoslavia, notably in Bosnia, as Serbian forces continued the sieges of Sarajevo and several other Muslim-held centers, while Croatian forces, in uneasy alliance with one side and then the other continued to pursue their own territorial aims. Tens of thousands were killed and millions were in flight from Bosnia. United Nations peacekeeping forces conducted off-and-on relief operations and, perhaps more important, by their presence somewhat deterred Serbian forces from openly accelerating their genocidal program of "ethnic cleansing" and mass murder. The Milosevic government was returned to power in Serbia, guaranteeing a continuing flow of armaments to Serbian forces in Bosnia. Several truces and "peace treaties" were made and broken by all sides, though international peacekeeping efforts continued, greatly hampered by the vagueness of repeated Western threats to intervene.

Low-level civil war continued in Northern Ireland, but substantial progress toward peace was reported for the first time in many years, as secret and then public direct peace talks developed between the British government and the Irish Republican Army. No truce, however, had eventuated at year's end.

attacks, increasingly in collaboration with South African army forces. On November 18, the ANC, the National Party, and 19 other parties agreed on a new constitution that would guarantee "fundamental rights" for all South Africans in the course of a transition to majority rule; national elections were scheduled for April 27, 1994. Willem De Klerk and Nelson Mandela shared the 1993 Nobel Peace Prize.

Angolan Civil War: Massive fighting continued in the resumed war. Jonas Savimbi's National Union for the Total Independence of Angola (UNITA) forces retook much of the territory they had held during the civil war, capturing Huambo (Mar.), Angola's second largest city, and then going on to take two thirds of the country, in a war that during 1993 took an estimated 50,000-100,000 lives.

The Intifada and the Hezbollah-Israeli border war continued. Hezbollah cross-border attacks into northern Israel intensified. Israeli air and artillery attacks forced an estimated 200,000 to flee southern Lebanon.

Government armored forces continued to attack Shiites in southern Iraq, forcing an estimated 200,000-300,000 into Iranian exile. Major United Nations air attacks on Iraqi ground batteries occurred (Jan.) and air and missile attacks were made on Baghdad (June).

Somali Civil War: American and other United Nations peacekeeping troops continued to operate in Somalia, with lessening effectiveness. Forces of Mohammed Farah Aidid killed 23 Pakistani soldiers (May) and 18 American soldiers (Oct.). As the Americans prepared to depart, full-scale civil war threatened to resume.

d. Kasdi Merbah (Abdallah Khalaf; b. 1938), Algerian opposition leader and former prime minister, assassinated on August 21; he had been a leading peace advocate as the fundamentalist-generated civil war continued to grow.

d. Oliver Tambo (b. 1917), African National Congress (ANC) leader, president of the ANC and leader of its guerrilla insurrection (1967-1990).

d. Chris Hani (Martin Thembisile Hani; b. 1942), General Secretary of the South African Communist Party, assassinated by rightwing terrorists on April 10.

period of indecision, P. V. N. Rao's government moved decisively to stop Hindu fundamentalist violence, arresting an estimated 75,000-150,000 demonstrators in New Delhi and en route to planned demonstrations in that city. Massive bombings killed more than 300 people in Bombay and Calcutta (Mar.), the beginning of long-term bombing campaigns by fundamentalists and other factions.

An undeclared Georgian-Russian war, coupled with covert Russian support for rebel forces in Abkhazia, ultimately forced Georgian leader Eduard Shevardnadze to take Georgia into the Russian-dominated Commonwealth of Independent States. Russian forces then intervened to quickly defeat rebel forces in western Georgia, while at year's end the fate of Abkhazia remained uncertain.

Afghan Civil War: Armed conflict continued among the several factions vying for control of the country, with the heaviest fighting occurring between Sunni and Shiite armed forces at the capital city, Kabul. A cease-fire (May) did not hold, and the agreement (Oct.) to hold free elections in 1994 was not expected to fare any better.

Tajik rebels in alliance with Afghan forces struck repeatedly across the Afghan-Tajikistan border against Tajik government forces and allied weak Russian border guards (June-July); but reinforced Russian forces under new commanders responded with artillery and air cover, bringing the engagement to a close (early Aug.).

Cambodian Civil War: Although the Khmer Rouge refused to participate in national elections (May), a strong government of national unity emerged, led by Norodom Sihanouk, once again a constitutional monarch. Government forces then attacked Khmer Rouge concentrations, forcing them out of their bases toward Thai sanctuaries, as a continuing low-level guerrilla war developed.

d. Ranasinghe Premadas (b. 1923), president of Sri Lanka, assassinated (May 1). The long three-way war among government forces, Tamil separatists, and Sinhalese guerrillas continued.

d. Wang Zhen (b. 1908), Chinese Red Army general, who joined the Communist Party in 1927, fought through the entire Chinese Civil War and Sino-Japanese War, held several cabinet-level positions after Communist victory in 1949, and was ultimately a hard-line Politiburo member and vice-president in the 1980s and early 1990s.

Peruvian Civil War: Although Shining Path leader Abimeal Guzmán Reynoso was in prison, and the Peruvian army continued its reign of terror, Shining Path forces mounted a continuing guerrilla war; a series of bombings occurred throughout the country during a speech by president Alberto Fujimori (June 5).

Muslim fundamentalist terrorists bombed New York's World Trade Center (Feb. 26), killing six and injuring more than 1,000. Several Muslim militants were ultimately convicted of committing the actual bombing, while fifteen, with roots in Sudan, Egypt, Iran, and Afghanistan, were charged with conspiracy to commit the bombing and a wide range of other terrorist activities. Among them was Egyptian Islamic fundamentalist cleric Omar Abdel Rahman.

Guatemalan Civil War continued into its 33rd year, despite the accession of human rights advocate Ramiro de Leon Carpio to the presidency. Many Mayan Indians who had returned from Mexican refuge early in the year were attacked by army forces.

d. Matthew Bunker Ridgway (b. 1895), American general who was allied commander in chief in Korea (1951-1953).

d. James "Jimmy" Harold Doolittle (b. 1896), American Army Corps general noted for his morale-building bombing raid on Tokyo (1942).

Intermittent guerrilla engagements between Chechnyan government forces and Russian-backed insurgents grew into civil war (Sept.). Divisional-strength Russian armored forces with strong air support invaded Chechnya (Sept. 11), encountering strong resistance from lightly armed government forces. Russian forces attacked Grozny (Dec. 31), the Chechen capital, taking the conflict to a new level and generating a strong Russian antiwar movement, along with powerful criticism from the Russian military and nationalist groups for the army's failure to crush the Chechens quickly. The conflict continued into 1995; Russian forces took Grozny, but could not win the war, as Chechen forces prepared for a long war of independence, probably from bases in the Caucasus Mountains.

In the former Yugoslavia, a group of related conflicts continued, as Bosnian Serb forces with Serbian sources of armament and air support fought poorly equipped Bosnian Muslim forces, while the United Nations played a humanitarian role and ineffectually tried to broker a peaceful end to the war. The Bosnian Muslim–Croat portion of the war ended at least temporarily (Mar.), with creation of a Croat-Muslim federation. The siege of Sarajevo was eased by a truce (Mar.), and a monthlong Bosnian Serbian–Muslim cease-fire was negotiated (June). But truce and siege violations were frequent throughout the year, with token NATO air attacks on Serb forces, coupled with threats of withdrawal directed at the Muslim side, proving no deterrent to the resumption of fighting. Sporadic Croatian-Serbian clashes restarted in Croatia (Nov.). Former U.S. president Jimmy Carter negotiated a dramatic four-month Bosnian War cease-fire (Dec. 23), but it did not hold and was not extended, as the multiple wars again intensified.

Following almost two years of intermittent negotiations, a cease-fire was announced (Aug. 31) in the Northern Ireland Civil War (1969-94). Formal peace talks between Sinn Fein and the British government began (Dec. 9).

Rwandan president Juvénal Habyarimana and Burundi president Cyprien Ntaryamira, both Hutus, were killed when their plane was shot down over the Rwandan capital of Kigali (Apr. 6). Hard-line Rwandan Hutus then organized genocidal attacks on the Tutsi minority and moderate Hutus in Rwanda, killing an estimated 500,000 to 1 million. Tutsi Rwandan Patriotic Front forces, operating largely from cross-border bases in Uganda, defeated the Rwandan military in the civil war that followed; an estimated 2 million Hutus fled to neighboring countries with the retreating Rwandan military, protected in part by intervening French forces, which later turned protection over to United Nations peacekeepers.

Palestinian-Israeli wars (1948-94) ended with the PLO-Israeli peace accords (May 4), providing for Palestinian self-rule in the Gaza Strip and Jericho. Yasir Arafat headed the first Palestinian government. A Jordan-Israeli peace treaty followed (Oct. 26); Syrian-Israeli negotiations were also proceeding. Terrorist incidents continued, as fundamentalist Hezbollah and Hamas Muslim factions and Israeli nationalist groups attempted to block the peace process. Arafat, Israeli prime minister Yitzhak Rabin, and Israeli foreign minister Shimon Peres shared the Nobel Peace Prize.

Angolan Civil War (1975-94): Fighting continued throughout much of 1994, while Angolan government-UNITA talks continued. Government forces attacked Huambo (mid-Nov.), shortly before a new peace treaty was signed (Nov. 20), establishing a very tenuous peace.

Sporadic north-south clashes in Yemen flared into full-scale civil war (May 5). Northern forces quickly defeated weaker southern forces, taking Aden (July 7) and effectively ending the war. An estimated 5,000 people died in the conflict.

Turkish forces numbering 40,000 mounted a largely unsuccessful spring offensive into Northern Iraq (Apr.), aimed at Kurdistan Workers' Party (KKK) insurgents waging a guerrilla war into Turkey from cross-border bases. An equally large Turkish cross-border offensive (Mar. 1995) would meet with little success.

Guerrilla civil war intensified in Algeria, as Islamic Salvation Front (FIS) and Armed Islamic Group (GIA) forces stepped up their terror campaigns, and army and police units pursued anti-terrorist actions.

Civil war intensified in Somalia as the failed United Nations peacekeeping mission wound down operations. Evacuation of remaining UN forces would be completed in 1995 (Mar. 3).

In Liberia, after sporadic fighting throughout the year, rival factions signed another peace treaty (Dec. 21, 1994), calling for a cease-fire and free elections in October 1995.

In Afghanistan, factional fighting continued, with several factions receiving financing and war materials from other countries, including Iran, Pakistan, Uzbekistan, and Saudi Arabia, with less direct American, Russian, Indian, and Chinese involvement. United Nations mediation efforts failed. Central government forces continued to hold most of Kabul, but had little control elsewhere. The Islamic fundamentalist Taliban faction accreted power (mid-1994), took most of southern Afghanistan, and defeated Hezb-e-Islami forces besieging Kabul, but could not take the city. Kabul was largely destroyed, most of its population fleeing the city.

Russian-Georgian treaty (Feb. 3) made Georgia a de facto protectorate of Russia. Georgia and Russian-backed Abkhazian rebel forces then agreed on a cease-fire (Apr. 4), and Russia sent peacekeeping forces to Abkhazia, which also became a de facto Russian protectorate.

Low-level guerrilla actions continued in Tajikistan, as Afghan-supported Tajik Muslim rebel forces repeatedly attacked Russian and Tajik border guards from cross-border bases in Afghanistan.

In Nagorno-Karabakh, fighting between Azeri and Armenian forces continued until a Russian-mediated cease-fire took effect (mid-May). The cease-fire held, while protracted negotiations continued.

In Cambodia, civil war between government and Khmer Rouge forces continued, as the opposing sides fought a series of inconclusive engagements throughout the year, the Khmer Rouge continuing to operate in Cambodia and from cross-border bases in Thailand. The Cambodian government formally outlawed the Khmer Rouge (July), in recognition of the existing state of war.

Sri Lankan Civil War: Fighting continued between Tamil rebels and Sinhalese government forces. With the election of Chandrika Bandaranaike Kumaratunga as prime minister (Aug. 16) and as president (Nov. 19), peace negotiations seemed promising. But the Tamils would withdraw from the negotiations (Apr. 1995), immediately making guerrilla attacks on government forces, as full-scale war resumed.

d. Kim Il Sung (Kim Jong Ju) (b. 1912), Communist dictator of the Democratic People's Republic of North Korea (1948-94), initiator of the Korean War (1950-53), who subsequently pursued a Cold War with South Korea until his death.

Tensions between the Haitian military government and the United States built throughout the year. U.S. invasion plans went forward, with authorization for a U.S.-led invasion force coming from the United Nations Security Council (July 31). Elements of an all-U.S. force of 20,000 were in the air on their way to invade Haiti (Sept. 18), the day that a last-ditch American negotiating team composed of former U.S. president Jimmy Carter, General Colin Powell, and Senator Sam Nunn reached an agreement providing for the peaceful occupation of Haiti by American forces and the resignations of generals Raoul Cedras and Philippe Biamby, who would later leave Haiti. Elected Haitian president Jean-Bertrand Aristide returned to Haiti (Oct. 15) and formed a new government.

In Colombia, guerrilla war continued. Now in its fifth decade, the insurgency was led by the Colombia Revolutionary Armed Forces (FARC) and the several factions of the National Liberation Army (ELN), in shifting alliance with the drug cartels.

In Peru, the Shining Path (Sendero Luminoso) guerrilla insurrection continued, despite considerable government gains in the long civil war and the unchecked activities of right-wing death squads.

Guatemalan Civil War intensified, as the several left guerrilla forces combined in the Guatemalan National Revolutionary Unity organization (URNG) accelerated guerrilla activities directed at toppling the military-dominated national government. Right-wing death squads affiliated with the military also intensified their activities; U.S. military aid to Guatemala would be suspended (Mar. 1995) because of human rights abuses.

In Mexico's southern state of Chiapas, low-level rural guerrilla insurrection mounted by the Zapatista National Liberation Army began (Jan.) and continued sporadically throughout the year, as repeated attempts to mediate the conflict failed.

d. Richard Milhous Nixon (b. 1913), as 37th President of the United States (1969-74), American commander-in-chief during the later stages of the Vietnam War. He resigned to avoid impeachment after his role in the "Watergate Affair" had been exposed.

Index

Index

Index